Architecture
and
Interior Design

The East Building of the National Gallery of Art, Washington, D.C., 1978. I. M. Pei & Partners, New York. (National Gallery of Art, Washington.)

ARCHITECTURE
AND
INTERIOR DESIGN

Europe and America
from the Colonial Era to Today

VICTORIA KLOSS BALL

A Wiley-Interscience Publication
JOHN WILEY & SONS
New York • Chichester • Brisbane • Toronto

Library of Congress Cataloging in Publication Data

Ball, Victoria Kloss.
    Architecture and interior design.

    "A Wiley-Interscience publication."
    Includes bibliographical references and index.
    1. Architecture—Europe—History. 2. Architecture,
Modern—Europe—History. 3. Interior decoration—
Europe—History. 4. Architecture—United States—
History. 5. Architecture, Modern—United States—
History. 6. Interior decoration—United States—History.
I. Title.

NA954.B34   720'.9   79-24851
ISBN 0-471-05161-6
ISBN 0-471-08722-X pbk.

Printed in the United States of America

10 9 8 7 6 5 4 3 2 1

To the memory of
my husband

GEORGE COLBURN BALL

Consultants

Dr. Anna Brightman, Professor of Interior Design
the University of Texas at Austin

Dorothy G. Shepherd, Curator of Textiles
the Cleveland Museum of Art
Adjunct Professor of Near Eastern Art
Case Western Reserve University

Dr. Mary L. Shipley, Professor of Interior Design
the University of Arizona at Tempe

Dr. Marion E. Siney, the Hiram Haydn Professor of History
Case Western Reserve University, Cleveland, Ohio

Dr. Charles W. York, Professor of Interior Design
the University of Texas at Austin

Preface

These paragraphs are an attempt to explain the what, why, how, and perhaps the whereto of these volumes. They have been written to refute the seemingly prevalent idea that architecture and interior design are autonomous arts. Rather they are skills that are joined in purpose and should have similar basic preparation. Possibly then they might be more aptly executed by different persons with differing talents.

Architecture is far more than empty frames and spaces: it deals with a structure and habitable volume. Architecture is great art only when its forms, setting, and contents make a whole as seen within its culture. In the present books we are concerned with buildings and their furnishings which involve all those heterogeneous artifacts, utilitarian as well as ornamental, that contribute to satisfactory interiors. How much of our valuable museum space is devoted to them!

To limit the compass further our focus is on the aesthetic concepts that bind the architectural complex. Construction and purpose are treated as they contribute to them. Architecture and its components are viewed in the light of their ability to create an interesting unity of space, color, and texture that will serve a mutual purpose. The intention—the *why*—of this work is to provide a coordinated history of those arts that have contributed toward such total architecture.

The organization—the *how*—is chronological. The usual division of art periods is followed for convenience. The subject matter emphasizes western civilizations. Other cultures, however, have been touched on whenever they have been influential or have become important ancillaries.

Each chapter is introduced by excerpts from contemporary thought because the writing of an age is one important index to its character. These quotations are followed by a brief summary of the salient facts of concurrent civilization. From there the course lies with architecture and the principal decorative arts. Here again the aesthetics of the total art form is held to be the determining principle. In this regard, as the leading style centers move west along the Mediterranean and then north across the Alps and over the Atlantic, it is both interesting and important to note the role played by regional genius.

The division into two books has been made for several reasons. In addition to the practical ones concerned with ease of handling and accommodation of production, ideational logic favors the separation. Book 1 explores the transition from an early Asiatic culture to an emerging European. This period is germinated in the crucible of Greece and Rome and develops through the seventeenth century. Then, despite the roots and the maturation that had taken place, a new coupling of elements occurs. Book 2 deals with changes since this time. It describes a culture that was bred from a New World view. America may have been the catalyst, but, as Greece led to Europe, so America stands at the gateway to horizons far more extensive. Both books may be purchased and read independently. Together it is hoped that they will throw some light on the reasons for the past and the expectancies for the future—in the arts with which they deal.

I chose my illustrations from the many possible ones because I felt that they were both significant and representative. Only concretely, by means of buildings and their interiors, can the story come alive. Other historians may prefer other choices: herein lies a challenge to further and deeper study.

We can reenter past cultures in the buildings that remain and the belongings placed therein. When carefully documented and examined, they give proof that the purpose of art (a purpose that is peculiar to art) is to bridge the islands of experience on an intuitive level. Works of architectural art convey an ineffable spirit of time and space. If these volumes serve to illustrate this truth, then the picture of sources, of roots, and of future directions will begin to emerge.

* * *

It has been my privilege to have known and worked with many who have understood the arts. I should somehow like to thank them all for the enrichment they have given my life. Among these friends some have put their shoulders to the wheel and have given these pages a shape that they never would have had but for such help. First there are those invaluable critics who have donated their time and their special knowledge. They have contributed suggestions for reorganization; they have corrected statements; they have spotted obscurities of expression. Although my work may fall far short of the critic's expectations, nevertheless what virtues it has are in no small degree due to the following scholars, from each of whom I have received thought-provoking criticism and excellent counsel: Dr. Anna Brightman, Professor of Interior Design, the University of Texas at Austin; Dorothy G. Shepherd, Curator of Textiles, the Cleveland Museum of Art, and Adjunct Professor of Near Eastern Art, Case Western Reserve University; Dr. Mary L. Shipley, Professor of Interior Design, the University of Arizona at Tempe; Dr. Marion E. Siney, the Hiram Haydn Professor of History, Case Western Reserve University, Cleveland; and Dr. Charles W. York, Professor of Interior Design, the University of Texas at Austin.

The kind help and encouragement of the following friends is also gratefully acknowledged: James S. Ackerman, Pietro Belluschi, Arthur H. Benade, Rita Blumentals, Lindsay O. J. Boynton, Ruth E. Bowman, Mrs. William P. Cordes, George E. Danforth, William B. Denny, Frances K. Dolley, Hope L. Foote, E. Blanche Harvey, Mr. and Mrs. Herbert Kemp, Mr. and Mrs. Donald MacCloskey, Nanno Marinatos, Frederick A. Miller, Thomas Munro, C. W. Eliot Paine, Ernst Payer, William Priestley, Richard A. Rankin, Bertha Schaefer, Mrs. Albert Schug, G. E. Kidder Smith, Martha Thomas, and Dorothy Turobinski.

I wish to acknowledge with special appreciation those friends who helped with funds in furthering the travel and research required for this work: A. Leroy Caldwell, Grace P. Neal, and John C. Pearson.

Recognition and gratitude should go to Gordana Ukmar, who organized the figures and executed many of them, and to Robert Lloyd, who helped with the photographic reproduction work. The remaining figures were drawn by Harriet and Allen Raphael. My gratitude and admiration is extended to Virginia Benade for her skilled and untiring effort in putting the text into presentable form and in pursuing the acquisition of the illustrations. Without her the book never could have achieved publication.

To my Wiley editor, Wm. Dudley Hunt, Jr., I am indebted for his belief in this sort of manuscript and for his guidance of it and me through the complexities of the publication process.

Obviously many museums, libraries, and historical foundations have assisted with data and with photographs. To them I wish to say thank you. The generous cooperation of the Cleveland Museum of Art, with whose collections I have long been in contact, was accorded to me by its director, Dr. Sherman E. Lee, and its excellent curatorial staff.

I want to express my appreciation for the assistance of my husband George Colburn Ball. He spent many hours on documentation and used his photographic skill in taking many of the illustrations.

VICTORIA KLOSS BALL

Chagrin Falls, Ohio
April 1980

Contents

What Are We Talking About?

HISTORY

History is the record of the passage of time, the story of changes in nature and in the human experience. It is the mind of man that has interpreted this chronicle and so in a sense each of us makes his own version of the past.

The historian tells us how nature impressed the transient eons in the erupted mountains, in the crustaceans solidified in rock strata, and in the ossified imprint of reptilian feet on the quarry bed. He clarifies the relation between a flint arrowhead and its cultural milieu. He explains how the facts of history are interconnected.

From such recording one thing stands out crystal clear—history foretells as it retells, and if we are sensitive to its nuances we can see the future written in the past. In no field is this so true as in art, where creation springs from the ability to dig below the immediate rationale to a deep well of accrued instinct and stored wisdom.

There is no art that so closely touches humanity as the art that has created its material environment. We are about to consider its phases. The story discloses much about human practicality, rationality, emotions, and ingenuity.

ARCHITECTURE

Building is one of the creative activities of mankind and architecture is defined as the art or science of building. Certainly both building and architecture are principal examples of environmental art. But what is the difference between the two terms? Surely the variance is something more fundamental than is conveyed in the idea of a long period of specialized training at school or in apprenticeship. History provides the answer to our question.

Primitive societies, when the need arose, learned to build, but they did not markedly develop the science, and especially not the art, of architecture. The reason is obvious. Three interrelated considerations are germane to architecture and these three develop slowly in a culture or indeed in an individual. Planning comes first. By this we mean the judging of spaces and their interrelations with respect to intended uses. Then appropriate construction techniques must be considered. And, while working on these problems, the aesthete will try to visualize the building in order to make it a delight to the senses.

A Roman architect, Vitruvius, during the first century A.D., named these three requirements: *convenience, durability,* and *beauty*—terms that have rung down the centuries as architectural standards. When Vitruvius elaborated the idea of convenience, he had something more in mind than the concept of suitability to overt purpose. For him an edifice needed to incorporate the idea of its purpose. A temple should induce a feeling of reverence; a palace should look as though it were a dwelling of importance. An architectural complex should not only be practically functional (suited to use and durable) it should be expressively so.

INTERIOR DESIGN

The unique business of interior design is to implement architecture by qualifying the spaces for occupancy in the manner intended by a preordained program. For this reason it is not only an anomaly to separate interior design from architecture; it is by definition impossible to do so. Therefore Vitruvius's mandates apply to building design, both inside and out. Materials, structure, spaces, colors, and textures may be slightly different but concepts must mesh. Because of the integrity of architecture, we frequently make no topical distinction in description between the exterior and the interior of buildings. At other times it may seem better to discuss them separately simply because at various historical periods the liaison between the two was not close.

Interior design is part of architectural design and it specifically handles interior furnishings. Anne Lindbergh, in *Locked Rooms and Open Doors,* speaks of her acquisitions, observing that ". . . beautiful possessions like silver, pictures, furniture, were tangible expressions of spiritual values you believed in. In a sense, then, they are creation too."[1] This statement definitely and accurately suggests an expressive value that resides in things quite independent of and beyond their intrinsic worth—a value that Mrs. Lindbergh with her special sensitivity would be the first to recognize. This meaningful factor need not have a high price tag, although history tells us that precious materials and talented artistry and craftsmanship are not cheap. Nor, on reversing the coin, can money guarantee intangible values. In short, furnishings are so integral a part of a larger, more comprehensive architectural setting that in order to ensure a well-tuned, smooth-running piece of environmental machinery all manner of correlations must mesh.

THE DECORATIVE ARTS AND DECORATION

Design, of course, whether one is speaking of it in relation to architecture or to interiors, is not the same thing as decoration, although it may include the latter as an instrument toward effectiveness. Decoration implies something added to an object for the ostensible purpose of augmenting its aesthetic quality. This definition is not meant as condemnation nor as any judgment of the inherent value of ornamentation. One of the most interesting lessons of history is the revelation of how early and in what manner mankind sought to embellish and enrich through decoration. Decoration, however, always remains an addition to something else. Design, on the other hand, is inherent in the relations between parts of a whole. Thus, when the designing sense is focused on creations intended for overt function, it must right-

fully include thought for use. In other words, decoration both in architecture and interiors must consider service.

PEOPLE

There is no way to evade the issue—design in the arts related to our surroundings must consider people and their needs, both obvious and hidden. Therefore the architect or the designer must try to understand man in his current state of culture. This is a tremendous commitment, yet it is amazing how well the leaders have often succeeded in suiting, as it were, the pattern to the cloth. This relationship between a culture and its buildings we shall be talking about. History may tell about buildings and artifacts, but the inferences drawn from them are what concern us. And inferences are about people.

YOU

Each person sees with his own eyes and understands with his own mind. Therefore any talk about people, decoration, interior design, architecture, or history must in the final analysis relate to personal interpretation, which, of course, will be different for every individual. May each of us augment the following pages by means of an ever-enlarging experience and an ever-enriched understanding and judgment.

CHAPTER ONE
America to the Eighteenth-Century

We, greatly commending, and graciously accepting of, their Desires for the Furtherance of so noble a Work, which may, by the Providence of Almighty God, hereafter tend to the Glory of his Divine Majesty, in propagating of Christian Religion to such People as yet live in Darkness and miserable Ignorance of the true knowledge and worship of God, and may in time bring the Infidels and Savages, living in those Parts, to human Civility, and to a settled and quiet Government; Do, by these our Letters Patents, graciously accept of, and agree to, their humble and well intended desires.

From the first Charter of Virginia, April 10, 1606

AMERICA BEFORE 1600

Renaissance Europe during the fifteenth and six-teenth centuries enjoyed an expansive culture. With the progressive breakup of the feudal age and its inward-looking economy, the rivalry be-tween newly consolidated states for wealth and power, and the improved facilities for navigation it is not surprising that the early discoveries of western lands by Christopher Columbus and Amerigo Vespucci in the closing years of the fifteenth century were followed during the next hundred years by a number of daring explora-tions of the newly found continent and of the sea routes to the Far East.

The Spaniards, who by virtue of various de-crees and treaties claimed all land lying 370 leagues west of the Cape Verde Islands,[1] were ambitious to capitalize on this wealth. In 1512 Ponce de Leon landed in Florida. A year later Vasco Nuñez de Balboa discovered the Pacific. By 1522 Magellan had circumnavigated the globe, and in 1519 Hernan Cortez and his conquistadors invaded Mexico and subjected the Aztec Indians. De Sota journeyed up the Mississippi and others forged Spanish possessions from vast tracts in South America. Spanish influence on the new continent was extensive. Her language and cul-ture have predominated in more countries in America than have those of any other European nation.

It was a compatriot of Columbus, however, Giovanni Verrazano (followed soon by Jacques Cartier), who sailed to the New World early in the sixteenth century, commissioned by Francis I. Landing in territory that is now Canada, he claimed it for France. From the St. Lawrence River, French Catholic missionaries and French fur traders penetrated the vast hinterland across the Great Lakes and navigated the Mississippi River.

Whatever aspirations the Valois had for a new world empire, they were countered in the north-east by the English. It was another Italian, John Cabot, sailing from England, who on two succes-sive voyages as early as the last decade of the fif-teenth century skirted the Newfoundland and New England coasts, thus arousing England's in-terest in the wealth of the Americas.

The newcomers had, of course, no apprecia-tion of the culture of the American Indians (Amerindians) and were certainly ignorant of any extinct American civilizations. The Indians whom the sixteenth-century explorers encountered be-longed to tribes and nations that had developed an agricultural subsistence in which hunting and fishing were supplementary. Among groups that were dominantly agrarian, dwellings were perma-nent. They ranged from the large pueblos of Utah, Colorado, Arizona, and New Mexico to the ingenious bark- and grass-covered wigwams (de-rived from an Algonkian word that means house[2]) which extended in size from the oval of 10 to 16 ft to the rectangular council house of 30 to 100 ft. In the north these structures provided shelter from the weather; in the south they were more open to the elements. Each type of habitation was well adapted to the conditions of a neolithic civilization confronted with a particular ecology.

The Indian cultures of Mexico, Yucatan, Central America, and Peru featured outstanding accom-plishments in engineering, art, mathematical sci-ence, and astronomy. The Incas worked bronze, but no Indian group understood the use of iron. Although the potter's wheel was unknown, many tribesmen, especially in the southwest, were skilled ceramists. Before the arrival of the white man, possibly before A.D. 700, the Indians of the southwestern United States had developed a re-markable artistry in basket making. Known today as the "basket makers," they demonstrate the same aesthetic sensitivity that the Indian has shown in his weaving, bark, and leather fabri-cation.

The latter part of the sixteenth century marked the beginning of permanent European settle-ments on the new continent and provided some conjectural landmarks and firsthand accounts of the people the settlers found. The first European colonies were in reality little more than small military outposts built to secure the land, to pro-tect trade routes, and to organize religious com-munities. St. Augustine, Florida, is the oldest. Be-fore its founding the Spaniards had established a foothold on the island of Puerto Rico, the earliest encampment in the New World. King Philip II of Spain ordered the founding of St. Augustine in 1565 because of the threatened encroachment of

Spanish-claimed territory by the French Huguenots at Fort Caroline only a few miles farther north at the mouth of the St. Johns River. In 1586 St. Augustine suffered at the hands of the British sea-rover, Sir Francis Drake, a fate almost as cruel as the extinction it had meted out earlier to the French. The grim circumstances which set nation against nation in the dispute for occupation were not alleviated by the presence of the Franciscan Brothers who had accompanied the Spaniards and had established a convent at St. Augustine or by the fact that the French settlement at Beaufort, South Carolina, had been established as a refuge from persecution in the European religious wars.

One house in St. Augustine claims to be the oldest on soil now owned by the United States. Although the documentation has not been entirely authenticated, it is fairly certain that some of its walls antedate Drake's visit. Part of the present building is believed to have been used by the Franciscan brothers when their nearby convent burned in 1599.

The date 1702, not at all venerable as American houses go, is now positively ascribed to the present Florida house, which incorporates the smaller "oldest house." It stands as an example of the earliest Spanish domestic structure. The plan of the oldest portion was simple, consisting of only two of the present rooms with a wide doorway between and with a smaller entrance from the street. The construction technique consisted of large framing members filled with shell rock formed by the fusion of tiny solidified crustaceans. This is referred to as *coquina*, which was also used to a depth of almost 2 ft for the floors. When cut into sizable blocks, it often served the Spaniards as a structural material.

If Spain acted with more force in the southeast than could an isolated group of French religious refugees or a small crew of roving buccaneers

from Tudor England, the situation along the northern coast was soon balanced in England's favor. In the late sixteen hundreds England harbored many groups who were receptive to the idea of colonization in a new land. Both religious and economic motivation played their part. The latter enticed men to buy land through one of the organized trading companies whose purpose was to capitalize on government patents. From 1578 Sir Humphrey Gilbert and his more famous half-brother Sir Walter Raleigh promoted colonies for England, one of which was the ill-fated "lost colony" of Roanoke, Virginia—the first English band to attempt to build a life in America.

The last colonization of the sixteenth century was Spanish and in the west. In 1598 Onaté, one of Cortez's men who had married a descendent of the Indian chief Montezuma, came with a group of settlers to the pueblo at Santa Fe, New Mexico, under Spanish royal patent. Coronado had preceded him but had left no community. After wide exploration Onaté returned to Santa Fe and on that occasion built the structure that through many vicissitudes has survived as the Palace of the Governors, or the Royal Palace (Figure 1.1). It now houses the New Mexico Museum. Its dates are variously given as 1598 to 1614. Like the St. Augustine house, only a few timbers of the original structure remain. The early form has been retained, however, and it takes much from indigenous adobe in construction and of Spanish political necessity in plan. The details were derived from Spanish and Indian folk building.

To understand the "Palace" as well as the later architecture of the Spanish "missions" of the

Figure 1.1 Palace of the Governors, Santa Fe, New Mexico, built in 1609, rebuilt 1680, restored in the twentieth century. (State of New Mexico Commerce & Industry Department Photo.)

west one needs to become familiar with the living quarters of the southwest Indian. Historically, they progressed from the habitations of the basket makers, who dwelt in organized communities of pit houses, to those of the cliff dwellers who lived in cavern ledges high above the valley floor, to the final stage of the classic pueblo—a type of communal dwelling built on the open plateau. The last dates from A.D. 1000 and reached its paradigm before 1300.

From their inception these dwellings consisted of a series of rooms built (with some use of wood for footing) of local sandstone or adobe brick (a mixture of sun-dried clay and straw formed into building blocks). The exteriors as well as the interiors were often washed smooth with clay. The walls in a classic pueblo extended above the roof, which was a framework of poles, at right angles to which were smaller ones covered with brush and clay. Water was drained by wooden spouts that projected beyond the walls. The underground (in some cases above ground) ceremonial chamber for group activities, known as the *khiva*, was approached, as was the pueblo, by a hatchway on the roof to which the only access was by ladder. With respect to materials and structural system the Governor's Palace duplicated the pueblos. It did, however, have certain Spanish refinements such as wood framing for doors and windows and a wooden portal colonnade with brackets and columns.

The Governor's Palace in political concept was a *presidio*. This is a settlement accompanied by a garrison, as a *mission* is one centered around a church. In later times San Diego, Santa Barbara, Monterey, and San Francisco began as presidios. The presidio building presented a fortress approach to the outside world. Built around an inner court with a well, it housed an arsenal and maintained quarters for the militia. In times of peril it sheltered a civilian population who otherwise dwelt in the surrounding countryside. Nearby there would be a church—at Santa Fe it was S. Miguel, standing today. Because Spanish policy dictated living in peace with the Indians, converting them to Catholicism, and employing their labor, many of these early Spanish buildings were built by Indian hands. Certain naïvetes in their

embellishment as well as vigor in their overall conception can be attributed to these early workmen.

AMERICA—1600–1700

Although the Frenchman Samuel de Champlain is said to have founded the lower riverside town of Quebec in 1608, this early community was in reality little but a trading post. Port Royal, the chief town of the maritime province of Acadia, Canada, was founded in a similar way in 1605. Small French-speaking settlements were established along the Mississippi, and Robert Cavalier, Sieur de La Salle, claimed "all land drained by the river and its tributaries" for Louis XIV. Nevertheless, little was done about colonization until the post of Biloxi was started in 1699, followed in the early years of the eighteenth century by New Orleans to which the seat of the French colonial government was removed. The 1600s had girdled the east, hemming in English and Spanish territory with a French cordon that was not to be completely broken for the rest of the century.

As previously mentioned, the British East India Company was chartered in 1600 for the purpose of trading in the lucrative Oriental market, in which the Dutch and Portuguese, followed by the French, were competitors. James I, persuaded that similar opportunities lay in the New World, granted a charter to two groups of capitalists under which one had the exclusive right to plant colonies south of latitude 38 (about in the position of Wilmington, Delaware) and the other north of 41 (near Norristown, New Jersey). Each might have 100 miles of coast and 100 miles inland. Neither might settle within 100 miles of the other. The ships chartered by the first group, "The Virginia Company of London," landed on Jamestown Island on May 13, 1607, and founded what remained for thirteen years the only English settlement on the Atlantic coast of North America.

The company to which the northern grant was assigned was less successful in making a permanent settlement. It was not until the Mayflower landed at New Plymouth, Massachusetts, in 1620 that the second effectual colonization by the English occurred. This group counted about one-third of its 102 passengers as Puritans, a religious separatist group from the Church of England. Many of them had been living in Holland since 1608 and had decided to come to the New World under English charter.

The only other nation to gain a foothold in America was Holland. In 1609 Henry Hudson, an Englishman in the employ of the Dutch, discovered the river that bears his name and claimed it for his sponsor. Dutch merchants established a trading post on the Indian-named island of Manhate. In 1623 the Dutch West India Company was organized and the first group of settlers was sent over in 1624. To protect the Dutch claims forts were raised along the Hudson as far north as Albany (Beverwyck), site of Fort Orange, and south as far as Fort Nassau. The Dutch New Netherlands encompassed New York, Long Island, New Jersey, and Delaware. Quite naturally its territory did not go uncontested and by 1664 quitclaim was made to the English. Soon after the Dutch town of New Amsterdam was renamed New York, in honor of the Duke of York, King Charles II's brother, and the future James II.

By the end of the century, although Spain had spent vast sums in fortifying her American territory (e.g., Castillo de San Marcos, St. Augustine) and France had autocratically sent out ecclesiastic and civic rulers to govern hers, the new frontier lands favored the progress of those people who had come to western shores in the hope of finding a utopia in which to create an ideal civilization. English colonies based on such aspirations were established along the Atlantic seaboard from New Hampshire to the Carolinas. It is the story of their architectural achievements during this formative or "provincial" period that we now consider.

AMERICAN ARCHITECTURE AND INTERIORS—1600–1700

It is customarily said that the seventeenth century in America was, architecturally speaking, an extension of Medieval Europe. Although this was true because the combination of hostile forces and the necessity for reliance on hand skills preordained stalwart, rough-hewn structures, nevertheless the artifacts of the two eras presented some striking differences. In America regional variations, which were the result of ethnic backgrounds as well as environmental conditions, were conspicuous. Likewise the rapid telescoping of cultural time which occurred during the seventeenth century caused the latest of European styles to appear in conjunction with antiquated tendencies on the same building or in the same locality (e.g., Bacon's Castle, the Adam Thoroughgood house, and the Pennsylvania log houses that coexisted within a small distance of one another).

The fact that the American pioneers were not European peers nor yet wealthy (although many were well born and well educated) gives us our first really good look at European building of the lesser nobility, middle-class merchants, farmers, and professionals.

In *New England,* after the first need for shelter was satisfied, houses of frame construction appeared (Figures 1.2 and 1.3). There is little evidence remaining of any building before 1650, although parts of the Fayerbanks House in Dedham, Massachusetts, and the old house at Cutchogue, Long Island, reputedly antedate the mid-century.

As most of the Puritans came from eastern England, from Lincoln in the north and Surrey and Kent in the south, and many had sojourned in Holland, their building in America reflected the indigenous structures of these districts. Although brick was used for pretentious homes in the east of England, much building was of wood and there is evidence that wood-faced buildings were frequently seen in Holland. London is said to have been a city of wood at the time of the Great Fire.

Given the stands of timber in New England, it is small wonder that the characteristic early house of New England was framed. It was known as a *fayre* house and was essentially similar to European post-and-beam construction. Unlike its European counterpart, it often began with a low cellar, excavated under a portion of the dwelling and frequently reached only by an external hatch-

Figure 1.2 The Parson Capen House, Topsfield, Massachusetts, 1683. (Photograph by Samuel Chamberlain.)

way. Sometimes, however, the cellar entry was placed under the flight of stairs that led to the second story. Although the cellar was unpaved, its walls and the foundations were of fieldstone. As in England, the sill on which the house rested was close to the ground and into the corners of this were tenoned large posts hewn from great oaks and measuring 8 to 10 in. by several more in the direction of the sill. Because land was not a problem, the structure was oriented broadside to the front. In a large house four additional posts, one on each side of the central chimney, were inserted in the front and rear sills to support large beams (known as girts) on the first- and second-floor levels.

Often, as abroad, the second story overhung the first. The first-floor posts then stopped at the second-story projecting girts (which were again large—8½ by 9 in. in the Fayerbanks house). Load-bearing posts were repeated at the second-story level.

A huge ceiling beam, known as the *summer beam* (possibly from the French *sommier*, "to rise"), measured about 9 by 11 in the house under discussion. It was let into the end girt and cross or chimney girt and lodged in place by a strong dovetail joint. The second-floor joists (smaller horizontal members) were framed into the summer beam and the front and rear girts.

6

Because the summer extended down into the room, the ceiling seemed even lower than its full height, which was at best less than 8 ft.

The steep roof was supported in the front and rear by a member smaller than a girt and known as a plate. Large girts were used at the ends of the house. The reason for this difference in size of members was to provide a strong extension to support the overhanging cornice. The roof, braced in a manner similar to the second story, was laid on high-pitched rafters, generally reinforced by collar beams and carrying horizontal purlins. The

Figure 1.3 Framing system, seventeenth-century New England house. (a) rafter; (b) rear corner post; (c) second end girt; (d) second chimney girt; (e) rear plate; (f) attic floor joists; (g) second summer beam; (h) rear girt; (k) front corner post; (m) front plate; (n) front chimney post; (q) first summer beam; (r) second floor joists; (s) sill; (t) cellar girt; (u) front girt; (v) first end girt; (w) first floor joists. (Adapted from J. Frederick Kelley, *Early Domestic Architecture of Connecticut,* Dover, 1952.)

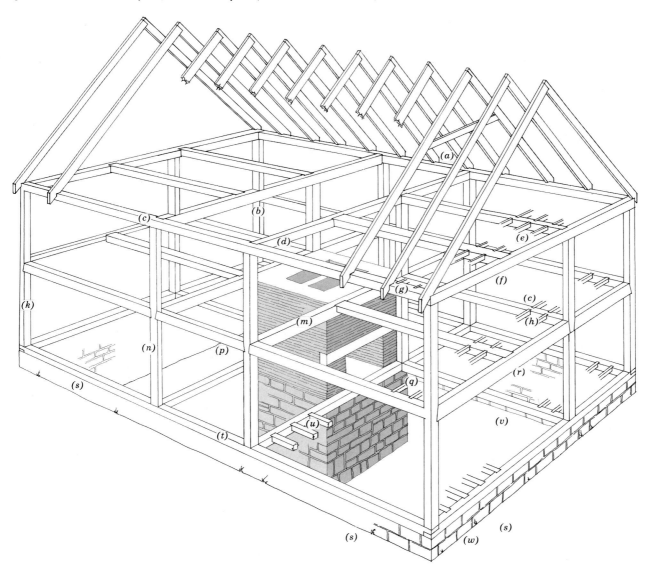

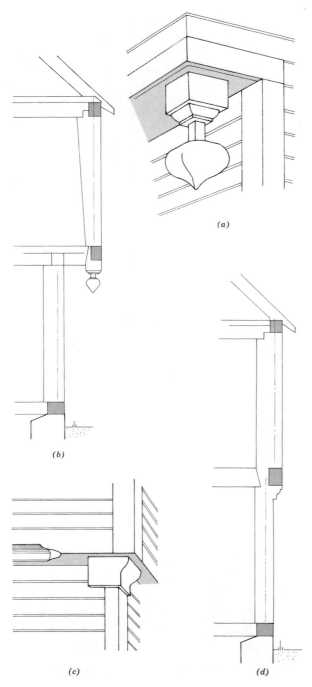

Figure 1.4 Two methods of carving structural bosses for framed overhangs: perspective (a) and section (b) of a boss as a projection downward from a second-story post; perspective (c) and section (d) of a boss hewn integrally with first-story post. (Adapted from J. Frederick Kelley, *Early Domestic Architecture of Connecticut,* Dover, 1952.)

finishing material was thatch or cedar shingles. Rafters were often merely tenoned in place at their upper joints.

This framing system had its minor variations from location to location. It was always sturdy and had its own aesthetic appeal beside which our present wooden structures made with two-by-fours and six-by-twelves seem puny, even though we must concede to them rapidity and ease of construction.

The earliest overhangs in the New England house were formed by inserting the second-floor front girts (Figure 1.4) into the projecting ends of the cross girts. A stout and stable overhang of possibly 2 ft could thus be accomplished. Sculptural bosses were carved from each of the four points where the second-floor posts projected below the transverse girts. Later overhangs were made by hewing back the first-floor posts to narrower dimensions and allowing them to extend to support narrow overhangs. Bosses, when present, had to be reduced proportionately in size. As in the modeled quality of the turnings on furniture, much is lost by later refinement which the practiced eye soon distinguishes.

The American builder used any one of a variety of clay and brush fillings (sometimes known as *cat and daub*) in the space between the supporting timbers. Here the rugged winters dictated an additional outer covering and weatherboarding and clapboarding were used. Weatherboards were white pine boards sawed slightly less than 1 in. thick. They were applied horizontally directly to the studs (smaller upright members) and were made watertight by rabbeting out their lower edges. Later applications were beaded at the joint. Clapboarding was more common than weatherboarding. For this the oak log was "riven" or split much as one would quarter and eighth an apple. The grain was thus of beautifully striped quarter-sawed wood, streaked across with whitish medullary rays. The resulting pieces were no more than half an inch at the widest section and feathered out very thin at the core or narrow edge. They were overlapped with this narrow edge underneath.

Hand-riven shingles were used for roofs and occasionally external walls, the latter being unique to building in America. In Connecticut these shingles were often white pine, although in most localities the customary woods were oak, chestnut, or cedar. Often of considerable length (14 in. to 3 ft), thicker than those in use today and having greater overlap, they provide an interesting rough texture to the few extant examples in New England.

Windows were few. The predominant form was the single or double casement which occasionally operated on strong iron hinges. The individual lights, of slightly elongated diamond shape (about $4\frac{1}{2}$ by $5\frac{3}{4}$ in.)[3] were held in their frames by lead calms (cames or calmes). Some homes, such as the Parson Capen house (Figure 1.2),[4] apparently had small rectangular panes from the beginning. The placement of windows was primarily dictated by comfort and security and the north side was avoided. Second-story windows were tucked up against the plate, and those on the first story were often set in the center of the walls of the front rooms. If hall and chamber were unequal in size, the effect was asymmetrical. Double-hung sashes were not in general use until the eighteenth century, but older houses were frequently given this fashionable dress at a later time. All windows were set close to the exterior wall, thus creating a deep interior reveal.

Seventeenth-century doors were sturdy, either battened or built of two thicknesses of boards placed at right angles. Long strap hinges of hand-forged wrought iron, studded with large flat-topped wrought nails, provided a decorative note. This form was gradually replaced by the butterfly hinge and H and L hinges, the names of which are descriptive. Latch handles are an enjoyable study in themselves because of the great variety of shapes given to them by individual craftsmen. Doors were bolted on the inside. Iron rings sometimes served as knockers and for lifting latches. Door surrounds were at first plain but later in the century, when an occasional nicety in the form of a paneled door appeared, molded architraves were seen.

Few masonry houses were built in New England during the seventeenth century. The Peter Tufts house at Medford, built of brick, came as late as 1677. Scarcity of lime is offered as the reason for the popularity of wood. There was the

idea, still found in provincial mores, that masonry was cold, damp, and unhealthy, which, if not properly structured it may well be. Only in Albany, where Dutch tradition and available building materials met to sanction stone and brick buildings, are they numerous. In Rhode Island and on the adjacent Connecticut shore lime from shells was more accessible, and masonry houses, such as the Whitfield house at Guilford (which was in reality an important community meeting house), were soon built. Hybrids sometimes occurred, however. The Morris house (1670) in New Haven incorporates stone ends with great fireplaces in the end walls in a homestead otherwise constructed of framing.

The usual (exceptions can be found to the following descriptions) New England plan (Figure 1.5) was rectangular, at first a single room with a

Figure 1.5 Progressive changes in plan of a seventeenth-century New England house: (a) one room with entrance porch and hall; (b) two rooms—a smaller parlor has been added; (c) further expansion with the addition of a lean-to containing a pantry, a kitchen, and a bedroom. (Adapted from Hugh Morrison, *Early American Architecture*, Oxford University Press, 1952.)

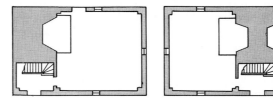

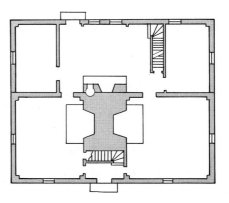

chimney. As opportunity provided, it was enlarged by a slightly smaller room which fitted its fireplace masonry in reverse. The first room was variously known as the hall, keeping room, or sometimes the kitchen. The second room, which contained the large bedstead, was designated as a chamber or, in the more advanced terminology then in vogue in the homeland, the parlor. When a full-height second floor was added, the rooms duplicated the first-floor arrangement and were invariably called chambers. This terminology was faithfully preserved, in some instances to the present. One early commentary on the home of the Philip Schuylers in Albany reads:

> One room, I should have said, in the greater house only was opened for the reception of company; all the rest were bedchambers for their accommodation; the domestic friends of the family occupying neat little bedrooms in the attics or in the Winterhouse.[5]

Bedrooms had room only for a bed.

The salt box shape so characteristic of old New England houses derives from the extension or lean-to on the back which reached in unbroken line from the rear roof. The present generation may not remember the form of the old salt cannister which had a slanting hinged lid extended from the main portion of the box for easy access.

Figure 1.6 Parlor of the Parson Capen House, Topsfield, Massachusetts, 1683. (Photograph by Samuel Chamberlain.) *P. Capen 1798* is carved in the back crest rail of the chair in foreground.

The lean-to, often a later addition, was customarily divided into three rooms: a large center room or kitchen with a fireplace opening into the central stack, a small bedroom behind the chamber, and a room auxiliary to the kitchen designated as a pantry or buttery. Custom often speaks of a small, somewhat isolated bedroom reserved for birth or illness to facilitate care. In such a room in John Alden's home in Duxbury both he and Priscilla are said to have died.

The stairway was situated in an enclosed space or porch which extended from the chimney and between the chimney girts to the front of the house. It began with a step and winders in the hall end of the space and ascended along the wall by a flight of steep steps until the second series of winders brought it to a position on the second floor at the opposite end of the porch. Occasionally the porch space projected from the front plane of the house and a porch chamber occupied the second-floor level, in which case the two-story enclosure has a gable roof at right angles to the main axis. Gables so placed were designated as *lucomes* and the dormer window assumed the same name. Presumably the word derives from the French *lucarne* (a small roof opening).

Pretentious homes soon discarded the lean-to in favor of a second story. As the stories tended toward duplication of space allotment, the result was a ten-room plan. It can be seen that with more rooms communication routes become a problem; rear space was accessible only by invasion of the privacy of the front. Hence rear

stairs were often added. Eventually this paved the way for the greater formality and convenience of the central hallway.

It is logical to describe the interiors of these seventeenth-century New England houses in the same breath as the exteriors because in materials, construction, and feeling they were of a piece (Figure 1.6). The earliest floors were made of 10- to 20-in. oak boarding laid at right angles to the joists. White pine came gradually into favor and was consistently found in bed chambers where its greater softness was an advantage. The first floor was laid with a subfloor but the upper ones had none. The floorboards were secured by decorative flat-topped hand-wrought nails or, on occasion, by wooden dowels.

Interior walls were clay daubed or lime plastered on wood laths. Pine sheathing was resorted to when lime was unavailable and often ran in random widths in a vertical direction on the front wall and horizontal on the inner ones. The simplest ceiling treatment left the joists and boards of the second floor clearly visible. Before a later vogue for enclosing the structure with a false ceiling of plaster was introduced girts and summers were left exposed or sometimes boxed in. They were often painted or given decorative treatment with carved chamfers.

Stairways were first boarded into a compartment (Figure 1.7), but soon well-turned balusters of short lengths began rising from a boxed stringer (Figure 1.8).

The earliest fireplace had no mantel; its place was taken by a large beam set flush with the masonry. The opening, at first solely of stone and later lined with refractory brick, was carefully shaped for efficiency and appearance.

On a projecting inner ledge, about 6 ft from the floor, rested a bar known as a *lug*, which was customarily made of green wood and subsequently of iron. Chains with hooks, called *trammels* or *pot hangers*, were suspended from it. The iron swinging crane, a Yankee invention, appeared a century after the first settlement, and a brick oven was set in the masonry at the side of the hearth. This operated on the principle of a fireless cooker, being heated with wood embers that were then removed for the long, slow baking process.

Figure 1.7 Staircase from the Samuel Wentworth House, Portsmouth, New Hampshire, 1671. Metropolitan Museum of Art, New York. (The Metropolitan Museum of Art.)

Figure 1.8 Staircase, ca. 1710, from the Samuel Wentworth House, Portsmouth, New Hampshire. House built in 1671, remodeled in 1710. Metropolitan Museum of Art, New York. (The Metropolitan Museum of Art.)

Holland held her extensive American territories in patroonships in which smaller plots were sub-let leaseholds. Likewise certain lands were directly assigned under freeholds which tended to become more quickly settled because of the incentive that land ownership provided. Dutch influence spread from Albany County in the north to Fort Nassau on the Delaware River, opposite Philadelphia. In Westchester County English prestige infiltrated from Connecticut and west of the Hudson, in Bergen County, New Jersey, as well as in Ulster County, New York, Flemish Huguenots bought land and left their mark.

After 1664 patroonships became English manors, often with no switch of governors, as exemplified by Kiliaen van Rensselaer, the third patroon of Rensselaerswyck. The result was a certain ingrown provincialism. In the freeholds, on the other hand, the communities attracted settlers from virtually all parts of northern Europe. This, in truth, became the melting pot of the New World. Father Jogues, a Jesuit priest from Canada, wrote in 1643:

> On this island of Manhate and its environs, there may well be four hundred men of different sects and nations; the Director General told me that there were men of eighteen kinds of languages; they were scattered here and there on the river, above and below, as the beauty and convenience of the spot invited them to settle.[6]

In Manhate no house that predated the English occupation survives. For source material one must have recourse to written description or look for etchings and drawings made at a later date. In the first category we read that Governor Andros, reporting to the Committee of Lords of the Colonies in 1678, said that New York contained three hundred and forty-three houses, with ten inhabitants to each, "most wood, some, lately, stone and brick."[7] Madame Knight, who described the city near the close of the century, says, "The buildings are brick, generally, in some cases of divers colors, and laid in cheques, being glazed they look very well."[8]

Etchings made by Samuel Hollyer in a series entitled, "Old New York Views" (New York Historical Society), all of which borrowed from old guide books of the early eighteenth century, record New York as it may have looked within the memory of men then living. We see brick houses with high, steep gables generally turned toward the street. They have pantile roofs. Pantiles were 13 by 8 in. hollow tiles with attached knobs for hanging over the laths. It is evident that the masonry tradition had been accepted.

Albany was the next freehold Dutch town of importance. Prints of similar brick-gabled houses of the seventeenth century exist (e.g., those of Domine Schaets and the house in which Philip Schuyler was born[9]). As in the English colonies, the surfeit of land often allowed the broad side to be placed parallel to the street. As the eighteenth century approached, the colonial Dutch house lost some of its typical native features, such as the high-pitched roof. Thus it made a smooth transition to the Georgian style of the eighteenth century, which in turn was indebted to the styles of Holland.

The earliest remaining Dutch houses of rural nature were built of local fieldstone, which was available in all the counties bordering the Hudson and Mohawk Rivers, at least as far west as Schenectady. Lime was secured from the ridges along the parent river. Stone building persists in these areas today, although greater precision in cutting the blocks is noticeable as time progresses. Brick making was an early industry along the Hudson, especially at Rensselaerswyck, the patroonship across from Albany. Brick buildings appeared sooner in the towns.

The Dutch house in America was also a simple rectangle. The early ones had large gables with unbroken slants to a low wall line. In most, especially around Albany, the roof was steep pitched, but it was lower and broader where Huguenot buildings penetrated. Steep roofs are to be seen on the Mabie (Figure 1.9), Hendrick Bries (Breese), and Peter Bronck houses.

The tiniest of dormers, often with one-slant roofs, open like little eye blinkers from side roofs. Early windows which were conspicuously few, had leaded casements. The Dutch still favored wooden-framed casements at a time when the English colonists had advanced to double-hung sash.

The Dutch door is also associated with these

Figure 1.9 The Mabie (or Van Antwerp-Mebie) House, Rotterdam Junction, New York, built before 1700. The enclosed porch is a later addition. (G. C. Ball.)

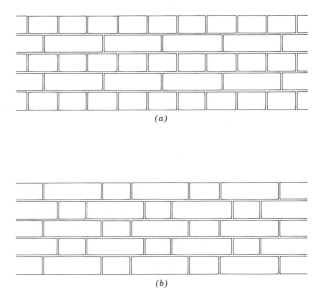

Figure 1.10 Types of brick bonding: (a) English; (b) Dutch or Flemish.

houses, although as a Medieval European transplant it is found as well in rural Pennsylvania. Set on the inner face of thick stone walls, it provided a sheltered entrance that recommended itself to practicality as well as for its play of light and shadow. Such a door can be seen at the Peter Bronck house.

Dutch brickwork differed from English in several ways. In the first place Dutch bricks are smaller, 1½ by 3 by 7 in. The header bricks were frequently fortuitously glazed because they were nearest the fire (head in) in the kiln. This glazing had a lovely bluish-gray color attributed to the saltpeter in the clay, which took on a luster in the intense heat of the oak fires.[10] The Dutch, unlike the English, did not use the elaboration of brick moldings, nor did they resort to embellishment by rubbing. Bonding, when done according to Dutch tradition, is cross bonding, sometimes known as Flemish bonding (Figure 1.10). It has alternate headers and stretchers in every course aligned so that in every other row a header would repeat its position. This created an interesting diamond pattern which is especially lovely when headers are glazed. Flemish bond can be seen in the Breese home, whereas Fort Crailo nearby is in English bond (Figure 1.10). English

bond is made with alternate rows of headers and stretchers. After 1700 many buildings in the Dutch territory and farther south used the English bonding for the foundations but resorted to the more interesting Flemish-Dutch patterning above the water table.

One essentially Dutch characteristic in brickwork was the treatment of the high gable in which coping bricks were placed at right angles to the edge. Not terminating on a straight line, a better seal was secured. The pattern formed is known as *mouse teeth*, or *muisentanden* (Figure 1.11). It can be seen on the gable of the Leonard Bronck house at West Coxsackie and it makes an interesting note on the gables of the modern administrative buildings at the west approach to the Rip Van Winkle Bridge over the Hudson.

The story that bricks for early American building came as ballast from abroad has largely been dispelled,[11] although it is likely that some may have been brought over in this manner because bricks represented a salable product. The number, however, could only have been meager in relation to the requirements. The designation of Dutch or English brick undoubtedly refers to size rather than to origin.

Dutch brick building technique often required iron tie rods or wall anchors to provide rigidity. These rods can be seen at Fort Crailo and the Leonard Bronck house. Portholes in the gables or walls are frequent and might indeed have been a matter of defense, although inner wall ventilation would also have been served. Gutters on Dutch houses, like those on German, were of wood and were used along the long wall. Extending quite a distance beyond the gables, the passerby had a precarious time in the event of a deluge.

In the interior the Dutch framing system differed from the English. In place of girder, joist, and flooring the Hollanders used heavy beams (varying from 7 by 12 to 16 by 20 in.) across an internal space, on top of which the upper floor was directly laid.[12] As the beams might be as much as 4 ft on centers, the flooring had to be wide thick planks. Heavy wooden brackets were the transitional support between beams and wall posts. The intervening spaces were filled with any suitable material and the wall was then concealed by vertical board sheathing, frequently with the

14

Figure 1.11 North wall of the Leendert (Leonard) Bronck House, West Coxsackie, New York, 1738. Brick, English bond, with iron wall anchors. Under the shallow eaves the bricks are laid in patterns known as *muisentanden*. (G. C. Ball.)

visible brackets painted white. Often the interiors were more simply treated with plaster, as in the Mabie house.

The plan of Dutch houses was unique, although certain details were shared by the dwellings of the French Huguenots. One room was the nucleus, as in the Peter Bronck house. It was then increased to two equal-sized rooms, a plan shared by the French in this part of the country. The upper story, easily tucked away in the gable, was reached by stairs that were narrow and steep, often no more than a ladder, located in the main room. In the Bronck and Mabie homes they are adjacent to the original front doors. The fireplace and chimney were on an external wall, flanking the entrance wall. This arrangement, however, was not universal, and in the Jan Martense

Figure 1.12 The north room in the Jan Martense Schenck House, Brooklyn, New York, ca. 1675. Reconstructed in the Brooklyn Museum. (The Brooklyn Museum.)

Schenck house (Figure 1.12; built in New Amersfort, Jamaica Bay, dismantled, and now in the Brooklyn Museum) and in the houses at New Paltz of a later date it is central to two rooms.

According to continental custom, the principal beds were enclosed in a *bed place,* whereas additional sleeping space, as well as room for auxiliary services such as drying flax, herbs, or clothes, was a function of the loft. In urban structures in the New World, as in the old, the garret might have been used as a warehouse and external pulleys carried goods through a large door in the gable.

Further discussion of building in Ulster County, New York, below Kingston, and in Bergen County in northern New Jersey must take into account the regional architecture of the French, who took out freehold patents as early as 1677. The New Jersey houses of these settlers are particularly lovely for their use of the local brown sandstone with muted yellow jointings. The French fre-

quently strung their equal-sized rooms along in a row and gave each a separate front door. The roof pitch was low, which may account for the broader, lower gables seen on Dutch homes in the Catskill valleys. In the French houses, such as that of Cosyn Haring, the slight extension of the roof evolves into the graceful sweep customarily termed Dutch colonial but which probably owes more to the Gallic style. On the other hand, the boarding of the gable ends above the wall line seen in French houses may have been borrowed from the Dutch.

It is interesting to note that the French "po-teaux-en-terre" construction (i.e., palisading with logs in an upright position), which is observed in the first home of Daniel des Marest west of Hack-ensack, was soon abandoned and is seen only in the French settlements in Canada and along the Mississippi.

In its interior a provincial Dutch house resembled a painting by Vermeer. Beams, left natural or colored, stood out strongly against the white-washed walls and brackets. The broad-planked floors were often painted in alternating light and dark lozenges to simulate the marble tiles of the affluent burghers of the homeland.

One interior feature was the large, hooded, open fireplace which projected into the room. Its ample mantel was placed near the ceiling to avoid (hopefully) danger from fire but low enough to allow the housewife to display on it whatever pottery or metal she might possess. A ruffled flounce traditionally hung from its edge; a surround of Dutch tiles and a fireback were decorative touches. Soon, however, in the smaller rooms the open hearth was enclosed and the flanking wall spaces were then taken up with cupboards.

Whereas the Hudson River guarded lower New York and upper New Jersey, it was the Delaware that opened the gates to *southern New Jersey, Delaware, and eastern Pennsylvania* which had harbored Swedish forts and Baltic traders since 1638 and an infiltration of Dutch who overran the garrisons in 1655. Finally, after transference to the English in 1664, the land was divided into eastern and western sections, which were subsequently allotted to crown favorites. In 1681 William Penn received a grant to the western section

and opened the property to people of all faiths: Quakers from England and Germany, Rhineland Germans, Welsh, and Scotch Irish from Northern Ireland were among them. Soon civilization pushed west to the Schuylkill and beyond the Susquehanna to central Pennsylvania and the foothills of the Alleghenies.

We retrace our steps to the first builders, the Swedes, who not only introduced their native log construction but also favored a plan that William Penn recognized as advantageous to the small pioneer builder. It has been dubbed the *Quaker plan* (Figure 1.13).[13]

At home in Sweden these people peeled large logs and round-notched them so that they might support others, cob-stacked—their ends protruding from the building. Later they split the logs or squared their sections to give the corners some sort of mitered or rabbeted joint. All forms were used in America and construction without benefit of nails became habitual among the westward-moving pioneers. The original log houses were raised directly on leveled land. In New England garrison houses were built in this manner as early as the mid-seventeenth century, but whether the idea developed from necessity, whether it was copied from the forts of the British army, or whether it was borrowed from Swedish immigrants is not known.

Swedish log houses had gabled roofs. Above the plate which held the rafters they were clap-

Figure 1.13 The Swedish two-room plan which William Penn advocated for use by the Quakers. (Adapted from THE DWELLINGS OF COLONIAL AMERICA, by Thomas Tileston Waterman, Copyright 1950 The University of North Carolina Press. Reprinted by permission of the publisher.)

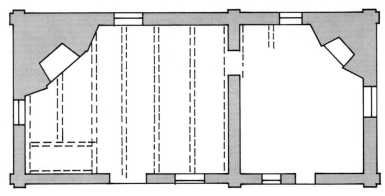

17

boarded on the gabled end, and joists were laid across the plate for ceilings and floors. An excellent example of Swedish log building is the Morton homestead in Prospect Park, Delaware County, Pennsylvania, the first part of which was built in 1654; another section, connected now by stone to the first, dates from 1698. The craftsmanship in a house of this sort was so perfect that no chinking was required for the oak and chestnut timbers.

The characteristic plan of the simplest Swedish house constituted one room with a corner fireplace, sometimes on a diagonal, sometimes along one wall. In Sweden this room was known as a *stuga*. It was later enlarged by the addition of a narrow passage in which the outer door was placed to protect the inner door from drafts. This *gang* was located along the fireplace wall. Often the gang was divided to provide a small inner space that could have several uses. The Swedes, like the Dutch, had built-in sleeping quarters and added a built-in table for good measure. Thus some ideas which seem so modern today were not the invention of the twentieth century.

This plan of stuga and gang was one that paternal landlord William Penn recommended to all

> Freemen, Planters, and Adventurers, and other inhabitants of the Province and Territories . . . build then a house of thirty foot long and eighteen broad, with a partition near the middle, and another to divide one end of the house into two small rooms.[14]

We find it wherever the Quakers went, sometimes as far west as the western part of Virginia and as far south as the Carolinas. We shall meet modifications of this plan frequently in the Philadelphia area; for example, Graeme Park in Horsham, Pennsylvania, which Sir William Keith, Secretary to the Province, built in 1722, has a space division of two stugas joined by a divided gang. The rear chamber has a corner fireplace.

When Penn decided to build his city on the site of an old Swedish settlement, he had the foresight to lay it out in a regular grid, in essence the plan made by Sir Christopher Wren (with whom, incidentally, Penn had been a student at Christ College, Oxford) after the London fire of '66. Thus Philadelphia became the first location in America to echo and keep pace with the foremost thought on English city planning. The gap across the ocean was shortening.

Penn's own home, Pennsbury, now seen only in restoration, is an architectural form abreast of seventeenth-century English building and foreshadowing the eighteenth century. It has a bisymmetrical brick facade and a hipped roof, not unlike Groombridge. Its rear elevation, however, presented the clapboarded, asymmetrical aspect of earlier buildings. As homesteads of this nature advanced along the Schuylkill and farther west into German country, local fieldstone took the place of manufactured brick and gave to this section of the new land another of its idioms.

In Philadelphia Penn had envisaged a community in which each landowner would have a home with a pleasant yard and garden in true English fashion. We have no authenticated example of Philadelphia houses of the seventeenth century. The first of the remaining buildings of the early eighteenth were erected when the phenomenal growth of the city had already necessitated the order (1687) by the Provincial Council that all inadequate habitations be torn down and replaced by others more suitable. This was probably our first instance of slum clearance by fiat, and it seems to have been couched in terms similar to today's, which took no great concern for the persons affected.

By 1720 the city population had reached 10,000, land values had skyrocketed, and the familiar row houses seen in most eastern cities had appeared. Penn had recommended that they be built of brick to escape danger of fire. Their plan was related to the London type, used in the extensive rebuilding after the fire. It may be visualized by the Letitia Street house (Figure 1.14),[15] now in Fairmount Park but originally and more suitably in a corner situation on a downtown street. Its name derived from that of Penn's daughter. The plan is two rooms deep, with one unbroken wall space, thus readily adaptable to common party walls. Certainly the bisymmetrical placement of its front windows, with double-hung sashes and flat segmental arches, as well as the paneled shutters, door, and bracketed porch roof, are indicative of the progress of Philadelphia architecture.

Figure 1.14 The Letitia Street House, Philadelphia, Pennsylvania, ca. 1683. Moved to Fairmount Park and restored in 1883. (Owned by the Fairmount Park Commission, City of Philadelphia; Photographed by the Philadelphia Museum of Art.)

One feature found in houses of the Penn settlement, seen in drawings of contemporary London and likewise often noted in Germany is the pent roof. This is a heavy shed overhang which may be repeated at each story or used alone over the doorway. The heavy wooden coved cornice is likewise one of the features that gives solidarity to the Delaware and Pennsylvania houses—again probably German in origin but serving as a unique expression of the architecture of the area.

Because no authenticated seventeenth-century interiors remain, we can but assume that they retained the characteristics of heavy beams, corner fireplaces, stairs winding up in a corner—indeed all of these are in the Letitia house. The basic feeling of sturdiness and weight remained in the homes of the German pioneers of the next century, vanishing only under the advance of the Georgian.

Moving farther south, we come to *tidewater Maryland and Virginia,* washed by the large inlets of the Chesapeake Bay which drains the Susquehanna, Potomac, Rappahannock, York, and James. Farther south the shores of the Carolinas are less navigable, indented by numerous small estuaries without substantial or safe harbors, until the tidal waters of the Cooper and Ashley Rivers join in

South Carolina at the site of the city of Charleston. Georgia in the seventeenth century might be described as a no-man's land or baffle area left uncontested by the Spaniards and English alike.

Maryland, on the upper Chesapeake, was founded by Lord Baltimore in 1632 as a refuge for Englishmen of the Roman Catholic faith. Adjacent Virginia land was bought under the aegis of proprietary companies and became a crown colony in 1624. South of this lay territory that had been granted preemptorily by Charles I to a favorite, Sir Robert Heath. In 1660 his son capitalized on this practice and purported to grant courtly titles in return for purchase and settlement; but the *Baronies, Landgraves,* and *Cassiques* of the New World were destined not to endure. Settlement, however, did flourish in and around the mouth of the twin rivers at Charleston. Englishmen of the state church, Quakers who were now unwelcome in their Maryland sanctuary and who pushed south through the Piedmont (i.e., the freshwater drainage of the southern rivers), Huguenots, fugitives from France, Scottish dissenters, and some Dutch importers made up a polyglot population.

The establishment of the first permanent English settlement at Jamestown in 1607 is well known, yet we can only imagine the buildings of this little band as it first faced the wilderness. According to the report of John Smith, one-time president of the provincial council, the first structures corresponded to those of all pioneers under similar conditions. These first homes were destroyed by fire and the entire town, as well as a neighboring one called Henrico, was razed in an Indian massacre in 1622. Jamestown did make a comeback, and it was probably the subsequent rebuilding that was unearthed in 1934 by the National Park Service.[16]

The brick foundations of six row houses were located in the excavation, but their upper stories may have been framed. Ralph Hamer, secretary of the colony, wrote of "Two faire rows" of houses built between 1611 and 1615 and mentions that they were "all of framed timber, two storeys and an upper garrett, or corne loft, high."[17] The excavated foundations show plans two rooms deep to a floor. The reason for the building with common party walls is conjectural.

However, the truth probably is that they were more economical, as well as safer, and that the majority of the settlers, who came from London and vicinity, were accustomed to consider the row house as the norm for city building.

As fate would be perverse, it was as farmers and not as cosmopolites that the Virginians were to succeed, especially after the introduction of tobacco growing around 1613. Thus, although Jamestown was soon deserted for the new capital at Williamsburg, there are Virginia plantations dating from the seventeenth century to be found in Princess Anne County across the bay from Norfolk and Newport News. Even so erudite a historian as Fiske Kimball doubted that any of these antedated 1650, but because careful research has authenticated the date of St. Luke's Church in Smithfield as 1632 some skepticism has been removed. The brick dwelling of Adam Thoroughgood (Figure 1.15) and the framed Brinson house are among the oldest.

The simplest of these tidewater examples, both in Virginia and Maryland, had the customary one-room plan (Figure 1.16) with a chimney on the outside of the end wall. When the plan was enlarged to two rooms (Figure 1.16), chimneys were placed on the outside of the two end walls, a scheme adopted because of the need to dissipate rather than conserve the heat of the South. These chimneys were broad at the base but receded by stepped tiers to smaller dimensions. Ceilings even in early southern homes were customarily higher than in the north.

Like most English plans, the two rooms were rarely the same size but assumed the relation of Medieval hall and chamber. In small houses, especially in Maryland, the stairs in a two-story house were sometimes placed adjacent to the chimney in the major room. In Virginia and Carolina they were more frequently found on the opposite wall. The next step was to create a passageway between the two rooms and to place the stairs there or in actuality to create a corridor to enclose the stairs. In a few instances a lean-to was built at the rear of a small house, but in general an extension in the form of an L or a T was preferred—again for reasons of better ventilation.

In the Rolfe house near Smithfield it is surprising to find classic bisymmetry in placement of

Figure 1.15 Doorway of the Adam Thoroughgood House, Princess Anne County, Virginia, last half of the seventeenth century. Brick, Flemish bond. (G. C. Ball.)

their rebellion against the royal governor on the allegation that he had neglected their frontier defense. Bacon's Castle is of brick, with a tall steep-gabled roof, and planned with the familiar English hall and chamber arrangement. The diagonally stacked chimneys are Medieval. The ends have the step and circular gable, and the tall, very narrow windows look backward in time. Quite medieval in style is the enclosed porch and stair tower, which projected from the center of the long axis. Some of these early characteristics have been modified over the years. Similar Jacobean houses are to be found in Barbadoes and

Figure 1.16 (a) One-room plan and (b) two-room plan as used in Tidewater, Virginia. (Adapted from THE DWELLINGS OF COLONIAL AMERICA, by Thomas Tileston Waterman, Copyright 1950 The University of North Carolina Press. Reprinted by permission of the publisher.)

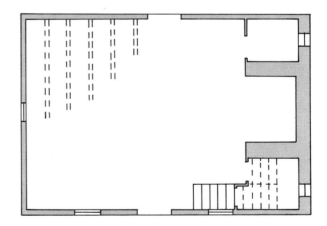

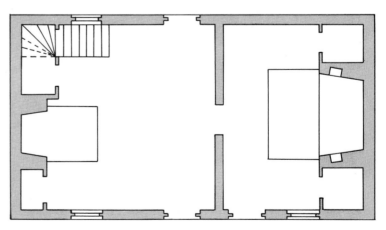

windows and doors. At the Thoroughgood a dentil cornice indicates that classical features were introduced here almost as soon as they were in the work of Inigo Jones.

The larger mansions of Virginia and the Carolinas reflect more of the major English Jacobean. Bacon's Castle (Figure 1.17), in Surry County on the south side of the James is one of the most important remaining examples in this category. It acquired its present name because it was used in 1666 as an arsenal by Nathaniel Bacon's men in

Bermuda, where early settlers engaged in the slave trade.

In construction many of the tidewater houses were framed and possibly weatherboarded without benefit of fill between the posts. The floors were supported by the lighter beam system and the interiors were probably pine sheathed. However, brick put in an early appearance, as shown in the Thoroughgood house and Bacon's castle. The characteristic bond was English, although one wall of Thoroughgood is Flemish.

Few relics of the seventeenth century remain in and around Charleston. The city itself was burned in 1740 and most of its wooden buildings were destroyed. Later houses, which preserved the old forms, remain and, as at Medway plantation, built by Jan van Arrsens near Charleston, indicate the presence of the Quaker plan in this region at that time. Another space arrangement is known as the French Huguenot plan. In two front rooms of uneven size the entrance was directly into the larger. At the rear was a stair hall flanked by two small spaces. This is a southern extension of the northern French plan of two rooms with an entrance to each.

The presidio of the Spanish southwest and a community building such as the Whitfield house at Guilford, Connecticut, remind us that under pioneer conditions the uses to which buildings were put were often not specialized. It is a constant source of amazement, nonetheless, to realize the antiquity of some uniquely functional structures such as *churches, civic centers,* and even *schools.*

In Hingham, Massachusetts, the "Old Ship" Meeting House (i.e., church) was begun in 1681 (Figure 1.18). Decrying elaborate ritual, the congregation built a simple cube structure in which the wooden seats were oriented toward the pulpit at the end opposite the door. This particular Palladian proportion was perpetuated in America in many civic buildings of four-square directness. With the addition of a pyramidal roof and the annexation of cupolas and spires, we recognize it in innumerable later county court houses and crossroad churches.

In Wilmington, Delaware, the "Old Swedes" Holy Trinity Church was begun in 1698. In Philadelphia, the "Gloria Dei," belonging to the Swedish Lutherans, was started in the same year.

In Virginia the almost incredibly early date of 1632 attributed to St. Luke's Church in Smithfield, with its brick Gothic architecture and its interior showing Jacobean forms, indicates that Englishmen wished to translate their old surroundings to their new homes as soon as feasible. Harvard will not forget that it was founded in 1636, nor William and Mary in 1694.

SOME PROVINCIAL AMERICAN HOUSES

NEW ENGLAND

Fayerbanks House	Dedham, Massachusetts	1636
Henry Whitfield House	Guilford, Connecticut	1639
"Scotch" Boardman House	Saugus, Massachusetts	1651
Pickering House	Salem, Massachusetts	1651
John Alden House	Duxbury, Massachusetts	1653
Stanley-Whitman House	Farmington, Connecticut	1660
Thomas Lee House	East Lyme, Connecticut	1664
Whipple House	Ipswich, Massachusetts	1669
Morris House	Near New Haven, Connecticut	1670
Samuel Wentworth House (Figures 1.7, 1.8, and 1.22)	Portsmouth, New Hampshire	1671 and 1710
Paul Revere House	Boston, Massachusetts	Before 1675
Jonathan Corwin "Witch House"	Salem, Massachusetts	1675

Figure 1.17　Gable end of Bacon's Castle, Surry County, Virginia, ca. 1650–1676. Brick, English bond. (Courtesy of the Association for the Preservation of Virginia Antiquities; photograph, G. C. Ball.)

SOME PROVINCIAL AMERICAN HOUSES (continued)

Peter Tufts House	Medford, Massachusetts	1677
Turner Ingersoll House or *House of the Seven Gables*	Salem, Massachusetts	1680
Parson Capen House (Figures 1.2 and 1.6)	Topsfield, Massachusetts	1683
Frary House	Deerfield, Massachusetts	1685
Buttolph Williams House	Wetherfield, Connecticut	1692

NEW YORK AND EASTERN NEW JERSEY

John Budd House	Southold, Long Island; moved to Cutchogue, Long Island	1649 1660
Peter Bronck House	Coxsackie, New York	1663–1685
Mabie House (Figure 1.9)	Rotterdam, New York	Before 1700
Des Marest House	Bergen County, New Jersey	1686
Fort Crailo	Greenbush, New York	1704
Haring House	Bergen County, New Jersey	1704
Breese House (second)	East Greenbush, New York	1722

PENNSYLVANIA AND DELAWARE

Upper and Lower Log House	Darby, Pennsylvania	1640
John Morton House	Prospect Park, Delaware County, Pennsylvania	1654 and 1698
Letitia Street House (Figure 1.14)	Fairmont Park, Philadelphia	1683
Brinton House	West Chester, Pennsylvania	1704

EASTERN MARYLAND AND TIDEWATER VIRGINIA

Lower course of Jamestowne houses	Jamestowne, Virginia	1640
Rolfe House (part restoration)	Surry County, Virginia	1651
Brinson House	Princess Anne County, Virginia	Last half of seventeenth century
Bacon's Castle (Figure 1.17)	Surry County, Virginia	1650–1676
Make Peace	Somerset County, Maryland	1663
Adam Thoroughgood House (Figure 1.15)	Princess Anne County, Virginia	Last half of seventeenth century

SOUTHEAST

Oldest House	St. Augustine, Florida	Before 1599
Medway Plantation	Mount Holly, South Carolina	1686

SOUTHWEST

Palace of the Governors (Figure 1.1)	Santa Fe, New Mexico	Built in 1609; rebuilt after 1680
San Estevan Mission	Acoma, New Mexico	1629–1642

Figure 1.18 Old Ship Meeting House (First Unitarian Church), Hingham, Massachusetts, built in 1681, subsequently enlarged and altered. (Historic American Buildings, Survey, Dorothy Abbe, Photographer.)

25

FURNITURE

General Development

By American furniture we mean furniture made in America. The question then is: which pieces found here answer this description, for undoubtedly many were imported. English colonial policy was based on advancing English home industry through consumption by a colonial market.

That the southern colonies were dutifully obliging may be inferred from the following quotation dated in the year 1633:

> . . . in neither of these provinces [i.e., Maryland or Virginia] are there yet any towns of considerable bulk or importance. For all the greater planters have generally storehouses within themselves for all kinds of necessaries brought from Great Britain; not only for their own consumption, but likewise for supplying the lesser planters and their servants etc. And while this kind of economy continues, there can be no prospect of towns becoming considerable in either province. Which is so far a benefit to their mother country that they must continue to be supplied from Britain with cloathing, furniture, tools, delicacies etc.[18]

That just one hundred years later the New Englanders were taking matters into their own hands is indicated in an account that the British Commissioners for Trade and Plantations laid before Parliament, January 23, 1733. Major Gooch, Lieutenant Governor of Virginia, had informed that

> . . . the people of New England, being obliged to apply themselves to manufactures more than others of the plantations, who have the Benefit of a better Soil and warmer Climate, such improvements have been lately made there is all Sorts of Mechanic Arts, that not only Scrutores, Chairs, and other wooden Manufactures, but Hoes, Axes, and other Iron Utensils are now exported from thence to the Plantations, which, if not prevented, may be of ill consequence to the Trade and Manufactures of this Kingdom, which Evil may be worthy of the consideration of the British Parliament.[19]

Because British export records do not antedate 1697, no accurate statistics that would relate American to British manufacture can be supplied for the seventeenth century. Claims to the former must be limited to observation of the remaining pieces that bear some guarantee of manufacture in New England.

The student of American furniture history is likewise confronted with the second problem of determining what furniture came with the settlers from the mother country. Conjecturally, chests to take the place of packing cases would have been the most obvious baggage and during the first lean months would have been useful as chairs, tables, and even beds.

Only one piece, the wicker cradle now in Pilgrim Hall, Plymouth, brought over for Peregrine White, who was born to William and Susannah White on the voyage across the ocean, can be positively authenticated as having arrived on the *Mayflower*. This cradle may have been made in Holland. A chest of deal is quite probably also of Dutch origin. It reputedly belonged to Elder William Brewster and may with reason be assigned to the famous voyage and ship. It is interesting because it is butt-joined but it also possesses some pretension to nicety in the carved bracket supports and the curved shaping of the legs.

On July 1, 1633, a law was passed in Plymouth, Massachusetts, which stated that

> . . . the wills and testaments of those that die be proved orderly before the Governor and Councell within one moneth after the decease of the testator. And that a full inventory duly valued be presented with the same.[20]

Because of this enactment, it has been possible to detail the possessions held by twenty-two members of this group of settlers. In the absence of similar records from other colonies the research done on these by Plimoth Plantation, Inc., and The Pilgrim Society, both of Plymouth, Massachusetts, has been extremely valuable. It is evident that although the group lived frugally it was not without the necessities and even the amenities of life; for instance, in addition to chests, stools, and forms—the simplest and earliest furnishings—there was mention of chairs, of which Samuel Fuller, the "surgion," owned five! Four cupboards are found in the "Joyned" category, possibly in the nature of court cupboards. "Lookeing glasses," possibly of the metal variety, do not bespeak ingenuous absence of vanity. One table is listed as "framed," as is one bedstead ("bedsteed"). Bedding, carpets, pots and pans, and tableware were recorded.

Types and Description

Supplementing this written record what can be learned from the furniture that remains from the first part of the seventeenth century? The total is small and must be sought in New England. Although certain pieces suggest by their crafting that they came from overseas, some of the supply is tabulated as American built.

The common seat was the stool or form, often elongated for placement beside the trestle table as a bench. American short forms from this era are scarce, probably because, being relatively unimportant, they have perished. Lockwood says that he has never seen a long form of American manufacture from the early seventeenth century, although the English ones are fairly common.[21]

Four types of chair are found. The earliest and possibly the most common is three-legged, two in front and one behind. The top of the chair back is as wide as the front and arms link it to the front supports. The legs are turned and the seats of rush or wood are dished out to hold a cushion. The Harvard chair, used for ceremonial occasions at Harvard for more than two centuries—but not known to have belonged to John Harvard, the first president of the college—is this type.

The wainscot or panel-backed "grait chayer" was the most pretentious. Although never seen in large numbers, it is noteworthy that one of the earliest American chairs, the possession of Edward Winslow who arrived on the Mayflower, may be characterized as a wainscot. Its original provenance is in question. Some feel that the relative crudity of its scratch carving indicates American craftsmanship. Lockwood assigns a date of 1614 and London as the location. This chair is now in Pilgrim Hall, Plymouth.[22]

Among the dozen or so chairs of this early date almost half are in the Bolles Collection of the

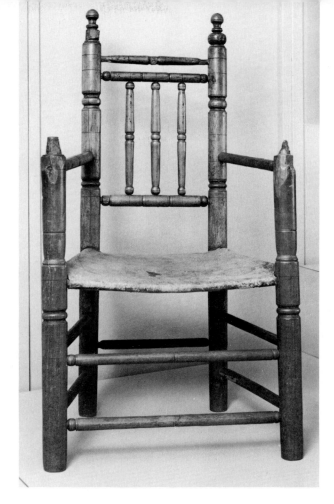

Figure 1.19 Turned armchair which belonged to John Carver, first Governor of the Massachusetts Colony, made around 1620. Pilgrim Hall, Plymouth, Massachusetts. (Pilgrim Society, Plymouth, Massachusetts.)

Metropolitan Museum of Art. Some display the open spindle back of the rural English Yorkshire or Derbyshire chair, and several have backs that can be drawn forward to form a table. Some important great chairs of oak have been located in Virginia and in all probability were imported.

The third pioneer-type of chair, the turned, was made locally of ash with hickory spindles. We find their prototypes in Pilgrim chairs. One is known as the *Carver chair* and was the property of John Carver, the first governor of the colony. As he died in 1621 following overexertion during the spring planting, it may well have come with him in 1620 and is probably from Holland. It also is in Pilgrim Hall.

A Carver chair is characterized by three horizontal rails and three vertical spindles in the back (Figure 1.19). These sturdy chairs have heavy

Figure 1.20 American slat-back chair of the Pilgrim type, with massive posts, ca. 1660. Wadsworth Atheneum, Hartford, Connecticut. (Courtesy Wadsworth Atheneum, Hartford, The Goodwin Collection.)

turned posts that became lighter as the century advanced. The pole lathe for turning was one of the first machines recorded in the colonies and it is frequently mentioned in documents.

Similar to the chair that bears the governor's name is one named for the good Puritan Elder William Brewster, which is also on display at Pilgrim Hall. If one can correlate characters with possessions, the exuberant array of forty-odd spindles on the chair tells us something about its owner. The back of a *Brewster chair* is composed of a double tier of four turned members. The arms duplicate this arrangement, whereas under the seat there were originally two similar tiers, on the front and on the two sides. This chair is one for which a passage on the Mayflower may be considered. Deviants of this many-spindled chair are to be found in seventeenth-century

America, several again being in the Bolles collection. These are assumed to be of English origin.

The fourth and last style of chairs copied and used in provincial America is similar to the turned chair, except that the back fill-ins, and occasionally the arm interlaces, are flat. The banister back has vertical members; the slat back is horizontal (Figure 1.20). Combinations are found, but characteristically each chair has three slats.

The areas around New York City often produced furniture that differed from the norm. There we may find elaborate ball turnings and even the quite novel spiral.

No bedsteads remain from the Pilgrim century. The oldest extant table, of the board-and-frame variety, is at the Metropolitan. This one, dated about 1650, is oak with a top of pine; pine replaced oak on most American trestle tables because it was not so heavy or so difficult to work. The piece at the Metropolitan has solid oak pedestal legs connected by a board that is piniored in place.

Passing from the few well-known pieces of authenticated American-made furniture antedating 1650, we enter the second half of the century, when articles as well as designs were more numerous and a definite maker can often be assigned. All the varieties mentioned continued in use, although often updated as later models arrived from overseas. The time lag between production abroad and in America continued to grow shorter.

Another kind, however, began to take its place. As the trek into the hinterland accelerated, the frontiersmen created furniture cruder in execution and less advanced in style. Often it possessed hybrid qualities as memory for detail became dim with the intervening miles. Media are local and indeed several kinds of wood sometimes appeared in one piece. Such furniture is known as "country furniture" today, but "provincial" seems a more accurate term.

Oak, maple, pine, and later some walnut are the characteristic woods of New England furniture, whereas walnut was favored farther south.

The chest of drawers was introduced toward the end of the century. It is mentioned in earlier inventories but is seldom seen. The Garvan Collection of American furniture at Yale University contains a chest which, with its cabochon bosses and strapwork paneling and split spindle ornamentation, steps out of the Jacobean world of a half-century before. It is of oak, with two low drawers, and was made in America ca. 1675.

As a necessary article with sales value, the chest was soon a product of New England cabinetmakers and regional types were developed. Into this category fall the Hadley (Figure 1.21),

Figure 1.21 Chest over drawers, Hadley type, Massachusetts, 1670–1710. Pine and oak. Height, 85.5 cm, width, 114 cm, depth, 47.5 cm. Yale University Art Gallery, New Haven, Connecticut. (Yale University Art Gallery, The Mabel Brady Garvan Collection.)

Hatfield, and Hartford (Wethersfield) chests and cupboards. These pieces of storage furniture, believed to have been made in the Connecticut valley, all have lower drawers and, in the case of cupboards, doors as well. The upper section of the Connecticut cupboard relates to the English court cupboard in that it is set back from the lower section to provide a shelf. These New England chests are taller than the usual early American models, often 4 ft against 2½, respectively. The Connecticut variety, however, may be less than 4 ft long, but the cupboards stand approximately 5 high by 4 long. Depth in all is about 1½ ft.

The similarities and differences to be noted in these pieces have led Clair Franklin Luther, who is the author of *The Hadley Chest,* a definitive work, to classify them under the three towns referred to above. Characteristic of all is the division of the top front into three panels which are carved with sunflower and tulip motifs.

We can then particularize by saying that the Hadley type is carved in low relief with scroll patterns that introduce tulips and leaves. Its central panel usually (although not always) contains a motif known as a sunflower which is often described as an aster and may be derived from the Tudor rose. The end panels of the Hatfields are tulips which stem from a central element resembling a low mound and called an earth motif. It is frequently seen on Jacobean embroidery. The Hartford type is designated as the Connecticut sunflower chest. It has a threefold sunflower in the center upper octagon-shaped panel which is flanked by tulip patterns in the end ones. Split spindles and cabochon bosses, made of finer grained wood than the oak of which the main body is composed and dyed to a contrasting color, make imposing pieces of this and other Connecticut chests.

The Hadley (Figure 1.21) and Hatfield chests, each of which contains the initial of the owner and of which there are only a few more than 100 remaining, were apparently the work of a commercial partnership between two generations of the related families of Allises (John, 1642–1691) and Beldings (Samuel, Sr., 1633–1691).[23] These chests resembled the "hope" chest variety and may have originated among the women of the two households for the purpose of dower storage. John Allis was noted as a millwright and carpenter; chests may have been only a pleasant hobby. The John Huntington collection of the Cleveland Museum of Art possesses the AA chest, said to have been made about 1680 for Abigail Allis, who was born on February 22, 1672. The MA chest of approximately the same date was made for Mary Allis. It was signed by Nicholas Disbrowe (1612/13–1683) of Hartford and contends with still another chest, the REB by Phineas Pratt (1593–1680) of Weymouth, Massachusetts, which may be dated 1650, for the title of the earliest marked piece of American furniture.

Nicholas Disbrowe and Peter Blin (active ca. 1675–1725) of Wethersfield are the names associated with the sunflower chests of the Hartford district. Disbrowe is acknowledged as the craftsman responsible for eight sunflower cupboards made between 1660 and 1700, the lower parts of which are similar to the sunflower chests. The upper sections, however, contain bold and unique strapwork and spindle and boss decoration. These important pieces are analogous to the English court cupboard, here called a *press cupboard,* which are rare and quite valuable. One outstanding example is the Prince-Howes press cupboard now at the Wadsworth Atheneum in Hartford. The majority of Hartford press cupboards have rectangular superstructures rather than the obtuse angled ones common in England.

A group of Plymouth cabinetmakers, of which John Alden (1599–1687) and Kenelm Winslow (1599–1672) were members, is responsible for a dozen or so fine oak cupboards[24] and an equal number of chests that bear close comparison with their English counterparts in design and in craftsmanship.

Painting, in America as in Europe, was a favorite method of adding pattern to case furniture. Thomas Dennis (1638–1706) of Ipswich, Massachusetts, made some of the most interesting samples which he embellished with the brush and with inlays of light on darker wood. Everyone is familiar with the Dutch (German) painted chest and the large Dutch standing kas, which originated in the seventeenth but found their best expression in the eighteenth and early nineteenth centuries (see Chapter 5). Pine is basic to painted wood in New York, whereas poplar is more frequently seen in Pennsylvania.

In addition to bible boxes, used to store the family bible and writing supplies, the colonists also made fall-front desks and secretaries.

Close to the century's end, perhaps some ten years after its introduction to England, William and Mary style furniture appeared in the English colonies (Figure 1.22). The high boy was known as the high chest at that time and American pieces followed the continental prototypes quite closely.

Framed tables became more common after 1650. Several varieties of smaller tables, such as

Figure 1.22 Room from Samuel Wentworth House, Portsmouth, New Hampshire, built in 1671, paneled ca. 1710. Floor joists of attic are concealed by plaster. Bolection moldings are used in the paneling of the fireplace wall, which is painted Indian red. Furniture, which is late Stuart, includes a highboy and lowboy in William and Mary style. Metropolitan Museum of Art, New York. (The Metropolitan Museum of Art.)

the butterfly, the tavern, and even the round gateleg are extant.

Among the chair types of the second half of the century the low-backed chair, which resembled the English Cromwellian, put in a rare and belated appearance. One in the Garvan Collection at Yale, dated 1650–1660, is in maple and is covered with the original woolen upholstery.

The high-backed chair, counterpart of the Carolean, began to appear. Those made in this country are simpler than the continental examples. Legs and stretchers were generally turned and the Spanish club foot was favored, even though it seems incongruous in its mating with sturdy turned legs. The central portion of the tall backs was often caned and had turned supports that ended in well-modeled finials or were capped with a carved arch.

Slat- and banister-back chairs of this era also took to height. The carved slats lent themselves to individual and regional differences. Northern examples are simpler, with curvature only on the upper edge of the slat. The chairs from the central states have more pronounced curvature and more plastically sculptured turnings. Seats are customarily rush. The slat- and banister-back chairs were never exclusively cottage chairs and may indeed be considered the first chairs of American handicrafting that presaged the kind of advanced work that was to come from American centers during the next century.

The French in America made a counterpart of the slat chair, called à *la capucine* (possibly from Capuchin monasteries). It is found along the Canada borders and in New Orleans and the bayou country. The French style is characterized by a reversed S curve, known as a *salamander slat*. French chairs join the arms back from the front of the seat and fit neatly into the era of Louis XV proportions of the eighteenth century.

Daybeds, known as couches, made from the middle of the seventeenth century until around the middle of the eighteenth, exhibit appropriate style character. Their headpieces were ingeniously adjustable and were regulated by a cord or metal chain.

TEXTILES

Necessity preceded luxury in dictating the textiles of early America. Except for stores brought with the immigrants and, toward the end of the century, some more elaborate imports for wealthier households, textiles were home-manufactured essentials.

Flax and wool were the two indigenous fibers and cloth woven from them (or a mixture, i.e., linsey-woolsey) constituted the bulk of the fabrics available. Cotton was not produced to any extent on the mainland during the seventeenth century. Nevertheless, cotton cloth or a combination of cotton and linen known as *fustian* had been manufactured as a home industry since the middle of the century when a cheap supply of cotton was imported from Barbadoes. Spinning this new fiber was the problem and we are not surprised to read of a court order in the Massachusetts Assembly on May 13, 1640, suggesting concern about

. . . what course may be taken for the spinning of the yarn, and to return to the next Court their

several and joint advice about this thing. The like concern would be had for the spinning and weaving of cotton wool.[25]

Oddly enough in a country so dependent on its own resources no mention of clothmaking devices appears in the inventories of the Pilgrims.

Dyes were also locally applied and generally locally procured—the hulls of nuts for browns; barks, onions, and various flowers yielded the yellows. It was necessary to buy the powdered root of the madder for red and indigo for blue. An indigo pot, once established, was kept in continuous use. Indigo was one of the early crops of Carolina planters.[26]

One mode of decoration, in use even before stenciling, was resist dyeing, in which sections of the pattern would be covered with a resist, or a discharge, in order to resist or void, respectively, some of the dye. Thus, although time was not available for elaborate needlework on textiles, simple monochrome patterns were not beyond the reach of the patient and imaginative housewife. *Hatchments* or embroidered coats of arms were prized possessions, probably in the family before coming to western shores.

Old inventories tell much about the uses of textiles, and it is clear that neither function nor type differed radically from custom in the homeland. Beds had linen sheets and pillowcases ("pillowbeers"). Thick wool blankets were common and wool coverings took the place of the European feather bed. Tables were equipped with white nappery. Floors were not covered, except with rush mats. Curtains were seldom provided but when used were simple hangings of wool or linen.

CERAMICS, GLASS, AND METALS

The colonists manufactured ceramics and glass, although neither industry was technically advanced. Eastern Virginia and its surrounding districts yielded an exceptionally fine potter's clay which the Indians called "unaker." It probably contained a high percentage of kaolin. Petuntze was also available. Therefore it should be no surprise that a salt-glazed stoneware was one of the first commodities produced at Jamestown. The museum there has a pitcher of red-glazed stoneware which was reportedly made during the first twenty-five years of the settlement. This utilitarian staple is found in shards of jars, pots, and dishes.

Despite the fact that on a list of the burghers of New Amsterdam in 1657 there is listed one Dirck Claesen, "Pot Baker," no marked piece can be credited to him or to any other ceramist of this period. James Kettle of Danvers, Connecticut, who was born in 1687, is the first New England potter of record. There are whole pieces of early New England pottery in red clay with a lead glaze in the Smithsonian Institution. Some are ornamented with a white slip. Only later did New England make stoneware.

Research into the subject of early glass manufacture in America is of recent occurrence. We know that the second expedition to Jamestown in 1608 had "eight Dutch and Polish" glassmen aboard, probably lured by Raleigh's account of silica and extensive forests in the new land. Jamestown's glass house was reconstructed for the 1958 celebration. Excavations of refractory brick, clay pots, and bits of glass had revealed its original location. It is believed that the output consisted of utilitarian objects for use by the colonists and perhaps for commerce—not so much with the Indian as with the European. There is little recorded of these shortlived establishments.

Hard metals were early commodities here. Iron for small utensils and for large cooking pots was forged in many places and became a favorite export of the New Englanders before the large Pennsylvanian furnaces of the next century came into existence, but pots and kettles were costly necessities. Iron kettles that weighed as much as 40 lb often stood on slender legs to raise themselves from the fire. A plate warmer was a luxury, and a "Dutch" oven or *bake kettle* was boxlike with an opening to the fire. The *peel* or *slice* was a long-handled shovel used for placing bread in the oven. Tongs and skewers for turning roasts on the spit were other essentials.

Wood was the usual material for platters, trenchers, dishes, and spoons. A message was sent back to England in 1629 from Governor Endicott, which advised those who planned to

come to the colonies to bring wooden utensils with them. Metal utensils, copper, brass, and silver were the greatest of rarities, bespeaking a considerable degree of affluence. There was very little tin and its place was taken by "latten," a kind of brass. The best of brass was imported for escutcheons only after 1690.

There is a record of pewter articles shipped to the colonies for sale during the second half of the century and a few pewter objects are mentioned in wills. Any naming of American pewterers is thought to refer to dealers and menders rather than to manufacturers, for no signed piece remains.

Silver presents a somewhat different story. As the colonists obtained foreign silver in trade and because colonial production of coinage was proscribed by the crown (a law often honored in the breach, as the pine tree shillings attest), the wealthy turned their metal over to a goldsmith for manufacture into plate, which became a prize possession. The first recorded silversmith, John Mansfield (1601–1674), came to Boston in 1634. Two whose works are best known are the partners, Robert Sanderson (1608–1693) and John Hull (1624–1683), whose small business was conducted in Boston (Figure 1.23). Jeremiah Dummer (1645–1718) was an apprentice of Hull. Captain John Smith reported silversmiths in Jamestown but in all probability they had come in search of gold, a metal that was rumored to be abundant. The first New York smith was Cornelis van der Burgh (1653–1699). Silversmiths, like pewterers and indeed like many craftsmen in the seventeenth century in this land where necessity ruled, seemed to have been masters of several trades. Engraving they could do and blacksmithing, too.

Because there was a dearth of vessels for church use, silver ones were not denied by the ascetic Puritans. Families often loaned their prized possessions for ecclesiastic use and as frequently bequeathed them to the church. They may have justified their wealth in this manner. Therefore many pieces that started life in a domestic setting became church property. Chalices and their patens, or covers, were an exception to this rule, and were made specifically for the purpose. Most of the typical European articles are represented in seventeenth-century America—standing cups, sal-

(a)

(b)

Figure 1.23 Silver dram cup by Robert Sanderson (1608–1693) and John Hull (1624–1683), American. Height, 3.75 cm, depth, 7.25 cm. (a) side view; (b) bottom. Yale University Art Gallery, New Haven, Connecticut. (Yale University Art Gallery, The Mabel Brady Garvan Collection.)

vers, beakers, tumblers, caudle cups, tankards and flagons, spoons, and candlesticks. It is somewhat a revelation to see the relatively fine American silver work of this period, even though existing pieces are not numerous.

34

Among general style influences we note that the first forms were plain. New York silversmiths were more likely to use engraving in greater extent than the New England men. Gradually well-rounded forms in the Carolean style began to supplant the flat tops and straight-sided pieces of earlier provenance. Elaborations such as twisted handles ending in scrolls and embossing with floral, human, and animal forms appeared. With these the main body of the piece might be quite plain. But more about silver in the next period when it becomes not necessarily more beautiful but more interesting in development and variety.

DESCRIPTIVE SUMMARY

The six chapters that preceded this one (see Volume 1) have dealt with architectural arts as they traveled from Italy north, west, and down three centuries. What could the art that was created for continental bankers, a wealthy church, and power-greedy monarchs have in common? And how could it relate to the needs of men who crossed an ocean and conquered a wilderness?

During the Renaissance and Baroque eras, important changes were being made in the way people lived: necessities took on the glow of amenities; visual refinements became style—a style cloaked in the dress of ancient Rome but certainly invested with the mien of the wearers.

The vagaries of history created differing time cycles within each of the four cultures under discussion. The West saw the sunrise while the East viewed the post meridian. But the West beheld a beginning on a cultural level where the classes were coming closer together and where the index of wealth was not so high.

The art of the eighteenth century was to be changed thereby. Noteworthy architecture descended from church and state to home, and possibly what may be considered one of the western world's greatest original contributions to a style for interiors was made.

CHAPTER TWO

Eighteenth-Century France

I have only twenty acres, replied the Turk. I cultivate them with my children; and work keeps at bay three great evils: boredom, vice and need.

Exalted rank. . . is very dangerous, according to the testimony of all philosophers; for Eglon, King of the Moabites, was murdered by Ehud; Absolom was hanged by the hair. . . .

I also know, said Candide, that we must cultivate our garden.

Your are right, said Pangloss, for when man was placed in the Garden of Eden, he was placed there ut operaretur eum, to dress it and keep it; which proves that man was not born for idleness.

Excerpts from *Candide*, Voltaire

CULTURE SPAN

Louis XIV, during the last years of his life, maintained a positive outlook, closely controlled the reins of government, preserved an affection for the young generations in his dynasty, and in no way lost his zest for building.

Nevertheless, the last quarter of the century had been austere. The war in the Palatinate had scarcely ended before the War of the Spanish Succession began, and although it placed Louis' grandson on the throne of Spain it forever destroyed any hope of uniting the two countries under one Bourbon ruler. It also gave England valuable concessions in the Iberian peninsula.

Tragedy struck the court in the new century when in a little more than a year (1711–1712) the Grand Dauphin, son of Louis XIV, the Grand Dauphin's son Louis, Duc de Bourgogne, and the Duke's wife, Marie Adelaide of Savoy, perished in an epidemic of measles that swept Paris and its environs. Miraculously the infant heir was saved.

Louis XV, great-grandson of the Sun King, was only five years old when he acceded to the throne. His uncle, Philippe d'Orléans, was regent (period known as Le Régence, or the French Regency, 1715–1723). The *duc* immediately whisked his young charge away from the vast golden palace, the only home he had ever known, and established him in the Tuileries and at the royal chateau at Vincennes, while he himself moved into the Palais Royal, the old *hôtel* of Cardinal Richelieu, just across the Rue de Rivoli from the Louvre. Here he set up a personal court, which, if not noted for its puritanical ideals, was nevertheless friendly and receptive to cultural influences.

Even during the last years of the old monarchy the nobility, first those of lesser rank and later of the very first, had begun an exodus from Versailles to Paris. There they built new *hôtels* and renovated the old in lavish style. High profits had been made in the wars, and those who were fortunate enough to have preserved theirs from the catastrophic losses of such speculative ventures as John Law's (a Scotch entrepreneur) Mississippi real estate deal were anxious to display their wealth and to live in a less restricted manner than had been dictated at Versailles.

In 1723 Louis achieved his majority and in the same year the Regent died. Returning to Versailles, the King gave his attention to his personal interests. He subsequently had the north wing of the palace drastically altered by tearing out the old and magnificent Staircase of the Ambassadors to make room for his small personal apartments. Here he preferred a quiet life with his successive favorites, among the first, the Marquise de Pompadour (Jeanne Antoinette Poissons, 1721–1764), and the last, the Comtesse du Barry—who was the prettiest, the youngest, and as certainly the least cultured. Louis had received a kingdom too ready-made. He sapped rather than strengthened the French monarchy.

Before the end of his reign other European wars, contests for a balance in European power, depleted the French treasury and returned her little in territorial advantage.

During the reign of this fourth Bourbon king social power not only moved from Versailles to Paris but in so doing acquired a broader and very different base. Money and talent acted as honey to attract the elite. Financiers such as Monsieur de la Popelinière, wealthy bourgeois women such as Madame Geoffrin (widow of a glass manufacturer), and even the déclassée favorite of the Regent, Madame de Tencin, presided over salons or gatherings where nobility, men of letters, and political figures met for that art in which the French excel—conversation.

A new tenor of thought, sometimes referred to as *the Enlightenment,* may be considered to have begun in these Parisian drawing rooms. By the end of the century the liberal, humanitarian, rational-scientific doctrines reviewed by these select groups had emerged and spread to become the property of the commonalty.

One of the subjects discussed, which is of principal interest to us, concerned the standards of judgment in the arts. The French academies had continued their endless debates of such topics as the relative values of color versus form and of abstraction of the ideal (the Greek theory) versus particularized realism (the moderns). These tiresome and futile arguments were countered by the lively discussions in such assemblies as those of Madame Geoffrin, who found that contemporary artists, of nonacademic station in particular, were excellent drawing cards. Moreover, free exhibitions were begun by these artists, which led to the counter move by the establishment of reopening the annual Louvre salons in 1737. All of these happenings charged the atmosphere with healthy public criticism of the rigid aesthetic standards that had prevailed since the days of Colbert.

Interrogation went beyond the arts and traveled outside the drawing room. In England the philosopher John Locke was contemporary with Wren and probably served in somewhat the same manner as one who could introduce the new in thought without dumping the old into the ashcan. He was followed by that famous Scotch mountain of skepticism, David Hume, and thereafter nothing could be claimed as a verity. The French method was that of the gadfly Voltaire and the romantic Rousseau. These men stirred up hornets' nests and, when they were finished, new words such as freedom, liberty, the people, equality, and natural rights were in the vocabulary. And much blood had been spilled.

The French revolution was an exposition of the new logic on a political plane, the more cruel because the belief in the infallibility of kings had bred such iniquities in French society. Louis XV did indeed forget to tend his garden at a time when the soil was heavy with weeds and thorns. The result, which his successor was powerless to prevent, was terrifying, and many parasitic and beautiful orchids were doomed in the process.

ARCHITECTURE

Architecture, always an expensive art, is slow to change, and in eighteenth-century France it retained a classic approach.

After Mansard's death in 1708 his brother-in-law and understudy, Robert de Cotte (1656–1735), succeeded to the post of *premier architecte*. Subsequent to de Cotte's retirement in 1734 the aging Jacques Jules Gabriel took command until 1742, when his very talented son, Ange-Jacques Gabriel (1698–1782), followed in his footsteps. These men mark the progression in the bâtiments through the reign of Louis XV; the younger Gabriel bridges to Louis XVI.

From the latter part of the Sun King's reign there was little building in the royal domain; new work was confined to interiors. This allowed the prominent architects time and freedom to work for other customers, both in Paris and abroad. De Cotte and another crown architect, Gabriel-Germain Boffrand (1667–1754), were employed by the Elector of Cologne, the Czar of Russia, and by Stanislas Leszczinska, father-in-law of the King and ex-ruler of Poland, who then lived at Nancy. The planning and building in this last city, with its long vistas and its expanded and contracted spaces, largely the work of the architect Emmanuel Héré de Corny (1705–1763), has attracted notice because of its advanced character.

The name *Rococo* is generally assigned to the aesthetic expression of the first half of the eighteenth century. The word is derived from *rocaille* (rock work) and *coquille* (cockleshell), both of which were used in grottoes at that time. It favors the Baroque characteristics of rhythmically moving shapes, of a centrally oriented asymmetrical balance, and of space interpenetration. But as the Rococo spirit differs from the Baroque in not being so essentially emotional or forcefully spiritual, it is no accident that the French Rococo is a style exemplified by smaller scale and linear rather than plastic traits. The term suggests an era of sparkling elegance, coquetry, and charming grace, but withall something restless and impermanent—a brilliant arpeggio, a frothy effervescence with which a waning society whiled away its hours of decline.

The Rococo came to France during the first half of the eighteenth century largely as a style of interior architecture. It was only in central Europe that Baroque space molding and Rococo curvilinear gestures developed as total architecture. This alliance resulted in a world-famous series of churches and palaces (e.g., the Church of St. Charles Borromaeus in Vienna by Fischer von Erlach, 1656–1723; the Episcopal Palace of the Schoenborn family at Würzburg by Balthasar Neumann (Figure 2.1), 1687–1753; the Zwinger Palace for Augustus, Elector of Saxony, at Dresden, by Mattheus Daniel Pöppelman, 1662–1732; the Belvedere Palace for Prince Eugene of Savoy, in Vienna, by Johann Lucas von Hilde-

39

Figure 2.1　Staircase in the Episcopal Palace (home of the Schoenborn family) at Würzburg, Germany. Balthasar Neumann, architect. (Bildarchiv Foto Marburg.)

Figure 2.2 Chateau de Jossigny, near Paris, 1743. (©
Arch. Phot. Paris/S. P. A. D. E. M., 1979.)

brandt, 1668–1745; and the small pavilion of
Amalienburg on the estate of the Palace of Nymphenburg, near Munich, for the Elector Charles-
Albert of Bavaria, by François de Cuvilliés, 1695–
1768).

In France some architectural changes took
place at this time in both exterior massing and
interior planning. These innovations were basically functional and not at all transitory. They
were most pronounced in urban dwellings. So
great was the demand for town accommodations
that the architect Boffrand built many houses on
speculation. Much of this construction centered
in the old Quartier du Marais on the right bank
of the river to the northeast of the Hôtel de Ville
and in the newer section on the left bank, the

Faubourg St. Germain, just outside the old university walls.

Such activity forced up land values and resulted
in the modification of the typically French urban
house plan with its low entrance wall, its inner
court or courts, and its *corps de logis* or living
quarters spread along the rear. In its place might
appear the block-type building forecast in the
earlier drawings of J. H. Mansard and P. Bullet, or
the owner might raise the customary low street
wall to include rental property, thus financing his
own pleasant living in a rear logis looking out to
a garden. Both plans produced a new order of
urban architectural stacking.

This tendency, however, was not universal;
both Boffrand and de Cotte erected buildings in
Paris in the old tradition. Again in the traditional
manner was the Chateau de Jossigny, built a
short distance east of Paris in 1743 (Figure 2.2).

The last serves to illustrate the general appearance of a conventional early-eighteenth-century country house. An exquisite iron gate and a small courtyard give it a setting similar to the *hôtels* of Paris. The French, whether in town or country, favor a view of their homes through such a *claire-voie*, whereas the English, when space permits, seem anxious to conceal theirs by means of winding roads. Rigidly bisymmetrical, Jossigny is given planar recessions by the use of three projecting pavilions. There is a high ground story relative to the second *étage*. The top floor of an eighteenth-century house often had dormers in a hipped or Mansard roof or *oeil de boeuf* windows in an attic. The Jossigny roof is less steep than was customary in the seventeenth century, but it still exceeds the slope of contemporary English roofs. Its principal windows are tall and of the French type, casement to the floor. The tops may be straight but are more likely to have elliptical heads. Shutters are optional. A strongly molded string course separates the main stories, a characteristic soon to disappear when designers resolved the conflict between horizontality and verticality in elevation and learned to unify the facade. At Jossigny, although the classic-inspired pedimented front is retained and a semblance of pilaster treatment is observed, hierarchical order toward the axis is not pronounced. Indeed, it never was so strong in France, where the end pavilions tended to detract from the central emphasis.

It has been customary to cite Ange-Jacques Gabriel as the leading architect of the midcentury transition to Neoclassicism, that complex art movement which negates both Baroque and Rococo in favor of a certain nostalgic, archaeologically correct, and idealistically conceived impression of the classic past. The refined and elegant nature of Gabriel's treatment of the classical idiom conceals his really innovative contributions. Viewed broadly, Gabriel's work goes beyond Neoclassicism to incorporate principles that are the quintessence of some of the modern. One of his earliest commissions, the Petit Trianon (1762) is an illustration of this talent.

This building belongs to architectural species that might well incorporate innovations. Although at this time large buildings were rarely commissioned, many *pavillons* were erected. These were small structures, planned in the spirit of play, situated on the grounds of an estate, and intended as a sort of hideaway from the formality of life in a large ménage. By courtesy the name *pavillon* is associated with any house belonging to persons of social importance, which house is less pretentious than the principal *hôtel* or chateau.

Specific type names were further extensions. *Hameau* was a small rural farm set down in a more formal landscape. Marie Antoinette's *hameau* on the grounds of Versailles is certainly the most famous (Figure 2.3). *Temples* were small classic-inspired buildings, not meant to be lived in, but intended for contemplation and perhaps for a rest during a walk or a meeting place of serene atmosphere. A *belvedere* was a place to go to look out from, as, with some purpose, Gertrude Stein said of museums. It was placed to command a favorite view and, on a large estate, made a good deal of sense. A *hermitage* was a secluded residence such as each of us longs for at times. A *folly* was a small building, extravagant or bizarre, contrived by an owner who thus declared that he was sufficiently wealthy to indulge in such romantics. It might suggest a tongue-in-cheek approach to life. All of these represent an escapist view, and it is significant that they mushroomed in the atmosphere of the late seventeenth- and eighteenth-century Bourbons.

The Trianons of Versailles fitted this picture. To the northern side of the park, the first, or *Trianon de Porcelaine*, was built by Louis XIV to gratify Madame de Montespan. It came by its name because the site had been the village of Trianon, which was destroyed to make ground for the small palace, and because the facade of the edifice was ornamented with plaques of blue and white faience much as the Chateau de Madrid had been with Della Robbia ware at the time of Francis I. The *Trianon de Porcelaine* was in due time demolished to make room for a larger palace, now known as the *Grand Trianon*, which still stands.

The popularity of the Grand Trianon with the kings and royal mistresses had its ups and downs. It was finally presented to Madame de Pompadour who, to amuse Louis XV, established there

Figure 2.3 Hameau, Versailles. Richard Mique, architect. (Giraudon.)

her practical dairy farm. This interest waning, the grounds were turned into a botanical garden. Louis conceived the idea of erecting the *Petit Trianon* in the center of this horticultural park (Figure 2.4). It was begun for Pompadour to whom he remained devoted until her death. Louis subsequently gave it to Madame du Barry. Still later it became the favorite residence of Marie Antoinette and is closely related to her life. Louis XVI is said to have given his queen the Trianons with the words, "They have always belonged to the King's favorites and should therefore be yours." She was just nineteen.

Opinions about the merit of the Petit Trianon differ. Fiske Kimball speaks of Gabriel's "gentle, refined, and somewhat facile academism." Reginald Blomfield finds in Gabriel's work "the expression of all the best and most characteristic qualities of pure French architecture." Emil Kaufmann calls it "a mature specimen of the new manner." Where was each directing his eyes?

An objective description of the little building would state that its form was an isolated block measuring 78 ft, 6 in. in width and depth by 50 ft, 6 in. in height. Its cubicle appearance is accentuated by a low roof surmounted by a balustrade and by the fact that all ornament is in extremely low relief. The building is far enough away from the usual tourist footpaths that, when viewed from a distance, it shimmers in the sun like a geometric toy left in the field by some careless child, a forerunner of the trylon and perisphere of the 1939–40 New York World's Fair. This obvious and simple form of Gabriel's creation strikes a new note among buildings of more subtle mass proportions. Kaufmann sees the "new manner."

Approaching the building by the southern facade, one becomes increasingly more aware of low courtyard appendages which serve to carry the eye toward the structure itself in true Baroque fashion. The western facade, the one most easily seen from the garden, is the most elaborate. Here a shallow portico features four Corinthian columns, a sweeping flight of stairs, and a wide platform. All corroborate Kimball's verdict of "facile academism."

As though to balance this richness, the eastern elevation is quite plain and the ground floor is

separated from the upper ones only by its rustication. The northern as well as the southern face are punctuated by Corinthian pilasters in low projection, which allows little or no play of Baroque chiaroscuro. By comparison the east front of the Louvre seems antiquated.

It takes a practiced eye indeed to recognize the complexities and subtleties of the rhythmic proportions that Gabriel combined in his little masterpiece. Blomfield is so right in seeing here the stamp of pure French architecture. Within the overall metrical space are found proportional relations that cause the eye to move. It is this singularity that leads the Rococo designer to place the most organic furniture ever produced in a rigidly architectonic arrangement. Both the rationality and the sensitivity of the French mind are demonstrated in eighteenth-century art.

Within Gabriel's total work the Trianon is unique in its use of the classical language in ways that seem fresh and new. His other buildings fit easily into some aspect of the Baroque-Rococo tradition. The *Pavillon du Butard,* a royal hunting

Figure 2.4 The east facade of *Le Petit Trianon,* Versailles, 1762–1768. Ange-Jacques Gabriel, architect. (G. C. Ball.)

lodge dating from 1750, had a large pedimented entrance, although proportions otherwise were cubicle. The Hermitage at Fontainebleau has Baroque wings. The Pavillon Français at Versailles is ornamented with parapet statuettes and elaborate consoles—Baroque conceits. The Ecole Militaire in Paris which Gabriel planned (although it was largely built by Alexander Brongniart from 1771 to 1773), has a high domical roof, quite orthodox; its giant portico is flush with the face and its colossal Corinthian columns rise from the ground. In 1753 Gabriel was called on to plan the Place de la Concorde at the west end of the Tuileries, superseding by royal command the designers who had submitted ideas in an academic contest. In its contrived vistas and terminal buildings it presents aspects of the Baroque.

Louis XV is said to have spent many hours in consultation with Gabriel over the plans for the Petit Trianon and to have told the architect that he wanted it to be in the "new style," which he pinpoints as that of Le Butard. By this Louis shows his awareness of the fashion that emerged during the last half of the eighteenth century—the new classicism or Neoclassicism. As already mentioned, Gabriel, possibly unknowingly, went further than this in his execution of Louis's wishes and created a form that in its very stark unorthodox simplicity leaped almost to the twentieth century while at the same time fulfilling in a thoroughly French and almost feminine way the mandates of the neoclassicism of the eighteenth.

Strangely enough it was Italy which first introduced the idea of a Greek classicism (i.e., neoclassicism) at this time. It was on Italian ground that archaeology developed its scientific procedures and that late Roman (Graeco-Roman) treasures were first unearthed. When Queen Maria Amalia, wife of the Spanish Bourbon King Charles IV of Naples (ruled 1735–1759, later Charles III of Spain), learned of certain finds within her dominion at Herculaneum and Pompeii, she approached the program of excavation with enthusiasm but with the archaeological expertise of a dilettante. It is really remarkable that no more damage was done before it proved irreparable.

Cardinal Alessandro Albani, nephew of the Albani Pope Clement XI (1700–1721), was a leading Roman humanist and collector of antiquities. His acquisitions, housed in his villa in the northern section of Rome, are still open to view by permit. The Cardinal had persuaded the German historian Johann Joachim Winckelmann (1717–1768) to become librarian of the Vatican library, which was in Albani's care. Winckelmann, as Raphael before him, was assigned the important charge of Superintendent of Antiquities for the territory around Rome. With scientific exactitude and thoroughness (acknowledging, may it be said, his indebtedness in this discipline to the French antiquarian Comte de Caylus, 1692–1765, called the father of the science of archaeology), Winckelmann took over the excavations and studies of the buried twin cities, Herculaneum and Pompeii, and the ruined temples at Paestum. The villa of the Emperor Hadrian at Tivoli came under similar scrutiny. Winckelmann's principal literary work, Geschichte der Kunst (History of Art), was published in 1764. His principal thesis stressed the superiority of Greek architecture to Roman copying. It is ironic that the fame and attendant reward of a gold medal which his writings brought were the cause of his murder at the hands of a thief, as the aging scholar was returning to his Italian post after a visit to his native country.

Pompadour, who has often been accused of nepotism, certainly favored her family in obtaining influential positions for them. Not only did she recommend her uncle Lenormant de Tournehem to the office of Superintendent of the Bâtiments, she subsequently in 1751 secured the post for her brother M. de Vandières, the Marquis de Marigny. In preparing the young man for the responsibility, she arranged an extensive Italian tour for him. His traveling companions were the Abbé Leblanc (1707–1781), known for his hostility to the Rococo, as spiritual advisor, and the famous graphic artist Charles-Nicholas Cochin, the younger (1715–1790), as art director. The architect Jacques-Germain Soufflot (1713–1780), later designer of the French Panthéon, was also a member of the group.

It would be natural for the traveling party to come under the spell of the archaeological and antiquarian atmosphere of Rome, not only at the French Academy but quite likely at Cardinal Albani's gatherings. Hence one route back to

France for neoclassic influence would be clear.

One characteristic of the new classicism has been described as a reaffirmation, following Baroque liberality, of fidelity to the classical canons. By the sixties this was focused on Greece and Greek buildings. The archaeological interest in the ruins of the Greek temples in southern Italy triggered this trend. Both Soufflot and Cochin sketched those at Paestum.

Greece itself had remained a difficult country to visit because of Turkish control of the land and brigandage at sea. Nevertheless, some daring young men, like the Frenchman David Le Roy (1724–1803), went to Athens. He published his *Ruines des plus beaux monuments de la Grèce* (Ruins of the Most Beautiful Greek Monuments) in 1758. James Stuart (1713–1788) and Nicholas Revett (1721–1804) published their *Antiquities of Athens* in 1762. Robert Wood had penetrated the really wild territory of Asia Minor to write the first accounts of the Greek-Roman ruins (e.g., the Roman ruins of Palmyra). Robert Adam, the Scotch architect, who had never been able to finance an expedition to Greece, was sarcastic about this "Gusto Greco"[1] and deprecated Stuart's work. Yet Greece, however superficially understood, was destined to rise on the fashionable horizon.

As a matter of fact, interest in Greece was not a mere surface ripple but rather the consequence of deep currents of thought. Certain philosophical writers had ascribed to Greek production a more forthright use of materials and structural systems and their more reasoned relation to function than the Romans had attained. In Vitruvius's injunction to regard *firmitas, utilitas, venustas* (structure, utility, appearance) it was felt that the last, the element of appearance, had been disproportionately emphasized during the Renaissance-Baroque. It was high time for firm structure and utility to take over—as it had in Hellas—or so they argued.

The first of these recalcitrant writers was a Venetian man of the cloth, the Franciscan Abbé Carlo Lodoli (1690–1761). We know of his teaching only indirectly through the labors of two of his disciples, Andrea Memmo and Francesco Algarotti.[2] To Lodoli good visual form is directly related to the expression of structure and function.

He has often been called the father of modern functionalist theory.

In France, as early as 1706, the Abbé de Cordemoy (J. L. de), about whom little is known, published his *Nouveau Traité de Toute l'Architecture*. In 1753 the Jesuit priest Marc-Antoine Laugier (1713–1769) produced his *Essai sur l'Architecture*. Both praised primitive and presumably Greek building as economical expressions of structure related to function and form. Laugier condemned all Renaissance and Baroque elements as superfluous and actually suggested that architecture return to simple trabeation and cease its dependence on supporting walls.

Such theorizing did not materialize as fact until new materials and structural systems almost two centuries later rendered it practical. It did, however, orient architects toward simplification and led inevitably to a preference for regular unadorned shapes such as the cube, the sphere, and the cone. We see less of the subtle root rectangle proportions, which paradoxically had been the essence of Greek art.

The most radical examples of the new architectural thinking occur on the drawing boards of the rising generation of young men. In those troublesome times they had little or no chance of materializing. Look at the Cenotaph of Etienne-Louis Boullée (1728–1799) or the Shelter for the Royal Guards by Claude-Nicolas Ledoux (1735–1806). Their rigid geometry and lack of classical ornament ran well in advance of the times.

Then, as always, most young architects kept one eye on commissions that would see the light of day. To mention a few, Jacques-Germain Soufflot (1713–1780), Jean François Chalgrin (1739–1811), François-Joseph Bélanger (1744–1818), Marie-Joseph Peyre (1730–1788), Richard Mique (1728–1794), and Charles de Wailly (1729–1798). Mique succeeded Gabriel as Premier Architecte in 1775 and is the designer of such later conceits on the grounds of Versailles as Marie Antoinette's famous *hameau* (Figure 2.3) and the classic *monapteros* or rotunda dedicated to Cupid. Thus romanticism and classicism formed another union as they have succeeded in doing in just about every epoch from the Baroque to the modern. Mique paid the price for his royal association and met his death on the guillotine.

Figure 2.5 The *Panthéon,* Paris, begun ca. 1757. Jacques-Germain Soufflot and others. (Giraudon.)

Soufflot designed the Church of Ste Genevieve in Paris, which occupies the site of the tomb of the patron saint (422–512) of the city. It was completed with some modification only after his death. In 1791 the church became the French Hall of Fame and was renamed the Panthéon (Figure 2.5). In its original form the building conformed to Baroque principles, with its details placed to make smooth transitions, its planar recessions, and its classical portico. A central dome and four subsidiary domes had been planned over a Greek cross, and it was intended that the dome rest on four colossal Corinthian pillars in conformance with the new ideas of visible columnar structure. Piers had to be substituted for reasons of safety. The windows were closed to make a simpler and stronger wall and a cylindrical form replaced the elaborate lantern of the dome. Two lateral towers were removed—in many ways the Panthéon favors that simplification which spelled the new (Figure 2.6).

The architect François-Joseph Bélanger, certainly not so great as Soufflot, was nevertheless

Figure 2.6   Interior view of the *Panthéon*, Paris, begun ca. 1757. Jacques-Germain Soufflot and others. (Lauros-Giraudon.)

complished in sixty-four days, an extraordinary achievement.

It was a far cry from its prototype, however. Its shape is similar—almost a cube—but it has none of the refined proportions that place the Versailles *pavillon* at the top of the examples in which linear divisions epitomize the French Baroque tradition. Finished in stucco, the Bagatelle could not hope to emulate the beautiful texture of the golden stone of the Petit Trianon. Its central hall is surmounted by a low truncated dome and the facade and corners are punctuated with horizontally coursed pilasters topped with novel capitals, a form of boldness that Gabriel used in the *Pavillon Butard* and in the *Pavillon Pompadour* at Fontainebleau. Between the pilasters are straight linteled windows, with a central door that in no wise dominates the entrance as one of the Baroque period would have done. The classic coinage of niches and garlanded recesses is present, but the whole conveys the impression of a new, streamlined, and cleaned-up appearance. Trianon is prophetic of tomorrow, while inhabited by the exquisite ghosts of the past. Bagatelle, although possessed of a charm of its own, scarcely knows how to handle ghosts.

Bagatelle is as famous for a later owner as it was for its first. The wealthy English Lord Hertford bought it in 1835. He had already made the major purchases of his fabulous collection of French furniture and he needed to house them. Lord Hertford's collection descended to his son Sir Richard Wallace. It was given to the English government to form the nucleus of the famous Wallace Collection to be seen at Hertford House in London. After various ownerships, Bagatelle was purchased by the city of Paris in 1904.

Among the younger men working with pared-down forms was Pierre Rousseau (1751–1810), whose Hôtel Salm for Prince de Salm-Kybourg in the eighties was reerected by public subscription after its destruction by fire during the Commune (1871). It is now the Palais de la Légion d'Honneur. It used the projecting cylinder as part of its design, which as a salient circular portico became a familiar element in nineteenth-century building. Claude-Nicolas Ledoux, on the contrary, employed the partly recessed doorway in the *Pavillon Louveciennes* for du Barry, much as Palladio

the darling of fashion among the declining aristocracy and thus his work represents some of the popular aspects of Neoclassicism. Bélanger was a man who led a curious life of license in a career that showed a personality of considerable imagination and skill. His building known as the *Bagatelle* (Figure 2.7), which stands in its country setting in the Bois de Boulogne in Paris, has many romantic claims to fame. Some time in the last quarter of the eighteenth century the youthful Comte d'Artois, brother of Louis XVI and later to reign as Charles X, placed a bet with his attractive sister-in-law Marie Antoinette that during her absence at Fontainebleau he could have a duplicate of the Petit Trianon built in Paris. It was ac-

Figure 2.7 The Bagatelle, Paris, 1777. François-Joseph Bélanger, architect. (© Arch. Pho. Paris/S. P. A. D. E. M., 1979.)

did. This preserved the building's cubicle form. It too became a popular feature in the Greek Revival movement of later years.

The greatest teacher of architecture in eighteenth-century France was Jacques-François Blondel (1705–1774), nephew of the Jacques Blondel on the roster of the original Academy. He observed a certain dichotomy of standards in his precepts—those looking back to the Academy with its Renaissance-Baroque tradition and those that condoned greater freedom of expression and less subtlety of form. He himself felt the necessity for a hierarchical formality on a building's ex-

terior, but he was willing to concede more individuality and, presumably, modernity to the interior: ". . . simetrie . . . est aussi peu essentielle dans l'interieur qu'elle est importante à observer dans les dehors. . . ."[3] This implied separation of the two parts of a whole has led to many a lamentable mise en scène. Nevertheless, a division between exterior and interior was indeed practiced in early eighteenth-century French design—a Renaissance-Baroque classic style on the outside, built to uphold the importance, the dignity, and the ego of the old regime, with a Rococo interior to charm the senses of a society that needed titillation. Such design polarity is often seen as an indication of a split culture or a legitimately divided architectural purpose. Blondel may occasionally have had reason on his side.

49

SOME EIGHTEENTH-CENTURY
FRENCH HOUSES

Versailles (Figure 2.9)	Versailles	1701, remodeling of king's apartments; Oeil de Boeuf; Cabinet de Conseil; decoration of the Chapel 1712, Hall of Hercules; Grand Trianon, Cabinet des Glaces; Lepautre, designer
Palais Royal	Paris	1716, for the regent, redesigning of interior; Oppenord, designer
H. de Toulouse	Paris	For Comte de Toulouse; de Cotte, architect; Vassé, interiors
H. d'Assy	Paris	1719, for M. Chaillou; Oppenord, designer
Versailles	Versailles	1722, apartments of the dauphin; de Cotte, architect
C. Chantilly	near Paris	1735, rebuilding for Duc de Bourbon; decorative artist, Christophe Huet
Versailles (Plate 1)	Versailles	1725, decoration of queen's apartment; de Cotte, architect; Vassé, designer; decoration, Hall of Hercules, Vassé, designer 1735, panels in queen's apartments; Ange-Jacques Gabriel and Jacques Verberckt, designers *Cabinets et Petits Appartements du Roi* (Figure 2.11)
C. Neuf de Luneville	Lorraine	For Dukes of Lorraine; Boffrand, architect
C. de Craon	Near Nancy	For Marquis de Craon; cabinet by Jean Pillement
H. de Soubise (Figure 2.10)	Paris	1735, for the Prince de Soubise; Boffrand, architect; Oppenord, Pineau, designers
C. Rambouillet	Near Paris	For Comte de Toulouse, remodeled apartments; Oppenord or Verberckt, designer
C. de Rohan	Strasbourg	1731, for Prince Cardinal de Rohan; de Cotte, architect
C. de Jossigny (Figure 2.2)	Near Paris	1743, for Claude le Comte, Seigneur des Graviers
Versailles (Plate 1) (Figure 2.11)	Versailles	1745, remodeling the *Cabinets de la Reine,* of the dauphin, of *Petits Appartements, Salle d'Opera;* Ange-Jacques Gabriel, architect
C. Champs	Bire	After 1745, for Mme. de Pompadour; chinoiserie by Christophe Huet
Hermitage	Fontainebleau	For Mme. de Pompadour; Ange-Jacques Gabriel, architect; Verberckt, decorator
Pavillon du Barry	Versailles	Built for M. Binet, acquired by Mme. du Barry
Le Petit Trianon (Figures 2.4, 2.8, and 2.12)	Versailles	1762, 1768, for Mme. de Pompadour; Ange-Jacques Gabriel, architect
Pavillon de Louveciennes	Louveciennes	Ledoux, architect
Pavillon de Musique de Madame	Versailles	1780, for Marie Josephine de Savoie, sister-in-law of Louis XVI; Chalgrin, architect
Bagatelle (Figure 2.7)	Paris	1777, for Comte d'Artois; Bélanger, architect
H. Salm	Paris	for Prince de Salm-Kybourg; Rousseau, architect

INTERIOR DESIGN

Plans and Space Organization

When Louis XV returned to Versailles, he gave orders for the installation of a series of small rooms in the north wing. The building of these additions, now usually known as the *Petits Cabinets* or *Appartements du Roi,* indicate a fairly universal trend in planning in domestic precincts.

Despite talk of functionalism and of limited funds, the real cause for the altered emphasis in planning for convenience rather than show, for comfort, intimacy, and privacy, rests with the *Zeitgeist*. There must have been a premonition of impending upheaval and a cloistered shelter provided a psychological refuge. The natural domesticity of the sovereign may have provided both cause and effect.

Versailles set the style. Everywhere vast spaces were cut up into smaller quarters; new accommodations were thus provided. It was general for an apartment of ten rooms to consist of an anteroom, a principal reception room and a secondary one, or *salon de compagnie*, a dining room, a small library, private sitting rooms, boudoirs (i.e., small intimate rooms in a lady's apartment), and clothes closets. Larger homes might include a coffee cabinet, where guests could retire for coffee after dinner, a *medailler*, or cabinet for the display of medals, music and writing rooms, and *even* a bath. Indeed it was quite civilized planning, although the multiplicity of divisions would seem foreign to us. The overall arrangement was such that the areas designed for social intercourse were separate from those intended for domestic privacy.

The plan of the Petit Trianon is an illustration (Figure 2.8). The ground floor is for service, although much of its space is given over to the sweeping flight of stairs to the rooms above. The disposition here on the north-south axis of the staircase and principal salon is not bisymmetrical, although on the west or garden front the large dining room is arranged to look out squarely on the avenue of the formal garden.

When the property came into Marie Antoinette's hands, a floor was inserted east of the stairway for apartments for the royal children. This level was known as an *entresol*, and it sometimes encroached on attic space. The rooms provided, both above and below, had lower ceilings, hence were much easier to keep warm, a circumstance that in the absence of central heating would have much to recommend it.

Stylistic Qualities of Interiors

Because many changes in interior space organization, architectural detailing, and surface treat-

ments were made throughout the eighteenth century, a chronological framework is adopted for their description.

Period I. Last Years of Louis XIV: 1700–1715

J. H. Mansard and Robert de Cotte, who followed him, were the first architects at the Bâtiments during the last years of the old monarch's reign. We must now determine who the designers were who were responsible for the interiors. In the usual procedure these men worked in collaboration with the ruling architect. Sometimes it was hard to separate the two bodies of accomplishment and it often happened that the designer was not given the credit to which he was due as a member of the team.

Pierre Lepautre (1648–1716), whom Fiske Kimball calls the "father of the Rococo," was the chief *dessinateur* (designer) and *graveur* (illustrator, draftsman, or graphic artist) in the last decade of Mansard's tenure. He was the son of the engraver Jean Lepautre, whose ornaments had so

Figure 2.8 Plan of the Petit Trianon, Versailles, 1762–1768. Ange-Jacques Gabriel, architect. (a) small parlor; (b) salon; (c) back parlor; (d) dining room; (e) sitting room; (f) cabinet; (g) hall; (h) ball room; (k) antechamber; (m) principal staircase; (n) reception room; (p) staircase. (Adapted from J. Arnott and J. Wilson, *Petit Trianon*, New York, 1913.)

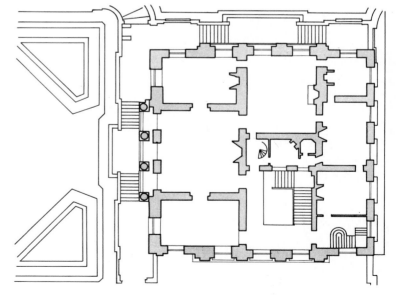

influenced Le Brun and under whom the latter had trained. Pierre's drawings are recognizable by a firm skilful line and freely but carefully executed wash shadows. His work can be seen in the remodelings around the turn of the century at Versailles palace and the Grand Trianon.

Here we observe certain changes that inaugurated the Rococo as distinct from the grand style of the seventeenth century. In the first place the French Baroque coved ceiling was eliminated, thereby reestablishing the rectilinear space. (The cove had been built on a false framework of wood which had been covered with plaster.) The extra height thus gained was transferred to the panels. Mirrors placed above the low fireplace were increased in height and extended to the cornice. Sometimes a single tall frame encompassed mirror and *trumeau* painting. Ceilings were plain,

Figure 2.9 *Chambre du Roi Louis XIV,* Versailles, remodeled in 1701–1714 by Pierre Lepautre, designer. (Lauros-Giraudon.)

often with a low-relief rosette at the center.

Not only were vertical divisions emphasized but the old horizontal divisions of panels were frequently discarded. Mirrors had arched tops without the break of an impost block (Figure 2.9) and all openings responded.

Another first for Lepautre was the abandonment of heaviness in architectural orders. Although he may occasionally have used slender pilaster strips to demark his proportions, their profile was low. His moldings were in relatively low relief and with them he incorporated delightful carvings—the inspiration for which may have derived from Berain—and used them in the spandrels where arch meets pilaster. The corners of the panels were sometimes truncated by C scrolls. Thus began with Lepautre the marriage of ornament and frame that is one of the principal trademarks of the Rococo.

No one should pass by this transition period in French decorative art without stopping to study

the work done at Versailles in the king's apartments, centrally located over the little oval court. In this instance the architect and designer could not start from scratch, for the enterprise was the result of decisions to shift the boundaries and change the purposes of some of the existing rooms and at the same time to give the ensemble a face lifting. The preserved designs for the *Chambre du Roi* are from the pen of Lepautre who succeeded in producing the new look by adding arched mirrors over the chimney pieces and bed enclosures and by carving the old heavily molded door frames and window casings to greater delicacy in his own light style. Here in the room where Louis died a very special architectural feat of combining the new and the old was accomplished. In the words of Fiske Kimball,

> . . . a union of qualities rarely seen together, nobility and splendour and moderation, richness and refinement, monumentality and delicacy, strength and lightness, in the vital synthesis of a perfect work of art.[4]

In the antechamber of the king, better known as the gallery of the *Oeil de Boeuf* because of its oval window, a similar amalgamation of traits can be noted in a merging of the two centuries. The delightful frieze by Van Clève and associates above the cornice, which depicts golden infants at play against a trellised background known as *mosaique,* should never be missed. It leaves one with a warmer feeling toward *Le Roi Soleil,* for it is said that it was done at the king's behest.

During the last decade of Louis's life the Versailles chapel, begun by Mansard, was completed under de Cotte and the designing hand of Lepautre. In its tones of white, gold, and pastels, its ceiling so illusionary of the noonday firmament, and its overlay of tall columns which surmount the structural arches in one of which Lepautre placed an altar of his own design—this work constitutes an epigram to the seventeenth century, Louis, and Mansard as well as an introduction to the eighteenth. When its antechamber, the Hall of Hercules, was completed in the first years of Louis XV's occupancy, a new era had arrived. Its inception, nevertheless, was the work of the designers of the preceding reign.

Several hands are perceptible in the actual carving in the chapel, among them those of the most important artist for the future, François-Antoine Vassé (1681–1736), said to have been the favorite sculptor of de Cotte. He was a provincial boy, schooled by his father in the sculptor's art. The prizes he won in academy contests were presented by the Duc d'Antin, then superintendent of the Bâtiments—hence his future.

Vassé's work in the Royal Chapel shows a plasticity not so conspicuous in Lepautre. The profiles of Vassé's moldings favor the cyma curves rather than the rounded bolection. Lightness is achieved by piercing. Thus Vassé assumed an important role even before the death of his predecessor. His significant contributions, however, date from the Regency.

In addition to the principal designers, the period made use of ornamentalists, the oldest of whom has been mentioned frequently—Jean Berain (1640–1711). Berain is known principally for his arabesques, a manner of panel decoration already waning in favor of woodcarving. His paintings of airy nymphs and acanthus foliage growing from the panels' central candelabra supports are charming. He made much use as well of flat bandwork connected with C scrolls. The publication of his designs by his son-in-law served to spread his influence. Berain was the favorite artist of Monseigneur, the Grand Dauphin, for whom he designed the Chateau Meudon.

Claude Audran III (1658–1734) also worked for Monseigneur at Meudon. He rested his claim to royal favor on his work on the ceilings, still done on a composition of cardinal and diagonal axes. Their chief and novel charm lies in the playful scenes in which birds and monkeys (*singeries*) are forced to share the stage with humans. Both Berain and Audran used their light-hearted skills in designing for the royal tapestries. The *Musée des Arts Décoratifs* possesses three ceilings attributed to Audran and possibly done for the little Duchess of Bourgogne, mother of Louis XV, at her Chateau de Ménagerie, after her arrival at the French court.

In the face of such panel painting the impressive ceiling frescoes of former years retreated. They remain only in churches and a few halls of state—witness the immense noncompartmentalized piece by François Lemoyne (1688–1737) in the Hall of Hercules and another in the adjacent chapel by Antoine Coypel (1661–1722).

Thus the major characteristics that differentiated French eighteenth-century interiors from the preceding Baroque were well established before the close of Louis XIV's reign. The architectural ordering by classical canons had been abandoned. Rooms were made to appear higher with tall arched panels, and, as in all French work, an architectural unity of height was established. Surfaces were largely of boiserie with linear patterning, which, shallow in relief, was already uniting part to part to make a unified whole without destroying the sense of architectonic character.

Period II. The Regency and Early Louis XV: 1715–1723 to 1735

During the term of the regent, Philippe Duc d'Orléans, and continuing to the last years of the *Premier Architecte* de Cotte (1656–1735) the Rococo style fulfilled its initial phase as a mode known to the French as *Le Style Régence.*

The principal architectural achievement of the Regency was the redoing of the old Palais Royal, but because only drawings remain to show what was done there at that time, we look to other works of the Regent's favorite architect, Gabriel-Germain Boffrand, to suggest his innovations. In the remodeling of the *Hôtel de Soubise* (1735–1740), now the *Musée des Archives,* Boffrand left one of the most treasured examples of the era. It was Boffrand's genius to be not only a skilled planner of interiors but also an artistic modeler of space. This was not the first time, as we know, that Baroque oval rooms appeared in France. Here, however, in the salon of the Prince and the *Salon d'Hiver* of the Princess (Figure 2.10) are nonorthogonal volumes that possess a continuous undulating rhythm of wall and ceiling. Whereas the *Salon d'Hiver* has over-panel decorations done by Charles-Joseph Natoire (1700–1777), the prince's chamber contained well-rounded figures which extended from panel to panel and were not retained within any one them—a new method of handling.

Working with Boffrand in much of this development was the designer Gilles-Marie Oppenord

(1672–1742). The younger man needs an introduction. Gilles was the son of a naturalized Hollander, Jean Oppenord, ébéniste to Louis XIV. He had studied in Italy but showed particular interest in the work of Bernini and Borromini rather than in the Renaissance artists to whom the French Academy was devoted. Therefore it is easy to understand how Oppenord, like Boffrand, became an artist who molded space and why, with this proclivity, he too became a favorite of the regent —and why the two, architect and designer, could work happily together.

The interior at the Hôtel d'Assy, adjacent to the Hôtel de Soubise, has been credited to Oppenord throughout. In d'Assy the design of the panels and interior openings promoted the illusion of flowing space. Corresponding arched tops are interconnected with spandrel patterns that reach out to one another. Overdoor paintings are enclosed in swelling cartouches which are easily articulated in the rhythm of the whole. Withal there exists a relative sense of rest and composure accomplished by the use of blank space and by a planned subordination and cohesion. Oppenord's wall treatment, inherited from Berain and Lepautre, is essentially linear, although its movement is a counterpart of Boffrand's shaping of internal spaces.

One other famous *hôtel* of this period belonged to the Comte de Toulouse, the legitimated son of Louis XIV and Madame de Montespan. This interior was done by the government architect de Cotte, working with Vassé. Here again we notice the latter's fondness for rhythmic contours, the free organic bow of the curves of the fireplace, and the frontal and diagonally placed consoles.

The Comte also renovated his Chateau de Rambouillet at that time. The carving in some of the rooms is of such quality and effulgence that it has long caused wonder about the artist. Ownership would undoubtedly implicate Vassé. Character points to Oppenord. Some have attributed it to a still younger man from whom we shall hear—Jacques Verberckt (1704–1771), a carver by profession and another of the fine craftsmen who came from Holland.

Some of these men were in a position to try their wings when the court returned to Versailles. The royal establishment of builders came back

Figure 2.10 *Salon de la Princesse* (*Salon d'Hiver*), Hôtel de Soubise, Paris, 1735–1740. Gabriel-Germain Boffrand, designer; over-panel decorations by Charles-Joseph Natoire. (Giraudon.)

into prominence with the immediate necessity of completing the Hall of Hercules, the readying of the apartments of the queen on the occasion of the marriage of the young Louis to Marie Leszczinska of Poland, the refurbishing of the suite of the Duc d'Orléans, and most particularly the first work on the suite of rooms that Louis had claimed for himself. This work done at Versailles illustrates the more conservative and most elegant aspect of the Rococo (Figure 2.11).

De Cotte and Vassé were responsible for the earlier part of these undertakings. Vassé's commitments were characterized by his mirror treatments which were delicately framed with sculptured palm stems that spread at the top into a decorative arch. Because both de Cotte and Vassé were aging, it was foreordained that younger men would take the initiative. Ange-Jacques Gabriel took over from Vassé in the creation of the queen's suite (Plate 1). Under him, and working from his designs, was the carver Verberckt.

By 1730 interiors had changed from the early eighteenth-century manner of Louis XIV to that of the Regency period in which space itself gained an undulating quality, a new and somewhat uncharacteristic French development. Linear decoration became freer, reaching out to ceiling and field. Carved boiserie and paint panels enriched the whole with all the fantasy that the most fertile imagination could project.

Period III. Culmination of the
Rococo: 1730–1750

In the second quarter of the century the Rococo reached its maturity in the exploitation of asymmetry, in which a panel at the right of a room answered another at the left. It should be borne in mind, however, that French decoration has never completely forsaken formality. Placements have always been bisymmetrical: large fireplace mirrors flanked by carved panels and double doors. Asymmetry occurred only in minor elements, in a framework of bisymmetry. Moreover, the designers for the king were always more conservative in expressing the mode. It is interesting to note that the word *symmetry* had lost its classical connotation of *proportion* and was applied in the sense of bilateral correspondence.

This last phase of the French Rococo is known as *le goût nouveau* (the new taste) or *genre pittoresque* (the picturesque style), something piquant and singular in nature's effects. It is precisely at this time that the word *rocaille* became a significant descriptive term in French design.

Several designers were its prime representatives. Juste Aurèle Meissonier (1695–1750), who succeeded Jean Berain and his son as private designer to the king, drew many illustrations of ornaments that appeared in several books of engravings about 1734. A native of Turin, he brought an Italian feeling for Baroque plasticity to his work. Endowing it with asymmetry, he produced patterns with such pronounced torque that several elevations were required to convey their total appearance.

Meissonier's style found ultimate favor only in central Europe, where the Baroque had put in such a belated appearance that it blossomed in the cultural atmosphere of the eighteenth century. This union favored the acceptance of precious objects conceived in the freest manner.

The artist who best exemplified the French aspects of the pittoresque Rococo was Nicolas Pineau (1684–1754). Returning to Paris in 1726 after years spent in Russia, he turned his sculptor's genius to designing. Many of his drawings remain at the *Musée des Arts Décoratifs*. Here we see extreme attenuation of moldings and ornament, which allows more space for a still more liberated play of decoration. This consists of interplay between tendrils and interlacing which invades the panels in such a way that even the edges are broken by curves. Often the dado strip is omitted and sprays of ornaments unite top and lower panels.

Pineau reintroduced the ceiling as an important element in the scheme. Large cartouches were placed at cardinal points and the upper molding of the cove that had come back into fashion undulated as a three-dimensional extension of the wall. Pineau broke with strict French geometry to the extent of placing fireplaces, windows, and doors in rounded niches and indeed conceded enough to plastic treatment of space to use rounded corners. Otherwise, however, French linear quality and delicacy of surface treatment was respected.

Figure 2.11 Window overlooking the *Cour de Marbre, Petits Appartements du Roi Louis XV,* Versailles, ca. 1735. Ange-Jacques Gabriel, designer; Jacques Verberckt, carver. (Giraudon.)

In closing the door to this exquisite, feminine, fairylike period of French decoration—a period that all of the world would at times like to embrace as an escape to Elysian fields—we note that the royal works in progress did include a few design innovations. In the *petits appartements* (Figure 2.11) the pastels were new—the *au vernis* to be detailed later—the carvings of Verberckt, more imaginative, the paintings, more windswept. This was accomplished always with that classic French reticence characteristic of the younger Gabriel—the innate quality that enabled him to bridge so successfully the period in the last years of Louis XV which forecast the coming of the Neoclassic.

In relating these two eras, a special place must be allowed for the lavish patronage of the Marquise de Pompadour. Wealthy now in her own right, she used her passion for houses and their furnishings to acquire fourteen. Among them were the Chateau de Champs, her hermitages at Versailles, Fontainebleau, and Compiègne, and the rental Hôtel d'Évreux (Palais de l'Élysée). Her per-

sonal architect was Jean Cailleteau (?–1755), called Lassurance, as was his father, and designated Lassurance II. The character of all that she touched veered toward exquisite elegance rather than novelty. Its quality derived from circumstances that are seldom duplicated in the world of fashion—a discriminating taste coupled with all the consummate artistry and finesse that wealth could command in a court and land in which these attributes were available.

Period IV. The Neoclassic

La Pompadour's style sense not only served to keep French design on a conventional keel, it was an influence in the direction of the Neoclassic. Her brother, the Marquis de Marigny, returning to France after his Italian tour as a capable young man of twenty-four, cast his weight as a proponent of a movement away from the excessive licence of the *genre pittoresque* toward the more circumscribed manner of the classic.

The early interiors of Gabriel's Petit Trianon (1762–1768) are among the best examples of this period of transition (Figure 2.12). Rococo characteristics existed in the retention of low relief ornament, much continuous paneling, and em-

57

Figure 2.12   Interior, the *Belvédère* at the Petit Trianon, Versailles, 1762–1768. Ange-Jacques Gabriel, architect. (Lauros-Giraudon.)

phasis on verticality that is part of the Louis XV era. Straight-line emphasis, however, began to intrude—moldings acquired classical profiles and ornaments were bisymmetrical and academic in inspiration. In most rooms ordonnance returned. Room shapes were rectangular and all ceilings were flat. The principal mantels were straight-sided with *gaines* (i.e., tapering pedestal supports often with human termini) at their corners.

The same character of conventional transition is seen in the interior architectural changes that occurred in the palace of Versailles itself. The rooms of the King's apartments at Versailles, which were first done in the thirties, were altered in the fifties and sixties under the guidance of Gabriel in a style that reflected the Trianon. Although the later Neoclassic style favored painted panels, either on canvas or wood, many of this period at Versailles were carved. Succeeding Verberckt as woodcarver was Jules-Antoine Rousseau, a royal artist.

Before Louis XV died in 1774—of smallpox, the scourge that for several centuries had been no respector of rank in its decimation of the population—a more robust phase of the Neoclassic was evident. In 1770 the Salle de l'Opéra at Versailles, work on which had been in progress since 1748 under Gabriel, was rushed to completion for the wedding of the Dauphin, the future Louis XVI, and Marie Antoinette.

The theater interior reintroduced colossal columniation and compartmental framework, as well as French classical ornamentation done in bas relief by the sculptor Augustin Pajou (1730–1809). The hall is now used by the French Senate and has undergone several drastic changes in decoration since its inception. In Louis's time it was painted a soft green to harmonize with the blue velvet hangings. In the later era of Louis Philippe it was repainted in red tones. *Chacun à son goût.*

Some rooms both at Versailles and in the Petit Trianon were redone by Gabriel for the Dauphine in 1770. The style of ornamentation is a mature and refined version of the Neoclassic which bears a relation to the style of Robert Adam in England, a lighter and more domestic classicism. By 1778 plates of Adam design began to appear in France and influenced such men as the architect Bélanger,

who has on occasion been dubbed the Anglophile dandy.

Working with Gabriel for Marie Antoinette was Jean-Simeon Rousseau de la Rottière (1747–?), the son of Jules-Antoine Rousseau. He is said to have been her favorite interior designer. The Cleveland Museum of Art owns the painted panels of a lovely little Neoclassic room taken from an old Paris hotel. Done by Rottière, they display arabesques on green canvas ground with musical symbols for motifs and bear close comparison with the boudoir of Mme. de Serilly by the same artist which is now in the Victoria and Albert.

Also at the Cleveland Museum is a charming small room in the Neoclassic manner taken from the Hôtel d'Hocqueville in Rouen which was extensively remodeled about 1780 (Plate 2). Its wood panels, its plaster sculpture, its parquet floor, and its blue, gold, and brown color scheme illustrate the vigorous phase of the style.

As the decade of the revolution drew near, even the impetus needed to redesign interiors was lost. When extravagant French interiors could again be created, they were in the heavy style of the Empire.

Painting and Sculpture

Many of the painters of the eighteenth century not only served as ornamentalists but also did portraits and easel and panel paintings, thus forming from these mixed media a new element in room decoration. The first in point of time was the Flemish genius Antoine Watteau (1684–1721). His wall vignettes are known from engravings made after his untimely death. Like his canvases, the subject matter was largely taken from the Italian *commedia dell'arte,* which were typed dramatic situations, well known since the sixteenth century. Otherwise they were of a genre with which Watteau was uniquely successful, known as the *fête galante,* thoroughly characteristic of the French seventeen hundreds. In these paintings, aristocratic persons were seen celebrating some sort of pleasurable occasion or pastime, usually in a rural setting. In *pastorales,* on the other hand, simple country folk are the actors. Whatever was touched by Watteau's brush carried an aura of atmospheric space which is well

Figure 2.13 *The Embarkation for Cythera,* Antoine Watteau (1684–1721). Louvre, Paris. (Cliché des Musées Nationaux—Paris.)

indicated in *The Embarkation for Cythera,* a fabled never-never land in a dream world (Figure 2.13). It was a tableau of Rococo people disporting themselves in unreality.

Nicolas Lancret (1690–1743), a follower of Watteau, worked much in his manner, although his figures are more precisely fixed, hence illusion is minimized.

The Chateau de Chantilly was rebuilt during the the Regency for the powerful Condé family. One of the Chantilly rooms, now known as the *Salon des Singes,* was done by the artist Christophe Huet (?–1759). Little is known of this painter and decorator (the two names are almost synonymous in Rococo France) except that he lived in Paris in presumably affluent circumstances. Although the subject matter of animals—of monkeys in particu-lar—acting as humans had been relished since

Medieval times and had been a favorite topic for French panels since Berain, Huet was the indubi-table master. The last work of his life was done at the Chateau de Champs in 1758 for Madame de Pompadour. There he painted panels for the large salon and for a small boudoir. The salon displays not only *singeries* but *chinoiseries*—oriental fig-ures in an occidental setting.

A friend and favorite of Pompadour was Fran-çois Boucher (1703–1770), fourteen years her sen-ior (Figure 2.14). He like Cochin is said to have instructed her in the art of engraving. By her favor he became *premier peintre* to the king and ulti-mately director of the Academy. His role as su-pervisor of tapestry production must remain for later telling. Although Boucher was greatly influ-enced by Watteau, it is evident that his genius was more virile. His scenes are realistic and his women sensuous flesh and blood as Watteau's never were. Boucher could straddle the worlds of fantasy and reality in a manner that made him the decorator of boudoirs par excellence. To do

Boucher justice, however, it must be acknowledged that he was an artist of prodigious facility and indefatigable industry and that his subjects ranged from religion to opera decorations.

Jean Pillement's (1726–1808) talent was largely of a decorative nature. The Chateau de Craon just south of Nancy boasts chinoiserie panels by him. Jean Honoré Fragonard (1732–1806), pupil of Boucher, may be studied in a series of partitions painted around 1773 and intended for Madame du Barry's Pavillon de Louveciennes but never accepted there. They are now in the Frick Museum in New York. As little as we might associate the style of Jean Baptiste Simeon Chardin (1699–1779), in its fondness for commonplace subjects, with salon painting, nevertheless there can be seen in his mastery of tonal gradations, of his quiet grouping of objects in a poetic light, the charm that enabled him to work with Charles Amadée Philippe Van Loo (1705–1765) on the decorations at Fontainebleau.

The favorite painter of the royal family was

Figure 2.14 *Cupids in Conspiracy,* François Boucher (1703–1770). Cleveland Museum of Art. (The Cleveland Museum of Art, Gift from the Louis Dudley Beaumont Foundation.)

Jean Marc Nattier (1685–1766). As the queen was more hampered by a lack of funds than the royal mistresses, Nattier's commissions were less frequent. It is reported that among the many artists in the employ of the crown who had to press for their pay Nattier was no exception. François Lemoyne, who did the ceiling paintings for the Hall of Hercules at Versailles, is said to have committed suicide in despair after failure to retrieve the cost of his paints.

Jean-Charles Delafosse (1734–1789) was the ornamentalist who bridged the Rococo and the Neoclassic. He was accustomed to offer his customers a choice between the two styles—a certain indication that revivalism and eclecticism were aborning.

Hubert Robert (1733–1808), who collaborated with Richard Mique, painted large canvases of classical scenes. Having spent most of his life in Italy, he had the ability to clothe Neoclassic statues and ruins with French grace.

Just as it is difficult to treat most of the eighteenth-century painters as divorced from their role as decorative artists, so the sculptors of the period cannot easily be discussed except in relation to their place in the scheme of complete de-

Figure 2.15 *The School Mistress,* Étienne Maurice Falconet, Royal Sèvres soft-paste biscuit porcelain group, ca. 1757. (Manufacture nationale de Sèvres.)

sign, for much of their work, either in terra cotta or hard stone, was intended for architectural settings. One of the earliest was Étienne Maurice Falconet (1716–1788). A poor boy who had attracted the attention of Lemoyne, he became the latter's pupil. Best known for his colossal statue of Peter the Great in St. Petersburg (Leningrad), which he executed between the years 1776 and 1788, he is certainly endeared to us for his series of decorative sculptures made under the patronage of the Marquise de Pompadour for the Sèvres porcelain factory, where in 1757 he took charge of the sculpture department. Some of these works are ceramic but many are in marble (Figure 2.15).

The taste for the terra cotta or biscuit figure was a characteristic of the age, and Claude Michel

(1738–1814), better known as Clodion, was a facile and an engaging practitioner of the art. He created a seemingly inexhaustible number of fat little cherubs, nowhere better seen than in the *Invention of the Balloon* at the Metropolitan (Figure 2.16). He also made many little creatures in the genre of the faun. Clodion was apparently a better artist than son-in-law and his autumn-summer marriage with Catherine Flore Pajou

Figure 2.16 Model for a proposed monument to commemorate the invention of the balloon in France in 1783. Claude Michel Clodion. Terracotta. Height 110.5 cm. Metropolitan Museum of Art, New York. (The Metropolitan Museum of Art, Rogers Fund and Frederic R. Harris Gift, 1944.)

(daughter of sculptor Augustin Pajou) was dissolved during the Revolution. An outstanding group of Clodion sculptures may be seen in the James de Rothschild collection at Waddesdon Manor, Buckinghamshire, near Aylesbury.

FURNITURE

Organization of Craft

The student of French eighteenth-century furniture can be at no loss for material. According to Mr. F. J. B. Watson in his catalogue of the famous Wallace collection of French furniture, more than 9000 pieces were recorded and described in the *Journal du Garde Meuble,* or record of the guardianship of royal furniture, in the hundred years following the initial entry in 1673.

Royal purchases, however, no longer count for all French furniture of the finest quality. During the eighteenth century many more people bought *les meubles* and they chose many more types. Not only the king and court and foreign aristocracy but also an affluent population constituted a potential market. This not only gave reason for the manufacture of pieces of provincial calibre, it introduced an entirely new method of merchandising. The *marchand-mercier,* who bought and sold furniture on speculation entered the picture. The customers of such a man as Lazare Duvaux, who kept a shop in the Rue Saint-Honoré where the craftsmen were centered, included fashionable members of the aristocracy and Mme. de Pompadour, whose patronage was the best advertisement any firm could capture. A new diversion of shopping had been introduced to amuse a bored nobility.

The coterie of French *menuisiers* was still further tightened by a type of quality guarantee. After 1741 a member of the furniture maker's guild was required to stamp his name, the initials JME (*Juré des Menuisiers-Ébénistes*), and the date of the jury inspection on every piece of furniture. Sometimes an ébéniste merely used his own initials, like the Germans, father and son, Bernard Vanrisamburgh, whose mark was B.V.R.B.

Royal protégés as well as certain *ouvriers libres* (free craftsmen) who might be working in religious institutions, were not subject to guild restrictions.[5]

The reason for such qualification lay in the fact that foreign craftsmen, then largely from central Europe, were coming to Paris, lured by the hope of gaining some of the lucrative French jobs and government positions.

Because guild members in France were registered and the date of their acceptance into the guild fixed, the JME marking, taken in conjunction with the guild records, became a clue to the authenticity and date of the piece, just as the royal records serve in locating articles made for the crown. Thus after midcentury it is easier to analyze style trends with chronological exactness in France than in England, where no such system of marking prevailed.

Chronology

We are justified in dividing French eighteenth-century furniture into at least three style groups. The first may be called late Louis XIV or, more commonly, Régence. It covers roughly the first quarter of the century. Then enters the full-blown Rococo which is traced to its final asymmetrical phase in the midforties to midfifties. The last period is the Neoclassic, known in France as *le goût Grèc* or *le style antique.* This was observable from midcentury.

Materials and Processes

The media for this spate of furniture were similar to those of the grand siècle. Oak and French walnut continued their dominance, but fruit and local woods were exploited for the provincial pieces. Elaborate articles were marquetried and given ormolu mounts as before. For such inlay exotic woods were used, often with the tones of the amaranth or *bois de violet* (Shakespeare's "purple amaranth") played against the dark purple to black of rosewood and the lighter tones of the tulip. As mentioned, ebony waned in favor at precisely the time that the wood inlayer, the maker of the finest veneered furniture, acquired the name of *ébéniste.* Woods used in Rococo furniture in general possess fortuitous color striations; Neoclassic woods such as mahogany and

63

French eighteenth-century furniture, which was left in its natural finish throughout the Regency, in later years was often painted. This was no ordinary work. It might have been the famous type of surface known as *vernis Martin*, a hard eggshell texture similar to that of the best Oriental lacquer, the trade secret of the five members of the Martin family of craftsmen (Guillaume, Étienne Simon, Julien, Robert, and his son Jean Alexandre). Not claiming to have invented the process, they developed it with such artistry that it has given their name renown. Their skill was in much demand for the decoration of furniture, small articles, and even carriages. The walls of the Dauphine's apartments at Versailles were in *vernis Martin*.

Another type of finish is known as *antiquing*. This consisted of an additional coat of some neutral pigment, such as umber, applied so that it appeared to soften the original color along the edges or over the surface. Gold was used in a similar manner.

Concessions to comfort dictated upholstery, supplemented by squab cushions filled with down. Elastic springs are said to have put in their first appearance. Caning was especially favored on Regency chairs, and wire mesh covered the doors of bookshelves. Silks and Chinese papers lined the interiors of cabinets.

Types, General Description, and Craftsmen

If it was difficult to determine all the type names of French seventeenth-century furniture, it becomes something of a game to learn those of the eighteenth. Again remember it is not necessary to know every new designation. Often the original records are ambiguous in this matter.

Storage Furniture. The *armoire*, the traditional standing piece of French storage furniture, persisted throughout the eighteenth century, although it became somewhat smaller in size. The example illustrated here, an *armoire-bibliothèque* (wardrobe-bookcase), is approximately 8 ft high, 4½ ft wide, and 1½ ft deep. It is one of a pair, made about 1720, and attributed to Charles Cressent (Figure 2.17).

Figure 2.17 Armoire-bookcase (one of a pair), attributed to Charles Cressent, France, ca. 1720. Cleveland Museum of Art. (The Cleveland Museum of Art, Purchase, John L. Severance Fund.)

satinwood have flashes of changeable light embedded in the grain of the material, a patterning that lends interest to straight-line pieces.

All varieties of marble were popular for table and cabinet tops. In Neoclassic pieces inlays of Sèvres porcelain took the fancy of the fashionable.

Cressent (1685–1765) may be accredited as the principal cabinetmaker of the early period and particularly of the Regency when he was employed by Duc Philippe. A pupil of André Charles Boulle, he practiced the crafts of cabinetmaker and *fondeur* (metal caster). This versatility got him into a great deal of labor trouble with the fondeurs' guild, which contended that the bronze castings should be turned over to one of their members—which Charles was not. Posterity nevertheless rates him as a good sculptor of ormolu, having learned from his father François, a sculptor in the service of Louis XIV. Possibly his dexterity in the arts gave his endeavors a unity of style sometimes felt to be absent when several men collaborated on one piece of furniture.

Whatever the cause, Cressent's work showed a refinement of taste above the average. The armoires under discussion illustrate the transition from the style of Louis XIV—which under Boulle was likely to be heavy, dark, and ornate—to that of Louis XV, its antithesis. The marquetry of the carcass is expertly devised of tulip and king woods mounted with bisymmetrical ormolu motifs. It forecasts the future in the restrained curve of its hood, the diagonally placed corner pilasters, and the truncated corners of its panels. Cressent did not at that time sign his pieces, but the evidence of workmanship, style, and provenance are reason for crediting these armoires to him.

Other varieties of the *armoire-bibliothèque* are germane to eighteenth-century France. A type that is wide and comparatively low is known as a *bibliothèque-basse*. Such a piece might have front elevation dimensions of 6 ft wide by 5 ft tall.

The Wallace collection contains a Regency commode. It is basically rectangular and has four tiers of drawers. The canted corner supports are modestly scrolled and terminate in *pied-de-biche* (foot-of-the-hind) feet—concessions to the incipient Rococo. The front is a serpentine curve, still another forecast. Its ebony wood on deal and its embellishment with Boulle *contre-partie* marquetry turn it toward the height of the Sun King's reign.

Another exquisite commode (Plate 3) is decorated with elaborate gilt bronze mounts which may have been commissioned from the atelier of Jacques Caffiéri (1678–1755). The importance of

ormolu in French furniture of the eighteenth century and the supreme position of the Caffiéri family as fondeurs (particularly that of the fifth son of the original Filippo who came from Rome to the Gobelins in 1660) make such an assignation reasonable for these superb examples of the art. The cabinet most likely came from the workrooms of Jacques-Pierre Latz (ca. 1691–1754), under whose direction the whole was designed and made. Latz was a naturalized German who became by complimentary title an *ébéniste du roi*.[6]

Looking at the commode with its subdued marquetry in tulip on oak and its warm variegated marble top, we see an article designed in three dimensions, the exposed elevations of which deviate from any one plane. The ormolu, so expertly chaste, is pronouncedly asymmetrical, although some bilateral reversions are required.[7] After long acquaintance it seems to transcend its materials and become the manifestation of its joyous aristocratic way of life, the full-bodied Rococo.

Thereafter, belts were tightened, sizes diminished, and strictures were called for. A commode by Jean Henri Riesener (1734–1806) in the Wallace Collection may be cited (Figure 2.18). Note that the veneering on oak is mahogany and that instead of marquetry patterning the natural wood grain is allowed to speak for itself. The mounts are in the manner of Pierre Gouthière (1732–1813/14). The straight lines of the body, the bisymmetry and indeed the rigidity of the bronze, characterized by wreaths and cornucopias, and the return to the acanthus leaves that encase the tapered feet indicate the classical influence. The splayed central panel is typical of the late production of this top-ranking ébéniste of the Louis XVI period.

Attention is merited for a similar chest of drawers made by René Dubois (1737–1799). Two sons of Jacques Dubois (1698–1763) were ébénistes, another example of the continuance of dynasties in French craftsmanship. The guilds pursued a policy of granting special privileges in the nature of lower entrance fees to descendants and thus continuity was encouraged. This Dubois cabinet is embellished with oriental lacquer combined with ormolu mounts. Ormolu laurel wreaths, lion masques, and profile medallions take the place of warriors' heads, scrolls, and interlacing L's. The

Figure 2.18 Commode, stamped J. H. Riesener. Mahogany veneered on oak; bronze mounts chased and gilt; Spanish brocatello marble top. Height, 89.5 cm, width, 137 cm, depth, 61 cm. Wallace Collection, London. (Crown Copyright, Reproduced by permission of the Trustees of the Wallace Collection.)

lacquer imagery, however, pursues its customary oriental asymmetry.

In order to wrap the French eighteenth-century periods into a neat and final package, let us observe a sideboard or *desserte,* again by Riesener. Only to say that in this mahogany piece with Sèvres plaques and regimented bronzes—characteristic of the artist's style in the last years of the monarchy—we see elegance and exquisite daintiness, but withal a lack of strength that had previously characterized a culture.

Size, of course, quite expectedly grew smaller with the intimate apartment. Many quite diminu-

tive pieces of storage furniture followed the trends of the time, among which are the *cartonnier,* designed to hold papers, an *armoire d'encoignure,* or corner cupboard, and a *chiffonier,* or high narrow chest of drawers intended for the boudoir. This was a feminine society and *les petits meubles* were filling in the small spaces in a miniature interior scene.

Tables. The eighteenth century had a legion of tables of all possible sizes, uses, and descriptions. Stylistically, they gradually lost their seventeenth-century stretchers, they decreased in size, and they assumed curvilinear contours and cabriole legs until the reentry of classicism brought back the fluted, straightened tapered ones with saltire or serpentine stretchers.

Before the latter part of the century large dining tables were almost nonexistent. Smaller ones

Figure 2.19 A carved wood console table that illustrates the story of Ganymede, French Regency style, first half of the eighteenth century. Height, 84.5 cm, length, 97.5 cm, depth, 51.5 cm. Cleveland Museum of Art. (The Cleveland Museum of Art, Gift of J. H. Wade.)

were designed to seat more intimate groups and large collapsible boards took care of the banquets. The imposing rectangular table continued to dominate the center of the salon.

The console, dating from the reign of Louis XIV, assumed its most graceful forms during the Rococo. One, for many years a great personal favorite, has all of the qualities that spell the Regency (Figure 2.19). In natural unfinished wood, its cabrioles, which turn into women's figures as caryatids but end surprisingly in hooves, are joined at the bottom by masks and dragons. Its perforated skirt is elaborately carved and pierced with roses, C swirls, mascarons, and a representation of Ganymede being carried aloft by the eagle. The top is old rose and ivory-striated marble. Attached to the wall below a boiserie or mirror, the whole is a consummate job of artistry that combines usefulness, decorative quality, and the romance of suggestive tales in one unusual composition.

Card and game tables, of course, were still in use everywhere—triangular ones for playing *tri* or *ombre*, four-sided, for *quadrille*, and even pentagonal pieces for five-handed *brelau*. Trictrac ta-

bles, many of which pivoted so that their boards might be stored when no longer needed, were required for backgammon. The *rafrachissoir* was a small round table with shelves, which stood near a larger table for serving guests. The *guéridon* was a small stand with a metallic grille railing. It was intended to hold statuary or plants. Sometimes a smaller version was the *jardinière*, whereas the larger *bouillotte* was intended for a card game of that name. And so on and so on.

The *bureau* continued in popularity with an endless variety of feminine pieces, among which are cylindrical and kidney-shaped examples. The *poudresse* was a toilet table, whereas the *bureau-toilette* combined the functions of desk and dressing table. The *bonheur-du-jour* was similar in shape but contained a small cabinet for bibelots as a superstructure.

Then followed the imposing desks, the *bureau plat,* the familiar *secrétaire,* and the cylinder or roll-top. The *bureau à cylindre* (roll-top) is a form that dates from the middle of the eighteenth century, the most famous of which is known as the *bureau du Roi Louis XV,* now at the Louvre (Figure 2.20). It was begun in 1760 by the illustrious ébéniste of the central phase of the Rococo, Jean François Oeben (1720–1765). At his early death it was completed by his pupil, Jean Henri Riesener, who married Oeben's widow. These two men represented the pinnacle of Rococo and the transition to Neoclassic. Both were Germans who came to France to seek profitable employment. Oeben entered the atelier of Charles Joseph Boulle, son of André Charles, and on the latter's death succeeded him as *ébéniste du roi.* In turn Oeben became the teacher of a generation of prominent cabinetmakers including, in addition to Riesener, Martin Carlin (?–1785) and Jean François Leleu (1728–1807). Oeben, possibly because of his German background, gave to the fanciful Louis XV style the firm, precise technique it required. He became the favorite ébéniste of Pompadour and was constantly in demand by her.

The *bureau du roi* was signed by Riesener in 1769; the affixation of the signature was customarily the final act of the ébéniste. Actually at least six craftsmen worked on this famous desk: Wynant Stylen who did the woodwork and Jean Claude Duplessis I (?–1774) and Louis Hervieux

Figure 2.20 *Bureau à cylindre de Louis XV* (back), Versailles, 1769. Jean Henri Riesener. (Cliché des Musées Nationaux—Paris.)

who provided the mounts were among them. Riesener made at least six similar *bureaux à cylindre*. Later ones possess the straight legs of the Neoclassic style. The original is typical of the transition from Louis Quinze to Louis Seize in furniture design. Its cabriole legs are already straightening and its bronzes are bisymmetrical in principal contours. Two reclining bronze figures hold girandoles or candlesticks at the corners and a clock occupies the center at the rear. The chief ornamentation is the pictorial marquetry which was probably designed by Oeben and completed by his assistant. Mechanical features

for opening the drawers are evidence of the growing interest in machinery.

Riesener came into difficulty with the crown as the period of financial troubles approached. Although he was always in high favor with Marie Antoinette and indeed continued to make furniture for her chateau at Saint-Cloud as late as 1791, other men who could produce at less cost were given commissions. Such was Guillaume Beneman who made a desk in the Rothschild collection. It was copied from the lower section of the *bureau du roi*.

Adam Weisweiler (*maître* in 1778) was a most skilful German craftsman who operated in France during the last quarter of the eighteenth century. He, too, was a favorite of the queen. His early work for her may be illustrated by a secretary now in the Wrightsman Collection at the Metropolitan, an ebony case embellished with lacquer plaques in the Chinese fashion. Weisweiler favored lacquer decoration and by the use of this medium effected a singularly happy union of decoration done in Rococo with straight-line pieces of Neoclassic.

Many desks had paraphernalia for locking up private papers. This fact serves to illustrate the growing importance not so much of *belles-lettres,* for which the smaller women's desks were adequate, but of business correspondence and desks for the executive. A cylinder desk by David Roentgen (1743–1807) is on display in the Kress bequest at the Metropolitan. Its elaborate marquetry in light woods with feminine swags and clusters of roses is fairly typical of Roentgen's taste. Born in Germany, his shop was in Neuwied, and he maintained branches in Paris, Berlin, and Vienna—another sign of the times.

The Kress collection has a fall-top upright desk, a *secrétaire à abattant* or *en armoire* (a type that dates from midcentury) on which is an elaborate marquetry pattern designed by Jacques-François Blondel, the architect, and lifted from his book of engravings. This desk is signed by Pierre Roussel (1723–1782).

Even in an era surfeited with fine furniture the name of Claude Charles Saunier (1735–1807) should be mentioned. His work, similar to Riesener's (Figure 2.18), looked forward in its simplicity to the next period of design in which a certain eminence is found in overall shape rather than in decoration.

Seating Furniture. The great divide in seating furniture, which has often been placed around 1700, forecasts lower height, broader seat, softer padding, and flowing curved lines. The cabriole leg, which resembles the underpinning of a graceful faun, joins the body with a cartilaginous transition and no longer appears as a disjointed member. Cyma and serpentine curves flow over arms and back.

Total scale continued to grow smaller. Some of the late century chairs seem so fragile in size and construction that they project some unhappy thoughts about the masculinity of the race. Nev-

ertheless, the great majority of examples are commensurate with a contemporary living room. Chair seats were 18 in. from the floor, a height that is anatomically comfortable but would seem to be too high for modern loungers.

With the Neoclassic the dominant line became straight, although arms retained a graceful curve. The often-used oval back was supported by extensions from the rear legs, a type of construction that forms a weak joint. Legs were tapered and four-sided or, more often in France, fluted and terminated in a thimble foot.

Types of seating furniture remained similar to those of the seventeenth century, although there were many specialized additions. The *fauteuil* was the standby. Its arms, however, were not upholstered except for *manchettes* or small pillows of padding where the arm rested. The *chaise* was a similar important chair without arms. A *bergère* (Figures 2.21 and 2.22), that almost too comfortable invention of the French, was a fully upholstered armchair with a squab cushion filled with the lightest down. The feeling engendered by sitting in a bergère is almost akin to being wafted by clouds of silk, as are Fragonard's cupids. The *tabouret* was the ubiquitous stool, still used by the court in the presence of royalty, although the etiquette was said to be losing some of its rigidity.

A series of *fauteuils* illustrates changing style character. A late Louis XIV chair in the Wallace collection will serve as the first example. The back is slightly lower; the curved lines preserve their Baroque C's; stretchers remain; and the upholstery is still three-dimensional in texture.

Compare it with a Régence fauteuil (Figure 2.23) designed by René Cresson (trademark—Cresson Laine, one of the members of the celebrated Cressent family and possibly the designer of the Ganymede console). Chair back and seat height has been reduced; outlines are continuous curves; scale is much lighter; arms join the seat a distance from the front; the finish is natural, the upholstery, a light cane, and the manchettes, a smooth brown leather. The carving has flattened in profile; feet are delicately terminated in a padded scroll; stretchers have disappeared.

A chair of about 1730 at the Metropolitan suggests some further changes (Figure 2.24). The framework has been painted and gilded; uphol-

Figure 2.21   A French *bergère,* period Louis XV. Formerly in the collection of the Cleveland Museum of Art, present whereabouts unknown. (Photo, Courtesy of the Cleveland Museum of Art.)

Figure 2.22   A French *bergère,* period Louis XVI. Formerly in the collection of the Cleveland Museum of Art, present whereabouts unknown. (Photo, Courtesy of the Cleveland Museum of Art.)

Figure 2.23   Regency arm chair (*fauteuil*), signed Cresson Laine, 1715–1723. Oak. Cleveland Museum of Art. (The Cleveland Museum of Art, Purchase, Dudley P. Allen Fund.)

stery is silk damask; the proportions have been broadened in relation to height and the arms sweep downward to meet the front seat. The curvature of all members is certainly more pronounced.

The Rothschild collection at Waddesdon Manor contains a *chaise* that bears the closed crown stamp allowed to princes of the blood. Here we see elaborate embroidery on a satin covering. The carving on the apron exhibits the asymmetry that marks the height of Rococo influence.

Next are *fauteuils* (Figure 2.25) made by Georges Jacob (1739–1814). Jacob was a Burgundian by birth. His parents, farmers in the district, died when he was young and the boy made his way to

Figure 2.24 Alcove, ca. 1730–1735, plus later additions. Design attributed to François Antoine Vassé. Carved oak, painted and gilded, with panels of the Four Seasons. Metropolitan Museum of Art, New York. (The Metropolitan Museum of Art, Gift of J. Pierpont Morgan, 1906.)

Figure 2.25 Two *fauteuils* from a set of six arm chairs and a sofa, French, signed G. Jacob. Height 100.3 cm, height of seat 43.8 cm, width 73 cm, depth 72.4 cm. Birch chair frames, carved and gilt; Beauvais tapestry upholstery. Wallace Collection, London. (Crown Copyright, Reproduced by permission of the Trustees, The Wallace Collection.)

Paris to learn the art of wood sculpture, a natural aspiration for a Burgundian. He set up an independent shop in 1765 and became the maker of some of the finest chairs in the Louis XVI style. Through his friendship with David, the arbiter of Empire decoration, he was one of the few pre-revolutionary designers to continue successfully into the nineteenth century. The Wallace Collection exhibits a set of six Jacob armchairs. Made of birch and *rechampi* (i.e., background painted, carved decoration gilded) in white and gold, their

proportions had not been radically changed but the carcass is straight-lined. They have weak construction because the side supports extend only as far as the base of the back, possibly for the purpose of making the whole appear lighter in bulk. Seats here are slightly bowed in front. The arms are straight and end in a curved upright to the front seat. Legs in this case are round fluted. Connections between seat and legs or between uprights and arms are square blocks on which are *paterae* (round or oval disks decorated with a rosette or other ornament). Arms are carved with a laurel chain or some similar bisymmetrical linear decoration. In the chairs under discussion the fluting returns to the classical acanthus. The upholstery on this set is Beauvais and features pastoral or musical instruments—then in great favor.

In addition to stools and single chairs there

were seats intended for use by several persons. A *canapé* is fundamentally a bench with a back. The name has become a generalized term for various forms of couch or sofa (see Vol. 1, Chapter 10). A *marquise* or *causeuse* was similar to an English settee or love seat—in reality an enlarged chair. A *sofa en gondola* is one in which the arms sweep around to form the back. A *chaise longue à Duchesse* is one in which there is a small *dossier* or back.

Among the many specialized chairs the following list is both provocative and suggestive of the multiplicity. A *voyelle* is similar to an English cock-fighting chair, designed for sitting astride with one's arms resting on the back. It was frequently used by gentlemen when observing card games. A confessional bergère, the counterpart of the English wing chair, had upholstered cheeks (wing flaps) and arms. Pivoting chairs were *de bureau*. A *coiffeur* was one with a leg in the center front, designed to fit under a dressing table.

Figure 2.26   Bed, attributed to Georges Jacob. France. Cleveland Museum of Art. (The Cleveland Museum of Art, Purchase, John L. Severance Fund.)

Exactness in terminology cannot be ensured. What is a Lawson sofa, a lounge chair, an occasional chair today?

BEDS.   With the Rococo the poster bed (*lit à colonnes*) tended to disappear. One with a high headboard or head and footboard, often carved and upholstered within a frame, took its place. Bed hangings, which were still customary were suspended from the ceiling or wall or projected from a headboard. The oldest form, the *lit à la duchesse*, popular during the reign of Louis Quatorze, had a tester with valance and curtains supported from the wall at the head of the bed. The *lit d'ange* had a shorter tester with two looped side draperies. A *lit à la Polonaise* had a dome with suspended curtains. The average family continued to place its bed in a wall alcove along which curtains could be drawn, a disposition properly known as a *lit à la Mauçaise*.

The Cleveland Museum displays a bedstead (Figure 2.26) attributed to Georges Jacob. It is even more interesting that by tradition it is the bed of Marie Antoinette from Versailles. The embroidered silk head and foot upholstery are re-

putedly the work of the queen and her court from the designs of the famous textile artist Philippe de la Salle. The precise strong carving of the framework, with its natural roses and stylized rosettes, its torches and spiraling wreaths, demands the exquisite raised stitchery to effect the necessary balance. The width of the bed is 58 in. and the length, 7 ft, although the whole is so well proportioned that it scarcely seems so large. I have often watched little children whose eyes fairly popped out of their heads when told that it be-

Figure 2.27 Clock, Germany, ca. 1750. Carved and gilded wood and faience. Cleveland Museum of Art. (The Cleveland Museum of Art, Purchase, John L. Severance Fund.) This clock is an example of German Rococo style. The design bears relation to engravings by François de Cuvilliés, architect of the Pavilion Amalienburg at Nymphenburg, Bavaria.

longed to a queen. They neither appreciated that "uneasy lies the head" nor that the bed was less physically comfortable than their own, for it had neither springs nor firm mattress.

Musical Instruments

The eighteenth century developed the finest harpsichords ever produced. Like the virginal and the spinet, the strings of this instrument were plucked with jacks. In the harpsichord the sets of jacks and strings were multiplied and stops were introduced. Its design therefore bore little relation to those of its predecessors and more closely resembled a long, narrow, winged piano with a small keyboard. The finest were made by the family of Burkhardt Tschudi of Switzerland and London. The characteristic artistic finish was of lacquer, gilt, and painted pattern, often in gay vermilion with black and gold.

The pianoforte, first seen in Italy in 1711, grew rapidly in popularity with the century and in the nineteenth appeared as the piano.

Timepieces

The newly perfected mechanism for recording time created its own extensive market. In France the unity of the eighteenth-century decorative scheme and the prevalance of elaborate wall paneling provided a small object like a clock (pendule) with an importance that could not be granted to large pictures. Thus, although French horologists such as the Le Roys (e.g., Pierre, 1717–1785) were renowned, it was the casemaker who was usually referred to in any description of the instrument.

The mantel clock (horloge de cheminée) and the bracket clock (cartel, when designed as one with its wall support) were ubiquitous. Often a floor pedestal (escabelon) was specifically planned for its small clock. The long case clock, or régulateur, was never so popular in France as it was in England.

Whereas central Europe and England were faithful to the tradition of wooden clock cases (Figure 2.27), France more often added bronze or a similar metal. Therefore names and styles are linked to those of the French fondeurs. Although designs followed the foremost decorative trends, they rarely lost contact with architectural form. Neighboring countries, on the contrary, frequently produced cases that incorporated all the exuberance of the Meissonier-Pineau epoch, often without a saving structural sense.

With the advent of Neoclassicism not only more rigid classical designs but new materials, such as marble and porcelain, appeared.

TEXTILES

One reason for the preeminence of French furniture is the supremacy of French textiles in this period. They graced chairs and beds and were used to cover walls and line cabinets. On the floors were French rugs. These fabrics were silks from Lyon, printed linens and cottons from Normandy, tapestries from the Gobelins, Beauvais, and Aubusson—and Savonneries.

French silks were the finest that the occident has ever designed or woven. Although they have frequently been called pictures on the loom, they were really representational designs for weaving. Men like Jean Revel (1684–1751), Philippe de la Salle (1723–1803), and occasionally a panel painter like Pillement created with an expert eye to the potentials of textile processes (Figure 2.28).

Weaves became progressively flatter and brocades and damasks predominated. They were made on a draw loom which enabled the weaver to create his delicate traceries with an artist's liberty because the pattern threads were the wefts that did not have to bear the tensions of the loom and thus could be fine and of many different colors.

In Louis XV's reign the textile designers transformed the floral ogivals of the late Baroque into graceful undulating curves or trellises for natural designs of flowers, ribands, and laces. Here the French decorative skill was again demonstrated in patterns integrated by climactic rhythms and punctuated by the careful placement of motifs that terminated a section and provided a visual rest.

In the period of transition during the Regency Jean Revel's designing was significant. He was a silk manufacturer as well and is also said—in the

Figure 2.28 Silk brocade, possibly designed by Jean Revel. Musée Historique des Tissus, Lyon. (Musée Historique des Tissus, Lyon.)

loose terminology of the day—to have been an architect.[8]

Certainly his patterns, although quite realistic, exhibit a structural sense. They show a degree of modeling and three-dimensional projection and have a breadth of scale and depth of coloring that allowed their use during the transition years from high relief to shallow linear carving. With considerable use of black and gold threads as highlights, the result was a sumptuous piece.

The gamut of pastel colors in vogue during the middle of the century was fully developed by Philippe de la Salle who has, with a high degree of reason, been called the world's greatest textile designer (Figure 2.29). His most famous work was done for Catherine the Great of Russia (ruled 1762–1796). No apology need be made, however, for the fabrics he designed for the bedroom of Marie Antoinette at Fontainebleau. A botanist as well as a weaver, he was capable of brocading on taffetas and satins the most natural of floral sprays, such as branches of laurel, often strengthened by black shadow outlines, though rarely with gold. We see exotic birds, cornucopias of largesse, and trophies of garden paraphernalia trellised on ogi-

Figure 2.29 The boudoir of Marie Antoinette, Fontainebleau, designed by Richard Mique. The wall silks were presented as a wedding gift to Marie Antoinette by the city of Lyon. (© Arch. Phot. Paris/S. P. A. D. E. M., 1979.)

val framework. Chenille thread incorporated in the pattern often provided a depth and softness not otherwise to be achieved.

During the last decades of the century patterns in silks, as in all textiles, became smaller. The ogival or wavy band was replaced by a supporting lattice of narrow warp stripes on which were twined diminutive floral sprays. The forces for flattening the textures and lightening the colors remained in operation. Watered silks were made in accordance with new techniques learned from

England. Plain, close-clipped velvets were also in vogue and were useful materials for covering *fauteuils* and *bergères*.

The silk men had suffered frequently because of enforced specialization. An event such as the death of the Dauphin in 1711 and the court mourning that followed closed out all orders for sumptuous fabrics and many thousands of silk weavers were thrown out of work. Because they were not allowed to emigrate for fear of divulging craft secrets, untold misery beset such weaving centers as Lyon.

Whereas silks were the fabrics of the rich, cottons and linens were used by the less affluent. When events placed a damper on lavish display and India offered new designs, brighter colors, and crisper textures, it is easy to understand the growing popularity of printed textiles among all classes. A character in one of Moliere's plays, the *Bourgeois Gentilhomme*, says, "I have had these Indiennes made. My tailor tells me that men of fashion wear such gowns in the morning."[9]

The process of manufacturing these *Indiennes* or *Persiennes* was tedious and time consuming. The paper design was transferred to cloth by pouncing charcoal through a pierced pattern. It was then outlined in black with iron filings. These outlines gave the early cottons a rich character. Resist chemicals were then applied to all parts that were not intended to take the blue indigo dye. When this deterrent was removed, certain white portions were treated with a mordant to assist in the registration of the red to violet hues, whereas the resist was left on other portions to ensure that they remained uncolored. The cloth was then immersed in a red dye bath. After removal of the resist, yellow was painted in over those blues that were to appear green. Green dye was not perfected until the nineteenth century. Because of the brush work done on them, these cloths are sometimes called *toiles peintes*.

In catering to the increasing demand for lower prices, the Eastern trade first complied by producing handblocked cottons, which were called *chints*, from the Indian word for *small spot*. The early chintzes were largely blue. Near Madras where they were manufactured was the little town of Calicut, which is said to have been the first place to have produced blockprinted cottons in tones of red, purple, blue, and yellow. This cloth was known as *calico*, similar to small-patterned printed cottons known today.

Cotton bedcovers, called *palampores* when blockprinted and *kalamkers* when made by hand-painted techniques, were exported to Europe. The designs consisted of a centralized *hom* or *tree of life* pattern on which the greatest inventiveness in auxiliary motifs was used.

Naturally the West was anxious to imitate these printed oriental fabrics. The art of blockprinting had been practiced in the Rhenish monasteries since Medieval days. Patterns had been printed on linen in Italy. Now France, England, and the Low Countries sought production on a larger scale. In France the center of this trade was in Normandy in such towns as Rouen, Elboeuf, and Louviers. One weaving town was Creton, which contributed its name to cretonne. In England the western towns such as Manchester are facetiously known as Cottonopoli. Cotton was not native to these northern countries and in the eighteenth century cotton material was imported *in the gray*, or unbleached, stage for further finishing.

One of the most interesting chapters in the French attempt to imitate the imported *Indiennes* is the story of the printed cloth known as *Toile de Jouy* (Figure 2.30). This industry was the result of the enterprise of a young man in a family of German dyers named Oberkampf. Dyeing was one of the chief problems of cotton manufacture, unsuccessfully solved in France and England. The

Figure 2.30 Toile de Jouy, *The celebration of the federation, July 14th, 1790*, after a design by Jean Baptiste Huet. Musée de l'Impression sur Etoffes, Mulhouse. (Musée de l'Impression sur Etoffes, Mulhouse.)

Oberkampfs were particularly well versed in the science of creating permanent cotton dye colors. The father of the Christophe Oberkampf (1738–1815), mentioned above, emigrated to Switzerland for religious reasons. The Swiss at this time supported a flourishing business that produced the more difficult printed fabrics. Oberkampf became financially successful by adding his knowledge of dyes to the Swiss printing procedures.

Christophe Philippe Oberkampf was born in Switzerland in 1738. Twenty years later he left his home for Paris, where he worked for a firm making colorful (incidentally, contraband) cotton prints. When the government ban was lifted in 1759, the young Swiss decided to open his own firm in the small village of Jouy near Versailles.

He had prodigious success, certainly for several reasons. In the first place he is said to have been an indefatigable worker, toiling almost twenty-four hours a day at his shop. Much of the labor of production he performed himself. He used the direct printing method learned from his father by which he was able to bypass the need for mordant application of colors in the red family. He also inherited his father's superior dye formulas. One of the reasons that the French government had closed numerous shops had been the poor quality of the dyes used and the fact that the colors soon faded.

The printing of some of Oberkampf's early toiles was done with a black outline and some painted detail. After 1770, when he had finally changed to the quicker woodblocking methods, Oberkampf made further progress by converting to copper roller printing.

In design the earliest *toile de Jouy* was imitative of the small Indian patterns. Later the current style trends were followed and chinoiserie, bucolic scenes, and classical subject matter were adopted. Often local vistas were used, and some cloth, intended for the American market, displayed Revolutionary ideology and views of American cities. The roller printing process had made fine line work feasible and thus delicate shading made for realism. The fine lines combined well with the fine texture generally used in eighteenth-century decoration, and the massing of the motifs created the illusion of large areas of color rather than small pictorial divisions. Colors were monotone blue, red, and mauve.

Jean Baptiste Huet (1745–1811), who also designed tapestries, made many of the best late Jouy designs.

The Jouy factory, which had been visited and honored both by Louis XVI and Napoleon, was all but destroyed by the Prussians in their advance on Paris in 1815. This was the year of Oberkampf's death.

Tapestries

Medieval tapestry makers were unequaled in their ability to use the potentials of tapestry technique to create representational wall hangings that conveyed the essence of religious and ideological feeling. Renaissance tapestries introduced pictorial storytelling. Baroque tapestries thrilled with their dramatic power. By comparison the eighteenth-century tapestries of France, although of fine weaving, featured escapist romance, circumscribed at the beginning and end of the century by classical fences and, at the height of the Rococo, by asymmetrical floral bowers.

The Royal Gobelins had been closed for a time after 1693 because of the financial slump contingent on war expenses. When they reopened in 1699, new men had taken charge. One of the first was Claude Audran III, whom we met with Berain at Meudon. As early as 1699 a set of tapestries of Audran's design, called *Les Portières des Dieux* (portals of the Gods), was put on the Gobelin looms (although additions were made much later) and with them the eighteenth-century style may be said to have begun. The Audran *Portières* included four that depicted the seasons (Figure 2.31) and four, the elements. In all the color is paler, the frame (i.e., *alentours*, the surround), narrower, and the central figure, vignetted on a bank of clouds. Indeed the background once more becomes as important as the main action.

French decorative art has often been enriched by families of artists, a phenomenon that the eradication of the guild system tended to destroy. One of these families was the Coypels. Noel Coypel (1628–1707) designed a seventeenth-century Brussels *Triumph of the Gods* for the Gobelins. It was he who painted the ceilings in the queen's suite and the Hall of the Queen's Guards at Versailles, and it was his son Antoine (1661–1722) who painted the central panel in the

Figure 2.31   *Bacchus: l'Automne,* tapestry from set *Les Portières des Dieux,* designed by Claude Audran the Younger. Cleveland Museum of Art. (The Cleveland Museum of Art, Gift of Flora Whitney Miller, Barbara Whitney Henry, and Major Cornelius Vanderbilt Whitney in memory of their mother, Mrs. Harry Payne Whitney.)

Versailles chapel. In the next generation Charles Antoine (1694–1752) designed one of the most popular Gobelin eighteenth-century tapestry sets. In it were scenes from Cervantes' tale of the adventures of that satire of a knight, Don Quixote. Coypel finished twenty-eight pictures in this set from 1714 to 1751. As was frequently the custom, several artists collaborated in the enterprise: the flowers were done by Louis Tessier and the animals by Claude François Desportes (1695–1774), each of whom was a master of his métier. Never have picture stories been more fun—the cowardice of Sancho Panza, who climbs a tree when the hunt becomes too thick, and the *alentours* of golden woven frames joined by peacocks—all spoofing the beloved hero who was trying so hard to do his thing.

The output of the Beauvais looms had never ranked with the Gobelins, and after the death of the manager Béhagle and the concomitant financial difficulties of the last of the seventeenth century the works faced bankruptcy. It was not until the painter Jean-Baptiste Oudry (1686–1755) was hired in 1725 that any decided upswing in performance was evident. Oudry was a marvelous painter of animals and has left us many canvases in the popular genre of the game of the huntsman's skill. Far more endearing are his Beauvais tapestries which illustrated the fables of the French raconteur Jean de La Fontaine (1621–1695). Needless to say that the portrayal of animals with human characteristics could not have found a better executor than Jean-Baptiste.

Oudry performed the stroke of practical genius that brought Pompadour's favorite François Boucher to Beauvais. This team of designers under the proprietorship of an able man, Nicolas Besnier, raised the reputation of Beauvais to a pinnacle at which it equaled, if it did not exceed, that of the Gobelins.

In 1733 Oudry was appointed head inspector at the Gobelins. For them he designed his most famous tapestries known as the *Hunts of Louis XV* in a country setting around Compiègne.

After the death of Oudry in 1755 Boucher was called to the Gobelins as chief inspector. During the period of his encumbancy he designed twenty tapestries now known as the Gobelin Bouchers. Because of crown policy at this time of willing-ness to sell to the foreign market, many of these Bouchers found their way to England. Six of the medallion tapestries adorned the dining room at Osterley Park. All low-warp weavings, they represent Gobelin's only period of low-warp use.

Boucher not only designed for Beauvais and Gobelins but continued to design for Beauvais after he had gone to Gobelins. One of his most unusual achievements in this last context was his Chinese set, six pieces of which were conveyed to the Chinese Emperor Ch'ien-Lung in Pekin in 1763. Their design is Chinese in subject but French in interpretation, as an example of the mishmash of chinoiserie then in vogue. The Chinese in return sent Chinese-made pieces to France. Here we see real Chinese interior scenery (e.g., in the *Family Gathering on New Year's Morning* tapestry, Figure 2.32), but little comprehension of the potential of large tapestry design.

Boucher also created designs for the Gobelins for the La Fontaine version of Cupid and Psyche which provided a background not only for French eighteenth-century eroticism but also furnished the excuse for a profusion of elegant interior detail associated with the court of Louis XV.

These midcentury works were composed on a somewhat different format than the earlier circumscribed patterns. Their framework was open, asymmetrical, and led the eye from groupings of animals and courtiers with their paramours back to an atmospheric idyll. Classical herms and vases might serve to keep balance between the extremes of romanticism and classicism, always so necessary to the French spirit.

Boucher died in 1770. The painter Jean Baptiste Huet, inspired by Boucher, then created pastorals for Beauvais. These were the last of the consequential tapestries to be made at either of the two principal factories during the eighteenth century.

The small factory at Aubusson, a town in southern France where rather coarse, less expensive tapestries had been woven since the fifteenth century, was struggling meantime with inadequate funds. In 1731 it received a shot in the arm when the government sent prominent dyers and painters from the Gobelins for a time each year in the hope of revitalizing production. Oudry and Boucher cartoons were loaned and Huet went to

Figure 2.32 *Family Gathering on New Year's Morning,* Ch'ing Dynasty, eighteenth century. Tapestry, silk and wool. Height 2.59 m, width 3.81 m. Cleveland Museum of Art. (The Cleveland Museum of Art, Bequest of John L. Severance.)

Aubusson for a brief period during the reign of Louis XVI. From 1740 to 1790 Aubusson showed the result of this blood transfusion, but the work became too painterly and lacked the quality that makes art great—design itself, the interaction of color, shape, and texture that provides some kind of interesting unity.

Among the effects of Aubusson are the tapestry and later the needlepoint rugs known by that name. Similar carpets were produced at Felletin, a small town nearby. Today the name Aubusson is (in loose terminology) likely to be assigned to a rug with no pile and with French eighteenth-century floral and scroll designs in pastel colors.

The Savonnerie factory continued to produce its pile rugs, which retained the stronger palette

and the bolder patterning of the seventeenth century, the time of their ascendency (see Vol. 1, Chapter 10). These tapestries, embroideries, and tufted weavings also served as eighteenth-century furniture upholstery.

WALLCOVERINGS

The eighteenth century opens the door to wallpaper as we know it today. In France it was Jean-Baptiste-Michel Papillon (1698–1768), of a family of dominotiers (the producers of small domino papers during the seventeenth century; see Vol. 1, chapters 7 and 10), who first used hand painting as an auxiliary to his woodblocking on small sheets of paper (approximately 14 x 18 in.) pieced together on a wall to form a pattern. In 1738 he wrote the article on *papier peint* for the encyclopedia edited by Didero and d'Alembert.

Near the center of the century the process of

roller printing, first with wood rollers and then copper, was introduced. Later the printing was done on rolls of paper rather than on the small sheets previously in use. The first invention made possible greater precision of outline, the second, the easier application to large areas.

The man who capitalized on these advancements was Jean-Baptiste Réveillon (?–1792), who added to the improvements the perfecting of size colors which enabled the printer to apply many colors to the same design. His papers often showed as many as twenty-six tones. Jean Baptiste Huet designed for Réveillon's Paris factory as he had for Beauvais and Jouy. Sometimes the same patterns were used for cloth and wallpaper.

Réveillon's establishment fell victim to the revolutionary mobs and, embittered, he departed for England, where he died. Jacquemart and Benard operated Réveillon's establishment from 1791 to 1840.

CERAMICS

During the eighteenth century European ceramics reached their peak achievement. This statement

Figure 2.33 *Cabaret* (tray with tea or coffee service), Chantilly factory, France, ca. 1730. Soft-paste porcelain *Kakiemon* ware. Cleveland Museum of Art. (The Cleveland Museum of Art, Purchase from the J. H. Wade Fund.)

will certainly not go unchallenged, for many will enter claims for fifteenth-century majolica or nineteenth-century porcelains. Nevertheless, for material, form, color, and the wedding of decoration to structural design, the favor lies with the best wares of the eighteenth.

To this excellence each country made its unique contribution. The second series of attempts to imitate Chinese porcelain occurred in France. A soft paste (*pâté tendre*—pottery clay plus frit glass) was made at Rouen, but it appears to have been a rather poor *blue and white ware,* done in imitation of similar Medici pieces. A small contribution was made by a factory at St. Cloud which seemed particularly interested in reproducing the patterns, some raised, of the oriental Fukien.

The most productive of the early French soft-paste firms was Chantilly, opened in 1725 by Louis-Henri de Bourbon, Duc de Condé and Lord of the Domain of Chantilly. The wares from this establishment may be taken as a guide to an understanding of the output of many other quite small and transitory endeavors. Chantilly and Rouen and St. Cloud endured only through three-quarters of the century.

The first Chantilly was treated to a tin oxide glaze, whereas the Chantilly made after midcentury used a lead glaze, which created a warmer cast and a thinner skin. Frequently Chantilly designs were patterned after Japanese *Kakiemon* (Figure 2.33) and used a yellow red for quaint sprigs of color in the style of the Japanese ceramic artist Sakaida Kakiemon.

Most factories used several different marks during even a short history and recourse must be to such a compendium as Chaffers[10] for positive identification.

From Chantilly we move closer into the aura of the court and to the soft paste of Vincennes and ultimately to Royal Sèvres. Vincennes may be considered an offshoot of Chantilly, for two brothers by the name of Dubois were discharged from Chantilly and took their ceramic secrets to Vincennes. A Chantilly workman, François Gravant, of more dependable character, secured the supervision of the Vincennes plant from the French Minister of Finance who had sponsored the enterprise. Product and management were vastly improved.

The enterprise then came directly under royal concession, and the king's jeweler and modeler, Jean Claude Chamberlain, called Duplessis, and other royal craftsmen, were deployed to its service. It was indeed a matter of great financial importance to the crown to be able to compete with the ceramic advances that had taken place in Germany. Vincennes, working under crown patronage, was assigned this responsibility. In 1753 Louis granted the factory exclusive porcelain rights in France and permitted the use of the intertwined L's as trademark. Beginning with that year, the use of the capital alphabet was adopted to signify the date: 1753 was A, 1754, B, and so on; W was omitted. In 1756 the kilns were moved to nearby Sèvres and the marks transferred to that famous ware. The double alphabet was inaugurated in 1777 but ceased with PP, the year of the revolution. The Vincennes product from 1753 to 1756 is highly prized for body and decoration. Vincennes produced hard paste later in the century.

Other early and noteworthy factories near Paris were situated at Mennecy-Villeroy and Bourg-le-Reine.

The French continued to make soft-paste porcelain long after the Germans had discovered and made the true hard-paste body. One reason for French tardiness lay in the fact that kaolin was not found in France until later in the century; but certainly the essential values of soft paste played a part. Although soft paste will not withstand extremes of heat and it is difficult to fire without kiln loss and despite the fact that the finished ware chips easily—all practical qualities that the French never overvalued—soft paste is more translucent and has a warmer tone than true hard paste. The two bodies are different also for the soft paste is more granular than the hard.

The Germans had stolen the march in regard to the discovery of what is known as the hard-paste porcelain body so revered in Chinese imports. The story of this accomplishment is, of course, well known, but its significance cannot be too strongly impressed. Johann Friederick Böttger (1682–1719) was a chemist in the employ of the King of Poland, Augustus II, who was also Elector of Saxony. Böttger was born in Thuringia under the rule of the King of Prussia, Frederick I. The story is told that he feared imprisonment and a royal command that would force him to practice the alchemist's skill—to turn base metal into gold —which every knowledgeable chemist was presumed to have. Be that as it may, it is certain that he crossed the border into Saxony, where nevertheless he found that his skills as an arcanist were still in demand. He was able, however, to persuade Augustus to put his trust in practical science, and the result, directed toward research in the field of ceramics, was the discovery of the kaolin body and in Germany the alabaster flux (rather than feldspar) of hard-paste china. Böttger thus bridged the years of magic and those of science.

Böttger's first successful experiment seems to have occurred about 1708 or 1709. In 1710 the king authorized the opening of the factory at Meissen, where the laboratories were located. The first Meissen white wares date from 1715. In the meantime the young chemist set himself the task of improving the production of a faience plant and evolved his famous red stoneware (Figure 2.34). Much of its decoration could be

Figure 2.34 Red stoneware vase, Meissen factory, Germany, 1708–1710. Johann Friederick Böttger. Cleveland Museum of Art. (The Cleveland Museum of Art, Gift of A. and R. Ball.)

Figure 2.35 Covered jar, Meissen factory, Germany, 1749. Gilt bronze mounts made in Paris, ca. 1750. Height 81.1 cm. Cleveland Museum of Art. (The Cleveland Museum of Art, Purchase from the J. H. Wade Fund.)

done with a glass engraver's wheel, so flintlike was the body. Applied decoration in the form of formalized leaf pattern and strapwork, derived from silver, was often seen.

The substance of the first Meissen (or Dresden—the two Saxony towns are adjacent) was very hard because of the alabaster flux (Figure 2.35). It was relatively opaque and somewhat yellow. Dainty sprig decoration was often applied to cover faults or pits. Most of these ornaments were of overglaze enamel. Thus the flowers stand out from the firm background in a manner not seen on soft paste. Honey gold was used for embellishment because the low enamel firing was sufficient to evaporate the carrier and leave the gold encrusted.

In 1720, after Böttger's death in 1719. Johann Gregor Herold took charge at Meissen. This is another story of circuitous piratage, for Herold was trained in a Vienna factory that had obtained its trade secrets from Meissen. Under Herold's leadership Dresden china became some of the finest and thinnest that Europe has produced.

Designs, which at first were largely derived from the Orient, began to borrow from Rococo painting. Shapes were derived from the contemporary arts. Colors were more numerous and higher fired, thus more integrated. Ground colors of canary yellow, apple green, lilac, and maroon were also incorporated into the body. After 1726 the two crossed swords became the Meissen mark, and many additions designated special periods and special wares.

For the long run between 1731 and 1775 Johann Joachim Kändler (?–1775) was model meister. The excellence of production subsequent to 1750 is often credited to another of those keen, artistic, but domineering ministers of state, Count Heinrich von Brühl of Saxony, who assumed directorship at Meissen in 1733. Kändler was a sculptor and modeled with a bold, almost Baroque, quality. He may be said to have inaugurated the art of porcelain figures as practiced in Europe. Even the plates of his celebrated "swan dinner service," (Figure 2.36), created for Count Brühl, were raised with sporting swans, dolphins, and nereids.

Whereas the early period of Meissen is characterized by Rococo forms, the Neoclassic style succeeded after 1770. The tendency then was to follow the lead of the Sèvres hard-paste patterns and to imitate the Sèvres colored glazes. In later years Meissen lost its unqualified lead and its design patterns became derivative. The Meissen factories sold seconds and put a mark through the swords to identify them. Numerous small concerns in the Dresden area imitated the mother establishment and used the Dresden swords with some addition as a distinguishing mark.

Other important mid-European factories may be listed as Vienna (1719–), Berlin (1761–), Hochst (1746–), Nymphenburg (1753–), Frankenthal (1755–1799), Fürstenburg (1758–1888), and Ludwigsburg (1758–1824).

And so back to France which we left near mid-century in the period dominated by Sèvres soft

Figure 2.36 Plate from the Swan Service, Meissen factory, Germany, ca. 1737–1741. Johann Joachim Kändler. Porcelain. Diameter 42 cm. Cleveland Museum of Art. (The Cleveland Museum of Art, Thirty-fifth Anniversary Gift.)

paste. The making of hard paste (*pâté duré*) had been delayed because no one came up with the chemical secrets. This deterrent was altered when in 1761 one Pierre Antoine Hannong of a factory near Strasbourg, a factory that had been able to experiment with the making of hard paste in crude commercial wares, sold his secrets to Sèvres. Pierre Antoine had occasion to regret his course of action for he was never paid by the French crown. The excuse had been shallow—the necessary ingredients demanded by the process were not then available in France. This was soon altered. During the sixties kaolin was found near Alençon and in the Perigord and by 1768 the

Sèvres *Manufacture royale de porcelaine* was making hard paste. For a time soft paste was also made, but after 1804 *pâté duré* was alone.

The verdict of time often rates Sèvres soft paste above its later achievements. This supremacy is due to several factors. First is the characteristic and already described beauty of the body. Second, because it is extremely difficult to throw soft paste on a wheel and even more so to mold it into intricate shapes, a simplicity of form necessarily results. Additional Rococo contours must be provided by the use of ormolu which adds interest and enrichment.

When all is said and done, however, French Sèvres soft paste owes its aesthetic quality to the patronage of Pompadour and the artists who had her favor—Falconet (Figure 2.15) and Duplessis, whom she backed for the positions of artistic responsibility. Her death in 1764, somewhat coinciding with the advent of hard paste at the factory, tipped the scales in favor of the earlier productions.

A soft-paste tureen made at Vincennes in 1752 and another made at Vincennes-Sèvres in 1756 are eloquent of this period of French supremacy (Plate 4). Notice the Rococo shapes with their restrained curves reminiscent of French silverware contours. In these, in lieu of ormolu mounts, the framing is done with gilded scrolls. Handles are invariably of naturally depicted vegetation. The background colors are *rose Pompadour,* a *bleu du roi,* turquoise, rare yellow, violet, two shades of green, and a soft purplish blue. The designs are frequently reserved on a white ground. In all examples the birds and verdure seem to merge with their surround without ever losing their identity.

Another important pinnacle for the Vincennes-Sèvres team is its production of soft-paste biscuit figurines (Figure 2.15), which were in answer to the Kändler output at Meissen. The two technical difficulties, those of firing the large pieces that the Germans favored and securing colors that would emerge true to natural palettes, were surmounted by making the figurines small in uncolored and unglazed biscuit. Thus "biscuit" or *bisque* was born. The name is said to have derived from the fact that bread baked hard for the soldiers was known as biscuit.[11] Sèvres biscuit fig-

urines ranged from 3 to 16 in. in height. They first appeared about 1750 and were made until supplanted by hard paste twenty-five years later. As many as 300 different models were cast. Often the mark of the *repareur* appears on them, not as might be supposed, a repair man, but rather one who joined together the separate parts. Made from drawings by such men as Boucher, Falconet, Jean Baptiste Pigalle (1714–1785), and Oudry, these statuettes are miniature masterpieces.

Although numerous other small ceramic factories, most of them under some form of royal patronage, flourished in France during the second half of the eighteenth century, they were not in any sense competitive with royal Sèvres and are largely of interest to those students who have made this period their specialty. Among these establishments were those at Tournai, Orléans, Strasbourg, Lille, Valenciennes, Caen, Limoges, Bordeaus, and Marseilles. Surrounding countries—Spain, Portugal, Switzerland, Russia, Holland, Belgium, and Scandinavia—also began to manufacture ceramics. Particular mention should be made of the Royal Danish factory at Copenhagen, in which Queen Dowager Juliane Marie took an active interest and in 1775 granted a fifty-year monopoly. It became a royal establishment in 1779. Its mark, carried to the present, is three wavy lines which represent the three principal rivers of Denmark. On a fine body of bluish white paste Danish artists painted the flora of the country on a service that the Crown Prince presented to Catherine the Great of Russia. Its patterns are continued today.

GLASS

France failed to take the lead in eighteenth-century glass manufacture, despite her earlier traditions. At late century the French glass houses that remain important today had their beginnings. Among them were Baccarat and Saint-Louis. Their output at that time was largely imitative of the cut glass of Bohemia, England, and Ireland. Following the Neoclassic fashion, milk glass cameos became a marketable product in France. Another novelty, tiny figures of sculptured enameled glass, known as *porcelaine en verre,* were made at Nevers.

METALS

Eighteenth-century French silver is of excellent quality but of meager amount. During the period of the Seven Years War (1756–1763) much of it was melted down to refill the royal coffers.

Paris, of course, led in production, although other mint towns such as Strasbourg, Lille, and Toulouse were becoming important. In the opening years of the 1700s cut-card work, typical of the late Louis XIV period, predominated. The Régence style, although marked by classical ornament such as the stylized acanthus motif, the repetitive strap-work seen in the engravings of Lassurance, and the diaper-designed background of Berain, introduced a delicate richness of curved outline scarcely noted before.

In 1729 Henri Nicolas Cousinet (1718–1788) made twenty-three pieces of *vermeil* (silver gilt) and porcelain to be presented to the queen in celebration of the birth of the Dauphin. The chocolate pot (Figure 2.37) from this set illustrates one of the first applications of French asymmetry of pattern. The entire collection, which consists of all the paraphernalia that could be required for the service of chocolate or tea while "on the road," is now at the Louvre. This compact, eighteenth-century traveling kit was called a *nécessaire*.

It is significant that this particular royal set included two chocolate cups of Chinese *blanc de chine,* a sugar bowl and teapot of Japanese porcelain, and Meissen pieces. Such precious foreign ware was often mounted in French silver.

Rococo patterns made use of embossing, engraving, and applied decoration. The designs of men like Meissonier would seem particularly suited to fashioning in a malleable metal such as silver. Indeed, that master of engraving is reputed to have been a silversmith, although it is thought that possibly this designation was an honorary one conferred by Louis XV in 1725 in recognition of his designs.

Although the names of many masters of this central period are worthy of study, those of Thomas Germain (1673–1748) and his son François Thomas Germain (1726–1791) are especially distinguished. The elder man was in the employ of Louis, Duc d'Orléans, son of the regent. The

Figure 2.37 Chocolatière de Louis XV, 1729. Henri Nicolas Cousinet. *Vermeil* (silver gilt). Louvre, Paris. (Cliché des Musées Nationaux—Paris.)

younger made many pieces for the courts of Portugal and Russia. François went backrupt because of the failure of his clients to pay.

The return to classical design in silver was not noticeable until around 1770. The work of Jacques Nicolas Roettier (1707–1784), who executed orders for Catherine the Great for presentation to her favorite Prince Orloff, was representative of the prestige of French silversmiths at that time. After Orloff's death Catherine bought back the service for herself.

Many silversmiths were also proficient in bronze. In addition to ormolu mounts on furniture and smaller objects such as candelabra and firedogs, mounts on precious porcelain were often of *bronze doré* (gilt bronze). Certainly Jacques Caffiéri (1678–1755), fifth son of Philippe

Figure 2.38 Pair of firedogs, Paris, 1752. Signed by Jacques Caffiéri. Height 44 cm. Cleveland Museum of Art. (The Cleveland Museum of Art, Bequest of John L. Severance.)

(1634–1716), was the most famous fondeur of the crown (Figure 2.38).

Oddly, Claude Michel, called Clodion, who patterned his delightful terra cotta statuettes with such Rococo coquetry, also worked in a more restrained manner, fashioning bronze chandeliers and similar objects with consummate skill. This professional dexterity seems to have been practiced by the three brothers Slotz, who, though prominent sculptors in the decorative field, designed many bronze fittings. Often a sculptor such as Louis Simon Boizot would create the model to be cast and chiseled by the fondeur.

The outstanding fondeurs of the last years of the monarchy (Figure 2.39) were Pierre Gouthière (1740–1806) and Philippe Thomire (1751–1843). Gouthière came to Paris sometime near the middle of the century from Troyes to become a *maître-doreur* in 1758. He was another man who married the widow of his employer, thus enabling her to carry on in her late husband's name and making the firm a tighter financial entity. A pretentious and charming Neoclassic house built in the Faubourg Saint-Martin belonged to the Gouthières (6 rue Pierre-Bullet). Gouthière typically lost his bills that were due from the crown. Bankrupt in 1788, he never recuperated his losses.

DESCRIPTIVE SUMMARY

Although French architecture of the eighteenth century remained essentially classic, interior design was notable for three accomplishments—first, advanced planning in domestic arrangements; second, the creation of a restrained, for-

Figure 2.39 Firedogs, France, style Louis XVI, ca. 1785–1790. Gilt bronze (ormolu). Cleveland Museum of Art. (The Cleveland Museum of Art, The Elizabeth Severance Prentiss Collection.)

mal, architectonic, yet flowing style of interior boiserie; and third, a happy feminine fashion in accouterments, all of which, of course, were altered toward the latter part of the century in ways described.

France had stood at the pinnacle where aristocratic taste, wealth, and an establishment of excellent designers and craftsmen joined to create regal yet comfortable interiors. With the Revolution the patrons and their subsidies vanished. Those craftsmen who survived served new masters. The style of the Louis was doomed. Eighteenth-century France was the last occasion when time, place, and circumstance united for creativity in the arts that we are studying. Adaptations and revivals mark the future, until?

CHAPTER THREE

Eighteenth-Century Italy

That man who appreciates the placid sky
and affects purity and simple garb . . .

Odes, Giuseppe Parini (1729-1799)

Impatient, riled, angry
Ever: I cause anguish to myself, and to others;
I yearn in peace for war, in war for peace.

Saul, Vittorio Alfieri (1749–1803)

CULTURE SPAN

Italy was a political satellite of the greater European powers throughout the eighteenth and first part of the nineteenth centuries. In Piedmont in northwestern Italy the Italian court of the Dukes of Savoy centered at Turin, that most French of Italian cities. Here the closest of blood ties with the French nobility served to carry the prestige of French styles southward. Because Savoy controlled the major passes over the Alps, she was able to play opportunist politics in a manner that usually proved to her financial advantage. As a buffer state she grew relatively wealthy and could afford one of the most elaborate of the toy courts of the region.

In Tuscany the last of the Medicis played out an ignominious existence as Grand Duke. The province was turned over to Lorraine and through marriage returned once more to Austria. At Genoa in the 1750s, when the young Scot Robert Adam was making a study tour of Italy, he was passingly interested in a pretty girl in a fashionable domino. After some inquiries, " 'We soon found her to be of no small rank, being the nearest surviving relation of the Medici family. . . . Her own name, Mary of Medici. . . .' "[1] She had probably been named after Duke Gian Gastone's sister, the Electress Anna Maria, who bequeathed the Medici art collections to the public of all nations on the stipulation that they were never to be removed from Florence. Thus by fiat was created a legacy that continues to speak to the many of all nations who throng the Queen City of the Arno.

Venice, stripped of her oriental trade but maintaining her seductive charm and her mercantile instincts, became the playground of Europe—an eastern and exotic mecca that attracted a restless European aristocracy newly introduced to travel. Some tourists remained to build their villas in the valley of the Brenta. The late Gothic centuries in Europe had witnessed that first internationalism which was of the church and church art; the eighteenth in Italy saw a cultural interchange on an aristocratic caste level.

Rome remained the prestigious capital and at that time had more of a cosmopolitan tone than any other in Europe. It attracted not only nobility and talent but also serious students of the classic scene—just that mixture of society so necessary to an intellectual and stimulating atmosphere. It was here that the patronage of Cardinal Albani and the work of Winckelmann gave status to romantic and serious interest in archaeology and Neoclassicism. In 1772 the Vatican Museum was established to house what is now the world's largest collection of material from the classical past.

Meanwhile the papacy, in an attempt to maintain neutrality in the power struggle that took place in the surrounding states between the Bourbons and the Hapsburgs, lost the support of both. Moreover, church policy split between the factions that advocated church reform from inner regeneration (Jansenism, from Cornelius Jansenius, Bishop of Ypres, who in 1638 published a book advocating that policy) and those who sponsored external reorganization (the Jesuits). These conditions served to sap the strength of the Vatican and its power fell easy prey to Napoleon's army at the end of the century. In the anticlerical atmosphere of the revolution the popes remained occasional prisoners, not to return to their native home until 1815.

In Campania the suzerainty of the Spanish Bourbons, although often interrupted, created periods of sufficient prosperity to allow considerable building in and around Naples. Sicily, too, a pawn of superior powers, became a playground for the southern Italian aristocracy.

Despite the general political and financial uncertainty, the arts flourished. It is not surprising that the opera was brought to a high state of perfection (Giovanni Pergolesi, 1710–1736) in the playtime atmosphere that prevailed.

It is more to be wondered that science made strides with such men as Count Alessandro Volta (1745–1827) in electricity, Antonio Genovesi (1712–1769) in physics, and Giambattista Vico (1668–1744) who laid the basis for the modern social philosophy of history.

In literature, so often the antenna of change—in the Academy of Arcadia with its outlook toward a sentimentalized past, in the calm and reasoned poetry of Giuseppe Parini, which again views social caste as an organ of *noblesse oblige,* and in the serious patriotic drama of Vittorio Alfieri with its impassioned cries—we find the chronicle of this individualized and changing society.

ARCHITECTURE

Social conditions certainly affected the what and when of eighteenth-century Italian architecture. The wealth of the Spanish Bourbons served to build the palace at Caserta (Figure 3.1), just north of Naples, which had undoubtedly been designed with an eye for Versailles. Its facade is a monotonous, bisymmetrical repetition of windows framed in classical aediculae with the alternating pattern of the Roman Palazzo Farnese. It has an ineffectual projection of end pavilions in relation to the central temple portico, a weak use of the colossal order, and a tame contrast of textures. This is Roman classicism, returned from its French sojourn, without the grace that characterizes Versailles at its best, without Gabriel's sense of proportion, and without the strength of membering in Perrault's Louvre.

The interior arrangement of Caserta is, however, remarkable. Laid out as a spacious rectangle with inner cross arms and four courtyards, its central axis provides that immense vista through three vestibules to a prolonged allée that outdoes the vastness of the Versailles gardens. In the central vestibule views are provided in eight different directions through an enfilade of rooms and out toward the courts. The Baroque characteristic of gigantic staircases and controlled sightings can boast no better manifestation. This is the serious, wealthy side of the eighteenth-century Italian scene, with its full pretensions to classicism.

The architect of the palace, Luigi Vanvitelli (1700–1773), although a Neopolitan by birth, was of Dutch parentage, the son of Gaspard Van Witel. After studying and working for Pope Clement XII in Rome he was commissioned to build Caserta in 1752. Vanvitelli is related to several utilitarian works of note, the prime one being the construction of the principal viaduct of Naples. This gives us a foretaste of the day when architects will be more concerned with structural engineering and will not consider it beneath their dignity to plan for straightforward functional design. Recall that Lodoli was an Italian. Vanvitelli's job at the Vatican included watchdogging for any imperfections in the structure. His architecture might have returned to the classical elements of the Baroque in appearance but his philosophy incorporated all good building techniques.

In the Imperial City there was little construction of enormous palaces but significant revitalizing of the old. If southern Italy, with its long history of Spanish rule, was understandably prejudiced in favor of tradition and its architectural badge of classical design, farther north the eighteenth-century buildings preened their Baroque feathers more openly. The Corso wing of the Palazzo Doria-Pamphili, with its play of light and shadow over its undulating facade and its curved-headed doorways and windows, is an illustration

Figure 3.1 The Royal Palace at Caserta, near Naples, begun in 1752. Luigi Vanvitelli, architect. (Alinari/ Editorial Photocolor Archives.)

from secular architecture. It was the work of Gabrieli Valvassori (1683–1761), done during the second quarter in the most productive years of Roman eighteenth-century architectural activity.

This was the time of civic planning of numerous city squares and their beloved fountains, such as the Trevi (completed in 1762 from a design by Niccoli Salvi but inspired by a Bernini drawing). A Roman landmark is the flight of steps which rises from the terrace where stood the old Spanish embassy to the Holy See. It was designed by Alessandro Specchi (1668–1729) and completed by Francesco De Sanctis (1693–1740). Known affectionately as the Spanish Staircase leading to the Trinità dei Monti, its swelling contours and vistas are consistent with Baroque planning of an architectural landscape in three-dimensional space rather than in the two of St. Peter's Piazza and in municipal rather than ecclesiastical or private terms.

Venetian palaces were even more imitative of their forebears. The P. Labia was in the tradition set by Longhena in the Pesaro. The villa boom in the Veneto was largely in the style of Palladio. The Pisani, Manin, and Valmarana emphasize the enclosing embrace of an entire farm building complex in one set of architectural arms, characteristics in which Palladio himself antedated the Baroque. A Venetian church of the eighteenth century, like Chiesa dei Gesuati by Giorgio Massari (1687–1766), shows Rococo embellishments on an essentially Palladian structure.

In Venice—and in more fanciful manner in Sicily—*villegiaturas* were built. These were small houses with accommodations for living on something like a vacation basis. They were situated in the country, to which there was a general exodus during the summer. In the *villegiatura* entertainment could be less lavish and activities akin to the garden party or present-day *al fresco* picnicking had their origin.

The financial impoverishment of the nobility was but another aspect of the rise of middle-class prosperity. The latter group is said to have taken up avidly the idea of owning a house in the country—but for slightly different reasons. Psychologically speaking, when the workers occupied their country homes they were divorced from their urban vocations and from those sumptuary laws

regulating their dress and deportment that were still in effect. For them traveling to a new location could mean the assumption of a different personality. Sometimes we of the twentieth century forget how rigid the class system of former periods and other lands could be. By comparison ours is indeed a classless society.

More transient than the small vacation villa were the *casinos,* both private and public, which mushroomed in the urban situation. Again we quote from the young Robert Adam, who did not fail to fall into the pleasurable life they afforded:

> . . . what they call the Casino, which is nothing but a public coffee house, open from morning to night for the best ranks of people and quality who game, dance, or walk about and see others do so.[2]

There were other social gatherings in private boxes at the opera where the hostess supplied refreshments in addition to the opportunity to see and be seen. It was a world apart, and it is small wonder that in the gay atmosphere of northern Italy adventurers, presentable young foreigners, and those who represented the established elite vied for invitations.

We must look to the Piedmont for another combination of Italian traditions into a typically Rococo picture. It is best exemplified in the architecture of Filippo Juvara (1685–1736). Coming from Sicily of a family of silversmiths, he was early destined for the church but in addition trained in Rome as an architect. He served both prince and pontiff in the latter capacity. He traveled much and by 1724 was employed by Victor Amadeus of Savoy, then King of Sicily. What may be regarded as Juvara's two masterpieces, the Church of the Superga (as well as the Chiesa del Carmine) and the Palace of Stupinigi (Figures 3.2, 3.3, and 3.4), were built near Turin, Savoy's capital.

Although both are classical in exterior appearance, each relies on space for a Baroque climactic effect. Superga, signifying "on the back of the mountains," is placed at the center of an ascending vista; Stupinigi, with its long avenue of approach and bowed arms, is on a level plain. In their interiors both show a masterful welding of

Figure 3.2 Palazzo Stupinigi, near Turin, 1729–1733. Filippo Juvara, architect. (Alinari/Editorial Photocolor Archives.)

Figure 3.3 Palazzo Stupinigi, the Grand Salon, 1729–1733. Filippo Juvara, architect. (Alinari/Editorial Photocolor Archives.)

Figure 3.4 Plan of the Palazzo Stupinigi, 1729–1733. Filippo Juvara, architect. (Adapted from A. Tellucini, *L'arte dell' architetto Filippo Juvarra in Piemonte,* Turin, 1926.)

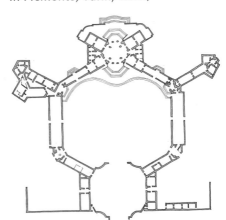

traditional plans with a manifestation of structure. In the Superga the Greek cross and the Latin round form are joined; in Stupinigi the cross centered on an oval rises to a cyma-shaped dome. Despite these complexities, the load-bearing pillars, which rise the full height of the building, so emphasize the structural framework that they seem like the sinews of a Gothic cathedral. In decoration the buildings are light and colorful; in form the emphasis is on space.

Juvara placed a new front on the Palazzo Madama in Turin, built for the queen dowager. Here the expanse of windows and the impressive handling of the staircase stress his love of light and his ability to manipulate space—this time in a more solid, sober, and classical manner.

Although a more exhaustive study would include the contributions of other architects, these few, taken from the south to the north of Italy, indicate once more the conflicting and individual qualities of the Italian genius—academic purism and reversion to austerity, tempered by reverence for functionalism with Baroque emphasis on unified space—and in the unique little buildings and (as we shall see) their interiors the lightest froth of the Rococo.

SOME EIGHTEENTH-CENTURY ITALIAN HOUSES

V. Palagonia	Bagheria, Sicily	1715, for Francesco Gravina, Prince of Palagonia
P. Labia	Venice	1720, for Labia family; architects, Andrea Cominelli and Alessandro Tremignon; ballroom frescoes (1745), Giovanni Battista Tiepolo and Mengozzi-Colonna
P. Stupinigi (Figures 3.2, 3.3, and 3.4)	Turin	1729, for Vittorio Amadeus II; Filippo Juvara, architect; ceilings, Giuseppe and Domenico Valeriani
P. Capodimonte	Naples (Figure 3.12)	1738, for Charles IV
P. Doria	Rome	Three separate palaces; main one, 1734, for Pamphili; Gabrieli Valvassore, architect
V. Pisani	Stra	1735, for Doge of Venice; Girolamo Frigimelica, architect; frescoes (1767), Giovanni Battista Tiepolo
P. Clerici (Figure 3.5)	Milan	1736, remodeled for Marshal Giorgio Antonio Clerici; frescoes (1740), Giovanni Battista Tiepolo
V. Carlotta	Lake Como	1745, famous for its gardens
V. Lechi	Brescia	1741–1745, for Pietro Lechi; frescoes, Giacomo Lecchi and Carlo Carloni
P. Reale (Figure 3.1)	Caserta	1752, for Bourbon Charles IV; Luigi Vanvitelli, architect; later furnishing of parts, nineteenth century
P. Reale	Naples	Begun 1600, refurnished for Bourbons; associated with Napoleon, nineteenth century
V. Valmarana	Vicenza	Begun 1669 but bought in eighteenth century by Valmarana family; frescoes (1757), Giovanni Battista Tiepolo and son, Giandomenico, and Mengozzi-Colonna
V. Chigi	Rome	1763–1766, for Cardinal Flavio Chigi; Tomasso Bianchi and Pietro Camporese, architects
P. Cinese	Palermo	1798, for Naples King Ferdinand; Patricola, architect
P. Mansi	Lucca	Seventeenth and eighteenth centuries; famous for eighteenth-century furnishings
V. Albani	Rome	For Cardinal Alesso Albani; Carlo Marchione, architect
V. Melsi	Near Lake Como	For Francesco Melsi d'Eril, vice-president, Napoleonic Republic of Italy; Giacondo Albertolli, architect

INTERIOR DESIGN

Materials; Space Organization

Interior design in eighteenth-century Italy, with a parallel in Central Europe, created spaces that seemed dematerialized, even though structure was not hidden.

It is very difficult to discuss these interiors in terms of the usual breakdown into ceilings, walls, openings, and floors. To do so would be to miss the point that their essence lay, almost like the Gothic, in a fluid relationship among them. In accomplishing this much was achieved by the art of the plasterer and painter. The former broke surfaces with linear, low-relief, three-dimensional pattern and the latter further adjusted his murals not only to create *trompe l'oeil* space but, with his pastels and shimmering gold, to produce an impressionist's vibrating atmosphere.

Description

Paint and stucco, then—although transitory media—remain significant in Italian decoration. Frescoed ceilings, and often frescoed walls, were customary in important rooms. The Italian thus preserved what had long been his heritage—realistic depiction—now imbued with a sense of fantasy and theatricality, sometimes centering, without intense conviction, around religious themes, often cloaked in classical garb, most exuberant when exploiting the social scene, and most fun when pure whimsy.

Giuseppe and Domenico Valeriani were the Venetian artists who painted the *Triumph of Diana* on the ceiling of the great circular salon at Stupinigi. Because this building was intended as a hunting lodge for the Savoys, Diana would be essential, and emblems of the chase—hunting horns, arrows, and boots—appear in all of the wall trophies, another suggestion of the relationship of the court to the customs of France. Stupinigi was one of the first buildings in which the French fashion for chinoiserie was shown and in which an entire room setting of it was created as a foil for richly ornamented Rococo furniture.

In the *trompe l'oeil* tradition one of the most famous and most deceptive interiors is that of the Villa Lechi in Lombardy. Here the Brescian artists Giacomo Lecchi (no relation to the owners) and Carlo Carloni painted the entire wall of the ballroom with a stage setting that depicts a grand Baroque staircase on which the eighteenth-century owners are descending to greet their guests. The gentleman turns to assist the lady as a small lapdog scurries on in advance. Incidentally, the famous stables of this villa, with their stalls surmounted by classical statues and urns, indicate the merging life of a country gentleman, proud of his academic leanings, with that of the practical manager of a working estate which had need for horses, dray and riding as well as war chargers (the Lechi were important supporters of the Napoleonic cause several years hence).

The greatest ornamentalist and an outstanding painter of this period was the Venetian Giovanni Battista Tiepolo (1696–1770). With him should be mentioned his gifted sons Giandomenico and Lorenzo. If ever there was a decorative painter who could utilize classical and religious subjects, handle them with a vigor of Baroque compass, and bathe them in an aura of eighteenth-century translucency, that painter was Tiepolo. He worked with strong hatched colors, dramatic contrasts of light and dark, unusual and low viewpoints, and linear spiraling of figures. In his best works, such as the *Chariot of the Sun* fresco (Figure 3.5) in the Palazzo Clerici in Milan with its memorable characterization of the dwarf charioteer or in the *Sacrifice of Iphigenia* (Figure 3.6) in the Villa Valmarana (Figure 3.7) in Vicenza, a decorative Rococo manner belies the strong revelation of human struggle.

In the murals done by Giandomenico Tiepolo at Valmarana we see a different temperament and most probably the expression of another era. This is patent in one of the rooms of the guest house or *foresteria* of the villa. (The main building is known as the *casa padronale* in a working villa of the Veneto.) Here is shown an oriental fantasia that might be likened to some of the murals of Salvador Dali. It is amusing but hard and brittle, possibly an example of the artist's viewpoint of a fractured or dissolving world. One more remark about Valmarana: note the background that the *quadraturista* Colonna provided for one salon—simulated Gothic arches and castles containing

Figure 3.5 Detail of the fresco *The Chariot of the Sun,* Giovanni Battista Tiepolo, Palazzo Clerici, Milan. (From *Italian Villas and Palaces* by Georgina Masson, London: Thames & Hudson; New York: Transatlantic, 1973.)

classical grisaille—it is an early example of this sort of romantic hodgepodge.

The output of Giovanni Battista Tiepolo was enormous, found not only in Italy but in the palaces of Würzburg and Madrid. Like Rubens, he was an international favorite.

Painted, stucco, or even ceramic rocaille ornamentation was used on the wall surfaces of many Italian interiors of the period. This was followed by Neoclassic work with Pompeian overtones. In Italy such decoration is frequently added to a framework of classic or Baroque paneling which has not been altered and thus a dichotomy results. This is a progressive condition whenever a culture cannot create at one "fell swoop." Seldom in history do bâtiments, Gobelins, assured authority, and artistry coexist. When they do a style is born.

In line with the thinking focused on pictorial embellishment, the small, framed picture played a role and became a popular adjunct to the Italian scheme. Advances in the graphic processes

Figure 3.6 *The Sacrifice of Iphigenia,* Giovanni Battista Tiepolo, 1757, Villa Valmarana, Vicenza. Fresco. (Marburg/Prothmann.)

Figure 3.7 Villa Valmarana, Vicenza, begun in 1669, based on designs by Palladio. (Photo Researchers.)

were in part responsible for this. One of the most interesting graphic artists of the time was the designer and architectural student, Giovanni Battista Piranesi (1720–1778). While studying in Rome, he sketched and engraved[3] the Roman ruins. A man of tremendous imagination, he did not hesitate to supply missing parts with his own designs and thus provided a rich and available, although not exactly accurate, treasure trove of illustrations for many ornaments. He was a friend and admirer of Robert Adam, possibly because,

Figure 3.8 One of a series of etchings titled *Carceri*, Giovanni Battista Piranesi, eighteenth century. Fogg Art Museum, Cambridge, Massachusetts. (Courtesy of the Fogg Art Museum, Harvard University. Purchase—Louise Haskell Daly, Francis H. Burr Memorial, George R. Nutter, William M. Prichard and Francis Calley Gray Fund.)

like the young Scotsman, he wished to build for his century in the grand manner of ancient Rome.

But where Adam turned out clean-cut niceties of reproduction, Piranesi roamed beyond the structural possibilities of Roman architecture to offer a weird medley of psychic scenes (Figure 3.8). His bridges that lead nowhere, his archways that end on a course they did not begin—all show a fractionated world but without the satirical bite of a Giandomenico Tiepolo. It is as though Piranesi was groping for structural potentials not yet fully envisaged. Other engravers of a less rich but more usable talent, such as Pergolesi and Cipriani, we shall have occasion to refer to later.

Among the painters of small scenes was Francesco Guardi (1712–1793). On a canvas slightly more than 11 × 14 in. he painted his famous *Piazetta S. Marco, Venice,* on which he conveyed a wealth of architectural detail and human activity, enveloped in a luminous blanket of sunlight. The eighteenth century which bought and enjoyed such pieces often framed them with a mat in order to add to their importance and to isolate them from their architectural surround. The French favored a soft blue and added a narrow gold frame. Possibly the blue was intended to enrich the velvety tones of a burred mezzotint or a drypoint technique. Certainly it complemented the lightness of the painted interiors.

An older artist than Guardi, Giovanni Antonio Canal, known as Canaletto (1697–1768), indicates full well why the Italians, and particularly the Venetians, became the "picture makers" of these salable scenic pieces. Canaletto, although he was born and died in Venice, painted in Rome and England. An English impresario by the name of Owen McSwiny underwrote the Italian's journey to Britain. McSwiny bought pictures on order for an English clientele. Canaletto brought the romance of Venice to the northern interior.

The French gave the world the fanciful and graceful existence of a Cythera, but no nation provided such a theatrical touch to reality as these eighteenth-century Italians. This was their genius in designing; they took the Rococo and the Neoclassic and contributed to it the lyrical sunshine of life.

In the illusions of the eighteenth-century Italian surrounds it is a moot question whether the roles of painters such as Tiepolo and Canaletto ought not to have been reversed. Scenic painting, such as Canaletto's, may create an illusion of space which, if not architectonic, is a pleasing substitute where space is cramped. Enlarged, the Venetian scenes of Canaletto could be untiring. Could the room-sized figures of Tiepolo's walls wear well as a permanent environment?

FURNITURE

Materials; Description

During the first half of the eighteenth century Italian taste came under the influence of the French Rococo style in furniture design; during the last half, although all furniture responded to the straighter lines of the Neoclassic, the picture was reversed. It was the more somber character of much Tuscan work that influenced the French. It is also considered to have been the immediate inspiration for that later French classicism, often known as the *Directoire,* based on the politics of the government at that time. Concurrently, in a phase of Anglo mania styles deriving from English Hepplewhite and Sheraton had their vogue.

Throughout the century two forms of Italian furniture may be observed. The first were colorful painted pieces; the second were unfinished natural wood designs which most frequently originated in the provincial capitals farther south. Some exceptions to such a sweeping rule are, of course, to be expected.

Whereas painted furniture was exactly the right accent for the transient life of northern Italy, it was less suited to the homes of the rising middle class or for that matter to the more ceremonial existence of Rome and Naples. Here carved and gilded ornament was more common. Walnut and fruit woods which predominated were supplanted later by mahogany and rosewood. The artistry with which these pieces were fashioned differed with the circumstances of the purchaser. Although all Italian furniture was well constructed, none of it at that time possessed the finesse of the work of the leading French ateliers.

Curves when present on Italian pieces were a bit more exaggerated than those of France, and

except for the painted pieces which were exceptionally attenuated with thin straight aprons, the proportions were sturdier. Italian chairs were rather thinly upholstered and caning was a great favorite, thus providing for coolness. Padded arms were seldom seen.

An entire repertoire of very small furniture designed for use in opera boxes or casinos presented a new type. Often amusingly decorated, the chairs were usually in suites of twelve or more, designed to fit a large table. Again in the words of Robert Adam, describing the Countess Salin on whom he danced attendance during the Florence carnival season:

> She was an old daft frolicksome jade, dressed out with wings and veils and Lord knows what all . . . [and he] took great care of her as she never failed to order a good supper every night at Mr. Mann's box, at which I fared rather plentifully.[4]

Thus the suite of chairs. The table used in such instances was round and one of the first designed for dining.

Italian beds were not generally canopied because every opportunity was seized to catch the elusive breeze. Madame de Sévigné's daughter complained about how naked this seemed to one reared in the cloistered atmosphere of the north. Actually the lack of curtains was the bedstead's only claim to uniqueness. Placed against a wall, it had a high, upholstered head- and footboard as in France (Figure 3.9). Iron bedsteads had been popular in Italy since the Renaissance and were now designed with fanciful Rococo or more sedate patterns—really quite appropriate in small rooms.

Musical Instruments

Percy Bysscke Shelley, who died in Italy in 1822, wrote:

> Music, when soft voices die,
> Vibrates in the memory—

and for many of us this is most true of Italy. Moreover, the music is eighteenth-century—Clementi, Mozart, Vivaldi. It is largely melody with accom-

Figure 3.9   Bedroom from the Sagredo Palace, Venice, ca. 1725–1735. Metropolitan Museum of Art, New York. (The Metropolitan Museum of Art, Fletcher Fund, 1925.)

paniment rather than the earlier interwoven voices of polyphony. For chordal compositions the plucking of strings on a harpsichord was not so satisfactory as the hammer action of a piano, which allowed more expressive dynamics and required less frequent tuning. Therefore it seemed foreordained that the first pianoforte (of a mere four-and-a-quarter octave range) would be designed in Italy in 1720 by Bartolommeo Cristofori, curator of the court instruments at Florence. Many, of course, have been the refinements made on the early instruments—the accomplishments of Germans, French, English, and finally Ameri-

cans. The first pianos were wing- or heartshaped, like the present "grand." In these the strings ran perpendicular to the keyboard. About 1758 a "square" or rectangular-shaped piano was made in Saxony with strings parallel to the keyboard.

About 1800 the piano largely replaced the older harpsichord and when industrialization lowered costs it became common home property.

The Metropolitan Museum of New York possesses a harpsichord made by Vincenzo Sodi in Florence in 1779. Its case is a stylistic hybrid, with heavy Rococo scrolls for its base and delicate Pompeian motifs in intarsia for its adornment (Figure 3.10). By contrast Cristofori's pianoforte of 1720, also at the Metropolitan, is plain and Tuscan in character (Figure 3.11). Eighteenth-century Italian furniture shows these two faces.

Figure 3.10 Harpsichord, Vincenzo Sodi, Florence, 1779. Metropolitan Museum of Art, New York. (The Metropolitan Museum of Art, The Crosby Brown Collection of Musical Instruments, 1889.)

CERAMICS

Italy remained until comparatively late in the twentieth century largely a country of individual craftsmen's workshops. In ceramic production, however, she had a greater part in factory production which began in Venice when in 1720 the *Casa Eccelma Vezzi* was established. This became the third venture into the mysteries of hard-paste china on the continent, although the factory, which continued until the early seventeen-forties, produced both soft and hard paste of good quality.

The designs on the Venetian china of the Vezzi period are more imaginative and spirited than those of their German neighbors. They were executed in a Pompeian red on a white ground and constitute another small and select body of work which is much sought.

Figure 3.11 Piano Forte, Bartolommeo Cristofori, Florence, 1720. Metropolitan Museum of Art, New York. (The Metropolitan Museum of Art, The Crosby Brown Collection of Musical Instruments, 1889.)

The next Italian venture might have been easily predicted. Queen Maria Amalia, wife of Charles IV of Naples, was the daughter of the Elector Augustus of Saxony. From her father she inherited a passion for fine hard-paste china and her husband was persuaded that its manufacture would prove profitable. On the grounds of his palace at Capodimonte, on a high eminence now in the suburbs of Naples, the famous *Capodimonte Porcelain Factory* was opened in 1745. It was closed in this location fourteen years later when Charles left Naples to become Charles III of Spain. Most of the knowledgeable workmen were transported to open a similar project near Madrid.

In 1771 Ferdinand IV reopened the Italian factory at his villa in Portici and it is this location that gave the famous ceramic-lined Portici room in the Capodimonte Museum in Naples its name (Figure 3.12). Its Rococo design is oriented more toward Spanish than Italian character. Early

Capodimonte is frequently modeled in bas relief of natural forms such as rocks, shells, and coral branches delicately tinted.

In 1773 the factory was finally moved to Naples but was closed in 1821 when the Ginori at Doccia, near Florence, secured its molds and presumably its formulas. The Capodimonte and Portici production was both soft and hard paste as well as biscuit. Ginori was hard porcelain. The Ginori factory was established by the Marchese Carlo Ginori in 1735 and has remained family property to the present. The family name designates all of its china. Another Italian factory, the Nove, which began in 1725, made very good faience.

OTHER CRAFTS

Within the limits of their individualized production the Italians found some profitable enterprise. Robert Adam, leaving Italy for his return home, writes of packing his collection of "virtu," which consisted of plaster casts of " '. . . antique vases, antique altars, and some lions' heads, capitals, pieces of friezes etc.' "[5] A brisk trade in antiques and of copies thereof had developed!

Likewise there was copying of the French. Pope Clement XI founded a workshop at San Michele in Rome for making carpets in the Savonnerie style.

When Italy finally awakened during this century to the potential of her own genius, it was to the tune of the corporation piper rather than to pope, king, marchese, or individual enterprise.

DESCRIPTIVE SUMMARY

Each country seems to have played its part in the architectural arts. Italy in the eighteenth century was the virtuoso, ringing the variations on many established themes from Gothic to Rococo. In all she played with drama, sometimes with superb

Figure 3.12 The Porcelain Room from the Royal Palace of the Portici, made by the Royal Factory of Capodimonte for Charles de Bourbon and intended for his wife Maria Amalia of Saxony. Eighteenth century. Capodimonte Museum, Naples. (Soprintendenza Beni Artistici Storici della Campania—Napoli.)

achievement within a genre, as in Stupinigi. Even in the accompanying furnishings she ranged from the Baroque-Rococo to Neoclassic circuit with great appeal. She was the original fountainhead of styles; she sent them to the north and they returned to her for thrills and again for country charm.

105

CHAPTER FOUR
Eighteenth-Century England

I think the full tide of human existence is at Charing Cross.

Samuel Johnson

CULTURE SPAN

The quotation from Samuel Johnson not only illustrates a particular state of mind it also describes an actual fact of historical significance. Dr. Johnson was right—London may have been considered the hub of the universe in 1737 when he arrived at the metropolis. It was then the capital of a nation that had proved her strength on the Continent a quarter of a century before and was to gain in colonial power by another series of encounters a quarter of a century later. After signing the Treaty of Paris at the end of the Seven Years' War (1756–1763) she approached her territorial summit. Nevertheless, the eighteenth century in England, as in France, was a period of regressive change. When the War for American Independence ended, a large section of England's western colonies became self-governing.

After the death of Queen Anne England invested her governmental functions in a responsible parliamentary system, and, independent of the outcome of foreign wars, was to enjoy stability. Even the Hanoverian kings, although at first often resented, became, in effect, the symbol of a united people to whom the crown was important.

The mercantile system through which colonial wealth was channeled to enrich the coffers of the mother country had kept the national finances healthy. Events soon gave it challenge and theoretical writing such as Adam Smith's *Wealth of Nations* (1776) voiced what pragmatism had foreseen. Its point of view of *laissez-faire,* which held that economic laws were self-regulating and should not be controlled, greatly aided the growth of capitalism which has figured so importantly in the nineteenth and twentieth centuries. This economic change occurred despite the lesson that England had been taught during the early seventeen hundreds when the South Sea Bubble—a financial cataclysm that paralleled the Mississippi venture in France—had made fortunes for some and impoverished others.

Smith had predicated wealth as deriving from labor applied to raw materials. A series of practical inventions, inaugurated principally in England, of which the first was the steam engine by James Watt, implemented what came to be known as the Industrial Revolution. This was a socioeconomic development in which powered mechanisms made possible a vastly increased production of economic goods and for which the capitalistic economy provided the necessary funds.

Machinery, labor, and money so modified the national finances that the old social structure based on a landed aristocracy began to falter. Today we are witnessing the prolonged aftereffects of this peaceful revolution.

Although change is rooted in many factors, it is both caused by and causes philosophical movements. The intellectual current called the *Enlightenment,* a period of liberal questioning of all kinds of values, operated in England as it had in France. A whole school of receptive writers, of whom William Godwin (1756–1836) became an early center, were spokesmen for an innovative society. They translated into cultural mores the empiricism that such philosophers as George Berkeley (1625–1750), John Locke (1632–1704), and David Hume (1711–1766) had translated into thought. (Incidentally, the intelligentsia in England, as in France, congregated in "bluestocking" drawing rooms like Lady Mary Montagu's and the coffee house fellowship of the first part of the century fell somewhat under feminine influence.)

England, once seventeenth-century classic tradition had taken root (e.g., the work of Jones and Wren in architecture), did not veer far from its central course. The Rococo never really became an English decorative style; it was rather a graft. Romanticism as a term for an intellectual movement is a different conception and one that may with some justification be said to have begun in eighteenth-century England. Classicism deals with the conventional, the proximate, and the clear; romanticism, with the relatively unorthodox, the distant, and the undefined, whether of time or place. The classic operates in a vise of preadjusted prescriptions and under the concept of reason; the romantic, in emotional terms where no set body of rules need operate. It is paradoxically true that the Enlightenment and romanticism seem to stem from a common font of liberal thinking.

Anthony Ashley Cooper, third Earl of Shaftesbury (1671–1723), a leading arbiter of artistic taste, said at the beginning of the century in his *Essay on Painting*:

Nothing is more fatal to Painting, Architecture, or the other Arts, than that *false* relish which is governed by what immediately strikes the Sense, than by what consequently and by Reflection pleases the Mind, and satisfies the Thought and Reason.

Sir Joshua Reynolds, first president of the Royal Academy of Arts, made this statement sometime between its founding in 1768 and his own death in 1792, in his *Discourses*:

I have strongly inculcated . . . the wisdom and necessity of previously obtaining the appropriate instruments of the Art in a correct design . . . before anything else is attempted. But by this I do not want to cramp and fetter the mind, or discourage those who follow . . . the suggestion of a strong inclination: something must be conceded to great and irresistible impulses: perhaps every student must not be strictly bound to general methods, if they strongly thwart the peculiar turn of his own mind.

The conundrum faced by the artist was only that common to thinking in general. The German philosopher Immanuel Kant (1724–1804) struggled with it. The human mind, he said, was the essential organizing factor for making deductions from sensory material. The working of the mind, he believed, went beyond human reason to an intuitive understanding. The romantic German poet Friedrich Schiller (1759–1805) interpreted art as play, a means of arriving at a spontaneous understanding of truth. The romantic point of view was beginning to make inroads.

How could the century that promoted these views be easily understood in its political, economic, social, and artistic changes? The eighteenth was one of great complexity.

ARCHITECTURE

The Swiss historian Jacob Burckhardt (1818–1897) warned against the tendency in modern historical writing to assign captions to styles. He called it "simplistic thinking."

This danger is nowhere more pronounced than when we speak of English eighteenth-century architecture as Baroque, Palladian, Gothic, or Neoclassic, for none of these modes is a clear-cut phenomenon. In any style that repeats an earlier inspiration its character is often altered and crossed with other predecessors. If, however, we allow our statements a little necessary freedom, names are like pin-up girls—something to hang ideas on.

Christopher Wren

At the beginning of Queen Anne's reign the career of Sir Christopher Wren was yielding to those of younger men. His old commissions such as the Greenwich Hospital complex and St. Paul's cathedral had not yet been completed. He was also designing one of his few city mansions—Marlborough House, adjacent to the old Tudor pile of St. James. None of these would be pacesetters for the new century. Wren with his methodical and refined mathematical mind had adopted the Classical and Baroque more for its rationale than for any personal feeling for its rhythms. With his immediate followers it was another story.

The English Baroque School

Two men, both quite exceptional in talent, must now be considered. The first is Nicholas Hawksmoor (1661–1736), who, having entered Wren's employ in the Royal Works as a young man, soon became the assistant on whom the master relied. This sort of position often afforded opportunity for personal enterprise, and Hawksmoor, when given the opportunity to solo, performed equitably in his own right. He is remembered as the architect of a small group of London churches, certain buildings at Oxford, and a few outstanding examples of country-house design.

One of his earliest and greatest works was Easton Neston (Figure 4.1), the country seat of Lord Lempster, scion of a wealthy Northamptonshire family, newly elevated to the peerage. After his third marriage, to the daughter of the Duke of Leeds, Lempster had decided to rebuild the fam-

Figure 4.1 Easton Neston, Northamptonshire, 1702–1703. West front. Nicholas Hawksmoor, architect. (Photograph courtesy of *Country Life*.)

ily home at Towchester in a manner more suited to his social position. As Wren was Lempster's cousin by marriage, he was undoubtedly instrumental in the appointment of Hawksmoor to the position of architect.

The choice was good. Easton Neston is a stone building of outstanding architectural character that fits into its milieu, yet stands significantly above it. Although not so truly prophetic as Gabriel's *Trianon,* it shares with it a clarity and austerity of volume. It is not a mansion on which one feels that the classical orders have been pinned in the hope of creating a prestigious facade. Rather these orders serve well to unify the design and to create movement from part to part

within the whole in a truly Baroque manner. This movement is toward the focal interest that pivots the composition bysymmetrically. Notice how the prominent stairs, projecting pavilion, and arched windows on the west front at Easton Neston lead the eye toward the central axis. Thus Hawksmoor directed attention where he wanted it, on the entrance to a great house of a wealthy landowner, thereby accentuating the owner's importance. Wren's erstwhile assistant, like his master, is said to have been a sincerely modest person; Easton Neston indicates that it was the modesty that accompanies stature.

Leaving Northamptonshire, we move south to Oxfordshire and Blenheim, the creation of the architect Sir John Vanbrugh (1664–1726; Figure 4.26). It was built as the gift of a grateful nation to the hero of the War of the Spanish Succession

(1702–1713), the first Duke of Marlborough. The architect of the largest of English private dwellings was British by birth, Flemish by family, and French by way of art-student days. On returning from the Continent, he was first a successful dramatist and a designer for the Queen's theater in Haymarket. In his late thirties he was introduced to architecture through an appointment as royal comptroller. The several examples of similar commissions developing into architectural careers serve to remind us that architecture was not then a profession that required years of preparation in the structural sciences and the arts.

Vanbrugh's association with Wren in the royal works may have prompted him to attempt the creative field of architectural designing, and his literary career may have suggested entree through the bookish route. This meant for the eighteenth century a study of the advice of the Italian Renaissance architect Palladio, with his strict insistence on the classical canons. Vanbrugh is known to have purchased a French edition of Palladio in 1703 and to have been among the subscribers to Leoni's first edition in English. Although always remaining too much the individualist and ornamentalist to be classified with the school of architects known as the English Palladians, he often showed an understanding of Palladio's principles while not becoming a slavish imitator of his forms.

In addition to Blenheim, Castle Howard, which Vanbrugh did for the Earl of Carlisle, and that marvelous pile he created for War Admiral Delaval on the Northumberland coast, Seaton Delaval (Figure 4.2), illustrate his manner and his creative potential.

Figure 4.2 Seaton Delaval, Northumberland, 1720–1729. Sir John Vanbrugh, architect. (British Tourist Authority.)

All three houses use a classic vocabulary. Vanbrugh, however, refused to articulate his buildings with one set of Palladian proportions. He arbitrarily varied the sizes of his orders—Corinthian and Doric at Blenheim—so that the eye, through similarities, easily picks up the separate movements in and out of the sections of the building, like voices in a fugue. All three houses climax the central axis in a more pronounced manner than did Easton Neston—Castle Howard with a central dome, Blenheim and Seaton Delaval with a heightened central hall. The last two illustrate Vanbrugh's handling of the giant pillared porch, often superficially thought to be an earmark of the Palladian.

This virtuoso architect also showed skill in handling his skylines by massing his separate and disparate units to obtain subordination and consequent eye movement toward the pivotal focus. In Castle Howard he grouped a series of sculptural ornaments—balls and crowns resting on volutes, like so many Greek acroteria—which lead to the dome. Blenheim has corner towers and ornaments in proportional relation to the center. At Seaton Delaval he obtained his end by vigorous and asymmetrical subordination with sharp antithesis of towers and pavilions. This house with its rugged force is like a Soulages or a Kline painting thrown into the Baroque waters of a Tiepolo era.

In one other exterior characteristic, in the contrived reaching out to embrace a defined portion of the landscape while teasing the imagination with a view toward infinity, these early-eighteenth-century houses illustrate a tendency that may be attributed to Palladio, to the Baroque, or back to late Roman days. At Easton Neston on the east a formal garden and parterres link the house to a small lake (of present manufacture) that leads to the original canal and the open scene beyond. At Blenhiem and Delaval we have the house with wings such as England had built since Jacobean days but now accompanied with Versailles-like vistas. In all there is high Baroque space planning, with varying topographical levels and ingredients gathered into a crescendo that has its climax in the house proper.

Clearly the men who immediately followed Wren, while keeping to the subject matter of the well-understood classic, handled it with the freedom that we have associated with the Baroque.

English Palladianism

Such individualistic treatment was not destined for a long period of popularity. More conventional solutions were in evidence by the teens of the new century, solutions that would have a more direct appeal to a new Whig (landed gentry and trade) aristocracy then coming to power. Architecture to be important architecture needed the letter-of-the-law adherence to established canon, and Vitruvius, as interpreted by Palladio and so much the idol of Inigo Jones, would alone suffice. Richard Boyle, third Earl of Burlington and Cork (1695–1753), emerges as the proponent of the new school of academicians. To what extent he actually designed the houses for which he assumed credit is not known. It is certain, however, that as a man of nobility and wealth who had traveled and studied on the Continent and had been a disciple of Palladio's writings and architecture, he became leader and patron of a group of architects in England who cherished Palladio's precepts.

It was Burlington who subsidized the publication of various editions of the master's *I Quattro libri dell' Archittetura,* first edited in 1570. It will be recalled that Palladio proposed writing more books on the subject, plans that were never completed. Many of his unpublished drawings were purchased in Italy by Burlington, and these, with others he secured from the collection owned by Inigo Jones, are now in the possession of the Royal Institute of British Architects.

The first English edition of Palladio was published in 1715, the work of Giacomo Leoni (1686–1746), a Venetian architect whom Lord Burlington introduced to England. (Leoni was the builder of Clandon Park, home of the first Lord Onslow, Speaker of the House of Commons under Walpole. He also built Moor Park, Hertfordshire; Figure 4.3). Apparently this initial translation was not accurately done and it was probably Burlington again who secured the services of Isaac Ware (d. 1766) whose graphic talent had been recognized earlier and an education proffered by patronage. Ware, later the creator of Chesterfield House in London (where the famous Chesterfield letters were written), wrote extensively on architecture and sensibly urged a comprehension of Palladio's contribution rather than a blind fol-

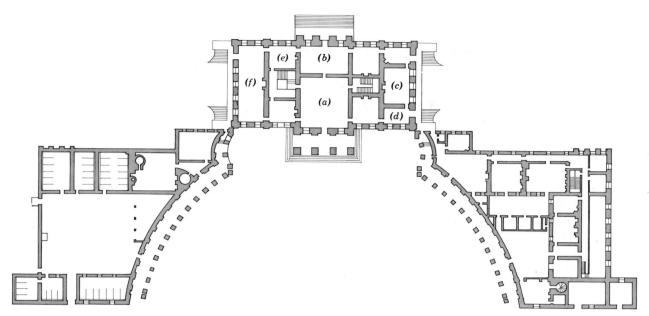

Figure 4.3 The original plan of Moor Park, an English Palladian-type dwelling, Hertfordshire, 1720. Giacomo Leoni, architect. (Adapted from *Vitruvius Britannicus* by Colen Campbell, 1715–1717.) (a) hall; (b) salon; (c) dining room; (d) bath; (e) library; (f) gallery. *Left wing,* stables and courtyard; *right wing,* kitchens, service quarters, greenhouse, and coach houses.

lowing of his rules. Ware's edition of Palladio, with its beautifully executed drawings, was published in 1738. It has recently been made available in reprint form.

Ware's liberal advice went largely unheeded in fashionable circles. What passed for strict Palladianism was followed in the designs of numerous large houses, among which was Burlington's own home, now considerably altered, in Piccadilly, and the more famous Chiswick House (Figure 4.4) at Chiswick, upstream from London, a replica of Palladio's Villa Rotonda. This he may have designed in collaboration with the architect Colen Campbell (d. 1729),[1] a Scotsman whose Mereworth Castle in Kent is another copy of the famous Vicenza house.

Neither of these English buildings is an exact duplicate of the Villa Capra. At Chiswick Burlington used the Corinthian order, rather than the Ionic, and only one pedimented portico, whereas the dome on a drum is raised much higher than in the Italian model. At Mereworth the chimney flues, so necessary in the northern climate, are

carried in a copper casing above the dome. Palladio stated that the purpose of his original four-porticoed plan was to provide a view in all directions from the knoll on which the building stood. As such an intent could not be achieved in the English locations; these buildings became mere pleasant pedantic exercises. Campbell is also well known for his work for Sir Robert Walpole at Houghton in Norfolk. He erected Stourhead for Henry Hoare in Wiltshire, an estate whose art collections and gardens are equally famous.

William Kent was Lord Burlington's most devoted protégé. He had come to London as a youth, running away from his apprenticeship to a coach painter. The dubious moral of this tale has been repeated many times in history. Securing patronage, he studied in Italy, where he came to Boyle's attention. Returning with him to England he lived at the Burlington country estate at Chiswick until his death some thirty years later and is buried in the Burlington family vault. Kent was a man of varied talents, not the least of which were in the fields of furniture and landscape design. He is known as the architect of Holkham Hall in Norfolk, built in 1720 for Thomas Coke, later Earl of Leicester.

The first part of the eighteenth was an extravagant era in English architecture and many country seats with Palladian pretentions rose through-

Figure 4.4 Chiswick, near London, ca. 1725. Lord Burlington and William Kent, architects. (G. C. Ball.)

out the land. Men such as George Dance, Sr. (1695–1768), of the Mansion House in London, the elder Wood, John (1704–1754), of Prior Park (Figure 4.5), Bath, Henry Flitcroft (1697–1769), of Wentworth Woodhouse in Yorkshire, are grouped with the English Palladian architects. James Gibbs (1682–1754), a Scotsman whose fame rests firmly on his steepled churches—to be considered in proper context—was also the architect of a number of houses, among which is the Palladian-style Sudbrooke Park in Surrey, completed about 1726 for the Duke of Argyll.

The claim of any English architecture to the title of Palladian, even to that of Baroque, must remain a matter of degree. A comparison of Holkham and Blenheim will mark the poles. Observe in both the same superficial insignia—the stone building material, the temple front, the bisymmetrical, and the threefold classically proportioned divisions with centrally directed emphasis.

Then calculate the differences—the restraint versus the restlessness, the simplicity versus the diversity of ornament, the clear and the complex organization. One is a firm statement; the other dangles its participles.

The Smaller Georgian Houses

The Baroque and Palladian schools of monumental designing created documents that inflated the importance of their owners and architects as they must have dwarfed the personalities of their inmates. The same zeitgeist produced the moderate-sized Georgian house, perhaps the most fondly remembered bequest of the first Hanoverians and even now to be seen dotting the English countryside and occasionally preserved in the fluctuating urban scene—wherever families with less than the wealth of Croesus were able to afford residences of some little accommodation. These buildings also reflect something of the face of Baroque classicism with overtones of Palladian import that once linked the Vicenza villas to their farms.

114

The middling houses of England domesticated the character of the great houses without losing their distinct proportional reasons for greatness. They looked back to Coleshill and Eltham Lodge (Figures 4.6 and 4.7) and forward to nineteenth-century Poleston Lacey and Arlington Court, to create, as they perpetuated an image of the British eighteenth-century middle class character, aesthetically discerning as it preserved a remarkably worthy way of life.

Many examples may be found. Let us look at Mompesson House in Salisbury (Figure 4.8), a house in Chelmsford, Essex (Figure 4.9), another at Burford in Oxfordshire (Figure 4.15), Eagle House in Surrey, the famous though no longer standing Hogarth House (reputed home of his father-in-law, the painter James Thornhill), which was in the then fashionable Soho district of London, and later the interiors of some of the row houses in Queen Square, Bath.

Actually the early Georgian house varied within a norm that depended on location and the circumstance of the owner. It is generally thought to have been built with brick punctuated by stone quoins at the corners in the Wren manner. It

Figure 4.5   Garden facade, Prior Park, Somerset, ca. 1735. John Wood I, architect. (Marburg/Prothmann.)

might just as likely have been stone, like the house at Burford with its pretensions toward Palladianism (Figure 4.15). With the progress of time stone

Figure 4.6   Sketch of Eltham Lodge, London, 1663–1664. Hugh May, architect. (Adapted from Sherban Cantacuzino, *European Domestic Architecture,* Dutton, 1969.) This is an outstanding example of a late seventeenth-century house. Such designs are forerunners of the bisymmetrical Georgian style.

Figure 4.7   (below) Ground floor plan of Eltham Lodge, London, 1663–1664. Hugh May, architect. (a) entrance hall; (b) staircase hall; (c) anteroom; (d) great parlor; (e) bedroom; (f) little parlor. (Adapted from Sherban Cantacuzino, *European Domestic Architecture,* Dutton, 1969.)

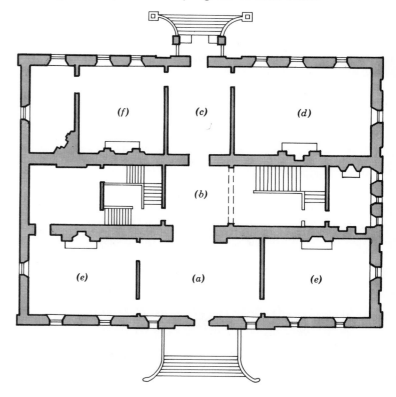

Figure 4.8   Mompesson House, Salisbury, ca. 1701. (G. C. Ball.)

quoins tended to disappear and corners to become sharply defined. On occasion a Georgian dwelling would be a single block standing free and independent, self-contained in a rise of several stories. In town it usually inherited a Medieval tendency to cling to its neighbor. Often it embraced bisymmetrically placed subsidiary blocks which were either conjoined or stood apart as independent pavilions. In America the latter were known as dependencies.

The design of the house would be clear as it duplicated itself on each side of an imposing entrance, which only in case of space limitation in the city would be shifted off center (Figures 4.10, 4.11, 4.12, 4.13, and 4.14). In many town houses the approach would be further extended by the vestigial remnant of a court or small yard with its usual neat fence and often beautifully wrought iron gate.

The smaller eighteenth-century house shared with its seventeenth-century prototype a difficulty with respect to organizing its horizontal and vertical movements. Rows of repetitive sash windows and stories often demarked by string courses resulted in strong lateral dominance. Which was accentuated by the ever-lowering lines of the hipped roof that had been in demand ever since its introduction in the last century. Moreover, horizontal balustrades either at the eaves or near the ridge pole cut off vertical extension.

Vertical emphasis, however, was not lacking, often asserting itself in a central pavilion that rose above a cornice line and was accompanied by doorway and window treatment that carried the eye upward. Many houses like the one at Burford had two-story pilasters that rose from a basement podium for this purpose. A soaring cupola sometimes added verticality as at Eagle House. High chimneys with flues grouped in encompassing

Figure 4.9   House at Chelmsford, Essex, ca. 1725. (G. C. Ball.)

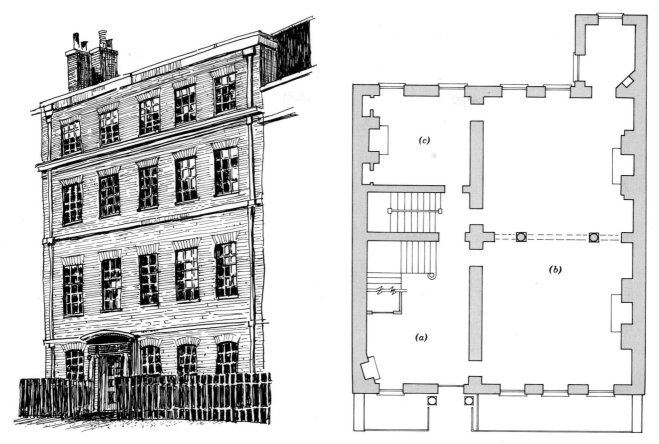

Figure 4.10 (above, left) Elevation sketch of early-eighteenth-century house (called Hogarth's House, no longer in existence), Dean Street, Soho, London.

Figure 4.11 (above, right) Plan of the ground floor of Hogarth's House: (a) entrance hall; (b) double dining room; (c) small dining room.

Figure 4.12 (below, left) Plan of first floor of Hogarth's House: (a) hall; (b) front drawing room; (c) small drawing room; (d) back drawing room; (e) powdering room.

Figure 4.13 (below, right) Plan of second floor of Hogarth's House: (a through f) bedrooms; (g) dressing room.

(Adapted from a brochure published by W. & J. Sloane and Co., New York, 1921.)

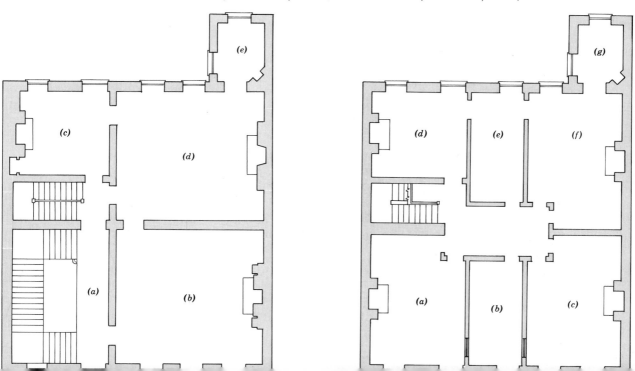

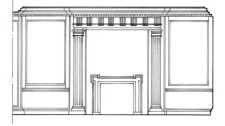

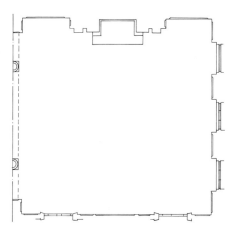

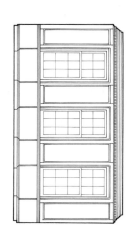

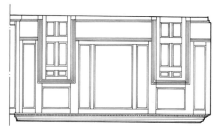

Figure 4.14 Plan and elevations of front dining room on ground floor of Hogarth's House. (Adapted from brochure published by W. & J. Sloane and Co., New York, 1921.)

stacks accomplished both bisymmetry and erectness.

The small Georgian house was not sufficient in size to fear a monotonous flat frontal plane. Nevertheless, there were times when center or end pavilions were used to break the facade. Dormer windows created Baroque projections, which, bisymmetrically placed, were not of necessity in line with the openings in the main body of the house. The dormers were frequently capped

with classical pediments even when the lower windows were untrimmed. A common way to handle the latter was in the arrangement of the brick surround. This was often done in a harder brick of slightly different tone. English texts refer to gauged trim which is made of specially dimensioned brick to create segmental and flat-arched lintels. Stone copings with projecting ears were also seen. Venetian (Palladian) and round windows are at times introduced, the former to give emphasis to a central pavilion, the latter to light an upper story.

The window opening grew broader and less tall as the period progressed (Figure 4.15). The double-hung sash predominated, although occasionally early houses still retained leaded casements on the upper stories together with sash on the first level. These last were regularly composed of twelve lights arranged in four rows. A size of 12 by 15 in. per light was not unusual. Glazing bars were substantial and generally of wood. They often distinguish a house of this era from its later replica. Although classical treatment of windows, with full entablature and pediment, can be found as the century grows, the later examples can scarcely lay claim to the artistry that places a restraining hand on the windows of the initial years, the better to display a doorway and to provide visual quietness to the smaller facade.

The doorway, together with the cornice, received the greatest emphasis and attention. Early facings were majestic in their use of carved stone. When wood became a substitute and more elaborate carving was possible, the ornateness was increased at the expense of impressiveness. The actual door was paneled with flush panels usually numbering six. The aediculae were bold eye-catchers, with moldings, pilasters, and consoles to bear heavy arched and often interrupted pediments. The treatment waxed more classical, with columns, entablatures, and even triangular academic pediments. Never, however, does the Georgian house lose its vigor or emphasize mere superficial prettiness.

English (London) Parish Churches

The state church of England had been Anglican for less than two hundred years. During that period the London fire wiped out eighty-seven

Figure 4.15 Two houses on High Street, Burford, Oxfordshire. (G. C. Ball.) The proportions of the windows in the house on the right indicate a later eighteenth-century date than those in the house on the left. The dates of the original buildings may not actually correspond with those of the windows. Burford is essentially a Tudor town that underwent much face-lifting in the eighteenth century.

parish churches and the phenomenal spread of the city to the suburbs created the need for additional accommodations. The responsibility for designing the first replacements fell to the lot of Sir Christopher Wren and depended on the provisions for rebuilding the city during the latter part of the seventeenth century. The designing of more than fifty new or reconstituted parish churches during the first half of the eighteenth century came under the Act of 1711, and its execution was vested in a commission. Nicholas Hawksmoor, as Surveyor, served that body for the remainder of his life. James Gibbs succeeded him in 1713. Although other architects, notably the Italian-trained Thomas Archer (1668–1743), designed some of the required churches, it is to Hawksmoor and Gibbs that we must look for the emergence of the type that has so greatly influenced the style of ecclesiastical building wherever the English language has been carried.

This type embodies much that emanated from the fertile brain of Wren. There had been little or no precedent for the problem of creating a religious edifice that, in the words of Sir Christopher, would allow a large congregation " 'to hear distinctly and to see the minister' "[2]—and, of course, at that date, to be designed in classical terms.

Wren, hampered by an increasing work load and by frequent circumvention of his authority by parish committees and local trade companies that supplied the cold cash, never effected the ultimate solution. Nevertheless, these eighteenth-century churches owe much to Wrensian proto-types.

We may take James Gibbs's church, St. Martin-in-the-Fields, as an example of the developed style (Figure 4.16). Its aisled interior has five bays and is almost symmetrical from east to west. Its obvious structural support is supplied by pillars and piers that elevate full entablatures which in turn support semicircular arches that intersect with a central barrel vault. In the side walls Gibbs used the round-headed windows often seen in Wren's work and, in addition, placed a focal Palladian window in the chancel.

The exterior of the building is a classical form, with a balustraded roof. Its portico is an early English example of a classical hexastyle and the side elevations are punctuated by equally spaced

Figure 4.16 Church of St. Martin-in-the-Fields, London, 1722–1726. James Gibbs, architect. (G. C. Ball.)

classical pilasters ended on the east by two semi-columns in antis.

The real problem, of course, was a matter of prestige—how to give a classical church the skyward aspiration and height that had been associated with Gothic architecture—in other words how to integrate a traditional Gothic spire with a classical tower in an aisled church. At St. Martin's the tower begins as a classical tempietto and is terminated in a pointed obelisk, the whole giving somewhat the effect, when seen from a distance, of a Gothic pinnacle.

This solution may appear to be a bit curious when viewed with fresh eyes and in a critical manner; but repetition and association has rendered it a beloved symbol to anglophiles. It must be acknowledged that the publication of many of Gibbs's designs in his *Book of Architecture* encouraged easy copying. Yet it is little short of miraculous that this earnest Scotsman, destined for the Catholic priesthood, should have provided a solution which, although a stylistic hybrid, was yet so pat for its occasion that its American counterpart, "the little white[3] church in the vale," should have gripped the emotions for centuries to come (Figure 4.17).

In Palladian fashion St. Martin's is painted white and is enriched in its interior by plaster fretting done by Signors Artari and Bagutti whose coming to England Gibbs arranged.

Gothicism

From the foregoing paragraphs it is clear that such a symbol as a Gothic spire associated with English churches could not be easily set aside; and we may claim with equal conviction that a preference for Medieval asymmetry and for the use of native building materials lay deep in the Anglican subconscious. With the advent of the historicism which emerged with the eighteenth century, these inclinations had an opportunity to surface.

Looking back toward the Middle Ages, oddly enough, is considered a phase of romanticism, whereas the copying of the classic ages does not usually bear that label. Yet both, insofar as they share an interest in the distant past, have much in common. They may be said to be blood relations

Figure 4.17 United Church, New Marlboro, Connecticut, 1744. (G. C. Ball.)

in a family of revival styles that emerged as the midseventeen hundreds approached.

Gothicism had never entirely died in Britain, as many examples of the repeated use of this style in ecclesiastic, scholastic, and law buildings will testify. In northern countries it has always seemed to express a continuity with the past, hence to have found favor in buildings that housed traditional institutions.

During the eighteenth century, however, Gothicism expanded into other types of structure and took on a more self-conscious attitude. One of the most famous early examples of its use was in the home of Horace Walpole, the gifted son of the first prime minister. Strawberry Hill (Figures 4.18 and 4.19), as it was known, was begun in 1747, with little more reason for being than the whim of its witty owner who used it at first as something of a scaffold on which to hang snips and snaps of pseudo-Gothic decoration; but Walpole's keen intellect, once engaged, found it difficult to treat the subject of revival with superficiality, and what began as a clever bow to the literary mania for Gothic novels (including its owner's *Castle of Otranto*) ended as a genuine interest in the history of Gothic artifacts. Strawberry Hill is used today as a Roman Catholic College affiliated with the University of London.

Figure 4.18 Strawberry Hill, home of Sir Horace Walpole, Twickenham, 1747. (Photograph courtesy of *Country Life*.)

In a manner similar to that used at Strawberry Hill the amateur architect Sanderson Miller in 1753 constructed the famous Gothic Hall at Lacock Abbey for his patron John Ivory Talbot. It had become fashionable to name one's home an abbey, as though it were one of the buildings of a Medieval religious complex.

The eighteenth century in these examples tackled the Gothic as it had engaged the Chinese—more as a circus acrobat would leap from one horse to another in order to amuse the crowd—and in so doing often sacrificed innate quality for showmanship.

Toward the end of the century, when accurate knowledge of all architectural styles was more available, James Wyatt (1747–1813) made considerable use of the Gothic. His Fonthill for the romantic writer William Beckford (e.g., the novel *Vathek*) is a case in point. It is in plan and size

Figure 4.19   Interior view of Strawberry Hill, home of Sir Horace Walpole, Twickenham, 1747. (By permission of St. Mary's College; Photograph courtesy of *Country Life*.)

and accuracy of detail a more learned example of Gothicism, but because its tower collapsed from faulty construction it can be said to have overreached its grasp, much as some Gothic cathedrals (e.g., Beauvais) are known to have done.

We cannot leave Gothic romanticizing without mentioning the sham castles and artificial ruins that became the fashion for estate owners to place in their English landscapes. Conceived to induce a plaintive melancholy, they fitted into any surroundings that glamorized life away from reality.

English Neoclassicism

Because the term *Neoclassicism* is somewhat ambiguous when used to cover the architectural complexities of the late eighteenth century, the names *historicism* and *archaism* have been suggested as alternatives. Historicism advocated a deeper knowledge and wider field of research as a basis for architectural studies. One result of this tendency was a more catholic taste, which led to a romantic interest in civilizations remote in time and place.

Archaism, on the other hand, followed such writers as Lodoli and Laugier in emphasizing the study of primitive (archaic) buildings. This aspect of Neoclassicism was concerned with structural necessity as the dictator of form, and with its exaggeration of function at the expense of visual design it became in its way another romantic fad.

Both tendencies are illustrated in the achievement of Sir William Chambers (1723–1796). The son of a wealthy Scots merchant, he was born in Sweden, where his father's business interests were centered. His first exploit, after a British schooling, was a nine years' journey to the Orient with the Swedish East India Company. In 1757 he published his *Designs of Chinese Buildings,* which proved an important lever for English buildings in the Chinese taste, for example, his pagoda in the gardens of Kew Palace.

Returning to England when he was twenty-five, Chambers determined to be an architect and to this end studied in Paris and Italy over the next six years. His natural bent for writing and drafting allowed him to publish in 1759 his *Treatise on Civil Architecture,* a book that enjoyed a widespread influence and gained for its author some of the most lucrative commissions. In addition, his pupil for drawing lessons, the heir apparent, later George III, gave his erstwhile teacher a rather fine apple by knighting him to the English peerage.

The largest and probably the most important work of Chambers's career (there were many others, private houses, etc.) was Somerset House in London, which, although completed after his death, was principally built according to his plans. Somerset House was a public building designed to bring together the various government offices. Actually, although it fell short of becoming a piece of monumental architecture that could have been impressive on its site, it has been praised as a building that serves its purpose well. It is a classical complex with a rusticated first story and upper ones punctuated by a rhythm of colossal Corinthian columns. Its great length is relieved by projecting pavilions.

Possibly Chambers's greatest importance lay in his professional character. As a member of the aristocracy his social position was unassailable. His position as a personage improved the public's concept of the architectural profession. It was he who in 1768 became one of the founding members of the Royal Academy of Arts. Chambers ran an architectural office in much the same manner as is customary today, established a regulated system of fees, took and trained pupils, and wrote critical treatises on current architecture.

The chief of his contemporaries was Robert Adam (1728–1792), who professed a similar reverence for Rome and the Latin heritage. The lives of Chambers and Adam coincided in time, and their backgrounds and indeed their temperaments were similar enough to build an ill-concealed rivalry between the two. Adam had come from a relatively well-to-do Scottish family, being the son of William Adam, a celebrated architect of Edinburgh and author of *Vitruvius Scoticus.* This was a treatise on the Roman master which, like Campbell's *Vitruvius Britannicus,* was an excuse for showing many of its author's creations.

Young Robert possessed an overwhelming ambition and, considering foreign study a prerequisite to big commissions, wagered his patrimony on an education in Italy. Spending the years between 1754 and 1758 on the Continent, he studied draftsmanship and measured and drew antiquities in the company of his tutor and traveling companion Charles-Louis Clerisseau (1721–1820), a talented student at the French Academy in Rome. Because of some breach of Academy discipline, Clerisseau had been forced to relinquish his post and so was in the market for just such an opportunity as the young Adam was able to offer. From 1760 to 1763 Robert's younger brother James was in Italy on a visit, also intended for architectural study. His elder brother John remained in Scotland, assuming the lion's share of the responsibility for the family business and for his widowed mother and sister. The youngest brother, "Willie," moved in and out of the subsequent Robert-James architectural partnership in London with something like phantom regularity.

It is a fairly well acknowledged fact that the architectural talent in the family was largely Robert's, and there is no question that his was the persistent drive to rise to the top. Both Robert and James had planned a course of conduct in Italy and London which they hoped would introduce their talents to the *bon ton.* Though well born, they were still outside the aristocratic circle on which grand patronage depended.

Adam could not hope to dislodge Chambers from his inner-circle standing with the crown (although in 1762 he did hold the position of Architect to the King, an office he voluntarily relinquished six years later to become a member of parliament). Nevertheless, as a handsome and likable young Scot with personal enthusiasms that were ingratiating, as the canny sycophant with his eye forever on the main chance, a daring adventurer willing to wager on his own abilities, an industrious worker and a sensitive and prideful genius, he was certain to prove a favorite with the new Tory aristocracy that returned to power with George III. The successful outcome of the Seven Years' War had given the country a new prosperity. Many large homes were built or redesigned and Robert Adam received his share of the big plums.

At this process of face lifting Robert Adam proved himself a master. He was exactly suited to giving a new air of "elegance" even to a Tudor mansion like Osterley, which belonged to the financier Sir Robert Child, or to the interior of Syon (Figures 4.20, 4.21), seat of the Duke of Northumberland.

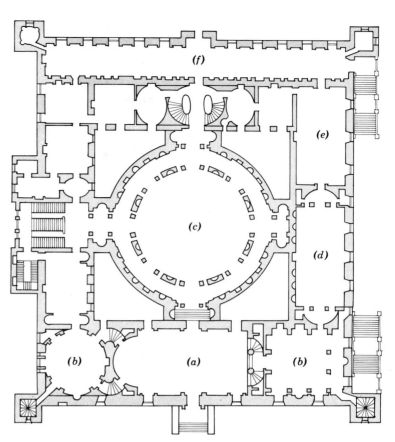

Figure 4.21 (below) The Gallery, Syon House, Middlesex, 1761–1762. Robert Adam, designer; stucco probably by Michel Angelo Pergolesi. (By permission of the Duke of Northumberland; Photograph courtesy of *Country Life*.)

Figure 4.20 (above) Plan of Syon House, Middlesex, 1761–1762. Remodeled by Robert Adam. (a) hall; (b) anteroom; (c) rotunda, not executed; (d) dining room; (e) drawing room; (f) gallery. (Adapted from Robert Adam, *Works*.)

Adam, it must be confessed, often collaborated with and frequently may have been instrumental in supplanting other architects on location. His first patron, the Earl of Harewood in Yorkshire, demoted John Carr for the younger architect. At Kedleston in Derbyshire he worked with and then replaced James Paine. The south front of this building stands as the most complete exterior of a large house ever designed by the Scotsman. Here he raised a giant order over a rusticated basement to tie together two upper stories. The face is crowned with a parapet behind which rises an attic story, the inspiration based largely on the theme of the triumphal arch. Garlands appear in low relief on a broad frieze, which indicate that Adam for all his talk of Roman classical architecture was at heart a decorator and ornamentalist who would find his greatest success as a designer of interiors, a role in which he showed much talent.

The Adam brothers suffered a severe financial setback but experienced a considerable artistic triumph in several of their planned civic enterprises. The chief of these was the venture known as the *Adelphi* (brothers), a series of streets built over reclaimed land along the Thames embankment. This incorporated wharf facilities for shipping at the lower level and groups of smaller houses enclosed in one continuous pattern on the upper. Here the designing was singularly successful and inaugurated a delicate style of facade for the smaller homes that had a lingering vogue on both sides of the Atlantic (Figure 4.22).

Some individual planning was evident even when the houses were in terrace form. The building that housed the Royal Society of Arts is typical of the norm. The ground story was of brick or rusticated stone. Windows and doors were often recessed into arches that were flush with the wall. The doorway was a lovely and characteristic feature. It was enclosed in an enframement that included two side lights and a delicately patterned fanlight. The entrance was sometimes extended by a pillared small porch in which all proportions were attenuated and the ornament daintily fashioned. Adam architecture shows a tendency toward flattened projections on windows and doors. Mullions and muntins are finer than in Georgian small-house design. A Palladian window often appears above the central door.

The principal and attic floor are frequently designed as one unit, tied by slender pilasters that support a full entablature. The low roof is surmounted at the eaves by balustrades, and fragile wrought iron balconies often enrich openings.

Actually the Adam style is highly individual. Its ultimate source was classical Roman architecture. It made use of the late Roman decoration that Robert had drawn at the Emperor Diocletian's palace at Spalato which he had visited after his Roman sojourn (publishing his results in 1764). He certainly gained a delicacy of handling from his French companion Clerisseau and he may have acquired a sense of dramatic imagination from his friend and fellow draftsman Giambattista Piranesi. But the ensemble culled from all probable sources was still the Scotsman's—classic with a slightly feminine touch and with a finesse that well suited the aristocracy on both sides of the channel. (The Louis XVI style bears comparison with the Adam.)

The Adam style, in its facial aspects, could be

Figure 4.22 House at No. 21, St. James Square, London, 1750. Robert Adam, architect. (Photo Researchers.)

easily imitated. James Wyatt, whom we have already met as a successful adapter of many manners, was one who followed in Adam's footsteps. Thomas Leverton (1743–1824) was another who should claim recognition for his sound designing of houses in one of those planned developments of which the eighteenth century boasts—Bedford Square in London. Here in narrow 20-ft dwellings we can see how remarkably effective the small-scale patterning of Adam and Leverton could be in creating the air of a palace in a modest building.

The first stage of urban residential designing in England occurred during the seventeenth century when men of wealth bought large tracts of land outside the city (i.e., London), built their imposing houses on the corner of a contrived square, and sold off the rest in smaller plots. This resulted at best in somewhat haphazard building. Such was Berkeley Square.

These eighteenth-century developments involved the buying of land for the avowed purpose of creating reasonably priced homes in a grouping that was architecturally unified by a common facade. One of the earliest and handsomest of these projects is seen in the work of John Wood and his son in the city of Bath. This provincial city, used since Roman times as a health resort because of its mineral waters, witnessed a fashionable return of visitors in the seventeen hundreds. Lady Chesterfield, wife of the second Earl, wrote in 1665 that she found ". . . the waters . . . less supportable than the payne."[4] The inadequacy of living accommodations no doubt prompted this opinion. It is said that Charles I and Henrietta Maria were housed in a tent when they frequented the city.

It fell to the lot of the elder Wood, on the suggestion of persons of wealth, to alter the situation. He and his son, with other entrepreneurs, devised and carried through to completion plans for the city and its dwellings which make it, even today, a civic expansion of great charm (Figures 4.23 and 4.24). John Wood I (1704–1754), finished Queen's Square (1729–1736) during his lifetime. This building complex has a demarked ground floor surmounted by two upper stories held together by three pavilions with massive semiengaged pillars topped with a pedimented entablature.

John Wood II (1728–1781) completed his fa-

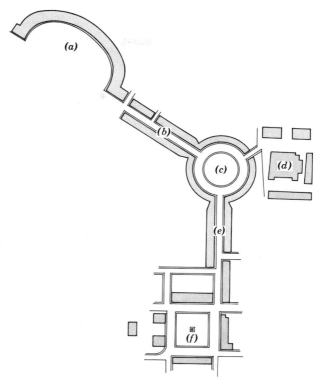

Figure 4.23 Plan of a portion of the development at Bath, England, designed by John Wood I and John Wood II: (a) Royal Crescent; (b) Brock Street; (c) Circus; (d) Assembly Rooms; (e) Gay Street; (f) Queen Square. (Adapted from John Summerson, *Architecture in Britain, 1530–1830*, Penguin, 1953.)

ther's plans for a semicircular development (the Circus, of which the full circle was never attempted). This was composed of thirty-three units designed with a common front that bore three superimposed orders—Doric, Ionic, and Corinthian. His more pretentious layout, the Royal Crescent (Figure 4.24), is shaped like one side of a huge ellipse and uses colossal Ionic columns above a high base to unify its stories.

Robert Adam designed the Pulteney Bridge at Bath as a link between the Pulteney estate and the city. Small housing developments near the bridge are in the Adam attenuated style and their interiors are as attractive a manifestation of the era as can be imagined.

Two additional variations of classicism in architecture occur toward the end of the century. The structuralist approach, as demonstrated in

Figure 4.24 The Royal Crescent, Bath, 1767–1775.
John Wood II, architect. (British Tourist Authority.)

England, appeared as an omission of superfluous decoration and in the intended exposure of structural systems. Both characteristics are seen in Sir John Soane's (1753–1837) Stock Office for the Bank of England (1792).

The second direction to appear in English architecture is seen in the return to the classic Greek canons. The strong archaic Doric is preferred to the examples that descended from Rome through Palladio and the Renaissance. This respect for the Greek often went no further than the adoption of the subtlety of the Greek profiles. As the influence continued into the next century, however, it took the form of the strong Greek-style porticoes raised by George Dance II (1741–1825) at Stratton Park, Hampshire, in 1803.

Obviously Greek mania, as it was called, which had sponsored both the structural and the canonical approach, was spurred by publications like those of Le Roy, Stuart, and Revett. James Adam wrote, after viewing the Greek temples at Paestum:

> . . . the famous antiquities so much talked of late as wonders, but which, curiosity apart, don't merit half of the time and trouble they have cost me. They are of an early Doric, that afford no detail and scarcely produce two good views. So much for Paestum![5]

And so much for sour grapes and changing tastes!

LANDSCAPE

Consideration of the trend in Baroque architecture to tie the buildings to the landscape arouses curiosity about the character of the terrain. Renaissance tradition, with its terraces, parterres, clipped hedges, formal vistas, and waterways, can be seen in many English paintings: Sir Philip Sidney in the garden at Wilton is an example.

At precisely the time with which we are dealing the movement that inaugurated the "English Garden" began. Its roots can be found in landscape painting which was developed as a separate genre in the seventeenth century by the Dutch painter Meindert Hobbema and the French Nicholas Poussin and Claude Lorrain, among others. The second source of this conception of the natural garden is located in the growing philosophy of romanticism which suggested that natural beauty gives rise to flights of the imagination in a manner not possible in straight-jacketed formalities. Joseph Warton writes effusively in 1744:

> Rich in her weeping country's spoils, Versailles
> May boast a thousand fountains, that can cast
> The tortured waters to the distant heavens;
> Yet let me choose some pine-top'd precipice
> Abrupt and shiny, whence a foamy spring,
> Like Anio, tumbling roars.

William Kent was the first to popularize the use of informal gardens as a complement to formal architecture, exemplified at Chiswick, Stowe, and Rousham. What Kent perceived was that landscapes planned on the principle of the Baroque S curve, which lends itself to surprise vistas, can be a welcome addition to the extreme regularity of a classical building. During the eighteenth century the British asserted themselves for asymmetry in landscaping while coming to terms with bisymmetrical influences in architecture.

One of the most famous examples of such scenery is to be seen at Stourhead, Wiltshire, where the owner Henry Hoare, with the help of Henry Flitcroft (1697–1769) and the sculptor Rysbrack, created the garden that has become known as Henry Hoare's Paradise. Flitcroft, Kent's architectural assistant and close associate, was the son of William III's chief gardener and so naturally thought in terms of flora as well as stone. The layout called for the use not only of various types of natural greenery but also of small classical buildings and sculpture, all of which were set to create a spiral plasticity disclosed by a walking tour, forever leading to and from its vortex at the house.

Whereas Stourhead was largely directed by the interests and sensitivities of its owner, Kent's planning of similar gardens gave sanction to the style and spawned the careers of landscape specialists, chief among whom was the famous Lancelot Browne (1715–1783), better known as "Capability," who gained his initial reputation under Kent at Stowe. The English garden gradually lost its dependence on its classical props. It grew more natural with time, more like a Ruisdael painting than a Poussin. Nevertheless, it remained one of contrived naturalism. Capability Browne is often facetiously blamed for the destruction of more artlessly beautiful English scenery than he ever succeeded in creating.

BOOKS ON ARCHITECTURE

To what extent was this architecture of the eighteenth century a heritage of the rule books of the past? Because an era of prodigious publishing of architectural treatises began at this time and has not yet abated, the following review is offered:

Ultimately the counsel which guided the English designers went back to the Italian writers Vitruvius, Alberti, Serlio, Scamozzi, and Palladio. Their texts infiltrated the eighteenth century on three separate levels. First there were the general books on architecture, such as Isaac Ware's *Complete Body of Architecture,* 1756, or the writings of Robert Morris in his *Lectures on Architecture, Architecture Improved,* and *Rural Architecture,* published about midcentury. These men give sound architectural advice which touched with astounding foresight on all three aspects—function, expression, and design—set down by the classical authorities.

Isaac Ware says:

> In studying a design of Palladio's, which we recommend to the young architect as his frequent practice, let him think as well as measure. Let

him consider the general design and purpose of the building, and then consider how far, according to his own judgment, the purpose will be answered by that structure. He will thus establish in himself a custom of judging by the whole as well as the parts; and he will find new beauties in the structure considered in this light.[6]

William Chambers's *Treatise on Civil Architecture* of 1759 marks a new period in architectural writing in which a man of considerable background, experience, and intellectual capacity offered to the professional public a work involving personal consideration of the orders and design factors of architecture.

The second group of books laid great stress on the translation of the classical writers and aimed at interpreting them to the local architect, construction carpenter, and mason. These volumes include advice on local materials, construction, plans, and detail drawings, especially of the orders. In the top echelon were Colen Campbell's *Vitruvius Britannicus,* 1715–1725, William Kent's *Designs of Inigo Jones,* 1727, and James Gibbs's *A Book of Architecture,* 1728.

In the third group of books were the best sellers of the day, the real how-to-do-its, written by the men who knew the problems and the intellectual stature of the clientele they were addressing. William Salmon, a carpenter of Colchester, published *Palladio Londinensis or the London Art of Building* in 1734. Subsequent editions followed until 1755. (Notice how the impressive part of the title comes first!) Another book of his was *The London and Country Builder's Vade Mecum; or the Complete and Universal Estimator, comprising the London and Country Prices of the Different Works of Bricklayers, Masons, Carpenters, Joyners, etc.,* published in 1745 and

again in 1773. This is one of the first price books, counterparts of which became so useful in an age that had left the guild system and had not yet invented a modern trade equivalent.

Abraham Swan published *The British Architect* in 1745, a work that brought patterns of the Rococo to the colonies. Francis Price (?–1763) published *The British Carpenter* in 1733, which despite its unpretentious title was by all accounts one of the best contemporary texts on the subject. In later editions he included a description of Palladio's orders, no doubt as an added sales appeal. Price was architect and surveyor of the works at Salisbury Cathedral, which accounts in part for the high-level, firsthand information the book contains.

The most prolific writer of guidebooks was Batty Langley (like Inigo Jones one wonders whence the baptismal name) who wrote upward of twenty volumes between the twenties and forties. Langley was a man who apparently had been trained in gardening by his father and had acquired a draftsman's skill through surveying. He wrote trade books on both subjects, works that at the time were often belittled by the architectural profession but were avidly bought.

William and John Halfpenny wrote most of their instruction books during the period after 1750 when the demand for interpretation of architecture was widespread due to the confusion that the wider style market had created.

All of these and many more make good reading in light of the cultural as well as the architectural scene. They became even more meaningful when they passed westward over the Atlantic and accounted in large measure for the Colonial, Federal, and later, to a lesser degree, the Greek Revival style in America.

SOME EIGHTEENTH-CENTURY ENGLISH HOUSES

Easton Neston (Figure 4.1)	Towcester, Northamptonshire	1702–1703, for Lord Lempster; Nicholas Hawksmoor, architect
Castle Howard	Yorkshire	1702–1714, for the Earl of Carlisle; Sir John Vanbrugh, architect
Chatsworth (north front)	Derbyshire	1687–1706, for the Duke of Devonshire; Thomas Archer, architect
Blenheim (Figure 4.26)	Oxfordshire	1706–1724, for John Churchill, Duke of Marlborough; Sir John Vanbrugh, architect
Stowe	Buckinghamshire	Eighteenth century, for the Dukes of Buckingham; gardens by William Kent

Marlborough House	London	1710, for the Duchess of Marlborough; Sir Christopher Wren, architect
Clandon Park	Surrey	1715, for Richard, Lord Onslow; Giacomo Leoni, architect
Old Burlington House	London	1717, for Lord Burlington; Lord Burlington and Colen Campbell, architects
Hogarth's House (Figures 4.10, 4.11, 4.12, 4.13, and 4.14)	Soho, London	Actually the home of Thornhill; paintings by Thornhill and Hogarth; dismantled
Stourhead	Wiltshire	1720–1724, for Henry Hoare; Colen Campbell, architect
Seaton Delaval (Figure 4.2)	Northumberland	1720–1729, for Admiral Delaval; Sir John Vanbrugh, architect
Moor Park (Figure 4.3)	Hertfordshire	1720, for Benjamin Styles; Giacomo Leoni, architect
Ditchley	Oxfordshire	1722, for the Lees; James Gibbs, architect; William Kent and Henry Flitcroft, interiors
Mereworth Castle	Kent	1723–1725, for Colonel Fane; Colen Campbell, architect
Chiswick (Figure 4.4)	Near London	Ca. 1725, for Lord Burlington; Lord Burlington and William Kent, architects
Sudbrooke Park	Richmond, Surrey	1726, for the Duke of Argyll; James Gibbs, architect
Holkham Hall	Norfolk	Ca. 1730, for Thomas Coke, Earl of Leicester; William Kent, architect
Prior Park (Figure 4.5)	Bath, Somerset	1734, for Ralph Allen; John Wood I, architect
Marble Hill	Twickenham	1725, for George II; Henry Humphrey, Earl of Pembroke, and Roger Morris, architects
Mansion House	London	1739, 1757, for the Lord Mayor; George Dance I, architect
Stoneleigh Abbey (south front)	Warwickshire	For Lord Leigh; Francis Smith, architect
Wentworth Woodhouse	Yorkshire	1740, for Lord Malton; Henry Flitcroft, architect
Chesterfield House (Figure 4.25)	London	1748, for the Earl of Chesterfield; Isaac Ware, architect
Bath Circus (Figure 4.23)	Bath, Somerset	1754, John Wood I, architect
Strawberry Hill (Figures 4.18 and 4.19)	Twickenham	1747; reconstruction for Sir Horace Walpole
Harewood House	Yorkshire	1760, for the Earl of Harewood; Robert Adam on work of John Carr, architects
Kedleston Hall	Derbyshire	1761–1765, for Lord Scarsdale; Robert Adam on designs of James Paine, architect
Osterley Park	Middlesex	1761–1763, remodeled sixteenth century house for Sir Francis Child; Robert Adam, architect
Syon House (Figures 4.20 and 4.21)	Middlesex	1761–1762, remodeled Medieval house for the Duke of Northumberland; Robert Adam, architect
Landsdowne	London	1765; Robert Adam, architect (room in the Metropolitan Museum of Art)
Heaton Park	Manchester	1772, for Sir Thomas Egerton; James Wyatt, architect
Somerset House	London	1776, 1786; Sir William Chambers, architect
Royal Crescent (Figures 4.23 and 4.24)	Bath	1769; John Wood II, architect
Adelphi Terrace	London	1769; Robert and James Adam, architects
Carlton House	London	1783, reconstructed for the Prince Regent; Henry Holland, designer
Buckingham Palace	London	Home of the Duke of Buckingham, bought by George III in 1761 and settled on Queen Charlotte; George IV called on John Nash to rebuild

INTERIOR DESIGN

Plans and Space Organization

A discussion of eighteenth-century English interiors must be subsumed under a few types and styles, with allowance made for crossing lines.

A brass knocker heralded visitors to the *Georgian house*, bells putting in a feeble appearance only in midcentury. On entering we are again greeted by those Baroque tenets of symmetry and transcendence. The spatial plan of a large central hall with a salon to the rear was in reality the descendent of those that had influenced Palladio and is to be seen in Giuliano da Sangallo's *Villa Medici Poggio a Cajano* of more than 200 years before. In a climate in which the open courtyard could not serve the social needs of a culture nor the Medieval living hall separate its various activities, this pretentious artery served both practical and formal demands. In smaller town houses, where for lack of ground space a free central area could not be maintained, the hall was pushed to the side and a view from the front door to the rear might be contrived by a back window placed on axis (Figure 4.11). Thus continuity of building and landscape was restored—a cardinal mark of the Baroque.

Although functional planning did not weight the scales too heavily, nevertheless the distribution of spaces in domestic architecture gradually became better disposed for privacy and efficiency. Secondary stairs for servants were frequent. The usual arrangement placed the principal staircase in the hall. Occasionally it occupied a side compartment, as Palladio advocated, in order to clear an imposing exhibition space. For the same reason the stairs were frequently found in a secondary room behind the hall from which it was separated by an arch order.

The actual flight sometimes climbed along the wall by small excursions. At Chesterfield House (Figure 4.25) Isaac Ware installed a modification known as the "imperial staircase" (a central flight leading to a landing, from which flights returned symmetrically on each side). Even in moderate-sized buildings flights were ample. They were characterized by broad treads and low risers (e.g., 6 in.). The percentage of available space al-

located to the central hall and its stairs was large—approximately one-third of the overall width. In the squared villa plan the central salon sacrificed somewhat more space, which reached through the crown of the building where it was top-lighted.

In addition to the hall and in keeping with the pretentions of the menage, the first floor was divided into reception rooms, variously called salons, saloons, drawing rooms, and parlors. Libraries, dining rooms, and even bedroom suites—especially those reserved for royalty—were prominently located.

In a small house the service quarters occupied the ground story, which is referred to as the English basement. In large country seats the wings contained services and offices (Figure 4.3). The rooms for ceremonious dining could be found on the first or second floor, bedrooms in the upper stories. The term "bed chamber" appears on the same plan with "bed room," which suggests more space for the former. From size and location it is clear that the chamber served its ancient role of sitting room as well. Some examples of adjacent dressing rooms exist.

Inasmuch as flushed sanitary facilities and inner garde-robes were equally nonexistent, these small isolated rooms provided some privacy. Although outdoor privies were customary, the drainage in congested areas was unsatisfactory and mortality rates were shockingly high. Recall that none of Queen Anne's many children except the Duke of Gloucester lived to adulthood. None of the nine children of the diplomat Sir William Temple and his wife Dorothy Osborne survived their parents. As realists, we cannot help but equate glorious spaces with Crane's plumbing.

These interior spaces were indeed large by today's standards. The great hall at Blenheim (Figure 4.26) overwhelms with its 45 by 70 ft in plan and its gargantuan 67 ft in elevation, quite close to the Palladian proportions of the Golden Sector. It is clear that many of the Palladian architects tried to incorporate volumes that con-

Figure 4.25   (opposite page) Entrance hall of Chesterfield House, Westminster, London, 1748. Isaac Ware, architect. (National Monuments Record, London.)

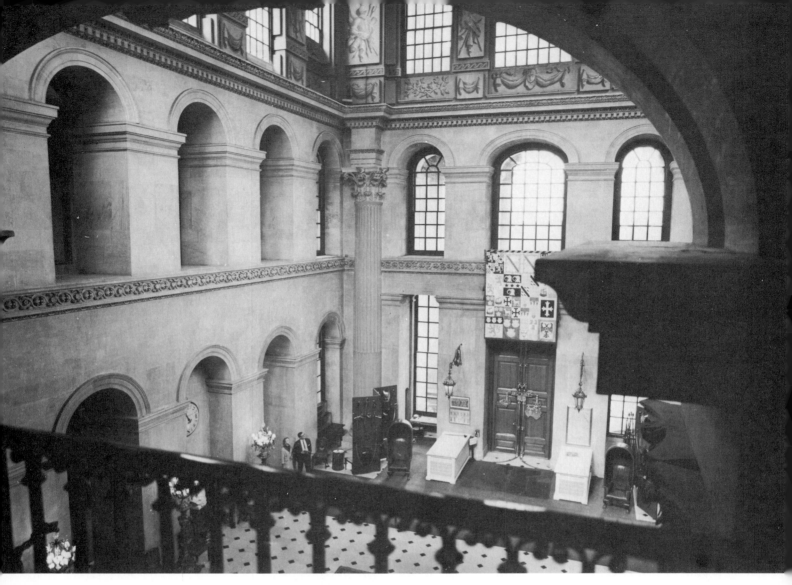

Figure 4.26 The Great Hall at Blenheim, Oxfordshire, 1706–1724. Sir John Vanbrugh, architect. (British Tourist Authority.)

formed to classically prescribed proportions. Sir William Chambers upheld the canon that the height of a room should equal its width.

In smaller houses the dimensions, although not so academically conceived, were pleasing and the sizes seem more than ample (Plate 5). The measurements of the drawing room in Thornhill's home were more than 20 by 22 by 13 (height) ft.

Adam halls retained their spaciousness, of which the architect wrote:

. . . intended as a room of access where servants in livery attend. It is here [i.e., Syon] a room of great dimension, is finished with stucco, as halls always are, and is formed with a recess at each end.[7]

With Adam, however, the principle of the oblique approach often supersedes the placement of rooms enfilade, which provided the long vista. One of Robert Adam's claims to fame lies in his exploitation of a variety of room shapes and angles of view. This is well demonstrated at Syon. When it is recalled that these shapes had to be created within the old Tudor framework, Robert's genius is apparent. It is even more astounding that he and, in his footsteps, Leverton and Wyatt could introduce this sort of spatial drama into their plans in some of the narrow houses on the London squares (Figure 4.27). Similar areas are found in the work of the late Neo-classicists—Henry Holland (1745–1806) at Carlton House and John Soane in his country houses of the eighteenth century.

Architectural Details

The tall, narrow windows of the Stuarts became shorter and broader with the Hanoverians (Figure 4.15). The double-hung sash above the dado was common to the middling house. As previously mentioned, the number of lights might decrease from eighteen to fifteen to twelve (12 by 15 in. each). In modest interiors they would rise to the entablature, but in large rooms they leveled with the door height. Round-arched windows and the Palladian version, both, of course, of greater size, were found in churches and important halls.

In early windows panes were customarily nearly flush with the outer wall. In 1709 an act of Parliament required that in London and Westminster they be set back a minimum of 4 in. The exterior painting of the surrounds then gave a characteristic and new appearance to the houses in these districts. On the inside the reveal was paneled. The frame at the wall was finished in a manner similar to the rest of the architectural dressing, which could mean anything from a simple molded surround with *ears* to an elaborate classical treatment with pillared and pedimented entablature.

Neoclassic windows reverted to the taller and leaner proportions, the height to the width being prescribed as two to one. They were frequently two-and-two-fifths to one. The substantial glazing bars of earlier windows became smaller scaled. Upper story windows were almost square or round in proportion. Architraves were often surmounted with a broad frieze and projecting flat cornice board. Doors, which were usually six paneled, were given architectural surrounds to correspond with the windows.

Any study of fabric treatment on bygone windows is difficult. Photographic records do not exist and paintings are not always to be trusted, although the satirical prints by such well-known arists as William Hogarth, Thomas Rowlandson, and George Cruikshank are revealing and some facts may be deduced. It seems fairly certain that

Figure 4.27 Entrance hall at No. 1, Bedford Square, London, 1780. Thomas Leverton, designer. (By permission of the Trustees of the British Museum; Photograph courtesy of *Country Life*.)

windows with impressive architectural features were left bare. Drapery might be hung over all or part of the glass.

Contemporary documents indicate that important chambers were curtained, often receiving a treatment duplicated in the bed hangings. From Chippendale's letters to clients and workmen we read:

—two blue Moreen window Curtains to hang in drapery and fringed at bottom with lines tassles. (My Ly Ante Chamber)
—two Cotton window curtains to Match the bed (Ly Bed Chamber)
—two green Mix'd damask window Curtains to draw in drapery and to be fringed &c two Venition Sund blinds for the window (Library)

—a Very Neat Mohogany Couch bed with an Oval Canopy on top a Cotton furniture to ditto of a very Neat Small running pattern (Library)[8]

Firms of cabinetmakers such as Chippendale could contract to do the complete job of interior design which included window and bed treatments. Curtains and coverlets of cotton were desirable in a time when drycleaning was unknown. They were referred to as "washing furniture."[9]

Almost any Georgian fireplace should be pre-served in the interest of eye appeal (Figures 4.28 and 4.29). They were intended for room focus and are worthy of the honor. Wren often placed his in a corner (Hampton Court) and the practice was not unusual thereafter (Mereworth Castle). The earliest fireplaces preserved some vestige of the seventeenth-century floor-to-ceiling treatment. When so done they were known as "continued" rather than "simple"; the latter extended only to the mantel shelf. The lower portion would be 5 to 6 ft high for a 7-ft length, with an almost square opening of a little more than 4 ft. The mantel and shelf often simulated a classical structure with pilaster or console to support an entablature with a cornice that would call itself a

Figure 4.28 Georgian marble mantel. Height, 1.66 m, width, 1.88 m. (Photograph courtesy of T. Crowther & Son, Ltd., Fulham.)

Figure 4.29 Marble Georgian mantel in French style. Height, 1.52 m, width, 2.18 m. (Photograph courtesy of T. Crowther & Son, Ltd., Fulham.)

shelf. Plainer fireplaces were graced merely with molding and projection ears. Variations on the theme were many but the result was universally handsome.

In addition to the smaller more ingratiating chimney pieces which fitted into the average home, there were those designed by the Palladians for enormous halls (Figure 4.30). William Kent has been held responsible for many of them but it is certain that others were involved. Sir Henry Cheere, the sculptor, is known to have designed and executed some. These imposing ornaments were made of marble or perhaps its counterpart, *scagliola,* a powdered marble combined with gypsum and other cohesive ingredients. These fireplaces were heavy and poorly proportioned but were imposing withal and suited to the pretentions of their locations.

The small Adam mantel is one of particular interest and beauty (Figure 4.31). Done in stone or wood, it was enframed in semiattached pillars, pilasters, or consoles, with a wide frieze and thin cornice shelf. The frieze was delicately trimmed with fluting, reeding, or laurel garlands with classical *paterae* (round or oval medallions) above the pilasters. Graceful classical urns often decorated these medallion accents.

Designs were heavier, bolder, and more tightly meshed toward the end of the century.

Although woodburning never became obsolete and brass andirons remained among the hand-

137

Figure 4.30 Marble mantel of Palladian or William Kent type, designed for a large space. Height, 1.68 m, width, 2.43 m. (Photograph courtesy of T. Crowther & Son, Ltd., Fulham.)

somest of household adornments, coal and coke were also used for fuel. Thus in the heart of many an eighteenth-century fireplace may be found an iron and brass basket for the harder fuel and possibly an iron fireback and hob. The latter was essentially a side shelf, frequently integral with the grate, on which a kettle could be heated—"the kettle on the hob." As an added detail we often find a wooden fire screen or "dummy board figure" which, in human or animal form, was used to ward off intense heat.

Interior Surface Treatment

Floors were stone or wood, depending on the importance of the building. As the use of carpets in domestic interiors increased the elaborateness of the floor treatment was reduced. The English never favored parquetry to the extent that the French did.

Oriental rugs were popular for coverings as can be noted from many contemporary paintings and from import accounts. The Adam brothers designed many of the handwoven carpets for their rooms. Machine-made carpets (see sections on textiles later in this chapter) were introduced during the eighteenth century and, wherever economy was essential, began to supplant the handwoven varieties.

The principal rooms during the first part of the eighteenth century continued to be paneled. The raised or Stuart panels were superseded by the flush or slightly sunken, with small ovolo (quarter round) moldings. The art of the carver still flourished and the cost of labor was not prohibitive for some very fine work. The wood was pine (English deal), oak, walnut, and later occasionally mahogany (e.g., No. 15, Queen Square, Bath). Softwoods were often painted, the middle-value, subdued colors growing lighter as the century advanced. In an average room, represented again by Thornhill's residence, the dado was 30 in. high and the wide panels might be 3 ft, 6 in. across. These fitted with the narrow ones filling the end spaces. Stiles were approximately 6 in. broad. Interior panels disappeared first in minor rooms and in stair halls where fitting was difficult. Often they were retained only below a dado.

Throughout the century many classical elements crept in. Halls bore their arched openings on pillars or piers and a classical aedicule furnished the surround. Pilasters or semiattached columns punctuated the space above the dado. Where great houses used niches to break the monotony of wall areas, small ones had cupboards or recessed shelving for the same purpose. Corner cupboards made an occasional appearance.

Entablatures during the Georgian period were full classical with architrave, frieze, and cornice, and their bold projections crowned the room with vigor. The work of Adam and of many later designers was less academic. Architraves were sometimes omitted in favor of a deep frieze. Profiles were reduced in projection except where a flat cornice crowned a door entablature. Adam occasionally brought an attenuated room down to human level by adding an attic story above a cornice.

Figure 4.31   Adam-type mantel. Height, 1.61 m, width, 2.18 m. (Photograph courtesy of T. Crowther & Son, Ltd., Fulham.)

Painting. Although mural and ceiling painting never gained a firm foothold in England, it had its advocates. The artist William Hogarth provided a conversation piece for the hall of his father-in-law's (Sir James Thornhill) home. It represents a gallery with a group of figures, somewhat smaller than life size, looking down on the spectator. It is said that Thornhill, whose daughter eloped with Hogarth, took an irascible view of his son-in-law until he discovered how well the young man could paint.

Small scenes were outlined by stucco wall frames, derived from the prototype at the Palazzo Spada in Rome. On a simpler note we find genre paintings done on panels, many of which have been discovered in recent years under numerous coats of varnish. They are often interesting vignettes of the contemporary scene—buildings, ships, people coming to life like an eighteenth-century Pompeii. Seldom is there record of the painter. Andien de Clermont, for instance, is the name associated with the panels at Woodcote which have a distinctive French flavor.

Stucco. In the work of Robert Adam, as in much Neoclassicism, panel divisions are simulated with low-profile stucco. In the richest halls the classical elements of the scene were marble. Much of the stucco decor was done by artists imported from Italy. Signor Amiconi is said to have been responsible for the work in Leoni's Moor Park; Artari at Clandon, Houghton, and Easton Neston. Bagutti was the sculptor of the stucco decorations at Mereworth. We have made mention of the last two men in the discussion of St. Martin-in-the-Fields. The Anglo-Dane Charles Stanley did the unusual work at Stoneleigh Abbey. Sculpture in the round, like the pieces over the door panels at Houghton done by Rysbrack, was often seen.

Some of the loveliest examples of English room plaster were the work of local talent; for example, the Bath builder, John Huchins, at the home of the Linleys. On the other hand, the competent work of Henry Flitcroft at Wentworth Woodhouse carries little aesthetic conviction.

Robert Adam also relied on Italian talent. Michael Angelo Pergolesi may have been sent over to England by James to work on the Long Gallery at Syon. Giambattista Cipriani (1727–1785) was hired by Robert for many commissions.

Angelica Kauffmann (1741–1807) and her husband Antonio Zucchi (1726–1795) were not only good artists but also interesting personages. Mrs. Zucchi was a Swiss who had studied in Rome and there had married Zucchi, an artist and engraver in the employ of the Adams. Zucchi reportedly preferred to live in Italy, and, after a sojourn in England, returned there in 1781 for the remainder of his life. Angelica Kauffmann assisted her husband in much that he did and likewise painted the delicate ceramic plaques with which Neoclassic furniture is often embellished. Mrs. Zucchi became the first woman painter to be appointed to the Royal Academy.

Ceramic medallions in unglazed bisque were made for furniture and wall decoration by John Flaxman who executed them at the Wedgwood factory.

What of the styles of the wall and ceiling decoration in stucco? Large ceiling compositions, as seen in the hall at Mompesson House, retained their popularity throughout the Stuart reigns. Progressing along classical lines, the stuccos nevertheless began to show the loosening of rigid compartmentalism that the Italian Baroque influences introduced. Artari at Houghton (1722) created surface decoration in the ceiling that was not only somewhat lower in relief but also less stereotyped. He skilfully followed the Baroque tradition of keeping part subordinate to part and building to a central climax. But how delightfully he allowed the composition to break its bonds with the putti, in real putti fashion, climbing out of their playpen and clinging to their floral swings to perform childish gymnastics. They remind one of the anteroom at Versailles but seem somewhat frivolous for England.

At Mereworth, Bagutti's stuccos bear little relation to the architecture and still less to the Renaissance-Baroque system of hierarchical proportions. Although the staccato accents here were prophetic of the future, an adequate substitute for the traditional had yet to be established.

The same criticism may be leveled against the stucco at Chesterfield, where enframements copied rather closely from French Rococo models were used in a disturbingly un-French manner. It has been said that the decoration here was done when the architect Isaac Ware was away from the location—the most charitable statement that could be made. Although the English naturally experienced a period of French Rococo mania, they never yielded to it innately and usually designed poorly in this style. Only when transformed by English genius, as exemplified by Chippendale furniture or by simple shell designs in niches and on ceilings, was it endowed with that indigenous quality that makes for fine art.

Adam ceilings are in low molded plastic often known as *Carton-Pierre* (stone cardboard). This was a mixture of whiting, resin, and size, amalgamated when hot and allowed to cool to the consistency of dough. It was then forced into molds to solidify, when it was fixed to the wall or ceiling with glue or small pins.

In style the designs for Adam treatment were Pompeian in inspiration. The compartmentalized patterns consisted of circles, ovals, and straight-line, often hexagonal forms, interlaced and held together in the manner of arabesques. The frames usually incorporated the painted or ceramic medallions just referred to. In the hall at Kedleston the designer, George Richardson, was a draftsman who was taken to Italy by James Adam and the executor was one Joseph Rose. Robert Adam speaks again and again of "putting movement into his designs." In space planning he may be credited with accomplishing this objective by altering shapes, but in decoration it is caused by linear tracery and accented motifs.

Applied Coverings. Following the Adam style, wall treatments became plainer, partly from designers' intent and no doubt because the personnel was not available to execute elaborate work. Holland in his plans for Carlton House (demolished in 1826) for the Prince of Wales was dramatically austere. The interior contained few concessions to paneling and relied on contrasts of light plaster and dark wood for effect.

Flat walls suggested covering with costly damasks and printed cloths, which were fashionable for the salons and smaller sitting rooms of important households. Wallpapers were a substitute used early by Chippendale at Nostell Priory; for example, "52 Yds Yellow Embossed Flock Paper."[10]

Large wall expanses invited pictures. Gentlemen who made the European Grand Tour brought home collections of European paintings which turned their estates into miniature art galleries.

Entrepreneurs like the Adams bought abroad with intent to sell at home. James writes from Rome:

> We have another excellent countryman at Rome who plays his cards there to admiration. Bob will remember him—his name is Jenkins. Last winter he sold no less than £5,000 worth of pictures, etc., to the English, of which every person of any knowledge is convinced he put £4,000 in his pocket.[11]

Family portraits have added much to the personalization of these buildings of a bygone age. Competent painters were to be found in England since the days of Holbein and Van Dyck, and the eighteenth century had many notable practitioners.

Colors. A word should be said about Robert Adam as a colorist. Following the vogue for lighter tones, which progressed with the century, Adam favored the pastels of Louis XV interiors but went further in clarity (saturation). This is the brilliant schema of the Venetian painters and it fitted well with the recommended Palladian white. Robert Adam made it his own and used these tones—for instance, pink and blue—for the entire outfitting of a room. It must have burst on the scene like a flower garden.

Adam, essentially a colorist, was versatile. One plan centered around Etruscan inspiration, such as the design for No. 26 Grosvenor Square (demolished), which was in Etruscan yellow, red, brown, and black—on a white ground.

Furnishings and Their Arrangement

If the classical eighteenth-century house is so important in the total scheme of things architectural, part of its preeminence is due to a style of furnishing to which the world of the English gentry was elegantly suited. The bisymmetry of room shapes and the pairing or tripling of objects—the latter allowing a central pivotal position (e.g., as in a mantel garniture)—would suggest that arrangements were formal. The many small accessories, however, indicate that any rigidity of placement would be inappropriate.

Figure 4.32   An early Queen Ann armchair. England, ca. 1710. Victoria & Albert Museum, London. (Crown Copyright. Victoria & Albert Museum.) The back supports in this example lack the broken-arched form.

FURNITURE

Among the finest furniture are the heirlooms of the eighteenth century. In England, as in France, many were exceptionally well made and, for their milieu, well designed.

Queen Anne Style Furniture

The walnut pieces of the first quarter of the century are alluded to as "Queen Anne," a comfortable and attractive style.

Materials. Good English walnut, which had played so important a role in late Stuart furniture, was growing scarce. French and American wood had often to be substituted, the former a light color and the latter streaked with dark veins. French walnut was restricted during the war years, and later export shipments were almost entirely cancelled in an attempt to preserve the native supply. English cabinetmakers responded to the scarcity by veneering walnut onto other cores, although arms and legs of pieces were solid.

Many writers have spoken of the year 1700 as the dividing line that separated the eras of show from those of comfort in furniture. The transition was not quite so abrupt: during the early years of Queen Anne's reign (1703–1714) one can find chairs that looked backward with scrolled legs and serpentine stretchers and forward with fiddle splat backs. When solid wood was available, and often it was elm or beech or some provincial substitute for walnut, the back might continue its Carolean carving; when walnut veneer was used, the splat was unadorned. All such hybrid pieces, whenever and wherever found, are as human documents the most fun and lead one into the realm of conjecture about their making.

Seating Furniture. Despite these ambiguous pieces, the typical Queen Anne chair does exist (Figure 4.32). Its vital statistics read—about 40 in. high, width around 3 ft for an armchair, less for a side chair, and both depth and height of seat, 18 in. Compare this with today's Barcelona chair of Mies van der Rohe, with its low seat and cube dimensions of slightly more than 30 in. People of Queen Anne's time must have been about as broad as we, but they sat up straighter and higher and insisted on the comfort of head and arm rests.

Ask anyone to describe a chair of this period and he will invariably start with its cabriole legs. This organic curve, as old as Egypt in furniture design, was customarily used in England for both front and rear legs of furniture in the Greek manner, where the animal from which the form is derived appears to be running forward and back at the same time. Occasionally this makes the chair appear somewhat bandy or bowlegged, as the Irish called it. Because its curvature cannot be regularly and easily plotted, the cabriole is a typical Baroque feature. Sometimes it was designed well and sometimes not so satisfactorily, if we may cite the latter as one of the factors that prompted Hogarth to analyze it in an attempt to ascertain "the line of beauty."[12] In Hogarth's self-portrait there is a chair that has been dubbed the Hogarthian chair. Its cabriole legs are extremely awkward and could scarcely have illustrated the perfection he sought.

When English craftsmen of the early eighteenth century learned how to secure a strong frame in spite of an inherently weak structural form (wood splits along its straight grain), stretchers were eliminated and the animal lost its harness. Its feet were varied—the slipper, the trifid, the hoof, the club (these often with the underpinning of a pad), and only later the claw and ball, which combination did not become important in England until at least the thirties. Both the ball and the claw change their silhouettes throughout their history, sometimes being tall, sometimes squat, again flattened on the bottom, the ball grasped firmly or loosely, occasionally by talons and then again by webbed feet. In America these variants suggest different schools of craftsmen; in England, in a more original situation, they seem to be dictated by time and fashion, the progress being from the simpler to the more elaborate forms. The rear legs were often club-footed when the front were claw and ball.

The back supports of the Queen Anne chair rise in a graceful curve to a place above the seat rail, where, with a break in continuity, they sweep in an elongated cyma or S curve to the central splat. This splat, topped with some characteristic motif, such as a shell, masque, scroll, or leafage, was drawn from a combination of C and S curves, which assumed the general overall shape that resembles a fiddle—whence the name *fiddle splat*.

The seat, tenoned into the back, was slightly narrower in that direction and had squared or rounded corners toward the front. The upholstery was slip-over or slip-in. Although a seat rail with shaped apron existed, some of the most imposing examples were broad and straight, often finished with fluting on the lower edge. The legs of the chair were sometimes "hipped," meaning that the knee projected up onto the seat rail. The knee was then ornamented and an accompanying motif was fixed to the center of the front with such designs as pendant husks, satyr or lion masques, or shells.

Arms, when present, had curves in several planes and inaugurated the earliest expression of what is known today as the silhouette chair because it is equally lovely when viewed from any angle. The arm finials, which projected beyond the uprights, varied from simple scrolls to numerous zoological images, of which the eagle's head was one of the most common. The uprights were often attached to the seat at some distance back from the front. Although chairs were frequently made in sets for dining, stools, similar in design, were also used in halls and salons to save money, to provide variety, and to conserve space. A stool and a chair often substituted for a day bed, a piece that tended to go out of fashion during the reign of George II, when the French "sopha" was introduced. Settees were fairly common but some on the market today are spurious, having been made from two chairs.

Chair backs descended in height and those that were upholstered were straight across the top, only to resume a graceful camel hump shape in the later mahogany era. An exception to this straight-top rule is the upholstered *wing* or *easy chair,* which, although it had its seventeenth-century counterparts, flourished prodigiously at this time. Like other chairs, it became lower and broader and wings and arms made one continuous flowing surface with ends of the *roll-around* or *roll-over* variety. Squab or loose seat cushions increased the comfort. Wing chairs were not considered appropriate for formal drawing rooms. Lord Chesterfield advised his son not to "welter in an easie chair."

Such was the typical Queen Anne chair, neither so prepossessing nor so uncomfortable as its predecessor, nor so elaborate and elegant as its Georgian successor. It would have been unseemly in marble Palladian halls but without peer in homely pine-paneled rooms. Notice those in the painting, "A Club of Gentlemen," by William Hogarth.

Speaking of simplification brings to mind that the perennially popular Windsor chair put in its first appearance at this time (Figure 4.33). It was often intended as a piece of cottage furniture, and was likewise used in gardens and halls. There is an unauthentic tale that King George I admired one in a cottage at Windsor and had it duplicated. It is certain that its lighter scale and

Figure 4.33 English Windsor chair, early eighteenth century. Victoria & Albert Museum, London. (Crown Copyright. Victoria & Albert Museum.)

graceful shape made it suitable for less formal apartments. It was originally made in provincial woods such as deal, yew, or beech and often in America in a combination of materials, each suited to specific parts of its anatomy. The English Windsor usually had a fiddle splat back and cabriole legs braced with recessed turned stretchers. The carving and the turning on a good old Windsor is one test of its authenticity. It should be vigorous and strong with a well-formed saddle seat, good rounded hand grasps, and pronounced bulbous turns to stretchers.

Other Furniture Types. Having once fixed the Queen Anne chair in mind, other furniture types

from this period will be easy to recognize. The tall double chest of drawers is about the only form that needs special mention. It was rightly known as a *tall boy* in England (*high boy* in America) because without doubt it required the tallest of youths to reach up into its top drawer 7 ft above the ground. In America it was made in styles from William and Mary to Chippendale, but in England no example has come to light in the Chippendale style, and Chippendale shows none in his "Director." The Queen Anne *tall boy* is a descendent of one common to the William and Mary period. It readily annexes the cabriole leg, the full-bonneted scroll top, and the bail handles with butterfly escutcheons. It is often seen as a stylistic hybrid, possibly with any one of the earlier characteristics of turned, stretchered legs, flat top, and pear-drop handles. The *low boys* often served separately as dressing or side tables. The very tall *chest-on-chest* is also referred to, somewhat incorrectly, as a *tall boy* (Figure 4.34).

Early Georgian Style Furniture

Materials. After the first quarter of the eighteenth century and in the reign of George II new stylistic trends became evident. In part they were due to the advent of mahogany, with its suggestion of suitable techniques of handling that led to different designs; in part they were due to the need for more imposing furniture to fit into grand halls.

Mahogany began to make inroads as a furniture wood in England after 1700. This wood had been known in Elizabeth's time and the fable—that Sir Walter Raleigh, who certainly used it to floor his ships, presented a table made from Jamaican "mahogotheny" to the Queen—is well known. The first reference to the wood in the statistics of imports was at Christmas in 1699, certainly an opportune gift to a nation that was to use it with such discernment.

The earliest imports came from the West Indies—Cuba and San Domingo, which belonged to Spain, and from Jamaica, which was a British colony. In 1722 and again in 1726 Parliament imposed a tax on the import of foreign woods. The traders, however, merely passed Spanish wood off as Jamaican, and so there seemed to be no immediate dearth of the Cuban and San Domingan varieties which had great hardness and a deep red color. Toward the middle of the century a fast-growing Honduras timber, lighter in color and larger in pores, became popular, no doubt because it was less expensive and supplanted the diminishing West Indies varieties. This softer wood, not so suitable for carving, reopened the style trend for veneering at the very time that straight-line Neoclassic furniture appeared.

Once introduced, mahogany was recognized as a superior wood for the fashionable furniture of the day. It came in large planks, often 4 ft broad and 48 long. It had a close, straight grain (large figures came later with the African mahogany), was free from imperfections, and was strong, with little shrinkage or sap. In addition to being good for joinery, it possessed just the right softness for carving. This virtue was apparently not immediately obvious to cabinetmakers, for there are countless examples of early mahogany chairs made with solid Queen Anne fiddle splat backs unadorned by piercing.

Mahogany is one of those woods that take a glistening polish due possibly to tyloses (a sort of natural gum) in the pores. Mahogany can be made to gleam simply by rubbing it with the palm of the hand. Although both an oil and the time-worn wax finishes are reported, the royal accounts speak of the application of shellac and rottenstone to eighteenth-century furniture. If these ingredients are used for many rub-down coats, the finish is similar to that known today as an *old French finish*. No other combines so well the qualities of durability with a satisfactory satin reflection which appears to come from the depth of the wood. By Neoclassic times an oil varnish was available.

Although mahogany was so basic to the period we are discussing that the historian Macquoid called it "The Age of Mahogany," other materials were used. Many of the imposing "Palladian" pieces were made of pine treated with gesso and gilt, an odd condonance of faking that all Baroque people seem to have tolerated. As French fashions became stylish, exotic woods appeared in marquetry. Ormolu mounts, although never so popular in England as in France, were applied.

Figure 4.34   Chest-on-chest. Mahogany. Victoria & Albert Museum, London. (Crown Copyright. Victoria & Albert Museum.)

General Character.   In the opinion of many this early Georgian furniture is the finest England has ever produced. In the work of some of its leaders it can hold its own with that of the best of the French royal *menuisiers.*

The furniture of the first Georges should be

considered in the nature of stylistic variations on a Baroque theme. For all of its often curved lines it is architectonic in a manner that Queen Anne furniture is not. One feels the rectilinear carcass under the undulations.

As in architecture which favored many Baroque devices to gain movement within its confines, to open up its form, and to cloud its contours, so this Georgian furniture used the serpentine line for its movement, opened its planes by piercing, and obscured its edges with carving. Its scale was masculine without being oppressive, its materials and techniques, elegant without being ostentatious, its color (largely due to the use of dark mahogany as opposed to light walls), providing the drama of contrast that can also cause eye movement. In its arrangement within an interior it is again climactic. It masses tall pier mirrors, case clocks, and cabinets as vertical centers of interest that punctuate a low level of horizontality.

One of the difficulties attendant on acquiring discernment with respect to Georgian furniture lies in the frequent allusions to "William Kent" design or to Palladian furniture. By this is meant furniture exceedingly large in scale, architectural in treatment, and expensive in execution. It was planned as a permanent adjunct to the palatial halls we have been considering. It included large cabinets, tables, and mirrors. The name accrues because William Kent was one of the first architects to consider the designing of furniture as the prerogative of the architect. "Kent's" furniture used classical and Baroque architectural features for its adornment; thus it seems wise to treat it as a pretentious manifestation within the coterie of fashions related to the main spirit of the Georgian.

Other diversions are the French, Gothic, and Chinese influences, each of which is affiliated with a corresponding architectural fashion within the general style. The word *fashion* denotes a more transitory and superficial phenomenon than *style*. It is one that we shall meet more frequently from this time. Merchandising, riding with the times, sustains fashion and in the end destroys it with too many cross stimulants.

In 1740 Matthias Lock, a carver and designer, published *A New Drawing Book of Ornaments* which contained many rocaille designs and was the first pattern book to herald Rococo taste. This meant the borrowing of such elements as the French scroll foot, the rocaille shell, a general lightening of scale, and asymmetrical composition, and more use of the French techniques of marquetry and lacquer.

The Gothic taste in furniture, which recurred periodically, was at midcentury the most transient of the current fashions. It was expressed in minor details such as Gothic frets and Medieval decorative motifs.

Likewise the Chinese taste moved along as an addition to many styles. A Chinese-inspired fret would appear on a classic table or a Chinese dragon would be perched on a Rococo bedstead. Few were asking for authenticity and fewer could recognize it.

The Cabinetmakers and Their Work. After the death of Gerreit Jensen, whose work is coterminous with the last of the Stuarts (for he died in the same year as Queen Anne), the royal accounts list a partnership (1714–1726) between John Gumley, a glass manufacturer and cabinetmaker, and James Moore (?–1726). Moore was the exceptional man who signed his furniture. Several of Moore's pieces have been documented[13]—one a gilt gesso table in the queen's audience chamber at Hampton Court, another at Buckingham Palace, two tables at Windsor, and several in homes of the peerage. His designs featured straighter lines than the usual broken Baroque forms.

Like Moore's tables, the mirrors of John Gumley were rectilinear. Their frames were beveled glass or carved or gilt wood. Those made for the Duke of Devonshire at Chatsworth, probably by Gumley, were 12 ft high, including their surmounting armorial cresting. For smaller houses 3 or 4 ft was more usual. One of the problems, as can be imagined, of supplying these tables and glasses to the country seats was transportation. When possible they were shipped by boat to the nearest port and then overland by "waggon."

It is with William Hallett (1701–1781) that we begin to stand on firmer biographical ground with respect to cabinetmakers. He was one of the most fashionable purveyors of George II's reign, and information about him mounts constantly. That prince of English gossipers, Horace Walpole, whom it is difficult not to quote, for his life (1717–1797) embraced so much of this century and his circle included so many of its important people, said, "I want to write above the doors of most modern edifices, 'Repaired and beautified; Langley and Hallett churchwardens.' "[14]

It is revealing of the social shifts of the time that Hallett bought the site of Canons, which had belonged to the Duke of Chandos, at a sell-out figure, and on the vaults of the old house had one built for himself. He had aspirations to the establishment of a gentleman's family and estate, ambitions which the twentieth century would find natural and praiseworthy but which the eighteenth did not understand and thought that the sale of this place to a cabinetmaker was " '. . . a mockery of sublunary grandeur.' "[15]

Hallett's style is imposing, like that of two other men, John Cobb (?–1778) and William Vile (?–1767), all of whom had business interconnections. Much of their work volume is in large architectural case furniture in the Kentian tradition with Rococo overtones. Cobb, the man, is apparently legend, a pompous individual with the ability and sagacity to create a small fortune and without the saving grace of humor that would have made the wearing of it tolerable. William Vile's skill is identified with top-rank cabinetry in the Rococo taste made during the first half of George III's reign.

Following Cobb and Vile, we can peg our knowledge of mid-Georgian furniture on Thomas Chippendale (1718–1779), who, although he has lost some of his kingpin position among eighteenth-century celebrities as recent knowledge about other prominent craftsmen has come to light, still remains the type figure of all that is significant in English furniture of the day. So much is this true that he eclipses the Georges in naming a style. Even he, who certainly made a bid for publicity when in 1754 he published his "Director," would have been amazed at his posthumous fame.

His contribution possibly needs some reappraisal for today's audience. Over a quarter century ago Oliver Brackett's then authoritative life of Chippendale was published. Since that time it was first popular to credit everything of merit produced in the mideighteenth century to his

workshop. Then it became equally the custom to discredit the genius of this man. Today we are in a better position to estimate his contribution and at the same time to evaluate that period in English cabinetry for which he is the legendary image.

We know little about the boy who was born in 1718 in Yorkshire of a family of wood craftsmen. It is thought that he came to London about 1727. He was thirty when he married Catherine Redshaw, who died in 1772. He married Elizabeth Davis in 1777, but the union was short-lived, for Chippendale died of tuberculosis in 1779.

He is known to have secured a house in Conduit Street, Long Acre, in 1749, in that section of old London then inhabited by similar craftsmen. His activities to this date are not authenticated but it is assumed that he plied his trade, rising through the various stages of apprenticeship until he finally became a master craftsman or entrepreneur for the service of others in allied occupations. This amounted to being the head of a firm in the modern sense. The mideighteenth century is the first period when such organizations are found.

Business establishments had the usual troubles along the way. Banking was not expedited then as it is now and money was often stolen en route from debtor to creditor. Clients were frequently in arrears on accounts. Chippendale was hard pressed to pay his bills. Customers complained—the producer overshot his estimate—the goods were late in arriving—the finished product was not as represented. Letters on both sides are often acrimonious. Truly the job of managing productive service enterprises such as those of Chippendale—Gillow (Robert, 1703–1773; Richard, 1734–1811; Robert, Jr., d. 1796)—Linnell (William, d. 1776; John, d. 1796)—Ince (William), Mayhew (John)—and Seldon (George, 1727–1802) and descendents—was fraught with troubles similar to those that have echoed down the years until today.

The part of Chippendale's career that becomes important to our history dates from 1753 when he opened a shop in St. Martin's Lane near Charing Cross. Fashionable London had been building in this west end neighborhood since the days of the Great Fire in 1666. There are clues to indicate that Chippendale was sufficiently astute to recognize the value of a good address. His studio, however, could not have been very large and much of his contracted work must have been sublet. Many of his biographers quote an announcement taken from the *Gentleman's Magazine* for 1755 to the effect that "A fire broke out in the workshop of Mr. Chippendale, a cabinetmaker in S. Martin's Lane, wherein were the chests of twenty-two workmen."

At various times there were partners in the Chippendale firm—James Rannie before 1766 and, several years later, Thomas Haig, who continued a partnership with Thomas Chippendale II after the death of Thomas I. The son died in 1822. Haig had withdrawn from the partnership in 1796 and in 1804 the firm went bankrupt. It is said to have kept high quality standards to the end.

Chippendale's renown rests on his book, *The Gentleman and Cabinet-Maker's Director* (1754), as well as on the quality of his known achievement. It is of interest that Chippendale named his publication as he did. He seems to have consistently made a bid for the elite trade (as would be natural) and his inclusion of the word "gentleman" in his title is noteworthy. The names of the Duke of Portland, the Earl of Northumberland (later the Duke), and the Duke of Beaufort (for whom subsequent commissions were executed) were among those of the original subscribers. Likewise the names of contemporary cabinetmakers appear, an indication that his designs served as inspiration for current furniture, a fact that makes it difficult to assign pieces to his workshop unless records of purchase remain. Although Chippendale probably did much of his own designing, it is believed that some drawing may have been by Matthias Lock, a consummate draftsman, and H. Copland, who had collaborated with Lock in publishing books of ornament.

Subsequent editions of the "Director" were published in 1755 and 1762; a French edition also appeared in the later year. The 1762 edition was increased by forty plates and gives us some clue to the changes that the decade had brought in style trends. Less emphasis is placed on the large rectilinear pieces, more on small objects such as pedestals, firescreens, and mirrors, and all are favored in the lighter French Rococo taste.

That Chippendale attained a modicum of social prestige is attested by the appearance of his autograph in the register of the Royal Society of Arts to which he was elected in 1760. It was in company with the names of Sir Joshua Reynolds, David Garrick, and Samuel Johnson.

Chippendale's firm can with reasonable certainty be connected with certain articles. Among some eighteen or more locations for which he executed commissions, the accounts of several are pertinent.[16] Two were in his home county—Nostell Priory for Sir Rowland Winn and Harewood House for Edwin Lascelles, Lord Harewood. One was in Kent—Mersham-le-Hatch for Sir Edward Knatchbull. The Nostell Priory papers, a series of letters between Chippendale and his patron, and a body of consecutive accounts date from 1766 to 1772. The Harewood archive dates from 1769 to 1777. Mersham-Le-Hatch covers the years 1767–1768, 1768–1770, 1772, and 1778. This chronology is well past the time of the "Director" and takes Chippendale's work into its final and Neoclassic period to which his best accomplishment is conceded. As this phase was often to order of Robert Adam, it is dealt with later.

Chippendale's establishment undertook all manner of interior work—upholstering, window curtaining, carpet designing, paper hanging, wood refinishing, and furniture moving, in addition to the cabinetry for which it is best known. Men were sent to make installations and "seamstresses" were employed on location for the draperies and bed coverings. This last throws some light on women in business.

Of the oddments picked up in reading the Chippendale accounts, the following few have been culled as interesting reading:

Nostell Priory

157 sham books for the upper part of the Library Door.

10 mahogany French arm chairs cover'd with blue morine.

3 small picture frames for water coloured pictures.

A ditto easy chair.

A Green and Gold Chymney Glass.

A mahogany Pembroke table with writing drawer.

12 rush bottom chairs [such might go in the
   servants' hall].
A turnup bedstead made to fit in a deal
   press.
Altering and repairing a large organ case.
A mahogany house for a monkey.
Taking down window curtains, cleaning
   them and putting up a bed.
To a slide for the front of the Crib bed with
   Ticken
To a field Bedstead.
A pair of mahogany steps with an upright
   handle.
Braid, brass rings, and plumets [curtain
   weights].

Harewood

Curtains with circular heads lined and
   fringed complete.
A very large State bedstead with a Dome
   Canopy decorated on the Inside with rich
   carved Antique Ornaments—a large Antique Vauze on the Top, with corner vases
   and sundry other ornaments, the Cor-
   nishes with Emblematic Tablets and Swags
   of Roses, with various other ornament exceedingly richly Carved—the whole Gilt
   in Burnished Gold, exceedingly highly
   finished.
A very large Pier Glass.
A large wrought brass Lamp with 12 burners
   for oil
2 large Barjaires [bergeres].
2 large Green Venetian Sun Shades.

Mersham-le-Hatch

Crimson Cheque Window Curtains in the Nursery.

"Colligut ut spargit" was the fabled motto of Chippendale. "He collects as he scatters"—among the many ephemeral fashions of the time, one recognizable English style.

Types: Seats. Taking its departure from the Queen Anne chair, the back of the Georgian was the first part to square itself (Figure 4.35). The break in the side rails was dropped along with the continuous top arch. The latter was replaced by a separate cross piece contoured in bow shape and often called the "cupid's bow." The occa-

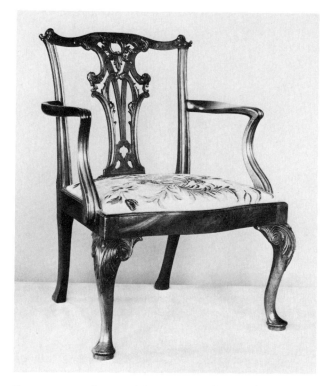

Figure 4.35 Chippendale-type armchair with pad feet. Victoria & Albert Museum, London. (Crown Copyright. Victoria & Albert Museum.)

sional three-dimensional swirls in the finials are alluded to as "swept whorls."

Arms were frequently engaged to the front of the chair by a long concave sweep. The back was pierced (Figure 4.36), its elaborateness running the gamut from simple ladder-back curves to the most amazing intertwined ribbands and bows. Sometimes, however, the entire width of the back was filled with Chinese or Gothic frets (Figure 4.37). Although carved and highly ornamented cabriole legs appeared, the straight-bracketed leg with recessed stretchers was more frequently used with the fretted fashions. But because chairs were made to order from pattern books, the most heterogeneous designs occurred (Figure 4.38): straight legs and French backs, French legs and Chinese backs, or simple ladder backs with claw and ball cabrioles. Some arms on Chinese-type chairs were straight and canted out from the seat. The latter were flat or dished; their contours straight or rounded, their upholstery slip-in or

149

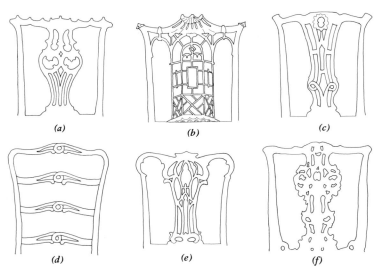

Figure 4.36 (above) Examples of Chippendale-type chair backs: (a) lyre shape splat; (b) Chinese fret splat; (c) pierced splat with swept whorl top rail; (d) ladder back; (e) honeysuckle-motif splat with arched top rail; (f) intertwined ribbands splat.

Figure 4.37 (below) Chippendale-style armchair in the Chinese manner, 1750–1770. Mahogany. Metropolitan Museum of Art, New York. (The Metropolitan Museum of Art, Kennedy Fund, 1918.)

Figure 4.38 Chippendale-style armchair with straight legs. Victoria & Albert Museum, London. (Crown Copyright. Victoria & Albert Museum.)

slip-on. Upholstered and wing chairs (more fully described in American context) followed the general patterns. The sofas were particularly attractive and noteworthy. Coming into being for the first time, they had long, upholstered seats with backs rising in a graceful swell known as the "camel's hump."

Types: Storage. Chests present a variety of interesting forms. The commode (so named in the "Director") took the place of the high and low boys. Many exhibited the French techniques of marquetry and ormolu. Some of the best and most English were done in mahogany (Figure 4.39). Fronts were often serpentine. The gilt brasses, the straight-bracketed feet, and the molded bases are English characteristics. The solid drawers were

150

finished with moldings rather than flush veneered. Some of the largest commodes with recessions in the center were used as library or desk tables.

Writing furniture, called, when low, by the French name *bureau* and, when topped by shelves, *bureau bookcase* or *secretary*, gained popularity. The upper sections yielded to the various styles and thus may be found with scroll or triangular pedimented or straight contours. One unique form of writing chest which could be opened to an enlarged flat surface was called a *bachelor's chest*. It was one of those practical double-duty pieces that could fit into smaller rooms. No doubt that interesting bachelor Walpole had a hand in its design for use at Strawberry Hill, concerning which he wrote to Horace Mann in Florence, enclosing a sketch of the interior:

> It is really incredible how small most of the rooms are . . . I could send it to you in this letter as easily as the drawing, only that I should have nowhere to live until the return of the post.[17]

Types: Tables. The round, gate-leg table continued in fashion, several often being required for a dinner party, although some were as wide as 40 in. Long trestle boards with cloths were still set up for state occasions. Done in characteristic Chippendale style, foldtop card tables, corner tables with letdown flaps, tea tables, tripod tables, and small writing stands are among the numerous items that this period bequeathed to ours.

The large walnut tables with Stuart characteristics which graced the reception halls were found far into the century. The Kentian tables, although their marble tops might be supported on scrolled consoles, were of straighter contour, which indicated more architectonic thinking. One example measures 7 ft in length, 2½ in depth, and 32 in. in height—a clue to the enormity of "Palladian" furniture.

Figure 4.39 Medal cabinet, William Vile, made for George, Prince of Wales, shortly before his accession to the throne in 1760. Mahogany. Victoria & Albert Museum, London. (Crown Copyright. Victoria & Albert Museum.)

Figure 4.40 Chippendale bed in the east bedroom, Harewood House, Yorkshire. (Harewood House, Yorkshire. By permission of The Earl of Harewood. Photo, B. Unné.)

Types: Beds. The usual bed of the era was the postered variety designed to display ornate pillar-shaped posts (Figure 4.40). They were exceedingly tall, those illustrated in the "Director" being 8 to 9 ft high. There were other designs for intricate domed and "duchess" beds, but they were the beds of state and assuredly not common. That all, with their elaborate festoons of material, could not be kept overly clean or free from vermin may be imagined. A recipe, based on mercury, from the *Gentleman's Magazine* of 1735 makes this suggestion:

> . . . after having taken the Bedstead to Pieces and brushed it very clean from Dust and Dirt, rub in all the Cracks and Joints the above Mix-

ture, letting it dry on; nor must the Bedstead be wash'd at any Time afterwards.[18]

Types: Mirrors. One smaller mirror dating from the early century was rectangular, in two sections of beveled glass, and surrounded by a molded wood frame with cyma curves top and bottom or by a frame made of beveled mirror glass (Figure 4.41). Typical Georgian mirrors, now broader in relation to their height and generally larger, were similar (Figure 4.42). Some took on Baroque embellishments and some of the handsomest contrasted dark frame veneers with gilt ornamentation. Toward midcentury, oval shapes were introduced. Both oval and rectangular forms had modeled or carved ornaments in gilded Rococo designs of fanciful imagery, C and S scrolls, ho-ho birds, and exotic animals (Figure 4.43). Thomas Johnson of Soho published several books of designs for girandoles and mirrors—*Twelve Giran-*

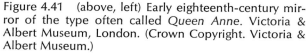

Figure 4.41 (above, left) Early eighteenth-century mirror of the type often called *Queen Anne.* Victoria & Albert Museum, London. (Crown Copyright. Victoria & Albert Museum.)

Figure 4.42 (above, right) English Georgian mirror. Victoria & Albert Museum, London. (Crown Copyright. Victoria & Albert Museum.)

Figure 4.43 (below, right) Georgian gilt mirror, ca. 1750. Victoria & Albert Museum, London. (Crown Copyright. Victoria & Albert Museum.)

doles, 1755, and *One Hundred and Fifty New Designs,* 1758. He was a carver of sconces, girandoles, and other accessories of the furniture trade. Matthias Lock has also been mentioned for his exuberant drawings of these decorative shapes.

Types: Clocks. Clock cases were made by the cabinetmaker, whereas the works were the specialty of the clock maker. The same situation prevailed in the manufacture of barometers, which were used extensively before the morning paper, telephone, or radio began providing weather reports. Because clocks were pendulum-regulated,

the tall case was prominent (Figure 4.44) and this was the age of the finest. Formal English paneling suited the use of the floor clock better than the contemporary Rococo background of France.

Justin Vulliamy (fl. 1730–ca. 1790) was a well-known clockmaker of Swiss origin; Benjamin Gray was clockmaker to George II. British clocks of this period are well represented in the Winthrop Collection at Harvard's Fogg Museum of Art, which contains examples by John Seymour, Aylmer Stoppes, and John Goodfriend. A discussion of their design is related to American models.

Late Georgian or Neoclassic Style Furniture

On September 22, 1765, Horace Walpole wrote a letter from Paris to his friend George Montagu. In it he makes many observations about French society and French taste. One note belongs to our story. He says: "In their dress and equipages they are grown quite simple. We English are living upon their old gods and goddesses." This can only mean that the Rococo had given way to the Neoclassic in France but was still in evidence in fashionable England.

Dating and General Character. Neoclassicism in furniture design was born in England in the early sixties and lasted until supplanted by its more rigid counterpart, the Greek Revival or Empire styles of the next century. Although Rococo influences were often conterminous and there was call for some concessions to Gothicism and the Chinese taste, nevertheless Neoclassicism was a style that showed a fair amount of uniformity.

In general its furniture displayed dominantly straight lines, vertical emphasis, smaller scale, lighter tone, and finer texture. English Neoclassic furniture owed much to the less pompous classical influences of Pompeii and the Graeco-Roman; it resembled Louis XVI furniture as done, for instance, by Jacob and Weisweiler but was less austere. More so than in France, it was the furniture of a consciously fashionable society.

Figure 4.44 English long-case clock, George Graham, London, ca. 1715. Walnut and pierced fretwork. Height, 2 m. Metropolitan Museum of Art, New York. (The Metropolitan Museum of Art, Gift of Irwin Untermyer, 1964.)

Designers and Cabinetmakers. In addition to the innovations that Robert Adam carried out in architecture and in the overall concepts of interior design, we must acknowledge that almost singlehandedly he introduced English Neoclassic furniture design.

His first big commission on his return from Italy was for Sir Nathaniel Curzon at Kedleston (1759–1760). James Stuart had already made some tentative classic-oriented designs for the interior to which Adam fell heir. He also inherited the accomplished Linnells as craftsmen inasmuch as they were already making furniture for this house.

Although Adam had had no experience with furniture designing, Kedleston forced him into immediate action. He met the challenge with heavy rectilinear pieces, often with cabriole legs, on which he hung his vocabulary of classic ornaments—sphinxes, rams' heads, and acanthus wreaths—to accentuate the terminals.

When, after the Seven Years' War (1763), titled Englishmen were again lured to France to purchase materials for their newly refurbished buildings, Adam had the opportunity to observe the products of French Neoclassicism firsthand. In a bid for English patronage the Gobelins had inaugurated a liberal policy of selling and to this end issued some illustrations of interiors that would be appropriate with a particular set of tapestries. These Parisian sketches may have been designed by the French architect M. Soufflot. In any event the outcome of this program can be seen in the tapestry room at Osterley and again at Croome Court (now at the Metropolitan Museum of Art). Certainly the illustrations gave Adam inspiration for designing a room ensemble—furniture to accompany the background.

Robert Adam's mature style was nevertheless an original creation, which we shall discuss in relation to the various categories of furniture. Here we review his connections with other late-eighteenth-century men.

Furniture firms operated most extensively at exactly this period and were responsible for a large percentage of the work done in prominent locations. The firm of Ince and Mayhew published the *Universal System of Household Furniture* (1759–1763) which was patterned after Chippendale's "Director."

Adam and Chippendale apparently had equitable business relations. Records indicate that at Harewood House and again at Mersham-le-Hatch, where Adam did the interior designing, the furniture in the first and all of the interior furnishings in the second were designed and executed by Chippendale. In other houses Adam and Chippendale seemed to have shared the responsibility of purveying the furnishings. Some freedom of choice appears to have been allowed the owner with respect to his engagements.

Certain other names repeatedly appear in the textbooks: Thomas Shearer (fl. ca. 1788), George Hepplewhite (?–1786), and Thomas Sheraton (1751–1806).[19] All owed their fame to their publications rather than to their craftsmanship, although the first two are known to have been furniture makers. With Shearer we make our first acquaintance with *price books* for the furniture business. These were virtually trade catalogs which detailed in cost of materials and labor the necessary price to ask for any article. Shearer contributed designs for the 1788 *London Book of Prices* (later editions, 1793, 1805, 1823). He also published his *Designs for Household Furniture* in 1788. No furniture has been positively identified as having come from his shop.

George Hepplewhite is a shadowy figure in the group that we associate with English Neoclassic furniture. Facts about his life are conjectural. It is believed that he was apprenticed to Gillow and that, after coming to London, he conducted his business in the parish of St. Giles, Cripplegate. Apparently he too contributed drawings which later appeared in the 1788 *Book of Prices*. The other book on which his fame rests, *The Cabinet Makers' and Upholsterers' Guide,* was published posthumously by his widow, Dame Alice Hepplewhite, who carried on his business under the sign of A. Hepplewhite and Company. Again, although no furniture can be credited to him, his designs illustrate a graceful style which has come to be associated with his name (Figures 4.45 and 4.46).

Thomas Sheraton provides the most interesting human document in the group. It is not known to what extent, if at all, he carried on the business of cabinetmaking. Born in Durham County, the son of a cabinetmaker, it is claimed that he was apprenticed as a youth to learn that skill. Whether true or not, it is certain that he spent much time in writing religious tracts and preaching in Baptist

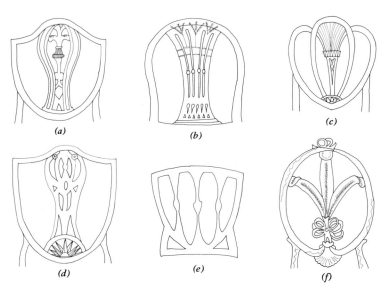

Figure 4.45 (above) Examples of chair-back types associated with the Hepplewhite style: (a) lyre shaped splat, (b) vase shape splat; (c) heart shape splat; (d) lyre shape splat; (e) splat in shape of crusader's shield; (f) splat using three feathers—decorative device of the Prince of Wales.

Figure 4.46 (below) Armchair in Hepplewhite style, eighteenth century. Victoria & Albert Museum, London. (Crown Copyright. Victoria & Albert Museum.)

chapels, endeavors not exactly related to carpentry. Sheraton came to Soho in London in 1790 and probably any furniture that he might have made antedated that year.

Subsequently he supported his family in a most meager way by writing, acting as a stationer, and by giving drawing lessons. As a draftsman he was singularly proficient and it is perhaps noteworthy that he called his first large publication *The Cabinet Makers' Drawing Book*. It appeared in 1791 and 1794, with a revised edition in 1802. In 1803 Sheraton brought out his *Cabinet Dictionary*, and in 1805 he published the first part of his unfinished *The Cabinetmaker, Upholsterer, and General Artist's Encyclopedia* (Figure 4.47).

Adam Black, the future publisher of the *Encyclopedia Britannica*, worked for Sheraton for a short time at his London address. He noted the poverty of his surroundings and a certain acrimony which Sheraton displayed in speaking of his confreres. Sheraton may have suffered from a slight mental instability and he certainly lacked financial acumen, but his drawings and designs indicate a sensitive artist who, despite the fact that he borrowed liberally from others, stamped his own with a simplicity that owed much to an elegant sense of proportion. As the *Drawing Book* went abroad as a pattern book, its designs became the inspiration for what we might again, with some licence, call the Sheraton style, a simplified straightline Neoclassicism that we shall study in relation to separate items (Figure 4.48).

Changes in Materials and Techniques. With the third quarters of the century it is interesting to note how such old-line men as Chippendale, Vile, and even Cobb fell into the new patterns of the craft. Customarily thought of as working in mahogany, they often turned to the lighter satinwood. They resort to marquetry rather than exclusively to carving. Chippendale's inlay is frequently on a rosewood ground. Gilding and japanning make his pieces more acceptable in Adam-style rooms. Adam favored painted furniture rather than japanned. Although both Chippendale and Vile made some of their finest pieces in Rococo taste, nevertheless Chippendale, who was prone to use the chamfered bracketed foot and bail handles, straightened their contours in his late furniture.

Types: Dining Room Furniture and Large Case Goods. We must begin our study of Neoclassic furniture here because it was precisely in this department that the Adams made their greatest contribution. In their *Works in Architecture* (1773–1779) they say:

> To understand thoroughly the art of living, it is necessary perhaps to have passed some time among the French. In one particular, however, our manners prevent us from imitating them. Their eating rooms seldom or never constitute a piece in their great apartments, but lie out of the suite, and in fitting them up, little attention is paid to beauty of decoration . . . as soon as the entertainment is over, they immediately retire to the rooms of company. It is not so with us. Accustomed by habit, or induced by the nature of our environment, we indulge more largely in the enjoyment of the bottle. . . . The eating rooms are considered as the apartments of conversation in which we pass a great deal of our time . . . they are always finished with stucco and paintings, that they may not retain the smell of victuals.

In the early sixties there appeared a grouping of dining room wall furniture used frequently by the Adams and probably designed by them, although execution may have been by other hands (Figure 4.49). This consisted of a large serving table with accompanying side pedestals surmounted by knife urns, the whole making an ensemble which, with a large picture or glass hung above, created an imposing as well as useful focal point. A low wine cellarette completed the arrangement. Adam pieces for Viscount Scarsdale (Sir Nathaniel Curzon) at Kedleston in 1762 are our earliest examples.

In Shearer's published designs of 1788 the first instance occurs in which pedestal ends were joined with the serving table and in which the use of the sideboard as it is known today was initiated. Other pieces of this order are shown in Hepplewhite's *Guide* and in Sheraton's *Drawing Book.* Although without historical sanction, common usage has assigned the name Hepplewhite to those with concave central panels and Sheraton to those that are convex.

This one type of article can illustrate the growth of Adam's personal style. With the passing of the years we note greater lightness and finer detail-

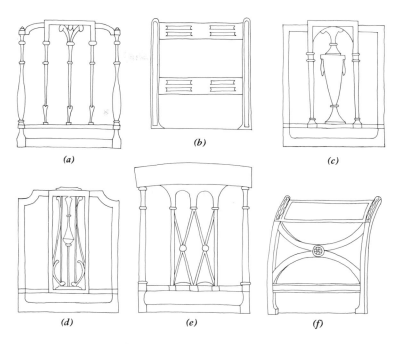

(a)   (b)   (c)

(d)   (e)   (f)

Figure 4.47 Examples of chair backs associated with the Sheraton style: (a) splat with three feathers motif of the Prince of Wales; (b) late form, horizontal splat; (c) splat with vase motif; (d) splat with lyre and vase motif; (e) splat showing early form of wide top bar; (f) late form, curved horizontal splat.

Figure 4.48 Sheraton-style armchair, 1780–1790. Satinwood. Formerly in the collection of the Cleveland Museum of Art, present whereabouts unknown. (Photo, Courtesy of the Cleveland Museum of Art.)

Figure 4.49 Adam-style dining room group: pedestal silver-chests, sideboard, and wine cooler. Executed by firm of Thomas Chippendale. Harewood House, Yorkshire. (Harewood House, Yorkshire. By permission of The Earl of Harewood. Photo, B. Unné.)

ing. The square tapered leg, or the round fluted one, often with thimble foot or some variety of spade foot, at times gave way to spiral turning.

Later Adam tables and consoles had curved fronts. They became stock items to combine with a tall pier glass as wall decoration.

Adam design was always well and classically proportioned. In the girandoles and mirrors, for instance, first by ornamentation strung on wires and then by pattern applied to the glass itself, a tripartite division of space was created that climactically moves the eye to the center of interest. Recall that Robert Adam always spoke of the "movement" incorporated in his work.

Another way of accomplishing the same result was in the positioning of the legs on large pieces.

When an article had a number of legs, as the tables frequently had, a wider space at the center was calculated for this purpose.

The movement was further enhanced by terminal accents carried out in painted or ceramic medallions done by such artists as Angelica Kauffmann, Michelangelo Pergolesi, and Giambattista Cipriani. The bisque plates were Wedgwood jasperware and were often modeled by John Flaxman (see the section on ceramics later in this chapter).

In addition to the dining room articles, other "room" furniture, for example enormous architectural bookcases, some more than 15 ft long and composed of as many as five sections, was in demand. Vile and Cobb produced masterful ones, often embellished with their well-known "oval of laurels" design in crisply carved mahogany. For these large pieces a classical architectural form was most fitting. Sometimes the central section protruded, the beloved "breakfront" cabinet. In England this was known as the cabinet-with-wings. Generally the lower portion is solid and the top is glazed. A number of similar cabinets built without wings were intended for the display of much prized china. It has been reported that Hepplewhite designs favored straight-line tracery on the glass; Sheraton showed more delicate oval forms.

Types: Tables. One of the most important contributions of the late eighteenth century to furniture types was the long dining table, or, more properly speaking, several tables which could be placed together to form one long, or *range*, table. The first step in its evolution was the joining of two units, each with five legs, one of which swung out to lift a wide flap. The next version was composed of three units, the center one a double flap table with six legs. Two end tables, with curved outer edges, could be detached and used along the wall or piers as consoles—the whole a handsome and useful trio for the service of family and many guests.

Complementing the range and pier tables was a host of small ones. Noteworthy introductions were the first of the nesting tables, named by their number, such as *quartetto* when there were four. Sheraton reports in his *Cabinet Dictionary* that the ever-popular *Pembroke* table was made for a lady of that name. This is a small oblong table with two drop leaves across the longer sides and a shallow drawer at the end. Although small tables varied in height, the most usual was the uniform dining height of around 30 in.

The immense and memorable library tables are rightly museum pieces. One made by Chippendale in 1766–1770 for Nostell Priory cost more than 72 pounds. They often took the shape of double kneehole desks. A table of this kind was intended to stand in the center of a spacious library, for it marked the time when a gentleman needed a large surface not only for laying out folio editions for reading but likewise for managing the estate accounts.

Mechanisms. Ingenious mechanical devices for expediting this executive work seem to have sprung up by the legion, like Camus's soldiers. End drawers sprouted writing shelves when opened. Ratchets lifted them to the desired

height and slant. Large circular tables, known as *rent tables*, had revolving drawers under a stationary top, for cataloging the separate accounts with which a landowner dealt.

Many designers interested themselves in mechanical gadgetry, Sheraton being one of the most diligent in that respect. In his publications were folding chairs and ladders, washstands that resembled tables, twin beds that could be joined or separated at will, twin sister desks that could revolve, timing devices to rock the baby's cradle, and thumb spring catches.

Many varieties of telescopic table emerged. John Cobb is credited with one that drew out and raised a standing-height desk which allowed its user to choose between a seated or standing position. The tambour front, an ingenious device made of narrow wooden members glued to a flexible foundation which rolled back to open, was introduced by Sheraton.

Types: Beds. State beds continued to be of the greatest magnificence and Chippendale, Hepplewhite, and Sheraton all illustrated models with canopies in the Gothic, Chinese, and French taste. The testers were elaborately draped with fabric.

One new variety of four-poster, possibly derived from the domed bed, was the simpler "field" bedstead with arched tester. A probable explanation of the name lies in the fact that presumably the frame, covered with a netting, would protect a sleeper from small flying creatures when in the field, or, in other words, while on a military campaign. One must remember that officers traveled with what would seem to us remarkable equipage for polite convenience.

The bed that Chippendale described in his Harewood accounts is undoubtedly the well-known one that remained there for so long. Robert Adam designed only seven beds, one of which is at Osterley. This was criticized by Walpole as being bedecked like a milliner's headdress, an observation as pertinent in relation to some creations today as it was 200 years ago.

Types: Seating Furniture. Chairs were conspicuously smaller in scale than the mid-Georgian models. Although the straight line was dominant, the oval, shield, or heart shape was often given to the back. Whenever a curve appeared in Neo-

159

classic furniture it was the graceful attenuated variety and generally a regular curve, easily plotted. The nervous cabrioles, C and S scrolls of former eras, had disappeared. Adam chair backs, which come closest to French models, were straight-topped or oval. Hepplewhite styles were predominantly shield or heart. Sheraton returned to straight contours. In the late Sheraton models we find the modified klismos and the curule, but as these led naturally to the Greek Revival styles they may be considered nineteenth century.

The oval and shield-back chairs had that weak type of structural support made from an extension of the rear legs which grasped and suspended the back above the seat.

The fill-in for those backs that were not upholstered was imaginative. In the shield back, which of itself had many variations, the carved splat consisted of interlaced hearts, a wheel pattern, a stylized vase, a lyre, the Prince of Wales' three feathers, or again the classic honeysuckle. Parts of this ornament usually converged into a lunette at the bottom of the frame. When similar devices were used on straight-backed chairs, they extended vertically from the top rail to a crosspiece near the bottom. A fine, classically inspired sense of proportion confined the decoration to the central third of the width, which section might be raised above the sides.

Seats, frequently tapered toward the rear, had slip-on or slip-in upholstery. When the latter was used, the seat rail was handsomely carved with reeding that terminated with paterae at the joining with the legs. Caning was often employed.

Arms made a sweeping curve to join the front legs or were attached to the side of the seat at a distance from the front. Some models had vertical vase-shaped baluster supports and others used graceful concave or cyma curves to connect with the arms. Those with upholstered arm rests, akin to the French *manchettes*, were known as *elbow chairs*.

Legs, especially on Hepplewhite models, were four square, with rectilinear block feet often referred to as *spade* feet. For some unknown reason they were frequently called *Marlborough* legs. On Adam-designed chairs the legs were often round and fluted, terminating in a *thimble foot*. Stretchers were not common on these chairs but might be found on the rectangular-legged variety. Hepplewhite straightline stretchers were vertical in extension and recessed or saltire. Even when front legs were straight, the rear ones might be gracefully curved.

Settees, sofas, confidantes (a sofa with armchairs attached at an angle to the ends), and stools designed for window placement, and more properly known as window seats, occur in many forms. The backs were straight, rolled over, or gracefully humped. The ends were straight, rolled outward, or curved inward. Legs corresponded to chair styles or reverted to animal shape such as the dolphin, sphinx, or winged lion—if these are to be considered animals.

Types: Mirrors. Mirrors were as important to the Neoclassic as the long case clock was to the mid-Georgian periods (Figure 4.50). The innovator in this case was certainly Robert Adam, who featured them so extensively in his wall decorations. Coupled with the pastel coloring of many of his interiors, the Adam mirrors helped to create sparkle and gaiety. Large enough to occupy a commanding position, they were rectangular or oval as the room design required. Their frames were made of painted wood of narrow dimensions, carved and gilt. They were crowned with a detached crest or incorporated that element within the body. Later mirrors were tripartite and divided by decoration to resemble a Palladian window. Stucco in the form of laurel leaf decoration strung on wires provided tracery of infinite variety. Many French sources such as J. F. Neufforge's *Receuil* and certainly Adam's own classic vocabulary were enlisted. In Adam's late mirrors the decoration was more important than the glass and, as has been remarked, it became the "epitome of his attitude toward furniture."[20] The mature period of Adam design lasted through the late seventies, after which his work became repetitious and effete.

TEXTILES

Mercantilistic English parliaments took every possible step to curb the passage of money to France in payment of luxury furnishings and particularly textiles. Embargoes and heavy duties were placed on the commodities that the French made supremely well, namely silks, tapestries, and carpets. Inventories still speak of French and Genoa velvets, damasks, and brocades.

It is interesting to note the English efforts to compete. Immigrant Huguenots who had received sanction at Spitalsfield in 1629 had greatly increased in number after 1685. Canterbury became another refuge for these weavers. Celia Fiennes, who is famous for her horseback ride through England on a side saddle, reports seeing in Canterbury in 1697 ". . . the great number of French people . . . employ'd in the weaving and silk winding."[21] A large-scale silk mill was started in Derbyshire by John Lombe who had learned his secrets in Italy.

In Chippendale's accounts at Nostell Priory, he makes constant reference to the use of silk, and says:

> Sir Rowland at the same time desired patterns of silks might be sent to Lady Winn to Chuse for her Drawing Room which would enable us to finish the furniture we have had so long in hand. At any rate whether Lady Winn at present chuses her pattern of silk or not, I must beg the favour that the patterns may be immediately return'd to us, as the Weaver has already been twice after them.[22]

In addition to continental and English silks, "indian" silks were imported. By this was meant wares from the East carried by ships of the East India Company. These silks were often embroidered and painted in patterns popularized by the Indian chintzes.

Although England had grown rich on wool, nevertheless the monopoly of fine tapestry weaving had been indisputedly in French hands ever since 1703 when Mortlake had finally closed. Englishmen went to France for the medallion tapestries that lined the walls and covered the furniture of Croome Court, Newsby, Osterley (Plate 6), and Moor Park. The Osterley set, for instance, was woven to order for Robert Child, although the ruse had to be resorted to by the Gobelins of selling it to Louis XV, who then returned it to the factory, thus encircling the statutory edict of the

Figure 4.50 An Adam mirror from Osterley. Victoria & Albert Museum, London. (Crown Copyright. Victoria & Albert Museum.)

Bâtiments du Roi to produce only for French royalty.

Embroideries with wool remained the English manner of duplicating the effects of the French tapestries. Always considered a gentlewoman's art, the techniques of needlepoint and point d'hongrie (Austrian flame stitch) were often practiced by noblewomen.

From the Chippendale archives at Mersham-le-Hatch for May, 1773, we quote:

> Your Chairs, Glasses, Table &c. is all ready to be sent away, but as Lady Knatchbull see'd to want 4 larger Chairs—what we call Barjaires, they must be made & in the meantime We must send her Ladyship patterns for the needlework which will be very large, consequently will take some time in working.[23]

161

The Cleveland Museum of Art owns a set of four armchairs, English, 1760–1765, done in Chippendale's French style. They are upholstered in needlepoint and illustrate scenes from Audley End.

Savonnerie-type hand-tufted carpets were supplanting orientals in large formal rooms. The English were successful in duplicating them. A charter was granted to émigré French weavers in 1702 and to weavers of the town of Axminster, slightly later, to manufacture these carpets in the French manner. By the middle of the century the English carpet industry was well launched and the Royal Society of Arts in 1756 and again in 1758 cited several factories for the merit of their products. The Moorfields Manufactory was used by Robert Adam and Chippendale recommended the Axminster to Sir Edward Knatchbull of Mersham-le-Hatch.

During the latter part of the eighteenth century machinery was gradually introduced to perform one function after another in the carpet industry. At first the mechanized process was used solely in making flat-weave carpets similar in structure to wool damasks. In 1735 such a carpet, known as the Kidderminster, for the name of the town, was produced in several colors. By 1749 an uncut pile carpet, known until recently as Brussels carpet (although made in England!) and the cut pile Wilton (named for the location of manufacture) were both machine manufactured. (The Wilton had also been hand produced). These carpets were made on narrow 27-in. looms and continued to be manufactured in this width until the advent of the contemporary broad loom.

The more humble cottons, linens, and wools were the staple fabrics of decoration. In the "linsey-woolsey" fabrics undyed linen and colored wool yarns effected a mottled pattern in the weaving. The names of many of these common textiles have gradually become obsolete. Chippendale refers to morine, callicoa, tammy, harrateen, Fustian, gawse, Scots cloth, buckram, serge, baize, oilcloth, Holland, and Persian (definitions for some can be found in Chapter 6).

Printed cotton and chintz continue to appear in the inventories. The English printing industry was at first concentrated near London but moved later to Lancaster and Scotland. Woodblocking, the earliest work, was followed in mideighteenth century by copper-plate registration. Numerous inventions such as that of the Scotsman Thomas Bell, who took out a patent in 1783 for an improved roller printing technique, made England one of the world's principal cotton printing centers. Woodblocking, however, was never discarded and, although more expensive, it continues as the method for fine English linens. It excels because overprinting which allows a depth of color not otherwise possible can be done.

Early woodblocking had a limited palette of black, red, purple, and brown. By the use of indigo blue plus yellow from the North American oak green later came into the picture. Among other patents, John Mercer (1791–1866) improved a process for discharging a light pattern on a dark ground, the whole then being overdyed. Overdyeing or printing with manganese created orange figures on a bronze field—a color scheme seen at the end of the century.

The English had considerable skill in the use of unusual colors in natural flora and fauna designs, first in free-flowing Baroque style and later in stripes or as pictorial vignettes. Indian-inspired patterns with crisp, swirling flowers on coiling stems are charmingly imaginative. Eighteenth-century English prints rank high from all angles.

WALLPAPER

The use of wallpaper for all varieties of purpose increased. Nor was this, as is often reported, solely a middle-class phenomenon. At Harewood, a deputy of Chippendale reports:

> Canvass and Paper Hangings to the State Bed Chamber . . .

Again in the same location:

> 2 round Screens covered with fine Crimson India paper . . .

Most important of all:

> 41 pieces of Paper of the Antique Ornament with Palms &c on a fine paper with a pink ground. The pattern cut on purpose and printed in various Colours.[24]

Improved English manufactory accounts for the bulk of the work. The man most responsible for the advancement of technique and design was Baptist Jackson (1701–?) who when young was employed by Papillon and thus came in contact with work of high quality. Returning to England he was engaged for a time in the manufacture of printed cottons and then undertook the production of wallpapers. By this time not only wood blocks but wooden rollers and metal plates were in use. Although English papers of the period show the influence of many of the current style trends, nevertheless it was in floral prints, and particularly those on a rich dark background, that Jackson found his forte. His sketchbook, preserved in the Victoria and Albert, gives evidence of his preference for naturalism, and he is said to have had little sympathy with such exoticism as chinoiserie.

CERAMICS

Chronology of China Production

Before the seventeen hundreds England's ceramic output was in pottery. Ambitious ceramists who had become acquainted with the oriental and continental high-fired wares were not satisfied that their product should lag behind. As Dickens would say, "Chelsea began it!" But historical opinions have vacillated about which of the several British factories—Chelsea, Bow, Derby, Plymouth, or Worcester—should have credit for being the first to manufacture English porcelain. The matter is largely of academic importance because near midcentury all of these houses made their initial bow.

Chelsea, a small factory in the west end of London, took out a patent in 1743[25] under the proprietorship of Nicholas Sprimont, a Flemish émigré and silversmith. Two others, Charles Gouyn, a jeweler, and Thomas Briand, a chemist, are cited as cofounders. Undoubtedly the last was responsible for the manufacturing process, whereas Sprimont influenced the design and seems to have had the necessary business acumen. Certainly it was he who secured the patronage of the Duke of Cumberland, younger brother

of George II, whose collection of Meissen china could be studied. Although the House of Hanover encouraged the production of porcelain, it is noteworthy that it did not subsidize the factories as did the European monarchs but left financing and management to private interests.

The Bow factory located to the east of the city down Lambeth way appears to have obtained a patent in 1745, granted to Edward Heylyn and Thomas Frye, a painter and an enameler, respectively. About the same time Thomas Briand and James Marchand became the first to try porcelain manufacture at Derby, the county seat of Derbyshire. William Duesbury, an enameler, became identified with Derby in the midfifties and it was to this event that the success of the factory is credited.

Worcester, nearby in Worcestershire, grew from a Bristol establishment of 1748. One of its leading promoters was Dr. John Wall (?–1776), who became its head in 1772, a position he retained until his death four years later. It had been Dr. Wall who, concerned about a regression in economic growth in the city, had interested industrialists in sponsoring a ceramic enterprise as a semicivic endeavor.

Plymouth, on the southern coast of Devon, is the last of the important early china centers. It operated under patent held by William Cookworthy, a Quaker apothecary interested in securing the secret of hard paste.

Wedgwood and Spode also made porcelain but it is for their refined pottery that they are noted and it is in this connection that their history is detailed. During the later years of the eighteenth century many English porcelain factories were established (e.g., Caughley, Coalport, and Minton).

Development in Management and Character of Paste

The first Chelsea and Bow china was soft paste (Figure 4.51). Chelsea ware, with its cream-white body reflecting a soft lustrous light, was probably the more meritorious. Decoration, when applied, which at first was seldom, was in enamel colors that tended to sink slightly into the glaze in a manner similar to that of French Mennecy and

Figure 4.51 *Sight* and *Hearing,* a pair of Chelsea soft-paste porcelain figurines, ca. 1755. Height, 28.3 cm. Metropolitan Museum of Art, New York. (The Metropolitan Museum of Art, Bequest of John L. Cadwalader, 1914.)

Villeroy. Many Chelsea pieces were in the form of figurines and often came in sets of three for garnitures.

Although the Bow factory made some modeled pieces with a body similar to Chelsea, it specialized in utility products. For this the soft paste was not suitable. Economy prompted experimentation, with the result that about 1749 Thomas Frye patented a body that contained added phosphates in the form of bone ash. This improved the practicality of the ware without making it as hard and white as the Meissen and oriental chinas. Later, when English porcelains had changed to hard paste, the ash, which continued to be added, acted as a flux and stabilizer and imparted greater translucency and a creamier tint—the famous English bone china.

Bristol and Worcester soft paste introduced soapstone or steatite as a flux. Wares that contained this ingredient were made in England until near the middle of the nineteenth century. The Bristol body is very hard and infusible and possesses a certain alabaster translucency.

In all of this experimenting the question of the kind of clay to be used was of paramount importance. The source of early clays is still a matter of conjecture, whether imported from the orient or America. There is ample evidence, for instance, that Chelsea used a superior type in terms of plasticity and firing. To William Cookworthy of Plymouth is conceded the honor of discovering kaolin and petuntse in Cornwall, possibly before 1750, although a patent for his formula was not forthcoming until 1768, too late to aid him in his Plymouth enterprise which was taken over by younger men from Bristol.

From this time English hard paste china, of kaolin and petuntse body, usually with the incorporation of bone ash in its formula, was the medium most used by English porcelain manufacturers. Its body was not so hard or opaque as the continental hard paste nor so soft as the previous English soft paste but much more durable than the latter.

The Chelsea factory, having gone through four marked periods (1745–1750, the incised triangle; 1750–1752, a crown and trident in underglaze blue or the raised anchor; 1752–1758, the painted red anchor; 1758–1770, the gold anchor), was sold to Derby (mark—the Chelsea anchor and a *D*). For a time the firm was called Chelsea-Derby.

On the front edge of Bow flat objects three spur marks in a triangle invariably appear. Their cause or purpose is not known; they may be merely the mark of glaze clips. Some form of cryptic anchor, dagger, or both are among the various indications found at times on the back of Bow. In 1778 William Duesbury of Derby also acquired Bow and the Derby interests had tied up three of the early establishments.

After a century of vicissitudes, during which time the firm passed to other hands, the Crown Derby Porcelain Company was organized in 1877, and to this day continues to produce quality china. Many early Derby pieces bear no mark except for an identifying figure scratched in the paste. Later marks are numerous but frequently contain a crowned D, with crossed batons somewhat suggestive of Meissen.

There is still Worcester. From its very first years, when its aim was to produce the most usable of table wares with a harder heat-resistant body, it is clear that Worcester was in possession of advanced formulas and experienced potters. Dr. Wall became the managing head of Worcester in 1772. The Dr. Wall period is considered to have extended to 1783 and to have represented certain fine standards rather than a period of leadership.

The Flight family bought the works in 1783 and in 1807 members of the Martin Barr family purchased interests. The first enlargement contributed the name of Flight and Barr and the second that of Barr, Flight and Barr. In 1829 the Barrs took sole possession. Finally, the original Worcester firm and a rival one nearby united under the name of Worcester Royal Porcelain Factory, which is still operating. The earliest Worcester mark was a script *W*. The crescent is associated with other designations. The initials or name of the factory owner often appeared after 1783. The marks of the original Worcester were surmounted by a crown after 1788.

China Trade Porcelain

First we must dispel the fallacious belief that Lowestoft as a factory town produced the vast amount of hard-paste china which was sold as *Oriental Lowestoft,* a name sometimes confused with that of china trade porcelain. The output of the Lowestoft works from 1757 to 1802 was soft paste and its decorative character was similar to Bow. Most of the later Lowestoft was utilitarian in nature and was designed for the average consumer. Examples can be seen at the Victoria and Albert and at the Fitzwilliam Museum at Cambridge.

China trade porcelain, on the other hand, was a mercantile phenomenon of some years standing, reaching down into the middle-class market only during the eighteenth century when wares were exported from China to Europe and after 1784, direct to America. In 1699 the English East India Company was permitted to enter Canton for purposes of trade, the port having been closed to the western nations because of the perfidious conduct of the early traders. The English, competing with other European nations, soon established a permanent business in Canton. The British Museum possesses a large Cantonese punch bowl which in its pictorial decoration illustrates the *hongs* (warehouses) in the Chinese port. Here the exchange of merchandise took place—sandalwood from Hawaii, ginseng (a native American root that claimed medicinal properties), and furs were unloaded for cargoes of tea, silk, lacquer, spices, ivory, and porcelain.

The method of handling this trade in porcelain was as follows: The East India Companies sent "pattern chests" of samples to their home offices. Often one plate in the chest might contain several decorative patterns from which the customer could choose. After an order had been placed with an entrepreneur shopkeeper or directly with the East India representative there was a time lapse of several years before the consignment could be delivered. The porcelain was actually made at the expert kilns at Ching-Te-Chên and was decorated at Canton. This specialized work appealed chiefly to those who wished armorial bearings or some other exclusive design. Generally it proved too expensive and time consuming. The Lowestoft factory was one of a number of factories that dealt with special orders from China.

At a lower price, pennies instead of shillings for a plate, large shipments of Chinese blue-and-white or undecorated white wares arrived at British ports to be sold at auction.

Potteries

To continue the list from the seventeenth century, the Staffordshire pieces of Thomas Whieldon (1719–1795) with their agate coloring are ingenious in technique but a bit on the side of aesthetic ingenuousness. The homely but expressive figures of the Ralph Woods, father and son, and the gamut of provincial but much loved Toby jars, give us the best of folk art. Salt-glazed tablewares of stoneware body are sturdy antecedents with characters that live. Lusters of the late eighteenth and nineteenth centuries, made by adulterating a metal with glass and lead and fluxing it onto the article, are, as they were then, substitutes for more precious materials.

Eighteenth-century pottery is not all folk tradition. In its annals Wedgwood and Spode head

the list because of their perfection of pottery body, the successful commercializing of medium-priced dinner services, and, incidentally, the manufacture of porcelain (from 1812 to 1816 and after 1878 for Wedgwood, after 1789 for Spode).

The Wedgwood factory had been in operation in a limited sense since the midseventeenth century. It was Josiah Wedgwood (1730–1790), however, who successfully brought the family industries out of the handicraft stage and from cruder pottery making into the production of the cream-colored wares, some porcelain, and a deal of bisque. Josiah Wedgwood and Thomas Whieldon were in partnership from 1754 to 1759, on which date Josiah entered business for himself. In 1769 Thomas Bentley became a partner but the contract was short-lived, for Bentley died the next year.

Josiah Wedgwood, a man of business acumen and high standards who also had a sensitivity to style trends, experimented constantly with his product to provide the average market with a good, salable commodity. One of his first achievements was the perfection of a black (by virtue of manganese) unglazed stoneware known as *basalt* because of its resemblance to the natural basalt rock. Given a lustrous polish, it was often modeled into ornamental vases and plaques. Resembling ancient iron pieces or Bucchero ware, it proved to be popular with Neoclassic customers. Another unglazed ware with a hard vitreous body was the famous *Jasper,* which was given a variety of colors by adding pigments to the clay or whiteness by adding barium sulfate.

Wedgwood's most significant contributions to ceramics lie in his refinement of the pottery body of dinnerware and in the character of its lovely creamy glaze, similar in surface appearance to *blanc de chine.* He designated this ware as semiporcelain and called it *Queen's Ware* in honor of Queen Charlotte, wife of George III.

The Wedgwood products have been marked since 1772; the identifying signature designates types and proprietorships. The name *Etruria* was added to the basalt pieces and recently to Queen's Ware. *Barleston* has been imprinted on the latter since 1940. Both are place names given to certain Wedgwood factories, all near Stoke-on-Trent in Staffordshire.

The Spode family is also famous in ceramic annals. Josiah Spode I (1733–1796), after serving an apprenticeship to Whieldon, began his business in 1770. It descended through three generations until in 1833 William Copeland bought the factory but kept the Spode name. In addition to a fine earthenware and to an unglazed type known as *Parian,* the firm made an ironstone china for which it is noted.

Design

You will have early-eighteenth-century English ceramic design in a nutshell if you remember that it came of age when the Rococo, the oriental, and the native flare for flora blossomed. Later, classicism gained momentum.

Some Chelsea dishes, molded as fruits and vegetables or even as animals, are full of Rococo whimsey. The earliest, called the *goat and bee jugs* because of their representational modeling, are without added color. Soon, however, the painters arrived. Long-tailed birds and magnificent botanically detailed flowers, sometimes copied from engravings in such books as Philip Miller's *Figures of Plants,* published in 1755, are freely rendered on the surfaces. The sweep of the drawing, the asymmetrical arrangements, and the exquisite coloring of these pieces can scarcely be equaled. Like English furniture of the mid-Georgian period, they possess a vigor not so usual in the continental examples. We cannot agree with Walpole, who wrote to Horace Mann in 1763:

> I saw yesterday a magnificent service of Chelsea china which the King and Queen are sending to the Duke of Mecklenburg. There are dishes and plates without number . . . , in short it is complete; and costs twelve hundred pounds! I cannot boast of our taste; the forms are neither new, beautiful, nor various. Yet Sprimont, the manufacturer, is a Frenchman [a footnote says he was a Fleming]. It seems their taste will not bear transplanting.

Chelsea figurines of a comparable period fitted nicely into the decorative scheme of eighteenth-century living. They are lighthearted in spirit, graceful in pose, and exceedingly pleasing in color. In the best of the sculptured objects there

is the finesse and expression of an integral rhythmic world that belongs to good sculpture. The Frenchman Louis François Roubiliac (1705?–1762) modeled many of these pieces.

Some of the early articles are panel painted and here the English have contributed beautiful body colors. Powder blue, although found elsewhere, is typical of Bow. Chelsea often used a rich claret tone as well as a pale green, a turquoise blue, and a deep sea blue. Cookworthy produced a lovely cobalt at Plymouth. The Worcester grounds are likely to be what is known as scale grounds, meaning that the pattern of a scale carries the color. The rich dark blue is most famous, but many others, such as pink, gold, yellow, and brick red, are present.

The English were proficient in panel painting on porcelain. It is known who some of these skilled painters were—John Bowen, Michael Edkins, and John Niglett of Bristol. Bowen's river scenes are almost in a class with Canaletto's, and it is unfortunate that they were not made on flat surfaces. We find a Mr. Boreman at Chelsea, William Billingsley at Chelsea-Derby, and Robert Allen at Lowestoft. Saqui, a French artist, from Sèvres, worked at Plymouth, and the bird paintings there were done by Henry Bone. Later work, for example, at Worcester, was done by an independent firm of specialists. William Giles (1718–1780) operated a similar establishment in London.

Much early Chelsea and Bow is entirely ungilded. Late gilding of English china was done with the moderation that makes it an accent to other embellishment. There were, however, periods when Walpole's harsh criticisms were justified—the gold was too lavishly and too poorly applied.

Transfer printing, developed as early as the fifties, facilitated the making of repetitive patterns. When carried out with sensitivity of color and pattern to shape, it enriched the end product at a reduced cost.

Repetitive molded decoration was often applied to the Neoclassic wares of Wedgwood and Spode. Both also manufactured figurines, medallion plaques, and modeled groups. The Wedgwood engagement of John Flaxman, R. A. (1755–1826; Figure 4.52), a Yorkshire sculptor, which began in 1775, gave us a series of interesting historic medallions which has enriched our photo-

Figure 4.52 Wedgwood ceramic vase with bas-relief of John Flaxman's *The Apotheosis of Homer*. Height, 45.4 cm. Metropolitan Museum of Art, New York. (The Metropolitan Museum of Art, Rogers Fund, 1910.)

How to cover, how to end, a necessarily abbreviated account of British ceramics of the eighteenth century? There is meat in the box for every taste and every pocketbook. This very fact makes it requisite to develop a discriminating eye for body, shape, and aesthetic quality.

GLASS

The English had a distinct commercial asset in their seventeenth-century lead-glass formula. This metal, softer, stronger, clear, and brilliant, became the norm for English glass. By the catalytic action of national taste and as a consequence of the new material the shape of English pieces changed to sturdy forms without the ponderosity or elaboration of decoration of the German models or the fanciful fragility of the Venetian.

Many of the early-eighteenth-century glasses (goblets) are called *balustered,* which is defined as a glass with one dominating knop in the stem (Figure 4.53). In these the bowl is often heavy and may have a thick solid base. In the earliest this bowl is U- or V-shaped (ca. 1690–1730). Sometimes the solid bases of the bowls contain the imaginative "how is it done?" tear drop. These are followed by a group known to collectors as the *balustroids* (ca. 1730–1760), which is similar but has a bell-shaped bowl.

In 1745 an ill-advised government decree levied an excise tax on the raw materials of the prospering glass industry. Economically, the result could be predicted—strong firms survived, weaker ones closed or moved elsewhere (more about this later). Stylistically, the result was an attempt on the part of the designers to make a little metal show off as more. Bowls became thinner and rounder, stems sometimes lost their knops and frequently were faceted to reflect light more easily. In the later times of the Napoleonic wars the goblets of this style shrank still further in size; often the straighter stems included the opaque *air twist* for greater impressiveness.

The location of the glass houses remained approximately the same. Newcastle-on-Tyne, in northeastern England, was the eventual home of the Lorrainers who had crossed the channel in

graphic gallery of the past. Flaxman's models were translated into workable molds by such Wedgwood experts as William Hackwood. The Italians Angelo Dalmozzoni and Camillo Pacetti copied from the Roman antiquities and often made models that were used in rooms done by Robert Adam.

Figure 4.53 Balustered goblet with V-shaped bowl and tear-drop of air in the glass; early eighteenth century. Victoria & Albert Museum, London. (Crown Copyright. Victoria & Albert Museum.)

Figure 4.54 Enameled armorial goblet (one of a pair), ca. 1760–1770, signed: Beilby invt. et pinxt. Height, 22.3 cm. Corning Museum, Corning, New York. (The Corning Museum of Glass, Corning, New York.)

the sixteenth century. One type of eighteenth-century glass is known as the Newcastle balustroid group—tall ones of comparatively slender proportions, without conspicuous knopping. In London the concentration near Greenwich remained as the locale of the Venetian sixteenth-century contingent of glass men. The plate-glass houses were at Vauxhall and Southwark, the former the site of the Duke of Buckingham's earlier venture. These continued to make the better mirror glass without which the large Georgian mirrors would have been economically impractical.

Although the loveliest of the lead glasses needed no further embellishment, some engraving was done in England, possibly to compete with the glasses sent to Holland and finished by Dutch engravers. Mid-European engravers settled in England after the midcentury wars and presumably taught their craft to Englishmen. Coloring and enameling came into vogue in the last half of the century with the higher price of glass. In this field the names of William and Mary Beilby are well known, although we may venture the statement that this renown often derived from the pride of possession that accompanied glasses emblazened with armorial crests (Figure 4.54).

169

The glasses made in the neighborhood of Bristol—the milk glass, the opaque opalene glass of waxy feel, the clear dark blue transparent glass—all have become collectors' items. Nailsea (closed in 1873), which was noted for glass bottles in two colors, possesses similar interest for antique hunters. All of these glasses, however, were somewhat in the tradition of French opalene and cannot be said to relate to the mainstream of British lead-glass manufacture.

The Irish Waterford story is another matter (Figure 4.55). The Waterford Glass House was established in Waterford, Ireland, a port on the south coast, in 1783 by George and William Penrose. Although small enterprises had already been opened in Ireland, it was not until England placed her second excise tax on glass materials in 1777 that the Penrose brothers brought over their own craftsmen from Stourbridge in west England to Ireland, where materials were tax exempt. The Irish free trade bill of 1780 removed an existing restriction on Irish export of glass. Thus collectors of old Waterford glass may have a better chance of locating it in America than in England or even in Ireland.

Actually, because of the fine quality of the glass of the Waterford factory, it is almost impossible to distinguish it from the English glass of the same period. It is a colorless lead glass of unusual purity.

Articles with a known documented lineage and the few decanters blown into a mold marked *Penrose-Waterford* are possibly all that can be authenticated. The latter are relatively thin and shallow cut. They usually have three rings around the neck and arched decorative face panels.

The Waterford firm changed hands several times before closing in 1851, only to be reopened later.

METALS

Metalcraft was another of the glories of the English eighteenth century. This expertise, however, was not in gilded bronze which, as ormolu, was not in demand until the invasion of the French fashions in the fifties. Robert Adam designed and used cast and chaste tripods in *gilt bronze,* as did

Figure 4.55 Decanter marked *Penrose Waterford;* eighteenth century. Victoria & Albert Museum, London. (Crown Copyright. Victoria & Albert Museum.)

William Chambers. London smiths—a Mr. Anderson and the Soho works (1762–1775) of Matthew Boulton (1728–1809)—are listed as producers.

Brass was used for fireplace accessories, clock faces, and, to a limited extent, lighting fixtures. Silver and pewter were more usual for small candlesticks and glass or even wood for domestic chandeliers. Brass was the metal for large civic and ecclesiastic fixtures.

Regal English stairs possessed *wrought iron* balustrades coupled with wood or metal handrails. Ironwork was first in the style of the Baroque-inspired scrollwork of the seventeenth-century designers Daniel Marot and Jean Tijou. Later designs showed Pompeian influence.

The superb iron gates at Westover in Virginia are thought to have been the work of Thomas Robinson, probably the most prominent smith of London. Although he fashioned his scrolls after Tijou, he designed in a simpler manner. It may be said that, like Wren with houses and Chippendale with furniture he took the European Baroque in iron work and rendered it exquisitely British. This was genius.

Figure 4.56 Inkstand: base, sander, inkwell, and bell, Paul de Lamerie, 1731. Silver. Length, 36 cm. Fogg Museum, Cambridge, Massachusetts. (Courtesy of the Fogg Art Museum, Harvard University.)

English *silver* of the eighteenth century exhibits a high level of silversmithing in metal and design. After 1719, when silver went off the high standard, the maker was allowed an option on choice of metal. Paul de Lamerie, a famous silversmith (1688–1751), for instance, used the Britannia metal for a considerable portion of his career when it seemed best suited to his designs.

Although the fluted and ruffled, as well as the cut-card, styles of William and Mary's reign persisted with surprising tenacity, nevertheless the plainer Queen Anne style evolved from the softer medium of the purer metal.

Following the revocation of the Edict of Nantes, the influx of Huguenot craftsmen soon turned the design tables in the direction of French-inspired design. Among them Pierre Harache, David Willaume, Paul Crespin, and Pierre Platel are often mentioned. The last was not only a master in his own right but is remembered as Paul de Lamerie's teacher (Figure 4.56). This famous silversmith, whose work is to be seen in most major museums, was born in Holland of French Huguenot parentage and was taken to England when he was less than a year old. His father's name was Paul Souchay de La Merie, the latter part of the name being contracted to its usual form when he crossed the channel. After a

seven years' apprenticeship with Platel, Paul obtained his papers as freeman of the London Goldsmith's Company in 1712. His work runs the gamut from the chaste Queen Anne design, to a classical one inspired by seventeenth-century France, to a Rococo form that often combined bold moldings and strapwork (Figure 4.57). There were likewise many competent English silversmiths of this era, among whom can be placed Benjamin Pyne and Anthony Nelme.

All of the divergent styles that impressed themselves on the silver market had the fortunate result of merging into what may be regarded as silver of the Georgian period. The shapes sometimes incorporated the fluting of the William and Mary, the restraint of the Queen Anne with engraving and chasing, the sturdy heavy gauge of the early Hanoverian pieces, and the exquisitely restrained curves and artistry of the Rococo. It is delightful household silver.

A few characteristic types indicate changing style trends. The tall straight-sided coffee pot remained during Queen Anne's reign. It derived from the straight-sided tankards and flagons which at that time had become larger and had gracefully turned handles. The teapot took on a globular form from oriental and Meissen examples or assumed the pearshape to be seen in pottery pitchers. By midcentury the pear was frequently inverted and substantially footed. Tea cannisters were at first straight-sided and then slightly bowed. Tea leaves, a luxury item, were at first locked in boxes and the containers were secured in some manner.

Sugar bowls were surprisingly large because sugar came in crystalline lumps. One type of bowl for sugar or condiments had a pierced frame with a colored glass liner. Tea urns for the heating of water were new and trays were a luxury item. They had reeded and gadrooned brims or pierced galleries. Complete dinner services with soup tureens and sauce receptacles abounded. The silver centerpiece with branched candelabra and sweetmeat dishes that surrounded a central flower container was called an épergne.

The earliest candlesticks of the century, called "chambersticks," maintained the shape of fluted columns. Many sticks were cast with shapes similar to goblets, with knops and bellshaped sockets

(Figure 4.58). Some assumed imaginative French forms and some were tripods. It became customary for a household to supply silver plate and the need for guests to bring their own was outmoded.

Silver cutlery became more common. Forks had three or occasionally four prongs. The handles duplicated those of the spoon. This was also true of knives, although the pistol-ended knife was often used no matter what the design of the other articles.

On spoons the William and Mary trifid handle developed a wavy pattern or some similar form. As it became broader it first curved upward and then down in accordance with the changing manner of laying the spoon on the dish. The bowl grew longer and more pointed and was attached to the stem by the *rattail* or by lobes or other decorative forms.

With Neoclassicism straight lines and more regular curves returned on hollow ware. In teapots, for instance, the plan became oval or octagonal, sides were straight, the body sat flat, and the spout was once again straight and tapering, rising from near the base. With the advent of Greek influence about 1790 the footed type, which is shaped like a Grecian urn, put in an appearance.

Neoclassic ornamentation was often what texts call bright cut engraving, or cutting with curving facets of various degrees of slant, thereby producing a multitude of reflections to arrive at an unusually sparkling effect.

The introduction of machinery and the specialization of processes to facilitate production occurred during the latter part of the eighteenth century. Matthew Boulton sold shaped parts of articles to silver craftsmen who then assembled them and completed their decoration.

The silver designer whose work most typifies the Neoclassic in England was Paul Storr, whose major period of activity fills the years roughly from 1792 to 1821 and thus takes us into the next century and the Regency style (under which he is

Figure 4.57 (opposite page) Sideboard dish by Paul de Lamerie, commissioned by the London Goldsmiths' Company in 1740. Silver gilt. Diameter, 78 cm. Goldsmiths Hall, London. (By courtesy of the Worshipful Company of Goldsmiths of London.)

173

discussed). The silver of Hester Bateman (entered her mark, 1774), head of a family concern that included Jonathan, Peter, two Williams, and Anne, is significant not only because of the introduction of a woman's name but also because the high quality of their output represents that of many small firms of the era.

Silver and silvergilt, despite their increase, were still on the top level of the social scale and few pieces were in the possession of any but the wealthy. Although wooden trenchers were no longer found except in the homes of the poor, pewter utensils were common. Eighteenth-century English pewter—an alloy of tin, copper, and antimony—was frequently in the desirable ratio called, without particular authorization, Britannia pewter, which reflected light in a soft, diffused manner.

The desire for a cheaper metal that might more closely resemble silver and the concomitant accidental discovery by Thomas Boulsover (1704–1788), a Sheffield cutler, that silver could be fused to copper and the whole rolled as one plate led to the manufacture of what is known as Sheffield silver. Although this discovery is supposed to have occurred about 1742, Boulsover used his ware only to make small buttons and boxes. About midcentury Joseph Hancock began to produce articles for table use in the new metal. At this particular period in the infancy of Sheffield plate there were no laws governing the signatures that the craftsmen might affix. Therefore an attempt to suggest solid silver marks was often made, a foolish expedient because the warm patina of Sheffield created a market all its own. Today old Sheffield patterns and techniques have been revived.

Figure 4.58 Four silver candlesticks made by Edmund Pearce, silversmith, London, 1720. Height, 16.7 cm. Sterling and Francine Clark Art Institute, Williamstown, Massachusetts. (Sterling and Francine Clark Art Institute, Williamstown, Massachusetts.)

DESCRIPTIVE SUMMARY

Some of this chapter has been devoted to the parish church and the middling dwelling that before the eighteenth century had not called for stylistic discussion. This description of the domestic and religious architecture of the gentry was quite purposeful because in these simpler types was spoken the genius of the land. This is not to disparage the imposing grandeur of the great mansions that stud the English countryside and rode the tides of fashion from Palladianism through Neoclassicism.

In such types as the Georgian house and the London churches, however, England fused time and place, exterior and interior architecture much as she had done on a wealthier scale under the Tudors. It was a unity France was unable to achieve. Moreover, in the England of the eighteenth century all former styles in the decorative arts merged and culminated in a demonstration of structural logic, formalism, and Baroque–Rococo verve to create a setting for the life of the gentilhomme—a setting possessed of plain majesty without austerity or triviality. This was no small achievement—one that has not yet been duplicated in our industrialized culture.

CHAPTER FIVE

Eighteenth-Century America

These names of virtues, with their precepts, were:

. . .

13. Humility—Imitate Jesus and Socrates.

Benjamin Franklin

CULTURE SPAN

The eighteenth century in America presents such a complex picture of political, social, and economic change that its progress must have amazed everyone, including those who assumed leadership.

The outstanding political fact was that France, Spain, and finally Great Britain lost control of the east central portion of the continent. England continued to dominate the north and Spain, the greatest territorial landlord in the new hemisphere, finally awoke to the necessity of trying to colonize her western territory.

The outstanding social fact was the quick spread of English culture. Britain in the third quarter of the eighteenth century ruled an empire that stretched from the Himalayas to the Appalachians and by 1763 to the Father of Waters, the Mississippi. The colonists took pride in this heritage—a veneration that caused them to look to England for their improvement, to seek an education there for their children, and to copy English styles of art. This anglicizing of the diverse peoples who had settled scarcely two generations before on American shores was in itself an amazing phenomenon.

In trying to understand it, we should not forget that England herself was the spearhead of the Western tradition we have been studying—a tradition that reached back to the social philosophies of the Near Eastern religions, particularly the Christian (e.g., Jesus), and on the other hand to the rationalism of the Greeks (e.g., Socrates). The fact that heterogeneous peoples in a new land could assume an English veneer merely proved that their roots went deep into the soil that had nurtured western European civilization in its trek from Mesopotamia, through Greece, Rome, Italy, France, Spain, and England to America; and although the fabric now had to cover the diversity of peoples from beyond the Rhine and the Baltic and stretch as far west as the New Land Ordinances permitted, the warp and the weft seemed strong.

It was the economic fact that finally separated the Old World from the New—economics and an awareness of strength. The colonies soon demonstrated their financial self-sufficiency. The Virginians, after an initial effort to manufacture and export such articles as pitch, tar, glass, frankincense, and soda ash, turned their land and labor into the wealth of tobacco. Rice and indigo filled the coffers of the Carolinas, and farming and musketry from the central areas and iron and lumber from New England produced capital. Friction developed, for one among several reasons, because the colonies felt that the parent country used these assets as a source of revenue while failing to provide sufficient military assistance against pioneer border dangers.

It is extremely doubtful whether men of the revolutionary century—Franklin, Washington, Jefferson, Madison, Adams, Hamilton, Jay, and countless others, would have possessed the courage and conviction to throw in the glove had they not unconsciously inherited that same brand of rationalism that was now based on scientific empiricism—that belief that man could master his fate by the application of reason.

Politically much of Europe was still struggling with the assumption of a perfection that handed down laws and was symbolized in the Divine Right of Kings. In the New World on the other hand, under pioneer conditions in which men faced dangers as equals, a new sociopolitical theory and the new rationalization found fertile ground. It had been proposed by such men as John Locke (1632–1704, *Essay Concerning Human Understanding*), who was convinced of the value and sense of the common people and felt that they had rights against any established rule that was not for the common good. In this respect his thinking fostered revolution. John Locke also preached tolerance and the right to diversity of thought. In this respect his ideas became the basis for the United States constitution.

Paradox in life is always the substructure of change. All these descendents of western classical-Christian thought made strange bedfellows. The eighteenth century in America managed very well in its attempt to reconcile conflicting ideals, a fact that is made evident in the course of the arts.

ARCHITECTURE

The Town and the City in the Eighteenth Century

The capital of Virginia was moved from Jamestown to Williamsburg in 1699. The new location had been known as Middle Plantation, where four families had located on the narrowest neck of land between the James and the York rivers. It was renamed in honor of King William III of England. Governor Francis Nicholson of Virginia established the plan for Williamsburg. He was fortunate in having new land and a free hand. He had behind him the type of town planning indicated in Christopher Wren's proposal for London drawn after the 1666 fire, as well as the layouts of such American towns as Philadelphia, Charleston, and Annapolis, and he plotted the city in wide parallel streets, intersected at right angles by others in multiples of one-half acre plots. The main thoroughfare, named after Queen Anne's son, the Duke of Gloucester, was terminated at one end by the capitol and at the other by the principal building of William and Mary College (founded in 1693).

Other growing metropolitan centers, such as Boston, New York, and Newport, hampered by irregular sites and rapid growth, were forced to retain their Medieval type of town plan with narrow and irregular streets. In respect, then, to city planning alone the American scene telescoped centuries of European techniques.

Williamsburg remained Virginia's capital until 1780 when it was considered safer to remove the offices to Richmond. The old town was restored during the early twentieth century, as stated by the Board of Trustees of Colonial Williamsburg,

> . . . to recreate accurately the environment of the men and women of eighteenth century Williamsburg and to bring about such an understanding of their lives and times that present and future generations may more vividly appreciate the contribution of those early Americans to the ideals and culture of our country.

It is an idyllic recreation of a life that can never return, but the purpose can merit nothing but praise, provided it can be made to work as a stimulus and not as an opiate.

Although city planners today are not unanimous in approving the viselike regularity of Renaissance-Baroque ideology, nevertheless, as seen in the homey small-town atmosphere of Williamsburg, which never reached beyond two thousand souls, we are not left with any feeling that life in its confines was cold or austere.

Building Materials of the Eighteenth Century

The major buildings of Williamsburg are built of brick, frequently laid in English bond below the horizontal water table and Flemish bond above. Headers were often glazed. Another Virginia custom, also practiced in England, was to rub the surface of the headers used for door and window trim, arches, and string courses to an interesting roughness. They were sometimes given a molded profile. The simplicity and dignity of this type of development can scarcely be improved. Stratford Hall (Figure 5.1), on that narrow peninsula that separates the Potomac and Rappahannock rivers, built by Thomas Lee, the grandson of Richard who came to Virginia in 1621, shows us the ultimate in quality to be gained from the use of

Figure 5.1 Stratford Hall, Westmoreland County, Virginia, 1725. (G. C. Ball.)

Figure 5.2 Christ Church (Old North Church), Boston, 1723. (Library of Congress.)

"Hang a lantern aloft in the belfry arch
Of the North Church tower as a signal light, . . ."

brick alone. Stratford was the ancestral home of Robert E. Lee, the celebrated Confederate general.

Although brick remained the principal building material of the South, wood as clapboarding was used on many simpler homes. Occasionally brick was covered with stucco as at St. Andrew's Episcopal Church in South Carolina as early as 1706 and again in 1751 when the handsome Georgian church of St. Michael's was begun in Charleston.

Brick was used for four out of five of Boston's principal eighteenth-century churches—the Old Brick Meeting House (1713, demolished 1808); Christ Church (Old North, 1723; Figures 5.2 and 5.3); Old South Meeting House (1729–1730); and the later Christ Church in Cambridge (1759–1761, by the architect Peter Harrison, newly arrived from England). Peter Harrison's King's Chapel (1749–1754), Boston, is of stone, a Quincy granite. *Meeting house* was the name given to the early square house of worship (Congregational). The Anglican (Episcopal) form was known as *church,* and this name became more general.

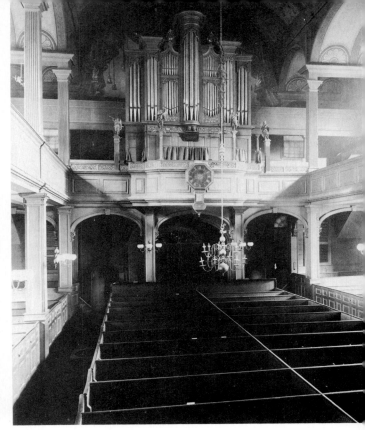

Figure 5.3 Interior view of Christ Church (Old North Church), Boston, 1723. (Library of Congress.)

There were masonry houses in New England even during the early years of the century, such as the brick McPhedris-Warner House in Portsmouth and the extinct stone Hancock House in Boston. Boston's second Town House (old State House), rebuilt in 1748, was brick, as was Faneuil Hall (1740–1742). The cost of brick, the abundance of wood, and the building tradition, however, fostered the more general acceptance of clapboarding.

The manner of working in wood was a modification of seventeenth-century methods. Although the large posts and girts, with exposed interior beams, were no longer economical, the eighteenth-century frame house was solidly constructed. The frame was of heavy timber, diagonally braced. Intermediate supports, not so frequent as the present studs placed on 16-in. centers, nevertheless occurred often and were reinforced for additional firmness. The spaces between were filled with soft brick nogging. The sheathing was clapboarding, now likely to be placed over a layer of horizontal boarding. As slimmer structural elements were not so pleasant

Figure 5.4 Cliveden, a property of the National Trust for Historic Preservation, Germantown, Pennsylvania. (National Trust for Historic Preservation Collections, Photo by John J. G. Blumenson.)

to view, one reason for interior paneling becomes apparent.

In the middle colonies, and especially in Pennsylvania, stone was a recurrent type of masonry. In finesse it was graduated from the rubble of Graeme Park (1721–1722) at Horsham, Pennsylvania, to the carefully cut and laid ashlar of Cliveden, Philadelphia (Figure 5.4), which was built after 1763. These dates indicate not only a difference in technique but also one in style, for with the general progress toward Palladian ideals at midcentury all surfaces were done in a texture as smooth as possible.

In the manner that Palladio faked textures the colonists ruled wooden siding to resemble stone, as at Mt. Vernon in Virginia (Figure 5.5), the Royall House (1733), the Jeremiah Lee House (1768), and the Wentworth-Gardner House (1759) in Massachusetts. This was done even in a building as important as the Redwood Library in Newport (1748–1749). Stucco over rubble masonry is scored to resemble finer stone dressing at Mt. Pleasant, Philadelphia (1761) and contrasted with pronounced corner quoins.

Because of the cost of stone and the scarcity of skilled cutters, exterior trim was generally executed in wood. There are notable exceptions, however, such as the door frames at Westover (1730) in Virginia (Figure 5.6), which are Portland stone (i.e., a cream-colored English limestone), at Mt. Airy (1758), which are native limestone, and at the Miles Brewton House (1765; Figure 5.7) in

Figure 5.5 (above) Mount Vernon, Fairfax County, Virginia. Original house, 1726–1735; additions, 1758; portico, 1784–1787; cupola, 1787. (Library of Congress.)

Figure 5.6 (below) Westover, James County, Virginia, 1730. (Library of Congress.)

Charleston. More important civic buildings often used stone trim: Washington's church, the Pohick Church in Virginia (1771–1772), the second-story entablature of Faneuil Hall, Boston, and the remarkable early stone embellishment in the

Figure 5.7 The Miles Brewton House, Charleston, South Carolina, 1765. (G. C. Ball.)

destroyed Foster-Hutchinson House in Boston (1688), the earliest classic building in the colonies.

Architectural Styles

The first quarter of the eighteenth century was a transitional period when classical details were introduced, although their principles were not always thoroughly understood. This era is sometimes called the *Early Colonial*. Quite conveniently the architectural styles of which we are now speaking can correspond to a neat 25-year progression in which, the years 1700 to 1725 may be called Period I.

The next fifty years would then be the *Late Colonial*. The first division is customarily 1725 to 1750; called *Early Georgian* with reference to its style of architecture, we call it Period II. The years from 1750 to 1775 or 1783 (Treaty at Paris)

become *Late Georgian,* often called *Palladian—* our Period III.

The fourth stylistic trend extends to and beyond the century and is known as *Federal:* Period IV. The very names of these divisions suggest the progression to the Christopher Wren tradition (II), the more academic Palladian (III), and the Neoclassic (IV).

Plans and Space Organization

American plans cannot be treated as standardized because American building followed early ethnic traditions, the pragmatic approach, and English styles.

Spaces grew larger but we will not find the size of Blenheim. Separation of activities and some specific designation of function became general. The Governor's Palace (Figure 5.8) at Williamsburg (Period I) and Berkeley, on the north bank of the James, which belonged to President Harrison (Period II), have back stairs for servants' use.

Figure 5.8 (above) The Governor's Palace, Williamsburg, Virginia. Original building, 1705–1720; wing added, 1749; burned, 1781; rebuilt, 1930. (G. C. Ball.)

Figure 5.9 (below) A portion of a remaining wall of Rosewell, James County, Virginia, 1726. Destroyed by fire, 1916. (G. C. Ball.)

Rosewell, on the north bank of the York (Period I), boasted a cross hall (Figure 5.9). Colonel William Byrd speaks of a room at Westover (I) which housed his 3600-volume library.

The growing tendency in space allocation in houses was toward the symmetry that locates the principal rooms, two wide and two deep, on either side of a central hall; but even within this norm some curious things happened. American designers have always had a tendency to disregard symmetry of plans if it interfered with interior function. At Westover the hall is off center, although its exterior portal breaks the facade in half (Figure 5.10). In the Hammond-Harwood House (II) (Figure 5.11) a rear dining room window camouflages an exterior door to the same purpose. Toward the end of the century architecture in America, as architecture abroad, became freer in the shapes of rooms, but necessity and convenience apparently dictated their placement, and it was only when a mature designer put his hand to the drawing board that the exterior told

Figure 5.10 Plan of Westover, James County, Virginia, 1730. (Adapted from THE DWELLINGS OF COLONIAL AMERICA, by Thomas Tileston Waterman, Copyright 1946 The University of North Carolina Press. Reprinted by permission of the publisher.) Note that the bisymmetrical exterior is unrelated to the interior divisions.

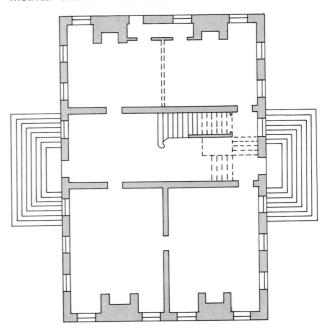

Figure 5.11 The Hammond-Harwood House, Annapolis, Maryland, 1770. (Library of Congress.)

the whole truth about the interior. In general it would seem that if the building worked well on the inside and looked as established styles said it was supposed to look on the exterior that was enough.

Vestigial persistence of Jacobean letter plans is characteristic of the early century and the more so as architecture traveled inland. The H plan at Tuckahoe (I), the T at Readbourne (II), the L in the Van Cortland House (II), and even the Medieval English scheme of large hall and small chamber remained popular.

The Dutch-Huguenot (i.e., Dutch Colonial) districts developed their two evenly sized spaces to include two quite small rooms to the rear, which a central passage opened to greater advantage. Without fireplaces these back rooms were cold in winter and thus became virtually summer pavilions.

Graeme Park (I) in Horsham, Pennsylvania, continued the Swedish plan with one file depth of rooms. The Swedish plan with corner fireplace, when organized around a central hall is best seen in the Trent House (I) in Trenton, New Jersey.

In the southern city of Charleston we first encounter the "single" or the "double" house, one or two tiers deep, respectively. To allay the excessive heat of the Carolina summer most of these houses were located with the narrow end toward the street (Figure 5.12). A wide two-story verandah, open to the prevailing winds, ran on the long side. The principal living rooms were then placed on the second floor on this axis, dining rooms were on the first, and the kitchens, in the basement. In the single house the hall was in the center of the long axis. In the double it was in the usual place and was entered from the street. In the single house the verandah, often a later addition, was sometimes shut off at the front by a false wall and a door. The latter was given all of the important architectural treatment that would have been accorded to the main entrance of any house. The Thomas Rose House (II) illustrates the single and the Heyward-Washington House (IV), the double.

Figure 5.12 This typical fine old Charleston house which stands with one end toward the street, has a pillared verandah and brick-walled garden. (G. C. Ball.)

New Orleans represents another special area in American eighteenth-century house planning. In the city (plantations are discussed later), the old European plan of offices on the first floor and living quarters above prevailed. Again a door, often of sufficient size to permit a horse-drawn vehicle to enter, opened to a side court or private yard. The surrounding second floor, and frequently the second floor front as well, was graced with a delicate wrought-iron balcony.

The origin of porches on the American scene has been the subject of historical conjecture. Some say they were seen in Canada as early as in the south and are thus a French introduction.[1] Actually they appear where the climate is suitable, as soon as the safety factor allowed, and wherever sociability and the academic precedent dictated. All of these factors were in favor of their introduction by at least midcentury. Van Cortland Manor (II) at Croton, New York, was begun in the

seventeenth century and possibly had a second-floor gallery from the beginning. The one-story porch appeared early at Tuckahoe. Perhaps the best forerunner of the full-fledged classical portico is at Kenmore (III) in Fredericksburg, Virginia, the home of Betty Fielding Lewis, George Washington's sister.

On plantations with their self-sufficient economy need was felt for dependencies and extra buildings. Almost any rural dwelling down to the present century had its contingent of kitchens, smoke house, wood house, poultry yard, and outhouse. The eighteenth-century mansion favored their placement (as Palladio had done in a similar necessity) in lateral arms. Toward the middle of the century these separate dependencies might be connected to the central block by quadrants, as at Mt. Vernon (II) (Figure 5.13) and Mt. Airy (III). When these connecting links to the outer buildings first occurred is in historical doubt. Both at Westover and again at Carter's Grove (III) where the dependencies are in line with the house the connecting passages were later additions.

In the post-Revolutionary era we see the extension of this idea in three-, five-, or even seven-part houses. This is represented by the Randolph-Semple House (III) at Williamsburg (Figures 5.14, 5.15), the Hammond-Harwood House (III; Figure 5.11) at Annapolis, and Brandon (III) in Virginia, respectively. Jefferson is credited with designing the Randolph-Semple House while he was a law student in the capital. He turned the gable end of the house to the front, thus creating a full temple form, and extended low wings to the side thus producing a small town residence with the classical dignity of a larger mansion.

Jefferson, both at Monticello (III) and at Bremo, introduced passages concealed by the slope of the land. Similar lateral walkways are at Mt. Airy (III) (Figures 5.16, 5.17), but the ultimate in grandeur returns to the separation of parts into three distinct and important buildings at Cliveden (III) and Mt. Pleasant (III), both in Philadelphia.

In all eighteenth-century house plans the disposition of the stairway was not so consistent with European chronology as might be expected.

Figure 5.13 (above) Entrance to Mount Vernon showing service buildings and connecting walkways. (Library of Congress.)
Figure 5.14 (center) The Randolph-Semple House, Williamsburg, Virginia, 1770. (G. C. Ball.)
Figure 5.15 (below) Plan of the Randolph-Semple House, Williamsburg, Virginia, 1770. (Adapted from THE MANSIONS OF VIRGINIA, 1706–1776, by Thomas Tileston Waterman, Copyright 1946 The University of North Carolina Press. Reprinted by permission of the publisher.)

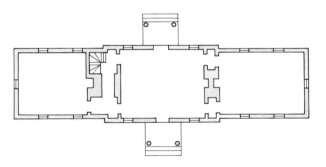

In Period I it was customary to locate the long, one-flight stairs in the central hall, as at Westover. A deviant location was in a compartment separated from the open front hall by a handsome keystone arch, as at the Williamsburg Governor's Palace (I), Royall House (II), and in the finest Georgian example, Carter's Grove (III). This was a derivation of English stairways like the one at Coleshill. Palladian tendencies in grand houses of midcentury often pushed the stairs to the side, as at Mt. Pleasant or located them in some lateral small area, as at Monticello. Tuckahoe (I) and Stratford (I) were derived from the H plan and have stairs in the wings, thus clearing the central bar for formal gatherings.

Plans of public buildings indicated a similar regard for pragmatism, although changing sooner to dictates of formalism. Churches advanced from the square meeting-house plan of the seventeenth century to the regular Wren-Gibbs inspired buildings of rectangular volume (Plate 9), which are found with and without transepts. The door was now in the west end, and the gallery was at the west or around three sides of the interior. The chancel with the choir and pulpit were arranged to the east. It is the progression from the plan of the old St. Andrew's Church (1706) on the Ashley River north of Charleston, to St. Michael's (1752–1761) in the city itself; from the Old South Meeting House (1729–1730)

in Boston to King's Chapel (1749–1754) in the same location, to Christ Church (1727–1754) in Philadelphia, and St. Paul's Chapel (1764–1766, spire and portico 1794–1796) in New York. It is curious to note that the plan of Boston's Christ Church (Old North, 1723; Paul Revere received his signal from its tower), which antedates Old South (1729) by six years, is more advanced. This is due to the availability of prints of Wren's churches, which it resembles. This again illustrates the unpredictable quality of American progressions. Non-Anglican churches often deviate

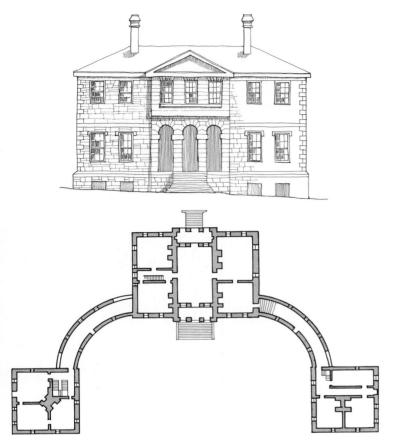

Figure 5.16   (top) Sketch of central building at Mount Airy, Richmond County, Virginia, 1758. This is one of the finest Palladian-type houses in America.
Figure 5.17   Plan of Mount Airy, Richmond County, Virginia, 1758. (Adapted from THE MANSIONS OF VIRGINIA, 1706–1776, by Thomas Tileston Waterman, Copyright 1946 The University of North Carolina Press. Reprinted by permission of the publisher.)

from the orthodox shape. In the next century many churches were given plans that permitted the seating of large congregations for which the Wren-Gibbs style was unsuited.

Public government buildings, for instance, the Old State or Town House at Boston (1712–1713, rebuilt after being gutted in 1711 and 1747 and restored in 1882), were based on the necessity of planning three chambers—one for the governor and council, a central one for the house, and another for the courts. As these important halls were often on the second story, the first was reserved for lesser offices. Wherever located, these

threefold divisions provided an opportunity for the introduction of bisymmetry and Renaissance-Baroque proportioning. On the other hand, Faneuil Hall (1740–1742; rebuilt 1761–1763 after destruction by fire) is an example of the pragmatic planning that places rooms where they are needed without due regard for appearances.

The Exterior Appearance

Exterior appearance rather than plans indicates the progression in styles along the Atlantic seaboard of America.

Transition Period, 1700–1725.   The Hazard House and the John Adams House (Figure 5.18), both in New England, are turn-of-the-century buildings. Both have light-scaled wood framing covered with clapboarding. Painting in red or white was a new feature. A side view of each discloses the lean-to outline. These houses were built higher on the ground than the seventeenth-century examples, although basements partly above ground were not yet widespread. Bisymmetry revolving around the door was achieved. The door itself has a classical tabernacle enframement and the windows at the Hazard House are double-hung sash, with pierced shutters. Throughout the century the use of shutters was variable. Some houses had them inside and out; some had none. Second-story windows in these early dwellings were placed close to the plate as they were in the seventeenth century. The fascia board below the roof line was still broad and bore no classical ornament.

A more developed classical style is illustrated in New England by Massachusetts Hall, Harvard University (1718–1720) or the McPhedris-Warner House in Portsmouth, New Hampshire (1718–1723). In both the principle of bisymmetry in the arrangement of external features has taken precedence. A certain provincial verticality rather than the classical Georgian horizontality is seen in the windows. Roof pitches remain steep and tall, with chimneys rising from the gabled ends. The roof is nevertheless truncated near the ridge pole with a balustrade. The McPhedris-Warner roof supports an embryonic central cupola. Most window tops on main stories remain flat, although

Figure 5.18   The John Adams House, Quincy, Massachusetts, 1700. (Library of Congress.)

occasional architraves are elliptical. Dormer roofs are flat or have triangular and arched pediments in Baroque projection. Door encasements are simple pilasters or half columns with entablature and pediment. The upper horizontal glass transom appears. The McPhedris-Warner House has a modillioned cornice along its front.

Dropping south to the middle colonies, Letitia House (1683), now in Fairmount Park, Philadelphia, but originally "downtown," invites attention as a regional transition piece (Figure 1.14). Here a string course demarking the two brick stories emphasizes the horizontality of the design. As a town house its original neighbors probably contributed to its appearance of breadth, whereas in its present location it appears too high and narrow. The double-hung windows are remarkably broad for their height and are more in agreement with later style proportions. The en-

framement here is bolder and the muntins, characteristic of the architecture of the central states, are heavier. Like such important English examples as Wren's Hampton Court, the trim is picked out in white.

Shutters are the solid variety more usual in the middle Atlantic colonies. Notice that the lights on the first floor are twelve over twelve and eight over twelve on the second, thereby inaugurating the graded proportions and vertical rhythms that counterbalance the horizontal of the string course and extended shutters. The Letitia roof remains simple gable, but it possesses a dormer that was all but universal during the first half of the century. At Letitia the inordinately deep fascia is typical of Teutonic-influenced styles. An early example of a *pent* extension with bold scroll brackets supports it.

Graeme park (1721) was built by Sir William Keith, secretary of the colony, possibly at the hands of John Kirk, a master mason. It finally found itself on the property of a vast United

Figure 5.19 The Jean Hasbrouck House, New Paltz, New York, 1712. (G. C. Ball.)

States arsenal. Regularity rather than bilateral symmetry obtains in the disposition of the door and of the early vertical six-by-three-light windows. The roof of Graeme is gambrel of high pitch. The entire silhouette is in proportions more common to Jacobean houses.

In the slightly earlier John Demarest House (1714) in Riveredge, New Jersey, we may see this gambrel-type roof as it begins to evolve toward the Dutch type roof with a break near the ridge and greater horizontality. The Dubois (1721) and the Hasbrouck (1712) houses (Figure 5.19) in New Paltz, New York, incorporate the long roof extension of the founding Huguenot settlers. Thus the low pitch of the Dutch roofs found along the lower reaches of the Hudson and the extended roof of the French combine to make a distinctive architecture known as Dutch Colonial in a new land where the two nationalities were neighbors.

Dropping south to Virginia at Williamsburg the dwellings of the "little people" show a continuance of transitional characteristics until far into the century—the development from the one-story quarter houses of English tradition with gabled and lean-to roofs of steep pitch, with high dormers often jerkin-headed, and end chimneys. Sash windows, both with and without shutters, side-front or central entrance as space dictated, and classical details as money and skill made them possible—these are the trademarks.

Virginia, however, boasted houses, indeed the most significant of the early century, that could rival the homes of the English gentry. Rosewell (1726) (Figure 5.9), on the north bank of the York, was demolished by fire in 1916 and only the remnants of the walls were left standing. It was built for Mann Page (1691–1730), son-in-law of the immensely land-wealthy King Carter, proprietary steward for Thomas, Lord Halifax, who possessed more than five million acres of northern Virginia under grant by Charles I as a place of refuge for some of his courtiers. Rosewell was the largest early-eighteenth-century house in the colonies and was completed only after the death of its owner. Its four stories, seen across the fields of Gloucester County, its early east-west pavilions, its straight-headed keystone window architraves, its tall-arched pilastered windows to the east, its skillful diminution of story heights, and a bi-symmetry around two handsome doorways of cut stone and brick reached by broad flights of Portland stone steps provide an unbelievable vision of Shangri-la. The roof to Rosewell was a deck-on-hip with a parapet and two cupolas. This item is an unexpected forecast of the Georgian on a building that otherwise might have stepped out of the best that late seventeenth century England could offer.

Thomas Tileston Waterman[2] suggested that some English-trained architect must have been in Virginia at the time and that possibly he was employed by the Carter family. He may have been responsible for the fine brick and wood work as well as the unified design of Carter's Christ Church (1732) in Lancaster County. English texts and pattern books contain clues to the origin of details but details do not make architecture any more than furnishings make interior design.

Tuckahoe (1710–1730), west in Goochland County, Virginia, where Thomas Jefferson received his early education, looks backward in its plan, its tall shuttered windows, and its quaint door hood and gabled roof. Its modillioned cornice and early porches and its belt course bespeak a later age.

The best claim to English derivation can go to the official buildings at Williamsburg—the Governor's Residence, William and Mary College, the Capitol, and the Bruton Parish Church. A cop-per plate in the Bodleian Library at Oxford suggests that the first three were taken from designs by the Surveyor General, Sir Christopher Wren. All were done in the first quarter of the century, although changes were made later, for the Palace was extended in 1749–1751 and the Capitol, rebuilt (1751–1753) after the first fire of 1747.[3]

Using the Palace (Figure 5.8) as an example, there is much that suggests the beginning of an architectural epoch rather than its zenith. Its overall squarish proportions, the vertical emphasis in windows, the high truncated hipped roof, the tall chimneys, the small jerkin-headed dormers (hip-on-hip, a provincial form of the gambrel), and the general austerity of its embellishment indicate that the designing hand was not sure in the Georgian tradition of a few years later. Nevertheless, the proportioning of the window spacing, the lights over the doorway, the water table, the beautiful hand-wrought iron balcony and rear gate, the modillioned cornice, the balustrade near the ridge pole, and the domed cupola with rectangular and arched windows show a sophisticated touch.

From personal preference we must stop at Stratford (1725), the home of the Lees. Here, despite its early H plan, the regular, almost bare, bi-symmetrical mass gives a sense of controlled strength rather than of Georgian finesse (Figure 5.1).

Moving to the deep south, few transitional buildings are left in Charleston, its largest colonial city. Fires, especially the great one of 1740, and hurricanes left nothing of the old standing. The Colonel William Rhett House (1712) is considered the patriarch. Now enveloped by the city, it was once a plantation home at the head of its own avenue and well outside the small town fortifications. The Colonel, vice-admiral of the province of Carolina, was largely responsible for freeing the seaboard from the depredations of pirates who plied the coastal waters. The Rhett House, as it originally stood, was an almost square building of stucco-covered brick with large ashlar quoins at the corners.

Although sash windows were used on the second and third floors, the Rhett House betrays its early date by its simple treatment of flat architraves with wedge keystones. Ground-floor windows have no enframement. Roofs of Charleston houses, after the fires, were required to be slate or tile and are more frequently the latter.

Mulberry Plantation (1714) on the Santee River is farther from Charleston and is in no danger of being incorporated even in the present extensions of the city limits. The South Carolina low country, comprised of that area that lies within the eastern section of the state, was, with its broad stretches of low-lying meadows called *savannahs,* covered with swamps and marshes. It was the home of the rice and indigo plantations, with their live oaks draped in Spanish moss, pine groves and slow, winding creeks. Most of the old homes did not survive the turbulence of the Civil War. Mulberry and later Drayton Hall (before 1758) are almost the only ones left intact.

Because of the intense heat and danger of malaria, the plantation houses were not occupied during the summer months and their owners lavished more money and care on residences in Charleston; therefore the somewhat retrogressive appearance of Mulberry, a low, two-story brick structure with a jerkin-head roof. Plantation buildings were low because of the danger of hurricanes. Mulberry is unique in the addition of four hip-roof corner pavilions with cone-shaped turrets superimposed. These turrets may be interpreted as due to the French Huguenot influence or they may be considered as survivals of the corner towers of late Tudor buildings. In any event they are reminders of the common sources of our architectural heritage. At Mulberry they make anachronistic juxtaposition with the early "piazza" and imposing flight of stairs to the front door. Windows, too, are tall and narrow—more seventeenth-century English and French than eighteenth-century colonial.

Early Georgian Period, 1725–1750. By the second quarter of the century the noticeably Medieval characteristics of the transition buildings were receding and the earmarks of Georgian architecture had become common. Proportioning was, of course, rather unevenly understood and embellishment was never elaborate.

A considerable number of examples are preserved. Because they are naturally somewhat less grand than their European counterparts, they have the easy grace of unpretentiousness. The Royall House (1733–1737) in Medford, Massachusetts, is chronologically in this list, although its four individually treated facades give it the air of a stylistic pattern book. Inasmuch as the separate embellishments are said to have derived from a house in Antigua, which the merchant Isaac Royall had admired and copied, their differences provide an interesting architectural conversation piece. The interior, to be discussed later, is homogeneous.

The Thomas Hancock House (1739) which stood on Beacon Hill illustrates the great need for historic preservation. Destroyed in 1863, the country lost one of its finest early Georgian landmarks.

Newport, Rhode Island, was the second largest city in New England at that time. Its early Georgian architecture is associated with the amateur architect, Richard Munday (?–1739), about whom biographical material is scarce. He is known by his works—several distinguished early Georgian buildings in Newport. He built the wooden Trinity Church (1725–1726), which is similar to Boston's Old North (Christ Church) of several years before. An aisled church with square box pews and balconies supported by squared pillars, it shows descent from Christopher Wren's London churches. The Old Colony House (1739–1741), which resembles the Boston Hancock, is also attributed to Munday.

Manhattan architecture that predates 1750 has all but vanished under the heel of progress. New York State architecture, represented by Dutch-Georgian pieces in the outlying districts, is, by fashionable English standards, quite retrogressive and somewhat regional in character. The Bronck houses (1738) in West Coxsackie near Albany were built by "immigrants" from the metropolis, indeed from the section that bears the family name, the Bronx.

Van Courtlandt House (1749) at the upper end of the Bronx overlooking Washington Heights is built of rubble in a seventeenth-century L plan, with a plain slant roof, portico, and some classically inspired ornament. Near Croton Point, Van Cortlandt Manor was originally owned by New Yorkers who may have used it as a station for trading with the Indians. When Pierre, grandson of the first owner, Stephanus Van Cortlandt, moved north to take up permanent residence, the house was rebuilt (shortly before 1749) to the condition to which the Rockefellers have restored it as a public landmark. Philipse Manor (1745), nearer the city at Yonkers, is somewhat more sophisticated in its use of the Georgian as it combines with the Dutch tradition of this section. It possesses a solid dignity that is characteristic of the best architecture of these years. The fanlighted doorway and the delicately pillared porch seem out of character and it is thought that they were later additions.

Surviving Pennsylvania buildings of this period are similar. Stenton (1728), in Germantown, the home of James Logan, a man of public affairs, is an example. Its simple doorway is among the first to incorporate a rectangular glass panel above it and narrow glass panels at its sides. It is interesting that only the front facade of Stenton is formally bisymmetric.

Construction of the Old State House, the most famous of Philadelphia's public buildings, better known as Independence Hall because the Declaration was signed there in 1776, was begun in 1731. The tower and the steeple were added in the fifties, the latter removed in 1781 for reasons of safety and not replaced until 1828 when it was rebuilt under the architectural direction of William Strickland. Andrew Hamilton, speaker of the Assembly, certainly an amateur architect, drew up the original design for the State House. It is basically Georgian and, with its outlying buildings, is one of the most significant assemblages of Georgian civic architecture.

Among the churches in the "City of Brotherly Love," the present Christ Church, whose architect is conjectural, was begun as an enlargement on the 1710 version and finished in 1744. The steeple was added a decade later.

In Virginia a group of houses, which extended slightly beyond the quarter of a century under discussion, exemplifies that consummate proportioning and skillfully pleasing brick wall treatment identified with the best Georgian architecture in America. Among them are Westover (1730; Figures 5.6 and 5.10), Berkeley (1727), Carter's Grove (1751; Figure 5.30) on the north bank of the James, the Wythe House (1752) in Williamsburg,

and Wilton (1754), formerly south of the river and now in Richmond. The last three, dated in the years following midcentury, indicate the caution necessary in pacing time by styles.

Carter's Grove is assigned to the master builder David Minitree, but the architect for all was probably Richard Taliaferro (1705–1799). Considered an amateur, he, like the supposed architect of Rosewell, presumably learned from pattern books like William Salmon's *Palladio Londinensis*. Taliaferro is known to have designed his own home in the capital, which later descended to George Wythe, his son-in-law, first law professor at William and Mary and Thomas Jefferson's instructor. We know that Taliaferro had a hand in designing the supper and ballroom wing of the Governor's Palace in 1749. On stylistic grounds and in view of the fact that he was currently alluded to as a "most skilful architect" and that he moved in prominent social circles, his was probably the guiding hand in all. It was obvious that, armed with the London books, he was capable of interpreting the Georgian in a manner that fitted Virginia culture.

On examination, these Virginia Georgian houses often differed from their English prototypes. Although in proportioning the overall horizontality of the classical supersedes the verticality of earlier periods, nevertheless it was accompanied here by a taller hipped roof that rose to a ridge pole and a lower lying mass of the building proper. In Berkeley the older gable was adhered to but in this case it was brought up to fashion by a modillioned cornice that extended around the ends as well as across the front.

Movement toward the central building and from there to the central door axis was made by all of the customary means, but it was particularly emphasized in Virginia by the fine layout of the house on the grounds. The immediate landscaped terrain in Virginia property was never very large, judged by the acreage of English estates, but the low-lying hedges or the iron fences at the extremities that enclosed the kept lawn and extended to the riverfront made an unusually pleasing space unity with the house. These were often pierced on the land side by a *claire-voyée* or gate through which one could obtain a view of the farmland beyond or by a *ha-ha* or dry moat over which a bridge gave actual egress to people but not to animals.

Exterior architectural details of embellishment are sometimes considered the *sine qua non* that gave these Georgian examples special grace. This position might well be argued. Nevertheless, the exceptional Portland stone doorways of West-over (Figure 5.6)—the north door equipped with full entablature and segmental pediment over Corinthian columns, the more famous riverfront doorway with scrolled pediment and entablature resting on pilasters—have been photographed so often that they seem almost to be a cipher of Virginia and the Georgian. The classical and exquisitely proportioned wood enframement at Wilton, the rubbed, gauged brick treatment of Berkeley, the Wythe House, and Carter's Grove are masterpieces that illustrate the twentieth-century doctrine written by Mies van der Rohe—*less is more.* For elegance with sturdiness, for grace with stateliness, for opulence without magnificence, these homes are unbeatable.

Late Georgian Period, 1750–ca. 1775. In the third quarter of the eighteenth century a wealthy and influential class had the means necessary to produce planned architecture. With architects available and architectural knowledge considered part of a gentleman's education, English books, such as James Gibbs's *A Book of Architecture* (1728) and William Adam's *Vitruvius Scoticus* (1750), were more in demand. With inspiration coming from England, the principles of English Palladianism were more in evidence and tended to alter the early Georgian toward greater discipline and more academic embellishment.

Formal organization of the exterior begins to mean more than bisymmetry and horizontality with the addition of classical dressings taken from a pattern book. The sort of planning that articulated exterior proportions with interior spaces into one welded unity was better understood and practiced. In general, it may be said that these midcentury builders were able to use relative scale to such advantage that they conveyed an impression of size and importance to buildings that were smaller than their European counterparts.

One means of accomplishing exterior–interior articulation was by the use of some modification of Palladio's temple-front formula. Frequently the main entrance and central hall were emphasized and associated by means of a projecting pavilion. Such appeared at Woodford (after 1756), the John Vassal House (1759), Mt. Pleasant (after 1761), the Chase House (1768–1771), Governor Tryon's Mansion (1767–1770), the Jeremiah Lee House (1768), and the Hammond-Harwood House (1770).

A recessed central portion like that James Gibbs used in England at Sudbrooke Lodge could accomplish the same purpose. This was done at Mt. Airy (1750) on the cliffs above the Rappahannock, the home of the John Tayloe family, and one of the most prominent "Palladian" style buildings in America (Figures 5.16 and 5.17). The south front of Mt. Airy is almost a copy of Plate LVIII in Gibbs, whereas the north derives from William Adam.

The porch, "piazza," or "verandah" (a nineteenth-century name) became general. Porches in the south soon adopted two-story aspects and became "double porches." Drayton Hall (before 1758), on the bank of the Ashley in South Carolina, is one of the earliest, as is Shirley (1769), belonging to the Carter family, adjacent to Berkeley on the James. The Miles Brewton House (1765; Figure 5.7) in Charleston certainly possesses the finest. In its first and second story elevations this portico has its Doric and Ionic orders superimposed.

The Miles Brewton House was built by the first Miles, the powder receiver for the colony, who willed it to his grandson and namesake. Many tragedies have befallen the men of this household. The younger Miles left by sea with his family bound for New York. No trace of his ship was ever found. Until recently the house was owned by the descendents of Mrs. Rebecca Motte, sister of Miles, whose husband was killed during the early days of the Revolution.

Although the common roof shape was still the hip (with local variations), the slant became lower and a roof deck surrounded by a balustrade was usual. Dormers remained and acquired academic caps, often alternating triangular and elliptical as well as semicircular pediments. On the nearly flat roofs they seem oddly out of place—more like antennae than eyeballs. Few cupolas are seen that antedate the Revolution; those of the Governor's Palace at Williamsburg, the Cupola House (1710) at Edenton, North Carolina, the Jeremiah Lee House (1768), and the one already mentioned on the McPhedris-Warner are the exceptions. The cupola at Mt. Vernon was not added until 1787. These lanthorns were the crowns of important buildings—churches, academic halls, and civic structures—rather than of domiciles.

Windows grew broader and proportionately less high. The number of panes was reduced as their positive size was increased. This is true, despite the rise in first-floor ceilings (see p. 207). It was made possible by leaving more space between the top of the window and the ceiling. Mullions remained sturdy until late in the century.

Doors were paneled, now with a greater number of divisions than the earlier six. Transom lights which arrived early at the Governor's Palace at Williamsburg and were augmented by narrow side windows at Stenton, were placed within the door aedicule itself. Occasionally a semicircular window is seen above the door, as at Mt. Pleasant and at the Miles Brewton House. The Palladian window and the round window grew more common, the former often used as a second-story prolongation of an elaborate central pavilion treatment or to light a back stairway and make an impressive rear elevation, as in the Chase House. Both Palladian and round had been common to important structures and especially to churches since early in the century. The Palladian window motif is used at St. Michael's in Charleston, King's Chapel in Boston, and St. Paul's in New York to illuminate the chancel. At Mt. Vernon it was wisely used to indicate the extra height of the large ballroom. The round window appeared as early as the Williamsburg capitol.

Decorative embellishment was most obvious on this midcentury architecture. With growing affluence it would be expected that the Schuylers, Van Rensselaers, Morrises, and Lees, as well as the Macphersons, Powels, and Chases, would wish to improve their houses. As most of the carving on doorways and windows was done in wood and as pattern books were available and

skilled carvers at hand, it is not surprising that adornment began to play its part. In more modest fashion this is seen in the many smaller houses grouped under the general title of Colonial Style.

Full classical enrichment became common. The Chase and the Hammond-Harwood houses illustrate the point. William Buckland (1734–?), who was brought to Virginia as an indentured draftsman to design Gunston Hall (1758), (the home of George Mason, author of the Virginia Bill of Rights), is considered to have been responsible for the two near-contemporary Annapolis houses. The doorway of Hammond House (Figure 5.11)—with its fanlight, temple surround of Ionic pillars, entablature with pulvinated frieze (with a convex profile), and triangular pediment set into a pedimented pavilion with full classical treatment including an elaborately carved central round window—is all the more lovely for the restraint used in designing the rest of the building. Matthias Hammond was a bachelor who had a thriving law practice and it is rumored that his concern for this house took precedence over the more usual human affections.

Not only triangular but also segmental and scrolled pediments are to be found. Often, as in the Wentworth-Gardner House (1759) in Portsmouth, New Hampshire, where triangular ones cap the windows, a broken scroll adorns the door. Here it carries a handsome gilded pineapple, an emblem seen in English works, and by tradition said to be associated with hospitality.

We can link the names of a few men as architects of these elaborate Georgian homes. Although Buckland might more correctly be called a decorator than an architect, certainly John Ariss (1725–1799), to whom Waterman[4] attributes fourteen important houses of the period, including Mt. Airy and a possibility of work on Mt. Vernon, merited the professional title. A native Virginian, he traveled to England, returning to advertise in the Maryland Gazette as an architect.

John Hawks (1731–1790), described as "a very worthy master builder," came from England in 1764 at the behest of Governor Tryon to build his palace (1767–1770) at New Bern, a building that served as the capitol of North Carolina and the governor's residence.

Ezra Waite (?–1769), who built the Miles Brewton House in Charleston, came to America on his own initiative. He advertised as "Civil Architect, House-Builder in general and Carver from London." "Just arrived from London" is frequently noted in the South Carolina Gazette and indicates the source of much of the current style influence. Gabriel Manigault (1758–1809), architect of the Charleston City Hall, designed the home (1790) that bore his name for his son Joseph.

In the north Peter Harrison (1716–1775), a Quaker turned Anglican and a native English Yorkshireman, planned such landmarks as the Redwood Library (1748–1750) in Newport, King's Chapel (1749–1754) in Boston, Christ Church (1759–1761) in Cambridge, and the Brick Market (1761–1772) in Newport. Possibly because of his early sojourn in England when that country was experiencing the full bloom of Burlington-Kent Palladianism, Harrison designed these American buildings with his eye close to English architectural books, a number of which he possessed. He also endowed what became the largest colonial architectural library in America.

Harrison may be credited with being the first to use the two-story columned temple front integral with a gable roof from front to back (the Redwood Library). The colossal order temple front on a pavilioned residence was seen first at Whitehall (1764–1765), the occasional home of Governor Horatio Sharpe of Maryland. The Jumel Mansion (1765), home of Roger Morris and later of Madame Jumel in New York City, possesses a towering porch appended to a four-square Georgian house. Jefferson used the two-story portico on the Virginia State Capitol (1789) and at Monticello (see p. 198). Such treatments were unusual before the Revolution.

At this point we recognize the architectural accomplishments of our third president as designer of the Randolph-Semple House (1770; Figures 5.14 and 5.15) mentioned earlier. His uniting of the front gabled building of one room in depth and two in height with two side wings each of one room and one story created the prototype for many modest homes of the post-Revolutionary period, especially as the population moved westward. The plan was capable of various interpretations and provincial idioms.

The characteristic late Georgian house which had low side wings or extensions was not Jefferson's creation unless he can be credited with designing such homes in the Piedmont as Brandon (1765). Here on a hip roofed Georgian-style building low appendages extend by still lower gabled connecting passages to two-story buildings, thus completing the seven-part late Georgian house which became the popular prototype for elaborate duplication during the affluent first half of the twentieth century.

The Federal Period, 1785–1820. Wars, insofar as they affect trade, cause a slowdown in style movements and frequently at their end a new cultural situation, often long in preparation, alters an artistic atmosphere almost overnight. Following the Revolution, America found herself confronted with two currents from abroad and adapted elements of each, sometimes favoring one or the other and eventually combining their essentials into one style. The period of this incubation may, for want of a better name, be called the *Federal style.*

From the England of Robert Adam and from the post-Renaissance France of Ange-Jacques Gabriel the first influence was derived. Two men in New England acted somewhat as liaison in its transmission, the first of whom was Samuel McIntire (1757–1811). He was at the very least a most gifted craftsman, born into a family of carpenters and woodcarvers, and himself most accomplished in the latter skill. We may also agree with those historians who credit him with possessing a remarkably receptive aptitude for new ideas.

In that expansive period when Salem merchants like Elias Hasket Derby loaded their clipper ships at the ports of China to trade with Europe and Cuba to great financial gain, McIntire was much sought by them to embellish interiors with fashionable woodwork and Neoclassic furniture.

In that day of unspecialization he was also engaged in architectural design, for his name is associated with several lovely New England Federal style houses. A characteristic McIntire structure is the Peirce-Nichols House in Salem, finished in 1782. Others are the Lyman House (after 1793) in Waltham, Massachusetts, and the John Gardner (Pingree) House (1805 on) in Salem.

These buildings may be regarded as transitional. In varying degrees they retained characteristics of the Georgian as well as the Neoclassic—the Lyman House is five part and low lying; we find belt courses, shutters, pilasters, refined but small classical porches, exquisitely etched fan lights, and a spate of low-relief decorative carving quite in the Adam fashion. Contemporaries of McIntire frequently kept the Palladian window motif above the central doorway.

Asher Benjamin (1773–1845), architect and writer, was in large part responsible for the widespread distribution of Adam forms in America. In *The Country Builder's Assistant,* published as early as 1796, he mentions that he modified the Adam details to make them more applicable to American craftsmanship and materials—thinner and more projecting cornices, slenderer orders, and freer molding decorations.

Certain characteristics of McIntire houses, such as their squarish forms, align him closely with the career of his near contemporary Charles Bulfinch (1763–1844) of Boston, whose work is more significant within the corpus of architecture. Bulfinch's background had fitted him for the role of gentleman architect. Born into a wealthy industrialist family, he was given the best education that America could provide and then went to Europe for the customary sequel. On his return he occasionally acted in the capacity of consultant in matters of architecture, a field in which most eighteenth-century gentlemen considered themselves well versed for the simple reason that such knowledge involved little more than a familiarity with the classical architectural library.

Having seen Wood's example of a unified housing development at Bath, England, Bulfinch decided to risk a financial enterprise along similar lines. With private capital he designed and sought to sell the "Tontine" Crescent, Boston's first housing development. It came on the market at an inauspicious time just before the Jay Treaty, when financial conditions between the United States and Great Britain were uncertain. Bulfinch's partners sold out and he went bankrupt even as the Adam brothers had almost done. The net result was that the Boston amateur had to earn a living and turned to architecture as a serious profession.

Three houses may be chosen to show Bullfinch as a man of pronounced architectural sense. They

Figure 5.20   The second Harrison Gray Otis House, 85 Mt. Vernon Street, Boston, 1800. Charles Bulfinch, architect. (Historic American Buildings Survey, George H. Cushing.)

were built successively for the same client, the Boston tycoon, Harrison Gray Otis. The first (1796) was on Cambridge and Lynde Streets in the west end of the city; the second, at 85 Mt. Vernon Street, was built in 1800 (Figure 5.20), and the third, at 45 Beacon, in 1806. These houses, perhaps more than Bulfinch's more public works, set the tone of Boston architecture around the turn of the century. In the first place, they were British and Adamesque classic in inspiration. From a flat wall plane tall windows were placed in receding arches, mullions were thin, cornices were horizontal and flat (No. 3), and grille work was delicate iron. The general proportions, however, remind one of the work of Gabriel. They paid little respect to low-lying Vitruvian rectangles with their appendages (the lack of land would have forbidden this even if stylistic feeling had not run counter). The bulk was tall, plain, and almost four square, but the sensitive placement of every functional detail gave the whole a self-contained rhythm that is as exquisite in its way as that of the Petit Trianon. Once the delicate detailing with which some of the porches, pilasters, and parapets were endowed was removed, the architecture was brick, simple, and bald. It had greater strength than its European counterparts.

The receding arches of many of these houses seem to invite the eye inward in a manner in which decorative excrescences do not. This is a signal of a growing tendency in architecture to reintegrate exterior and interior spaces. Oval-shaped rooms, for instance, are indicated in curved exteriors even as regular curved porches suggest interior shapes (Figure 5.21 and 5.22). It marks the skill of these turn-of-the-century men that they could coordinate a well-designed and flowing exterior with an eminently utilitarian interior. For all of this facility, however, it is symbolically true that in Bulfinch's architecture dynamic force was contained within walled entrenchments from the surrounding world, natural as well as human.

McIntire and Bulfinch, Salem and Boston, were not isolated phenomena. Much that was done there found duplication in principle throughout the country during the first twenty years of the nineteenth century. Designs such as those of Alexander Parris (1780–1852), from Maine but practicing in Boston, as well as those of Asher Benjamin, represented the New England states. Such houses as Decatur (1818–1819) by Benjamin Henry Latrobe (1766–1820) in Washington and the work of Gabriel Manigault (1758–1809) in Charleston, South Carolina, as well as the later Federal-inspired buildings of the Northwest Territory, indicate that the Federal style was not a local occurrence.

In the region of New York in the area occupied early by the Dutch and French the lovely idiom known as Dutch Colonial reached its most characteristic phase at exactly that time, when its lightness of scale was an offshoot of the Federal inspiration with which we have been dealing. The old Dyckman farmhouse on upper Broadway

is an outstanding example of this genre (Figure 5.23).

Where the northern states inaugurated a post-Revolutionary style, which, whatever its forward-looking aspects, nevertheless had antecedents in Neoclassic England and France, the middle south with Washington and Jefferson as representative spokesmen expressed the new America in still another way.

Jefferson led the way with Monticello (Figures 5.24 and 5.25). This American shrine, begun in 1770 and completed in 1809, looked architecturally backward and forward. What to call it stylistically has always been a puzzle. Its beautifully textured deep-pointed brickwork can vie with the handsomest of Georgian examples. It embraces the spirit of the late Georgian with its concealed quadrants and its porticoes reaching out to the surrounding land. Its tall central hall capped with a low, octagonal dome, its rear salon, and its unimportant stairway would have pleased Palladio. This is likewise true of its high principal story plus small and relatively unimportant second-floor quarters. The illusion of an attenuated first level was created by windows that, like the French, reached almost to the floor, whereas those of the second story were partly concealed behind a frieze.

A new note in American architecture was sounded by the colossal order used with full Roman Doric treatment. It was designed in proportions that, in relation to the mass of the building, made the strongest of statements. This aspect is basic to the Greek Revival of the next century. At Monticello there is a monumentality coupled with strength and simplicity that Jefferson felt was expressive of the present and future spirit of the new nation. This was not arrogance—rather confidence and dedication.

These qualities are best known to us in the designs for the government buildings in Washington, the work of a coterie of architects, each of whom may be said to have made his contribution.

After New York had served first as the capital of the new nation (1785–1790), the government moved to Philadelphia (1790–1800) and then to Washington. The plan of the city was laid out by Major L'Enfant, a well-trained French engineer, along radial lines known to him in Versailles and Paris.

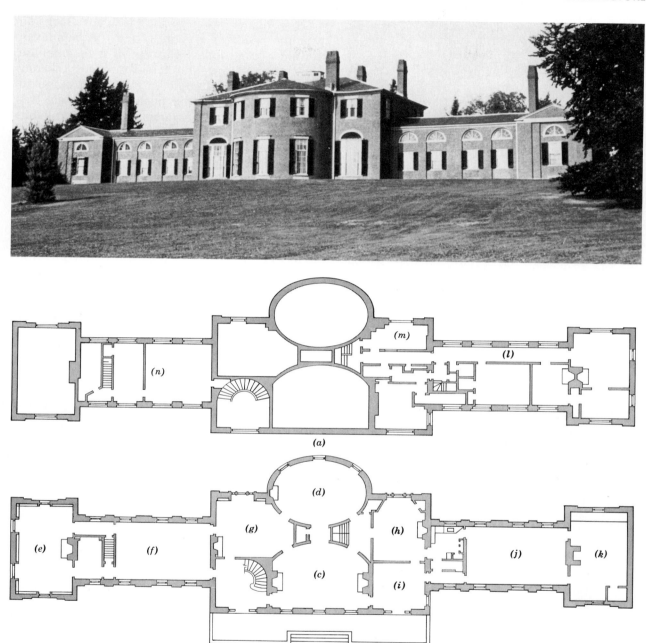

Figure 5.21 Garden facade, Governor Gore House, Waltham, Massachusetts, 1799–1804. Attributed to Charles Bulfinch, architect. (G. C. Ball.) Note how the simplification of the ornament suggests the future, whereas the triangulation of the masses reflects the past.

Figure 5.22 Plan of Gore House, Waltham, Massachusetts, 1804. Attributed to Charles Bulfinch, architect. (a) *second floor:* (*l*) servants' wing; (*m*) sewing room; (*n*) nursery. (b) *first floor:* (*c*) reception room; (*d*) oval room; (*e*) music room; (*f*) billiards; (*g*) library; (*h*) breakfast room; (*i*) butler's room; (*j*) servants' hall; (*k*) kitchen. The third floor contains bedrooms. (Historic American Buildings Survey.)

The original design of the President's mansion was the result of a contest, and the munificent reward of 500 dollars plus the right to supervise the construction went to James Hoban, a Kilkenny Irishman who had come to this country and to Charleston hard on the heels of Yorktown. Despite the continuous argument over the probable source of his design, it was English Palladian in inspiration and not forward-looking. Washington, who had insisted that the building be sizable and who appeared throughout his career to maintain a belief in the ultimate importance of the Union he administered, lived only long enough to see the walls rise. The cornerstone was laid in 1792. The second President, John Adams, was the first to live in the "White House." He entered as resident in November 1800, to call it home for only a portion of his term.

Before the building was gutted by fire at the hands of the British in 1814, Thomas Jefferson and his surveyor (i.e., architect Benjamin Henry Latrobe, 1766–1820) had planned the two colossal

Figure 5.23 (above) The Dyckman House, New York City, 1787. (G. C. Ball.)

Figure 5.24 (below) Monticello, home of Thomas Jefferson, near Charlottesville, Virginia, 1773 and 1796–1809. (Library of Congress.)

order porticoes, the rectangular to the north and the semicircular to the south. These structures were erected in 1824 and 1829, respectively—Jeffersonian porticoes on a late Georgian building with delicate Adamesque decoration—what better could weld an astonishing whole from the preceding fifty years of history!

The capitol is another story that merits more study than is given here. We view it as conditionally finished in 1831, after its initial conception displayed in the plans of the Englishman (Virgin Islands) Dr. William Thornton (1759–1828) and the Frenchman Stephen Hallet (1755–1825). Its construction was supervised by George Hadfield (ca. 1764–1826) and it derived its adult stature, after burning in 1814, from Benjamin Henry Latrobe, both of whom also came from England. (Thomas V. Walter was the architect for the construction of the wings and raising of the dome, 1855–1865). The original building was finally brought to completion under the American Charles Bulfinch, its architect from 1817 to 1831. It is a definite statement in the classic ideal with a central dome over a rotunda and with two adjacent spaces to house the two branches of the government (plus the Supreme Court, which until 1935 was in the north wing). Thus its exterior

Figure 5.25 Plan of Monticello, Albemarle County, Virginia. (Adapted from Frederick D. Nichols and James A. Bear, Jr., *Monticello: A Guide Book,* Thomas Jefferson Memorial Foundation, 1967.)

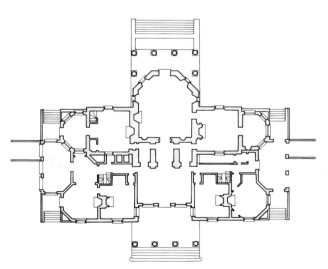

form majestically discloses and expresses its interior functions.

The Settlement of the West in the Eighteenth Century

Growing pains and grabbing pains, which seem to be the inalienable lot of the human race, pushed Americans west of the Appalachians, along the lower Mississippi, into Texas, New Mexico, and even California territory. Each settlement was in major part the result of pioneering by different groups of people, so that at the century's end the English, Germans, and Scotch-Irish were located in the midwest, the French and Spanish in southern Mississippi and Louisiana, and the Spanish in the southwest and California.

Faced with more primitive conditions, the buildings of the settlers were of necessity crude. Even in the East certain religious communities built in outmoded ways—for instance, the Seventh Day Baptists at Ephrata, Pennsylvania (ca. 1728), or the Moravians at Bethlemen, Pennsylvania (ca. 1773) and Winston-Salem, North Carolina (Salem, 1766). The first two communities hark back to Medieval construction and architectural style, whereas the Carolina group built largely in the English Georgian.

For much of the pioneering westward the Swedish type of log cabin proved suitable, for it required only manpower, limited equipment, and available forests to erect. Along all the main overland routes such as the Cumberland Trail these small houses can be seen today, often disguised beneath a later sheathing of weatherboarding, enlarged into a more commodious plan, and quite frequently sporting that American necessity, the front porch (Figure 5.26). In some of the earliest of these western communities, such as Schoenbrun and Gnadenhütten in Ohio (1772), Christianized Indians lived peacefully in log cabin settlements until they were wiped out by soldiers prompted by the fear and distrust enflamed by the French and Indian War.

Gradually style influences from the east made themselves felt, as conditions proved more suitable for their adoption. An example is the group of Georgian buildings at New Harmony, west of Pittsburgh, where another religious community

Figure 5.26 A converted log cabin near the Cumberland Trail. (G. C. Ball.)

was established. As the settlers pushed farther west, time telescoped, and later designs, such as the Federal and Greek Revival (the classic revival of the nineteenth century), took over. The Georgian was manifest only in isolated details.

The settlement of the region along the Mississippi from Illinois south retains few of its earliest structures, here built in the French tradition, sometimes with vertical log siding "poteaux-en-terre."

French plantation houses begin to assume their characteristic form which is quite different from the later ones of the English and Scotch who came into the district from the Carolinas and western Virginia in the early nineteenth century. Parlange Plantation (Figures 5.27 and 5.28), erected in 1750 by the Marquis Vincent de Ternant, is an example. Built of brick made on the plantation, the outer surfaces were stuccoed to withstand the

weather. With a two-storied gallery supported by wood pillars sometimes surrounding all four sides of the house (as at Parlange), the upper level was reached only by a flight of outer stairs. Here tall French doors with louvered outer blinds gave immediate access to separate rooms. The roof, in this case hipped, was covered with cypress shingles, a wood frequently used in the south for floors. Somewhat later in date but of similar style is Connelly's tavern in Natchez, Mississippi, the town that owed its nineteenth-century prosperity to King Cotton when it was the northernmost dock for large ocean-going vessels.

After the Treaty of Paris (1763) the Spanish filtered into New Orleans and the resultant Creole aristocracy further developed the typical early French house. These homes are to be seen in the Vieux Carré, the old section of the city that lies roughly in the great bend of the river. Lafitte's Blacksmith Shop, still standing, again really a house complex, was built between 1772 and 1791. It is supported on upright structural posts with brick nogging between, a construction system known as briquité-entre-poteaux.

Domestic architecture was all above-ground construction. It was built on brick flooring because of the ever present possibility of inundation and the certain dampness that forbade cellars. Constructed right to the street, slender columns carried two-storied galleries. Plans are as detailed earlier in this chapter. Windows were shuttered, tall, and narrow and, in the French fashion, interchangeable with French doors.

Early balconies, and by far the loveliest, were wrought iron, quite probably imported from the Spanish forges of Mexico. After 1835 the balustrades were cast iron, much more regular, and heavier in their design (source of manufacture and character are discussed in Chapter 6).

Figure 5.27 Parlange Plantation, Pointe Coupée Paris, Louisiana, 1750. (Library of Congress.)

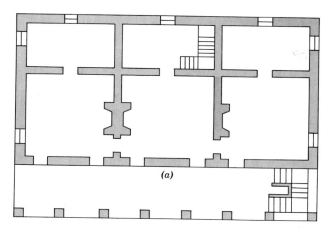

Figure 5.28 Plan of an eighteenth-century French plantation house built along the southern Mississippi River. (Adapted from Hugh Morrison, *Early American Architecture*, Oxford University Press, 1952.)

New Orleans houses were usually painted green, which with age has mellowed to a changeable blue that contrasts pleasantly with the old Spanish roof tiles.

New Orleans civic architecture—the Cabildo or Customs House (1795)—and the ecclesiastic—the Cathedral (Figure 5.29) with its Presbytère (1792–1794)—are Spanish in conception with French characteristics such as scroll-headed dormers and Mansard roofs, the work of imported French builders.

The major part of the Spanish story belongs to Texas and points farther west, for although Spanish occupation of Florida was continuous, except for brief domination by Britain from 1763 to 1783 until it passed to the United States in 1819, little Spanish architecture remains.

Following the building of Spanish missions in New Mexico and in Texas at El Paso in the early seventeenth century and their subsequent desertion caused by Indian uprisings, a renewed upsurge in mission building did not occur until the end of the seventeenth and the eighteenth centuries. Churches of the missions of this later period are at San Estevan at Acoma, San José at Laguna, San Tomás at Trampas, and at Taos. Little is left standing of the domestic buildings associated with the missions and their form can only be suggested as similar to Spanish buildings of a later date. These houses generally assumed

the Mediterranean courtyard plan and were built in the structural manner and with the decorative adjuncts that we associate with other surviving Spanish buildings of the southwest.

Missions in territory which would now be eastern Texas owe their existence to the threat of French forts along the Mississippi River. Likewise a number of Franciscan missions were authorized in the neighborhood of San Antonio, among them the Alamo and San José. A presidio was established at San Antonio in 1731, and the modern city may be said to have originated as the seat of the Spanish civil government. Near the middle of the eighteenth century San Antonio built its Governor's Palace, a combination of blank stone walls with concentrated Baroque decoration and the cipher of the Spanish Hapsburgs over the door.

The Arizona missions, that survive in the southern part of the state were constructed by the priests of the Jesuit order in the early seventeen hundreds. When the order fell out of favor with the Spanish crown, the missions were deserted and were not rebuilt until late in the eighteenth century by Franciscans. San Xavier (1784–1797) exemplifies the most advanced mission architecture. San José at Tumacácori bridges the last years of the eighteenth century and the first of the nineteenth. Ill-fated as most of them were, the missions of Arizona were still the reason for the establishment of the Presidio at Tucson; hence aided the settlement of the west.

Some California colonization was begun by sea and thus was independent of the New Mexico,

Figure 5.29 New Orleans Cathedral, 1792–1794. Jackson Square with its statue of Andrew Jackson is in the foreground. (G. C. Ball.)

Texas, and Arizona developments. The California area was discovered and claimed in the sixteenth century by the Spaniards (in 1542 Juan Rodriguez Cabrillo entered the Bay of San Diego) and the English (in 1577 Drake, on his voyage around the world, entered some of the California harbors and claimed the land, Nova Albion, for Queen Elizabeth). The Russians, too, had sailed down the coast from Alaska and made a third competitor. In 1602 Sebastian Vizcáino entered Monterey as the nominal viceroy for New Spain.

Three factors promoted the development of California during the eighteenth century. The first was the Jesuit missionary movement northward from southern (Mexican) California (the Jesuit missions were transferred in 1767 to the Franciscan order and subsequently increased in number). The second was the opening of the California harbors as ports of call on the trade routes to the Philippines. The third was Spain's plan to consolidate her lands after finding herself in legal possession of territory west of the Mississippi after the French and Indian War.

As a consequence of the last, an official enterprise from New Spain involved the organization of two land companies to settle upper California, territory that, except for the lower missions and the harbor communities, had been left virtually undisturbed. In 1770 one company, which had reached San Francisco Bay and had then returned to Monterey, took possession of the land for "the Glory of God, the honor of the King, and the security of New Spain." Thus began the Mexican-Spanish period of colonial California, the period in which a well-organized string of twenty-one Franciscan missions was built from San Diego de Alcala (1769) north to San Francisco de Solano (1823). In 1769–1782 the presidios of San Diego, Monterey, San Francisco, and Santa Barbara were established, and the pueblos or civilian towns of San José, Los Angeles, and the present Vera Cruz were founded. Some ranchos or cattle farms existed outside the presidio or pueblo compounds.

After Mexico separated from Spain in 1821 the missions were secularized and their millions of acres finally repossessed. Thus began the golden age of the ranchos, when as many as 10,000 acres belonged to a single tenant.

To cite further history—the United States secured upper California in 1848 after the Mexican War. Almost on the heels of the Treaty of Guadelupe Hidalgo gold was found in the west and California overnight became a mecca for the gold rushers. At once the era of Colonial agriculturalism was a thing of the past.

Whereas a discussion of the architectural beauties of the Colonial houses of California is best postponed until the next chapter because it was in the last half of the nineteenth century that a more normal settlement occurred and characteristics inherited from the period of the Colonial architecture crystallized into a more recognizable style, it must be mentioned that the California missions, crumbling into extinction, were not restored until the twentieth century. Differing from one another in elaborateness, they were alike in being load-bearing walled structures, covered with stucco and roofed with tiles. They were interconnected by long, arcaded corridors and accented with bell towers where each arch in the belfry held a bell. Classical details in the form of pilasters and entablatures were frequent and towers were often domed. Some softly modeled Baroque features speak eloquently of a Spanish heritage. Their variety within a natural unity created one of the outstanding architectural beauties in America.

SOME AMERICAN HOUSES, 1700–1800

Wanton-Lyman-Hazard House	Newport, Rhode Island	1700
John Adams House (Figure 5.18)	Quincy, Massachusetts	1700
Governor's Palace (Figure 5.8)	Williamsburg, Virginia	1705–1720
Wing added		1749
Burned		1781

Tuckahoe	Goochland County, Virginia	1710–1730
Samuel Wentworth House (Figures 1.7, 1.8, 1.22)	Portsmouth, New Hampshire	1671 and 1710
Jean Hasbrouck House (Figure 5.19)	New Paltz, New York	1712
Colonel William Rhett House	Charleston, South Carolina	1712
Cupola House	Edenton, North Carolina	1712
The Mulberry	Charleston, South Carolina	1714
Morattico	Richmond County, Virginia	1714
John Demarest House	Riveredge, New Jersey	1714
Ludwell-Paradise House	Williamsburg, Virginia	1717
McPhedris-Warner House	Portsmouth, New Hampshire	1718–1723
Trent House	Trenton, New Jersey	1720
Warner House	Portsmouth, New Hampshire	1720
Graeme Park	Horsham, Pennsylvania	1721
Dubois House	New Paltz, New York	1725
Stratford	Westmoreland County, Virginia	1725
Rosewell (Figure 5.9)	James County, Virginia	1726
Berkeley	James County, Virginia	1727
Ephrata Cloister	Ephrata, Pennsylvania	1728
Stenton	Germantown, Pennsylvania	1728
Westover (Figures 5.6 and 5.10)	James County, Virginia	1730
Readbourne	Queen Anne's County, Maryland	1731
Royall House	Medford, Massachusetts	1733
Hancock House (demolished 1863)	Boston, Massachusetts	1737
Leendert Bronck House (Figure 1.11)	West Coxsackie, New York	1738
Bryce House	Annapolis, Maryland	1740
Nelson House	Yorktown, Virginia	1740
Westervelt House	Tenafly, New Jersey	1740
Philipse Manor	Yonkers, New York	1745
Charles Pinckney House	Charleston, South Carolina	1746
Van Cortlandt Manor House	Croton, New York	Rebuilt just before 1749
Van Cortlandt House	New York, New York	1749
Parlange Plantation (Figure 5.27)	Pointe Coupée Paris, Louisiana	1750
Kenmore	Fredericksburg, Virginia	1751
Carter's Grove (Figures 5.10 and 5.30)	James County, Virginia	1751
House of the Miller	Muelbach, Pennsylvania	1752
Wythe House	Williamsburg, Virginia	1752
Wilton	Richmond, Virginia	1754
Hunter House	Newport, Rhode Island	1754
Ralph Izard House	Charleston, South Carolina	Before 1757
Woodford	Philadelphia, Pennsylvania	After 1756
Drayton Hall	Ashley River, South Carolina	Before 1758
Gunston Hall	Fairfax County, Virginia	1758
Mt. Airy (Figures 5.16 and 5.17)	Richmond County, Virginia	1758
Elsing Green	King William County, Virginia	1758
John Vassal (Longfellow) House	Cambridge, Massachusetts	1759
Wentworth-Gardner House	Portsmouth, New Hampshire	1759
Schuyler Mansion	Albany, New York	1761
Mt. Pleasant	Philadelphia, Pennsylvania	After 1761
Fraunces Tavern	New York, New York	1763

Cliveden (Figure 5.4)	Germantown, Pennsylvania	1763
Moffat-Ladd House	Portsmouth, New Hampshire	1763
General Herkimer House	Herkimer, Pennsylvania	1764
Whitehall	Anne Arundel County, Maryland	1764
Robert Morris (Jumel) Mansion	New York, New York	1765
Miles Brewton House (Figure 5.7)	Charleston, South Carolina	1765
Brandon	Prince George's County, Virginia	1765
Governor Tryon's Palace	New Bern, North Carolina	1767–1770
Powel House	Philadelphia, Pennsylvania	1767
Chase House	Annapolis, Maryland	1768–1771
Van Rensselaer Manor (removed)	Albany, New York	1768
Jeremiah Lee House	Marblehead, Massachusetts	1768
Mt. Clare	Baltimore, Maryland	1768
Shirley	Charles County, Virginia	1769
Ridout House	Annapolis, Maryland	Before 1770
Randolph-Semple House (Figures 5.14 and 5.15)	Williamsburg, Virginia	1770
Hammond-Harwood House (Figure 5.10)	Annapolis, Maryland	1770
Montpelier	Prince George's County, Virginia	1770
Ashlawn	Albemarle Co., Virginia	1771–1775
Gracie Mansion	New York, New York	1771–1775
John Stuart House	Charleston, South Carolina	1772
Winston-Salem Settlements	Winston-Salem, North Carolina	1766
Monticello (Figures 5.24 and 5.25)	Albemarle County, Virginia	1773; 1796–1809
William Gibbes House	Charleston, South Carolina	1779
Jerethmeel Peirce (Nichols) House	Salem, Massachusetts	1782
Dyckman House (Figure 5.23)	New York, New York	1787
Joseph Manigault House	Charleston, South Carolina	1790
The President's House	Philadelphia, Pennsylvania	1792
Lyman House (The Vale)	Waltham, Massachusetts	After 1793
The Crescent	Boston, Massachusetts	1793
Harrison Gray Otis House (1)	Boston, Massachusetts	1795
Elias Hasket Derby House (Oak Hill)	Peabody, Massachusetts	1795
Roelof Westervelt House (main section)	Tenafly, New Jersey	1798
The Octagon	Washington, D.C.	1798–1800
Gore House (Figures 5.21 and 5.22)	Waltham, Massachusetts	1799–1804
Harrison Gray Otis House (2) (Figure 5.20)	Boston, Massachusetts	1800
Nathaniel Russell House	Charleston, South Carolina	1803
Wayside Inn	South Sudbury, Massachusetts	ca. 1700–1800
Mt. Vernon (Figures 5.5 and 5.13)	Fairfax County, Virginia	Original 1726–1735
Additions		1758
Two story		1758
Portico		1784–1787
Cupola		1787

INTERIOR DESIGN

It is tempting, in speaking of the interiors of American buildings of the eighteenth century to say, "ditto England." Although this is not quite true, it is sufficiently so to warrant minimal description that will be concentrated on analogies and differences.

Space Organization

Because of varying shapes seen in American architecture within a stylistic norm, exterior and interior are discussed jointly.

Bearing in mind the fact that American interiors could not emulate the very large size of the greatest English and continental ones; nevertheless their relative dimensions were similar. Height was especially noteworthy. Ceilings moved from the seventeenth-century low of less than 8 ft to an average of 11 ft for the first story and nine for the second during the Georgian period. Toward the end of the century the first floor was often as high as the 18 ft found at Monticello; the second ranged from 9 to 12 ft. Occasionally heights varied within a single area when both public and private rooms were combined.

Architectural Details

Doors and windows follow closely their exteriors and prototypes, the former being paneled and both gradually taking on the aedicule of the classic surround. With the late century, the deep Adam frieze and thin flat projecting cornice board are to be found.

Fireplaces and mantels progressed in elaboration. Early ones were constructed with a simple panel surround. Often the fireplace was merely outlined with molding (Plate 8). Mantels with shelves, especially those with classical treatment, were common by the fifties. Completely independent mantels, often of marble but customarily of painted wood, belong to the post-Revolution years.

The stairs in eighteenth-century buildings, independent of the spaces in which they were built, are worthy of admiration. In contrast to those of the seventeenth, their angle of rise decreased and the treads became wider, making an easy ascent such as that experienced in the long flight at the Royall House. The straight flight was altered to include other varieties, even as early as the Governor's Palace at Williamsburg. At the Chase House the centrally located entrance flight subdivides into two parallel ranks from a mid-floor landing. This example was originally a complete *tour de force* with no support at the outer edge of the upper ranges. A slim column was later installed for greater safety. At Drayton Hall the plan, in effect, is the reverse of the Chase structure. Here, a double flight unites at a landing leading to the main salons on the second floor.

The post-Revolutionary circular and elliptical flights are the apogee of this spiraling tendency. At the same time we must not forget that Jefferson seems to have considered stairs a necessary nuisance and to have tucked them away from his imposing central halls whenever possible. In the limited space of such interiors as the Randolph-Semple House narrow winding stairs necessarily staged a return.

The design of the stairs proper also indicates a progression with a number of deviations. First was the closed string, which remained for quite a long period in smaller houses. At the Governor's Palace at Williamsburg, although the open string is used, the newel abutting four square with the stair ends is carved in characteristic Carolean fashion. As early as Tuckahoe, Westover, and Rosewell (perhaps the most advanced Colonial model), the open string and molded top rail swung into a graceful curve as they approached the newel. Strings were carved in elaborate foliated scrolls. Bannisters were frequently of three different varieties per step. The Rosewell masterpiece was done in mahogany and carved columnettes replace lathe turnings.

When the string course was omitted, it was usual to carve the soffit to match the side of the risers. It was often paneled, as in the Jeremiah Lee House. Several unusual balustrades, such as the Chinese fret design at Brandon, illustrate the care given by Georgian designers to their entrance halls and stairs.

Interior Surface Treatments

Domestic floors were wood, some wide-planked and many of narrow, matched hardwood boards. Occasionally they were ornamented with painted designs. Very few parquets existed, the stair landing at Carter's Grove among them.

Marble was not quarried on a commercial basis until after the Revolution. Outer hearths and the floors of important buildings were of imported

Figure 5.30   Hall and stairway at Carter's Grove, James County, Virginia, 1751. (Library of Congress.)

stone; those of the aisles of King Carter's Christ Church were dark Purbeck marble from the peninsula of that name on the Dorset coast. The hall floors of the Miles Brewton House and Governor Tryon's Palace (a restoration) are marble. In the era of government building that followed the Revolution marble and patterned wood were more usual.

With the turn of the century all important walls acquired floor-to-ceiling paneling. Occasionally the woodwork extended only to the dado on surfaces such as stair halls, bedchambers, or rooms in which flock paper was used. Carter's Grove serves as an example of the finest midcentury paneling (Figure 5.30). Here the wood was walnut of the dark variety fast disappearing from the scene. The carpenter, Richard Bayliss, was brought from England by Carter Burwell, grandson of

"King." Similar walnut was used for the magnificent interior of King Carter's Christ Church. Mahogany was more often seen in America than in England. In the Jeremiah Lee House it appears in the wainscoting and stair rails. Hard pine was common and often painted—at the second quarter of the 1700s in soft intermediate tones. It was on occasion grained to imitate marble or figured wood. A room from Marmion, Virginia (the home of the Fitzhughs), now at the Metropolitan, possesses panels painted with urns and landscapes. The museum suggests that although the woodwork probably came from England the painting was more than likely at the hand of some itinerant local artist.

As in England, the panels were large and disposed to form a balanced room arrangement. American moldings were generally simpler than their foreign counterparts and few examples of bold Restoration bolection moldings are to be found (e.g., the McPhedris-Warner House). The customary panel face was flush with the stiles and rails, although examples of receding panels do appear.

Embellishments were at first nonexistent and classical motifs tended to be slow in showing. Occasionally keystone shapes were centered on door surrounds and on the enlarged arches of the niches that offset the wall planes. Gradually such classical items as pilasters and full entablatures appeared. Fireplace areas took on their quota of Baroque scrolls, ears, and broken pediments of bold contour. Even chinoiserie was to be found as in the interior of Gunston Hall, where William Buckland designed one room in Palladian, one in the oriental manner, and even affixed a Gothic-arched porch—certainly the beginning of eclecticism!

With the post-Revolutionary trend toward Neoclassicism, paneling was on the way out, although classical treatment of opening surrounds continued—now of lower profile and flatter cornice or frieze (Figure 5.31). In the Peirce-Nichols House McIntire did the paneling of the west parlor in early Georgian, and shortly afterward, on returning from a trip to England and in preparation for a wedding in the client's family, designed the east parlor in the post-Georgian fashion.

Advanced architecture introduced plaster ceilings even before 1700 (e.g., Bacon's Castle). Provincial architecture continued to build with exposed beams until much later (e.g., the House of the Miller, Muelbach, Pa.). Ceilings of important rooms were often coved (e.g., Stratford, the Miles Brewton House, and the William Gibbes House). Stucco ornament was favored here as in England; one of the earliest examples is Westover, another, the Miles Brewton House. These were in the French rocaille style and probably derived from handbooks like Isaac Ware's. Later works at Mt. Vernon and Kenmore are in a more geometric and classical tradition which progressed to examples in the true Adam manner (e.g., the Nathaniel Russell House) and which also came from English sources. Post-Revolution ceilings generally reverted to plainness.

Furnishings and Their Arrangement

In number and quality the standards of furnishings in America were not lavish, although the in-

dex rose as wealth increased. European levels were approached as the era advanced. Abigail Adams (wife of John Adams and mother of John Quincy Adams), who had lived abroad for almost a decade, wrote that

". . . we approached much nearer to the Luxury and manners of Europe, according to our ability,

Figure 5.31 The Stamper-Blackwell parlor, 1764. Philadelphia Chippendale-style furniture; sixteenth-century Caucasian *kuba* carpet. Winterthur Museum, Winterthur, Delaware. (Courtesy, The Henry Francis du Pont Winterthur Museum.) This is the parlor of a house built for John Stamper, mayor of Philadelphia; the house was later occupied until 1831 by the Reverend Dr. Blackwell.

than most persons were sensible of, and that we had our full share of taste and fondness for them."[5]

Undoubtedly the arrangement of furnishings was dictated by a preference for formality, although written and visual contemporary evidence is hard to find.

FURNITURE

General Style Character

American furniture from 1700 until nearly 1750 followed progressively England's William and Mary and Queen Anne styles. These designs only gradually gave way to the Chippendale manner, largely as it was known through the third edition of the *Director*, published in 1762, the first to be well publicized on the western shores of the Atlantic. Chippendale inspiration predominated during the late Georgian period, just as surely as Adam, Sheraton, and Hepplewhite (to give these styles their usual cognomens) succeeded after the Revolution. French influence then loomed in importance.

Sources

Throughout the eighteenth century and even during the war years wealthy families were importing furniture from England. In the continuous accounts of the London Public Record Office from 1697 to 1780 figures for upholstered goods directed to America are available. Although the nature of the imports may be variously interpreted, nevertheless it is clear that upholstered furniture pieces were brought over in considerable numbers.[6] In addition, immigrants and travelers carried consignments. Judge Samuel Sewall of Boston wrote the following letter to London in 1716. The goods made up part of the dowry of his youngest child, Judith:

> Send curtains and vallens for a bed, with a counterpane, headcloth and tester, of good yellow watered worsted camlet and trimmings as may be enough to make covers for the chamber chairs; a good chintz bed [chintz here refers to the bed furnishings] well-made; a true looking glass of black walnut frame as good as can be bought for five or six pounds; a dozen of good walnut chairs, fine cane with a couch; a dozen of cane chairs of a different figure and a great chair for the chamber, all black walnut. . . .[7]

Simple and provincial furniture was locally made. Toward the middle of the century northern craftsmen rivaled or exceeded the skill of cabinetmakers in the mother country and much furniture from the New England states, New York, and Philadelphia was exported to the south, despite English pronouncements against this sort of trade.

Materials and Construction

Corresponding to English taste, walnut was the fashionable wood during Period I, later giving way to mahogany. Blond materials were much in demand during Period IV. Cherry became an alternative to mahogany in New York and New England, although much mahogany furniture of the finest sort was made in America. Hard maple is an American substitute for satinwood. Cabinetmakers combined materials, seeking for each part timbers that possessed the requisite qualities. Thus, in making Windsor chairs, hickory or oak was used for the spindles and bent wood members to give strength and resiliency; maple was used for the underpinning and hard pine, usually in one piece, for the seat.

Carving was the chief method of embellishment on Georgian pieces. Painting and japanning on early case goods imitated the coveted oriental lacquer. John Pimm (worked 1736–1753) of Boston was probably the maker, if possibly not the japanner of the William and Mary highboy at Winterthur, which he signed. He may have done the similar one at the Metropolitan (Figure 5.32). Post-Revolutionary furniture often relied on inlay or paint for its enrichment.

Taking chairs as an index, it is interesting to note how construction and design were partners (Figure 5.33). Philadelphia, seconded only by New York, was most directly influenced by the

English style books. This meant that front curvature on chairs was adopted early. In Philadelphia the front and side rails were carved from broad, heavy boards of longitudinally grained wood, the two pieces being rounded into each other and firmed by a rabbet joint and dowels. An extension of the leg fitted firmly into this section. At times a strong underbracing abolished the need for stretchers. Rabbeting also played an important part in the jointing of the back stiles with an extension of the rear legs. Seat rails were tenoned into the leg projection. A molding was applied to chairs where an upholstered seat needed to be secured in place.

In the North (New York sometimes included) a simpler and less extravagant construction solution was found. The front of the frame was made from a vertically grained board that contained its own molding. This section, as well as the side rails, was mortised into a square extension of the leg, which then formed the corner. When, especially in New York, the leg extension was smaller and wedge-shaped, due to the curvature of the seat, it was necessary to reinforce the joint with a triangular brace within the compass of the frame.

Although various woods were used for this underbracing, white pine was common both in New England and New York. Shiploads of this wood entered the ports of the south earmarked for the

Figure 5.32 (above right) Highboy with japanned decoration, William and Mary style, New England, ca. 1700. Note the pear-drop handles, baluster-turned legs, serpentine stretcher, and bun feet on pad. Metropolitan Museum of Art, New York. (The Metropolitan Museum of Art. Joseph Pulitzer Bequest, Purchase 1940.)

Figure 5.33 (below) Construction of front seat rail of Chippendale-style chair: (a) northern type (New England and often New York); (b) southern type (Philadelphia and occasionally New York). (Drawing based on furniture in the collection of The Metropolitan Museum of Art as pictured in their publication *American Chippendale Furniture: A Picture Book*, New York: 1940.)

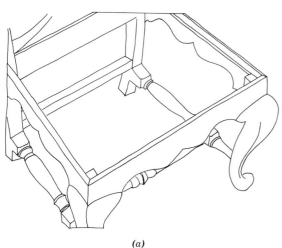

(a)

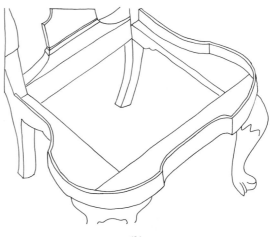

(b)

same purpose. A secondary wood was poplar, and in New England oak and beech or red pine. In Charleston cypress, which like chestnut is a strong, light, porous wood, was considered suitable for carcasses of large-scale case goods and was frequently used as a base for veneers.

The Windsor chair type, an American favorite, used spindles more frequently than its English counterpart. For this reason it was colloquially known as the *stick chair*. Washington ordered two dozen for the verandah at Mt. Vernon in 1796. In the American Windsor the legs were inserted invariably by means of wedge joints and thus were placed nearer to the center of the seat to effect a triangular and more stable form. Green wood, used for the seat, shrank as it dried, thereby tightening the joint.

Before entering the realm of "high style" furniture we must dispose of the construction of that typically American article—the rocking chair, a few of which, with slat backs, may date as early

Figure 5.34 Armchair, Salem, Massachusetts, 1765–1780. Mahogany with maple seat rails. Height, 98 cm, width, 74 cm, depth, 61.6 cm. Winterthur Museum, Winterthur, Delaware. (Courtesy, The Henry Francis du Pont Winterthur Museum.)

as 1725, although 1750 is more often assigned. Presumably a rocking chair was one of the first "comfort" inventions of the Yankee and derived from the European cradle, thereby accommodating both ends of life. The first rockers were added to chairs already in use. If evolved in this manner, they are marked by the lowness of their stretchers because the legs would have been shortened to compensate for the height added by the rocker. In a chair that from its inception was designed as a rocker the back legs thickened toward the bottom to take the thrust of motion. Early rockers are short, with front and rear projections, similar in shape, fitted into grooves in the legs.

Like the Windsors, rockers were utilitarian pieces and were made largely by local craftsmen. This is one reason for the lack of authentic information about their origin. They have remained in the American scene into the twentieth century, when those of behemoth size were placed on the porches of many a seaside hotel. Combining the penchant for motion with that of sitting, they antedated the automobile as an institution—one fraught with fewer problems.

General Regional Differences. The general statement that styles in America have followed English prototypes with a diminishing time lag is essentially true. An experienced eye, however, soon detects the differences that may stamp an American piece; for instance, the block front on a Newport chest was probably a Dutch or German import. The Spanish club foot that frequently appeared on William and Mary pieces in England may possibly be found on Queen Anne style furniture in America. Many early and often most provincial items were delightfully hybrid—rush seat, cabriole legs, straight, tall back with fiddle splat a mongrel seldom seen in metropolitan furniture.

The principal centers of craft production throughout the century were Boston and environs, Newport, New York, Philadelphia, and, after the war, the southern cities of Annapolis, Baltimore, and Charleston. A general rule indicates that New England furniture is, by comparison with work in other areas, straighter in profile and more attenuated in proportions (Figure 5.34). In

Figure 5.35   Armchair, New York, 1765–1775. Mahogany and pine. Height, 1 m, width, 79 cm, depth, 61 cm. Winterthur Museum, Winterthur, Delaware. (Courtesy, The Henry Francis du Pont Winterthur Museum.)

Figure 5.36   Armchair, Philadelphia, 1740–1750. Mahogany. Height, 104.8 cm, width, 81.9 cm, depth, 55.9 cm. Winterthur Museum, Winterthur, Delaware. (Courtesy, The Henry Francis Winterthur Museum.)

this category Connecticut wares were heavier and had a lower center of gravity.

New York items, of ample size, suggested a broadness of outlook and possibly of physique common to such as the Beekmans and Van Cortlands. Early New York furniture can often be spotted in such European reminders as broad and irregularly curved back splats (Figure 5.35). Newport furniture may be said to constitute a mean between Manhattan and Massachusetts. Philadelphia, the really elegant capital of the coastal area, provided distinction in furniture not so much by means of its breadth, which was only a little less than that of New York, but rather in suavity of outline and detail (Figure 5.36).

Colonial: Early Georgian (William and Mary,

Queen Anne) Type Furniture.   This diffuse heading is needed to cover the many ill-defined style names in American furniture during the first half of the eighteenth century. To pinpoint the beginning of this era we note an example of the "Boston" chair that was exported from the city port in such numbers that it merited the name. Now in the Boston Museum of Fine Arts, it is dated ca. 1700–1725 and indicates the persistence of earlier William and Mary forms. The wood is maple, the upholstery leather.

In the Peyton Randolph House at Williamsburg we can see a set of Queen Anne chairs of slightly later Massachusetts vintage. They have spare, narrow backs with little surface decoration and lack the step-up side rails customary in advanced English examples. They do, however, bear a version of the central fiddle splat. Low-slung stretchers are characteristic.

Three side chairs from the Rhode Island seacoast illustrate further developments of the style around 1740. The top rail had the well-carved shell motif toward which Newport moved soonest and the fiddle splat had attained advanced dimensions. Newport stretchers were likewise low slung, often serpentine, as seen in a Winterthur example. New England chair feet were customarily club (pad), trifid, or web pattern, with stump rear legs (Figures 5.34 and 5.37).

Moving south to New York (Figure 5.35), we note that the claw and ball foot was prevalent. The New York craftsmen followed the London pattern books closely. The rear legs on New York chairs were usually rounded with club (pad) feet.[9] The absence of stretchers and the sharply pointed cyma of the back is also observable. Notice the broad proportions, the thick seat rail, and the wedge-shaped extension of the foreleg.

The finesse and suavity of Philadelphia furniture (Figure 5.36) has long been acknowledged and some of this quality, dependent on its linear rhythmic character, is thought to have been due to the natural propensity in this direction of the many Irish craftsmen who immigrated to the area.[10] Details that appeared often in Philadelphia as well as in Irish furniture are the trifid, slipper foot, and collared sock. Rear legs were customarily stump (Figure 5.37). The serpentine stretcher was as prominent as in Newport. Recall that the curvature on Pennsylvania slat backs had the double curve top and bottom, which produced the flavor of the French ladder backs of the Bayou.

In addition to side and arm chairs, wing or "easie" chairs were much in demand.[11] They appeared in America with the William and Mary through the Federal styles. The "great chair,"[12] which Sewell requested for his daughter's dowry, was winged.

With the comfort provided by upholstery, with the back high enough to give a headrest, and with side cheeks to screen the draft, wing chairs were not only handsome but useful and so expensive that they were primarily intended as a luxury for the sick, to be placed in the bedchamber. The earliest variety had tall and narrow proportions; later ones and those from Philadel-

phia and New York were more ample. Early pieces, and more particularly those of the North, had "roll around" arms (Figure 5.38), whose front stiles were cone-shaped uprights which in reality capped the seat rail. Later, especially in Philadelphia, models possessed "roll-over arms." Here the wing was continuous with the arm and was then connected with the arm stile by a Baroque C scroll which "rolled over" in three dimensions (Figure 5.39). The last development, which also occurred in Federal straight-legged styles, placed the wing outside the arm rest. Because it was an independent member, it was capable of being formed in exaggerated curves (Figure 5.40).

To return to the "stick" chair (Figure 5.41) the American models forswore the fiddle splat and only rarely used the cabriole leg. Their backs were often braced. Popular versions were the low-backed "captain's" chair and those that had spindle additions to the low back, then called the *comb back* or *sack back*. The *fan back* resembled the *comb* without the back support at arm height. A *hooped back* had a continuous bentwood piece that extended from the arms up and over the back. It was also known as the *bow back*.

Figure 5.37 Types of feet frequently seen on Queen Anne style American chairs: (a) slipper; (b) trifid; (c) pad; (d) club.

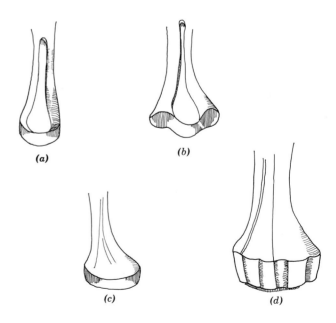

(a)   *(b)*

(c)   *(d)*

Figure 5.38 (above left) Wing chair in the Queen Anne style, New England, ca. 1725. Walnut and maple; covered with original needlepoint fabric. Height, 118.7 cm, width, 80 cm. Metropolitan Museum of Art, New York. (The Metropolitan Museum of Art. Gift of Mrs. J. Insley Blair, 1950.)

Figure 5.39 (above right) Wing chair, Philadelphia, 1740–1750. Height, 119.4 cm, width, 98.4 cm, depth, 69.5 cm. Winterthur Museum, Winterthur, Delaware. (Courtesy, The Henry Francis du Pont Winterthur Museum.)

Figure 5.40 (below) Wing chair, Philadelphia, 1780–1790. Mahogany. Height, 117.5 cm, width, 84 cm, depth, 81.9 cm. Winterthur Museum, Winterthur, Delaware. (Courtesy, The Henry Francis du Pont Winterthur Museum.)

Good stick chairs of the period, like their English prototypes, were strongly modeled. They appeal very much to a wood craftsman's aesthetic sense: George Nakashima, for instance, has made them the inspiration for certain of his contemporary chairs.

Couches or daybeds, and later settees and sofas, followed the usual style trends. As houses grew larger and rooms more numerous, fewer couches were used as beds. Nevertheless, the in-

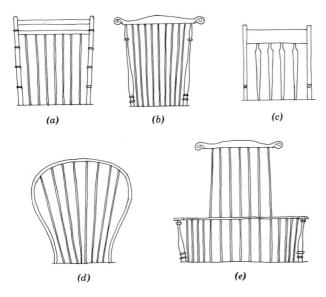

Figure 5.41 Popular names for types of Windsor chair back: (a) rod; (b) fan; (c) arrow; (d) bow; (e) comb.

ventory at Wilton listed a disproportionate number in relation to the number of bedchambers, which suggests that large rooms often had multiple occupancy and sleeping facilities.

Few beds—four-poster in style—have survived. The measurements of one are height, 8 ft, width, 4 ft, 11½ in., and length, 6 ft, 8 in. Later Chippendale-style beds were slightly less tall. Low post beds were common, but being less important they were fill-ins for children and servants and were usually single rather than double width. Provincial ones have come down as the "hired man's bed," but this name is but a romantic limitation placed on their many uses. Half-tester beds with a canopy over the headboard were sometimes designed to fold up against a wall. They were then known as *deception beds*. Beds that simulated a chest of drawers when folded were *press beds*.

There was, however, the usual inventory of chests of the type with drawers. Undoubtedly the most impressive was the highboy (Figure 5.42). In the *Boston News Letter* of May 14, 1714, these pieces were listed as "new fashioned chests." Recall that the popular name is a late nineteenth-century one, although "lowboy" was an occasional eighteenth-century term. The William and Mary highboy arrived in America hard on the

heels of its English counterpart but soon was displaced by pieces in the Queen Anne style, which for a long time had immense popularity, even after Chippendale styles were in vogue in the metropolitan centers. No records list a highboy in a first-floor room. It was a storage piece fre-

Figure 5.42 Tall chest of type commonly called a highboy, Queen Anne style, Boston, 1714–1774. Walnut and cherry (the finials and drops are modern replacements). Height, 2.19 m, width, 1.11 m, depth, 59 cm. Winterthur Museum, Winterthur, Delaware. (Courtesy, The Henry Francis du Pont Winterthur Museum.)

quently located in a bed chamber or in an upper hall.[13]

Queen Anne style desks had a history similar to the Georgian and are discussed under that context. The same can be said of small tables. The most useful dining table was the drop-leaf variety. Several placed end to end increased the seating capacity.

We have alluded to John Pimm as one of the few documented craftsmen of this period in connection with the lacquer highboy. The account book of John Gaines III (1704–1743) of Portsmouth is preserved in the Joseph Downs manuscript collection at Winterthur Museum and has provided valuable information on craft practices. Robert Crosman (1707–1799) of Massachusetts was connected with furniture on which a delicate vine tracery is carved, as seen on a chest at the Detroit Museum of Art. Within the last decade or so of extensive research the veil of obscurity that had surrounded the earliest American craftsmen is being pierced.

Late Georgian: Chippendale Type Furniture. Although much of the furniture of the early eighteenth century is anonymous, that of its later years is associated with the work of individual craftsmen. In America, therefore, even though the Chippendale pattern books from 1762 dictated the overall form, different and imaginative changes were rung on the basic conceptions. In skill of execution, as well, America during the last of the eighteenth century was producing furniture equal to much that was done abroad. At this period we shift our attention to the work done in key cities—to Newport and again to New York and especially to Philadelphia—and estimate others in relation to it.

Newport was a prosperous city before the British blockades destroyed its control of the three-cornered commerce with Africa and the West Indies. In this prewar Newport the third generation of the Townsend family—descended from Christopher and Job—and the second generation of the Goddard family—from the patriarch Daniel—made the superb block-front furniture to be seen in our leading museums. Examples of the work of John Townsend (1732–1809) are at the Metropolitan in New York, the Boston Museum of Fine

Arts, and the Winterthur. John had five cousins and a brother who were cabinetmakers. Therefore Newport furniture can be considered the product of a family monopoly. John's brother was Jonathon (1745–1772), and his cousins were Job, Jr. (1726–1818), Edmund (1735–1811), Robert (d. 1805), James (d. 1827), and Thomas (1742–1822). Hannah, sister of the five brothers, married John Goddard (1723–1785), who was born at Dartmouth, Massachusetts, and had been apprenticed to Job Townsend, Sr. John Goddard and John Townsend are rated as the outstanding craftsmen of this school. As the Townsends and Goddards were Quakers they did not bear arms in the Revolution. Their sympathies, however, were certainly not in doubt, for John Townsend was captured and held prisoner by the British. After his release he is thought to have worked for a time in Middletown, Connecticut, a circumstance that in small part may account for the furniture of that state that occasionally bore the Newport imprint.[14]

The Goddard-Townsend output, largely made between 1750 and 1785, was in the Chippendale style, although some Queen Anne details such as the carved shell motif were evident. The wood was thus customarily mahogany, although other varieties were used. The central splat, which often retained the fiddle shape, was pierced, and the seat was generally slip-over rather than slip-in. Carving was prominent on all Chippendale-type furniture, possibly due here, as in England, to the suitability of the wood for that purpose.

The shell motif that appeared on Townsend-Goddard work was bisymmetrical, with its outer lobe turned down in a *cyma reversa* curve. The anthemion motif was frequently placed on the knees of the chairs and was characterized by an unusually sharp, crisp edge. In all furniture of this period the claw and ball foot predominated. In Newport pieces the ball was full-rounded and the webless claws grasped it firmly, leaving a deep undercut space between the ball and the rear claw (Figure 5.44).

The earmark of Newport furniture is, of course, the block front (Figure 5.43). In cabinets it was designed with two convex outer blocks and one concave inner, thus forming an undulating curve.

Figure 5.43 Chest-on-chest, Townsend-Goddard School, Newport, Rhode Island, 1765–1780. Mahogany and chestnut. Height, 2.44 m, width, 1.02 m, depth, 57 cm. Winterthur Museum, Winterthur, Delaware. (Courtesy, The Henry Francis du Pont Winterthur Museum.)

Although many block fronts were carved from solid timber, the shells as well as the block in Newport pieces were at times done separately and attached. Drawers were flush with the frame and finished with a narrow bead molding. The finial on Newport desk secretaries was distinc-

tive, being a shallow urn with a tight corkscrew flame emerging from its center. On Goddard-Townsend cases the blocking extended through the cyma-bracketed feet which were finished with a characteristic decorative scroll on the inner side.

Block-front furniture was made elsewhere in New England. Benjamin Frothingham, Jr. (1734–1809), of Massachusetts, a major in the Revolutionary War and a friend of Washington, made pieces in this style and in the later Sheraton and Hepplewhite. Similar to those of most Boston craftsmen, his cabinets terminate in a sharp, corkscrew-turned finial. Joseph Hosmer (1735–1821) came from a family of cabinetmakers in Concord. His work shows similarities to Frothingham's. Massachusetts-style cabinets were quite likely to have full-bonneted tops and the fan or shell embellishment confined to the center drawer in the upper and lower sections. In the Massachusetts claw and ball the bird's claw lightly grasped the ball and the flanking ones turned backward in a diagonal line (Figure 5.44).

A specialty of New England cabinetmakers was the case furniture of bombé and kettledrum outline. So expert were these craftsmen that they were capable of creating shapes that not only possessed serpentine or bombé horizontal curves but at the same time curved up and down in kettledrum shape. John Cogswell (d. 1818) of Boston is credited with some of the most elegant examples. His pieces stood out from their more staid Bostonian companions because of their unusually gay bits of rococoish carving.

Connecticut furniture was likely to be heavier and certainly more curvilinear than its more northern counterpart. The enterprise of Aaron Roberts (1758–1831) is recognizable by the details of pinwheel rosettes, a notch in the full-bonneted scroll, a dentiled cornice, an inverted shell on the plinth, and fluted or roped columns at the sides.[15] As with the Townsend-Goddards some of these attributes brushed off on nearby contemporaries and not all similar pieces can be assigned to their originator. Roberts most frequently worked in cherry.

The cousins Aaron and Eliphalet Chapin (1753–1838 and 1741–1838, respectively) of East Windsor, Connecticut, did cabinetry conjointly and

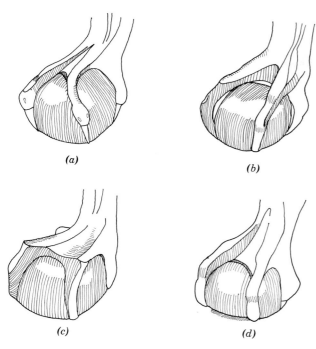

Figure 5.44 Some styles of claw-and-ball feet found on American furniture: (a) side claw extending back in diagonal direction (Massachusetts); (b) space between claw and ball (Rhode Island); (c) claw squared at the knuckles (New York); (d) ball firmly grasped by the claws (Philadelphia). (Drawing based on furniture in the collection of the Metropolitan Museum of Art as pictured in their publication *American Chippendale Furniture: A Picture Book,* New York: 1940.)

separately. Eliphalet spent four years training in Philadelphia and naturally some Philadelphia characteristics were noticeable in his furniture, such as the pierced center finial found on many of his cabinets. The scale of the New England pieces, however, was generally lighter, the wood, cherry rather than mahogany, spiraled rosettes terminated the scrolls of the arches, and fluted quarter columns appeared at the corners. Elijah Booth (1745–1823) was another Connecticut man whose work fitted the general pattern but with individual details such as beading along the edge of cabriole legs and a distinctive carved shell. Benjamin Burnham (active 1769–1773) of Colchester crafted the impressive Connecticut block-front desk at the Metropolitan Museum of Art.

The Dunlaps of New Hampshire were most interesting provincial cabinetmakers (Figure 5.45). Here in the less cosmopolitan area, near Chester

Figure 5.45 High chest of drawers made in the shop of Major John Dunlap, Bedford, New Hampshire, ca. 1780. Maple and white pine. Height, 2.11 m, width, 1.06 m, depth, 53 cm. Winterthur Museum, Winterthur, Delaware. (Courtesy, The Henry Francis du Pont Winterthur Museum.)

and Salisbury, Samuel Dunlap settled with his family in the early years of the eighteenth century. His son, Samuel II, seems to have been the first Dunlap to take up the trade. There was also a contemporary John Dunlap, but of the family

219

connections and enterprises not too much is known at present. All furniture attributed to the group is easily recognizable by its short legs, correspondingly high backs, and tall proportions. Pediments are upswept open-laced scrolls; the aprons are unusually deep, and they have a central motif resembling intertwined snakes or a crude caduceus. Although much of the work was in cherry or maple, many pieces were painted. It is said that the first Dunlap came from Ireland and here married Martha Neal. The magic of St. Patrick seems to have guided the chisels and awls of their descendants.

In New York chairs represented the major furniture contribution. Although tall chests and case goods were also made, few American highboys can be attributed to this area. Fretted cornices and broad fluted and chamfered corners are found on other pieces. Gilbert Ash (1717–1785) and Samuel Prince (?–1778) were well-known cabinetmakers of the district. The chairs of Gilbert Ash are a cross between Queen Anne and Chippendale in style, another of the American hybrids. Although only one known chair bears the Ash label, we are fortunate to possess several groups that are attributed to him through similarity. They are to be seen at Winterthur, at the Metropolitan, and in the Garvan collection at Yale.

Ash's chairs have the customary New York Queen Anne rounded seats, but have stump rear legs rather than the club variety found on most New York Chippendale chairs. The claw and ball on his chairs was sinuously curved, whereas in most allied pieces the profile was the block variety squared at the knuckles (Figure 5.44). The rear talon on New York chairs is often poorly articulated and the ball foot is grasped by claws that form almost a right angle with the leg. Ash falls in line with other New Yorkers in respect to the heaviness of the foliated carving as it appears on knees and top rails. It has neither the tightness of the New Englander nor the looseness of the Philadelphian. The tasselated motif and gadrooning on the bottom of the seat are additional New York details.

Samuel Prince is known by several isolated pieces, of which the most recognizable is the desk at Winterthur.

The Philadelphia school during the late Georgian period is characterized by a predilection for fine woods, graceful outlines, and profuse carving in the freest Rococo patterns, separately made and glued to the finished body. The exuberance of this ornament is so outstanding that it cannot be mistaken for that of any other group of artisans, and the more one observes it the more one is inclined to acknowledge at least a temperamental relation to Ireland.

Philadelphia pieces were relatively large but not so expansive as those from New York. With none of the primness of the North, Philadelphia chairs flaunted a bow top rail which often ended in a pagoda-shaped upward swing and undulated in the third dimension into the scrolled finial occasionally called a *swept whorl*. The back splat sometimes combined Chinese and Gothic details in an overall pierced fiddle shape which indicated remarkable imagination in forging a unity from many borrowed scraps. The feet consisted of a slightly flattened ball firmly grasped by the claws (Figure 5.44) and the rear legs were stumped. Aprons were elaborately shaped and, as in New York, frequently edged with gadrooning. Philadelphia retained many of these characteristics until well into the later, straight-legged period.

The Philadelphia school produced some of America's most famous highboys and lowboys at a time long past dating this type in England (Figure 5.46). These and other comparable Philadelphia chests were characterized by loose, flame-shaped, and urn finials, an asymmetrical open-pierced central motif, a vigorously curved bonnet, loosely conceived applied ornament, and the finest of matched veneers displayed on a flat front.

Knowledge of the men who created these masterpieces has been the result of comparatively recent investigation. Not so many years ago William Savery (1721–1788) was almost the sole craftsman whose work had been documented in a lowboy at Van Cortland Manor. Since then some twenty or more pieces bearing his label have been identified. His work still holds merit for well-proportioned design and good craftsmanship.

The present field of study is much more ex-

Figure 5.46 High chest known as the Van Pelt highboy, Philadelphia, 1765–1780. Cuban mahogany, tulipwood, white cedar, and oak. Height, 2.29 m, width, 1.16 m, depth, 65 cm. Winterthur Museum, Winterthur, Delaware. (Courtesy, The Henry Francis du Pont Winterthur Museum.)

tensive. It is convenient to consider some of the men in alphabetical order. Thomas Affleck (d. 1795), who was born in Scotland, is thought to have been trained in England. He did some of the most elaborate carving ascribed to the Philadelphia group. Much of his Chippendale furniture was characterized by the use of the Marlborough straight leg on which he lavished decoration that was more formally disposed than the usual Philadelphia work.

John Folwell's claim to fame rests in the making of the Speaker's Chair for Independence Hall in 1779. It is an imposing, oddly proportioned object with a high Chippendale-style back and straight legs reinforced by stretchers.

James Gillingham (1736–1781), a Pennsylvania craftsman, was best known for his chairs. Examples on display at the Metropolitan and again at Winterthur make use of a distinctive trefoil pattern in the fretted backs, taken in essence from the first edition of the Director.

Jonathan Gostelowe (1745–1795), another native Pennsylvanian is famous for his serpentine-front chests which could rival the New England pieces (Figure 5.47). The Philadelphia Museum possesses one, another is at Cliveden (now a National Trust property), and a third, at Winterthur. These are masterpieces in the late Chippendale style where Rococo ornament gives way to the beauty of pure form.

Benjamin Randolph (active 1750–1780), about whom there are few vital statistics known other than that he was born in New Jersey, is often acclaimed the greatest of the Philadelphia cabinetmakers. Certainly he was one of the most accomplished carvers. Many of the chairs attributed to him are so designated because of undeniable

Figure 5.47 Chest of drawers, attributed to Jonathan Gostelowe, Philadelphia, 1775–1780. Mahogany, tulipwood, and pine. Height, 91.7 cm, width, 120 cm, depth, 66 cm. Winterthur Museum, Winterthur, Delaware. (Courtesy, The Henry Francis du Pont Winterthur Museum.)

likeness to a set of six pattern chairs that descended in his family. The Chippendale wing chair at the Philadelphia Museum, which contains a carved masque conjectured to be a likeness of Benjamin Franklin(?), has furred paw feet and much shallow carving over legs and apron. Jefferson commissioned furniture from Randolph, and it is thought that he made the table on which the Declaration of Independence was drafted.

Randolph's work is another example of the belief that elaboration frequently commands the market price. It is said[16] that the Philadelphia easy chair just mentioned was sold at the Reifsnyder auction in New York City in 1929 for $33,000, the highest price paid up to that time for an American-made armchair. The Reifsnyder highboy, which changed hands at this same auction, was scarcely a cheap piece of storage furniture.[17] It was an outstanding example of the elaborate veneering and carving of which the Philadelphia group was capable.

Daniel Trotter (d. 1800) worked in a style transitional between that of Chippendale and the later Neoclassicists. He shared a shop in Elfreth's Alley (that charming street in Philadelphia of small eighteenth-century houses) with his son-in-law Ephraim Haines (1775–1811). Their specialty was a type of ladder-back chair that is familiarly known as a "pretzel" chair because the back slat had a small open center with intertwined curves.

Last of all we must include Thomas Tufft (1740–1788) who made a pair of labeled chairs now at Winterthur and a lowboy at the Philadelphia Museum. His work bears some relation to that of Gillingham, whose Second Street shop he eventually took over. His use of carving was more restrained.

Much New Jersey and Maryland furniture of the Chippendale style was related to the Philadelphia center. The southern city of Charleston was a hub for the making of the large architectural goods needed to fill the spacious high-ceiling rooms of the south. Free negroes and slaves were often the hands that fabricated these artistic pieces.

One known cabinetmaker was Thomas Elfe, Sr. (1719–1775), who was born in London, came to Charleston, and entered into partnership with Thomas Hutchinson. His pen earned him more fame than his cabinetmaking. The Charleston Library displays Elfe's account book for the years 1768 to 1775 which indicates that he catered to an influential trade. Nevertheless, not a single labeled piece of his has been found. In the archives of museums are treasured the ledgers of several craftsmen. Randolph's is at Winterthur.

Studies of southern cabinetry are still in their infancy. Organizations such as the Museum of Early Southern Decorative Arts (MESDA) at Winston-Salem, North Carolina, are furthering research in the work done in southern locales.

Federal: Hepplewhite-Sheraton Type Furniture. The first center of Federal craftsmanship was around Salem and Boston. The M. and M. Karolik Collection at the Boston Museum of Fine Arts (Martha Codman Karolik was a great-granddaughter of Elias Hasket Derby, the Salem shipmaster who ordered much of this furniture) possesses what is rated top rank in this field. Here we enter the epoch in which diversification and specialization allowed a piece to be assigned to several craftsmen; for example, Samuel McIntire did the carving on the chest that William Lemon (?–1827) made for Derby (Figure 5.48). It was placed at Oak Hill in Peabody, Massachusetts, the home that McIntire designed for Elias's daughter, Elizabeth Derby West.[18] This chest is now at the Boston Museum with rooms from the mansion.

In a similar manner Stephan Badlam, Sr. (1751–1815), made an elaborate chest for the same patron. Its carving was executed by John Skillin (1746–1800). It is now in the Mabel Brady Garvan Collection at Yale. McIntire also carved furniture for Elijah and Jacob Sanderson (worked 1779–1820), whose Salem accounts are at the Salem Essex Institute.

There has been considerable discussion about what, if any, complete articles of furniture Samuel McIntire did make. The consensus seems to be that in certain instances he did the carving on pieces that were executed by competent cabinetmakers. In others, in which carving and body seemed integrated, he may have been entirely responsible. In any event, the style that is associated with his name is to be seen in Hepplewhite's *Cabinet Maker's Guide* and in the early edition of and by a superbly carved vine motif running down the tapered rectilinear legs. Known for his expertise with the chisel, we look for his insignia—the stylized baskets and cornucopias of fruit and flowers, festoons, shocked wheat, and fluting that alternates with representational motifs.

The Boston firm of John Seymour (ca. 1738—ca. 1818) and his son Thomas (1771–1848), who came from Devon, England, by way of Portland, Maine, embraced a wider spread of styles. Beginning with the delicate Federal, Thomas's late work includes a few articles in the early Greek Revival manner. Like McIntire, the Seymours worked principally in mahogany and figured maple but they also used more exotic and expensive

Figure 5.49   Chair from a set of furniture made for the Derby family, attributed to Samuel McIntire, Salem, Massachusetts, eighteenth century. Height, 97.1 cm. Cleveland Museum of Art. (The Cleveland Museum of Art. Purchase from the J. H. Wade Fund.)

Figure 5.48   Chest-on-chest, William Lemon, cabinetmaker, and Samuel McIntire, carver, Boston and Salem, Massachusetts, 1796. Museum of Fine Arts, Boston. (Courtesy Museum of Fine Arts, Boston. M. and M. Karolik Collection.)

Sheraton's *Drawing Book*. When an entire chair is attributed to McIntire, like the shield-back mahogany example at the Cleveland Museum of Art (Figure 5.49), it is characterized by a sharp base to the shield which almost touches the seat

Figure 5.50 Tambour desk, Boston, 1794–1804, labeled John Seymour & Son. Mahogany. Height, 1.05 m, width, 95.9 cm, depth, 50.2 cm. Winterthur Museum, Winterthur, Delaware. (Courtesy, The Henry Francis du Pont Winterthur Museum.)

woods like rosewood and satinwood. Mahogany, for hidden parts, is frequently found in place of cheaper timber. Their craftsmanship in handling veneers and inlays is astounding and their joinery shows clearly their fine English training (Figure 5.50). Special, although not unique, earmarks are tambour shutter closings of alternating dark and light strips and inlay recognized by several highly individual patterns such as the lunette, pilaster, feather, and a series of alternating husks and dots enclosed in an arched frame. When the straight tapered leg was used, the Seymour pieces were usually braced with a characteristic scrolled bracket. When their furniture had tapered fluted legs, the knop was accompanied by three turned rings or groups of rings. One easily recognizable trademark is the light blue-green lining of paper or paint, which was customarily given to their cabinet or drawer interiors. Battersea enamels

were sometimes used as escutcheons on Seymour case goods. Wedgwood was used similarly on English pieces, Sèvres on French. Certain bow-shaped commodes were among their handsomest articles. Another type was the pedimented tambour desk of which there are three known examples.

Affleck, Gostelowe, and Haines continued to work in Philadelphia into the post-revolutionary period—later production that is well-represented at the Philadelphia Museum. The *field bed* was designed by but by no means exclusive to Haines.

One truly Federal piece was the graceful armchair commonly called the *Martha Washington* because it is associated with Mrs. Washington's chamber at Mt. Vernon. It was also known as the "lolling chair" and indeed it occasionally had an adjustable back and footrests—our first "recliner." Like the seat, its tall back was upholstered. The delicately turned arms swung forward to connect directly with the spiral legs.

Henry Connelly (1770–1826) was a designer who, like Ephraim Haines, counted among his patrons members of the Philadelphia elite such as Stephen Girard and Henry Hollingsworth. His pieces were lavishly carved and their shield backs were well rounded. Sheraton straight backs have a wider central splat and are not so tall as their English counterparts. The fretwork in the splat often simulates intertwined garlands in Chippendale style.

Connelly is famous for having made some of America's most beautiful range tables (Figure 5.51) both in Sheraton and in the slightly later Regency style (i.e., with splayed legs from a central support; see Chapter 17). His were three-part pieces, the central table having two drop leaves, the rounded end tables having one each.

Because of the expansion of the shipbuilding industry, Baltimore and Annapolis were prominent post-Revolutionary cities. The cabinetmakers of these two localities produced some late Chippendale-style furniture and are especially renowned for their Sheraton and Hepplewhite-inspired items, which had crossbanding and inlays of lighter woods. They also managed a brisk trade in "fancy chairs" and painted furniture.

Such men as John Shaw (1745–1829),[19] who came from Scotland, and his onetime partner

Figure 5.51 Du Pont dining room. American furniture, late eighteenth century: pair of inlaid sideboards, probably made in New York, which illustrate the early combination of several pieces (used earlier by Robert Adam) into one article; a three-part table known as a range table; urn-back chairs, New York; secretary and bookcase, Massachusetts. Winterthur Museum, Winterthur, Delaware. (Courtesy, The Henry Francis du Pont Winterthur Museum.)

Archibald Chisholm were Baltimore cabinetmakers. Shaw was an ardent American patriot and served his state in many capacities. In much of his furniture the new ciphers of the Republic, such as the eagle, were displayed.

Craft Organization

In America, although the crafts were organized in a manner similar to the European, no furniture guilds existed. During the seventeenth century furniture makers were joiners. As their work became more diversified and specialized these craftsmen divided into chairmakers and cabinetmakers, whose specialty was case goods. Carving was done by the carver. The learning system was similar to that of the guilds—a master craftsman and his apprentices who when trained became journeymen. During the eighteenth century an enterprising cabinetmaker often set himself up as a jobber and, opening a shop, employed others, or he contracted for work and availed himself of

225

the services of others on a fee basis. This same entrepreneur sometimes owned a warehouse from which he sold not only his own stock but many imported items.

As early as 1757 joiners (the generalized name continued in use) in Providence, Rhode Island, drew up a price list for their work. This was patterned on the *London Book of Prices and Design of Cabinet Work* previously mentioned. In 1796 *The Cabinetmakers Philadelphia and London Book of Prices* was published. After the Revolution, in an era of economic unrest, the journeymen formed societies to better their positions with their master craftsmen, who at that time established a code of fair wages, a cost-of-living wage, and an eleven-hour day.

As had been the custom abroad, craftsmen located their shops in proximity to one another. In New York the furniture trades were located at Broad and Wall streets. In Philadelphia it was Second Street. The cabinetmaker frequently lived above or adjacent to his shop. The names of these establishments were picturesque: "The Sign of the Chest of Drawers" or "The Golden Eagle." In turning an honest penny he did not limit his work to furniture. Wagon wheels, rolling pins, wooden buttons, and coffins were among the articles he sold. A considerable capital was required to finance such a shop and, when put up for sale, an inventory worth 1500 pounds in coin of the realm, as indicated for Benjamin Randolph's liquidation, was not unusual.

Apparently the southern centers had difficulty hiring workmen. Charles Watts (d. 1811), a cabinetmaker, advertised in New York City for

> . . . 8 to 15 journeymen to go to Charleston S.C. where they will receive generous encouragement. . . . I will oblige myself to pay any workman, who is capable of doing the general run of cabinetwork, seventy five percent on the New York, London Book of Cabinet Prices established in 1795. I will also advance in passage money whosoever chooses to come in the above line; and find work for any or all of the above number, for 6, 9, or 12 months without board, or find them it at three and 1/2 dollars per week.[20]

There is no record of the number of takers.

AMERICAN CLOCKS, EIGHTEENTH AND EARLY NINETEENTH CENTURIES

America boasted a number of important clockmakers and also forged to the front with inventions that placed good clocks within the financial reach of the average man.

Although William Cottey (1655–1711) set up in the clock business in Philadelphia in 1682 and one of his pieces survives, nevertheless the tall clock, known here as the grandfather clock, was seen earliest in its Queen Anne version which long retained its popularity. One of the prominent makers of this type was David Rittenhouse (1732–1796) of Philadelphia. Recall that the name on the clock was customarily the name of the maker of the works rather than of the maker of the case. Cases followed the working styles in furniture of regional craftsmen. Sometimes the case carried the name of the dealer, which fact, inasmuch as brass works were often imported, was not intended as a misrepresentation but rather as a guarantee of quality.

In addition to the case, the face and dials help to identify a clock. Until about 1770 the face of an American clock was brass sometimes with attached silver circlets or dial rings and spandrels or corner pieces. After this date a white-enameled iron plate became common, although brass and silver were not entirely discarded. During the last quarter of the century painted wood also appeared as a substitute for the less available costly materials. About 1837 painting was done on thin pieces of metal and thus durability and economy were served.

The face, at first square shaped, added an arched top early in the century. This addition included the ornamentation which around the year 1760 was often the moon in circuit.

Hands were steel but in early clocks there were neither minute marks nor minute hands. Roman numerals with their feet to the center were adopted for the hour marks.

About the year 1800 (it must be understood that many of the dates in this section are approximate), when all American industry was awakening to the pulse of mass or factory production, clock making was no exception. Simon Willard (1753–1848), the Massachusetts clockmaker, represented a generation that bridged handicrafting and machine manufacture. He made superlative clock works and his reputation was so high that he was frequently counterfeited.

Simon's brothers—all sons of Benjamin Willard, Sr.—were clockmakers: Benjamin, Jr. (1743–1803), Ephraim (1775–ca. 1835), and Aaron (1757–1844). His own sons, Simon, Jr. (1795–1874) and Benjamin F. (1803–1847) were also horologists and several distant cousins must be included in this specialized group. John Doggett of Roxbury, Massachusetts, was the man engaged by Simon, Sr., to make most of his cases.

Although Simon was by inclination the inventor and craftsman, it was Aaron, the business opportunist, who grew wealthy by manufacturing clocks in large numbers in a type of production-line enterprise. Most of this output was in mantel clocks sometimes known under the Willard name and sometimes called the Massachusetts shelf clock. Mantel clocks had been manufactured throughout the eighteenth century. They were occasionally called half-clocks because they resembled half a grandfather clock and were intended to stand on a mantel or shelf. The general dates assigned to the Willard mantel clocks are 1800 to 1820. Some had painted glass fronts, an innovation attributed to the Willards. The *banjo clock,* shaped like a banjo, is another type invented by Simon Willard on rights patent in 1802 (Figure 5.52).

The best-known name in mantel-clock manufacture is that of the firm of Eli Terry. Eli (1772–1852) established factories in New Windsor and Plymouth, Connecticut. He was one of the first advocates of that fundamentally American principle of trying to make something good for less money and watching people beat a path to his door. He is said to have taken out the first American patent for the improvement of clock works. These sold for four dollars each without their cases and fifteen with. Eli took his two sons, Eli, Jr. (1799–1841), and Henry (1802–1877), into his business and most of the extant Terry clocks postdate that union.

Some of the Terry-type clocks were made by Seth Thomas (1785–1859) who bought the right to copy the Terry clocks. The Seth Thomas firm is still in business. To Chauncey Jerome (the firm of C. and N. Jerome, Bristol, Connecticut) goes the

Figure 5.52 Wall clock (known as a banjo clock), Simon Willard, Roxbury, Massachusetts, 1802–1810. Height, 1.05 m, width, 26.3 cm, depth, 9.5 cm. Winterthur Museum, Winterthur, Delaware. (Courtesy, The Henry Francis du Pont Winterthur Museum.)

honor of exporting the first American clock to England in 1824. He applied the principle of adding the inexpensive wire pinion to the brass one-day clock. Thus began the revolution in American clockmaking that gave it the lead in inexpensive and accurate manufacture.

The Terry or Thomas clocks are marked by a scroll top, a square face with a round dial, and some sort of scrolled legs. Below the dial a scene was painted on the glass, no doubt one of the selling points. Face numerals were arabic and vertical. Early Terrys were likely to have wooden works but after 1837 sheet brass was used. The appearance of these later clocks follows closely the current style phases.

TEXTILES

Types

America, which moved quickly into the field of fine furniture production during the eighteenth century, was equally opportunist in manufacturing textiles. In 1700 native weavings were still largely linen and wool and some West Indian cotton.

It is well known that the colonists attempted to grow the mulberry and to cultivate the silkworm. The priceless gnarled tree on the Palace Green at Williamsburg is a mute reminder of this enterprise. In Georgia land was granted to the settlers on condition that they plant one hundred of these food reservoirs for the silkworm for every ten acres. In 1749 the British Parliament exempted from duty all raw silk certified to be the product of Georgia or Carolina. Connecticut developed a surprising home industry in sericulture after mideighteenth century. A blight which affected the mulberry finally put the quietus to silk manufacture in the United States.[21]

Thus all the natural fibers were available for cloth production during the greater part of the eighteenth century. It can be conjectured, however, that supplies were limited and that cotton and silk were not extensively made into cloth for home consumption. Homely textiles are often mentioned in inventories. The big problem, of course, relates to the interpretation of their names, and the historian finds that errors have occasionally been made by assigning a new cloth to an old name. A few interpretations are listed here. Wool materials were first the plain weave *tammy* and *durant* which derived both their names and character from the old cloths of Europe, such as the English *stamen* and the French *étamine à voile*. Often both frabrics were glazed to render them more highly light reflective and to change their texture. They resembled present-day voile in being made of highly twisted yarns and so possessed the quality of relative sheerness with strength.[22]

For upholstery material *calamanco* was used. This was a wool in a satin twill weave, meaning that its warp overshot was over more than three binding threads and that it had a regular progression to right or left with each throw of the shuttle. A close, compact cloth resulted. To glamourize calamanco it is known to have occasionally been brightened with some silk in the overshot. *Moreen* held its own as an upholstery fabric until well after the Revolution. This was a plain weave mohair-woolen which came from England. It was roller engraved by a process designed to flatten portions of the surface (*watered cloth*). Sometimes the marking was in designs that gave the superficial appearance of a damask. Among the linens, *holland* was a plain and *huckaback* a diapered weave. Linen damask was costly and most of it came from abroad.

Even though homespuns were used by the wealthy, especially in rooms of lesser importance, imported fabrics nevertheless played their part in the economy. Undoubtedly silks such as damasks, brocades, and brocatelles were imported from Lyon and Spitalsfield. The colorful Indian cottons, both printed and painted, along with their English cousins, quickly found their way to the American market. They were advertised as being sold from a Boston warehouse in 1738.

Nor did the American shrink from attempting fabric decoration. One "Callender Mill and Dye House" in the *Boston News Letter* for 1712 speaks of printing "All kinds of linnens."[23] Printers and engravers often offered to place patterns on fabrics. Occasionally an enterprising housewife publicized that she ". . . stamps linen china blue or any color that gentlemen and ladies fancies."[24]

One of the first professional cloth printers was John Hewson who came from England in 1773 when Benjamin Franklin assured him that calico printers were needed. Mrs. Washington is said to have worn dresses of the fabric he printed.[25] Before the Revolution, however, English competition forced such enterprises almost out of existence.

The weaving industry in America was one of the first to be organized. In the beginning a man who owned a loom, like Manasseh Minor (1647–1728) of Stonington, Connecticut,[26] would receive the spun yarn from a housewife and weave it into cloth. This local weaver was often a farmer who moonlighted in this manner to increase his earnings. Sometimes itinerant weavers worked on local looms which could have been the property of one householder. In plantation country the plantation hands were the weavers.

By 1788 cotton mills with powered machinery were set up in Philadelphia and in Beverly, Massachusetts. Many others soon followed. Sample books of these companies are extant with samples and handwritten inventories.

Cotton materials here, as abroad, became increasingly fashionable in Neoclassic years. References to such cotton fabrics as *cords* and *dimities* were more frequent, the former possibly being a heavier material of broken twill suited to upholstery and bed coverings and the latter probably resembling what we call dimity today.[27] When Jefferson returned from France in 1789, he brought with him "eight cords with crimson tassels" and a bundle of "mixed chintz and a piece of Toile de Jouy." Seersucker, which was then a cloth of alternating silk and cotton stripes, was imported from India.

Uses

The manner of using these materials in the interiors of eighteenth-century buildings must be deduced from inventories, wills, and personal notations. It is apparent that, in addition to upholstery, textiles were intended for bedcoverings, bed curtains, and possibly bedroom window curtains. Although it is almost heresy to say so, elaborate window draperies seem to have been a phenomenon of the latter part of the century and

then only in the homes of the wealthy and in the most important rooms. Elizabeth Delhonde, whose Boston estate was valued at £11,000 in 1749, had no window curtains, although she owned such costly furniture as her

> . . . work'd Camblet [a material made of camel's hair and silk] Bed, Counterpane and 8 silk chairs.[28]

Even at mid-century only one in five of the household inventories of wealthy Boston citizens mention any window curtains at all.[29] Exceptional is the oft-publicized listing of such a rich Bostonian as Peter Faneuil, in which several sets of matching bed and window curtains are noted.[30] The South, without puritanical inhibitions, may have indulged a taste for grandeur in a manner not usual to the North.

Later in the century elaborate draperies were more customary. In Tazewell Hall, the home of John Randolph, a deed of trust of 1775 mentions "handsome crimson curtains."[31]

Trade books such as those of Banting and Son of London showed patterns for window and bed treatments then in fashion. One Banting design, followed for the nursery field bed at Stratford, called for forty-three yards of dimity, seventy yards of binding, and two yards of calico tape and thread. Jefferson speaks of using seventeen yards of dimity for one window at Monticello, which must have been one of the tall ones on the ground floor.

Jefferson not only brought fabrics from Europe, a not unusual custom in those days, but he also took notes about the manner of making this material into curtains—first for his house in Philadelphia occupied when he was Secretary of State, and thereafter at Monticello. Meanwhile, when he became president, he broke with the tradition of using silks in important rooms and furnished the White House with chintz in the public rooms and dimity in many private apartments, including the large dining room. Many hangings were merely valances in shaped silhouettes, the edges of which were decorated with braid. When used in bedrooms, they closely duplicated the valances of the beds. Curtains of varying lengths, often only over the upper part of the window, were festooned or hung straight under them.

In contemporary English pictures we occasionally see single broad window curtains hung from metal rings or tape loops. This one curtain was then either drawn to the side, shuttled across the window, or hooked up in a swag. That they were used in America is evident from the fact that many inventories list an odd number of curtains and therefore they could not have been hung in pairs.

It should not be forgotten that Venetian blinds were as popular in America as abroad. George Washington writes:

> Desire Matthew to give me the exact dimensions of the windows . . . of the dining room; with the casement . . . that I may get a venetian blind, such as draws up and closes and expands, made here, that others may be made by it at home.[32]

Thus, although we must revise our ideas downward about the elaborateness of the use of textiles during the first part of the eighteenth century, the latter half provides full warrant that fashionable England and France set the tone.

FLOOR COVERINGS

What did affluent eighteenth-century America use on its floors? Oriental rugs to be sure. Merchant ships from the Orient and probably from embarkation points in the Near East found a ready market for their goods in warehouses along the Atlantic. In 1761 a Boston advertisement reads "Rich Persian carpets, 1 × 4 and 4 × 5 yards square."[33] In the refurnishing of Governor Tryon's Palace during the nineteen fifties, which took its clues from a 1773 inventory of the Governor's belongings, a large Ispahan measuring 34 ft square acquired from the Braganza Palace in Portugal was installed in the Council Chamber. Such large pieces, if indeed they were procurable outside the courts of Europe, could only have been an item for a hall of state. More likely would have been the ". . . large Turkey carpet measuring 11½ × 18 feet" included in the 1754 auction of the properties of Mr. Ebenezer Holmes of Boston.[34]

As mentioned in Chapter 4, considerable ambiguity existed in carpet nomenclature. We recall that before the middle of the century the bulk of

the weaving at Wilton and Axminster was by hand. Washington writes for:

> . . . new carpeting as will cover the floor of my blue parlour. Wilton 'if it is not so much dearer than Scotch carpeting—a suitable border, if it is to be had, should accompany the carpeting.[35]

Scotch carpeting, which superficially resembled *inlaid* or *Kidderminster carpeting*, was thicker than the latter and was a double cloth, meaning a flat weave with two warps and two wefts made on a hand draw loom. It was produced extensively in Scotland where hand weavers were readily available.[36] The Governor's bedroom at Tryon has been furnished with one Turkey-pattern English Wilton carpet woven about 1750.

In addition, various English embroidered pieces must have been used for eighteenth-century interiors on both sides of the Atlantic. French looms were manufacturing Aubussons and Savonneries. It is reputed that the carpet now (but not earlier, for Washington would not accept state gifts for personal use) in the Banquet Hall at Mt. Vernon was woven on a French loom at the order of Louis XVI as a gift to General Washington. It has the coat of arms of the United States in its center.[37]

Carpets in eighteenth-century semantics were floor coverings. A rug (equivalent to a bed rug) was similar to the seventeenth-century wool-on-wool coverlet and was intended as a warm covering for a bed or table or as a hearth rug to be placed over a more valuable carpet for protection near the fire. In a bequest to a young Virginia girl, Mary Ball, later mother of George Washington, we read of a bed with "One suit of good curtains . . . one Rugg, one quilt, one pair of blankets."[38] Undoubtedly the small rug was meant.

Between the soft small rug and the large heavier carpet came the "floor cloths." We know them as oil cloths—or canvas covered with a coat of oil paint. In the *Virginia Gazette* in 1769 there appeared an advertisement of one Joseph Kidd, "Upholsterer in Williamsburg," in which he made the following statement:

> Hangs rooms with paper or damask, stuffs sophas, couches, and chairs, in the neatest manner, makes all sorts of bed furniture, window cur-

tains and matrasses, and fits carpets to any room with the greatest exactness . . . and paints floor cloths . . . according to directions.[39]

These floor cloths sometimes imitated marble tiles or foreign carpets. Even in Jefferson's time many of the floors of the White House, including the large entrance hall, were covered with painted canvas.[40]

EMBROIDERIES

The eighteenth century with its wealth and city living allowed women some leisure. In addition to the ubiquitous sampler on which girls were taught stitchery, the making of various types of embroidery became fashionable for the first time in America. It was considered a fit occupation for the daughters of the well-to-do and was often a part of boarding school curricula. The "Fishing Lady" embroideries were undoubtedly made at some such institution. It is known that a Mrs. Susannah Condy conducted a school for embroidery in Boston. The "Fishing Lady" embroideries were all done in a fine wool tent stitch on canvas and portray a lady fishing in a park pool while a cavalier stands beside her. The Boston Museum owns several of these interesting pieces. The famous needlework picture of the Boston Commons made by Hannah Otis (1732–1773) is privately owned.

Needlework became even more important as a feminine occupation during the nineteenth century when hooked rugs and patchwork quilts, as American as apple pie, were made. They were often the result of group effort, done at sewing bees which offered periods of sociability for women stranded in small settlements.

So city dwellers and western pioneers contributed their bit to the aesthetic folk lore of a new country. It should also be remembered that the hatchment, or embroidered coat-of-arms, was a favorite symbol of a family's importance and a reminder of a cultural system it had left behind forever but which it was loathe to relinquish.

WALLCOVERINGS

As soon as wall sections were plastered, painting and stenciling were used to enrich them. Good examples of these crafts, dating from the eighteenth and early nineteenth centuries, can be seen at the Shelburne (Figure 5.53) and Cooperstown Museums of Folk Art. Work of this sort is attributed to itinerant painters such as the shadowy figure named Stimp who would decorate both walls and floors in exchange for room and board.[41]

Wallpapers were at the other end of the economic ladder. Coming into popularity in America around 1750, the earliest came from England and later from France. "Painted papers" predated "stampt papers in Rolls for to Paper Rooms," as an advertisement in the New England Journal of 1730 read.[42]

It appears to be a matter of some question just when the first wallpaper was manufactured in America, but it was undoubtedly made by Plunkett Fleeson of Philadelphia some time after the mideighteenth century. Fleeson advertised in 1761, "American Paper Hangings, all kinds and colors, as good as the imported and at the same price."[43] Other names of manufacturers began to appear at about this time. The principal centers were Boston and Philadelphia, with secondary ones in Albany and Baltimore.

The quality of the foreign papers, however, was unexcelled. The English examples indicate the artistic influence of Baptist Jackson and the most charming are those depicting natural foliage. Thomas Hancock of Boston, who incidentally was a bookseller, stationer, and importer of fine English wallpapers, when ordering from a London manufacturer in 1737 asked for a paper with a ". . . Great Variety of Different Sorts of Birds, Peakocks, Macoys and Squirrels, Monkys, Fruit, Flowers, etc."[44] He might conceivably have imported Jackson papers.

It is known that the wallpaper in the second Van Rensselaer Manor House in Albany (built by Stephen Van Rensselaer in 1765–1768 and dismantled in 1893; its hall is now at the Metropolitan) was ordered especially for this location from Jackson of London in 1768 (Figure 5.54). It is a painted paper with remarkable scenes taken from engravings of European eighteenth-century paintings and surrounded by scrolls and grotesques. This example represents the high point of English wallpaper design used in America.

French papers were understandably popular

Figure 5.53 Room in the Stencil House with designs stenciled directly on the wall boarding. House originally built in Columbus, New York, ca. 1790; moved in 1953 to Shelburne, Vermont. Some of the stencil patterns are attributed to Moses Eaton. Note the rocking chair, Windsor chairs, and Queen Anne-type side table. Shelburne Museum, Shelburne, Vermont. (Courtesy of The Shelburne Museum, Shelburne, Vermont.)

Figure 5.54 Entry hall, Van Rensselaer Manor, Albany, New York, 1765–1769. Jackson of London wallpaper; Queen Anne style chairs and tables; Chippendale-style sofa. Metropolitan Museum of Art, New York. (The Metropolitan Museum of Art.)

after the War for Independence. The first might have been those of Réveillon, but credited ones are more likely to have come from the factory of Jaquemart and Benard. Governor Gore of Massachusetts (Gore Place) writes of ordering French paper in 1806. The Metropolitan has a French paper from Eagle House in Haverhill, Massachusetts.

Although the wallpaper patterns followed current style trends (even to the costuming of the figures), they may be grouped in two categories. The first included the geometrics which copied the textiles of the time and the second was comprised of the pictorials (Figure 5.55). Often they were combined as scenics within smaller medallions—known as landscape medallions. A few were embossed to resemble satin.

Although most Chinese-style papers that reached America were made in France, several houses in the port of Salem were papered in Chinese tea papers and Salem's Assembly House had painted paper from China on its walls.

CERAMICS

The early beginnings of the ceramic and glass industries in America were retarded because of the

Figure 5.55 Library cross hall, Winterthur. French wallpaper, *The Monuments of Paris;* Persian Joshagan carpet; chairs by Stephen Badlam, Boston, and Stone and Alexander, Boston; desk, Boston: Simon Willard tall clock. Winterthur Museum, Winterthur, Delaware. (Courtesy, The Henry Francis du Pont Winterthur Museum.)

cost of equipment, the preference for continental products, and the proscriptions of the mother country against American production. Nevertheless, both industries were begun in the first half of the eighteenth century.

The second American tradition (following the seventeenth-century "redware") began in a small way and was the result of the character of some of the clay found from the Carolinas north to New Jersey, the "unaker" known to the Indians. This produced a whiter and harder body and pro-

vided the basis for American stoneware. Before the discovery of kaolin in Vermont this southern unaker may have been imported for the manufacture of stoneware in New England. This northern stoneware is to be found in larger jugs and pots, salt-glazed and often decorated with freely drawn designs in blue. These pieces have a distinct charm because of the easily appreciated alliance of hard body and sturdy shapes, the seemingly integral character of the glaze, and the freedom of the brush work.

Samples of the pottery of the Pennsylvania Germans date from the late eighteenth century (Figure 5.56), although some of their most famous pieces are nineteenth century. Made from red clays, sgraffito, slip-trailing, and painted techniques were all used for decoration.

Designs on all American German folk art derive ultimately from Germany, homeland of the Pennsylvania Dutch. A people with strong religious–family motivation, they were accustomed to commemorate such occasions as births and weddings with pictorial and written documents that were often framed and kept as family heirlooms. These pieces have descended under the

Figure 5.56 Glazed slipware pottery with sgraffito decoration, Pennsylvania, ca. 1790. Diameter, 29.8 cm. Metropolitan Museum of Art, New York. (The Metropolitan Museum of Art. Gift of Mrs. Robert W. de Forest, 1933.)

name of "fractur" painting. *Fractur* is the German name for the Medieval Gothic type of writing used in their calligraphy. The name derives from the Latin and signifies broken or angular lettering. The alphabet was formed by a heavy, broad downward stroke connected by a thin upward one, a form particularly suited to a quill pen. It has been the traditional German script·almost to the present.

The pictorial patterns as well as the script included in fracturs found their way to furniture, metalware, and ceramics. Almost too numerous to tabulate, they showed the heart, the star, the parrot, the small thrushlike bird sometimes called the *Distenfinken* or goldfinch, foliage, and especially the tulip.[45] Many of these designs were provincially bisymmetrical; again they were executed with the greatest freedom and with consummate skill to form a body of early American ceramic art that ranks aesthetically not only high but in reality the finest done.

By midcentury the dominant culture in the colonies was English, and affluent households favored the best of English pottery, known as "creamware," from Staffordshire kilns. Much of this was made with the American market in mind and was ornamented with American scenes and later with political heroes such as Franklin and Washington, done with transfer printing, an astute but not very patriotic move on the part of the English manufacturers.

Because of the cost, comparatively little porcelain found its way from Europe before the second half of the century. When, following the ratification of the peace in 1784, American ships—such as the *Empress of China* and the *Grand Turk*—traded with the Orient, the decorations were specifically directed to the American market and often consisted of facsimiles of the ships, coats-of-arms, and ciphers of the United States. One favored pattern displayed a view of Mt. Vernon surrounded by borders of flowering branches, Greek frets, and possibly star-encrusted blue bands.

Beyond the American folk pottery and stoneware few manufactories attempted to come into conflict with the pre-Revolutionary English embargoes. Neither were the American potters sufficiently knowledgeable to enter the competitive

market. One exception was the pottery firm of Gousse Bonnin and his partner George Anthony Morris which flourished in Philadelphia between 1769 and 1774. Bonnin was a French potter who had worked at Bow. The enterprise failed for reasons not clearly expressed, but adequately guessed at, and Bonnin returned to England. Theirs, however, was the first bone china made in America and was the forerunner of later enterprises.

The most famous pre-Revolutionary pottery, known as Bennington, has had a long and complicated history. From a small operation at Litchfield, Connecticut, where he made both red pottery and stoneware, came Captain John Norton across the border to Old Bennington, Vermont. There in 1793 in his first kiln he produced wares similar to the Litchfield. It was his son and grandson, Judge Lyman Norton and Julius Norton, respectively, who in 1831 began making their "yellow ware" in an attempt to rival the Staffordshire cream wares. Indeed, by stepped up production and clever advertising they succeeded in offering some competition.

This original output had a pottery body on which various glazes were imposed. These glazes generally had a yellowish-to-brown cast and sometimes mottled combinations of the two. One is known today as Rockingham ware probably because a similar output came from a ceramic factory on the estate of the Duke of Rockingham in England.

Modeled pieces caught the public fancy. Theophile Fry and Daniel Greatbach were the principal sculptors for the factory, and in addition to more pretentious pieces they made molds for such whimsies as hound-handle pitchers, cow creamers, and Toby jugs—done in variations of the yellow pottery body (Figure 5.57).

After 1839 Judge Norton took his son-in-law, Christopher Webber Fenton, into the business. As so often happens the younger men wanted to branch out into newer types of production and into the making of finer china. Fenton was one of those men who combine considerable artistic ability with a penchant for scientific investigation. He is said to have worn out the patience of his partners by his expensive testing. It was, however, because of his initiative that a separate divi-

Figure 5.57 Bennington-Rockingham type pottery, Connecticut. Height, 27.9 cm. (Courtesy, Mrs. Albert Schug, Monroeville, Ohio.)

sion of the original company embarked on the task of producing what is known as Parian ware, a hard, flintlike white body which superficially resembled white Parian marble. Generally unglazed, it was formed into numerous art objects and done in a variety of colors.

The diversity of Bennington production was great and the artistic quality somewhat devious, but, in addition to its sometime appeal, it became noteworthy as one of the first American potteries to embark on profitable production and to succeed in launching American attainment along the lines of folk art, less expensive table service, and "aesthetic" sculpture. In 1852 the company combined its various interests under the title of the United States Pottery.

GLASS

The American glass industry entered the field by the back door, so to speak, by manufacturing the homely necessities of window and bottle glass rather than fine tableware. For many years production of American glass had fallen behind demand. The first documented enterprise to cope with the problem was that of a German immigrant, Caspar Wistar, who had already shown his business acumen by developing a brass button manufactory in Philadelphia. He expanded his ventures by opening a glass house in Alloways-town, New Jersey, in 1739, which remained in operation for more than forty years. For expertise he obtained knowledgeable glass men from the Continent.

From this small beginning trained workers left to open their own glass houses (e.g., the Stanger factory in Glassboro, New Jersey, ca. 1780) which eventually spread north to New York and through New England.

Glass that resembles Wistar glass, wherever made, is spoken of as belonging to the New Jersey tradition (Figure 5.58). It was almost without exception a blown glass of potash-lime alkali

Figure 5.58 Lily-pad pitcher (New Jersey type glass) possibly from Lancaster or Lockport Glassworks, ca. 1840–1860. Height, 18 cm. Corning Museum, Corning, New York. (The Corning Museum of Glass, Corning, New York.)

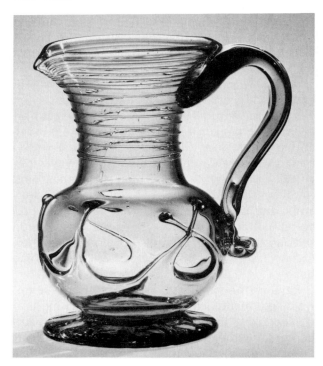

composition. It is an unwritten law that glass blowers may have the fag end of the pot for their own use. Thus Jersey glass is found in a number of objects besides the salable bottles. Included are candlesticks, pitchers, and bowls. The metal was never clear and may vary from the greenish tones of the Jersey examples to the often blue of New York and the occasional amethyst and frequently amber of New England. No group is too closely defined.

Because few pieces can be authenticated, identification must remain conjectural. Objects seldom traveled far; therefore location provides one clue and documented ownership another.

Shapes of this early glass were sturdy, somewhat irregular, and frequently alluded to as American folk art in glass. The traditions of decorating were as old as European glass history and include the crimping of edges, threading of necks into ridges, and the application of heavy swirling patterns made by twirling the gather on the pontil. Occasionally swags or tear drops were immersed in the body. The added prunts are most typical, however. Their shaping at first consisted of vertical streaks ending in a beadlike pad, which later evolved into what is characterized as the Jersey "Lily Pad." The second type of design was similar but had broader stems and oval pads and was connected with the output of the later New England and New York houses. The last version resembled a freely modeled lily pad with a curved stem terminating in a rather flat ovoid leaf.

Wistar glass still left the field open for the making of table glass of better quality, not all of which could be imported. Certainly the most romantic name in this history is that of "Baron" Stiegel (1729–1785), William Heinrich by given name, an immigrant from Germany (the title of "Baron" was as much a courtesy as that of "Colonel" for southern gentlemen). Although originally an iron worker, with a background in that industry in Germany, and the owner of ironworks at Elizabeth Furnace, Pennsylvania, he started his first glass house at the last location (1763) and added two more at Mannheim (1764 and 1768) in the same state. His first products were window glass and bottles.

Always the impetuous promoter, he decided to branch out into the making of "flint" glass (or

Figure 5.59 Polychrome-enameled mug of clear glass, Stiegel type, late eighteenth century. Height, 17.1 cm. Metropolitan Museum of Art, New York. (The Metropolitan Museum of Art. Gift of F. W. Hunter, 1913.)

glass containing lead) in competition with the European markets. This enterprise was never intended to be local in character. Stiegel imported experienced blowers from the Bristol district in England and enamelers and engravers from the Continent. He also advertised extensively in the New York papers.

Stiegel standardized the output of his factory carefully. He made both lead and nonlead glass. The decoration of Stiegel glass was varied but consisted in large part of enameling, engraving, and pattern molding (Figure 5.59). The factory was an American first which had a sizable output of good quality glass.

The personal history of the owner is well known. Because of his profligate spending, he became bankrupt and was sent according to rather illogical custom, to debtor's prison. After his realease he never recovered his "drive" and a few years later died at fifty-six.

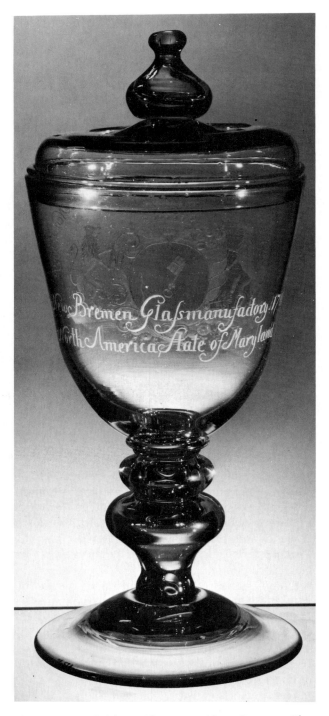

Figure 5.60 Goblet with cover, New Bremen Glass Manufactory, John Frederick Amelung, proprietor, 1784–ca. 1794. Metropolitan Museum of Art, New York. (The Metropolitan Museum of Art. Rogers Fund, 1928.)

Although the tradition of fine glass making in America did not gain momentum until later in the nineteenth century, several attempts to this purpose were begun before the Revolution. One about which most is known (and that is precious little in view of unexplored terrain) is the New Bremen, Maryland, glass works (1785–1794) of John Frederick Amelung. Amelung's fame is due in part to the fact that his was the rare eighteenth-century glass house to leave inscribed and dated examples (the moral of this is likewise clear).

Amelung, like Wistar and Stiegel, was born in Germany and his establishment was started with capital from certain German enterprises. Little was known of this house, which was forced to close in 1794 because of financial difficulties, until in 1928 the Metropolitan Museum of Art acquired a covered pokal, or presentation goblet, and subsequently a similar one, both made in the New Bremen factory. One had been fashioned for the city of Bremen in Germany (Figure 5.60), the other for Governor Thomas Mifflin of Pennsylvania. Other Amelung pokals like the two engraved with the name of George Trisler have come to light since.

In 1962 exploration on the supposed Amelung site, undertaken by the Corning Museum of Glass, the Smithsonian Museum, and the Colonial Williamsburg archaeological staff, yielded great quantities of glass—most of it nonlead crystal—and almost a complete range of current types. The entire output suggests that Amelung, although perhaps never having acquired complete control over the clarity of his glass, often embellished it with engraving of top quality.

Having alluded several times to window glass, it should be mentioned that two methods of manufacture were practiced: the traditional called for twirling small panes from the pontil and the second consisted of opening blown cylinders. Soon the improved French technique of increasing the size of the panes by forcing compressed air into these drums (hand pumped at this time) was adopted. One advertisement from the Franklin Glass Company, Massachusetts, 1813, reads:

The Franklin Glass Company in Warwick, is now in complete operation where may be had Window Glass of all sizes, in sheets or cylinders, or cut to any pattern. . . .[46]

Plate 1 *Chambre de la Reine,* Versailles. Ange-Jacques Gabriel and Jacques Verberckt. France, ca. 1738. (Clichés Musées Nationaux Paris)

Plate 2 (*Opposite*) Boudoir from the Hôtel d'Hocqueville. Rouen, France, ca. 1785. Length, ca. 14 ft, width, ca. 9 ft, height, ca. 13½ ft. The Cleveland Museum of Art. (Cleveland Museum of Art, Purchase, John L. Severance Fund)

Plate 3 Commode. Attributed to Jacques-Pierre Latz, Paris. France, ca. 1750. Width, 61 in. Oak, tulipwood, marquetry, with gilt-bronze mounts. The Cleveland Museum of Art. (Cleveland Museum of Art, Gift of Flora Whitney Miller, Barbara Whitney Henry, and Major Cornelius Vanderbilt Whitney in memory of their mother Mrs. Harry Payne Whitney)

Plate 4 Two soft-paste porcelain tureens. France. *Left,* Vincennes, ca. 1752. Height, 10¹/₈ in. *Right,* Vincennes-Sèvres, 1756. Height, 9¹/₂ in. The Cleveland Museum of Art. (Cleveland Museum of Art, Purchase, John L. Severance Fund)

Plate 5   English Georgian interior. Dining room from a house at Kirtlington Park, Oxfordshire. England, ca. 1748. Length, 36 ft, width, ca. 24 ft, height, ca. 20 ft. The Metropolitan Museum of Art, New York. (Metropolitan Museum, Fletcher Fund, 1931)

Plate 6　Interior at Osterley Park. Remodeled by Robert Adam. Greater London, 1761–1763. (Victoria and Albert Museum, Crown Copyright)

Plate 7   Watercolor design for the west wall of the Music Room at the Royal Pavilion, Brighton. Firm of Frederick Crace, London, 1818–1819. Cooper-Hewitt Museum, New York. (Cooper-Hewitt Museum, the Smithsonian Institution's National Museum of Design)

Plate 8   Marlboro Room from Patuxent Manor, Maryland, home of Charles Grahame, 1744. Philadelphia furniture, leather or brocatelle upholstery, wood and gilded tin chandeliers, brass candle brackets, *Fishing Lady* embroidery over fireplace, Feraghan carpet. Winterthur Museum, Winterthur, Delaware. (Courtesy The Henry Francis du Pont Winterthur Museum)

Plate 9 (*Opposite*)   Interior of Christ Church Congregational, East Haddam, Connecticut, 1794. Builder, Lavius Fillmore. New England Wren-Gibbs type design. (Wilson H. Brownell)

Plate 10   The Oval Music Room of the Nathaniel Russell House, Charleston, South
Carolina, ca. 1809. Harp, Sébastian Erard, 1803; American "Empire" couch and Balti-
more lyreback chairs, ca. 1810; Karabagh rug, ca. 1800; Chelsea candelabra. (Historic
Charleston Foundation; Louis Schwartz, photographer)

Plate 11 The Double Living Room with sliding doors, ca. 1860. *Rosalie,* Natchez, Mississippi. Belter-type furniture. Mississippi D. A. R. (Mary Conn McCord)

Plate 12 The Peacock Room, 1876–1877. Designed by James McNeill Whistler. Freer Gallery of Art, Washington, D.C. (Courtesy of the Smithsonian Institution, Freer Gallery of Art)

Plate 13   The Worgelt Study. Designed by Alavoine. New York City, 1928–1930. The Brooklyn Museum, New York. (Brooklyn Museum, Gift of Mr. and Mrs. Raymond Worgelt)

Plate 14   Baptistry of Church of the Sacred Heart, Audincourt, France. Designed by
Jean Bazaine, ca. 1951. (Photograph courtesy of Ernst Payer)

Plate 15 Rothko Chapel interior. Houston, Texas. Building designed by Philip Johnson to house 14 of Mark Rothko's paintings. Paintings (late 60s) and building (1973) commissioned by Jean and Dominique de Menil. (Copyright © 1973 by The Condé Nast Publications Inc.)

Plate 16   Central courtyard of the East Building of the National Gallery of Art, Washington, D.C. Architect: I. M. Pei and Partners, New York, 1978. Mobile by Alexander Calder; sculpture by Aristide Maillol. (National Gallery of Art, Washington)

Panes as large as 14 × 18 in. were made by the Albany Glassworks in 1792.

Improvement in the clarity of glass was constantly advertised and a comparison with imported glass both in this respect and in cost was invited. Gone would be the crown glass or twirled centers that the old factories produced and vanished is the violet tint (manganese introduced to counteract the oxide of iron coloration) which is the charm of the windows of so many of Boston's Beacon Hill houses.

METALS

Silver

The eighteenth century was the golden era of silver crafting in America. The work of the first half of the century, although less robust than the silver of the seventeenth, maintained a hearty character to which was added an urbane grace. The mastercraftsmen were many and their line of apprentice trainees was fairly well established. Often, as in the Winslow and Hurd families, at least three generations of famous men gave an aura of distinction to a name.

Most of the extant pieces have come from New England (Boston) and New York, although such men as the Huguenot Cesar Ghiselin (1670–1734) and Philip Synge, Jr. (1676–1739), have boosted the fame of Philadelphia. Well-known New England smiths of the early Georgian period whose work is displayed in many museums are John Coney (1655–1722), Edward Winslow (1669–1753), John Edwards (1671–1746), John Burt (1692–1745), and Jacob Hurd (1702–1758).

In New York we find Cornelius Kierstede (1675–1757—who later practiced in Connecticut), Simeon Soumain (ca. 1685–ca. 1750), Jacobus van der Spiegel (1668–1708), Jacob Ten Eyck (1704–1793), and Peter Van Dyck (1684–1751) and Charles Le Roux (1689–1745), both apprentices of Bartholomew Le Roux (Figure 5.61). Many Frenchmen appeared on the New York scene. Soumain, London-trained, represented that large group of religious refugees who came to America from France via London. New York pieces were capacious and elaborate.

Figure 5.61 Teapot, Peter Van Dyck, New York, 1720–1735. Silver and pearwood. Height 18 cm. Yale University Art Gallery, New Haven Connecticut. (Yale University Art Gallery. The Mabel Brady Garvan Collection.)

In the next generation in New England only a beginning is made by naming the two sons of Jacob Hurd (1702–1758), whose portrait was painted by Copley—Nathaniel (1729–1777)—and Benjamin (1739–1781) as well as John Coburn (1725–1803). Then came the group that centered around the Revolutionary war years: the famous patriot Paul Revere (1735–1818), John David (1736–1798), and John Richardson (1752–1831), the last two from Philadelphia (Figures 5.62 and 5.63).

Figure 5.62 Silver teapot, Paul Revere, Boston, late eighteenth century. Museum of Fine Arts, Boston. (Courtesy Museum of Fine Arts, Boston. Thayer Collection.)

239

Figure 5.63. Silver teapot, John David, Philadelphia, late eighteenth century. Height, 16.8 cm. Cleveland Museum of Art. (The Cleveland Museum of Art. Purchase from the J. H. Wade Fund.)

Benjamin Franklin in his autobiography says:

We kept no idle servants, our table was plain and simple, our furniture of the cheapest. For instance, my breakfast was a long time bread and milk (no tea), and I ate it out of a two-penny earthen porringer, with a pewter spoon. But mark how luxury will enter families, and make progress, in spite of principle: being called one morning to breakfast, I found it in a China bowl, with a spoon of silver! They had been bought for me without my knowledge by my wife, and had cost her the enormous sum of three-and-twenty shillings, for which she had no other excuse or apology to make, but that she thought *her* husband deserv'd a silver spoon and China bowl as well as any of his neighbors. This was the first appearance of plate and China in our house, which afterward, in a course of years, as our wealth increas'd, augmented gradually to several hundred pounds in value.

During the eighteenth century silver vessels intended from the first for household rather than church use made their appearance. These objects were a man's pride of possession, a usable artifact, and his bank roll, all in one. First came the serving dishes. Salvers and trays without feet became more numerous, although never plentiful. Patens grew feet, but were not called *tazzas* until the nineteenth century.

Silver knives and forks were seen infrequently; the latter when they did appear were the two- or three-prong variety. Spoons can be dated by their shape, which follows English precedent. The rounded bowl and round-stemmed *Puritan spoon* gave way to the more ovoid bowl and flatter stem. The notched end, trifid or wavy, and the rattail support of bowl to handle characterize the spoons of the early Georgian era, possibly descriptive of the one bought by Mrs. Franklin. Gradually the end of the spoon rounded and was first turned up and then down. The rattail support likewise lost its sharp contours and was frequently ornamented with wheat sprays, shells, and florals. Finally, with the budding nineteenth century, the American spoon assumed the fiddleback shape, made by firms such as Davis, Palmer, and Company of Boston. This pattern was fairly common and many families whose silver descends through several lines will find that the spoons are similar.

American silver had no hallmark for its identification. Frequently the maker's initials were enclosed in a device for advertising rather than legal purposes; for example, John Coney's mark in 1705 was a heart-shaped punch that displayed his initials over a fleur-de-lis; by 1710 he was using crowned initials in a shield above a pictorial coney as a rebus on his name. After 1720 the full surname frequently appeared because the initials were not always sufficient identification. A few makers added marks similar to the assay marks on English pieces to suggest British origin.[47]

To denote ownership some colonists followed the English custom of personalizing their silver with their engraved initials. Family silver often bore the initials of husband and wife, surmounted by the surname, to mark joint possession of valuable objects.

As "wealth increas'd" many were the articles fashioned of silver: low, open salt cellars; candlesticks (first in the form of columns and then balustered) which were equipped with a pricket to impale the candle; porringers (bowls with one handle) or caudle cups (with two); shakers; casters; dredgers or muffineers to cover a waffle with sugar; and such superluxuries as pitchers, sauce boats, snuff boxes, and monteiths (punch bowls with rims for cups).

It was the tea and coffee sets, however, that

were the distinguishing marks of a really wealthy and aesthetically discerning society. In form they all but duplicated English styles. Although complete tea sets with trays were not in use until after the Revolution, tea caddies and various containers for such items as preserved ginger and condiments were not uncommon. English Sheffield trays often accompanied American tea sets.

With the late Georgian and the advent of Neoclassic styles, the lines of tea services become straighter. And so we come to Paul Revere (1734–1818). Revere was of French lineage, the son of Apollis Rivoire who came as a boy to America from Bordeaux, France, and served an apprenticeship under John Coney. Young Paul was taught by his father and at twenty-two became a master silversmith. Because there were, in all, three generations of Reveres who were silversmiths in America, the youngest having died before his father, the famous Paul is often referred to as The Patriot.

His professional career covered periods in design from the late Georgian through the Federal. In his portrait done by Copley in 1765 he is holding a teapot of inverted pear shape embellished with a pineapple terminal and with curved spout and handle, typically Rococo Georgian. Although Revere moved with the fashion for straight-sided pieces, it is noteworthy that he retained the older tradition for his tea and coffee sets (Figure 5.62).

The famous *Sons of Liberty* bowl made in 1768 and now at the Boston Museum of Fine Arts is a restrained example of this stylistic order. With a height of 5½ in. and a diameter of 11, its beautifully contoured sides are pleasingly proportioned to its convoluted base. Quite plain except for its central oval bearing the insignia of the Magna Carta and of the first Bill of Rights, it inscribes for all who care to read the defiance of the group of fifteen young patriots toward the English restrictions on free commerce. By having their names engraved on a silver bowl they placed themselves openly against the laws of the mother country, and if matters had gone adversely, the future could scarcely have denied the incriminating evidence.

As a footnote on eighteenth-century silver the California colonial period merged Spanish wealth and metal craft in family plate of high value.

Other Metals

Although William Byrd sent to England for the wrought iron gates of Westover, iron foundries became an early part of colonial economy. Many iron furnaces were started in Pennsylvania—Carlyle Furnace, Laurel Forge, Cumberland Furnace, and Pine Grove—during the early colonial period. One of their well-known products was the iron stove that divorced the American kitchen from the hearth. The Franklin stove for heating was a product of the 1740s. Ornamental ironwork is a story best deferred until the next chapter.

Pewter was necessarily an indigenous craft with articles that follow on the heels of silver in style.

Brass, although not important in the early seventeen hundreds, became more so toward the late. In his day Paul Revere was as well known for his bell and cannon factory, where he cast bells and brass cannons, as he was for his silver.

DESCRIPTIVE SUMMARY

As a postscript to the American eighteenth century this review has attempted to show that the environmental arts, which at the beginning were certainly localized in style, by the end had become more recognizably unified. The result was by no means a homogenized version of the arts of Europe. It was a stratified, composite organism, richly diversified, yet stamped by a recognizable and vigorous spirit. It had every reason to be proud of its accomplishments. Especially in the domain of housing it left an abundant and dignified legacy, the exact counterpart of the rational thinking of those who forged one of the first nations of this continent.

CHAPTER SIX

The Nineteenth Century

Building and decoration cannot be separated from one another; they are intimately connected, and if appearances seem to disapprove this there is something wrong with one or the other.

Percier and Fontaine
*Recueil de Décorations intérieures comprenant
tout ce qui a rapport a l'ameublement*

CULTURE SPAN

The nineteenth century is now almost one hundred years ago and thus is beginning to be relished in popular retrospect. It is entering that aura of romance which, though it may often distort, probably just as frequently helps us to understand. The nineteenth century fulfilled the basic promises of the eighteenth. Political systems had been toppled, industrialization became a way of life, certainly some fluidity existed in society, and a sentimental concern for the underprivileged developed. In the increasing plurality of the world, however, the good life for all did not materialize. The operational machinery for its acquisition had not yet been developed and men had learned how to manipulate the new to their own advantage.

In many ways the nineteenth century was a more fractionated existence than any before. The interdependent industrialized and scientifically oriented culture required specialized skills that threw up barriers by their very complexity. In the process art had no opportunity to put down roots. It was inevitably splintered into compartments, and although Vitruvius's functional and message-bearing divisions did well by the segregation, the sensuous—the design element—came off poorly.

NINETEENTH-CENTURY ARCHITECTURE

Neoclassicism, 1800–1840

Neoclassicism continued its hold on architecture until well into the nineteenth century. Because the new developments, such as budding mechanization and industrialization, were little understood, art continued to wear the cloak of the old and tried.

Nineteenth-century classicism had an augmented standard of respect for archaeological correctness due to advances made in this new science. As the classical sources of reference multiplied to include Greece and the Hellenistic and Greek-Roman east, Vitruvius and Renaissance writers lost some of their authority. Because of the novelty of the new kernel within the old

matrix, it was preferred. The name *Greek Revival* was used to designate an avowed adherence to Greek principles.

Nineteenth-century classicism also remembered Ledoux and his insistence on structural logic and Laugier and his respect for functional form. Greek architecture was considered to have exemplified these mandates. In its temple form it allowed a clear-cut and forceful statement to be made, which accorded well with the new type of social and political thinking that was evident in much of the area under discussion. In all of these ways the new Neoclassicism made a neat, viable package.

Only a few examples can be cited. The British Museum (1823–1847) by Sir Robert Smirke (1781–1867), with its portico comprised of forty-eight Greek Ionic columns, comes first to mind, a majestic building whose exterior gives little evidence of the space purposes of the newly rising type—the museum. The Altes Museum (1823–1828) in Berlin by Karl Friedrich von Schinkel (1781–1841) comes off better. Here interior elevations and interior space allocations are more clearly indicated by the two-story Greek stoa with which it is fronted. In Paris the Church of the Madeleine (1807–1845) by Pierre Vignon (1763–1828) faces down the Rue Royale and, with its Greek Corinthian temple front, its Roman podium, and its inner Byzantine dome on pendentives, is truly a classic eclectic building. Nevertheless, it may also be said to have used the Greek to demonstrate structural integrity, the Roman to allow for an impressive expression of importance, and the Eastern to create a necessarily large space.

One English architect who had a more lasting influence on the future was Sir John Soane (1753–1837). His style was characterized by a tendency to strip the classical elements of design to their structural essentials, to invent his own manner of linear decoration, and to handle interior space in an ingenious and often highly utilitarian way. Shallow domes associated with clerestory fenestration introduced light as a functional and design factor in his work. Soane is said to have given copies of Laugier to his pupils, and his own pared-down London home—now an architectural museum—demonstrates his personal and comparable architectural theory.

Because of the spate of building required by a

new political complex and a phenomenally burgeoning country, America was ripe for architectural expansion. Two generations of professional architects and scores of provincial builders carried this forward. The English-trained Benjamin Latrobe (1764–1820) was certainly the first leader. In his design of the Bank of Pennsylvania begun in Philadelphia in 1798, which featured the pro-style portico from the Erectheum, and his somewhat prescribed work on the capitol at Washington he was entirely a devotee of rational simplification. Jefferson and Latrobe were not only friends but, in matters of architecture, sympathetic confreres. Together they sponsored a reaction toward simple and forceful styling in the classical idiom, coupled with functional planning and the use of the newer aspects of engineering.

Latrobe was an engineer, as were two of the next generation who were his pupils. Robert Mills (1781–1855) designed monuments to Washington in Baltimore and in the national capital, as well as several outstanding churches and government buildings. He used masonry vaulting for its fireproof qualities as well as for its space potential. Mills was most serious about his profession and

Figure 6.1 Tennessee State Capitol Building, Nashville, 1845–1849. William Strickland, architect. (Courtesy, Department of Tourist Development, State of Tennessee.)

may be said to have been the first architect who was American-trained in engineering as well as in architectural precepts.

William Strickland (1787–1854) illustrates, in his ambience, the aspect of a practicing architect's service that took him to widely separate areas of this country. He built the last of the temple-form capitols in Nashville, Tennessee, in 1845–1849 (Figure 6.1).

America initiated functional planning for the several types of building that sprang into demand. John Haviland's (1792–1852) Eastern Penitentiary in Philadelphia (1823), with its radial cellular plan, was an example much copied in Europe. Hotels like the Tremont House (1820–1829) in Boston and the more famous Astor House in New York (1832), both by Isaiah Rogers (1800–1869), set standards of luxury (and bigness!) unknown at that time abroad.

Houses were the principal vehicle for carrying the idiom of the Greek Revival across America. In them we find a capsule view of the quality of originality within the stylistic pattern of the past which was so notable. The printed word furthered this approach. Architectural books, like architects, proliferated on the new soil. In addition to the English tomes that appeared after 1775, America began to publish. The first text was written by a

Figure 6.2 Arlington, Arlington, Virginia, 1826. George Hadfield, architect. (G. C. Ball.)

Massachusetts architect, Asher Benjamin (1773–1845)—*The Country Builder's Assistant,* published in 1797. This was followed by six others from his pen, all widely circulated. Asher, apparently self-taught and coming from a provincial environment, possessed talent and an unusually alert and inquiring mind.

John Haviland was among the few who came from England after the Revolution. Arriving in 1816, his architectural training enabled him to write *The Builder's Assistant* (1818), in three volumes, the first work in America to show plates of the Greek orders.[1] *The Young Builder's General Instructor,* published in 1829, was the first of five by Minard Lafever (1798–1854). His renderings reveal that he was a meticulous draftsman. He was also an imaginative interpreter who boldly and sensitively altered the Greek precedents to make them applicable to the materials, the processes, and the workmen for whom they were intended. It was the works of these men rather than the English architectural classics which were the bibles

of the builders, who, by and at large, were responsible for the numerous houses, town halls, taverns, and even railway stations that dotted the country with reminders that we are all children of Greece.

Aside from the embryonic Greek-style Semple House in Williamsburg, the first temple design is seen in Pavilion IV of Professors Row at the University of Virginia, again the work of Jefferson. Here is an orthodox Greek Revival, with four columns, full pedimented entablature, and gabled roof extending over the entire depth. The Greek Revival never displayed its imposing grandeur to better advantage than at Arlington, by George Hadfield (ca. 1764–1826), built for George Washington Parke Custis, stepgrandson of George Washington (Figure 6.2). Its imposing portico was copied from one of the Greek temples at Paestum. Greek Doric entablatures were often simplified by omitting triglyphs and metopes, thereby making a less expensive undertaking and at the same time a more vigorous one.

Greek Revival architecture spread west, even, in isolated instances, to the Pacific coast, as settlers inundated the regions beyond the Appalachians after the War of 1812. The colonists invaded the hinterland from New England and upper New York, over the Mohawk Trail; from Pennsylvania, lower New York, and the South, over the Appalachian Trail through Pittsburgh and down the Ohio River, and over the Cumberland Trail. After ratification of the Louisiana Purchase, a vast area was made available for cotton cultivation, and many hit the Natchez Trail southwest or approached this vast area from the Mississippi.

In any event, homes were built, and as soon as possible this wave of settlers, fully cognizant of classical architecture in the East, sought to emulate it in the West.

All of this new building represented idiomatic interpretations of the Greek Revival. In the North this coincided with a rural and small-town existence on tree-lined streets on which were located somewhat uniformly designed dwellings characterized by pleasing proportions dictated by eyes accustomed to traditional rhythms. These northern dwellings were for the most part comparatively modest, although the Lanier Mansion in Madison, Indiana, and the Taft home in Cincinnati were exceptions to the rule. Most were like the small jewel of a house on the village green at Monroeville, Ohio, where one could defy any contemporary architect to invent a more pleasing shell for an immensely workable plan (Figure 6.3).

It was only to be expected that carpenters and even builder-architects would modify much of the prescribed vocabulary to suit local needs. One common change was the alteration of a bi-symmetrical plan to one that was asymmetrical. This placed two gabled buildings at right angles and in the set-back of the wing allowed space for the desirable "front porch." Wide friezes were planned to accommodate second-story windows. These windows were frequently covered with iron or wood grilles, which in their imaginative use of Greek motifs such as the anthemion became an idiomatic decoration of considerable aesthetic interest. A photographic record across the country is like taking a page from Lafever and with it in hand tabulating the course of the colonists westward.

In the cotton-raising Deep South and especially in the Mississippi territory Greek Revival architecture was cast in an indigenous mold which was

Figure 6.3 Greek Revival type home, Monroeville, Ohio, early nineteenth century. (Courtesy, Mrs. Albert Schug; photograph, G. C. Ball.)

often far afield from its prototype. Important architects from the North participated in this post-treaty building. Latrobe had his hand in the creation of the Pontalba Apartments (1848) in New Orleans, the first complex of its kind in America. This was a collaborative effort between James Gallier, Sr., and James H. Dakin, who worked from designs by James Gallier, Jr., of New York.

Although there is much evidence of Greek Revivalism in the old quarter (the *Vieux Carré*) in New Orleans, one must cross into the section farther north, the Garden City District, to find examples less colored by French and Spanish tradition. It was in the homes of the newer American aristocracy, both in the city and up river, that Neoclassicism took its firmest hold. Even then it was influenced by local building practices which in turn were designed in answer to local needs. As plantation owners grew wealthy, their vast acres of cotton tilled by slave labor, houses reflected that affluence and grew stately, tall-ceilinged, large-roomed, and open-halled, based on symmetrical plans. Slender colonial pillars were changed overnight to enveloping Grecian colonnades (generally of stucco-covered brick) freely interpreted in style. Second-story railings continued to be made of iron. Low windows added a

French feeling. Stairways were internal and often featured the best sweeping Federal curves for their ascent.

These houses and their many modifications throughout the Deep South were built to withstand the hot climate on shaded piazzas and in cross drafts and to provide a capaciousness for housing and entertaining many persons. Their charm, when analyzed, can scarcely be attributed to Greek proportions, although it may have had something to do with tall pillars. It was compounded of all these things, plus their evident suitability to their lush backgrounds and way of life.

Perhaps in a story that is concerned with the observable facts of architecture some little space should be given occasionally to its human side. There is scarcely a part of the South that so delights in calling itself "old" as the fabulous community around Natchez, Mississippi. This river town at the head of the ocean-going channel reincarnates its antebellum history in a series of pageants given each spring during the garden festival week, when young men in frock coats and belted swords and young women in hoop skirts and crinoline are such real ghosts of the past that it is easy to forget the paper companies and pecan factories adjacent to the district today. Among the 100 Greek Revival mansions owned by Natchez families one can easily find oneself living in two centuries. Yet the picture seems to be truer when the play-acting is over, when a building speaks for itself, when today's family gathers around the dinner table, when a descendant still lives in the house, or when it has been restored but relegated to some appropriate contemporary use.

Rosalie, built in 1820, is a five-bay cubicle, hipped-roof mansion with colossal Doric pillars front and rear (Figure 6.4). Notice the thinness of the entablature, which has neither triglyphs nor metopes in the frieze.

The galleries of Dunleith (the many Scottish names reflect the large number of plantation owners of that ancestry who moved from the Carolinas to this more fertile land) completely surround the inner core (like a Greek peripteral temple). Observe the dormers projecting from the roof—a pox on the Greek Revival style!

Melrose, Monteigne, Monmouth with its square pillars, Devereux, Stanton Hall, Hawthorne, and

Figure 6.4 Rosalie, Natchez, Mississippi, 1820. (Photograph, Mary Conn McCord.)

Burne—all must be visited, for no location offers such a kaleidoscope of the Greek Revival. Nevertheless, Natchez is not only testimony to the freedom with which the American builder adapted a style to suit his need; it is also an anachronism in its bracketing dates. Born in the diaphanous-gowned Grecian years of the early century, it continued to build into the hoopskirt era right down to the Civil War, a circumstance that must be understood when handling its interiors.

Today we look in vain for the finest of the plantation homes, so great have been the ravages of fire. In Louisiana Belle Grove, home of the Andrews, and Greenwood, owned throughout its life by the Percys, have succumbed (Figure 6.5). Natchez under the hill, the seamier side of river life, has also been washed away with the tide that laps its banks. It is all a phantom of the past.

The plantation homes of the lower Mississippi have regional derivatives in Texas as in the Varner-Hogg home of 1835–1860 near Houston. In the Rockies later pioneer villages, left as ghost towns by the exodus of trappers and miners, become picturesque subjects for artists and scenario writers. But in California a few old houses tell as much about the Spanish in America as about the Yankee.

Dates of the Mexican Colonial Period are usually bracketed by 1821 and 1848. The American Colonial Period, beginning in 1848, blends into the present. The Colonial epoch originated with the purchase of vast ranches or *ranchos,* for the most part by Spaniards, after the land holdings of the missions were put up for sale. In the more cosmopolitan areas the extended oriental trade proved a boon to pueblo and presidio ports. San José, Los Angeles, San Diego, Santa Barbara, Monterey, and San Francisco grew apace. Americans began to arrive by sea and by overland trails opened by hardy bands of beaver trappers. The people of two widely separated nations thus created California's pioneer stock; and with California, to a lesser degree, may be grouped the entire Southwest.

During the Colonial period adobe construction remained and the *casa de rancho* (ranch house) or the *casa de pueblo* (town house) were essentially Spanish in plan. A long rectangle or a house with

Figure 6.5 Greenwood, St. Francisville, Louisiana, 1830. (Destroyed by fire. Restoration in progress.) (G. C. Ball.)

wings surrounding a patio, contained open corridors and second-story verandahs which served as passages and porches. In Southern California the single story was common, but in the North the two-story with outside stairs and rooms directly off the porch was customary (Figure 6.6). With Eastern influence, windows which were originally filled with Spanish grilles or heavy outside shutters and a single shutter within, graduated to double-hung sash on the outer face of the deep (often as much as 33 in.) walls. Panes were small; sashes had twenty or more lights. Americans introduced the interior stairs and fireplaces, often framed by a simple Adam mantel brought by ship from the East, in a complex that could be strangely refreshing: the austerity of Yankee taste combined with the dramatic simplicity of Spanish walls. In 1849 came the addition of clapboarding, and Thomas O. Larkin, President Polk's consul at Monterey, lived in a California-type house modified in the direction of Georgian compactness and regularity.[2]

By the fifties, on the heels of statehood and the gold rush, building and eastern architectural influences catapulted. Where Neoclassic detail had prevailed in domestic work, a few distinguished civic Greek Revival buildings, such as the United States Mint and the Montgomery block, rose in San Francisco. Other buildings of laxer academic standards by that very fact emphasize the distance in culture as well as in miles and years

Figure 6.6 Casa Amesti, Monterey, California, early nineteenth century. (Library of Congress.)

from the Acropolis. European civilization had moved as far west as it could go with purity.

Nineteenth-Century Gothic Modes: 1830–1870

Mechanization and industrialization are of necessity geared toward impersonalization—and thereby drain life of its romance. It was inevitable that the panacea would be a sentimental return to the past in all of the frills of living. The Gothic, with its decorative fan vaulting, its colored light, its linear traceries, its mystical effigies, and its ethnic appeal, naturally returned to popularity. It catered to a sensibility that had forgotten, if it ever knew, the order behind the relationships of Greek art or that any regulated arrangement was found in Medieval structure (*see* Volume I, Chapter 5).

The academic Gothic of the nineteenth cen-

tury had two phases, the first roughly from 1830 to 1850 and the second extending in England until 1870 and in America slightly longer. The Continent was little affected, although its presentation is designated the *Neo-Gothic*. The entire opus by prominent architects is customarily called the *High Gothic* to distinguish it from its vernacular counterpart, the work of local builders. Again many writers (and we shall adopt their precedent) subdivided the High Gothic into *Early Victorian Gothic* and *Late Victorian Gothic*, the latter sometimes found as *High Victorian Gothic* (which phrase is ambiguous and is not used here).

The two leverages of the early period were "correctness" and its logical accompaniment "structural honesty." Its most famous prophets were the Pugins in England and Viollet-le-Duc in France. Eugène Viollet-le-Duc (1814–1879) first. Reared by an uncle who was an ardent liberal, Eugène shunned the usual *École des Beaux-Arts* schooling and instead spent some time in travel, including Sicily where he studied Norman and

Islamic buildings and developed a passionate love of the Medieval. In 1846, having returned to France and spoken out in his praise of French Gothic architecture, he was chosen by Prosper Mérimée (author of *Carmen*), then Inspector General of Historical Monuments, to assist with historical work in France. During his life Eugène became the restorer and often the savior of many French landmarks; to mention the merest few— Notre Dame and the Palais de Justice in Paris and Pierrefonds in l'Oise. The battle over the accuracy–inaccuracy, inspired spirit–letter dullness of his work has raged ever since. Certainly in his writing he influenced many subsequent Gothic architects by emphasizing the structural honesty as well as the historical accuracy of Gothic revivalism.[3]

Another Frenchman, an émigré to England, was Auguste Charles Pugin (1762–1832), who wrote at length on the subject.[4] His son Augustus Welby Northmore Pugin (1812–1852) became architectural assistant to Charles Barry (1795–1860), who built the Gothic-inspired British Houses of Parliament between 1836 and 1852 with erudite attention to architectural purity (Figure 6.7).

With respect to domestic architecture, the *Early Victorian Gothic* approach is demonstrated in A. W. N. Pugin's (he is often known by his initials—for reason) remodeling of Scarisbrick Hall in Lancashire. In this he, in turn, had the help of his son Edward Welby Pugin (1834–1875). Scarisbrick is significant as the precursor of the return of the "living hall" in domestic planning. In appearance, however, it somehow looks as though it had come from a machinist's die rather than from the skilled hands of Medieval craftsmen.

Although many types of building subscribed to Early Victorian Gothic principles, it was in the field of ecclesiastic architecture that it has lived the longest. This was due in great part to the fact that the Church of England adopted canons that accepted the English Gothic two-aisled church as the norm for ritual fulfillment.

In America Richard Upjohn (1802–1878) built Trinity Church in lower New York in 1846 (Figure 6.8), and from that time on many churches of all denominations were erected in this style on the Continent, in England, and especially in the United States.

The *Late Victorian Gothic* stressed the decorative character of its prototype by concentrating in particular on the coloristic and symbolic aspects. It is this period that was influenced by the writings of John Ruskin (1819–1900; see p. 263) who expressed his esteem for the kaleidoscope of Venice, for the Pre-Raphaelites with their rich imagery, and for the technique of light effectively portrayed by Turner in England and by the Impressionists in France.

Although correct detailing was not discarded, practitioners adopted more vigorous plasticity to replace the lacelike delineation of much early work. The conception was bolder and possibly more appealing to the intrepid civilization that was forging a commercial empire during the last

Figure 6.7 Big Ben Tower, a part of the Houses of Parliament, 1836–1852. Sir Charles Barry, architect. Fourteenth-century Westminster Hall on the right. (G. C. Ball.)

Figure 6.8 Trinity Church seen from Wall Street, New York City, 1846. Richard Upjohn, architect. A canyon of twentieth-century skyscrapers and a glimpse of an older building make up a typical contemporary cityscape. (G. C. Ball.)

century. We may cite the Church of All Saints, London, built in the decade after 1849 by William Butterfield (1814–1900), with its integral exterior polychromy of brick and stone and its interior of marble and tile.

Provincial Gothicism, often known as Carpenters' Gothic, of the forties and fifties, must be passed over with a pictorial account. In America this was the backwash of romanticism which followed the more austere Greek Revivalism in up-country areas. It was an era of "gingerbread" decoration made by the bandsaw and likely to appear on structures whose architectural lineage was suspect. Nevertheless, it represents a treasure trove of impossible creations. One delightful example is "Longwood," which was begun in Natchez on the eve of the Civil War and never completed. Another is the "Wedding Cake House" in Kennebunk, Maine, which has excrescences pasted on a plain Neoclassic exterior. Curious examples can be found in many sections of the country; their dates become later, the farther west one travels (Figure 6.9).

Renaissance Revival and Second Empire Style: 1850–1870

The face of the nineteenth century put on many masks, several of which were worn concurrently. One is known as the Renaissance Revival, which bore a close similarity to the Second Empire Style. Actually the Renaissance as a phase of the classical revival had been continuous in France since its introduction; for example, many expensive houses built around 1825 in the area between the Champs Elysées and the Seine during the heyday of Neoclassicism are characterized by French Renaissance detail.

Even in England the Renaissance ideal was

Figure 6.9 A house in New York State with ingenious architectural decoration. (G. C. Ball.)

never completely taken over by the newer classicism. If Barry's Travelers' Club in London of 1829 is compared with the Neoclassic terraces in Regent's Park of about the same year, it is evident that the wall surface is not so flat, the organization of visual elements places greater emphasis on the horizontal, and the stress is on elaboration of the aediculae of the openings rather than on pillared entrances. Quoins are exaggerated and the classical cornice, deep.

It might have been expected that Napoleon would try to consolidate his gains by civic programs. In fact, he inaugurated an urban project that involved the extension of several prominent Paris streets and planned the erection of contemporary buildings along their flanks; but time ran out for him and much of the work begun then was not completed until the sixties. Some facades of crisp, monotonous Neoclassic colonnades were the work of his time and his favorite architects Charles Percier (1764–1838) and Pierre François Leonard Fontaine (1762–1853).

Although Napoleon was fortunate that his successors, in particular Louis Philippe, carried his plans forward, it remained for his nephew, the emperor Louis Napoleon III, to instigate new and important building projects—hence the style name, Second Empire. Chief among these enterprises was the lengthening of the arms of the Louvre (L. T. J. Visconti, 1791–1853, followed by H. M. Lefuel, 1810–1880) to connect with the Tuileries. This work had been proposed long before by Catherine de Medici. To effect a similarity of parts it was only natural that this particular venture should have Renaissance overtones.

Louis Napoleon appointed Baron Georges-Eugène Haussmann (1809–1891), his Prefect of the Seine, to execute this vast urban renewal project, which involved a further widening of the radial avenues that terminate at the Place de l'Étoile and the erection of the flats with which they were fronted.

Superficially, the distinguishing mark of the *Second Empire Style* was the tall Mansard roof, which in its straight, concave, or convex sided form was used to give maximum interior space in the limited height allowed by the building ordinances.[5] In addition, there was a strong feeling for the plastic effects characterized by central and end pavilions, as in the Baroque of Louis XIV. Thus we find a style which in its general symmetry and ornament was in the classic vein but in its high roofs was not out of spirit with the Gothic.

The most spectacular of the palaces of the French Second Empire was the Opera House (1861–1875; Figures 6.10, 6.11, and 6.12), designed by Charles Garnier (1825–1898). Characterized by highly plastic Baroque planning, classical Italianate detailing, elaboration through marble sculpture, and gold and velvet decoration, it set the norm for all opera houses of the near future. It is withal acoustically well planned and serves its purpose as a parade ground for social intercourse. Moreover, its interior spaces are explicitly apparent in its exterior masses. Perhaps no other building so epitomized its times by summing up the basic qualities of functional core and Baroque flamboyance, classic propriety, and pseudo-Gothic spirit of exaltation.

In England hotels were particularly affected by the Second Empire style and many London facades owe their pomposity to the period. Houses, too—Waddesdon Manor in Buckinghamshire, home of the Rothschild Collections, done by the French architect G. H. Destailler (1822–1893), is a private dwelling in the Second Empire manner. Any visitor to Hyde Park has seen the tall truncated roofs of the terraces of Grosvenor Place which form the Victorian (or Second Empire) skyline.

In much that was done in America the Late Gothic and Second Empire combined to produce a style that pushed one facet or another to the fore, depending on the type and uses of the building as well as on the training of the architect. Throughout the country pretentious, free-standing houses of red brick or Connecticut brownstone had high mansards and windows with pointed arches surmounted by a carved barge board or a hood mold. As an example, we cite Olana, home of the artist Frederick Church, built high above the east bank of the Hudson near the Rip Van Winkle Bridge (Figure 6.13). Somewhat atypical of the usual run of such houses in its insertion of colorful tiles in the facade, it may be said to be allied more closely to late Victorian chromaticness.[6] The Palmer House

Figure 6.10 Paris Opera House, 1861–1875. Charles Garnier, architect. (© Arch. Phot. Paris / S. P. A. D. E. M., 1979.)

in Chicago, built in 1872 by J. M. Van Osdel (1811–1875), is an ostentatious display piece of Second Empire Style, as is the State, War, and Navy Department building built by A. B. Mullet in 1871–1875. The financial panic of 1873 put an end to building in a fashion so imposing.

When the Renaissance was again revived, it was as a serious archaeological study. Hitchcock has called it the *Academic Reaction*.[7] Its principal exponent was the firm of McKim, Mead, and White [Charles Follen McKim (1847–1909), W. Richard Mead (1846–1928), and Stanford White (1853–1906); Figures 6.14 and 6.15]. As they began their New York partnership, the United States was entering an era when vast fortunes like the Vanderbilt's and the Frick's demanded New York mansions that would carry prestige similar to that of the Cinquecento pa-

Figure 6.11   Grand staircase of the Paris Opera House, 1861–1875. Charles Garnier, architect. (© Arch. Phot. Paris / S. P. A. D. E. M., 1979.)

lazzo. This young architectural firm was capable of supplying an exact replica while filling the interiors with the fabulous richness of antiques.

Richard M. Hunt (1827–1895) was the first American to study at the *Ecole des Beaux-Arts.* He designed buildings in the academic French tradition during the latter half of the nineteenth century and should be listed as a successful architect who with competence provided America with regal European styles (Figures 6.16 and 6.17).

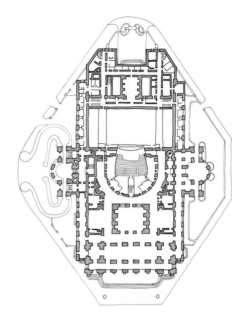

Figure 6.12 (right) Plan of the Paris Opera House, 1861–1875. Charles Garnier, architect. (Adapted from Charles Garnier, *Nouvel Opéra,* I.)

Figure 6.13 (below) Olana, New York State, 1870, home of the artist Frederick Church. Designed by Richard Morris Hunt in collaboration with Frederick Church. (G. C. Ball.)

Figure 6.14   The Villard Houses, Madison Avenue, New York, 1883–1885. McKim, Mead & White, architects. (Historic American Buildings Survey.)

Other Revivals

McKim, Mead, and White fostered other revivals, in particular, the Colonial Revival Style of such palatial mansions as the H. A. C. Taylor House in Newport. Needless to say, this sort of revivalism lapped over into the twentieth century, filtering down and climbing up the social scale; the former was characterized by an eclecticism of an often amusing variety and the latter by a fidelity frequently cold and unrelated to the patterns within.

Eclectic and Romantic Styles of the Nineteenth Century

In one sense all styles are revivals; all have borrowed something from tradition and have added some element of the new. When borrowing has seemed self-conscious and copying has been from many different styles bound into one piece, the result is known as eclecticism, a malady readily contracted by mechanized production. When the fiction created is of something idyllic, of faraway and long ago, the style may be called romantic—an escape psychosis.

Figure 6.15   Entrance hall staircase, the Villard Houses, Madison Avenue, New York, 1883–1885. McKim, Mead & White, architects. (Historic American Buildings Survey, Steven Zone.)

257

Figure 6.16 (above) Vanderbilt House—The Breakers—Newport, Rhode Island, 1895. Richard M. Hunt, architect. (Photograph, Wayne Andrews.)

Figure 6.17 (left) State dining room, The Breakers, Newport, Rhode Island, 1895. (Budek.)

To head the list of eclectic-romantic buildings, we all know about Neuschwanstein, that preposterous castle built by the king of Bavaria, mad Ludwig II. We can also point to the Pavilion at Brighton (Figure 6.18). This last work, observable now in careful restoration, possessed the virtue of having been well and expensively put together. In a rather sensational way it was the creation of the Prince Regent (1762–1830), son of George III of England. Never in complete rapport with his parents, blessed with too much money and too little work and aided and abetted by his adventurous uncle, the Duke of Cumberland, he led a life that certainly was lacking in discretion. Settling at the gay seaside resort of Brighton, ostensibly to take the waters for his infirmities, he abandoned Carlton House, his London residence, after his coming of age, and resided at Brighton until his Regency (1811–1820).

In Brighton he bought a modest farmhouse and hired the architect Henry Holland to make it suitable for the royal household. It was ready for occupancy in 1787. The style of Holland's building was influenced by French Neoclassicism.

The second rebuilding of Brighton was not accomplished until the Prince, in temporary command of some additional funds, turned the job over to the architect John Nash (1752–1835), that often inspired but not always meticulous designer of Regent's Park in London. The entire

Figure 6.18 The Royal Pavilion at Brighton, 1787–1818. Architects: Henry Holland succeeded by John Nash. (The Royal Pavilion, Art Gallery and Museums, Brighton.)

concept of this preserve in the center of the city with its natural areas and borders of unified Neoclassic terraces is a combination of housing and planned land use well ahead of its time. At Brighton Nash indulged his most imaginative romantic manner to create a fantasy of oriental domes and castellated towers built on armatures of iron.

Such a capricious product was not unique. On a lesser scale several East Indian conceits were built by nabobs on both sides of the Atlantic, and picturesque castellated mansions in a style known as *Scottish Baronial,* after Sir Walter Scott's home at Abbotsford (1816), traveled to America. Many were built on the high bluffs overlooking the Hudson River. When, in this location, wide porches with roofs supported by broad brackets were added, the name *Hudson River Bracketed* was attached. Alexander Jackson Davis (1803–1892), partner of Ithiel Town (1784–1844) and a

successful New York architect, is credited with many houses done in the bracketed style.

It is in the more numerous and less expensive homes that we find the true picture of an era that belonged to the commonalty. Andrew Jackson Downing (1815–1852) (Figure 6.19), a friend of Davis, a landscape gardener and writer on architectural subjects, published his *Cottage Residences* in 1842 and his *Architecture of Country Houses* in 1850. These books are truly compendiums of the eclecticism of the romantic and picturesque, geared to the purse strings of the many who could not afford the services of expensive designers. Covering what was generally a usable plan, an exterior facade, most often asymmetrically arranged, could be called Italian Villa, Rustic Cottage, Swiss Chalet, Gothic Pointed, English Tudor—all of an eclectic nature.

There were common denominators—a low-pitched roof with broad eaves, probably board-and-batten construction, some turreted extrusion, often bay windows, and always the wide verandah, joined to its roof with elaborately

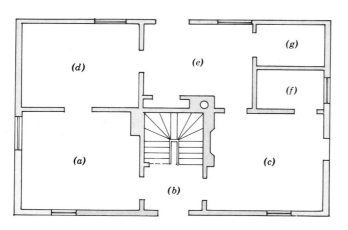

Figure 6.19 Sketch and plan of house by Andrew Jackson Downing: (a) parlor; (b) entry; (c) living room; (d) bedroom; (e) kitchen; (f) pantry; (g) storeroom. (Adapted from A. J. Downing, *The Architecture of Country Houses,* Dover, 1969.)

scrolled brackets. The typical Downing-illustrated house frequently sported carved barge boards, the ornamental designs of which have constituted the photographer's paradise. Needless to say, this style emphasized the natural setting and even justified some features as vantage points from which to survey nature's handiwork. In spirit this was the forerunner of the domestic work of Frank Lloyd Wright, but more than that it was the eternal expression of the observation of Tacitus that northern people loved the land.

Certain later expressions of these indigenous

types have been assigned names by art historians (e.g., Vincent Scully). One was the *stick style,* which prospered on the American scene in the seventies and eighties. Its name derived from the fact that the houses were framed on the quickly executed American system of studs and joists placed close together and braced but paneled with boarding in narrow uprights and horizontals to present an effect similar to half-timbering.

On a far more lavish scale the movement included the *shingle style* built for their clients by fashionable architects like Richard Upjohn and the English-trained Calvert Vaux (1824–1895), often in locations most unlikely for a rustic oriented "cottage"—namely Newport, Rhode Island. This style, too, was predicated on the use of native materials and featured free planning.

English Innovations

England produced a number of architects of eclecticism who nevertheless introduced some novel, forward-looking, and imaginative elements. Here the contribution was often stylistic rather than ideological or constructivist. The name "Queen Anne Style" has been rather loosely applied to some of the architecture of Richard Norman Shaw (1831–1912). If any analogy is to be found it is in the fine brick construction, with stone trim, in the return to facades of the regulatory principle which was the essence of early Georgian, in the use of the tall verticality of sashes, and in the homely aspect of some of the country houses (Figure 6.20).

Shaw was an eclectic who worked in many styles, but he stood with other designers, such as his sometime partners, William Eden Nesfield (1835–1888), Philip Webb (1831–1915), and E. W. Godwin (1833–1886), in his respect for the use of native materials, processes, and styles and for a basic feeling for the essence of English design stripped of all unnecessary adumbration.

Shaw, however, looked farther into the future than this resumé would imply. He introduced several innovations into his architecture near the three-quarter mark of the century. One notes an increase in fenestration and its grouping which almost foreshadows the modern ribbon window. Shaw, moreover, was interested in suiting con-

260

struction to materials, which he demonstrated in his handling of new components, such as metal frameworks; for example, in the 17 Chelsea Embankment building the iron structural members cantilever out to hold the weight of the upper stories. The logic of having appearance indicate the give and take of bearing stresses, a logic that satisfies a deep empathetic physiological need to know what is holding a building up, began to assert itself in terms of the twentieth century.

American Innovations and an Originator

Henry Hobson Richardson (1838–1889), the outstanding American architect of these years, made his contribution to great architecture in his thoughtful handling of native materials in relation to their design potential and to the functional expression of the building. It was extremely fortunate that his own virile personality coincided with the forceful energy shown by the captains of industry in this new America.

Born on a Louisiana plantation, a grandson of the English scientist, J. B. Priestley, he enjoyed the advantages of an affluent background. He was educated at Harvard and sent to the *Ecole des Beaux-Arts* to complete his architectural training. He returned to America after the Civil War to begin practice in the East, his family having lost its Louisiana holdings. It was natural that some of Richardson's first clients, the big business men of the region, should react favorably to his initial Second Empire-inspired style, particularly to that tautly organized and strong but refined version that houses the Beaux Arts itself, with its arched openings, pilaster-punctuated facade, and larger windows. Richardson's Greenleaf House in Cambridge is a good example of his ability to deviate from this style of architecture by adding a Mansard roof, classical detailing, and an American porch in a well-ordered hybrid design. In his own Staten Island home he again used the French style as a point of departure, but created its image in wood framing in which the structural elements were nicely detailed and evident (i.e., stick style). In his costly domestic work, such as the Watts Sherman House (1874), he fully demonstrated his ability to handle wood structure, often wrapped in shingles, in a style

Figure 6.20 Old Swan House, London, 1877. Richard Norman Shaw, architect. Marburg/Prothmann.)

characterized by comfortable informality and carefully calculated inconspicuousness.

The signature of the mature Richardsonian is a building of rough-hewn stone, with reveals of the round and segmental openings that clearly indicate the depth of the load-bearing walls. It has often been dubbed Romanesque Revival because of its powerful handling of masses, its

261

Figure 6.21 Marshall Field Company Warehouse, 1885–1887 (no longer in existence). Henry Hobson Richardson, architect. (Budek.)

strong, uncomplicated surfaces, and its rough granite or brownstone texture. Richardson's designs, however, were almost totally free of carved ornament, and those that existed were often of a character derived from periods other than the Romanesque.[8] Moreover, his skillful handling of the large windows required for the Marshall Field Company warehouse (1885–1887, since demolished; Figure 6.21) placed him in the first rank of embryonic modern architects.

Richardson articulated his interior spaces to exterior masses, as made apparent, for instance, in his libraries that incorporated stack rooms, reading rooms, entrance desk spaces, and galleries, all clearly indicated in the asymmetrical exterior.

Toward the Modern

The quality emphasized in the work of Shaw's generation in England and Richardson's in America was one of respect for materials with regard to their visual character and their technological potential. With this came an attempt to create an architectural form that could use the media in ways suited to the functions of building. This ideology has since been enormously complicated by the emergence of new and more efficient media for the jobs that the twentieth century needed done—notably the enclosing of more usable space per comparable architectural envelope and equipping the interior with desirable machinery.

The new materials, ancient in existence but recently perfected on an economically usable scale, were at this time restricted to iron (steel), concrete, and glass. Steel (a generic name for any of the various durable and malleable alloys of iron combined with a small percentage of other metals to give special properties for particular purposes) can be heavily loaded because it possesses to a high degree the ability to support weight like a swing—in other words, tensile strength. Concrete carries loads like a pillar, without crushing (Figure 6.22) and has great compression strength. The two in combination, with steel rods buried in the concrete, called ferroconcrete, can raise a building story on story, as it increases the span between the supports to a hitherto impossible measure. Moreover, this can be accomplished with the thinnest of supporting members and exterior coverings. When done under the advanced techniques of modern engineering and with the use of scientific knowledge of stresses and strains, the most daring plastic forms can result.

Glass can now be made in large sheets and a variety of shapes; it also possesses the desirable qualities that relate to insulation and optical management. It can assist in creating an architecture in which volume is apparently all space. Outdoors and in can be visually one.

It was the fate of the nineteenth century to struggle with this dichotomy of new structural potential and old emotionalized styles. John Ruskin discussed the issue in his essays. His reasoning seems strange to us today. In his *Seven Lamps*

Figure 6.22 Steel and concrete: (a) tensile strength of steel; (b) compression strength of concrete; (c) beam showing compression strain on upper surface and tension strain on lower surface.

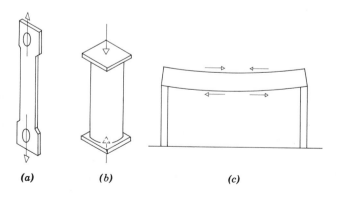

(a)   (b)   (c)

of Architecture (1849) and the *Stones of Venice* (1850) he claims that art derives its standards from society and that only an ideally unfractionated and virtuous society, which for him was the Gothic, could produce good art.

Ruskin had watched the tentacles of industry grip Britain and quite rightly felt that the divorce of the laborer from his product was at the root of the aesthetically unpalatable result spewed forth by the machine. To regain lost virtues, he argued, art must revert to the manufacturing methods of an unspecialized, hence a handicraft, society. Although he was a privileged member of a wealthy family, he nevertheless used some of his private fortune to further socialist activities.

If Ruskin, from his ivory tower, saw clearly that architecture in his age was in a quandary, it was his younger disciple William Morris (1834–1896) who took practical steps to place the world of architectural design on a creative path. Because he had studied architecture in a superficial manner, his main contribution was related to craft artifacts, in which connection he is further considered. Nevertheless, his own house, known as the Red House (built with the architectural help of his friend Philip Webb), was in a simplified and asymmetrical English vernacular style in which the exterior was dictated by the functioning of the interior spaces. It was of native red brick, devoid of the white stucco covering that the Regency style had insisted on and of any plastic ornament or polychromy, which the other current styles of historicism affected. The Morris creed considered that good art in the environment resulted from the use of local materials and handicraft and the belief that every article intended for use should be made as beautiful as possible.

Ruskin's ideology of a unified approach to the arts was one instigation for the art movement of the last decade of the century known as *Art Nouveau*. This title was adopted from the name of a new Parisian shop, *La Maison de l'Art Nouveau*, which was opened in 1895 by Siegfried Bing, an art connoisseur and dealer. Here articles styled in the newest form were displayed. The movement, called *Jugendstil* in Germany and Holland, from the title of a popular avant-garde magazine, became European international. It was called *Sezessionstil* in Austria and *Stile floreale* or *Stile Lib-*

erty in Italy; the latter designation was derived from the British firm of Liberty, which stocked materials associated with Art Nouveau designing. Today the short cognomen Art Nouveau serves to indicate a trend that incorporates something new in concept and includes all of the arts, fine and applied, involving objects large and small, machine-made and hand-crafted. The very ambition of its creed made the fashion difficult to maintain for any length of time as a creative force.

Notwithstanding, it is an important mode. If popular acclaim for its superficial aspects is the test, it was comparatively shortlived, but enduring, if judged by the persistence of its spirit. By its proscription of all art of the past—spelled out in a stipulation at Paris Art Nouveau Exhibition of 1900 that no work that showed any evidence of traditional design be admitted, it created a revolution in art, one that even today is far from being resolved.

Despite the fact that Art Nouveau was most successful in the areas of small artifacts and in the field of decoration, its relatively few achievements in architecture are significant. Here, two visual approaches can be detected—one that used the rectilinear carcass which is normally associated with traditional architecture, the other the organic

curves that are the earmark of Art Nouveau. The first is characteristic of the output of Scotland, Austria, and Germany; the second, of Brussels and Paris.

Scotland, with its background of austere Gaelic architecture, provided stimulus to a native son, Charles Rennie Mackintosh (1868–1928). In his Glasgow School of Art Building (whose east wing was finished between 1897 and 1899 and its west, just ten years later; Figure 6.23) he created a simplified, straightforward stone structure, which stripped away traditional turrets and small window slits and opened up studios to vast sheets of glass.

Other English architects of the last decades of the century—Charles Francis Annesley Voysey (1857–1941; Figures 6.24 and 6.25), C. R. Ashbee (1863–1942), M. H. Baillie Scott (1865–1945), and Sir Edwin L. Lutyens (1869–1944)—were followers of the tradition of Pugin and Webb but are important to our study because of their functional planning, their sensitive consideration for materials, and their simplified forms. Voysey, who designed houses with broad eaves, bands of windows, and asymmetrical massing, came closest to the Frank Lloyd Wright approach to architecture. In the generally light tone and absence of undue ornamentation, the structures of all these men provided a pleasant new note on the English scene.

In contrast to the English production of straightforward architecture which is significant for its

Figure 6.23 The Mackintosh Room at the Glasgow School of Art, Glasgow, Scotland, 1897–1899. Charles Rennie Mackintosh, designer. (Photograph: Clive Friend F11P, Woodmansterne Limited; Prothmann.)

Figure 6.24 Broadleys, Lake Windermere, Westmorland, 1898–1899. C. F. A. Voysey, architect. (Marburg/Prothmann.)

new-old architectonic quality, Belgian architecture of the period strove to be and was more innovative in style and handling of materials. In this it came at times perilously near the borderline where architecture ceases to be architecture and becomes mere decoration. Undoubtedly the most original Belgian architect was Victor Horta (1861–1947), who was trained in the Brussels Academy. Like his British contemporaries, he subscribed to the Art Nouveau principle of the unity of the arts and of the prerogative of the architect to design every detail of an architectural complex from framework to tableware.

The most evident as well as the most novel characteristic of Horta's architecture is the blending of decorative and structural iron in a pattern that combined straight lines with curves that seem to have originated with organic growth.

The iron tendrils that branch from the posts in the hall of the Tassel house (1892) and the Van Eetvelde house (Figure 6.26) and the painted decorations of the walls seem too junglelike for real enjoyment. On the other hand, the restraint shown in his interiors at the Hotel Solvay (1895), built for one of Belgium's immensely wealthy chemical industrialists, and in the auditorium of the Maison du Peuple (1897–1899), built for a group of cooperatives of working-class organiza-

tions, creates graceful spaces that are integrated with their anatomy.

The second Belgium architect to be connected with Art Nouveau is Henri van de Velde (1863–1957). Starting his career life as a painter, he turned to the designing of useful artifacts and ultimately to architecture. Once more the writings of Ruskin and Morris appear to have been the motivation. Architecture was not prominent in his early assignments and except for his own house and its contents (Bloemenwerf) at Uccle near Brussels in 1895–1896, which is a streamlined version of local rural dwellings, he built lit-

Figure 6.25 Plan of The Orchard, Chorley Wood, Hertfordshire, 1899. C. F. A. Voysey, architect. (a) hall; (b) porch; (c) study; (d) dining room; (e) lavatory; (f) water closet; (g) school room; (h) bicycles; (k) coal; (m) water closet; (n) scullery; (o) kitchen. (Adapted from an article in the magazine British Architect around 1900.)

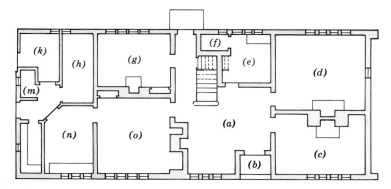

Figure 6.26   Salon, the Van Eetvelde House, Brussels, 1895. Victor Horta, architect. (Marburg/Prothmann.)

designed lounge were sent to the Decorative Arts Exhibition in Dresden. Many commissions in Germany followed and later he became the head of the Weimar School of Applied Art, which developed into the famous Bauhaus.

With the exception of Hector Guimard (1867–1942), who represents much the same idiom as Horta, the French architects of the late nineteen hundreds do not seem to merit inclusion in a story that must all too briefly relate only the most significant architecture to styles in interior design. Guimard, in his designs for the Paris Métro and the Castel Béranger (an apartment building) used iron, terra cotta, and glass in characteristic Art Nouveau shapes to achieve a total architectural conception, much as Horta had done. The French reclaimed their former importance in the twentieth century with Perret and Le Corbusier.

The fascinating architecture of Antonio Gaudí y Cornet (1852–1926), a native of Spain, must be considered even though it falls outside the geographic course we have set ourselves. The Chapel of Santa Coloma de Cervelló (1898–1914) and the Casa Milá (1905–1910; Figure 6.27) are fantastic, yet they display such knowledge of media potential, such spatial freedom, such unbelievable formations of masses and invention of ornament as to make one aware of the presence of a primal creative force. They remind us of the twisted columns seen in Medieval Iberian cloisters, of the excrescences on Plateresque and Churrigueresque architecture, of Baroque torsion, and of Art Nouveau curvature. Although not overtly functional, Gaudí's buildings stand as one more testimony to the volcanic eruption of human energy, catharsis for any unmitigated deference to logic and precept.

In Italy architecture was flourishing. Art Nouveau appeared there as a style of decoration grafted on the Renaissance idiom of rectangular mass. Lush naturalistic ornament was seemingly preferred and novelty for its own sake appeared as its *bête noir*. Giuseppe Sommaruga (1867–1917) in his Palazzo Castiglioni (1901–1903) is a fair enough example.

Both Germany and Austria assumed a more architectonic approach to building than can be attributed to the other nations of the Continent. Otto Wagner (1841–1918), the eldest of the Vien-

tle of significance until he did the 1913–1914 theater for the Werkund Exhibition at Cologne and the Rijksmuseum Kröller-Müller, Otterlo, Holland.

Between the dates of the earliest and the latest of van de Velde's achievements came his accomplishments as an artist whose name was closely connected not only with Art Nouveau but with the twentieth-century modern movement in Germany. As a result of the advertising derived from the furnishing of his own home and because he was clear and persuasive as a writer, he was invited to design a suite of four rooms for M. Bing's new Paris shop. In 1897 these rooms and a newly

Figure 6.27 Casa Milá, Barcelona, 1905–1910. Antonio Gaudí y Cornet, architect. (Photograph, Courtesy The Museum of Modern Art, New York.)

nese architects, conceived in a streamlined classical mode, making concessions only to the curve in his ingenuous wall decoration, which has about it something of the character of the provincial design seen on Alpine chalets. This is a major decorative feature on the exterior of his block of flats known as Majolika House because of the tile plaques that coat its thin planar wall.

In Wagner's Vienna Postal Savings Bank (1904–1906) we find none of the curvilinear rhythms that Horta had used. Here the iron frame was left exposed and it defines an equally formal and functional space. Nor are lightness and refinement absent. Indeed, these are qualities that seemed to touch everything that came from the queen city of the Danube. Wagner's pupil Joseph Maria Olbrich (1867–1908) brought a foretaste of the European style to America when he designed the court in the German Pavilion at the St. Louis Exposition of 1904. American soil, however, was not too suited to the generation of Art Nouveau. The culture it had spawned was too steeped in British tradition, too conventional, and paradoxically too vigorous for a style that was often unorthodox in a slightly theatrical way.

With Josef Hoffmann (1870–1955), Olbrich helped to found the Vienna Secession movement in 1897, which drew together a group that held exhibitions in Vienna relating to modern work in

267

Figure 6.28 Stoclet Mansion, Brussels, 1905–1911. Josef Hoffmann, architect. (Photography, Courtesy The Museum of Modern Art, New York.)

the arts. In 1903 Hoffmann, with the Austrian artist Koloman Moser (1868–1918), organized the Vienna (Wiener) Werkstätte. This school-shop-business complex was based on the Morris concept of an accord between architecture and the crafts and was designed to negotiate complete architectural projects from the largest to the smallest detail. The Wiener Werkstätte became one of the first organizations to present a commercial team and a unified design concept to the public. The Austrian Pavilion at the Werkbund Exposition of 1914 in Cologne and another in Paris in 1925 were outstanding examples of the completeness that could be achieved. The school's curriculum, based on a thorough grounding in core courses and allowing for higher echelon di-

versification of training, seems to be the only type that makes sense in the attempt to attain consistency in the environmental arts.

Most art students know Josef Hoffmann as the architect of Stoclet Mansion (1905–1911) in Brussels (Figure 6.28). This building is certainly a strange example of the invasion by the straight line into the camp of organic curves. Although Hoffmann's *Palais* was traditionally constructed, its exterior facing of thin marble slabs framed by gilded bronze moldings created a clean-cut surface that could not fail to explain the interior volume. Likewise the concentrated use of glass in the tower tier of windows and in the balcony, as well as the open iron railing, provided an aspect of seeing through, of interplay of exterior and interior, that was prophetic of much of twentieth-century development. Incidentally, the patterning of dark against light which extends even to the choice of neatly boxed foliage preserves the Austrian penchant for visual drama.

If any one of the most outstanding works of the Germans, such as the Atelier Elvira of August Endell (1871–1925), were stripped of its supercharged Art Nouveau decoration, it would turn out to be a building of almost square facade (no Greek proportions!) outlined by thin planes in a manner similar to Stoclet.

Beyond the spatial interest, Stoclet is important as a shining example of the Austrian preference for luxurious materials. Whether the fabric were marble and gold or pewter and wool, it was handled with a restraint that spells elegance simply by the attention to finesse in execution of each detail toward the unity of the whole.

The progress in contemporary architecture which resulted in the present world of steel, concrete, and glass structures is discussed in Chapter 7. It should be mentioned here that certain of the giants and pioneers in this advance had made noteworthy achievements during the last decade of the nineteenth century. Louis Sullivan (1856–1924) had completed his twelve-story Carson Pirie Scott Department Store in Chicago in 1899–1903. Charnley House by Frank Lloyd Wright (1869–1959) was finished in 1891 and his Winslow House, in 1893. Actually, his Robie house of 1908 came as a paradigm and a climax to his style of domestic building. The firm of Burnham (Daniel H., 1846–1912) and Root (John W., 1850–1891) began their remarkable Reliance Building, an all-steel skeleton skyscraper in Chicago in 1890 and their Monadnock Block was done in 1889–1891.

The architecture of the nineteenth century, which extended from the time of the wearing of satin knee breeches to that of stove pipe hats, from the revivals that stretched from classicism through Medievalism only to swing back, and which included the first popular attempt to throw historicism overboard and to create a new visual style—such architecture presents a difficult era to understand. That its forms were often mere surface artificiality that hide fundamental inner changes we can now both acknowledge and forgive.

SOME NINETEENTH-CENTURY HOUSES

ITALY

V. Marlia	Lucca	Built in the sixteenth century and rebuilt and refurnished by Princess Elisa, Napoleon's sister; frescoes by Prud'hon and Tosanelli ca. 1800–1809
P. Reale (Figure 6.30)	Caserta	Northern wing refinished and furnished by Queen Caroline, Napoleon's sister ca. 1807 and finished after 1815
P. Castiglioni	Milan	1901–1903; architect, Giuseppe Sommaruga (at present stripped of some decoration)

FRANCE

Malmaison	Near Paris	Built in the seventeenth century, used as a hospital; bought by Napoleon in 1799; redesigned by Percier and Fontaine
Chateau de Ferrières	Seine-et-Marne	1857, for Baron James de Rothschild; architect, Joseph Paxton

269

THE NINETEENTH CENTURY

SPAIN

Palace Güell	Barcelona	1885; architect, Gaudí

ENGLAND

Highclere Castle	Hampshire	1837–1857 remodeling; architect, Sir Charles Barry
Cronkhill Villa	Near Shrewsbury, Shropshire	1802; architect, John Nash
Stratton Park	Hampshire	1803–1804; architect, George Dance II
Brighton Pavilion (Figure 6.18)	Brighton	On nucleus of old farmhouse; first reconstruction, 1787, architect, Henry Holland; replanning, not executed, architect, James Wyatt; redesigning of stables, 1803, William Porden; redecoration of interiors, 1802, by P. F. Robinson, pupil of Holland, and London firm of John Crace and Sons; final architectural reconstruction; 1815, 1818, architect, John Nash; interiors, Frederick Crace and Robert Jones
Abbotsford	Roxburghshire	1816 and 1822, for Sir Walter Scott; architects, Edward Blore and William Atkinson, respectively
Windsor Castle	Windsor	1820–1830 remodeling; architect, Sir Jeffry Wyatville (1776–1840)
Scarisbrick Hall	Ormskirk, Lancashire	1837 and 1867, remodeling; architects, A. W. N. Pugin and Edward Welby Pugin, respectively
The Grange	Ramsgate, Kent	1841–1843; architect's own house, A. W. N. Pugin
Hughenden Manor	High Wycombe, Buckinghamshire	1847, for Benjamin Disraeli; architect, E. B. Lamb (1805–1869)
The Red House	Bexley, Kent	1859; architects, Philip Webb and William Morris
Elvethan Park	Hampshire	1861; architect, S. S. Teulon (1812–1873)
Cloverley Hall	Shropshire	1865; architects William E. Nesfield and Richard Norman Shaw
Castell Coch	Wales	1865, restoration; architect, William Burges
Glen Andred	Near Withyham, Sussex	1866; architect, Richard Norman Shaw
Eaton Hall	Cheshire	1870, enlargement; architect, A. Waterhouse (1830–1905)
McConochie House	Cardiff, Wales	1875; architect, William Burges
Kinmel Park	Near Abergele, Wales	1871–1874; architect, William E. Nesfield
Old Swan House (Figure 6.20)	London, Chelsea Embankment	1876; architect, Richard Norman Shaw
Smeaton Manor	Yorkshire	1878; architect, Philip Webb
Waddesdon Manor	Buckinghamshire	1880–1883; architect, G. H. Destailleur
Wightwick Manor	Wolverhampton, near Birmingham, Staffordshire	1887; architect, Edward Ould
Broadleys (Figures 6.24 and 6.37)	Lake Windermere, Westmorland	1898; architect, C. F. A. Voysey
The Orchard (Figure 6.25)	Chorley Wood, Hertfordshire	1899; architect, C. F. A. Voysey

Tigbourne Court	Witley, Surrey	1899; architect, Edwin Lutyens
Blackwell House	Lake Windermere, Westmorland	1900; architect, M. H. Baillie Scott
Windy Hill	Kilmacolm, Scotland	1899–1901; architect, Charles Rennie Mackintosh
Hill House	Helensburgh, Scotland	1902–1903; architect, Charles Rennie Mackintosh

AUSTRIA, GERMANY, THE NETHERLANDS

Neuschwanstein	Bavaria	1869–1881, for King Ludwig II
Linderhof	Bavaria	1870–1876, for King Ludwig II
Tassel House	Brussels	1893; architect, Victor Horta
Solvay House	Brussels	1895; architect, Victor Horta
Van Eetvelde House (Figure 6.26)	Brussels	1895; architect, Victor Horta
Bloemenwerf	Near Brussels	1895; architect, Henri van de Velde
Stoclet Mansion (Figure 6.28)	Brussels	1905–1911; architect, Josef Hoffmann

UNITED STATES

Governor Gore House (Figures 5.21 and 5.22)	Waltham, Massachusetts	1799–1804
Connelly's Tavern	Natchez	1799
The Octagon House	Washington, D.C.	1800; architect, William Thornton
Harrison Gray Otis House (2) (Figure 5.20)	Boston	1800; architect, Charles Bulfinch
Timothy Ford House	Charleston	1800
Watson House	New York	1800; architect, John McComb, Jr. (?)
Nathaniel Russell House (Plate 10)	Charleston	1803–1811
Pingree (John Gardner) House	Salem, Massachusetts	1804; architect, Samuel McIntire
Absinthe House	New Orleans	ca. 1806
Harrison Gray Otis House (3)	Boston	1807; architect, Charles Bulfinch
Valentine Museum (Wickham) House	Richmond	1812; architect, Robert Mills
Thomas Amory (Ticknor) House	Boston	1804; architect, Charles Bulfinch
Bremo	Fluvanna County, Virginia	1815–1819; architect, Thomas Jefferson
Decatur House	Washington, D.C.	1817–1819; architect, Benjamin Latrobe
Hyde Hall	Near Cooperstown, New York	1811 and 1833; architect, Philip Hooker (1766–1836)
"Wedding Cake House"	Kennebunk, Maine	1820
Sinton-Taft House (Taft Museum)	Cincinnati	1820
Montmorency	Warrenton, North Carolina	1822
Casa Estudillo	San Diego	1825

Starbuck Houses	Nantucket	1835
S. P. Lloyd House	Rensselaerville, New York	1825
Arlington (Custis-Lee) House (Figure 6.2)	Alexandria, Virginia	1826; architect, George Hadfield
Beauregard House	New Orleans	1826; architect, Francisco Correjolles
Casa Soberanes	Monterey, California	1829
Varner-Hogg Plantation	Near West Columbia, Texas	1830
Shadows-on-the-Teche	New Iberia, Louisiana	1830
Greenwood (Figure 6.5)	S. Francisville, Louisiana	1830 (destroyed by fire; in process of rebuilding)
Andalusia	Near Philadelphia	1834; architect for portico, Thomas U. Walter
The Hermitage	Nashville	1834; architect, Joseph Rieff
The Larkin House	Monterey, California	1834
Washington Irving House (*Sunnyside*)	Tarrytown, New York	1837; architect, George Harvey
Belle Meade	Nashville	1835; destroyed by fire and rebuilt 1853
Colonnade Row (Lafayette Terrace) (Figure 6.33)	New York	1836; architect A. J. Davis
Berry Hill	Halifax County, Virginia	1835–1840
Hugo Reid Adobe	Near Los Angeles	ca. 1840
Devereux	Natchez	1840
Rosalie (Figure 6.4 and Plate 11)	Natchez	1820
Melrose	Natchez	1840
Lanier House	Madison, Indiana	1840; architect, Francis Costigan
Fitch-Brooks House	Marshall, Michigan	1842
Dunleith	Natchez	1847
Pontalba Apartment	New Orleans	1849, designer, James Gallier, Jr. (1829–1870)
Stanton Hall	Natchez	1851
Trussell Winchester Adobe	Santa Barbara	1852
Longwood	Natchez	1855; architect, Samuel Sloane (1815–1884)
Monteigne	Natchez	1855
Pauling Manor	Near Tappan Zee Bridge, Hudson River	1838–1870; architect, A. J. Davis
Architect's House	Staten Island	1868; architect, Henry Hobson Richardson
Olana (Figure 6.13)	Near Rip Van Winkle Bridge, Hudson River	1870; architect for initial building, Richard Morris Hunt
Andrews House	Newport, Rhode Island	1872; architect, Henry Hobson Richardson
N. Watts Sherman House (Figures 6.29 and 6.30)	Newport, Rhode Island	1874; architect, Henry Hobson Richardson
The Breakers (Figures 6.16 and 6.17)	Newport, Rhode Island	1892, for Cornelius Vanderbilt II; architect, Richard Morris Hunt
Biltmore House	Ashville, North Carolina	1890–1895, for George W. Vanderbilt; architect, Richard Morris Hunt

James Charnley House	Chicago	1891–1892; architect, Frank Lloyd Wright
Marble House	Newport, Rhode Island	1892, for William K. Vanderbilt; architect, Richard Morris Hunt
W. H. Winslow House (Figure 7.16)	River Forest, Illinois	1893; architect, Frank Lloyd Wright
Isadore Heller House	Chicago	1897; architect, Frank Lloyd Wright
Warren Hickox House	Kankakee, Illinois	1900; architect, Frank Lloyd Wright
Laurelton Hall (*Tiffany House*)	Cold Spring Harbor, New York	1906

INTERIOR DESIGN

Plans and Space Organization

A continuing evolution toward freer and more functional interior planning marked the nineteenth century.

In Neoclassic interiors bisymmetry predominated as the answer to classical tenets as well as to current needs. We have noted that the width of the central artery diminished—less emphasis on Palladian proportions, less available space.

Great ingenuity was practiced in suiting all manner of stylistic exteriors to inner functional necessity. In designing their House of Commons the English built a Medieval hall within which they placed two opposing banks of seats for the two parliamentary parties. The French devised the semicircular plan at the Palais du Sénat (Luxembourg) in which many factions could be located in sectors without a sharp line of demarcation.

In cottage-type interiors some astonishing modern space arrangements have cropped up (Figure 6.19), such as the placement of the kitchen off the hall to the front (Downing: design X for a bracketed cottage) and bedrooms to the front (Downing: design III for a bracketed cottage). Formalized interiors are found as late as mid-century.

With the advent of the late Gothic after the middle of the century, some compliance with Medieval disposition occurred. Pugin at Scarisbrick used the Gothic Great Hall, but neither he nor comparable designers located it in the same relation to other spaces that it held in the past. It was Richardson in America, cueing in from

Webb in England, who made this two-story hall not only a central artery containing the stairs but a large living area as well—the return of the "living hall."

Some new design aspects are associated with these livings halls. In the Sherman House (Figures 6.29 and 6.30) Richardson opened the stairs by gradual flights to a third-dimensional view, seen through balustered grilles. Webb in 1863 provided his two-story hall with a gallery off which rooms were grouped. Some time before, at Highclere, Barry built a picturesque castle in which the rooms were gathered around a glass-roofed central cortile in the manner of an inner patio. Nesfield and Shaw, at Cloverley, planned rooms that led off the living hall at different levels, thus providing a view in several directions.

Another innovation was the abolishment of the small door between the living room and hall in favor of a wide opening made part of the group by a frieze that continued around the rooms. Space seemed to flow from area to area, as expressed in the twentieth-century pronouncement, "flow of space." Moreover, when spaces become integrated with a central core and small openings tend to disappear, we have "open planning," as demonstrated later in Frank Lloyd Wright's Warren Hickox House (1900).

One more ingredient which is part of the twentieth-century concept is the relation of the placement of a building to views of the surrounding landscape. This the nineteenth century produced in two details. One was the side verandah which, in addition to its sometime function of balancing the design bisymmetrically and creating an interesting rhythm of voids and masses, could extend the inner space into the outer. Verandahs on

273

Figure 6.29 (above) N. Watts Sherman House, Newport, Rhode Island, 1874. Henry Hobson Richardson, architect. (Budek.)

Figure 6.30 (below) Plan of the Watts Sherman House, Newport, Rhode Island, 1874. H. H. Richardson, architect. (a) vestibule; (b) living hall; (c) dining room; (d) library; (e) living room; (f) service; (g) butler's pantry; (h) back stairs. (Adapted from *The Architecture of H. H. Richardson and His Times* by Henry Russell Hitchcock. © 1961, The Shoe String Press Inc., Hamden, Connecticut.)

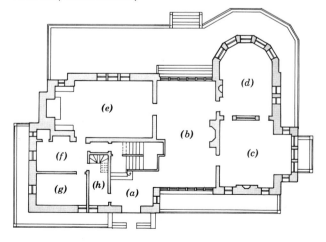

American houses became almost ubiquitous from midcentury, wherever land permitted.

Visual extension was also made possible by increasing the window areas. Both Shaw in England and Richardson in America used windows grouped as ribbons or window walls, anticipating once more the work of Frank Lloyd Wright.

The kind of thinking that developed these theories of spatial flow, open planning, and extension into the surround was not always skillfully or aesthetically translated into reality. Open plans grow monotonous when the spaces themselves are uninteresting. Flow of space depends on its creator's sensitivity to progressive proportions. Extension into the surround entails a planned relationship between interior elements and exterior expansion. Bay windows and inglenooks, which proliferated in nineteenth-century plans, can become both bumpy and fussy when poorly designed.

The skillful avoidance of these ills is remarkably demonstrated in the artistry of Victor Horta (Figure 6.26). Horta made use of wall plasticity, tinted glass dividing screens, and larger than usual clear-glass planes for openings to create an airy feeling within spatial limitations.

The role that dimensional restrictions attendant on urban conditions played in this new planning is a fascinating tale. Land restraint was common to most city development, but in New York City the size of the lots had originally been plotted foolishly at 20 or 25 by 100 ft. Hence builders had no choice but to go up and back. The off-center house of three or four stories, with service and nursery in the basement, formal rooms and dining rooms on the first level, and family and bedrooms from there up, became customary (Figure 6.31).

Figure 6.31 Plan of four stories of a New York row house, 27 East Fourth Street, 1832. (a) basement; (b) first floor; (c) second floor—bedrooms (third floor is similar; (d) fourth floor—servants' quarters and storage; (e) nursery and family room; (f) kitchen; (g) parlor; (h) dining room. (Historic American Buildings Survey.)

By the eighteen twenties houses reached north of Washington Square for twenty or more blocks. A new planning expedient permitted the retention of the earlier functional specialization of space yet gave it the flexibility to expand for large social groups. In the opening between the two "parlors," which occupied one floor of the house, large doors, which slid into the walls when not needed were added. This opening was embellished in the current styles and became one of the principal architectural features of the rooms. Such innovations became adjuncts of larger houses in other parts of the country (Plate 11). The two spaces at Stanton Hall in Natchez extended the area to 72 ft.

The planning programs of these affluent middle-class homes were not simple and, in addition to the necessity for enlargement there remained the need for specialization of spatial uses. A sitting room and a nursery were required. Servants were necessary and accommodations had to be provided for them. Offices were frequently maintained under the same roof, for the alternative of "downtown" tenantry was not yet universal. Li-

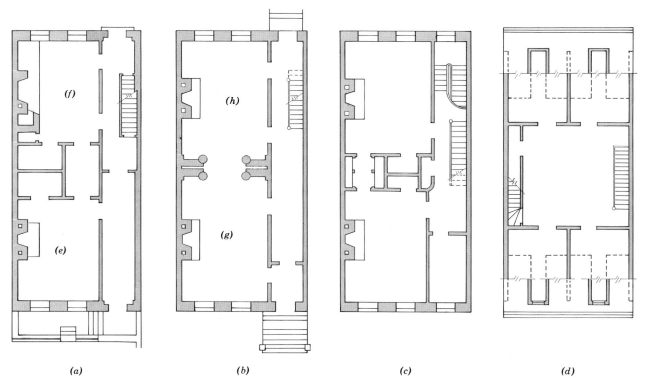

(a)　　　　(b)　　　　(c)　　　　(d)

braries and music rooms abounded. The parlor was not the exclusively formal room that is frequently implied. It was often the only place for the young people of the family to entertain. Recall that in Henry James's *Washington Square*, a brilliant delineation of New York life of this era, Catherine's suitor was not able to persuade her to meet him in the park and was "forced to see her on her terms in the parlor."

The row houses in New York, like the terraces in London and the *maisons de rapport* in Paris, crept out from the original central districts. With the advent of fireproof framing, elevators, sanitary plumbing, central heating, and gas stoves, they turned into apartments or flats. Old brownstones were converted into cold-water walk-ups for multiple use and the problems of functional obsolescence in the urban environment began.

In its break with classical tradition, the nineteenth century offered some remarkable solutions to its planning problems, solutions that embraced novel functional and aesthetic schemes. Underneath the surface of the stylistic window-dressing for which it is criticized, it gave the twentieth century some bold answers to cope with the growing need to preserve the amenities of life under spatial restrictions. The space problem is now more acute and is complicated by the fact that the modern world believes that benefits must spread to groups beyond the privileged few.

Architectural Details and Interior Surface Treatment

Nineteenth-Century Neoclassic French Interiors. Texts frequently subdivide French interiors of the first half of the nineteenth century according to political alignments; that is, Consulate, Empire, Bourbon Restoration, and Louis Philippe. All may be called Neoclassic as they progressed from the early to the late phases.

Napoleon intended to create a style by fiat when he commissioned Charles Percier and Pierre François Leonard Fontaine to be his court designers and architects. They worked under the aegis of Jacques Louis David (1748–1825), court painter in charge of the art of the realm and director of the *Manufactures Nationales*—in short a nineteenth-century Le Brun.

Both Percier and his younger friend Fontaine had been Prix de Rome students in architecture. Fontaine was the first to return to Paris and was later joined by Percier. Through their acquaintance with the cabinetmaker Jacob they were brought to official attention. Asked to design some furniture appropriate to the National Convention, the designers willfully decided to return to an "antique" style. Much of their decorative vocabulary is to be found in J. F. Blondel's *Maisons de Plaisance.*[9]

So great was the success of the two young men that they were diverted from their careers in architecture. They received commissions to design all manner of utilitarian and decorative objects. This separation from his planned profession disturbed Fontaine and he went to London to resume his career. But fate had sealed his future. Percier, meanwhile, had become director of decorations for the Opera and sought the aid of his former partner. While thus engaged they met David, who introduced them to General Bonaparte.

Much that Napoleon demanded was of the nature of restoration and refurbishing. This was true at Malmaison, the old chateau and seventeenth-century hospital, rebuilt during the eighteenth century. Josephine bought this property in 1799, three years after her marriage to Napoleon, and here she lived the happiest years of her life. She died there in 1814. For her the facade was redesigned in Neoclassic taste. Pleased with the work at Malmaison, Napoleon named Percier and Fontaine his architects, a position they retained for the duration of the Empire. In this period they restored and embellished St. Cloud, Versailles, Compiègne, and Fontainebleau, although the Emperor respected and retained most of the original interiors.

After the retirement of Percier in 1814 Fontaine became court architect to Louis XVIII, and during the reign of Charles X he held this preferential position to the House of Bourbon/Orléans for whom he restored and enlarged the *Palais Royal*. Indeed, he was in charge of the royal buildings until 1848 when he tendered his resignation.

Court designs, with their best and weakest manifestations, may thus be used to represent the entire period. For the worst—the team fitted one room at Malmaison as the Council Chamber. Its interior is formed from striped silk to resemble a tent supported by spears. Nothing could be farther removed from the structural anatomy of this lovely and chaste chateau. The walls of Josephine's chamber are somewhat similarly draped. To indicate how far these ideas traveled, we quote from a letter that Washington Irving wrote to his friend George Harvey in 1835: ". . . and beneath, at the slope of the roof, it might be papered with striped paper, so as to resemble the curtain of a tent."[10]

It is difficult to relate this kind of work with the testimony of the royal architects quoted at the beginning of this chapter. Possibly their official roles necessitated some artistic doubletalk. Fortunately the Empire designers usually did better.

The design of Empire interiors took its point of departure from the cleaned-up architecture of Neoclassicism. Interior walls were handled as large expanses. The dado was abolished and pilasters or semidetached columns of real or simulated stone often rose from baseboard to cornice. The wall coverings were stretched cloth, paper, or painted designs. The frieze was deepened and, like the rest of the wall treatment, was frequently faked by paper imitation on which Empire emblems such as garlanded wreaths, sphinxes, Napoleonic bees, fasces, key frets, and anthemions were arranged in tight composition. The source of inspiration for most of these motifs was Imperial Rome, the grandeur of which Napoleon emulated, and Dynastic Egypt, with which country he felt an affiliation because of his successful Egyptian campaigns.

Fashionable French windows were floor-to-ceiling casements. Always they were architecturally simplified, possibly with only an architrave surround, with molding of simple profile, and often surmounted with a deep frieze and straight, thin cornice board. Some windows were roundheaded. Glass was divided into fewer and larger panes and muntins were narrower. Doors were treated similarly with paneling in large sizes.

As rooms were likely to have originated in an earlier epoch, the low straight-lined fireplaces made the walls seem tall. Mantels were frequently black marble supported by round, unfluted colonettes, above which large mirrors were commonly hung, designed for the allotted space in straight-line gilded enframement. Floors were marble or parqueted wood, covered more fully than before with carpets. Colors tended toward strength, darkness, and great contrast of tone.

This archetype interior was modified in the service of members of Napoleon's family who took up magnificent residence in many of the capitals of western Europe. In Naples where the Palazzo Reale in the city and a section of Caserta to the north had been redesigned the initial shells contributed to the majestic effect. The Italian designer Antonio de Simone, assisted later by the French architect E. C. Leconte (1762–1818), was responsible for two handsome rooms at Caserta, the Sala di Astrea and the Sala di Marte (Figure 6.32). Here the tall, somber, punctuating pilasters, rising from a darker marble stylobate, support a frieze decorated with gilded griffins, above which a dentil border and cornice molding are surmounted by a tall attic. This is interior architecture in the Versailles sense. Large white marbles in bas relief occupy the intervening spaces.

We are in possession of innumerable paintings of the nineteenth century which illustrate the *mise en scène*. It is made clear by them that the Bonapartes and Murats of Naples, as well as the later Neapolitan Bourbons, possessed ". . . the Biedermeier taste"[11] in regard to the furnishings of their intimate apartments.

In accounts of the period between 1800 and 1850 the word *Biedermeier* occurs frequently. It has overtones of derision not always deserved. The Biedermeier style—or more properly the Biedermeier taste—was a name given to domestic interiors known especially in central Europe. It connotes a considerably modified version of the French court styles. Not only was it adapted to middle-class interiors but the Hapsburg rulers, Francis I and II (1792–1835), are said to have preferred this comfortable, homey version of the ostentatious Napoleonic mode.

In the last decades of the eighteen hundreds a series of poems, which had appeared at least forty years before in the German periodical *Fliegende Blätter*, was reissued. These verses were purportedly written by Herr Biedermeier (*nom de plume* for Samuel Friedrich Sauter), an ingenuous, affably bigoted, and pompous burgher, whose very name —meaning honest Mr. Smith—indicated what to

Figure 6.32 The Sala di Marte at the Palazzo Reale, Caserta, 1807. E. C. Leconte, architect; Antonio de Simone, designer. (Alinari/Editorial Photocolor Archives.)

expect from his pronouncements on life and art. The interior design of this epoch was given this title by late-century critics.

In summary we can say that continental interiors of the first part of the nineteenth century were patterned on Neoclassic ideals, modified toward the heavier, bolder, and more masculine when men like Napoleon played the tune and toward the more festooned and cluttered as the times became more bourgeois and romantic.

Nineteenth-Century Neoclassic English Interiors. In loose terminology the counterpart of the French

Empire Style is the English *Regency*, the historical limits of which are 1811 to 1820, when George III was judged insane and the Prince of Wales, later to become George IV, reigned as Regent. Its actual term is more expansive and even the greatest stickler will allow an extension to 1830, when George IV died.

The interior surrounds for the Regency style echo rather closely those of the Continent. This is true if we neutralize color schemes, bold stripes, and contrasting textures. The English effect is quieter, in many instances less gauche, and possibly less dramatic.

Within any general description the Royal Pavilion at Brighton must be the far-out thing. It was started before the Prince's tenure as Regent and was almost abandoned by 1820. Yet its atmosphere of exoticism within the confines of a trend makes of it the museum piece of the era. In spite of, or perhaps because of, its extravagant designs, it inaugurated patterns and color schemes that found an echo much later in such modern works as the Russian ballet and the paintings of Matisse and which appeared in Persian and Indian miniatures unknown to the western world of a century ago. Whatever connections there may have been remain a riddle.

We know little about the first interiors at Brighton which were the work of architect Holland's pupil P. F. Robinson. It is assumed that they were in the Neoclassic style of the late eighteenth century.

The second (1802–1804) and third (1815–1822) reconstructions are a matter of history and illustration. The London interior design firm of John Crace and Sons was apparently in the act in 1788 but then only to understudy the architect. In the second and third Brightons John Crace's son Frederick seems to have provided the designs (Plate 7) and to have carried out most of the interior work, although in the second Brighton Robert Jones, about whom too little is known, was paid separately for some of the rooms.

Unlike Napoleon, who was too preoccupied to take an active hand in the progress in his palaces, Prince George, as heir apparent, as Regent, and to a lesser extent as king, became to a degree unprecedented in the Hanoverian annals a patron of the arts and an exacting taskmaster to those who attempted to carry out his wishes. A letter from the resident clerk of the works, J. Watier, to Crace on January 1, 1818, states:

> The Prince Regent wishes you to come down as soon as you can and bring with you everything necessary, also what you have done. The P.R. wd rather see your progress here, he is fearfull that you will not understand him unless he has you on the spot—therefore make your own arrangement as I cannot put him of [sic] any longer.[12]

The Crace renderings, along with other documents pertaining to the interior work at the Pavilion, are now the property of the Cooper-Hewitt Museum, New York (the Smithsonian Institution's National Museum of Design). A final series of engravings and aquatints is preserved in the works of the architect John Nash.

The Prince's taste was quite in sympathy with the trend toward the romantic and picturesque. The painted elevations show a mixture of exotic elements that mingled the Chinese, Indian, and Moorish in their fabric. Note the music room—the crimson and yellow-reds of the panels on the west wall, the dragons entwined on backdrops of blue, and the lilac-toned dadoes. This palette is all the more interesting because another proposed design for this wall was in pastel blues and pinks, a typical French Rococo spectrum. Who goaded the decorators to the final, almost barbaric drama?

Queen Victoria sold the Pavilion to the town of Brighton in 1850 as not being suited to the needs of her family (an understatement). As restored today it stands as a stage setting that could have happened at no other place and at no other time—tinsel and real gold, gas light but no plumbing, the Prince and a wife (Mrs. Fitzherbert) he could not acknowledge, Aladdin's lamp but no real ability to create the happy state that its magic suggests. Yet what a divertissement in defiance of Neoclassic reason!

Nash redesigned Buckingham Palace in 1826 in a more somber version of the prevalent classicism.

Nineteenth-Century Neoclassic American Interiors. Grouped under the name *Greek Revival*, the American interiors of the first half of the century run the same gamut of delicate to robust Neoclassicism. Because the southeastern seaboard was not a style pace setter, we find in such an interior as the Nathaniel Russell house in Charleston (Plate 10) what is probably the most ingratiating example of combined retrospective and forward-looking tendencies. The subtly curved walls of its interior spaces, its unadorned wall surfaces above a simply paneled dado, its beautifully executed woodwork in low relief, and its most graceful of spiral stairs, spell Adamesque. We note, however, that the American Federal is modified here toward greater use of plain surfaces, toward more rigidity in the carved design, and toward bolder projection in the cornices. The entrance hall to Decatur House and the interiors at Gore are ex-

279

Figure 6.33 Facade of Colonnade Row, New York, 1836, showing row houses united by a classical colonnade. A. J. Davis, architect. (Budek.)

amples of these introductory years of the century. The interiors of many churches, such as the First Congregational in Bennington, Vermont (1806), with its clean white surfaces almost devoid of embellishment save for semiattached unfluted columns, are typical of this stripped, transitional aspect of Neoclassicism.

The later Greek Revival style, which can be illustrated by the capitol of North Carolina (Town and Davis, 1833–1840), Colonnade Row in New York (Figure 6.33), or a row house in Washington Square (Figure 6.34), places greater emphasis on the structural use of the orders, more vigor in profiles, stronger colors contrasted with white on the walls, and a generally more robust effect.

Nineteenth-Century Eclectic, Revival, Romantic Interiors. Interiors from 1850 to 1900—what do you call them? They were not of a piece, yet they possessed common traits. Revivals, even though pure in intent, slide imperceptibly into eclecticism, that free borrowing from many styles of the past. And what is revivalism or eclecticism but a climate tinged violet with romanticism? Utter revivalism there will be none—electricity and plumbing get in the way. Still there are degrees.

The French Second Empire style sparked many of the less authentic backdrops of this era simply because the Empress Eugénie, the attractive wife of Louis Napoleon, emulated Marie Antoinette in her surroundings, hoping, no doubt, to acquire some of the social caste of that ill-fated queen. Eugénie's apartments at St. Cloud, for instance, retained much of their original setting and were refreshed by a keyed-up color scheme and new decoration. White, gold, crimson, and blue dominated. Fabrics were rich but heavy. Motifs were ossified revivals of a classic catalog.

Prominent Europeans redesigned and refurbished old chateaux, castles, and palaces in kindred nostalgia; for example, the fabulously wealthy Rothschilds built the Chateau de Ferrières, and had it revivified and personalized, under the direction of the artist Eugène Lami (1800–1890), with a combined French and Italian exterior and something resembling a Second Empire interior.

England did not break with classicism until after the Queen's marriage to Prince Albert of Saxe-Coburg in 1840, when continental influences were felt. The refurbishing of the Prince Consort's rooms at Buckingham Palace set the tone for a style that at least took its name from the reigning monarch—Victoria—although in actuality it was a rather heavy-handed version of the French.

The same title is customarily given to the interiors in America of corresponding years (ca. 1850–1865). *Antebellum* is occasionally suggested as defining an age and a way of life that disappeared under the guns of the Civil War.

A composite picture of these midcentury years can be used if one will allow that it is merely a suggested norm from which time and place ring changes. Many characteristics of Neoclassicism remained (Plate 11)—high-ceilinged rooms, generous spaces, dividing screens, tall windows, and French mantels. Inner shutters were occasionally seen. Flat or coved ceilings were bare except for large central medallions from which the lighting fixture was suspended. Walls with unbroken areas or with moldings demarking dados and panels carried fabric, paper, or ornament. Floors in domestic interiors favored full, highly patterned carpeting. Accent colors were often strong, and the brilliant tones of the motifs combined with gold, white, and, even in the carpets, rich black.

In essence this midcentury interior was never much altered. Colors grew darker, beautiful wood was left in its natural finish rather than painted, textures became heavier, and simpler and bolder moldings were found. When done with grace, it was dignified and on the domestic scene, homely (Figure 6.35). A curious but not discordant quality often evolved.

Toward the century's end the Queen Anne Revival style in England (Shaw, Nesfield, Webb) and the Colonial Revival style in America (McKim, Mead, and White) represented, probably just as Eugénie's efforts did, an attempt to return to the

Figure 6.34 Stairway hall, Washington Square row house, New York city, ca. 1840. (Library of Congress.)

past. English versions emphasized simplification and the vernacular, the American, a restrained classicism. President Theodore Roosevelt's Long Island home, built in 1887 by the New York architectural firm of Lamb and Rich, with its plain pastel papering and light woodwork, damask draperies and net curtains, an Aubusson covering much of the floor, and its unassuming upholstered furniture, created an atmosphere, if not a duplication of the refined Georgian. It has remained a conventional, popular norm ever since.

All of these *isms* can easily shift from the pure to the spurious, from the genuine to the artificial, and from sincerity to cant. Mr. Downing said:

Figure 6.35 *The Hatch Family,* Eastman Johnson, America, 1871. Metropolitan Museum of Art, New York. (The Metropolitan Museum of Art. Gift of Frederick H. Hatch, 1926.)

When a villa is designed by an architect, he generally superintends and directs the finishing of the interior; and in the villas of considerable importance, interior decorators, who devote themselves to this branch of the profession, are called on to complete the whole, as the builder leaves it. Some of these, like Mr. George Platt of New York . . . , possess talent enough to take . . . a suite of apartments . . . , design and execute the decorations, add color, and furnish them throughout in any style.[13]

Not a style, but styles, are recommended; not creators with a common purpose, but two creators who work alone, arbitrarily, and consecutively. Blondel countenanced the separation of exterior and interior; now the interior can divorce itself from the present. It has taken a century for the fallacy of this mode of thinking to be recognized.

Reform Style Interiors. Henry Hobson Richardson and his followers during the seventies and eighties created a type of interior that they would be surprised to have us consider a reform style. It was reform because of its difference from the otherwise current fashion, which featured some phase of romantic, eclectic revivalism.

Richardson was physically a big man who maintained a vigorous outlook on life. He created an architecture in which coarser textures and the honest expression of materials played a significant role. In his buildings, such as the Sherman House (1874–1875; Figures 6.29 and 6.30), the Ames Memorial Library (1878), the New York State Capitol (1878), the Reverend Percy Brown House in Marion, Massachusetts (1881), the Paine House in Waltham, Massachusetts, or the Hay House in Washington as late as 1884, we have a composite picture of fine woods left unpainted. There is also the magnificent stone fireplace in the Senate Hall in the capitol at Albany, whose ornament was not archaeological and which, with its verdure carving, was inspired by the work of the Morris firm.

Richardson used ribbon windows (a band of windows also favored by Shaw) which he subdivided into separate double-hung sashes with small regular panes and heavy muntins, thus preserving their character as part of the textural fabric of the building. He often inserted stained glass, in tune with the polychromatic tendencies of the Late Victorian. John La Farge designed the hall glass of the Sherman House.

Richardson left much of the detail of his interiors to his assistants and in particular to Stanford White. Subscribing to the Ruskin–Morris principle of the unity of a piece of architecture, he made use of contemporary sculptors like Homer Saint-Gaudens, glass artists like Morris and La Farge, and men with the painter's touch, like White.

Stanford White was, in his tastes, much akin to Richardson. He may be said, however, to have possessed a greater decorative sense and a love for intricate detail and richness of pattern. Color, for him, played an important role. In the Sherman House the green and gold of the library and the

white and gold of the drawing room contribute not a little relief from what might have been an overwhelmingly somber tone. The plaster walls of buildings in the Richardson style were often painted by White to harmonize with the tones of rich pink marble or tawny orange sandstone.

White did his best work under Richardson. He demonstrated his capability of enriching the scene without detracting from its essential structure. When in the late seventies he branched out on his own, he often forgot the restraint that Richardson demanded. It cannot be denied, however, that he understood the wishes of those end-of-the-century Americans whose coffers apparently had no bottom. Before his untimely death in 1906 Stanford White became the most famous and sought-after "decorator" and one of the wealthiest.

In England a *William Morris* interior (Figure 6.36) represents a reform style akin to that of the Richardsonian in America. It is difficult to speak of it apart from its furnishings because Morris also advocated the indissolubility of art. At Wightwick Manor, near Wolverhamton in Staffordshire, we come close to viewing a William Morris period piece. This is a National Trust property dedicated to preserving and adding to the original purchases of Morris artifacts by Theodore Mander, ancestor of the donors, Sir Geoffrey and Lady Mander. The architect was Edward Ould but Charles Kempe (1837–1907) was responsible for its decoration.

Figure 6.36 Wightwick, Manor, Wolverhampton, Staffordshire, 1887. Edward Ould, architect. (Courtesy of Lady Mander, Wightwick Manor.) This interior illustrates the designing principles of William Morris.

Another example of a Richard Morris and Philip Webb interior is perhaps closer to hand in the decoration of the refreshment room in the Victoria and Albert Museum, done in 1867.

In line with the prevailing return to Medievalism, the woodwork in these two examples is paneled to a high dado, above which there could be a deep plaster frieze touched with gold or some ornamental panel relieved by painted pictorial inserts. These were customarily done by a member of the Pre-Raphaelite Brotherhood (see p. 304). Panels of Morris textiles or wallpaper substitute for the frieze if the room is exceptionally high-ceilinged. Ceilings are plastered within a wooden structural framework or designed as a set composition, thereby imitating those of an earlier age. Despite this sort of throwback, the actual ornamentation would have Pre-Raphaelite overtones, being a blend of nature's forms entwined at times with maidens' heads. Stained glass, a specialty of the firm, is often used in interiors. Handmade tiles by the potter De Morgan (see Ceramics) are conspicuous in chimney locations. Morris carpets of pronounced oriental character cover the floors (for Morris color schemes see p. 287). In all this

we see again the operation of the Morris creed of handicrafting and self-participation as a means of developing artistic surroundings. In addition we note that no detail is considered too small to be unimportant for this end.

Other reform movements in the last quarter of the century were related to the buildings of Voysey (Figures 6.24, 6.25, and 6.37), Baillie Scott, and Lutyens. We may illustrate with The Orchard, C. F. A. Voysey's home at Chorley Wood in Hertfordshire. Its first-floor space incorporated a living hall with inglenooks. The latter, which were frequent in the cottage architecture of the time, possibly served as shadowed foils for light and promoted a romantic image of Darby and Joan seated on adjoining benches. If inglenooks appear as reversions, the w.c. and lavatory on the plan are welcome portents of the future. Both were to be found at The Orchard.

The most significant aspect of this house lies in the manner in which Voysey created a simple, fresh interior where all imitation of the past is forgotten, where walls are flat planes without ornament, where colors are light and cheerful, and the whole has a bare, well-swept look. The hall is painfully straight-lined. It uses natural elements in its green slate floor and delicate green Dutch fireplace tiles. A rug of Donegal tuft in peacock

Figure 6.37 Interior view, Broadleys, Lake Windermere, Westmorland, 1898–1899. Home of C. F. A. Voysey, architect. (Marburg/Prothmann.)

blue covers only a small portion of the space. Curtains are turkey-red twill. The walls are covered below the molding with purple silk fiber paper above which the woodwork and plaster is white. As compared with other interiors of the time, it is uncluttered, colorful, clear, and textured.

Whereas the English school of designers leaned heavily toward a trimmed-down version of the cottage style, the Scots—Charles R. Mackintosh and George Walton—created at once more architectonic and more dramatic interiors. Lines were dominantly straight with pronounced verticality. The color schemes were light but always spectacularly accented with dark detailing. The sense of abstraction and rigidity, so necessary in architectural interiors, was prevalent even in the tea rooms (and what could lure a designer more toward the picturesque?) that were done for Miss Catherine Cranston in Glasgow. Margaret MacDonald Mackintosh, the wife of C. R., collaborated with her husband on most enterprises and it is tempting to think that some of the suave elliptical curves that crept in are due to her influence.

Art Nouveau Interiors. Art Nouveau, described as primarily concerned with decoration, nevertheless made important contributions to buildings and their interiors.

Because of the cost of designing in a new manner, Art Nouveau interiors are both expensive and sometimes precious. They may be said to begin with Victor Horta either at the Tassel House in 1892 or at the Hotel Solvay several years later. These Horta-designed apartments possess graceful movements that go beyond the Parisian Hôtel Soubise many years before in making extensive use of organic curves. In the halls the posts are exposed metal—polished forged iron—which uses to the full its potential for assuming tortuous shapes. Every decorative detail was designed by the same hand, thus preserving a unity that cannot be denied. The damask covering on the walls, the screens of stained glass which act as room dividers to make space visible, flexible, and flowing, the flowerlike clusters of electric lights, the furniture covered in the most sumptuous silks, the pieces of ornamental hardware, all present a study in curved-line elegance.

If this finally tires the nerves because of its never-ceasing movement and irritates the intellect because of its unarchitectonic character, at least it seems emotionally warm and rationally organized. An interior of Horta's defies reproduction, yet it can point the way by its creative character, its espousal of the potentials of new and old materials, and its expression of charm without loss of power to the twentieth century. Consider the TWA Air Terminal at Kennedy airport designed by Saarinen (Figures 7.31 and 7.32).

In Austria, which was much influenced by British designers like Mackintosh, architecture and interiors remained straight-lined. Nevertheless, they maintained an elegant sensuous appeal, acquired through expensive materials and the utmost attention to detail. Stoclet mansion in Brussels, done by the Austrian, Josef Hoffmann, is an outstanding example. In the high interiors are warm-colored marbles (when used as walls, the plates are framed by moldings of gilded bronze), tiles, mosaics, and handsome floors demarked with extensive use of straight-edged metal. Here Hoffmann abandoned dark tones and admitted much light. The tall, slim windows in the stair tower have become almost a cliché of modern builders. Mechanical apparatus in Stoclet was advanced for its time and structural elements were emphasized. Furnishings are not abundant. Thus an unusual degree of simplicity prevailed which might prompt the saying that it is not simple to be simple.

In Stoclet the murals of Gustav Klimt—cofounder with Hoffmann of the Vienna *Sezession* Movement of 1897—and the thin-wall revetments emphasize the idea of volume defined by planes. Space rather than mass is created. The subject of the mosaic murals is allegorical and deals with the "tree of life" motif. It is treated in a flat pattern of dominantly curved lines and is fashioned of glass and semiprecious stones, metal, and enamel—again the Austrian love of richness of effect. It was the Austrian architect Josef Urban who, coming to New York at the beginning of the twentieth century, created the fabulous apartment interiors that gave America a foretaste of the modern, and unfortunately created the idea that modern design was intended for extravagant pocketbooks.

285

East Germany, with the exception of Dresden, came rather late on the scene. West Germany, and especially Munich and Darmstadt—near France and close to Austria—became disseminating centers for Art Nouveau tendencies that skillfully combined the influences of Vienna, Brussels, and Paris.

In Munich a group of painters, converted into craftsmen and architects, exhibited at the Dresden Exhibitions of 1897 and 1899. Subsequently the Grand Duke of Hesse invited seven artists, among them Joseph Olbrich (1867–1908) and Peter Behrens (1868–1940), who had studied at the Vienna Werkstätte, to form a colony on his estate at Mathildenhohe. Their 1900 exhibition opened the gateway to the twentieth century.

We call attention to the interior work of two of the Munich men. Richard Riemerschmid (1868–1957) designed a music room for the 1899 Dresden exhibition. It was a well-planned space in which the curved embrasure of the window did not detract from the structural scheme of the room as a whole. Although a quiet wallpaper covered the lower section up to door-height level, a stenciled frieze, as deep as those of Morris, decorated the upper portion. With its sparse table and chairs arranged as immobile pieces, the room is both restful and interesting. The flood of light from the large clear window is significant of the emphasis on it in twentieth-century architecture.

Behrens in his later work at Darmstadt designed along similar lines—the exterior in streamlined traditional with some of the tonal drama of Vienna; the interior more tectonic than Horta's or even Riemerschmidt's, with all the wall planes kept intact and with curved line ornament segregated in its own compartment.

Color in Nineteenth-Century Interiors

Although mention has been made of nineteenth-century color, it remains to be emphasized that color science with conscious attention to its psychological aspects was of that period. Building on the seventeenth-century theory of Sir Isaac Newton on the refraction of light, Hermann F. von Helmholtz (1821–1894) expounded a theory of color vision, and Johann Wolfgang Goethe (1749–

1832), as well as the master dyer at the Gobelins, Michel Eugene Chevreul (1786–1859), experimented with the effects of colored light as mixed in the eye.

Psychology was also awakening to the emotional potential of color. Goethe in his *Zur Farbenlehre* (Theory of Chromatics, 1810) quotes a Frenchman as saying:

> He maintained that his tone of conversation with Madame had changed since she had changed the color of her drawing room furniture from blue to carmine.[14]

This consideration moved into the laboratory with the work of William Wundt (1832–1920), the German physiologist and psychologist. In 1856 W. H. Perkin, the British chemist, synthesized the first pigment, known as Perkin's mauve. Subsequently the first successful artificial green—viridian—was made public in 1859. Many architectural and painting manuals were free with advice about fashionable color harmonies. Often these ideas were accompanied by carefully hand-tinted charts, a far cry from Downing's recipe of 1850:

> The addition of a little blue-black . . . to the whitewash will produce a gray; add to this a little raw umber, and the result is a drab, or mix a little blue-black, Indian red, and yellow ochre, and you have a fawn color. The extra cost of these tints for a room fourteen feet square will, perhaps, be 15 cents—and the superiority of effect, to those who are not fond of the intolerable glare of white, is incalculable.[15]

It was this sort of counsel that was considered in the recent redecoration of Washington Irving's home, Sunnyside (1837), and that resulted in the tinted furniture of some of the bedrooms.[16]

During the second half of the century a different kind of color picture has been conjured for us. One of its chief commentators was the writer Lewis Mumford, who named his book and the period "The Brown Decades"[17]:

> Brownstone [Connecticut sandstone] began to be used in New York on public buildings, and just on the eve of the war [the Civil War] it was first used as facing for brick houses. With this alteration came dark walnut furniture, instead of rose-

wood and mahogany, sombre wallpapers and interiors whose dark tones swallowed up the light introduced later by the fashionable bay window. By 1880 brown was the dominating color.

For the historic record—the period of the brownstone row houses in New York bracketed the years 1865 and 1895 and reached north from Greenwich Village. The white sandstone favored by McKim and Company changed the complexion as well as the style of New York buildings.

Although the truth of Mumford's statement about the prevalence of brown can be verified by innumerable family portraits painted "at home" (Figure 6.35) in this era, the dark tones were often rich and the period was, if anything, characterized by a renewed interest in color on the part of its artists.

Polychromy is the distinguishing feature of Late Victorian Gothic in interiors as well as exteriors. This is first seen in the use of materials with distinct hues. Colored tiles and marbles were introduced in churches, and mention has been made that H. H. Richardson favored a similar use of spectral tones in the stones and woods of his buildings.

The artists of the English Pre-Raphaelite Brotherhood, whose creed, following the inspiration of Ruskin, was to emulate the styles of the Italian painters before Raphael, enlivened many an interior with their colorful decoration. Sir Edward Burne-Jones created the apse mosaic for St. Paul's in Rome. William Morris, who was affiliated with the group, designed the painted ceiling for the Union Debating Hall at Oxford. American painters soon joined in when John LaFarge painted the decorations and designed the stained glass for Richardson's Trinity Church in Boston. The French muralist Puvis de Chavannes and the Americans Edwin A. Abbey (1852–1911) and John Singer Sargent created the wall decorations in the Boston Public Library, all of which serves to indicate how color was considered essential at least to interiors of important buildings.

Pre-Raphaelite colors were rich and strong. In technical language they ranked Munsell value five and chroma eight. Holman Hunt's allegorical painting, which is now at the Wadsworth Athenaeum in Hartford, illustrates Tennyson's poem "The Lady of Shalott." Full blues and greens, as seen in the dark velvet, interweave with the colors of the peacock plumage to fortify the symbolic moment when dramatic emotionalism triumphs over the stern acceptance of duty—a welcome theme to the times.

A typical Morris room, one whose color scheme influenced much of the work done during the latter part of the century, included blues, greens, reds, and gold. Morris carpets were woven in the vibrant hues of the Caucasus. His wall chintzes and papers were often on dark blue backgrounds, for he was addicted to experimenting with indigo dyes. Chair upholsteries were in lighter tones of the primaries. Colorful friezes and some marqueteried woodwork enlivened the scene.

The preferred Morris color, however, was green, established from nature and used in Medieval *millefleur*. At Wightwick Manor the bannisters are in "orthodox green."[18] William Morris's earliest wallpaper, the *Daisy*, was yellow on a green-flecked ground. This focus on yellow and green may have led Gilbert and Sullivan, in their opera *Patience* (1881), which lampooned a certain current preciosity, to describe an aesthete character in verse:

A pallid and thin young man,
A haggard and lank young man,
A greenery-yallery, Grosvenor Gallery,[19]
Foot in the grave young man.

Notice that this presents a compound color conception as well as a psychological association, both of which would have been unthinkable in earlier centuries.

Yet another color scheme favored by the group of artist-designers who were considered aesthetes was inspired by Japanese art. The first large-scale exhibition of Japanese articles was shown in London in 1862 (the subsequent vogue for Japanese-inspired artifacts is currently known as *Japonisme*). Commodore Perry opened Japan to the West in 1859 and from that time Japanese prints came on the market. The expatriate American artist James McNeill Whistler (1834–1903) was an avid collector of oriental blue-and-white ware, prints, screens, and fans. This inspired another verse in *Patience:*

A Japanese young man,
A blue-and-white young man.

Whistler's own home was decorated in soft-color harmonies, such as lemon yellow, flesh tones, and silver greys. His nocturnes were symphonies in near monotones with a touch of vividness for accent. In 1863–1864 he painted the charming *Princesse du Pays de la Porcelaine,* using Japanese motifs in his design. Purchased by a wealthy London shipowner, it was hung in surroundings that Whistler felt were detrimental to the painting. Undoubtedly Whistler was the first interior designer to obtain permission to replan the interior space to fit the picture. Unfortunately the painter seems to have gone too far with his ideas and the owner instigated a lawsuit. For our purpose, however, the end justified the means. The famous room, which featured the peacock and its coloring as its central motif (Plate 12), may now be seen in the Freer Art Gallery in Washington, D.C. This belies any notion of brown decades.

The first exhibition of the French impressionists was mounted in 1874. Their experiments with broken color in an attempt to create greater intensity by mixing light rays in the eye must have had something to do with changing the interior palette from dark to light. The postimpressionists even borrowed from the Japanese those color rhythms that independently move the eye.

Many *fin de siècle* painters found their livelihood in designing furnishings and murals. With some color played a significant role. Edouard Vuillard (1868–1940) and Pierre Bonnard (1867–1947), members of an avant-garde group that called themselves the *Nabis* (from the Hebrew word for prophet), with their sunny pigments, created some most charming designs. They destroyed the barriers between outdoors and in by introducing flat-painted garden and village street scenes to grace interior walls. There is, however, an inherent danger in all this and it comes close to operating when we recall that Maurice Denis (1873–1943), one of the Nabis, said "There are no paintings, only decorations." Walter Crane calls Art Nouveau "That strange decorative disease." It was, of course, much more, but there is risk when painting is indiscriminatingly added to walls that decoration will be substituted for architecture.

It remains only to mention the late nineteenth-century concern for the effect of colored light in interiors. John La Farge, in his stained glass, revived the old technique of making translucent glass mosaics rather than paintings on glass. This produced much greater brilliance. There is scarcely an important building of the last of the century that did not use colored transmitted light for decorative effect. Frederick Church, the American painter, who was so interested in the broad expanses of color seen in lowering light, created stenciled color transparencies for many of the windows in his Hudson River home, Olana (Figure 6.13) through which tinted light entered the room. He also planned and oriented the house so that various effects such as diffused light, slanting direct light for accenting art objects, and light reflected off mirrors could function.

By 1900 the concern for color and light was shared by scientist, architect, designer, and artist.

Furnishings and Arrangement

All aspects of furnishing and arrangement are considered chronologically.

FURNITURE

Furniture of the First Third of the Century

Sources and Influences. One might begin this period with the furniture style commonly known as *Empire* and then agree that its backward glance might extend to the reign of Louis XVI and its transitional phase embrace the political periods known as *Directoire* and *Consulate.* The forward look, in addition to the years of the French empire, extends at least to 1830 and the reign of Louis Philippe. By this time it had reached almost every country and court of Europe and might with justification be called the *Napoleonic* style. In England a similar mode is customarily known as *Regency,* inasmuch as the Prince Regent popularized it by his purchases for Carlton House and Brighton. In America the blanket name is *Greek Revival,* the *Greek* or *American Empire,* the latter phrase certainly an anomaly. These terms, however inaccurate, are so well entrenched that they will have to serve.

The furniture involved, made in the early part of the nineteenth century, may be initially described as impressive in scale, of straight or geometrically curved lines, and of mirror surfaces relieved, in expensive pieces, by the glint of rigid ormolu decoration.

However remote the origins of Empire furniture may be, it is to the Emperor's architects, Percier and Fontaine, that crystallization of the fashion must be attributed. Their opus *Recueil de Décorations intérieures,* published in 1801 and again in 1811, was an album of designs largely of the furniture they had fashioned. Likewise the manager (Pierre la Mésangère) of the French magazine *Journal des Dames et des Modes* published a series of some four hundred plates that bore the title *Collection des Meubles et Objets de Goût,* from 1802 to 1835. The role of the periodical as a style propagandist had begun.

Once called into being, the superb quality of Empire furniture gave it repute. In France this was in large part due to the fact that, despite the extinction of the furniture guilds by fiat, a number of ébénistes and menuisiers of the Old Regime were still practicing and maintaining a body of work every bit as fine as any done for the late Bourbons.

Certainly the foremost of these craftsmen was François-Honoré-Georges Jacob-Desmalter (1700–1841), the second son of the famous late-eighteenth-century ébéniste Georges Jacob. The name Desmalter had been added to designate some of the family holdings in Burgundy. François-Honoré-Georges inherited, at first with his brother and after 1803 on his own, the family furniture enterprise. During his active years he was constantly sought by the emperor, first to make furniture for his private use and then for the imperial palaces—the Tuileries, St. Cloud, Compiègne, Fontainebleau, the Louvre, Versailles, and the Élysée.

Napoleon, be it to his credit, paid his bills in a manner that the Bourbons were not always known to do. Nevertheless, the House of Jacob went into bankruptcy in 1813. The recovery of the firm was due in part to the fact that Jacob-Desmalter, despite the blockade in force since 1806, was granted permission to trade with En-

gland and subsequently supplied furniture to Prince George. Jacob-Desmalter had married the daughter of the important furniture maker and dealer, Martin-Elroy Lignereux, who had succeeded to the influential position of the dealer Dominique Daguerre, erstwhile purveyor to the English throne. Thus influences traveled.

Other competent cabinetmakers had worked for the monarchy and remained to produce fine pieces for the new aristocracy. The German Guillaume Beneman, who had been *ébéniste du roi* under Louis XVI, continued under the Consulate to make furniture for Napoleon. Jean-Henri Riesener, Adam Weisweiler, Jean-François Leleu, and Jean-Baptiste Sené could be cited in the category of old masters serving a new clientele. Georges Jacob was, of course, their dean. Among the younger men, still trained under the guild system was Pierre-Antoine Bellangé who became cabinetmaker to Charles X.

Designers and makers may have been the catalytic agents, but Napoleon himself, in his role as Mycaenas and even more in that of Zeus, was the spiritual father of the Empire style. Indeed, it would not require a great stretch of the imagination to associate him with much nineteenth-century furniture. Madame de Stael (1766–1817), daughter of the Swiss Secretary of the Treasury under Louis XVI and one of the most brilliant women of this era, was an incisive critic of the Emperor and always regarded him as a foreigner to France. Notice these quotations:

During the twelve years of exile to which Napoleon condemned me, I often reflected that he did not have the misfortune of being barred from France. He did not have a single memory of France in his heart. Only the rocks of Corsica recalled to him the days of his childhood but the daughter of M. Necker was more French than he.

And:

. . . the fear that he inspired was caused only by the extraordinary effect of his person upon nearly all who approached him.

. . . every time I heard him speak I was struck by his superiority: yet it had no resemblance to men educated and cultivated by study or by social intercourse, such as may be found in England or in France. But his speech showed a feel-

Figure 6.38 Throne room of Napoleon at Fontaine-bleau. The magnificent ceiling dates from the time of Henry IV and the structural interior is from the time of Louis XIV and Louis XV. Most of the furnishings are of the Napoleonic era. (© Arch. Phot. Paris / S. P. A. D. E. M., 1979.)

ing for the situation, like the hunter's for his prey. . . .

Last of all:

And, changing the conversation because he no longer wanted to hear about this subject, he spoke to me of his love for seclusion, for the countryside, for the fine arts, and he took the trouble to reveal himself to me in ways appropriate to the kind of taste he supposed me to have.[20]

What could speak more clearly of the Empire style in France (Figure 6.38), one built on tradition, masculine in all its emphasis, imposing and forceful rather than urbane and gracious, in last analysis more akin to the pomp of Rome than to the feminine courtliness of France—and the hand of a new driver on the reins!

Napoleon established headquarters in many locations on the Continent. Whenever he took up residence in an old palace, it was refurbished. He is said to have insisted on as much duplication of accoutrement and arrangement as possible so that in the interest of efficiency he might feel at home wherever he went. In Milan it was the Villa Montevello, in Rome the Quirinal, which he gave to his infant son in 1811, the Villa Pontici in

Naples, and the old palace and Villa Marlia at Lucca.

Napoleon's family, especially his three beautiful and aspiring sisters—Elisa, the Princess Bacciochi, in Tuscany, Caroline Murat in Naples, and Pauline Borghese in Rome—equipped their palaces with sumptuous display. Although much of their furniture came from the *Garde-Meuble* in Paris, each had her coterie of local men. Elisa used the Florentines Giuseppe Benvenuto and Giovanni Socchi (often called "the Florentine Jacob"). She also employed Jean-Baptiste Youf, a Parisian cabinetmaker (in Italian *stipettaio* or *ebenista*) who went to Italy at her invitation.[21, 22] Pauline and Caroline, as well as Napoleon himself, favored French craftsmen but supplemented them with local workers.

In England Regency furniture ran the gamut from modified and lighter Sheraton to heavier George IV (Figure 6.39). The first important designer was the wealthy amateur architect Thomas Hope (1770–1831), who in 1807 published his *Household Furniture and Design*. Hope was born in Holland of an expatriate Scottish family which had made its fortune in merchandising. He had traveled extensively on the Continent, sketching architectural subjects with the view to practicing architecture. With a collector's instinct and plenty of what it takes to buy, he returned to Holland and subsequently to England with antique *objets d'art* from Greece, Egypt, Syria, and Turkey. He furnished his two houses, one in Surrey and one in London, as quasi-museums, designing much of the furniture from pieces seen on old coins, vases, and sculpture. Some bore a family likeness to the engravings of his friend Percier. The important circles in which he moved and his developed taste in antiquarianism lent much prestige to his archaeologically reasonable drawings. The Prince Regent is known to have relied on his judgment in making French purchases. Hope's contact with France was indeed so close that the style is sometimes dubbed Hope-Percier-Fontaine.

On the second level of designing was the cabinetmaker George Smith's *Collection of Designs for Household Furniture and Interior Decoration*, published in 1808, and his *Cabinet Maker and Upholsterer's Guide*, published in 1826.

George IV, both as prince and king, was a col-

lector of French artifacts, in which taste not many former British monarchs had shared. Through his agents he took full advantage of the sales of the sequestered property of the French royalists to purchase the furniture, porcelain, sculpture, and paintings of the Ancient Regime. This familiarity with the traditional probably sharpened his appreciation for the new. He bought one desk from the elder Jacob-Desmalter, which had presumably been made for the Emperor, and as late as 1825 secured another made by Desmalter's son.

The furniture known to have graced the Prince's residences, in addition to Neoclassic pieces of the late eighteenth-century style, included many delightful articles from China, some of which

Figure 6.39 A typical English Regency chair. Victoria & Albert Museum, London. (Crown Copyright, Victoria & Albert Museum.)

were in light bamboo. Therefore it was natural that similarly designed wares were made in England of typical occidental construction and of beech painted to simulate bamboo. These were executed for the Prince by the firm of Elward, Marsh, and Tatham (a firm that had undergone several reorganizations and from 1795 to 1809 assumed that title).

Although Brighton mingled the Oriental, the French, and the English in a lighthearted manner, the more sedate quality of British designing and the tread of heavy military boots (the return of the armies that had fought on the Continent from 1803 to 1815 is said to have had its coarsening effect) leavened the composite Regency style in England. It became more ponderous as seen in some of the most cumbersome "magistrate" furniture ever to burden a community hall, but it also showed its graceful aspect in collections in great houses like Major Samuel Whitbread's Southill and many homes of middling character.

Design influences made themselves felt in the early century in America by way of the English manuals. Smith's *Household Furniture* (1808) and his *Guide* (1826) can be claimed as the source of individual motifs.

In the new republic there was no dominant personage to create an atmosphere that might inaugurate a style. Possibly only one chair (in the Louis XVI manner) remains from the furnishings of the President's house in Philadelphia, and it is not known what furniture the Adamses left in the White House after their brief sojourn. Jefferson was the first president to have lived in the official mansion throughout his term, and he made an acknowledged effort to create surroundings comparable to the courts he had known in Europe as Ambassador to France. But we still know little about the character of the furniture because Jefferson merely states that the pieces were "elegant" or "fashionable."[23]

The architect Benjamin Henry Latrobe was responsible as Surveyor of Public Buildings for building operations at the White House. After a government appropriation for furnishings, he worked with the fourth president's wife, the attractive Dolly Madison, in selecting the necessary equipment for the official and private functioning of the mansion. The designs that Latrobe made

to this purpose have been preserved by his descendents.[24] They are in the *American Empire* style. He obviously borrowed several from Hope's storehouse. The fate of all this fine furniture was sealed when the British fired the building on August 24, 1814.

President Monroe, when officialdom moved back after rebuilding, used his own possessions, largely Louis XVI, bought earlier in France when he, in turn, was the American ambassador. Additional furniture came from Paris. One piece, a handsome pier table, ordered in 1817 from the Parisian cabinetmaker Pierre-Antoine Bellangé, is now in the Blue Room. Some articles from the administrations of John Quincy Adams and Andrew Jackson are in the late Empire style.

Perhaps the best known of a number of French-trained cabinetmakers who emigrated to America after the French Revolution is Charles-Honoré Lannuier (1779–1819). Of his ten brothers and sisters, only one, Nicolas, was an ébéniste and he may have trained Charles-Honoré, who with two of his brothers came to America around 1800. From 1805 to 1819 Honoré was listed as a cabinetmaker in the New York directory. His early American ventures were in the Louis XVI style but he soon progressed to restrained Empire design. A small table that bears his label is in the White House collection. Several beds from his workshop at No. 60 Broad Street are known, and other articles are attributed to him on the basis of style and quality of workmanship. The Lannuiers usually stamped their production according to the French custom and one of the beds bears the *H. Lannuier* imprint.[25]

Although New York was the most fashionable style center of the early eighteen hundreds, Philadelphia was not far behind. Among the eminent craftsmen of that locality were Michel Bouvier (1792–1874)[26] and Antoine Gabriel Querville[27] (1789–1856) (Figure 6.40). Both were of French descent and both established fortunes by their alertness to industrial production.

After the Louisiana Purchase and the influx of Americans New Orleans, the metropolis of the Mississippi, was a particularly attractive haven for French craftsmen. François Seignouret is the best known. Coming from Bordeaux, he arrived in 1800 to establish some of the first and most direct

French Empire influences. Understanding the needs of his clients, he made rich and massive furniture to fit their mansions. Among these pieces his handsome armoires are particularly impressive. Made of mahogany and rosewood, they often stood 10 ft high, and they or their counterparts may be seen in many a lower Mississippi home today. Denying the specializing customary to Frenchmen, Seignoret also made chairs. In 1853 he returned to France.[28]

Few need to be told that the Empire style came to America by the Scotch route (as well as by the French) in the person of Duncan Phyfe (born Fife, 1768–1854). In 1783 he came to America with his parents and numerous siblings, two of whom died in the crossing. Duncan, the second son, was trained in Albany, where the family took up residence. In 1790 he left for New York, the land of promise. Fortunately the young craftsman came to the attention of the daughter of John Jacob Astor and more than likely it was because of her influence that Phyfe acquired a wealthy clientele.

With the growth of his business he enlarged his establishment at 35 Partition Street and by 1816 owned three adjacent properties on that thoroughfare, the name of which had now been changed to Fulton, after the inventor of the steamboat. The exteriors of his properties, as shown in a watercolor at the Metropolitan Museum of Art, were of typical Federal (Adam) style. After 1815 he lived in a building across the street. Fulton Street had become a main artery, and today Phyfe's shops would have been at the terminus of the Holland Tunnel.

In 1837 the firm was known as Duncan Phyfe and Sons (Michael and James), and, after Michael's death in 1840, as Duncan Phyfe and Son. When Duncan retired in 1847, the business was dissolved and the stock of furniture was sold at auction. Much of Duncan Phyfe's production is at the Metropolitan (Figure 6.41), and a superb collection in an equally exquisite setting can be seen at the Taft Museum in Cincinnati. Its maker is said not to have entirely forsaken his skill after his retirement and to have taken delight in fashioning pieces for his family in his own little workshop at home.

Although Mr. Phyfe was apparently a modest

Figure 6.40 Pier table bearing the label of Antoine Gabriel Querville, Philadelphia, 1825–1830. Mahogany and marble. Athenaeum, Philadelphia. (The Athenaeum of Philadelphia.)

and unassuming person, a prodigious worker, and quite irrelevantly an equally insistent smoker (reportedly always drawing on a short pipe), he was also an astute businessman. Through sharp investments with money saved from his labors, he left an estate of nearly half a million dollars, plus considerable property. His furniture creation ran the entire gamut from the graceful Regency types to the crudest designs in the late Empire styles.

Within an equivalent time span Michael Allison, Phyfe's neighbor, produced in the Hepplewhite as well as the American Empire manner.

Materials. One inevitably thinks in terms of rich red mahogany disposed in large surfaces as matched veneers or as full-grain solid wood when considering French Empire furniture. But with the European blockade attendant on the war and because of the Napoleonic decree of 1806 which prohibited the importation into France of British-controlled San Domingo wood, French furniture used many variants. One was Honduras mahogany, a lighter wood. Others were the native fruits, along with the indigenous hardwoods. Exotic tim-

Figure 6.41 Lyre-back side chair from the workshop of Duncan Phyfe, America, nineteenth century. Metropolitan Museum of Art, New York. (The Metropolitan Museum of Art. Gift of the Family of Mr. and Mrs. Andrew Varick Stout, 1965, in their memory.)

for instance, used brass mounts as casters (which now appeared) and door pulls, he relied more on clean-cut reeding and patterned ornament. Provincial furniture often substituted wood or glass knobs for brass. The typical shape for the escutcheon in brass was the lion's head holding the ring pull.

It is not so generally known that Empire furniture was at times made of iron or steel. This allowed for lightness of structure, ease of folding or dismantling, and adaptability to military campaigns. The taut linear quality and sheen of these pieces blended well with the reflective surfaces of other furniture, forming contrasts in shape while maintaining alliances in texture.

Painted furniture, fashionable since the eighteenth century, remained in favor and also offered a less expensive equivalent to the other smooth surfaces. Imperial objects were often gilded and less frequently silvered. Marble surfaces were prized.

Description of Types: Seating Furniture. With the nineteenth century a knowledge of historic styles in furniture design begins to pay off, for the goal of conformity to some antiquarian past was never so rigidly prescribed, although by the time the standard had been lowered to the sights of untutored designers and watered down by several removes of pattern books the result was often pastiche.

Chair forms return first to the Roman rectilinear throne, the Roman curule, and the Greek klismos. The straight-line chair descends from Louis XVI. Its increasing weight was not unbecoming, and what it lost in grace it made up in sturdiness (which incidentally it could stand).

When, as in the Sheraton designs of his 1804 *Encyclopedia,* the back began to roll gently toward the rear and the entire form eased into that of a true klismos, then the idea of suave continuity dominated. This was particularly true of the early Regency style. Curved backs melted into seat rails and were continuous with scimitar legs. Duncan Phyfe camouflaged any joinings with carefully carved waterleaf and acanthus motifs.

The ultimate extension of the idea of smooth transition was to be found in the chair that approached the curule design. It seemed almost like

ber such as rosewood and amaranth was used when available. Although inlay was reserved for expensive detail, ebony and pewter were in demand for this purpose.

Embellishment on these handsome surfaces took the form of characteristically chiseled *bronze doré* (ormolu) mounts, placed and designed to accentuate by contrast. English and American makers, farther removed from the French ormolu tradition, clung rather tenaciously at times to their carved decoration. Although Duncan Phyfe, a molded concave enclosure for the human form. The possibility of obtaining thinner and larger sheets of veneer, due to mechanical improvements in the circular band saw, created pieces that could effectively conceal joints in the carcass. When these curule-type chairs included a smooth curve over the back and down to the seat, they were called *en gondole* or gondola chairs.

The general character of all these early nineteenth century chairs was so undeviating that one is scarcely conscious of the variety shown within the uniformity. Numerous changes were made in the backs—grille patterns, kidney shapes, lyres (a particular favorite of Duncan Phyfe in which the strings were customarily of whalebone or brass and the key, inserted through the top, was ebony), and even oval tops that resembled the headrests in modern automobiles.

Arm supports and legs also presented changing patterns. Prototypes might be unfluted Tuscan columns or figures stolen from antiquity, such as swans' heads, eagles, griffins, and sphinxes. The human form was used as caryatids, and atlantes and as a pedestal term. Chair legs ended in lions' feet or dogs' paws.

Here not only Rome but Egypt also counted. The scholar Dominique Viviant, Baron Denon (1745–1825), who as Director-in-Chief of the Musée Napoleon was arbiter of the fine arts during the Napoleonic regime, had accompanied one of the French armies on its Egyptian campaign. In 1802 he published an album of engravings entitled *Voyage dans la Basse et Haute Égypte pendant les capagnes du Général Bonaparte* based on sketches he had made of Egyptian temples and their details. Appearing in several countries, it became a useful storehouse for decorative motifs and it spurred the fashion for Egyptian modes.

Types of seating furniture remained traditional. Napoleon preserved the etiquette of the stool and the crossed-leg folding ones were preferred. Fauteuils and bergères were available in sets and the two-seated *causeuse* remained popular.

Canapés, sofas (English couches) grew longer and became wall fixtures. The *paumier* was a new model with a high back and arms. The *récamier*, or *chaise longue*, one end of which was higher and curved, took its name from Juliette Récamier

whom David painted on one in a gracefully reclining position. This piece is closely associated with the period. The *méridienne* had a lower foot than headboard and the back curved smoothly to connect the two. In England the upholstered round ottoman was favored.

Beds. Sleeping furniture showed no new types. Beds were still the *lit à la Duchesse, lit d'ange,* or *lit à la Polonaise,* differentiated by the character of the tester and side draperies (see Chapter 2). Beds were now customarily placed parallel to the wall. Few beds were bare of curtains, which were hung, looped, and decorated in various ways. Even the post bed which had extremely tall pillars was seen occasionally. The four poster remained a favorite in England and America, and the arched tester variety (the field bed) gained in popularity.

The shape of the bedstead, which offered fanciful variety, was often characterized by some romantic notion of how people slept in faraway times and places. There was the boat bed (en bateau), which took its point of departure from the Venetian gondola or Nilitic barge. The *lit à l'impériale* was mounted on a dais so high that it seemed like a catafalque. In America beds with high-rolled head and footboards were known as *sleigh beds.*

Tables and Storage Furniture. The console table became an important adjunct of Empire furnishings. It was handsomely embellished and was often given the addition of a lower shelf and a mirror between the two rear legs, which provided both the illusion of depth and a visual duplication of whatever ormolu mounts were on the front legs. Sideboards of imposing dimensions were extensions of the former Hepplewhite and Sheraton models in the Empire style. The same may be said for the extremely handsome bookcases and secretaries.

In addition to the many small varieties, the round dining table gained in importance. It was now ingeniously equipped with extension apparatus in the form of dropped sides or extension leaves. The Empire style imitated the late classical monopodium and the *guéridon,* or pedestal table, was a favored piece, especially in its round form.

Queen Hortense of Holland, a Beauharnais, and

wife of Napoleon's brother Louis, says in her *Memoires:*

> I was the first in France who established, in the drawing room, a round table to be used for work or for evening entertainment . . . as is common in the countryside. Previously French hostesses arranged groupings near the fireplace, all the ladies in a circle with their gentlemen standing up in the center of their group. Sparkling conversation, in which each tried to show his wit, was the only occupation of the evening.[29]

And again:

> I went to great trouble to persuade my officers not to remain standing as if they were carrying weapons but, instead, to take part in the conviviality. I wanted my home to be like a family gathering where the good always reigned and where a pleasing gaiety did not exclude respect for the hostess.[30]

One thinks back to the household of another Louis of a century before and notes the changed mores.

The *athénienne* or tripod stand was a variation of the Roman tripodium and was used for many purposes: a plant holder, a stand for washbowl and pitcher, or simply to show off an *objet d'art*. The *psyche* was a floor-length mirror pivoted between two uprights. Oval as well as rectangular in shape, it was favored more in France than in England or America.

Beyond all these the usual pieces were to be found in abundance. As rooms grew smaller, space was swallowed until the situation prompted Jane Austen to describe the parlor of Uppercrost in her novel, *Persuasion,* in this wise:

> . . . an old fashioned square parlor with a small carpet and shining floor to which the present daughters of the house were gradually giving the proper air of confusion by a grand pianoforte and a harp, flower stands, and little tables placed in every direction. Oh, could the originals of the portraits against the wainscot, could the gentlemen in brown velvet, and the ladies in blue satin, have seen what was going on, have been conscious of such an overflow of order and neatness.

Furniture of the Thirties through the Fifties

The character of French Empire furniture persisted well into the forties of nineteenth-century Europe. Its later versions were frequently known by the names of rulers—Louis Philippe in France and William IV or, after 1837, early Victorian in England. American versions were occasionally dubbed "pillar and scroll" or John Hall furniture (reasons anon). Madame de Stael said of Bonaparte, "His face, at that time lean and pale, was rather pleasant. Since then he has become fat which ill suits him."[31] So with his belongings.

To understand these phenomena of the years dating roughly from 1830 to 1860 one must recognize that because of the Industrial Revolution, the era of hand crafting was in its twilight, not to be resuscitated except in sporadic attempts at arts and crafts movements. In the late thirties cabinetmakers began closing their doors. A carriage-trade business remained for a few, but even here phases of construction were mechanized and the process developed the production-line technique that eliminated the personal touch.

The power that drove this machinery was steam, which had been harnessed to the band saw as early as the thirties. This saw, which operated on an endless belt, facilitated the cutting of curved surfaces. Other improvements came rapidly. Finer and larger sheets of veneer were possible and intricate scrolls could be easily duplicated. Michel Bouvier opened his own steam mill for sawing wood and cutting imported Italian marble.

Not only the process of manufacture but that of distribution was radically altered. It was possible to produce more cheaply and to market more widely. The first need was for catalogs that would illustrate the available patterns. Earlier books, of the nature of Chippendale's *Director,* illustrated the components of articles so that the buyer might choose among them and create his own design. The new ones advertised a total piece that could be bought without alteration and without loss of time. For this there was a fixed price, a practice anticipated by the price books of former years. A series of lithographic plates issued by the New York firm of Joseph Meeks and Sons in 1833 proved to be the entering wedge to a series of fascinating trade brochures.

Distribution was also facilitated by the advent of the merchandise store. This differed from the eighteenth-century establishment, say of the French *marchand-mercier,* such as Lazare Duvaux, in being in fact a "store" rather than a "shop." It was a storage place for the goods of a firm, held pending shipment or sale. Large inventories were apparently kept on hand so that orders might be handled speedily as they arrived. This policy of the large inventory has succumbed today to the principle of limited production, which operates continuously on estimated need. In the nineteenth century there was an almost inexhaustible demand for industrially produced furniture by people whose circumstances no longer permitted the purchase of handmade items.

Selling was not left to chance; for example, J. and J. W. Meeks had an organized system of sales outlets along the Atlantic seaboard, and the Meeks wholesale and retail store on Broad Street (1829–1835) and on Vesey Street (1836–1855) in New York was the center for this trade.[32]

Other firms in America operated on similar bases. Indeed it is difficult to draw the line between the old and the new in practice. Phyfe, for instance, used one of his buildings as a warehouse, employed as many as 100 workmen, took orders from far afield, but did not issue a merchandising catalog.

Various names have been arbitrarily assigned to some of this late classical revival furniture of the thirties and forties. John Hall, a cabinetmaker and architect, came to America from Devonshire, England, where he was born, probably in 1809. In 1840 he published his *The Cabinet Makers' Assistant.* The designs shown in this pattern book were heavy versions of *Empire.* Hall, however, had reduced the elements to their simplest forms and to those that were easily duplicated on the band saw. These pieces had regular geometric shapes and the supports used for adornment were either round pillars or scrolls (hence the name *pillar and scroll*). This was a formula that could produce in large quantities. Fortunately its very simplicity was its saving grace, and the country was flooded with furniture, not particularly elegant in shape,

Figure 6.42   Furniture of the 1840s in the living room of Miss Frances King Dolley. Note the John Hall-type scrolls on the table and the balloon type chair backs. (G. C. Ball.)

but redeemed by broad expanses of mahogany, walnut, maple, cherry, or their combinations. As a class it is sometimes known as "John Hall furniture" (Figure 6.42).

The Hitchcock chair is another of the popular factory-produced articles of this period (Figure 6.43). Made under the entrepreneurship, principally, of Lambert Hitchcock (1795–1852), it was intended for a wide market. Hitchcock expanded an industry at Barnhansted (Riverton, Hitchcockville are alternate names) which in 1818 was making chair parts, to the point that the complete

Figure 6.43 Chair signed by Lambert Hitchcock, Connecticut, ca. 1835. Western Reserve Historical Society, Cleveland, Ohio. (The Western Reserve Historical Society.)

object was manufactured. It then sold for the munificent sum of $1.50; anyone owning a signed piece today could realize many times that amount. They were stenciled on the back, "L. Hitchcock, Hitchcockville, Connecticut Warranted."

The design of these chairs is light and well proportioned, resembling some of the simpler Phyfe models. The front legs and stretcher are turned; they have horizontal back splats, to which collectors assign such descriptive terms as *pillow top,*

turtle back, and *cut-out.* The back uprights are a continuation of the legs; and the seats, wider in front, have straight sides and rolled front edges. The frames were of birch or maple and the seats were solid or filled with rush or cane. It is the painting and stenciling of the Hitchcocks, so adroitly and sensitively done by women and children, that has given them their particular charm. The use of two layers of color, red or yellow plus black, resulted in a rich depth of tone, and the painted stencil—baskets of fruit, cornucopias, and the usual vocabulary of flowers and birds done in soft colors and picked out with gold—has enlivened their somberness. The factory, which after bankruptcy and reorganization as Hitchcock, Alford and Company, closed in 1846, has been reopened to make accurate copies of the very usable Hitchcock chair.

Other firms manufactured comparable pieces. We read of Seymour Watrous, William Moore, Jr., Holmes and Roberts, J. K. Hatch, and the Union Chair Company in New England.

The Windsor chair was still ubiquitous, now grown more fragile as industrial processes were substituted for the sturdy hand work of the eighteenth century. Rocking chairs in this manner are among the rarer examples of Hitchcock work. Descending in style from the Windsor and Hitchcock, they are known today as *Boston rockers* or, when without arms, *Cape Cod rockers.* As a type they prospered well and have endeared themselves as comfortable articles in rural America.

As mentioned under ceramics in Chapter 5, the Pennsylvania Dutch variety of furniture, which the Germans of the rich Pennsylvania farmlands have made since the seventeenth century, reached a high peak of aesthetic perfection during the first of the nineteenth. Ultimately its worth is dependent on its decoration and in this the output of Christian Seltzer (1749–1831) and John Peter Rank (1764–1851) rates high.

Another type of provincial design bears the cognomen *Jenny Lind furniture* in America (the reason for any resemblance between the style and the exquisite voice of the popular coloratura, the "Swedish Nightingale," is certainly not apparent). It is to be seen in the many beds and chairs with spool and ball turning that flooded the market and found ready acceptance on both sides of the

Atlantic. Some were quite simple and fitted fairly well into Downing's country houses. In fact he dubbed them *Elizabethan* and recommended their use.

Probably the most sought-after and unavailable of the out-of-the-run varieties of nineteenth-century furniture is that made by the Shakers (Figure 6.44); (a small religious group, founded in 1747, and dying out in the twentieth century). This furniture was used in the communities of the Shaker sect, like the one at New Lebanon, New York, and was also offered for sale. Its lean form, its excellent crafting, and its well-proportioned spacing created wares that would blend well with much of the country type of living today. Mother Ann, spiritual leader of her flock, joined the Shaker cult in England in 1758 and then set sail with eight followers for the promise of America. She raised as her motto, "Do all your work as though you had a thousand years to live, and as you would if you knew you must die tomorrow."

Shaker furniture had an added advantage of being patently functional. This was due to the designers, the women of the community, who strove to make all implements labor-saving in order that more time might be devoted to the glory of God. It was the Shakers who are credited with the invention of the turbine water wheel, flat brooms, metal pen points, and pea shellers. They are responsible for the washing machine, the clothes dryer, a practical bread cutter, and a safety knife rack. They became part of the band of furniture designers who analyzed a need and then did something for its alleviation; for example, they put strips of pegboard on the walls on which to hang both clothing and chairs, and gave every room its built-in cabinets planned for specific commodities.

Unfortunately the Shaker communities died abortive because their belief in celibacy was social suicide. Today much Shaker furniture is to be found only in museums. Some Shaker architecture fortunately has survived. It was generally of a simplified Georgian style, although their large stone barns (seen at New Lebanon, New York and at Hancock, Massachusetts) are models of forthright structural logic. The interiors of Shaker dwellings were plain and sparsely furnished. The walls were white plaster and the

planked floors were painted a yellow-red. Simple carpets covered only a part of the area. Dark brown moldings at the windows and doors provided interesting tonal contrasts.

Revivals of Traditional Styles. In 1835 Augustus Welby Pugin published a pattern book called *Gothic Furniture in the Style of the Fifteenth Century* which made an attempt at historical accuracy. Pugin designs were difficult to execute and survived only in the work of some of the most expert craftsmen. Gothic furniture was at best largely an English phenomenon and even there most pattern books, although bowing to fashion, produced drawings that were Gothic by courtesy: pointed arch fretwork, crockets, quatrefoils, and pendant bosses for distinguishing character.

It is often difficult to lift the business of furniture making out of the realm of domesticity. The

Figure 6.44 Shaker furniture, United States, nineteenth century. Dunham Tavern Museum, Cleveland, Ohio. (Courtesy, the Trustees of the Dunham Tavern Museum. Photograph by Carlton Spearman.)

Gothic ecclesiastic revival, however, did spur the production of church furniture. The best known firm in this line was Hardoman and Cox, which maintained an establishment on Wardour Street in London. Thus the title "Wardour Street furniture," often seen in connection with church furniture in this style, takes on meaning.

Several Pugin designs, one for a Gothic *priedieu* and another for an oak cabinet, both executed by Crace, were shown in the Medieval Court of the Great Exhibition held in London in Paxton's Crystal Palace in 1851 (see p. 306). The Prince Consort and Sir Henry Cole, the idealist educator, planned this first international show in a combined spirit of praise for Victoria's reign and of publicizing the material progress made by industry. An attendant motive involved the improvement of taste by exposing manufacturers to the best international products.

Much of the furniture on display at the fair was called *Renaissance*. England slanted her Renaissance revival (often called Elizabethan and today parodied as Jacobethan) toward the English seventeenth century, whereas the French looked back to the time of Francis. The sideboard, as a grand piece of display furniture, was particularly favored in these styles, probably because its broad rectangular panels made an excellent framework for the carver's skill. The basic contours of the Exhibition sideboards were rectangular, embellished with colonettes, caryatids, terms, and scrolls as supports and with elaborately graven panel backs.

Woodcarving as an art may have been practiced longer in England than elsewhere. Among the midcentury chiseleurs, such as the Rogers family of London (father W. G. and two sons) and Thomas Tweedy of Newcastle-on-Tyne, was Gerrard Robinson, also from Northumberland (Figure 6.45). Robinson made the famous Chevy Chase sideboard designed in the sixties for the Duke of Northumberland.

The 1851 show was truly universal (in respect to Western culture) as claimed. The French exhibited much that had an ornate Renaissance dressing. The designing firms of Henri Fourdinois and Emmanuel Ringuet Leprince were well represented. Their pieces revealed a sensitivity for formal arrangement that is noticeably absent in the work of other countries. The Austrian and German Renaissance articles can be characterized as exuberant and heavy in scale; the French have greater simplicity and more noticeable finesse in the execution of their carving; the English pay attention to realistic detail and are lower priced, whereas the American are marked by mechanical ingenuity and production expertise.

Although critical essays on the 1851 exhibition designated the Renaissance as the prevailing fashion, it is not the style for which the fifties will be remembered. The *Victorian, Second Empire,* or, as it was more correctly called, *Louis XV Revival* or *Neo-Rococo,* although less publicized at the time, developed into the mode for which the period will be rather fondly recalled. It should be clear by now that none of these resurrected styles were ringers for their prototypes. They were frequently executed in different materials, heavier in scale, with more rigid carving, and often with overpowering upholstery. The last qualification is particularly characteristic of some of the Second Empire pieces, either those that leaned toward the Louis XV Rococo or toward the renewal of the Louis XVI, which has been alluded to as *Style Louis XVI-Imperatrice* because of the Empress Eugénie's infatuation with Marie Antoinette. What appears to us as "overstuffed" in the seating furniture of the period was largely due to the comfortable inclusion, for the first time, of spring construction.

Before detailing the Victorian (Second Empire, Louis XV) furniture, it is interesting to note that it was at times made in *papier-mâché.* This was not a new medium, for it had been used on both sides of the Channel during the preceding century. It consists in obtaining a rigid and equally strong framework by the use of paper pulp pressed with a binder into a mold, or of superimposing layers of paper onto a form and acquiring rigidity by the application of glue, resin, and flour—a weird kind of stucco.[33]

An interchangeable title for papier-mâché during the time of its greatest popularity (1840–1870) was *japanned furniture.* Indeed the process was said to have been invented in 1772 by Henry Clay of Birmingham, a japanner by trade. Articles of furniture, as well as the ubiquitous tray and panel, were prime for decorating with painting, gilding, and inlay, often with gems and mother-of-pearl, in floral and narrative patterns.

The bulk of the English papier-mâché industry

Figure 6.45 The Chevy Chase sideboard depicting a military skirmish, Northumberland, ca. 1860. Gerrard Robinson, carver. Grosvenor Hotel, Shaftesbury. (Photograph by courtesy of Trust Houses Forte Limited. © Trust Houses Forte Hotels Limited 1/9/79.)

centered at Birmingham where the firm of Jennens and Bettridge employed meritorious painters like John Breakspear, Philip McCallum, and Edwin Booth.[34] In the 1870s a brief revival of eighteenth-century styles produced more restrained decorative patterns in the classical manner in work in this medium.

Here it is timely to introduce another nineteenth-century industry that converged around the midland city—the production of cast-iron furniture. This originally appeared in imitation oak or was painted black or bronze. Tubular brass bedsteads were among other specialties. All constituted export ware. Price was the principal inducement for a mass market.[35]

We return to the Neo-Rococo as a style. In France the prototype had never really gone out of fashion. It had been preserved in the grace of provincial examples and in the genuine originals of a hundred years before. As a new vogue it began early, contemporary with the decadent Empire style. In this form it found great favor in the surviving courts of Europe, especially in Austria and Italy. It may be that its aura of regality also kept the original Louis XV much in favor in England and its revived forms with curvilinear legs and backs began to appear as early as the forties. It was in America that the loveliest and most usable of the Louis XV expressions came within the reach of the many. It is therefore in relation to that country that their production is described in more detail.

Some designers were still operating on a craftsman-to-customer basis. Many of these men had been trained abroad and had come to America as immigrants. In New York there were the Frenchmen, Alexander Roux (ca. 1813–1886) Charles A. Baudouine, Leon Marcotte (from France 1854, son-in-law of Emmanuel Ringuet Leprince of the New York-Paris-based firm of that name), and the Germans, Christian and Gustave Herter and John Henry Belter (1804–1863). George Henkels, Daniel Pabst, and Gottlieb Vollmer were Philadelphians. Augustus Eliaers, a Frenchman, was a prominent Boston cabinetmaker. In Cincinnati the name of S. S. Johns, whose manufacture of excessively large and ornate furniture for the passenger boats

that plied the Mississippi and Ohio rivers gave rise to the cognomen *Steamboat Gothic*, was highly publicized. In New Orleans the distinguished name was Prudent Mallard, who had been trained in Paris and came to America in 1838.

John Belter stands out in this group not only for the perfection of a medium but for the fact that he possessed the talent that produced a sufficient number of fine examples of Neo-Rococo to force it to emerge as a distinct style (Figure 6.46).

John Belter's furniture is noteworthy for its use of a laminated bentwood technique that presumably he learned in southern Germany, his homeland. Other cabinetmakers came as close to duplicating the Belter process as they could without infringing on his rights. Belter took out the first of several patents in 1846, just six years after his arrival in America. At that time he was operating from his shop at Third Avenue and East 76th Street, New York, having consistently bettered his original location at Chatham Square.

His process consisted in glueing together thin layers (about $\frac{1}{16}$th in.) of rosewood, mahogany,

Figure 6.46 Settee (part of a parlor suite) in the Belter style, midnineteenth century. Attributed to J. Weeks. Rosewood. Length, 1.65 m, height, 1.23 m, depth, 90 cm. Metropolitan Museum of Art, New York. (The Metropolitan Museum of Art. Gift of Mr. & Mrs. Lowell Ross Burch and Miss Jean McLean Morrow, 1951.)

oak, or other ebonized hardwood, with the grains running alternately at right angles. This part of the procedure gave added strength and minimum warpage. The number of layers was usually seven but might rise to sixteen. These finished laminated panels were then steamed in molds or cawls to achieve a unified surface and the required curvature. When necessary, small wooden blocks were added at points intended for deepest carving. Most of the carvers were men from Alsace-Lorraine where they had been trained in their craft.

Inasmuch as the final chair-back panel, which was curved to fit the body, was made of several staves or pieces that had been joined in the steaming mold, small hairlines at the joints were likely to show. These would be especially noticeable along the rear face of the back, which was left free of upholstery in the Belter chairs. Claims have been made that the presence of such breaks would authenticate true Belters. As a matter of fact neither the occurrence nor the placement of such cracks is significant, for some chairs were so small that they required only one stave, hence had no joints.[36]

Belter did not grow rich with his industry. Having taken his wife's brother into partnership in 1865, the firm finally went bankrupt in '67. It is said that as a disappointed man Belter broke his molds before retirement to insure against theft. His furniture is now to be seen in many museums and famous homes of the period.

The Neo-Rococo style which Belter took for his own had begun in America in the thirties with a model that had a hooped top and straight-turned or modified cabriole legs, a chair called a *balloon back* (Figures 6.42 and 6.47). From this initial departure from the Greek vocabulary the Neo-Rococo became more like its prototype Louis XV in its curvilinear outlines, cabriole front legs, and extensive use of carving. It differed in its heavier proportions, in its choice of mahogany or rosewood, and in its tendency toward higher seat backs and lower seats than the eighteenth-century pieces.

Drawing room sets consisted of chairs, sofa, and elaborate marble-top tables which varied from examples created for simpler tastes and pocketbooks to the elaborate and expensive, with

Figure 6.47   Chair with balloon back, 1840s.

filigree and deeply undercut carving of grapes, roses, pomegranates, and intertwined tendrils of morning glories. At one end of the line was upholstery of scratchy horsehair cloth; at the other, silk damask and brocade. Where the chair extended in three planes, it was essential to tuft the upholstery to keep it in place.

The remainder of the furniture of the revival age in America is not detailed here. The Neo-Renaissance and Gothic, which continued to be popular, were followed by a plethora of eclectic influences, called by numerous subtitles, each resurrected in several fashion cycles during the half-century. At its best, when an exacting clientele was the patronage, it resulted in some well-made and not too gauche specimens. At its worst it could appeal only through novelty and its variety can be described only by illustration. It was understandably the only possible kind of furniture that could be made by entrepreneurs who were dealing with new techniques, a new clientele, and a profit motive. Any retrospective catalog of American manufacture, such as the *Furniture World* (since 1871), illustrates succinctly the changes (without progress) that took place.

Pioneers for Reform in Furniture Design. Belter and Henkels and their contemporaries were, in the language of today, merely doing their thing. Equipped with craftsmen's skill, given the need to earn a living in a new land, they worked in the fashion then in favor on both sides of the Atlantic. Coupling hand-fabrication with the industrial mechanization of the future, they created furniture that had more to recommend it than much that is made today.

Certain men, however, felt that rehashes were not good enough for a creative age. William Morris (1834–1896), of course, was the most outspoken. Because he believed that craftsmanship was the route to originality as well as to social benefit, this seems the place to tell more about him as a person in order to understand him better as a designer and philosopher. Like Ruskin, he was a young man of some means and also like the older man was an Oxford scholar. His long friendship with the painter Edward Burne-Jones (1833–1898) began at the university. The chain of events which led the two, who had originally intended to enter the church, to take up art careers is not clear. Certainly introduction to the gospel according to Ruskin played its part along with the ideology of the Pre-Raphaelite Brotherhood of artists who were inspired by the symbolic painting preceding the Renaissance and Raphael, exposure to the Medievalism of the Oxford scene and the cathedrals of Europe, and possibly the doctrine of socialism published in Marx's *Communist Manifesto* of 1848. Morris pursued art with strong convictions of its ethical overtones and its potential for salutory and therapeutic experience.

William Morris was a stocky, likable, and energetic individual, and one who quickly turned his beliefs into action. In 1861 he supplied the major capital for the firm of Morris, Marshall, and Faulk-

ner, advertised as "Fine Art Workmen in Painting, Carving, Furniture, and the Metals." Charles Faulkner was, if anyone could be so designated, the business manager of the establishment. Actually the finances of the concern seem to have been rather loosely handled, for Morris dipped into his pocket whenever extra funds were required. In 1890 the firm name was changed to Morris and Company and a certain amount of mechanization and industrialization took place at that time. Ironically, the output became more elaborate, and many of the principles to which the group had been dedicated were lost. The firm, however, prospered and was in existence until World War II.

It must be acknowledged that much of the historic importance attached to the output of this group of friends is due directly to the personality of the founder himself, and especially to his writings. In addition to his poems [e.g., *The Earthly Paradise*, 3 vols., 1868–1870 and his socialist story *A Dream of John Ball*, 1888], Morris is remembered for a series of five lectures he gave between the years 1878 and 1881, rather late in his life. These talks were subsequently published in book form as *Hopes and Fears for Art*, from this his most famous quotation is: "Have nothing in your houses that you do not know to be useful or believe to be beautiful."[37] Thus he preached a doctrine against the useless clutter of knickknacks and for the taste by which each person can learn to evaluate beauty.

This artist's Utopia—and there was much more of Sir Thomas More than of Karl Marx in Morris's creed—would be brought about by the participation of workmen in the creative process. Indeed such communion would not only be a pleasurable act but it would also be the only means of healing the wounds of a fractionated society. This belief by Morris we are now beginning to accept as a valid diagnosis of the ills of the twentieth century:

I know by experience that the making of design after design without oneself executing them, is a great strain on the mind. It is necessary—unless all workmen of all grades are to be permanently degraded into machines, that the hand should rest the mind, as well as the mind the hand. And

I say this is the kind of work the world has lost, supplying its place with the work which is the result of the division of labor.[38]

Morris practiced what he preached, largely, may we say, because it would have been unthinkable for him to keep his hands away from the crafts. He loved creating textiles, glass, wallpapers, and, in his later years, graphics. His design for an edition of Chaucer's *Canterbury Tales,* which was executed at his Kelmscott Press (founded in 1891) near Chiswick, is world famous.

William Morris was a master artist of flat design, but it is questionable whether he ever made furniture or whether, if he did, it had aesthetic quality. The small amount that was made while the firm was handcrafting was done largely by the architects Philip Webb and George Frederick Bodley (1827–1907) and by the painter Ford Madox Brown (1821–1893). Morris, of course, remained the instigating force, and the type of furniture produced recalled his slant toward Medievalism and strong, honest construction as a prime requirement. In *The Dream of John Ball* he describes his ideal:

> . . . so strange and beautiful did this interior seem to me, although it was but a pothouse parlour. A quaintly carved sideboard held an array of bright pewter pots and dishes and wooden and earthen bowls; a stout oak table went up and down the room, and a carved oak chair stood by the chimney corner.

The "quaint sideboard" may be said to have come first (Figure 6.48). Several large cabinets and settles with high backs and overhanging canopies were made by the firm and seem to answer this description. They were obviously planned to display the painting of members of the group. One, designed by Webb, made in mahogany and pine on an oak stand and enriched by paintings by Morris of incidents in the story of St. George, is now in the Victoria and Albert. Some wag is said to have suggested that the furniture be destroyed but the paintings saved! At Wightwick is a settle of similar nature, designed by Bodley and decorated by Charles Kempe, the stained-glass craftsman who was associated with Bodley in designing the interiors of this Staffordshire manor.

Figure 6.48 Cabinet designed by William Morris; panels painted by Sir Edward C. Burne-Jones. Metropolitan Museum of Art, New York. (The Metropolitan Museum of Art. Rogers Fund, 1926.)

The construction of these pieces was straight yeoman's work, as was that of several types of chair designed by Ford Madox Brown. One was a modified ladder-back with rush seat and slender uprights extending above the cross pieces, for all the world resembling the Italian *chiavari* chair produced even today. Another, known as the Sussex chair, was a modified Windsor and sold for as little as five shillings. Most of the work of the firm, despite its attempt to bring good design with the reach of the masses, was expensive, as hand production is bound to be.

The decoration of the early pieces was largely in carving and painting. Later pieces, which were more elaborate, made much use of inlay. With no concessions to comfort, this furniture is totally masculine, but done with an artist's visual sensitivity.

It is said that Morris, who left the Great Exhibition of 1851 at first glance, castigated the whole as unredeemably ugly. He knew that something was terribly wrong and probably placed his finger on the cause, but he was unable to concede that the remedy involved the very machine processes he scorned.

The fallacy inherent in Morris's blindness to any art accomplished by industrialized methods had no greater illustration than in London's Crystal Palace. The building itself, designed and erected for the exhibition by Joseph Paxton, who was not an architect but a builder, was a modular prefabricated iron framework enclosed in glass. Assembly was quickly and economically done on location and the result was an immense open hall, superbly suited to the acres of display. The machine, which had wrought such poor taste within, showed that it was capable of creating better forms when its potential and limitations were understood. Morris, the craftsman and essentially the reactionary, was not the man to appreciate this.

The best-known counterpart of the Morris enterprise in America was that of the Roycrofters at East Aurora, New York. Work here was done anonymously and by hand. It was a community project, although one worker often carried an individual piece to completion. The Roycrofters were the creation of an unusual character. Elbert Hubbard (1856–1915; he met his death in the sinking of the Lusitania) had visited Morris in 1892 and had become a devotee of his principles, modeling his enterprise after the English firm. The adopted motto was, "Not how cheap it is, but how good it is." And again, "Get happiness from your work or you will never know what happiness is."[39] Hubbard was a shrewd businessman as well as a socialist and made a considerable fortune from his writings (e.g., "A Bushel of Diamonds," "A Message to Garcia"). These were essays that carried a moral.

The firm of Gustav Stickley in Binghamton, New York, also held to the traditions of handmade furniture, much of which was heavy, straight-lined oak. The Grand Rapids (a rapidly developing regional center) factories copied this honest-appearing style and named it *Mission*. The Roycrofters made similar pieces but refused to use that advertising name. "We would ask you not to classify our product as Mission. . . . Ours is purely Roycroft."[40]

During the eighties the English Arts and Crafts Movement developed from the Morris doctrine. It took the form of guilds, organized to sponsor community handiwork. In 1881 Arthur Heygate Mackmurdo (1851–1942), a highly original artist, and Selwyn Image established the Century Guild. In 1884 Walter Crane (1845–1915) followed with the Art Workers' Guild and in 1888 Charles Robert Ashbee (1863–1942) formed the Guild and School of Handicraft. The Arts and Crafts Exhibition Society (1888) had for its purpose the planning of yearly exhibitions of local crafts. These shows were effective in stimulating craftsmanship and indirectly improving standards because the exhibitors were given full credit and remuneration for their work.

The expense of handmade furniture militated against its use by the less affluent. Sir Charles Lock Eastlake (1793–1865), one of the earliest authors to be concerned with writing about taste and for the middle class market, said:

> Anyone can get drawing room chairs designed by an architect and executed by private contract for six guineas per chair. . . . What the public wants is a shop where such articles are kept in stock and can be purchased for 1 to 3 £. Curiously enough in these days of commercial speculation there is no such establishment.[41]

Eastlake was an architect and furniture designer for machine fabrication. It was the popularity of his writings, however, that established the "Eastlake style," which became attached to factory-produced furniture of rather monotonous character generally adorned with a fumed small bird or flower motif.

As a step toward providing guidelines for teaching individuals who would be capable of designing for industry, the British government schools of design began to train craftsmen in art as well as technique. Finally progressive firms sought the tutored designer who had a well-rounded education in both fields. In America certain architects such as Henry H. Richardson and Frank Lloyd Wright (see Chapter 7), designed sturdy furniture to be included in their custom-made interiors. The Grand Rapids furniture industry employed men like David Wolcott Kendall (1851–1910) and T. S. Handley, who had credentials from schools of architecture or design.

The creative work of some men in England stands out as innovative. Here, too, the architects often planned furniture to suit their needs. William Burges (1827–1881) and T. E. Collcutt (1840–1924) were disposed toward heavier, more rustic pieces, but Edward W. Godwin (1833–1886) designed what has been called *Art* or *Esthétique* furniture.

This last style, which used walnut, oak, or ebonized wood on a large overall scale, obviously derived from straight-line Gothic forms. Nevertheless its slender, turned uprights and its mode of decoration produced an appearance of preciosity that rendered it adaptable to country-type interiors and to more urbane surroundings. Inlay with woods and metal, frequent insets of enamel, and chaste metal fittings made the work both expensive and distinctive. Bruce James Talbert (1828–1881) derived many of his designs from his own book *Gothic Form Applied to Furniture* (1867), but the result was certainly more nineteenth-century "esthétique" than Medieval. Christopher Dresser (?–1904) belonged in the same category. A sideboard of his, made by the firm of William Watt, is now in the Victoria and Albert Museum. Like much of the Art furniture it bears a delicate restrained Japanese quality that calls to mind the influence of Japonisme at this time.

During the late eighties and the nineties in England the demand for furniture of cleaner line was expressed in pieces of lighter tone that would blend with the interiors created by Ashbee, Baillie Scott, Voysey, and Mackmurdo. These designs may be considered the forerunner of Art Nouveau tendencies.

The furniture of C. R. Mackintosh had a more lasting influence on the European scene, funneled through the channels of the Viennese showings. With its exaggerated tall chair backs, its slim proportions, its straight-line supports that rose through the entire carcass, often with additional internal decorative elliptical struts or painted embellishment done by his wife Margaret, the Mackintosh style (Figure 6.23) was, although mannered, at once acceptable to the sensitivities of the Austrian taste and to the tectonic rationale of the German.

Belgium acted as a bridge between England and Europe through its sales outlets for English goods. Gustave Serrurier-Bovy, architect and furniture designer, had a shop of international character in Liége. His own furniture assumed the straight-lined, flat, oriental quality of Mackintosh's work. Its tautness and attenuation conveyed some of the feeling of the Godwin taste. He, too, used the rectangular module as an enclosure for curved braces in the manner of, but less structurally than, Mackintosh.

Van de Velde (Figure 6.49), although not so delicate in his touch, nevertheless used curves as sturdy framing members. His creed was rooted in Ruskin's writings and thus he ultimately veered toward the organically conceived tract. This line, often known as the *whiplash*, became distinctive to the Art Nouveau style and was responsible not only for much of its charm but for its extravagances. In a manner similar to van de Velde's, Victor Horta produced urbane furniture for his houses.

In France Hector Guimard (Figure 7.38), whom we have met as an Art Nouveau architect, felt that architecture and interiors should be unified, and it is not surprising that he designed articles with straight supports and curved braces that seemed almost to grow from the tree. Louis Majorelle (1859–1926) of Nancy introduced such plasticity into his furniture designs in the form of plant stalks and flowers that it detracted from their desirable strength. The output of such men of Nancy as the glass manufacturer Emile Gallé (1846–1904), Eugène Vallin, and Eugène Colonna is often subject to similar criticism.

Austria, represented by Josef Hoffmann, joined the straight-line ranks. Hoffmann's chairs, however, do not appear to have been stretched vertically like a rubber band and they make concessions to comfort by being upholstered in leather (in the Stoclet dining room).

Figure 6.49 Side chair, Henri van de Velde, 1895–1896. Oak frame and rush seat. Height, 94 cm. Museum of Modern Art, New York. (Collection, The Museum of Modern Art, New York. Purchase.)

Germany took the most prophetic course, and although her architecture before 1900 gave little suggestion of the lead she was later to take the furniture she made and showed at her exhibits was well conceived for its combination of structural potential, comfort, and pleasing visual qualities. Bernard Pankok (1872–1943) of Munich and Stuttgart designed mahogany chairs of broad sturdy contours, whose patterns created by the vacant spaces were curvilinear in the familiar Art Nouveau tear-drop shape. August Endell (1871–

1925), as might be expected from his architecture, concentrated his ornament in carved anthropomorphic forms, which at points of structural articulation he played against plain sturdy surfaces. Peter Behren's chairs left ornamentation behind and presented flat surfaces made from shaped boards. He designed furniture for the German Pavilion at the St. Louis (US) 1904 Fair.

It was Richard Riemerschmid whose skill was most avant garde in his oak side chair of 1899 (now at New York's Museum of Modern Art; Figure 6.50). Here the back and diagonally oriented front leg brace are one subtle curve that could rival the later Barcelona of Mies van der Rohe. Legs rise gracefully into the seat which is canted for comfort. Riemerschmid was a Munich man,

Figure 6.50 Side chair, 1899. Richard Riemerschmid, designer. Oak with leather upholstery. Height, 78 cm. Museum of Modern Art, New York. (Collection, The Museum of Modern Art, New York. Gift of Liberty & Co., Ltd., London.)

and in this area so near to Austria in urbanity, to France with its clarity and sensuous delicacy, and to Germany with its rational scientific bent, we shall leave furniture for future development.

Other Articles

Clocks. Although little advance in the mechanics of horology occurred, the handsome character of the glass and brass mantle clocks of the early nineteenth century should be noted. It became fashionable to place precious objects of art under a glass dome which was fitted to its base. This covering was known as a *cloche* and the name was transferred to a mantle clock so treated. Earlier such turn-of-the-century *fondeurs* as Thomire had made bronze cases for expensive clocks and it was easy to transfer their expertise to the casings of later timepieces. Some of the loveliest, if not quite plain, at least retained the rigor and dignity inherent in the best of the tall case clocks and of the Neoclassic clocks of the preceding century. As the works were entirely visible, the swing of the pendulum or the turn of the balance weights created visual interest. Striking, when held within glass and metal, is often of the finest sonority. Throughout the later years of the century cases followed prevailing style trends and were frequently porcelain or wood.

Pianos. The piano replaced the harpsichord in popularity during the nineteenth century. The harp shape of the piano (now the *grand*) was common until about 1760 when the rectangular or "square" piano vied with it. The harp shape was used extensively during the First Empire. The Erard Brothers of Paris made one for Queen Hortense of Holland which is now in the Royal Dutch Collection at Amsterdam. It has an elegant mahogany and ormolu case with *verre églomisé* plates. The upright piano was introduced by Ignace Pleyel of France about 1815.

Although many of the names connected with the development of the piano were European, England and America led the way in commercial production. William Mason of York, England, was an inventor rather than a manufacturer. He perfected the piano mechanism (about 1755) to provide more resonance, thus giving it currency. Two English firms—Broadwood & Sons and Stodart—produced their famous-name pianos during the last quarter of the eighteenth century. This was synchronous with the manufacture of the first pianoforte in America by John Behrent of Philadelphia (1775). Firms which have continued in business throughout the twentieth century are Knabe (1834), Jonas Chickering of Boston (ca. 1815), Steinway (1851), Baldwin (1862), Krakauer (1878), and Mason and Hamlin (1883). Chickering made the first grand piano in America in 1840.[42]

Mirrors. One type of Empire, Regency, or Greek Revival mirror is rectangular and may be surmounted with a classical entablature without a pediment. The side panels usually affect some form of classical pillar. A scenic or patriotic painting may grace the frieze. These mirrors are frequently framed in gilded wood relieved with touches of black paint.

Girandole mirrors (Figure 6.51), round with convex surfaces, continue from the eighteenth century. The lighting brackets which are appended to them give them their name. The glass is often surrounded by a narrow black border to simulate ebony, which in turn is edged with a concave molding decorated with small gilded balls. Some of the handsomest of post-midcentury mirrors have mahogany or black walnut frames with bold, broad, concave-convex profiles.

Pier mirrors, to accompany a low table and hung on the wall between two tall windows, were features of mid-Victorian interiors. Ornate and gilded, their elaborate cornices favored a similar window treatment—a welcome brightness in heavily draped fenestration.

TEXTILES, CARPETS, TAPESTRIES, WALLCOVERINGS

France, which from the seventeenth century had been queen of the silk industry, was all but deprived of her preeminence at the time of the Revolution. The destruction of the aristocracy had been the obliteration of a clientele not soon replaced. Napoleon, as consul, took steps to improve the situation. At his order the walls of his various palaces were covered with the damasks,

Figure 6.51 Girandole mirror, America or England, 1810. Wood and glass. Height, 1.07 m, width, 66 cm. Winterthur Museum, Winterthur, Delaware. (Courtesy, The Henry Francis du Pont Winterthur Museum.)

the lyres, vases, and cornucopias, prevailed at first but grew stiffer and more formal until near the middle of the century.

One recognized drawback experienced by the French textile industry was the superior mechanization of the English processes (e.g., invention of the power loom by John Cartwright, 1788). The French countered by perfecting innovations that ultimately led to complete pattern manipulation by machine power. One of the most important developments was the invention by Charles-Marie Jacquard (1752–1834), son of a Lyon weaver, of the loom that bears his name. Here the design is made by raising of warps as dictated by a series of holes in punched cards. As so frequently happens, Jacquard was persecuted by the weavers of Lyon who destroyed his property in the fear that the new processes would jeopardize their jobs. It is pleasant to record, however, that in 1806 his patent was bought by the state, which rewarded him with a small pension and royalties. The long feud with his fellow workers was at an end.

Once again the French monopolized the luxury trade in silks. Quality remained excellent because of the somewhat illegal and clandestine organization of journeymen to preserve standards after the breakup of the guilds during the Revolution. Patterning, however, could never be the same because warp control could not provide the thousands of small color changes previously made by the weft. Although intricate patterns became impractical, ingenious tricks to obtain similar results by cheaper means, such as watered effects and the printing of patterns on warps before weaving, were in order.

In 1876 a severe frost killed the mulberry trees of southern France, source of the chief supply of reeled silk to the French factories. Hence it was really a fortunate portent when in 1884 Count Hilaire de Chardonnet presented a paper before the Académie Française entitled "Imitation de la soie naturelle." Five years later at the World Exhibition in Paris a demonstration of Chardonnet's apparatus launched an industry that has developed, through many improvements, to the vast takeover by synthetic fibers today. This development belongs to other studies. It has progressed along lines of greater practicality, less cost, and

brocades, and velvets of Lyon and his officers were told firmly to arrange for the same. We can see some of these silks in the contemporary paintings of Malmaison.

His various victories were reproduced in woven cloth by his designer Jean François Bony (1754–1825). Thus details of Egyptian architecture, Roman war emblems—fasces, eagles, and wreaths—appear. We find the imperial "N" encircled and the rubric of the bee woven in terra cotta on a background of black satin. The gentler patterns, due attention to what is known as the "hand" of the material. On the other side, the silk industry has become a luxury field, the province of the Orient and, to a limited extent, of Italy.

The vogue for cottons and linens continued meanwhile. The availability of Indian fabrics and the advances in the dyeing and printing processes ensured the popularity of the colorful dimities, seersuckers, chintzes, and cretonnes. England, France, and, in a manner limited by type, India—these were the fountainhead of textile printing. In England the finest work reverted to the wood-block process of such operators as Charles Swainson of Bannister Hall, centering around Lancaster. By the first decade of the century roller engraving done by the firms of John Lockett of Manchester and John Potts of Derbyshire[43] began to supply the world market.

Designs at first were good, often done in the new discharge printing technique by which the discharge chemical, printed in small dots, caused tonal gradations according to the spacing of the whites. The eighteenth-century patterns on dark grounds eventually gave way to flower and bird designs done with broader strokes and imprinted on a more varied series of muted tones. The Audubon *Birds of America* series came out in 1830.

French patterned cottons and linens followed the English styles rather closely. Centers of production were Rouen for the less expensive and Alsace for more sophisticated work.[44] Needless to say, Napoleon took an interest in cloth printing as well as in silk weaving. Prints of his career were made long after his death.

In the late 1830s patterns deteriorated. Pictorial roller prints with a certain quaint charm but no real design merit prevailed. Even the few establishments that specialized in wood blocking, which had managed to maintain a higher standard reached an aesthetically low ebb.

It was into this sort of situation that William Morris intruded. He sent his first floral design, "Tulip and Willow," to Bannister Hall for printing, and it is reported that he was so horrified with the Prussian blue they used for the background rather than the indigo he had intended that he withdrew the project. Instead, he collaborated with Thomas (later Sir Thomas) Wardle of Leek, an authority on silk cultivation and dyeing who was generous

enough to subsidize, in part, some of Morris's use of commercially outdated techniques. The two men were partners between 1875 and 1881 during which time sixteen fabrics were produced to Morris's order.

Morris was a difficult man to harness in tandem and his remaining twenty-eight patterns were printed at his own works at Merton Abbey in Surrey. In his last he was able to use the indigo discharge process that had long been his particular enthusiasm. The Surrey factory continued in business until 1940 and produced the more popular of Morris' designs, whereas the firm of Wardle at Leek and later that of Bernard Wardle of Bridgnorth, Shropshire, printed the work he did during his association with Sir Thomas. Stead, MacAlpin, of Carlisle, now holds the Morris woodblocks and continues to produce with them on order. Some are the *Honeysuckle,* the *Strawberry Thief* (Figure 6.52), and, his last design, the *Diagonal Trail.*

Morris's textiles combine a bold sweep of florals with a much more delicate background of similar motif. In this they bear a certain relation to the silk patterns of the heyday of Louis XIV textiles: large-scaled boldness of pattern executed with refinement of line. Even though the field is well covered, much as in a Medieval millefleur, dominance and subordination are well understood. Patterns are stylized and there is no slippage from one degree of abstraction to another. His work was a direct inspiration to Voysey and Mackmurdo and a forerunner of Art Nouveau.[45]

The firm likewise made tapestries. This was a natural revival of a Medieval technique. Using the Gobelin method of high-warp weaving, Morris made his second full-sized tapestry, the *Woodpecker,* in 1885. For this his friend Philip Webb drew the birds and he did the flora himself. Done in shades of bluish green and gold, it used the usual swirling leaf patterns on which the vertical element of the trunk and the round fruits and birds are superimposed. The latter are so graded in size that they create accent points along which the eye must travel. These foreground details, however, are simple forms and do not seem to accord with the complexity of the design as a whole. Later Morris tapestries include human figures drawn by Burne-Jones.

311

Figure 6.52 Textile, *Strawberry Thief*, William Morris, designer, England, 1883. Height, 89 cm, width, 97 cm. Cleveland Museum of Art. (The Cleveland Museum of Art. Gift of Mrs. Henry A. Chisholm.)

Art Nouveau created all manner of textiles—woven, painted, embroidered, and printed. Tapestries and carpets were not its chef-d'oeuvre because of the laborious time consumption and expensive material they entailed. Art Nouveau de-signing in England was intended for execution by the manufactories in the environs of Manchester, the center of cotton production. On the Continent the Viennese, with their Werkstätte approach, specialized in woven fabrics. Van de Velde, inspired as he was by Morris, is represented by wall hangings. Following in his footsteps were Germans like Otto Eckmann (1865–1902). Much of the German weaving emanated from the tapestry workshops at Scherrebek, France. The French sculptor Aristide Maillol (1861–1944), a member of the Nabis group, designed Art Nouveau type tapestries done in the workshop in Banyuls-sur-Mer.

These men greatly simplified the details of Morris' fabrics and designed with bolder, flatter swings of the brush. Mackmurdo's printed cotton fabric, *Cromer Bird* (ca. 1884) is typical of the play of bold design against a low-keyed swirling background. The same principle, but with less contrast of tone, is to be seen in Voysey's woven silk and wool fabric of 1897 at the Victoria and Albert. Less complex is van de Velde's (1893) wool and silk appliqué wall hanging entitled *Angels' Guard*. Other examples merely serve to accentuate the Art Nouveau stamp.

When we leave the upper echelons of nineteenth-century textile designing, we uncover a wealth of homely and hand-done products of the loom and embroidery needle and of combined forms of household technology which often possess charm and artistry. As such they are material for the collector's interest.

Woven coverlets come first to mind and, because they flourished in that limbo in which hand work was translated into machine power in precisely the era when the American Midwest was in the throes of growth, they illustrate that unique transition from pioneer to urban, from homespun to factory, which occurred concurrently in a number of places.[46]

The earliest of these weavings to have survived the hard use they received as bed covers are dated around the turn of the century. At that time many were woven in the home or by itinerant weavers with local wool and linen. They are sturdy, warm, patterned cloths with sufficient body to lie flat on a bed and provide a substantial focus of decorative interest. The size of these coverlets was fixed by the width of the loom, and many had to be made from several narrow strips. Later ones were more often in one piece.

The loom potential also limited the patterning—at first the simple, twill-like "Summer and Winter," the more complex single-weave overshots, or the thicker double-weave patterns. The last required a more complicated loom and were more likely to be the work of professionals.

Following advances in the spinning of cotton, that fiber was often substituted for linen and wool. Colors, too, became more numerous, and red, green, and yellow were added to the former indigo blue and natural.

In the eighteen twenties the Jacquard attachment was added to the draw loom and introduced to America. After that decade and down to the Civil War, when the heyday of these woven pieces was almost over, the work was largely done by experts, many of whom were men who had been trained in Europe—in Scotland, Holland, or Germany. The looms were community-owned and the weavers itinerant, or, if an area warranted, a weaver would set up his own shop with private capital. Many of their names or trademarks have come down to us (Michael Eichman in Pennsylvania, Harry Tyler in New York, David Haring in New Jersey, and Dennis Cosley in Ohio), for it was the weaver's name and date that remained irremovable in the warp and weft at the corner of the fabric. Occasionally the owner's name was added. Some weavers showed their trademarks—a house, a boat, a lion, or a bird.

The best of the coverlets, from the standpoint of freedom of patterning, came with this professional practice. Designs no longer needed to be small repeats; florals worked around a center, as in an oriental medallion, could be executed. Some of the more interesting but frequently less artistic patterns were representations of national emblems and landmarks. Possibly the most exciting patterns to a collector are those that can be traced from the weaver's drafting books to the loom or those that indicate patterns brought from the homeland. Pennsylvania and New Jersey motifs, for instance, show traces of the German rose. Picturesque names, such as "Chariot Wheels" and "Cat's Tracks," abounded.

There was a late renaissance of the woven coverlet at the time of the Philadelphia Centennial of 1876, which was associated largely with patriotic patterning. The old art had perished, however, and comparisons are really not valid. The Chicago Institute of Art has one of the finest collections of masterpieces.

Quilts were made in colonial days, although few in existence antedate the late seventeen hundreds. Under pioneer conditions the motive for

313

their manufacture was that of economy because cloth was costly and small scraps could be utilized. Later when appliqué quilts were created, the aesthetic motif must have loomed large. Trapunto ornamentation and tufting satisfied the same psychological need. Because large frames were necessary for the quilting operation, the enterprise became a social event, frequently undertaken by a church community for the purpose of raising funds.

Both practical and artistic prompting underlay all the different forms of small rug making before the industrialized products were readily available. Some hooked rugs of the nineteenth century were well designed and skillfully made, although the opposite could just as easily be true. Braided rugs were household items. The bias strips were accumulated until ready for firm hands to form into thicker ropes of material, sewn in turn into an oval or round carpet.

Textile Uses

As industrialization flooded the market with more easily accessible yard goods it was natural that the average household would "dress" its windows and cover its furniture to the point of stuffiness. Even the "cottage" views as shown in Downing indicate an elaboration unsuited to the character of the building.

High Victorian windows represented the epitome and had an array of hangings. First came one and sometimes two sets of sheers, which were often machine-made lace (a net called *Nottingham*). Over them hung lined draperies crowned with a highly ornamented hand-carved or gilt cornice. The draperies themselves were completed by an elaborately festooned valance, usually called a lambrequin. Fringes, tassels, ornamental ropes, and fancy metal tiebacks added to the ensemble. Similar dressing would accompany upholstery.

Toward the century's end the trend toward simplicity is noted in the interiors done, for example, by Voysey. Oriental justification for this unpretentiousness is frequently called to our attention in the early periodicals:

The India silks manufactured for Mr. Louis Tiffany, by a well known firm in Connecticut, from

cocoons imported by themselves, are delightful for lighter draperies. These are chosen by artists in preference to French and Italian silks with all their sheen and stiffness.[47]

Although silks suggested richness, the use of cloth of other fibers naturally followed the vogue for informality and accompanied limited purses. Their names continue to proliferate—scrim, India mull, momie cloth, and butcher's linen (a mixed fabric of linen and cotton)—to mention a few. An excellent variety of linen was called "Silesia" and was woven so wide that the broadest window could be covered without a seam. Chintzes and glazed calicoes were found in bedrooms and "summer" rooms. Both calicoes and ginghams, combined with a matching valance, were used as blinds.

Wool-felted material and baize were popular as coverings for living room tables. Hair cloth made of linen or cotton warp and horsehair weft was a novel upholstery fabric used during the eclectic decades.

A final word about the cashmere and Paisley shawls that were not only worn as cloaks but became "throws" for lounge and piano. The real cashmeres, worth a king's ransom, were woven in India of fine cashmere wool, in narrow strips, in a tapestry twill weave. They were then embroidered into one piece. Queen Victoria is said to have owned several. The ordinary imitation, a brocade known as "Paisley," was woven in the Scottish town of that name. They were of fine soft wool, done in patterns of the palmette and cone, imitative of the Indian. Writings of the last century suggest they were cut into strips for portiers!

Carpets

A parallel case may be drawn between machine-made carpets and furniture. Neither took over the mass market completely until near midcentury. During the Neoclassic period wealthier households still relied on the handmade rugs of France, England, or the Orient. Less important installations retained domestic handmade fabrics— hooked and braided rugs or painted canvas (used as floorcloths in the minor rooms of the White House for many years).[48] Later, inexpensive coverings of straw matting (*China matting,* an imported material made of grass), or green baize (a wool, similar to felt in appearance but woven in construction—its name derived from Baza, Spain) were popular. These fabrics were frequently tacked in place over a pad of paper (and taken up every spring and beaten clean!).

Machine construction of carpets (see Chapter 4), like the making of patterned cloths, developed gradually from improvements and power additions to the loom. England, of course, took the lead. In the *House and Home Papers* written by Harriet Beecher Stowe and published in the *Atlantic Monthly* (July 1864) we read:

> But, dear Mr. Crowfield, said Miss Featherstone, a nice girl, who was just then one of our family circle, there is not, positively, much that is fit to use or wear made in America,—is there now? Just think; how is Marianne to furnish her house here without French papers and English carpets?

The denouement of this story is that Miss Featherstone was apprised of the fact that an American, Mr. Bigelow, had gone to England in the hope of studying the English process. Denied entrance to the factories, he returned to America and worked out a loom (the Bigelow loom, in operation by 1851) that was capable of producing eighteen yards of *moquette* a day. Moquettes were uncut pile weave fabrics of the necessary measure of coarseness. The name described a French upholstery material of the same order.

Nineteenth-century machine-made carpets were known by names seldom recognized today. An *ingrain* (the earlier *Kidderminster*) was merely a wool damask of a weight that could be used on a floor. *Brussels* (uncut pile) and Wilton (cut pile) were types that embedded a limited number of colored yarns in the fabric and brought them to the surface only as dictated by the pattern. These processes were followed by another (and its loom) that was less expensive—provided enough production was available to offset the cost of setting up the apparatus. This produced the *Axminster* carpet, which had a high pile of numerous colors. The winding of each row of tufts on a separate spool allowed the use of an exceedingly small amount of wool for any one weft shot. The spool Axminster loom was invented by Halcyon Skinner in 1867, working on developments that

had been made by Alexander Smith at an earlier date.

Another process of obtaining a floor covering of many colors involved dyeing the pattern warp yarn before it was woven into the pile. This invention preceded that of Axminster weaving and in principle was as old as the Louis XIV upholstery moquettes. Carpets made in this manner on the Wilton loom were known as *Tapestry Brussels* (uncut) or *Velvets* (cut). The name Tapestry was appended because the tuft yarn, never entering precisely into the pattern, resembled the irregular hatchings of a tapestry. It was these Tapestry Brussels and Velvets that were the popular floral carpets of the mid-Victorian era. Their background was often black and their large bouquets of red flowers with vitriolic green leaves were in a sense gay and becoming to Victorian interiors, holding their share of attention in ornate high-ceilinged rooms.

As an illustration of the principle of industrial obsolescence it should be noted that carpets today are more likely to be knitted and tufted than woven.

Orientals. As mentioned, the nineteenth century benefited by a brisk trade in oriental weavings. The native industry found it profitable to conform to some of the Western demands in respect to size, color, and standardization. The territory just south of the Black and Caspian Seas produced room-size *Gorevan, Serapi,* and *Herez* carpets with large, interconnected medallions in soft colors.

Oriental rugs are the product of the wool-growing belt of the East, lying roughly between latitude thirty and forty. Here are situated the countries that produce the principal types—Turkey, Persia, the Caucasus, and the Turkoman (between the Caspian Sea and the Himalaya mountains), Indian, and Chinese. The last two varieties were rare, the latter because of unsettled trade conditions and the former being largely palace weavings.

Take a trip around Persia. The territory to the southeast, known as Kerman, lies adjacent to India and favors the natural flowers found in Indian textiles. The designs, however, more closely stud the field and the equivalent emphasis on the plant

Figure 6.53 Feraghan rug, Persia, ca. 1860. Length, 1.91 m, width, 1.22 m. Allen Art Museum, Oberlin, Ohio. (Allen Memorial Art Museum, Oberlin College. Charles Martin Hall Bequest, 15.7.)

often with the motif known as the pear or the fish. These rugs are the *Sarabands,* the *Lorestans,* the *Bakhtiari,* and the *Kurdish,* extending north to the borders of Kurdish territory. They are the smaller rugs and runners that the natives used to adorn their tents. Again the colors are Persian with saffron yellow appearing in the weavings of the Kurds.

The northern caravan routes from east to west served the more urbane districts that made the best-known of the Persian carpets. Here larger sizes, extensive use of the central medallion design, and a sophisticated sense of abstracting the pattern can be found. The *Khorassans* were made in the old eastern capital and have, in their overall brownish tones, an indescribable oriental twang in their makeup. Slightly south, on the border of the salt desert, the priceless *Kashans* were made, and their somewhat more practical sisters, the *Saruks,* came from the neighboring plateau to the west—all medallion carpets. In the north central is found the *Feraghan* (Figure 6.53), again a carpet with deep blue ground whose medallions are smaller and interlaced with foliate leaves and Chinese cloud bands (this was the route the Mongols traveled) in a complex that spells the pattern traditionally called the *Herati* (see Volume 1, Chapter 6). Feraghans are frequently found as runners. The *Hamadan,* made in towns that border on the Caucasus, places its more angular medallion on a camel's hair background and adds arrow motifs on the ends, the whole being known as the *pole medallion* (see Volume 1, Chapter 6). Strangely, the mountain tribes centering around the southern city of Shiraz produce a similar rug with three interconnected pole medallions.

Such are some of the more important of the numerous patterns of the Persian carpets. There are many more and curiously enough they begin to fall into recognizable categories after a little observation. Recognition by name, however, is of minor importance when compared with recognition by quality. The Persian carpet, most often done on a cotton warp with the finest of wool pile and generally using a Sehna knot (see Volume 1, Chapter 6), is characterized by an expert sense of stylization from natural flora with such fine line work that the whole combines with dec-

in its entirety is lacking. Colors may be deeper Persian ruby and blue.

To the west of Persia rise the high Zagros mountains, and this territory with its warlike tribes came less under the influence of occidental merchandising than did the more settled plateaus to the north. Mountain rugs here are characterized by small, neat patterns arranged in rows, oration of delicate scale, curved tracery, and blue, ruby-red orientation.

Turkish, Caucasian, and Turkoman belong to bolder schemas. Colors range from the vivid reds, yellows, and greens used by the Turks and Caucasian tribesmen to the more somber tones of blood red and black of the Turkoman. Turkish rugs such as the *Ghiordes, Bergamo, Anatolian,* and *Oushak* have straight-line geometric designs, the most favored of which are those of the prayer rug with its representation of the *mihrab* or prayer niche (see Volume 1, Chapter 6). The Caucasian, which springs from the territory between the ridges of the Kara Dagh mountains, usurps numerous tribal names such as *Kazak, Karadagh,* and *Beshir.* On one hand, the flamelike swastikas that shoot from their medallions suggest the mid-Eurasian origin of the Kazaks—the Cossacks or wild horsemen of the plains; again the Caucasians are the only rugs in which stylized animals and humans appear.

Much more prescribed are the Turkomans (Figure 6.54), which have given their name to a basketful of family goods, the *Tekke Bokharas,* the *Princess,* and the *Royal Bokharas,* with their octagon tribal *guls* or devices. The touch of yellow that tinges both their reds and blacks calls up visions of Mongolian nomads who used them as coverings for their tentlike yurts. The Turkoman knot is Sehna, partaking of the weaving technique of many of the Chinese. The knot predominating in the Turkish and Caucasian is Ghiordes. This renders a coarser body. Caucasian and Turkoman are all wool, and this is true of the majority of the Turkish carpets except those allied closely to the Persian.

Because most oriental weavings today come under western supervision, there is a demand for these articles manufactured almost one hundred years ago, when native talent flourished.

William Morris approved of using artifacts from unrelated sources insofar as they were aesthetically good and created a lovely ensemble. Thus he favored oriental rugs and particularly those of the Caucasus. His own enterprises involved carpet designing and weaving, which he undertook in 1878 at looms at Hammersmith. His designs have much in common with the Turkish and Caucasian.

WALLPAPERS

During the early Napoleonic era, when the consul was setting the vogue for the use of luxurious silks on the walls of his Bourbon palaces, the new proletariat was turning to wallpapers as a means of gaining an individualized background for living. One alternative lay in the use of cotton fabrics for walls and upholstery. Striped patterns in wallpapers favored the resemblance to the rooms done for Napoleon by Percier and Fontaine and were a natural development from the narrow striped patterns of the late eighteenth-century textiles.

About the time of the Bourbon return monotone papers came back into favor. These were capped with deep, friezelike borders and occa-

Figure 6.54 Carpet, Turkoman, Yomud tribe, nineteenth century (detail of upper left quarter). Fogg Museum, Cambridge, Massachusetts. (Courtesy of the Fogg Art Museum, Harvard University. Gift of Elizabeth Gowing, Harborne W. Stuart, Peggy Coolidge, and the Estate of W. I. Stuart in memory of Mr. and Mrs. Willoughby H. Stuart, Jr.)

sionally were framed within real or simulated panels, which provided a better background for the fashionable hanging of many pictures. Monochrome papers may have been related to the undercurrent reactions to the entire subject of the psychology of color.

We have mentioned that the firm of Jacquemart and Benard took over Réveillon's business. The new star on the horizon of wallpaper manufacture, however, was Joseph Dufour (1752–1827), a native of Macon, France, who conducted a business in Paris from 1804 until his death. He was then succeeded by his son-in-law, Le Roy. To Dufour is attributed the famous and fashionable sequences that created a panorama. His colors at times were almost a grisaille; at others they showed a pastel, chalklike character. Some of his best-known scenics are his famous "Monuments of Paris," "The Twelve Months" (designed by Fragonard, fils, in 1804), "Paul and Virginia" (designed by Brocq, from the story in the best-seller by Bernardin de St. Pierre), and "Telemachus on the Island of Calypso." These were placed on American walls. Andrew Jackson's home, the Hermitage, in Nashville, Tennessee, had the entrance hall papered in an American version of the Telemachus.

The work of Jean Zuber, of Alsace, was in imitation of Dufour. One of his best-selling papers was "Scenic America," with views of New York, West Point, Boston, and Niagara. Dufour's papers were the last of the hand-printed compositions. Soon machines had learned to register many colors from a continuous cylinder.

American firms were organized at the beginning of the century. In 1795 Ebenezer Clough opened Boston's "Paper Staining Manufactory." One of his noteworthy designs was the Washington Memorial pattern brought out in 1800. The firm of Asa Smith, operating in Baltimore for the short span 1800–1810 produced some conventional landscape medallions. By midcentury wallpaper, like other commodities, had deteriorated aesthetically. Curvilinear florals, imitation damasks, trellis and diagonal frames to support foliage, and pictorial vignettes were predominant.

When Morris produced his first paper, "Daisy," in 1862, a freshness of coloring, an almost folk quality of pattern, and good organization returned. Morris's friend, Metford Warner (1843–1930), headed the firm of Jeffrey and Company which printed the papers designed by the master. Walter Crane in England, van de Velde in Belgium, and Otto Eckmann and Walter Leistikow in Germany all had a hand in the better productions of Art Nouveau.

Nineteenth-century wallpapers demonstrate the best and worst of mural design. Setting aside all questions related to architectonics, some made use of the finest quality in media to effect a patterning that was complex but controlled; others were cluttered examples of disconnected details or tight compositions of rigidly dictated monotony.

CERAMICS

Ceramic histories frequently end with 1800. In France there is a soupçon of justification for this. Sèvres, for instance, was declared royal property and was all but eradicated by the Revolutionists. Molds were smashed. Some of the wares were destroyed by the staff who feared implication as royal sympathizers. Much unfinished china found its way to England where it was completed for sale and often passes for Sèvres today. One English firm, that of Thomas Randall at Madeley, Shropshire, was founded in 1825 on the premise of imitating the much sought-after Sèvres. Randall, however, never forged the Sèvres mark. Napoleon, seeking the emoluments of royalty, revived the official Sèvres patronage and for him a hard-paste body was made into pieces that glorified the Empire.

Most European factories looked backward to eighteenth-century patterns and later, when industrialization took over, produced sets of tableware to supply the foreign market. New firms to this purpose sprang into existence, such as Haviland at Limoges, which produced a fine hard paste. Dinner services were extensive and usually contained a dozen each of service plates, dinner plates, service dishes, cups and saucers, and who knows what all—a supply of articles largely considered expendable today.

In England new factories came into international prominence. The Nantgarw and Swansea factories of South Wales were established in 1813. The former moved to Swansea, probably in 1814, because of the peregrinations of that none too stable porcelain genius William Billingsley. The Nantgarw body resembles that of Sèvres and much of the decoration was London-done in the manner of the French.

Rockingham, in Yorkshire, began in 1820 but continued only until '42. Doulton was organized in 1818. In addition, of course, the old establishments of Spode, Wedgwood, Royal Worcester, Coalport, Royal Crown Derby, and Minton continued to produce bone china and fine pottery.

Beleek china was made on the Castle Caldwell estate west of Belfast (1857). The pearly luster of its paper-thin body was based on a prescription of J. J. H. Brianchou, a Frenchman who had patented it in England. Pieces are small art wares such as sugars, creamers, and bonbon dishes.

Potteries were connected with the Morris movement. The most celebrated potter was William Frend De Morgan (1839–1917). Morgan's factory was also on the site of the old Abbey of Merton. A resemblance in technique, color, and pattern to the luster wares of Persia is noticeable, although exact copying is not the case. The colors of plates, bowls, and vases were peacock blue, turquoise, green, pink, and mulberry, whereas his tiles—often used for the decoration of mantels—were green or oriental blue and white.

The first real porcelain in America was manufactured between 1825 and 1854 by the *Jersey Porcelain and Earthenware Company*. This was a business enterprise pure and simple, and none of its five owners had ever been potters. So many organizations since then have had similar histories—a circumstance that must take some of the blame for the character of design and media. The Jersey factory, however, apparently delivered the goods and was awarded several "Oscars" for laudatory performance (by the Franklin Institute for the Benefit of Science and Industry!). Although constrained to abandon porcelain manufacture because of foreign competition, fine pottery was made. The firm later became D. & J. Henderson and Company, which again demonstrates the shifting sands of American enterprise.

William Ellis Tucker, whose father had introduced him to fine china at his china shop in Phila-delphia, opened a kiln of his own in 1826. Here he made a gilt-decorated bone china that was harder than the English. It appears now that many of the sepia landscapes and floral bands that were its decoration were done by his brother Thomas. The output was predominantly large urn-shaped vases with griffin handles, bowls, pitchers, and sundry. William at first was sabotaged by English workmen. His financial difficulties led to a partnership with Judge Joseph Hemphill. Under this management men were imported from the Continent and wares in imitation of Sèvres were made. William Tucker died in 1832 and Hemphill lost his fortune in the financial panic of 1833. The factory closed in 1834.

Southern Ohio in the vicinity of Liverpool developed as an important ceramic center around midcentury. Pottery, creamware, and stoneware were products. A formula for the last was similar to an 1813 English patent in the name of Charles James Mason. Accordingly, a hard earthenware, light in color and suitable for tableware, was made. This is often known as *dinnerware*. The firm of Knowles (Isaac W.), Taylor (John), Knowles (Homer S.) represents the reorganization of smaller corporations begun in 1840. American firms were highly industrialized and many of excellent reputation flourish today.

Art Nouveau left its mark on American ceramic production. The Rookwood Company of Cincinnati, begun in 1880 by Maria Longworth Storer, produced vases and bowls with Art Nouveau shapes; their highly reflective glazes had opalescent overtones that resembled the variegated colors of Tiffany glass. The wares of the early-twentieth-century (1908–1931) R. Guy Cowen kilns, near Cleveland, with their sinuous forms and diagonally poised figurines of gazelles and fauns, bridged the production of Art Nouveau and Art Deco (see Chapter 7).

GLASS

Nineteenth-century glass was innovative in some of its production methods and in the work of a few artist creators. Bohemia continued to engrave its soda-lime metal. The country is also noted for its low-relief carving of ruby red and amber glass.

Colored glass appeared to be a nineteenth-century favorite. French opalene was one variety, a milk-white and pastel mixture. Among other colors, Bristol (England) made several shades known as Bristol blue. In America such names as amberina, peachglow, and Burmese helped to sell a good deal of colored glass.[49]

One must appreciate the fact that the nineteenth century is a rich source of collector-mania, the odd disease that is no respecter of pocketbooks and thrives on limited availability. Although much of the glass to which we have referred has distinct intrinsic merit, many collectors items prey greatly on the sap of uniqueness and technical adroitness. Fanciful paperweights, some of which combined opaque ceramics within crystal, produced at the firms of Baccarat, St. Louis, and Clichy, were dated up to midcentury and fit into this category.

Another oddity was silver nitrate glass, made by treating the interior of a double-walled vessel with metallic salt. Sometimes the outer layer would be flashed with a colored glass and then cut through to the silver to give the appearance of a cameo encrustation.

Creative forces were not all turned off in the search for novelty. In the heart of Lorraine, near Nancy, the aforementioned Baccarat and companions produced glass of excellent quality. Emile Gallé opened his workshop in Nancy in 1874. He had been prepared for his enterprise by a special study of botany and by work not only in his father's glass and ceramic factory but also in other glass establishments in the Saar valley. Being inspired, it is said, by a collection of Chinese snuff bottles in the Victoria and Albert Museum, he began to manufacture an overlay glass for which his name is famous. Many layers of colored glass were lowered to a sculptured layer by means of acid etching and wheel cutting. Often other substances such as mother-of-pearl would be fused into parts of the design. Inasmuch as Gallé understood the growth of the many natural forms he engraved on the metal, they carry a conviction often missing in those of other designers. Daum Frères were runners-up in the same kind of glass technique.

England clung to and performed wonders with her specialty, the cutting of lead glass. Steam driven wheels enabled the men to cut deep and complex patterns from which the light was refracted and reflected to make a chandelier or a decanter seem afire with darts of glitter. When patterns became more intricate and cutting shallower, the elaboration lost the essence of glass character. Nevertheless, it fitted well into the scintillating pattern of the jeweled society of the period.

The great number of pieces included in household glass services are often a shock to contemporary understanding. Specialized types for each wine, sugars, creamers, decanters, dessert services, sweetmeat dishes, wine coolers—many selling by the dozen and often bearing an armorial coat of arms—such are truly fabulous mementoes of an age long disappeared.

America, over the last century, has been noted for the birth of many glass companies, for the invention of new techniques of shaping, and for the circumstance of manufacturing almost every type of glass known to Europe—a true melting pot.

Glass houses which had multiplied rapidly after 1800 fought a losing battle against English subsidies until an American tariff put new life into the industry after the War of 1812. From a beginning of nine known furnaces about 100 had been founded by 1833.

Certain factories may be singled out as typical. The Bakewell Factory (1808–1882, through several reorganizations and changes of name) of Pittsburgh is indicative of the growth in this Middle West area. It is said to have been the first to have made cut glass in America. It held a prominent place in the industry for many years and eventually manufactured wares of every conceivable metal and process.

From 1818 to 1888 the New England Glass Company of Boston assumed a position second to none in the production of fine flint (lead) glass. One of its youngest organizers was Deming Jarvis (1790–1861). It is interesting to note that his position with the firm was the equivalent of the present-day sales manager, a job, like that of the salesman, which came in with industrialization.

The Mount Washington Glass Works of South Boston was established in 1837 by Deming Jarvis for his son George D. Jarvis. Deming's sons never seemed to have the business acumen of their father, and in 1866 Mr. William Libbey, who had been trained on location, took over the Washington works. After several further shifts of ownership and consolidations William Libbey transferred to the New England Glass Company, where his son Edmund Drummond Libbey was employed. Later, the elder Libbey leased the New England firm. William died in 1880 and in 1888 Edmund moved his business to Toledo. This Ohio city has taken a lead in the industry ever since, and the Toledo Museum of Art contains world-famous collections of glass.

Some years before, Deming Jarvis had severed his connection with the mother firm (the New England Glass Company) and in 1825 founded the Sandwich works in the Massachusetts town of that name. Jarvis was the English translation of the French Gervais, which added one more to the list of French names that have lent distinction to the New World culture. Although he inherited a considerable fortune from his father, Deming seemed to enjoy a career in business, first in dry goods, then in ceramics, and last in glass.

Figure 6.55 Cut-glass compote, attributed to Christian Dorflinger, New York, 1855–1860. Lead glass. Height, 24.6 cm. Metropolitan Museum of Art, New York. (The Metropolitan Museum of Art. Gift of Stuart P. Feld, 1969.)

It is still a mystery why Jarvis left the Sandwich factory and organized the Cape Cod Factory in 1858. It is thought that he believed that his son John might take over. Here again was disappointment, for John died in 1863, his father six years later, and the fires at the Cape Cod were drawn. The Sandwich firm continued until 1888, having made every variety of glass with respect to metal, forming process, and embellishment.

It is tempting to detail other glass houses of the century which rose to prominence and which in several cases are still flourishing businesses. The following is a restricted list:

1. The Libbey Company, Toledo, Ohio.
2. The Tiffany Company, Corona, New York. 1892–. Louis Tiffany's work will deserve special attention.
3. A. H. Heisey and Company, Newark, Ohio. 1893–.
4. The Steuben Glass Works, Corning, New York. 1903–. Sold in 1918 to the Corning Glass Company. Art wares operated as the Steuben Division.
5. The Dorflinger Glass Works (Figure 6.55), White Mills, New York. 1865–1918. Finest of cut glass.[50]
6. Redford and Redwood, New York State. 1835–1853–1877.
7. The Stoddard Glass Company, New Hampshire. 1842–1850–1873.
8. The Lancaster Glass Works, Lancaster, New York. 1849–1890–1908.

In 1825 Bakewell took out the first patent for pressed glass. Although it is not at all certain that this process of shaping glass between two dies was a Yankee invention, it certainly was more highly exploited in America than elsewhere. Previously glass was shaped by *off-hand blowing* (blowing and shaping by hand) or by *mold blowing* (blowing the initial shape by expanding the bubble into a mold). Off-hand work has always been expensive and was little done as a run-of-the-mill commercial enterprise during the nineteenth century.

The problem of inexpensive work was that of creating form and pattern at the same time, which was accomplished first in blown molded glass.

Figure 6.56 Blown three-mold decanter, America, 1820–1850. Height, 23.5 cm. Metropolitan Museum of Art, New York. (The Metropolitan Museum of Art. Rogers Fund, 1936.)

Blown three-mold glass and blown expanded are the distinctive collectors' items in this field. Three-mold glass was made from the 1820s to well into the thirties. It was probably made to provide a substitute for the expensive English and Irish blown glass with cut designs. Full-sized metal molds into which to blow glass were not used in America until the end of the eighteenth century, and those that shaped the pattern as well as the structural form are conceded to be of the nineteenth. At that time the molds hinged in two or four parts as well as three. The period of quantity and quality production began with the twenties and was synchronous with the three-hinged mold (Figure 6.56).

It is not easy to distinguish molded glass. Mold marks generally show on the outside of the glass in the form of a slight swelling. However, inasmuch as the piece often needs reheating, these marks all but disappear. The pattern impression on blown-mold glass lacks the precise clarity of pressed glass patterns. The former patterns, however, have a unique brilliance due to the fact that much three-mold glass is lead metal.

To collectors the three-mold category is fairly well known by its patterns which include the geometrics of ribbings, flutings, circles on ovals, and diamonds such as the sunburst. Again there is the arch group with its Roman and Gothic varieties and the frequently found arch and fern. The last belong to a larger category sometimes called the Baroque group, which includes shells, stars, hearts, palm leaves, and horns of plenty.

Lead metal was used for the best of the first pressed glass, of which the *lacy glass* is the prized prototype. When pressed glass is made from a fine quality refractive metal, the patterns seem to stand out with a clarity neither found in cut blown glass nor in pattern molded. If closely examined, it is often found that both sides of pressed glass appear relatively dull. The glass becomes brilliant only because of the refractions of light from the precise and numerous facets of the patterned surface projected from the smooth inner one. Therefore the smoother the inner side and the more facets on the outer, the more scintillating the result. Additional stippling of the intermediary surface between the major patterns was a method used to obtain this effect. *Pressed lacy glass* was the consequence.

Much of the early pressed glass, say between 1827 and 1840, was the lacy type, although non-lacy was also made at that time. The number of patterns is legion, most in the beginning showing an understandable similarity to those of cut glass (Figure 6.57). Such was the strawberry diamond, whose little diamonds may first have suggested the potential of stippling. Other designs were the American eagle and American pictorial, the baskets of flowers, the peacock feather, the anchor and shields, the scrolled eye, the princess feather, the daisy, and the heart—a collectors' paradise.

In France and Belgium (the Belgium Val St. Lambert factory opened in 1825) pressed glass was made as early as 1829. In French pieces the metal was heavier and the designs were in higher relief than the American counterparts. The Europeans were quick to take advantage of the stippling refractions, and it is thought that European houses inaugurated many of the Renaissance and Baroque patterns that were snatched up by American producers and altered to suit their material.

William Leighton of Wheeling, West Virginia, has the questionable distinction of perfecting a formula by which a lime glass could be substituted for the fine lead that had been used for the best of the brilliant lacy and three-mold output. This occurred around 1860 and after that date the early glass with its admirable qualities was destined to be largely a thing of the past.

Stained glass enjoyed well-deserved recognition during the closing years of the century. The prevailing Medievalism, as well as the arts and crafts movement and Art Nouveau conceptions, aided a rebirth of the skill. John La Farge has been mentioned in this respect. Burne-Jones and Ford Madox Brown designed windows for the Morris firm, which included those of St. Martin's in Scarborough and of several churches in Brighton. It is said that Morris himself determined the color schemes. He seemed to possess an unerring sense of what color would do to transmitted light and refused to put new glass into old church windows for purposes of restoration because he felt that new productions lacked the illuminating magic of the old.

Stained glass became the preferred medium of several Art Nouveau artists, including the Englishman, Sir Frank Brangwyn (1867–1956) and the Frenchmen, Maurice Denis (1870–1943), and Pierre

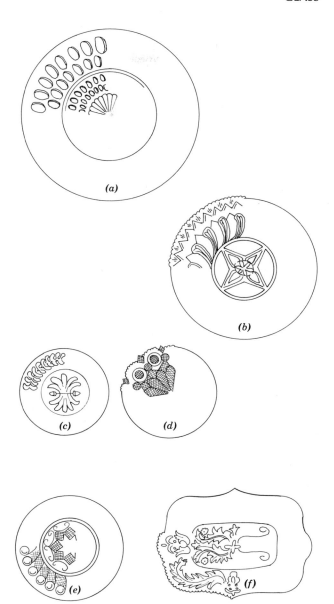

Figure 6.57 Pressed glass pattern types: (a) thumb print; (b) saw tooth or feather border; (c) plume; (d) Roman rosette; (e) peacock feather; (f) scrolled leaf and fleur-de-lis. (Adapted from photographs in *American Glass* by George S. and Helen McKearin. Copyright, 1941, 1969, by Crown Publishers, Inc., used by permission of Crown Publishers, Inc.)

Bonnard (1867–1947), and Edouard Vuillard (1868–1940). These men designed under the aegis of Louis Comfort Tiffany (1848–1933). Tiffany was another scion of a wealthy family, the son of the famous New York jeweler. He studied art under the American painter George Innes and completed his education in Paris. On his return to America he decided to seek a career in the decorative arts and to specialize in the production of art glass. Unlike Morris who stubbornly refused to learn his craft from anyone else, Tiffany went to the Heidt glass works in Brooklyn for preliminary training and delved into the study of glass chemistry. In 1876 he made his first windows in opalescent glass. In 1879 the Louis C. Tiffany Company, Associated Artists, was formed.

Much of their work was in interior decorating in that meaning of the term which suggested the creation of an interior that would stand on its own merits without reference to the architectural space for which it was intended. President Chester A. Arthur sold off much of the White House furnishings in 1882 at auction (a privilege that has fortunately been rescinded by law). Louis Tiffany was given the commission to redecorate, which he did in a fashion that approximated the nascent Art Nouveau. Tiffany placed a huge opalescent glass screen in the hall which reached from floor to ceiling and was blazened with a motif of interlaced eagles and flags. It remained in position until 1902 when Theodore Roosevelt had it removed at the time of the McKim, Mead, and White restoration.

Much of Tiffany's fame rests on his *favrile glass,* a handmade iridescent fabric used in lamps, vases, and table ware. It was blown from fine metal in an exuberant romanticism of flora such as lily clusters and wisteria vines. Such glass he included in the interiors he created for American multimillionaires Hamilton Fish, Henry Osborne Havemeyer, and W. S. Kimball. The effect was a strange mixture of Gaudi, Horta, and Stanford White, conveying not so much a fresh wind of creativity as one of collected opulence. Nevertheless, one must credit Tiffany with a number of modern features—gimmicks if you will—ornamentally pierced screens, organically modeled freestanding chimneys, and clusters of globular-shaped lamps. Despite such melodrama, Louis Comfort Tiffany (Figure 6.58) often showed a truly sensuous taste that could embroider the architectonic without completely destroying its form. In 1885 Sir Richard Francis Burton's (1821–1890)

Arabian Nights was published; with Tiffany its essence was revived.

METALS

Silver

Around 1840 electroplating of silver over base metal of copper, zinc, and nickel became practical after experimentation by the Italian scientist Volta (1745–1827). Paul Storr (1771–1844) in 1805 had produced the first "galvanic goblet" in the Royal Collection. In 1847 the American brothers, William, Asa, and Simeon Rogers, launched the process on a commercial basis.

Other inventions and their effective management reduced the price of silver articles. The screw press could cut out thin metal with great rapidity and force it into any desired shape. It could then be electroplated. The firm of Matthew Boulton of Birmingham again took the lead in these newer developments, as it had in the manufacture of Sheffield plate.

At the beginning of the century, when, although large business enterprises were being formed, the methods of manufacture had not yet entered the machine-crafting era, we note two important firms then practicing in England. One was the silversmithing establishment of Rundell, Bridge, and Rundell (successors in 1805 to the firm of Rundell and Bridge which had recently been appointed jewellers, gold and silversmiths to the English crown). Another was that of Robert Garrand which had enjoyed sovereign patronage since 1830. In 1808 Rundell employed a thousand hands, which is not a meager establishment even by today's standards. Among these men were Digby Scott and Benjamin and James Smith who had made the major portion of a state service that was placed on exhibition in 1807.[51]

This was the year that Paul Storr joined the firm and was given the assignment of making four large soup tureens of Egyptian design to add to this plate. His work was so well received by the crown that he was chosen by the Prince of Wales (later George IV) to add continually to his "Grand Service." Storr left the Rundells in 1819. In 1839 that establishment was bought by Francis Lambert.

Figure 6.58 Living room, Laurelton Hall, Oyster Bay, Long Island, New York, ca. 1902. Country estate of Louis Comfort Tiffany, designer. (Historic American Buildings Survey.)

To understand the design of silver at this period it is revealing to study two magnificent pieces made on opposite sides of the English Channel. The Cleveland Museum of Art possesses two soup tureens and trays, one by Henri Auguste (Figure 6.59), son of Robert Joseph Auguste, goldsmith to the erstwhile French king. This article was made between the years 1798 and 1809, at which date Auguste fled to England to avoid bankruptcy. The second piece, identical in type, was made by Paul Storr in 1812 (Figure 6.60).

The English piece indicates the strong hold that Georgian classicism kept on English design. Aside from the decorative motifs, such as fluting, beading, and gadrooning, one sees the typical Baroque classical emphasis piling up toward the center. Carefully studied are the rhythmic proportions of all details as they carry the eye toward the climax. On the other hand, Storr's work illustrates the aspect of English taste that looks backward toward the Rococo in the ogival outlines and the asymmetrical floral bosses where sea serpents and scrolls curl in volutes. That the lion mount shows signs of stiffening recalls the designs of Jean-Charles Delafosse (1734–1789) in his *Iconologie Historique*, where Rococo couples with sharp geometric. It must be remembered that refugees from the French revolution were coming to England and that often they brought only the jewelry and silver they could carry as viable goods. Such firms as Rundell were eager buyers because they had difficulty supplying the increasing demand for silver by the English gentry. This eighteenth-

Figure 6.59 Silver soup tureen and tray, Henri Auguste, France, 1798–1809. Height, 26.2 cm, diameter, 49.2 cm. Cleveland Museum of Art. (The Cleveland Museum of Art. Gift of James H. Hyde.)

century French silver provided inspiration for work by such men as Storr.

In the Auguste piece of a few years earlier there is displayed a more advanced style and typically the best of the French. The near-round top handle and the two curved side ones make an almost horizontal line. Interesting dramatization rather than transition is worked out between the plain and the decorated surfaces. The handle, a woman's head crowned with an inverted cornucopia ending in twisted serpents' tails, is fantasy itself. Decorative motifs in both pieces are from the past, but the Auguste piece is prophetic of the twentieth century with its apposite geometric shape and its refusal to bow to hierarchical positioning.

In Napoleon's France gilt silver, known as *Vermeil,* was favored. In the designs of Percier and Fontaine classic motifs were given imperialistic significance, which can also be seen in the Auguste

silver in the frieze of vases, laurel bands, and griffins, all stiffly bisymmetrical but gaining much by high relief with contrasting shadows. Here the result is satisfactory, but in less skilled hands on both sides of the channel the new heaviness, the low center of gravity, the rigid contrasts, and the bag of ill-assorted ornaments often posed problems for even such experienced craftsmen as Martin Guillaume Biennais (1764–1843) who worked during the first part of the century.

At this time in silversmithing America tended to follow Europe. Smiths prominent in the handicraft era were Benjamin Burt of Boston, Samuel Johnson of New York, and Joseph Lownes and Abraham Dubois of Philadelphia.

In 1850, with the introduction of at least partial mechanization and consequent lower prices, table silver proliferated, and the pattern simplicity of such early designs as the fiddle spoon changed to the wealth of those offered by most silver companies. Many designs claimed a spurious connection with a historical past. In hollow ware the repoussé technique was favored, especially in the

Figure 6.60 Silver soup tureen and tray, Paul Storr, London, ca. 1812. Height, 35 cm. Cleveland Museum of Art. (Cleveland Museum of Art. Gift of Thomas F. Grasselli in memory of Thomas S. and Emilie S. Grasselli.)

era of Rococo taste. Samuel Kirk of Baltimore (ca. 1793–ca. 1872) is an exemplar (Figure 6.61).

Christopher Dresser (1834–1904) designed silver for the English firm of Hujin and Heath of Birmingham, which in its geometric shapes and absence of ornament looks surprisingly modern. Voysey patterned silver and glass in a simplified style. Once again, Riemerschmid is noted for his functional outlook—everyday silver in streamlined pattern, forks with cutting edges added, knives with shorter blades.

Charles Tiffany, father of Louis Comfort, was instrumental in legalizing the United States silver standard that required the mark *Sterling* for metal of 18 dwt. (pennyweight) of alloy to 11 oz, 2 dwt. of pure silver.

Other Metals

Pewter suffered a setback as silver plate and ceramics became more readily available. White or Britannia metal, and a similar Tutania (patented in 1870 by William Tutan), were to be found in cheaper tableware. Both were harder than pewter but with less moonlight glow.

Handcrafting—usually combined with some use of the machine—returned with the Morris move-

327

Figure 6.61   Silver pitcher with repoussé decoration, Baltimore, late nineteenth century. Samuel Kirk, silversmith. (G. C. Ball.)

ment and Art Nouveau. W. A. S. Benson (1854–1924) designed and made ornamental hardware for furniture produced by the arts and crafts groups.

Much Art Nouveau metal was aesthetically weakened by its swirling patterns which allowed only monotonous movement to no purpose and without rest. Bronze, often silvered or gilded, was a favorite medium for small useful objects such as candelabra, light fixtures, and umbrella stands. Tiffany created typical Art Nouveau pieces such as bronze lamps with leaded glass shades. His reasoning here was quasi-functional. These shades, with their molten colors of Favrile glass, diffused the glare from incandescence and Tungsten filaments.

Iron had now moved from the era of wrought to that of cast. This replacement in the ubiquitous New Orleans galleries occurred in the thirties. Cast iron, because of its relatively high carbon content (ca. 4%) is hard and brittle and cannot be forged in the fine linear shapes of the wrought. The center for the English iron industry remained around Matthew Boulton's Birmingham, from which, despite important New World centers in New York and eastern Pennsylvania, many of the cast-iron stoves, much of the furniture, the fire grates, and utensils emanated. Although it is thought that the New Orleans cast-iron balustrades came from New York, data are constantly being discovered to indicate that local founderies and forges had been able to supply the demand in many localities.[52]

LAMPS AND LIGHTING

An easy transition is made between metals and lighting because of the use of the former in the service of the latter. Until the early years of the nineteenth century, candles in candlesticks were universal. The styling of candle holders belonged to England and to Europe, where such bronziers as Pierre Philippe Thomire (1751–1843) fashioned ormolu candelabra for the Emperor. The portable French *bouillotte* lamp with a shallow metal shade was designed for the small galleried *bouillotte* table. The lamp held multiple candles.

When fuel oils were burned in lamps, chimneys and shades were essential. Outer ones made of tin, known in France as *tole*, were the most common in the average household. Painted dark green on the exterior and a reflecting white on the interior, they spread light downward in a highly satisfactory diffused manner.

A Swiss chemist, Ami Argand, in the late eighteenth century devised a lamp that consisted of two concentric tubes (separated by a cylindrical wick) through which a downdraft of air was passed. The rate of combustion was thereby increased. Oil was in an adjacent reservoir. Because one fuel tank could supply several burners, an efficient light source was created. A number of American firms made these Argand-style lamps.

The introduction of heavy whale oil as the illuminant created other changes in form. One whale oil lamp incorporated a pump to force the heavy oil into the wick. The short whale-oil era, terminated by cheapness of kerosene or coal oil after the discovery and opening of the Pennsylvania oil fields in the sixties, was one of the most romantic in American history. Not only did it prompt such literary masterpieces as Melville's *Moby Dick,* but it was responsible for a fabulous business and the making of fortunes. Such Greek Revival houses as those of the Starbucks on Nantucket Island tell the story.

The highly volatile coal oil had to be enclosed in a protective reservoir. Over the wick went a glass chimney, on top of which was a shade. The latter was frequently ornamented in a manner scarcely related to the utilitarian purpose of light dispersion for which it was intended.

Gas lights were introduced in London in 1807, and by 1820 much of the city was so illuminated. In America gas lighting did not become common until after the Civil War. The first incandescent electric light was also an English invention (1840). Because both gas and electricity required installment expenditure, neither came into general household use until the end of the century, although they appeared earlier for commercial and civic installations.

With the widespread use of high levels of artificial light we enter the twentieth century.

DESCRIPTIVE SUMMARY

The culture that had developed from Mesopotamia westward was, during the nineteenth century, shaken to the core. In an exceedingly short span it had broadened its social base, extended its territorial vision, and become reoriented to an industrialized existence. Small wonder that art, which usually is a distilled barometer, showed erratic changes. Its bewildered front was a ruse to hide the distressing fear of being lost in a strange world. The real surprise lay not in its reaching out for an ephemeral foothold in the past but rather in its effort to find one in the future.

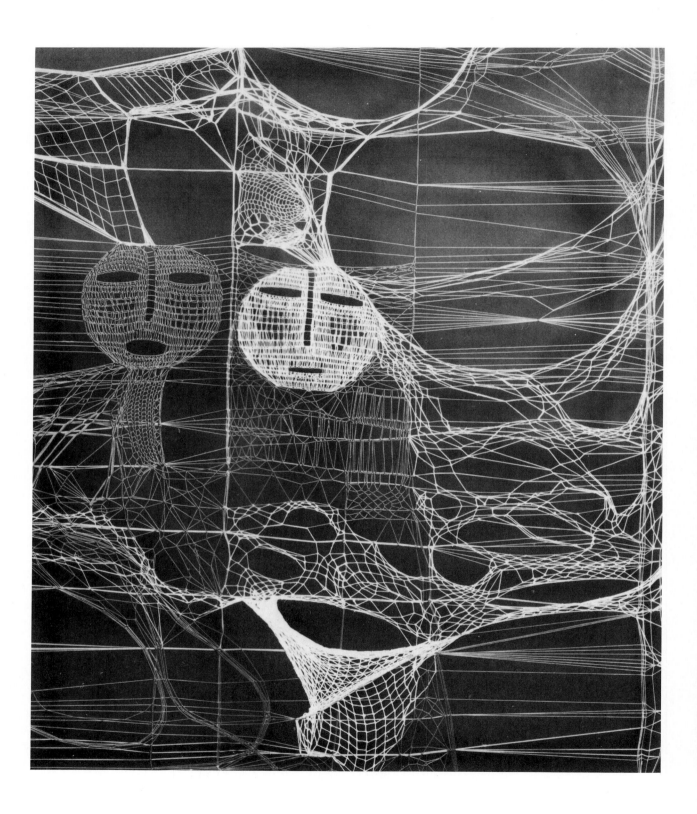

CHAPTER SEVEN

The Twentieth Century

The evolution of music, and everything else for that matter, depends on people who are gifted enough to understand that change is an absolutely irreversible process.

Pierre Boulez, quoted in *Time*, September 27, 1971

It is an oversimplification to assume that any age presents a homogeneous pattern. Ours being, more than most others, an age of transition, it displays a bewilderingly stratified picture: medieval beliefs still held and overlaid by eighteenth-century rationalism and mid-nineteenth-century Marxism, rocked by sudden volcanic eruptions of prehistoric fanaticisms and primitive tribal cults. Each of these components of the cultural pattern of the age finds its characteristic artistic expression. The Theater of the Absurd, however, can be seen as the reflection of what seems the attitude most generally representative of our own time's contribution.

The hallmark of this attitude is its sense that the certitudes and unshakable basic assumptions of former ages have been swept away, that they have been discredited as cheap and somewhat childish illusions.

Martin Esslin, *The Theater of the Absurd*

Some physicists, among them myself, cannot believe that we must abandon, actually and forever, the idea of direct representation of physical reality in space and time; or that we must accept the view that events in nature are analogous to a game of chance.

Albert Einstein, *The Fundamentals of Theoretical Physics*
Science, May 24, 1940

The crux of philosophy is to retain the balance between the individuality of existence and the relativity of existence.

Alfred North Whitehead

CULTURE

Anyone who has a memory for history may be granted the privilege of some clairvoyance. What can be the prediction for the segment of western culture that we have been following?

The first prophecy is a certainty. Western culture is now world culture and the world is reciprocally at its threshold. The overwhelming fluidity of motion disclosed by science has opened sliding doors of extent, now horizontal as well as vertical.

This has been accompanied by the development of power so great that it not only carries the threat of leveling the physical earth but the possibility of stretching the mind beyond the limits of its age-long parochialism. Like the heat of the sun, the harsh developments of the twentieth century may pose the danger of scorched earth or the benefit of a fruitful harvest.

What does this portend? Ancient classical culture was slanted toward reason, medieval toward theology, and modern toward science as an explanation of truth. What new synthesis? Can art— which owes its very existence to liaisons between the mental, emotional, and physical—provide any clue? Yes, evidence suggests that it can. Modern art, like most endeavor, is specialized. By focusing on intrinsic design values it has revealed their existence and potency in all great historic art. In this way it can give the future a firmer conviction of the worth and purpose of man's potential for creativity within cosmic change.

ARCHITECTURE

Structure

Old and new materials and structural systems dictate the direction of twentieth-century building. At first architecture exploited the efficiency of new media rather than of new structure. Steel and concrete and specialized glass were emphasized. Later developments tested new alloys, desirable for lightness, strength, and permanence. The process of pre- and poststressing the ferroconcrete parts in which steel cables embedded in the ducts are tensed before and after the curing of the concrete provides greater strain potential.

New methods of bonding have given new character to old material: thus, for instance, the use of laminated wood, which consists of thin layers adhered to make shaping and increased strength feasible. Impregnated and reconstituted woods provide certain new roles.

The structural performance of many materials can now be determined with increasing accuracy, although scarcely with absolute certainty. Like a good cook with a tried recipe, the engineer must still play it a little by ear.

Buildings today are given special consideration with respect to lighting, acoustics, climate control, and safety and sanitary features, which call for the organization of highly specialized knowledge.

During this century structural systems have often moved from those described as passive to those known as active. *Trabeation* is a passive system because the post and beam translate the load directly into the earth. Active systems change the course of their loads. They advance from *planar* structures (e.g., the trussed or the arched), where the transfer is in one plane, to *stereo* systems (e.g., space frames, bent plates, thin shells, stretched skins), where stresses are charted in several directions.

All are based on the principle that thrust counters thrust to produce rigidity. A plate, slab, or skin distributes a load economically because it is monolithic. This efficiency of three-dimensional extension can be demonstrated by the simple examples of strengthening a piece of paper by folding or by stretching cloth as in a tent or an open umbrella, where lines of force travel uniformly in all directions.

Not only may the course of the load be redirected but its ultimate support may also be that of suspension (i.e., tension) or upholding (i.e., compression). The building can be hung as a hammock or underbraced as a table. Some combination of these materials and modes of structure will explain the forms of modern building.

Their relative economy depends on the cost of staples, manpower, and structural necessity. Some merit consideration only when vast expenditures and intricate problems are faced. The simplest solution to a structural issue is generally the most desirable. Therefore much twentieth-century building continues to use trabeation, often, however, with ingenuity.

Pioneering

At the turn of the century the core of cities had need for commercial space and, because transportation to distance was difficult, there was nowhere to go but up. The practicality of vertical extension was expedited about 1850 by the invention of the power-driven elevator. The tall building, or skyscraper as it came to be known, was the result.

Stone load-bearing walls were impractical for great heights and a metal framework grid appeared to be the only answer. The outer sheathing, whether masonry, glass, or enameled plates, was carried on metal shelves or ledges bolted to the building at each story. Contemporary advancements on this principle speak of outer coverings as *curtain walls* or *screen walls* because they act in the capacity of sheathing but not of support. At the same time that buildings could be raised high, they could span larger interior spaces without internal props, thus opening up an enlarged space potential.

One can readily appreciate that any sensitive structuralist (e.g., the Greek and Gothic builders) would prefer that the construction should be explicit in the building's design. This is the structural honesty that Lodoli and Laugier were talking about (see Chapter 2).

In America William Le Baron Jenny (1832–1907) was one pioneer working with the new materials. His *Home Life Insurance Building* in Chicago has been called the first skyscraper.

Louis Sullivan (1856–1924), one of America's great architects, created some of the finest of the early tall business blocks. In his *Carson Pirie Scott Department Store* (1899–1904) (Figures 7.1 and 7.2), which is still standing in Chicago, the narrow vertical and broader horizontal supports, sheathed in tile, are clearly evident as holding up the building. Farther recessed, the window glass (Chicago windows with a central, wide, fixed pane and narrower opening sashes on either side) seems to create an illusion of volume (rather than mass) which flows around the stationary solidarity of the piers and beams.

Louis Sullivan was most probably the author of the famous adage: "Form follows function." Writing of himself in the third person, he said,

> In this wise the forms under his hand would grow naturally and express them frankly and freshly. This means that he would put to test a formula through long contemplation of living things, namely that *form follows function,* which would mean that architecture might again become a living art. . . .[1]

Sullivan is speaking here as a builder probably more than as a planner. The overt function performed by the parts of a structure should play its part in determining the appearance of a building. Thus in high structures that use trabeation, repetitive modules inevitably result. These could then be grouped into overall rhythms.

Sullivan is also echoing the principle set down by an earlier art critic, the American sculptor Horatio Greenough (1805–1852). It is astonishing to read in Greenough's essays a doctrine which insists that from within the complex architectural problem—the site, the material, and the uses—will come the right form for its artistic solution. Indeed, does not this idea trace its lineage to the Vitruvian triad and vaguely to the thoughts of Plato in regard to the ideal form for a thing?

Sullivan was a unique combination of artist-scientist. We use the term *artist* in its broad sense to mean a creative temperament sensitive to interrelations. His writings, especially his *Autobiography of an Idea,* would substantiate this statement. The ornament that he placed on his buildings indicates his logical regard for architectonic unity. In its intricate Celtic imagery it also reveals both his French and his Irish ancestry.

What steel was to Jenny and Sullivan, ferroconcrete (see Chapter 6) was to the Frenchman Auguste Perret (1874–1954). Coming from a family of engineers, he was intrigued by the economy of this new medium. He learned to understand its structural logic and its space contingency, which he demonstrated in the block of apartments erected in 1903 at 25 Rue Franklin in Paris (Figure 7.3). Here the ferroconcrete skeleton is not disguised; upper stories are cantilevered into space in a manner that shows the weight-lifting power of the material and gives a feeling of weightless-

Figure 7.1 Carson, Pirie and Scott Department Store. Chicago, 1899–1904. Louis H. Sullivan, architect. (Library of Congress.)

ness to the whole. A ground floor that makes extensive use of glass accentuates this property.

Three visual results accrue. A glance at the ground-floor plan of Perret's block shows the solid squares as the only supporting posts, around which flexible and often transparent dividers are located as walls. This is an arrangement known in contemporary architectural parlance as *open planning*. It is also evident that it is difficult to separate the exterior visually from the interior of the building, an aesthetic ideal called *interpenetration of space*. When viewed in another light, the phrase *flow of space* becomes apt. In the strange way that art has of preceding the physical fact, nineteenth-century space planning (pages 273 to 276) forecast these conceptions at a time when their rationale was really not part of their structure. What underlay this idea of space importance, the architectural corollary of the art movement known as *futurism*?

The Bauhaus

The famous *Bauhaus,* the twentieth-century German school for the building arts, attempted to

Figure 7.2 Detail of main entrance of the Carson Pirie and Scott Department Store, Chicago, 1899–1904. Louis H. Sullivan, architect. (Budek.)

nineteenth-century aesthetic movements. The new ethics, however, went beyond personal integrity to the role played by art in social expression and even in social reform. The housing developments at Stuttgart (1927) and at Frankfort-on-Main were direct forebears of similar low-cost housing today. Thus German twentieth-century architecture began on a democratic principle.

Wars precipitate cultural and aesthetic crises as well as political. Henri van de Velde, called in 1902 by the Grand Duke of Sachsen-Weimar to be director of the Weimar School of Arts and Crafts, relinquished this position at the outbreak of World War I because of his Belgian heritage. His post was taken by Walter Gropius (1883–1969), one of the youngest of the Werkbund leaders and a former pupil of Behrens. From 1914 to 1918 Gropius saw service at the front, and from this experience may have come his awakened perception of a changed world. After the war Gropius was approached by the provisional republican government to head the second Weimar Ducal School, the School of Design. He was able to unite the craft school with the design school, and from this union the *Bauhaus,* or school planned around the building arts, was born.

Figure 7.3 Open planning as seen in the plan of a dwelling at 25 Rue Franklin, Paris, 1903. Auguste Perret, architect. (Adapted from S. Giedion, *Space, Time and Architecture,* 5th edition, Harvard University Press, 1967. Reprinted by permission of the publisher.)

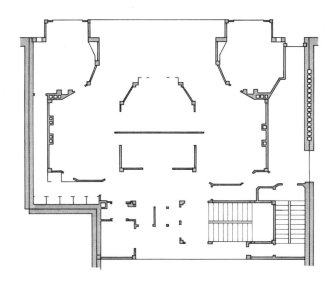

link architecture and sociology to industry. Germany, which had been emancipated from trade guilds only during the nineteenth century, was comparatively a latecomer on the accelerated modern market. She came quickly, however, to advanced organizational decisions. She had her Werkstätte (see Chapter 6) and in 1907 the architect Peter Behrens arranged the first German Werkbund. This was an association of manufacturers and designers who banded together to attempt a synchronization of art and industry. Recall that Behrens had worked in Austria before going to Munich.

From their inception the Werkbunds possessed a distinct social awareness that no doubt reflected the moral tone which had resided in all

Its purpose focused on technical and fine arts training was dual. After experience with the mechanization of twentieth-century war Gropius envisaged the harnessing of the school's curriculum to machine productivity. When, in addition, the program was, theoretically at least, centered on society's needs, all of nineteenth-century experimentation—the arts and crafts movements, the teaching theory of the Werkstätte, the Werkbund alliance of designer with industry, the sociological polemic—was bound into one instructional package.

It cannot be emphasized too strongly that one of the most important concepts of the Bauhaus was that architecture, interior design, furnishings, and even fine art could be coordinated because the system of education began with common disciplines to which every branch was subject. An architect could design a chair—and did. A painter could plan a building and make its furnishings, as Rietveld and Le Corbusier did. No doubt they could criticize one another because their thoughts were based on a common foundation. They spoke the same language.

The touchstone of Bauhaus doctrine was the experimental study of materials and of the most advanced methods of their fabrication. The media that were handled included such unorthodox materials as paper, synthetics, glass, new metals and alloys, wire, and thread. Moreover the involvement included more than an understanding of their practical qualities. It extended to the sensuous.

Gropius brought such artists as Vasily Kandinsky and Paul Klee to teach at the Bauhaus. Other artists chosen had already demonstrated their divorce from a conventional academic approach and their devotion to some aspect of contemporary art. László Moholy-Nagy (1895–1946), Josef Albers (1888–1976), Johannes Iiten, and Gyorgy Kepes were among the teachers who continued to exert an important influence on art in their experiments with the phenomena of movement and light (Moholy-Nagy), color (Albers and Iiten), and textures (Kepes). Thus materials were studied as spatial, color, and texture components of design.

The Bauhaus met with much opposition in the budding world of Nazism. Forced to leave Weimar, it moved by invitation to the town of Dessau in 1925. Here Gropius built new and expanded buildings. When Gropius retired to private practice in 1928, Hans Meyer, a Swiss architect, head of the enlarged architectural department of the Bauhaus, took over until 1930, when Mies van der Rohe (1886–1969) became its director. In 1933 the Nationalist Socialist Regime closed the school. Many of the leaders relocated in England, France, Switzerland, and America.[2]

Mies van der Rohe was born at Aix-la-Chapelle, moved to Berlin at an early age, became a pupil of Behrens, worked in the shop of Bruno Paul (one of the forerunners of modern furniture design), and served in the war before going to the Bauhaus. He had already begun the consistent chronology of his architecture by being interested first in the cleaned-up clarity of the German nineteenth-century classical architect Karl Friedrich Schinkel and the structural logic of Hendrikus Petrus Berlage of the Netherlands. At the time of his directorship he was master of the materials, structural technique, and clarity of form of the Bauhaus idiom.

In much of the building that Mies did both in Europe and America he introduces no new features beyond those planned by Gropius. In the long record of his achievement he proved himself the more versatile personage, the more exacting technologist, and the greater and more original artist, but a less dedicated social worker. His range extended from exhibition pavilions (the German Pavilion (Figure 7.4) of the International Exposition at Barcelona in 1929), to skyscrapers (the Seagram Building (Figure 7.5) in New York, 1956–1958), to private residences (Tugendhat House, Brno, Czechoslovakia, 1930; Figures 7.6 and 7.7), and to later residences in and around Chicago (the Farnsworth House, 1950).

He was as messianic as Lodoli in his preachment that structure was all-important and should never be disguised. He erred in his claim that the honest expression of structure was sufficient to create visual satisfaction, just as Sullivan had erred in insisting that functional adequacy could provide this result. Both men, however, put building art back on the right track and both were fortunately acutely sensitive to visual relations. Great works of art came from their hands.

The outstanding contribution of Mies van der Rohe to modern architecture came through his ability to master the aesthetics of movement in

Figure 7.4 The German Pavilion, International Exposition, Barcelona, 1929. Mies van der Rohe, architect. (Photograph, Courtesy The Museum of Modern Art, New York. The Mies Van Der Rohe Archives.)

space. This he accomplished by the manipulations of planes in three dimensions. To humans the new extension of space can be satisfying only if exterior space complements interior, if the eye is compelled to travel this space and find plateaus for rest, if the expanse is scaled to human comprehension, and if its symmetry is interesting.

Mies's German Pavilion has been destroyed, one of the real architectural tragedies of this or any age. It was a sparsely furnished structure intended as a spot where the traveler could pause and contemplate beauty, a miniature fairyland where rich onyx, black-pooled water, a marble statue by Georg Kolbe, provided glory for the eye wherever it came to rest. The visitor was teased into looking from one volume to another because of the exquisite low, horizontal proportions of the space itself and the placement of the very few items that defined it. It would be too complex a problem to analyze the contrived means. The fundamental reason lies in a visual fact often forgotten, that interrelations of color and texture as well as shape can operate as visual forces. With planned movement and total asymmetry Mies obtained a classical repose in his exhibition hall.

A close examination of the Tugendhat House (meaning *model* but actually done for a Mr. and Mrs. Tugendhat) will further demonstrate how Mies had mastered his art of controlling movement in space by the manipulation of planes. The house is built as a fairly regular cubed volume with floors once more cantilevered from regularly spaced steel columns. It owes its exterior beauty to its precision detailing, its quiet wall of glass, and its comprehensible, although certainly not customary, proportions.

Mies once said that there is an aesthetics of the plan (Figure 7.8). Anyone looking at the plan of Tugendhat can understand what he meant. The main living space, an enormous rectangle 50 by 80 ft, has only two opaque partitions, the one a straight slab of onyx marble which demarks the more private from the general living functions. The nature of this material is such that it allows light to infiltrate much as does alabaster; it makes of the division not a harshly opaque object but a transmitting ornament. The daily pleasure derived from experiencing this soft transmitted light prompted Tugendhat to say to a friend that, although the price of the screen was out of proportion to that of the house, he felt that it was more than justified.

The other divisional barrier is a large circular partition which partly shields the dining area.

Figure 7.5 (opposite page) The Seagram Building, New York, 1956–1958. Mies van der Rohe and Philip Johnson, architects. (Ezra Stoller, © ESTO)

Figure 7.6 The Tugendhat House, Brno, Czechoslo-vakia, 1930. Mies van der Rohe, architect. (Photograph, Courtesy The Museum of Modern Art, New York. The Mies Van Der Rohe Archives.)

It is made of macassar ebony which has a lovely play of brown and black in its patterning to con-trast richly with the warmer tones of the marble. It is in the size and placement of these walls that the artistry lies. One can visualize from the plan the proportional rhythm that relates the two and leads the eye from one to the other and even-tually outdoors. This is indeed plastic designing within a regular transparent volume.

Several of the walls at Tugendhat were flexible velvet curtains, and windows made use of many yards of raw silk. It is said, and it is believably re-lated to his love of detailing, that Mies van der Rohe never liked to skimp on the textures that added so much to his interiors. The fabrics were

Figure 7.7 Interior view, the Tugendhat House, Brno, Czechoslovakia, 1930. Mies van der Rohe, architect. (Photograph, Courtesy The Museum of Modern Art, New York. The Mies Van Der Rohe Archives.)

woven of fine threads but with piles or nodules that broke the light and provided just the needed foil for hard glass and steel. In such economy housing as the apartments built for the married students at Illinois Institute of Technology he proved that expensive materials alone do not constitute his wizardry; but they help and without them some find the form cold and uninteresting.

Among contemporary architects who have been followers of the Bauhaus master is Philip Johnson who collaborated in the architecture of the Seagram Building. He is the distinguished architect who built the group of modern houses in New Canaan, Connecticut (including his own well-known glass house; Figure 7.9) and a body of superior work throughout the country.

Despite his many-faceted architectural expres-

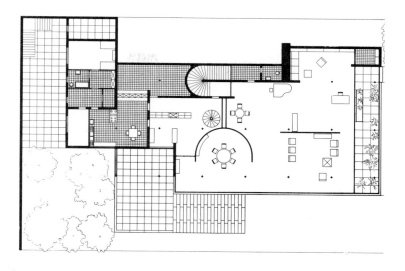

Figure 7.8 Plan of the Tugendhat House, Brno, Czechoslovakia, 1930. Mies van der Rohe, architect. (Collection, The Museum of Modern Art, New York, The Mies Van Der Rohe Archives.)

Figure 7.9 Interior view, the Philip C. Johnson House, New Canaan, Connecticut, 1949. Philip C. Johnson, architect. (Ezra Stoller, © ESTO.)

Figure 7.10   The stairs in the main lobby of the General Motors Research Laboratories, Warren, Michigan, 1955. Eero Saarinen, architect. (G. C. Ball.)

sion, one must count Eero Saarinen (1910–1961), as designer of the General Motors Research Laboratories and Technical Center, Detroit, a Miesian. In this building, within a rectangular framework, the example of a large circular element is introduced by the stairs (Figure 7.10). Circular stairs built without risers have become a commonplace of new architecture. They are used to conserve space, to minimize the effect of mass, and to suggest weightlessness. In the lobby of the Research Laboratories the individual travertine treads are hung from a single central beam by stainless steel suspension rods which radiate from one focus like spokes of a three-dimensional wheel. They resemble a dramatic abstract piece of sculpture, faintly reminiscent of a giant harp, perfectly tuned to the thin, skeletal structure of the building.

The International Style

The use of regular geometric forms—the repetition of supports and windows in modular sizes to obtain clarity and order, the use of transparency to acquire spaciousness, the manipulation of planes in conjunction with open planning to secure movement in space, the glint of steel and glass as principal materials—these are the visual characteristics that we associate with Bauhaus architecture. Henry Russell Hitchcock and Philip Johnson, when they examined its monuments in 1932, dubbed its expression the *International Style,* believing that by the thirties its theory of architecture, its social reason for being, and its design had received broad acceptance.[3] By the midseventies it has created the image of metropolitan civilization, if only because it provides the least expensive answer to high-density use. Today the term International Style is given to those buildings that make use of the new materials, such as glass and ferroconcrete, in a modular manner.

The French development along lines of the International Style introduced some new concepts. The greatest of the pioneers was Charles Edouard Jeanneret (1887–1965), generally known as Le Corbusier and affectionately called Corbu (as Mies van der Rohe is remembered as Mies). Le Corbusier was the name of Charles Edouard's maternal grandmother, and he assumed it in order to avoid confusion with a cousin who was also a painter and architect. Le Corbusier was born in Switzerland and, after study there as well as in Vienna, in Paris with Perret, and in Germany with Behrens, he traveled extensively in Mediterranean countries and finally settled in Paris.

Among his houses done before the thirties, and demonstrating the early phases of his work, is the famous Villa Savoye (Figures 7.11, 7.12, and 7.13) located at Poissy northwest of Paris, built for Pierre Savoye, a Paris insurance man. It survived the vicissitudes of World War II when it was looted by the Germans. When the townsmen attempted to buy the property from M. Savoye's widow and to remove the uninhabited structure for the erection of a much-needed high school, such a hue and cry went up from lovers of architecture that the city fathers relented.

Le Corbusier, like Gropius, was social minded. He addressed himself to the problem of man's habitation and from that reached out toward doctrines concerned with the total social environment. Like many twentieth-century architects he was a prolific writer and in his *Toward a New Architecture* he set forth his thesis that architecture and the dwelling in particular had not kept pace with technological developments. We should not forget, however, that Le Corbusier's house could not have performed for Louis XIV. Machines are designed for specific functions.

Two factors in the design of Villa Savoye should be noticed. Although it is a regular and clearly defined volume encompassed largely by glass and built of steel and concrete, its internal space evolves in four rather than three dimensions. The eye is moved not only on a two-dimensional horizontal level with vertical extension but space is opened on the diagonal by the use of ramps that give simultaneous vistas on two horizontal planes. To explore these potentials further would require movement in time—the fourth dimension.

The second novelty in Villa Savoye is that it is raised off the ground on concrete stilts, which Le Corbusier called *pilotis*. This hovering in the air was as premeditated by Le Corbusier as embracing the land was by Frank Lloyd Wright. Le Corbusier thought that man was becoming divorced from his anchorage to the earth and that his buildings should reflect this fact. It should be mentioned, however, that in 1919 Le Corbusier designed a house, Maison Monol, which clings to the earth in undulating lines as supinely as anything done by the American architect. This he called "female architecture," in distinction to the *pilotis* male principle.

Figure 7.11 Villa Savoye, Poissy-sur-Seine, 1929–1930. Le Corbusier, architect. (Photograph, Courtesy The Museum of Modern Art, New York.)

Figure 7.12 View from living room to stair hall and court, Villa Savoye, Poissy-sur-Seine, 1929–1930. Le Corbusier, architect. (Photograph, Courtesy The Museum of Modern Art, New York.)

No less than Mies, he appeared to grope between the irregular and regular as denoting the true concept of his style. Le Corbusier ultimately espouses the cause of tall, off-the-ground plans for city dwellings as the most economical means of efficient ground use. That his solution is raising many psychological questions today is perhaps beyond the point. The fact still remains that land cost in a city is prohibitive. With Le Corbusier's scheme utilities would be placed underground and gyrodomes built on flat roofs. Le Corbusier came close to realizing his ideal in the *Unité d'Habitation* apartments at Marseilles in 1952.

In this connection it is curious to note that Le Corbusier, like the Renaissance man, professes concern for human significance in his art, and as a true descendent of classical rational tradition he expresses himself in the realm of mathematical ideas. He places man in the center of the art world when he advocates his proportional gauge which he calls the *Modulor*. This is actually a return to the geometry of the Golden Mean Rectangle, with an initial square taken as 3 ft, or the measure from the top of the head of a 6-ft man to his solar plexus.

His proposition is that all good art should be restrained within this system. Put forth as a new premise, it is in fact the age-old symmetry of the Greeks, given Renaissance human interpretation. The very fact that Le Corbusier emphasizes the enclosure within an equilateral figure (the square) gives to the whole a current interpretation akin to the repetitive module of mechanization. Good modern architecture, like the human body, has its repetitive (heartbeat) and progressive (limb movement) rhythms. It merely differs from traditional architecture by altering the amount of their relative emphasis and the locations for their use.

In designing the Chapel of Notre Dame du Haut (Figures 7.14 and 7.15) at Ronchamp, France (1950–1955), Le Corbusier followed Wright in placing the emphasis on the character of the internal space. Le Corbusier, however, isolated interior from exterior. His conception of the interior of this inspiring hilltop church is that of a cavernous womb which is protective of the earthbound character of man. Yet the prow-shaped upturned end of the exterior suggests a rising toward the heavens. The shapes throughout are rounded and in harmony with a twentieth-century concept of the universe.

It is in his use of light as a design factor, however, that the architect of this building shows him-

344

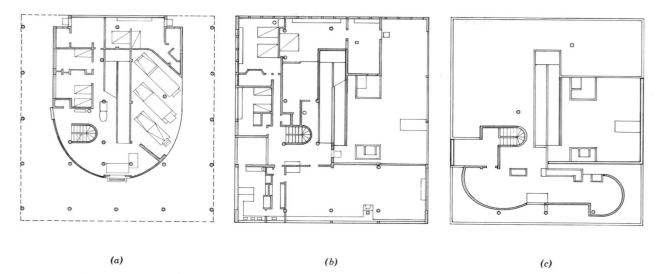

(a)   (b)   (c)

Figure 7.13 Plan of Villa Savoye, Poissy-sur-Seine, 1929–1930. Le Corbusier, architect. *Ground floor:* driveway, garage, service, guest rooms. *First floor:* living quarters with terrace. *Upper floor:* sun patio. (Adapted from Maurice Besset, *Le Corbusier,* New York: Rizzoli, 1976; Geneva: Skira Art Editions.)

self as an outstanding contemporary artist. Here luminant shafts creeping over the interior walls and revealing the great curve of the ceiling create the emotional atmosphere and provide the necessary movement. It is right that none but the starkest interior forms be permitted and that except for the fortuitous and sequential spotting by the slanting rays from the small, isolated windows there is no climax except at the altar. This is revealed in the twentieth-century manner of using contrast—bright against dark. The apprehending of the shaped walls and roof provide the only contact between exterior and interior.

The code of International Style architecture set forth with academic strictness was interpreted as proscribing any applied ornament. Even the charm of the shadow lines created by traditional moldings was replaced by that of the bolder shadows caused by the building planes. For ornament Mies van der Rohe allowed only sculpture if it was freestanding and thus juxtaposed to the building.

This starkness has provided a distinct air of drama to most International style buildings. Contrast rather than the obvious traditional transition is a *modus operandi* which has grown in importance in this agitated century. The surprising fact

remains that in the hands of van der Rohe even contrast remains somehow classical, serene, and restful.

Le Corbusier, himself a painter, made allowance for mural painting if it were flat design. He speaks in his usual aphoristic and enigmatic manner when he says:

> The mural paintings brightened only the most unpleasing walls of the house. The "good walls" remained white. The paintings created space in cramped spaces; within the entrance, within the porch, and at the bar.[4]

Le Corbusier's statement, of course, acknowledges the unthinkable premise that architecture could ever be "unpleasing" or that there could ever be any "bad walls." But he does allow for such splendid clamor as Juan O'Gorman placed on the walls of the Library of the University of Mexico. What is all right here would, of course, have been all wrong with Mies at Barcelona.

The Bauhaus men shunned chromatic color in their architecture as they did ornament. Van Doesburg's isometric color constructions, with their vivid planes intersecting in space, were more related to Le Corbusier's architecture than to that of Gropius and his followers. Josef Albers, for instance, says:

> stable yet dynamic,
> flat yet deep, uncolorful yet colorful,
> simple yet complex.[5]

345

Mies was one of the strongest proponents of the achromatic palette. He often paints his steel piers black and his followers allow only the liberty of white or near neutrals. Even for Le Corbusier the "good walls" remained white.

As time went on the influence of Frank Lloyd Wright's advocation of the muted colors of nature:

> Yes the group will look like some kind of desert fleet. We painted the horizontal boards with cold-water paint. . . . I chose dry rose as the color to match the light of the desert floor.[6]

changed the Bauhaus and International Style concept in ways that seemed more sympathetic to both oriental and Scandinavian color schemes. Bauhaus architect Marcel Breuer in his *Sun and Shadow*[7] advised color to define planes in space much as Van Doesburg had demonstrated on canvas. Today Luis Barragán, in Mexico, is changing the Corbusian black and white buildings to clear color to make the walls perform spatially at his command. Color saturations are also pepped up in this frenetic postfifties world.

America and Frank Lloyd Wright

The first American architect of international reputation was Frank Lloyd Wright (1869–1959), a dis-

Figure 7.14 Notre Dame du Haut, Ronchamp, France, 1950–1955. (From *The New Churches of Europe* by G. E. Kidder Smith.)

ciple of Louis Sullivan. The idea of divorcing himself from the land would have been unthinkable. In all that he said, as well as in much that he did, there ran one theme song, an ode to the strength and courage that comes from living in close contact with nature. Writing (like Sullivan) of himself in the third person, he describes the dedication that came out of his adolescent experience on his Uncle James's Wisconsin farm:

> Muscles hard. Step springing. Sure-footed, and finger as swift as thought. Mind bouyant with optimism that came from seeing sunshine follow clouds and rain, working out success following failure. It had come to himself consciously, out of his daily endeavors, as an underlying sense of the balance of forces in nature. Something in the nature of an inner experience came to him that was to make a sense of this supremacy of interior order like a religion to him. He was to take refuge in it and grow in it.[8]

Frank Lloyd Wright was born in Richland Center, Wisconsin. His father, of Irish descent, was a musician and a preacher from New England. His mother, whose ancestry was Welsh, had been a school teacher. Although Frank practiced as an architect from the time he was eighteen, there was much about him that remained the evangelist and the pedagogue. Like the Bauhaus men and Le Corbusier, his voluminous sheaf of writings may

remain his most significant contribution to the twentieth century.

As a visible symbol of his back-to-earth doctrine, Wright's earliest houses, such as the Charnley House in Chicago (1892) and the Winslow House (Figure 7.16) in River Forest, Illinois (1893), are low and have their emphasis on their ground stories. They are dissimilar from much of his later work in being conspicuously solid and statically bisymmetrical. The Winslow House was grounded by a low roof and broad eaves. Wright often called attention to the manner in which he had "brought down the house," forgetting that he had ample precedent in much of Richardson (see Chapter 6).

By the second decade of the century he had all but abandoned bisymmetry (Vosburgh House, Grand Beach, Michigan, 1916), and even earlier

Figure 7.15 Interior, Notre Dame du Haut, Ronchamp, France, 1950–1955. (From *The New Churches of Europe* by G. E. Kidder Smith.)

he had introduced a visual system that was characteristically his own (the Isabel Roberts House, River Forest, Illinois, 1907, and the Robie House, Chicago, 1909; Figures 7.17 and 7.18). Here intersecting planes, dominantly horizontal, interact to create the directions and proportions that keep the eye in synchronized strong outflowing movement. Wright thus began to be concerned with the accelerated and clashing power of the age. He dwelt in the vanguard of the most restless civilization that the world had known and became its true disciple in architecture.

An experience with the Robie or the Roberts house will conclusively show another trait of Wright's development. The dispersed motion that interested him seems to belong to space as well as to mass. To understand, one must study the plans of his houses (Figure 7.19). Rooms begin to flow together and a high-ceilinged living hall, in which dining and living area are one, came into

Figure 7.16   The Winslow House, River Forest, Illinois, 1893. Frank Lloyd Wright, architect. (Photograph, Courtesy The Museum of Modern Art, New York.)

being. From this large area—where incidentally Wright placed a molding or gallery at ordinary ceiling height so that space would not be dehumanized—other lower rooms extended, often in cruciform arrangement. (William Morris—see Chapter 6: ". . . the rational ancient plan . . . a high hall, with a few chambers tacked on to it for sleeping or sulking in."[9]) Thus two volumes of dif-

ferent heights, interpenetrate, moored by a large central chimney and service core. It is this pinion that is of sufficient visual and psychological importance to the entire plan of the house and its environment to become the dynamo from which generates all of Wright's spatial charges. Here is just the reverse of the schema of the Baroque ideal of such homes as Easton Neston in eighteenth-century England (see Chapter 4), where exterior space flows toward the house.

Wright used long bands of windows similar to those of Shaw and Richardson to carry the eye outdoors. He also used the clerestory window

Figure 7.18   The Robie House, Chicago, Illinois, 1909. Frank Lloyd Wright, architect. (Budek.)

Figure 7.17 Interior, the Isabel Roberts House, River Forest Illinois, 1907. Frank Lloyd Wright, architect. (Budek.)

oriented to capture the slanting rays of the sun and to create movement through space with light. In many of his buildings there are slots of glass that allow surprising pools of light and unexpected accents to appear. Beyond this clever use of illumination to emotionalize a setting, he envisages it in conjunction with his roof and eaves to move space outward horizontally.

That Frank Lloyd Wright also considered inner space important is clear. He speaks of the room (i.e., *raum* or space) in connection with his "Natural" or "Usonian" houses of the late thirties— homes that were planned for moderate incomes:

> The room must be seen as architecture or we have no architecture. We have no longer an outside and an inside as two separate things. Now the outside may come inside and the inside may and does go outside. They are of each other.[10]

—Quite in a different way, however, than the outside and inside of Tugendhat House or Villa Savoye are of each other (possibly more akin to Barcelona).

Falling Water (Figure 7.20), the home of Edgar Kaufmann at Bear Run near Pittsburgh (1937),[11] clearly indicates Wright's architectural tempera-

ment. This famous house dramatically summarizes Wright's contribution to nature communion, to modern technology, and to the concept of a controlled dynamic pattern of forces in space and of space. Certainly his treatment of mass here is

Figure 7.19 Plan of the Isabel Roberts House, River Forest, Illinois. Frank Lloyd Wright, architect, 1907. (a) living room; (b) reception room; (c) furnace room; (d) storage; (e) laundry; (f) hall; (g) kitchen; (h) dining room. (Adapted from S. Giedion, *Space, Time and Architecture,* 5th edition, Harvard University Press, 1967. Reprinted by permission of the publisher.)

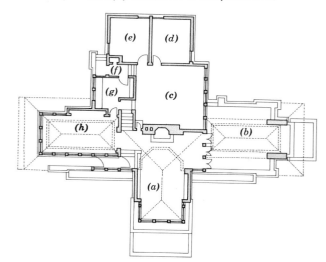

349

Figure 7.20 Falling Water, Bear Run, Pennsylvania, 1937. Frank Lloyd Wright, architect. (G. C. Ball.)

and his concrete block houses in California in the twenties, he enclosed New York's art treasures in a structure of predominantly spiral shape. He had gradually begun to conceive of movement as continuous rather than interrupted and after using intermediary shapes (hexagons and triangles), had finally seemed to prefer some phase of the volute. We see it in his V. C. Morris Store in San Francisco (1949), in his Johnson Wax Factory Administration Building in Racine, Wisconsin (1936), and now in the Guggenheim Museum (1942–1960; Figures 7.21 and 7.22). Erasing Manhattan, he opened up the interior of the Museum in a continuous rotation reaching toward the sky.

It was a building to house the art of the twentieth century, and with this in mind Wright added no ornament of his own. There was little need. The space has been rightly criticized on the grounds that it does not easily display its collections, but it does proclaim its architect as one who possessed a vision of a world that looked upward. Frank Lloyd Wright has envisaged a unity in these buildings that binds mundane things with an expansive universe. How different from the centripetal space concept projected by the Roman Pantheon.

Despite the plain surfaces of the Solomon R. Guggenheim Museum, Wright could not deny his ancestral love of ornament, nor did he look on it as an inexcusable evil. He used it in carved stone and terra cotta and drew on fonts as separate as the Celtic and the pre-Columbian (which was becoming known through such sources as the Mayan exhibits at the World's Fair at Chicago in 1893). In the furnishing of his own homes he was catholic and discriminating in his taste. The finest of rugs from the Orient graced matchless wood floorings and Japanese prints and Chinese sculpture adorned the walls and pedestals.

The art of Japan had interested Wright long before he built the Imperial Hotel in Tokyo (1920–1922, now in large part destroyed to allow the construction of a modern building). As early as 1905 he journeyed to Japan. Undoubtedly the native Japanese architecture, its alignment with nature, its use of elemental materials, its modular and open planning, and its grasp of its own traditions must have struck a deep, sympathetic chord. He appreciated its agreement with structural necessity and its low-key aesthetics.

phenomenal. The tumultuous positioning of the cantilevered concrete slabs is eloquent of the fact that all of the tensions that come out as twentieth-century genius were tied into Wright's psychic. More importantly, the spaces in this building, as they spread out under the decks, become a vital part of the total envelope. Twentieth-century space, part in, part out, here becomes a palpitating reality, even more significant than its superb lodging.

Preferring to live in the prairie and the desert (Taliesen—Shining Brow—the two homes and schools he built in Wisconsin and Arizona), Wright finally had to come to terms with the city. In characteristic fashion he shut it out. Echoing the monolithic form of his remarkably early concrete Unity Temple in Oak Park, Illinois (1906),

Figure 7.21 The Solomon R. Guggenheim Museum, New York, 1942–1960. Frank Lloyd Wright, architect. (Photo: Robert E. Mates.)

The Oriental Influence on Architecture

The one world that is talked about today is scientific and technological. It is becoming an expansive and aesthetic one to which the Orient has made significant contributions.

The Orient, as Dr. Sherman Lee has pointed out in his book *A History of Far Eastern Art,* is not one but several civilizations.[12] Within this heterogeneity the architecture of China and the southern Oriental countries possesses a kinship with western classical architecture in that it is bisymmetrical, enclosed, and centripetally oriented. That of Japan in the north is traditionally asymmetrical, open, and centrifugal in its arrangement. It is more in tune with Nordic European traditions.

It is regrettable that because of the exigencies of contemporary history Chinese architecture and furnishings have had so little chance to influence the West (Figure 7.23). In its relation to nature,

which is in a sense more intimate and less dominating than that of the Japanese, the Chinese have had much to teach. This cult of quiet respect for natural phenomena derives from the Taoist religion (Lao-Tzu, 604–531 B.C.) which was fused with the Hindu idea of contemplative acceptance—"He who is content has enough."

The religion introduced by Confucius (551–475 B.C.) at a time of political upheaval preached a sagacious and pragmatic doctrine of protocol. It was essentially an ethical doctrine designed to bring the country back to order and government through reverence for tradition and authority. The Chinese creed of family and ancestor worship owes much to its precepts. Because of these restraining influences, Chinese architecture has changed little with time.

China's third religion was imported by Buddhist priests from India during the Han dynasty (206 B.C.–A.D. 205). Concerned with a contemplative spiritual life of self-renunciation and supported by the subsequent Tartar emperors, it became the court religion and dictated much of Chinese re-

351

ligious art. It was introduced into Japan in the sixth century.

The Japanese house is as closely associated with the earth as is the Chinese. The Nipponese love of nature has its roots in the native Shinto worship. Shinto, however, did not teach passive acquiescence. It created spirits of nature who could be propitiated only by adeptness in shaping natural materials. This belief provided motivation for fine craftsmanship which has remained a qualifying characteristic of Japanese art.

Indigenous architecture has demonstrated this talent by converting some of the forests that abound (covering more than 90% of the island territory) into buildings that are both sympathetic toward their surroundings and characterized by the most elegantly precise wood technique. The tall evergreens, the hard maple, imported sandalwood, and bamboo have dictated a form which, when most native, makes use of predominantly straight lines. Even after the introduction of Chinese influences—Buddhism and curved roof silhouettes—the native Japanese restraint has modified any tendency toward architectural exuberance.

The prototype that indicates the appearance of the early Japanese house can be seen in the oldest Shinto shrine at Izumo. As Greek temples probably derived from the megaron (the formal building in Greek domestic architecture), so the Shinto shrines preserve the design of ancient dwellings. Indeed the Izumo shrine is supposed to have been the home of one Okuni-nusi-no-Mikoto to whose spirit it is dedicated. Being of wood, these holy structures would be impermanent were it not for the Japanese custom of faithfully reconstructing them every twenty or so years and thus preserving the ancient monuments.

When traffic with the mainland was closed from 894 to 1195 because of the unsettled conditions during the late Chinese T'ang regime, Chinese influence, which had remained somewhat foreign, had an opportunity to settle in and mingle with the traditions of the native islands. The resulting amalgamation has become the mark of the later Japanese.

During the eighth century and continuing until the rule of the emperor Meiji during the nineteenth, Japan has in reality been ruled by shoguns

or military leaders. The emperor held only titular power, for some military clan wielded the real authority behind the throne, and the administration of the government therefore was always oblique. The Fujiwara dynasty of military dictators ruled in this manner from 897 to 1185; the Kamakura (Minamoto, then Hojo families) until 1333; the Ashikaga (Muromachi) until 1553; the Momoyama, 1553 to 1615; Tokugawa, early and late Edo, until 1868.

In this dual administration the court at the time of the Fujiwaras became largely a place of ceremony. In its architecture it favored the Chinese style which had been associated with court life. At the capital city of Kyoto the palace was in the style of Shinden-Zukuri. Zukuri means building. Oriented toward the south—one of the relics of Chinese (and Grecian) superstition—the Shinden-Zukuri preserved a Chinese character in its bisymmetry and colorful gardens. Instead of being built around a series of enclosed courtyards, like the Chinese, the Shinden was in open U form. The taste was for great restraint in decoration. Natural materials in an unfinished state were put together with a nicety of proportion in characteristic understatement called *wabi, sabi,* or *shibui* to denote a highly esteemed unobtrusive elegance.

Contrarily, the military clans needed great strongholds for the purpose of defense. These castles were built in the style of Buke-Zukuri and can be seen in Japan today. Within the ramparts, in addition to the warriors' hall, a unit for the lord and his family was built in modified Shinden style. This transformation led, in turn, to the usual house form, known as the Shoin-Zukuri, which has existed since the Ashikaga.

To understand completely the Shoin-Zukuri one must know something about the influence of Zen Buddhism on Japanese architecture. Even before the Fujiwaras the Japanese Buddhist ritual, which took its lead from certain esoteric cults that came from India and China, became complex and elaborate. Its practice required the intercession of a numerous priesthood which stood between the

Figure 7.22 (opposite page) Interior view, the Solomon R. Guggenheim Museum, New York, 1942–1960. Frank Lloyd Wright, architect. (Photo, Robert E. Mates.)

Figure 7.23 Hoop-back armchair of the Lohan type, China, late Ming Dynasty, seventeenth century. (Cleveland Museum of Art. (The Cleveland Museum of Art. The Norweb Collection.)

people and their deity. Zen Buddhism, imported from China in the thirteenth century, promising reform, became in the hands of the Japanese a religion of contemplation, learning by intuition, and the practice of a simple, stern life. Its very austerity recommended it to the warrior class who embraced it as the state religion. In course of time Zen changed so that its ways became elaborate and subtle and its vaunted simplicity became a complex, albeit ascetic, ritual. The tea ceremony, certain prescribed garden arrangements, and the essential household shrines are derived from this source.

Several other factors owe, if not their inception, at least their adoption into Japanese household tradition to Zen. The first is the asymmetry of the plan (Figure 7.24). Monasteries, taking to the mountainous country around the capital at Kyoto, were forced to suit their disposition of space to the terrain. Hence the bisymmetry of the Chinese

plan was forsaken, and the asymmetrical, which had been native for years before the Chinese intrusion, was generally adopted.

At the period when it began to be known to the West Japanese building was thus a derivation from many sources. Because it introduced a concept in building quite in tune with phases of the modern movement, it should be understood.

Native Japanese architecture is simple in structure. It is modular, post and lintel, with all supporting members made visible. The wooden posts are set into stone footers and the cross beams are mortised and tenoned into the posts. The roof may be supported to a prodigious width by the simple expedient of projecting ever-widening beams from brackets and ornamental supports. Roof forms, of wood or tile, are slanting and include many shaped gables. The *irimoya* or hipped gable has been given a prominent place in the western architecture that emulates the Japanese. It is similar to the German pent roof but in quite different proportions.

The wide eaves, which form a verandah or *genkan,* act as air conditioners. The island climate is oppressively humid during the heat of summer. The eaves are given a width that successfully cuts out the high summer sun before it can enter the building but allows the low winter sun to sweep the interior. Making the sun a climate ally in this manner is called solar heating or cooling, as the case may be.

The plan of a traditional Japanese house contains a number of rooms dictated by the elaborateness of the establishment. Some areas are isolated according to the need for privacy or convenience. Baths and toilets are situated off the porch, for western plumbing systems are still unusual except in large cities. The total space may be divided into an all-purpose room, a dining area, a kitchen, and a guest room. Bedrooms are not demarked because the custom prevails of packing away the bedding—soft, thick, silk coverlets—during the day. At night they are stretched on the floor in lieu of mattresses. Concessions to western furniture are, of course, usual in hotels that cater to travelers.

The plan is flexible (Figures 7.24 and 7.25) and may be said to conform to the principles of open planning. One wall, in the total inner space, may

354

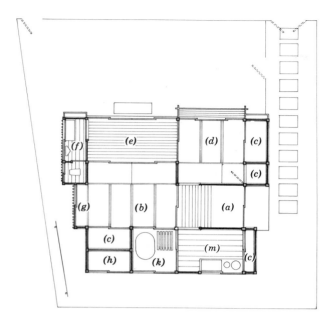

Figure 7.24 Plan of a Japanese house: (a) entrance hall; (b) living room; (c) wall cupboards; (d) reception or guest room; (e) verandah; (f) privy; (g) *tana* or wall shelves; (h) storeroom; (k) bath; (m) kitchen. (Adapted from *The Japanese House and Garden* Tetsuro Yoshida. First published in the United States of America in 1955 by Frederick A. Praeger, Inc., Publishers. Reprinted by permission of Holt, Rinehart and Winston.

Figure 7.25 Japanese Exhibition House, Museum of Modern Art, New York, 1954–1955. Junzo Yoshimura, architect. (Photograph, Courtesy The Museum of Modern Art Photographer, Ezra Stoller, © ESTO.)

alone be permanent. Stationary walls are finished on the inside with bamboo, lath, and plaster and on the outside with clapboards. In China they are brick and roofs are invariably tiled.

The movable walls in Japanese buildings (the *fusuma*) are constructed on modular wooden frames and filled with translucent paper. They are installed on slides and can be opened to the outdoors. In complete installations several sets of sliding screens face the exterior, one set made of solid material, another possibly louvered. If frames are used as windows, the modular divisions are smaller. These are the *shoji*. Above the level of the *fusuma* are the clerestory grilles known as *ramma,* which provide vertical extension to the interior space. A flat wooden ceiling is hung just below the pitched roof.

The floor is also modular, inasmuch as it is defined by grass mats, each 3 by 6 ft, which are arranged in a prescribed manner, their number thus dictating room or house size. These are the *tatami* and with the natural wood of the building, the white paper of the screens, their own olive green with darker binding they set an unusually subdued color scheme. This again differs from the colors of the principal architecture of the mainland, with its painted wood, blue, red, and green

Figure 7.26 Guest house in the Japanese style designed for a collector of oriental art, northern Ohio. Ernst Payer, architect. (By courtesy of Ernst Payer, A. I. A.)

tiles, colorful upholsteries, and gardens. Some of the Japanese religious shrines approach this tonal richness.

The *shoin-zukuri* house took its name from the room known as the *shoin,* a small bay or library with a fixed nook found in a Zen complex. The *toko* (*tokonoma*), (Figures 7.26 and 7.27), usually located in the section reserved for guests, is said to be a transferral of the small shrine containing a religious picture that is located in the home of a Zen priest. Today the family's most precious scroll painting is hung there. Changed with the seasons, it is accompanied by an appropriate floral piece, arranged according to prescribed rules (the *ikebana*). Thus the space has a center of visual interest, although it is not the usual bisymmetrically arranged mantel of western custom. The *tana,* another alcove adjacent to the *toko,* contains several built-in shelves and drawers.

The Japanese house contains little furniture. In this respect the Chinese interiors differ. Their beautiful appointments have been an inspiration to western designers since the eighteenth century. Scarcity of accouterments has emphasized a sense of space in Japanese building, whether it be dwelling, restaurant, or civic structure. This is another tie that binds it to many advanced theories of modern architecture.

The tea ceremony (*tya-no-yu*), also a legacy from Zen, and its ritual that involves the use of skillfully made articles such as stoneware tea bowls and iron kettles at once illustrates the dual character of Japanese genius with a nicety of refinement and an earthiness that dwells close to nature. Possibly it is this dichotomy that appealed to the generations that were breaking away from undue convention in western culture. If Japanese art had nothing else to offer the world, it would deserve an accolade for demonstrating that coarser textures can have their own type of finesse and distinction.

The gardens of the East are integral with the architecture. On occasion they are merely symbolic and intended to be viewed in contemplation. This is the case at the famous Daisen-in in Kyoto. These "meditative" gardens in Japan are inherited from the Shinden style which in turn is symbolic of the Buddhist conception of the mountains of the blessed with the sacred lake in the foreground.

Although the larger gardens are made to be walked in—with their stone bridges, stone lanterns, and washbasins placed for cooling and cleansing before entering the house—they can be symbolized where space is limited. Carefully raked sand can suggest water; long stones, bridges; small stones, hillocks; and dwarf trees, forests. The Chinese garden, equally lovely, calls for active participation, a contemplative trip walked in space. Paths, trees, shrubs, moon aperture gates, all are contrived to pull one along the

unraveled path, just about the loveliest of man's creations with nature.

No word can convey the spirit of Japanese traditional architecture. Toshiko Takaezu, one of the finest of American potters of Japanese ancestry, traveled extensively in Japan and spent three months in a Zen temple. Having been born in Hawaii, she wished to learn more about her racial heritage. In her pots, which so well illustrate the point, one finds the essence, "I always felt that in anything that was good there dwelt a sense of serenity no matter how alive the form might be."[13]

Rest with movement—the time-old adage for art. Takaezu said that from her visit to Japan came a realization that she could not find the answers to her quest from a country nor from a people but only from within herself. Japanese art may demand more of serenity than western civilization has to offer. The millions of persons caught up in the turbid mesh of today may find

Figure 7.27 Interior, guest house in the Japanese style. Ernst Payer, architect. (By courtesy of Ernst Payer, A.I.A.)

much to disturb the pools of their tranquility. "Because it happens inside me"[14]: this is the mandate which if sensitively and not arrogantly followed will bring forth new art.

Scandinavian Influence on Architecture

During the thirties architecture inspired by Frank Lloyd Wright and the Bauhaus International Style seemed incompatible and due for a confrontation. Bauhaus was created on a rigid post-and-beam modular structure of steel, concrete, and glass; Wright's designs were more flexible in structure, more natural in materials. The Bauhaus architects backed rigid geometric self-contained space; the Wrightians favored interpenetration of planes leading outward, with vast, low-hanging roofs overhead. Japanese aesthetic conformed to the modular dictum of the International and the use of indigenous media, as seen in the work of Frank Lloyd Wright. Something of a compromise was presented at this time by the introduction of the Scandinavian influence.

Eliel Saarinen (1873–1950), already an architect of renown in his native Finland, came to America and by his work at the Cranbrook Academy of Art in Bloomfield Hills, Michigan, opened American eyes to Scandinavian genius. Here, in curriculum as well as in product, Bauhaus doctrine combined with contemporary methods to create forms which were often humanly appealing.

The sculpture that Saarinen used at Cranbrook, done by Sweden's Carl Milles (whom Frank Lloyd Wright called "the greatest"), opened up a whole new world of stylization in spouting sea gods, trolls, and dryads. Eliel Saarinen's son Eero (1911–1960), was one of America's most famous younger architects and the creator of one of the century's largest architectural syndicates before his untimely death.

After World War II the Finnish architect Alvar Aalto (1898–1976) became world-renowned. He had built the Villa Mairea (Figures 7.28 and 7.29) in Noormark for the Gullichsens, a home that deserves to stand alongside Tugendhat House, Villa Savoye, and Falling Water as a landmark of the modern. He had been the architect of the Finnish Building at the Paris Exposition of 1937 and duplicated his success at the World's Fair of 1939 in New York.

Figure 7.28 Villa Mairea, Noormark, Finland, 1938. Alvar Aalto, architect. (GEKS)

Figure 7.29 Interior view, Villa Mairea, Noormark, Finland, 1938. Alvar Aalto, architect. (GEKS)

City Architecture in America during the Second Quarter of the Twentieth Century

While the movements which have just been re-counted were taking place, cities were certainly not standing still. Necessity created many tall buildings, of which two have been selected as particularly significant. Both are in New York.

First, the Chrysler Building (1926–1930), for which the architect was William Van Alen. The phenomenon in the decorative arts to which the term *Art Deco* has been applied (see p. 371) is seen in its form. The Chrysler Building, with its setback stories rising like so many flutes of a giant organ to the sky, certainly strains at the concept of functional accomplishment (the setbacks are for the purpose of obtaining light and air) married to decorative means.

The Rockefeller Center complex (1930, principal architect, Raymond Hood), remains a giant token of urbanism with its immense acreage and its symbolic need to carry the world on its back. Indeed, Radio City Music Hall and its precision dancers seem quite in keeping with the visual style trends of the times. Rockefeller Center can boast one achievement that even the most advanced later buildings cannot quite effect: in its outdoor square, shielded from the elements by tall winged arms, it becomes a real world neighborhood meeting place. Visitors from everywhere sit on its benches, parade, peer into its shop windows, watch its skaters, dine in its restaurants, and oddly enough converse with one another. It is in a way significant that it even dwarfs the cathedral which stands facing Atlas across Fifth Avenue.

More Recent Architecture

Frank Lloyd Wright, somewhat as Karl Marx, maintained that social rather than individual man was the power center of the modern world. A look at recent architecture would scarcely refute this. Staggering organizational complexes were built, some as early as the fifties—the Seagram Building (Figure 7.5) at 375 Park Avenue, New York (Mies van der Rohe and Philip Johnson, 1956–1958), within the tenets of the International Style but with considerable attention paid to innovative sensuous materials, curtain walls of bronze, fenestration of glare-reducing, pink-grey plate glass from floor to ceiling. Lever House, Seagram's near neighbor (Gordon Bunshaft, of Skidmore, Owings and Merrill, 1952), has a stainless steel grid curtain wall. Then the ultimate in Babel,

the World Trade Center (Minoru Yamasaki and Associates, 1970).

Tremendous areas are covered with space frames on the principle of Buckminster Fuller's geodesic dome (Figure 7.30). In 1959 the U.S. exhibit in Moscow used such a structure to cover an area 200 ft in diameter. Today the dome has covered more square feet of the earth than any other type of shelter:[15] marine barracks, radar stations, trade fair exhibits, auditoriums, astrodomes, and low-cost housing. It is a most economical coverage for large areas.

Much new construction, not always determined by the rectangular plane or the right angle, can enrich the architectural scene. Thus saddle shapes, elliptical, parabolic, cylindrical, torus, hyperbolic parabolic, and many others can be created geometrically, if the program warrants. Curves can introduce a built-in vitality and rhythm not accorded straight lines. Therefore the use of such complex figures, generated by points in motion, has been heralded as a return to organic proportions and principles. Curves bear close relation to living things and satisfying experiences. Their return engagement in architecture suggests, however valid, more humanitarian concern. Is it pure circumstance that Eero Saarinen made use of biomorphic shapes—the Ingalls Hockey Rink at Yale University (1959), the TWA Terminal at Kennedy International Airport (1962; Figures 7.31 and 7.32) and the Dulles International Airport building (1960–1963).

It is unrealistic to confine this type of designing to the United States—witness the Madrid Hippodrome (architects, M. Dominguez and C. Arniches, engineer, E. Torroja; note the importance of this last member of the team), as well as Oscar Niemeyer's work in Brazil, Juan O'Gorman's in Mexico, and Joern Utzon's in Australia—surely one technical world.

All, however, is not smooth and curved. The spectacle of chunky, rough-cast intersecting slabs, now colliding and thrusting through one another, is seen in the work of Louis Kahn [Richards Medical Research Building (Figure 7.33), University of Pennsylvania, 1957], Paul Rudolph (School of Architecture Building, Yale University, 1961–1965, since gutted by fire), and Le Corbusier (Secretariat, Chandigarh, India, 1951–1956). The term

Figure 7.30 Diagram of a space frame.

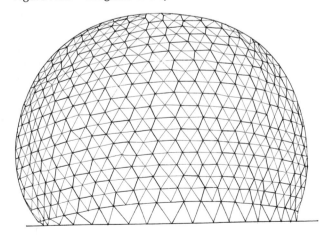

Figure 7.31 TWA Terminal Building, Kennedy International Airport, New York, 1962. Eero Saarinen, architect. (Courtesy of Trans World Airlines.)

Figure 7.32 Interior view, TWA Terminal Building, Kennedy International Airport, New York, 1962. Eero Saarinen, architect. (Courtesy of Trans World Airlines.)

Figure 7.33 The Richards Medical Research Building, University of Pennsylvania, Philadelphia, 1957. Louis Kahn, architect. (John Ebstel.)

"brutalism" was coined in England in 1954 to describe the style of Le Corbusier at the moment of his building *l'Unité d'Habitation,* his large apartment complex in Marseilles. These structures are dramatic and display visual force akin to that projected in action painting. It is not out of keeping with many aspects of today's story. One cannot forget that although Einstein described the great electromagnetic field which bends all matter in the macroscosm into vast curves, he felt baffled by the seemingly fortuitous clashes between the atomic particles of the microcosm.

Whereas variability of aesthetic conception would thus seem to be written into today's architecture, variability of function is also germane. It is becoming apparent for reasons of economy that one building may need to serve several related and interchangeable purposes. In 1960 specialists collaborated (Vern Knudsen and George Izenour) on Grady Gammage Auditorium, which had been designed by Frank Lloyd Wright for Arizona State University in Tempe. The solution has been effected several times since. It consists in walls that are a movable blanket of curved surfaces, each planned to enclose a requisite space for certain prescribed needs. In a world where desirable space is at a premium and requirements

Figure 7.34 A twentieth-century cityscape. (G. C. Ball.)

highly specialized the principle of flexibility is one that cannot be overlooked.

Most of the foregoing developments are related to group activity rather than to family or individual. In the area of architectural planning one of the touchiest, probably least remunerative, but certainly most essential areas is that of housing (Figure 7.34). Housing and schools underwrite our social consciousness. In New York one of the most recent developments is a school/apartment combine (Bronx P.S. 126). It may make some sense.

When financial conditions have warranted, some endearing homestead problems have been resolved by some of the most noted architects. These range from the glass-enclosed Farnsworth House (Mies van der Rohe, Fox Run, Illinois, 1946) to the many regional types, largely in natural materials. Many names come to mind—to

mention a few is to omit a score (Figures 7.35 and 7.36). From economic necessity the building industry has been responsible for much of the lower cost independent work that has been done and is often surprisingly close to people's needs.

Types of design are the row house (now often called town house), the house isolated on its own ground (often known as the ranch house which evolved from the nineteenth-century cottage or "bungalow" (a word of Eastern Indian derivation), or the apartment complex (whether high rise or low). The mobile home is understandably growing in popularity because of its adaptability to location.

One design experiment was demonstrated at the Montreal Exhibition Housing Development of 1967, the brainchild of Israeli architect Moshe Safdie (Figure 7.37). This finds acceptance because the individual family prefab units of which it is composed are quickly assembled onto a mas-

363

ter-planned nucleus. Each is designed to open on its neighborhood street, piled high in the air rather than spread out over the land. Although it bears a slight resemblance to ghetto crowding and the houses of the cliff dwellers, it may be a timely idea. This bears out Le Corbusier's contention for the principle of concentricity for modern dwelling. It also carries a unique aesthetic, possibly similar to that of abstract agglutinated sculpture.

It should be emphasized that none of the foregoing descriptions relates to the method of financing, which can be discussed under headings of private ownership, rental, and condominium or joint ownership. The important answers should be in terms of land use and of human needs in relation to economics.

Each age is commemorated in the building type that crystallizes its values. Several centuries hence the twentieth may be remembered for its commercial buildings, its stadiums, its air terminals, and its museums. It is a prediction that the twenty-first will express itself in urban communities within which people will dwell pleasurably. A strange forecast? The signs are already here.

The following list of twentieth-century houses shows the progress from those designed by the first generation of architectural leaders to those built by distinguished men of the second generation and then to the most recent examples often presented as experiments for the future.

Figure 7.35 The Coats House, Tillamook, Oregon, late 1940s (no longer in existence). Pietro Belluschi, architect. (Courtesy of P. Belluschi.)

SOME TWENTIETH CENTURY HOUSES

The Hickox House	Illinois	1900; architect, Frank Lloyd Wright
The Willitts House	Highland Park, Illinois	1902; architect, Frank Lloyd Wright
Casa Milá (Figure 6.27)	Barcelona, Spain	1905–1910; architect, Antonio Gaudí
Stoclet House (Figure 6.28)	Brussels, Belgium	1905–1911; architect, Josef Hoffmann
Pitcairn House	Pasadena, California	1907; architects, Charles S. Greene, Henry M. Greene ("oriental bungalow style")
Isabel Roberts House (Figures 7.17 and 7.19)	River Forest, Illinois	1907; architect, Frank Lloyd Wright
Coonley House	Riverside, Illinois	1908; architect, Frank Lloyd Wright
Cuno House	Eppenhausen, Germany	1909–1910; architect, Peter Behrens
Robie House (Figure 7.18)	Chicago, Illinois	1909; architect, Frank Lloyd Wright
Scheu House	Vienna, Austria	1912; architect, Adolf Loos
Barnsdale House "Hollyhock House"	Los Angeles, California	1920; architect, Frank Lloyd Wright ("concrete block type")
Millard House	Pasadena, California	1923; architect, Frank Lloyd Wright ("concrete block")
Schröder House	Utrecht, Holland	1924; architect, Gerrit Rietveld
Taliesin North	Spring Green, Wisconsin	1925; architect, Frank Lloyd Wright
House at Garches	Seine-et-Oise, France	1927; architect, Le Corbusier, Pierre Jeanneret
Villa Savoye (Figures 7.11, 7.12, and 7.13)	Poissy, France	1929–1930; architect, Le Corbusier
Tugendhat House (Figures 7.6, 7.7, and 7.8)	Brno, Czechoslovakia	1930; architect, Mies van der Rohe
Headmaster's House	Totnes, S. Devon, England	1931; architect, William Lescaze
House at Rugby	England	1934; architect, Serge Chermayeff
House in Chelsea	London, England	1935; architects, Erich Mendelsohn and Serge Chermayeff
Loomis House	Tuxedo Park, New York	1937; architect, William Lescaze

Figure 7.36 Interior of a house near Portland, Oregon. Pietro Belluschi, architect. (Courtesy of P. Belluschi's photograph, Phyllis Dearborn-Massar.)

Figure 7.37   Habitat, a housing complex built for Expo 67, Montreal, 1967. Moshe Safdie, architect. (*Plain Dealer* Photo, April 22, 1979.)

Kaufmann House, "Falling Water" (Figure 7.20)	Bear Run, Pennsylvania	1937; architect, Frank Lloyd Wright
Villa Mairea (Figures 7.28 and 7.29)	Noormark, Finland	1938; architect, Alvar Aalto
Taliesin West	Phoenix, Arizona	1938; architect, Frank Lloyd Wright
Gropius House	Lincoln, Massachusetts	1938; architects, Walter Gropius, Marcel Breuer
Breuer House	Lincoln, Massachusetts	1939; architects, Walter Gropius, Marcel Breuer
Farnsworth House	Plano, Illinois	1951; architect, Mies van der Rohe
Unité d'Habitation	Marseilles, France	1946–1952; architect, Le Corbusier (multiple housing)
Kaufmann House	Colorado	1946; architect, Richard J. Neutra
Wasserman House "Square Shadows"	Chestnut Hill, Pennsylvania	1934; architect, George Howe
Pardee House	Midland, Michigan	1937; architect, Alden B. Dow
Miller House	Carmel, California	1935; architect, William Wilson Wurster
Cole House	New Hope, Pennsylvania	1936; architect, Kenneth Day
Troy House	Needham, Massachusetts	1936; architects, Hugh Stubbins, Royal Barry Wills
Belluschi House	Portland, Oregon	1937; architect, Pietro Belluschi
Cahn House	Lake Forest, Illinois	1937; architect, George Fred Kech
Curtis House	Belmont, Massachusetts	1937; architect, George W. W. Brewster Jr.
Kohler House	Wisconsin	1937; architects, William F. Deknatel, collaborator G. Deknatel

Bauer House	Glendale, California	1939; designer, Harwell Hamilton Harris
Perkins House	Brookline, Massachusetts	1938; architect, G. H. Perkins
Koch House	Cambridge, Massachusetts	1938; architects, Edward D. Stone, Carl Koch
Manor House	Orinda, California	1938; designer, Clarence W. W. Mayhew
Sutor House	Portland, Oregon	1938; architect, Pietro Belluschi
Bogner House	Lincoln, Massachusetts	1939; architect, Walter F. Bogner
Eames House	Pacific Palisades, California	ca. 1940; designer, Charles Eames (steel fabrication experiment)
Goodyear House	Old Westbury, New York	ca. 1940; architect, Edward D. Stone
Hiatt House	Modesto, California	ca. 1940; architect, Gardner A. Dailey
Stonorov House	Phoenixville, Pennsylvania	ca. 1940; architect, Oscar G. Stonorov
Yeon House	Portland, Oregon	ca. 1940; architect, John Yeon
Johnson House, "Glass House" (Figure 7.9)	New Canaan, Connecticut	1949; architect, Philip C. Johnson
Holt House	Stockton, California	ca. 1950; architect, Joseph Esherick
Kirby House	Belvedere, California	ca. 1950; architect, John Funk
McDonald House	Seattle, Washington	ca. 1950; architect, Paul Thiry
Miller House	Carmel, California	ca. 1950; designer, Gordon Drake
Moore House	Portland, Oregon	ca. 1950; architect, Pietro Belluschi
Smith House	Stockton, California	ca. 1950; architects, Wurster, Bernardi, & Emmons
Tremaine House	Montecito, Californa	ca. 1950; architect, Richard J. Neutra
Little House	Pepper Pike, Ohio	1950; architect, Robert A. Little (one of a group of houses by the architect)
Windermere House (Figure 7.59)	Seattle, Washington	ca. 1950; designer, Hope L. Foote
Case Study House	Los Angeles, California	1950; designer, Raphael Soriano
Irwin Miller House	Columbus, Indiana	1953–57; architect, Eero Saarinen; interior, Alexander Girard
Davis House	Wayzata, Minnesota	1954; architect, Philip C. Johnson
Noyes House	New Canaan, Connecticut	1954; architect, Eliot Noyes
Hiss House	Lido Key, Florida	1954; architect, Paul Rudolph
Payer House (Figure 7.52)	Moreland Hills, Ohio	1957; architect, Ernst Payer
Married Students Housing	Yale University	1958–61; architect, Paul Rudolph
Moore House	Orlinda, California	1961; architect, Charles W. Moore
White House	Chestnut Hill, Pennsylvania	1963; architect, Romaldo Giurgola
Stubbins House	Cambridge, Massachusetts	1966; architect, Hugh Stubbins
Exhibition Housing Development (Figure 7.37)	Montreal, Canada	1967; architect, Moshe Safdie
Rotating House	Connecticut	1968; Richard T. Foster

INTERIOR DESIGN

Architectural Details and Interior Surface Treatments

No one can read the saga of twentieth-century architecture without realizing that treatment of space and its accompanying indoor-outdoor relationship are basic and planned for the building.

Therefore doors and windows are conceived as part of the wall planes and their individual character is not emphasized. Even auxiliary treatment would presumably be designed to further this effect. The same treatment holds true for fireplaces, although they may become accent items if their placement does not hinder more important spatial considerations.

Contemporary designers have been imaginative

in using design components in new ways to qualify interior surfaces in a manner consonant with architectural purpose. The careful use of texture looms important. Wood or slate may possess requisite similarity, yet sufficient contrast to offset steel and glass. Textured fabrics appear on floor and wall to the same end. Paintings that convey a texture impression, such as those of a Tobey or a Pollock, may be considered as enrichment. Obviously, upholstery fabrics and such articles as pottery and plants serve dually as texture modifiers and shape accents. Sculpture produced, for instance, by a Giacometti or a Bertoia qualifies space in similar fashion.

In spite of attempts by the original leaders to prescribe color treatments, designers and painters have been creative in the use of this element. One aspect is the work that results in color changes in the eye. The "op" and "hard edge" artists like Richard Anuskiewicz or Bridget Riley can cause uncanny and painful eye movements with their color juxtapositioning. The "supremists" and "soft edge" men, like Kasimir Malevich and Mark Rothko (see Plate 15), can alter "feeling tones" through large areas that operate in relation to the position of the viewer. All provide flexibility and movement within the visual field.

This relates well to modern scientific concepts, which apparently have revealed a "chancy" character in the physical universe. We are told that the collisions of particles within the atom are fortuitous. This knowledge has proved to be a disturbing factor in a belief in predetermined order. Design has reacted with various expressions; mutable color is only one. Another is the use of mobiles like Alexander Calder's (see Plate 16)—often a prominent feature in a space ensemble.

Light, too, can be manipulated as a design factor in an interior. The background can be kept in similar tones, thus helping to render the light all-pervasive, a factor in an all-glass interior. Movement may be fostered by merging dark colors into light. Both can be manipulated by wall colors or by lighting.

Furnishings and Their Arrangement

We now enter the domain where shape is the most important visual consideration and texture,

color, and light become its modifiers. In respect to the arrangements of interior shapes, the leaders of modern architecture were divided into two somewhat separate schools. Since their day the rigid disciplines have mellowed.

Mies van der Rohe featured a tightly compacted, bisymmetrical grouping of space furnishing, often marked by two Barcelona chairs (see p. 372) on each side of an area rug, centered on some decorative feature and surrounded by as much space as possible. This tectonic organization is inward and statically oriented. It is, moreover, a private and cloistered area—a tight little island in a large and open sea. Any psychological comfort that it may possess depends more on its exclusion than on its seclusion.

Within its larger surround a closed furniture arrangement performs the service of dividing space into comprehensible and, hopefully, functional subdivisions. This kind of designing can be what the famous dancer Martha Graham describes as continuing to "move inside" while holding still. The area is classically calm, but the group placement charges the surrounding atmosphere. It is a quiet, contained power used as a foil.

The second spatial arrangement used in contemporary interiors is more open and informal. It is associated with the designing of Frank Lloyd Wright. Here the individual furnishings rather than their grouping are counted on to further interior movement. Although such a distribution is often quite in harmony with the space presented to view, it is not always helpful from the standpoint of overt functioning because it frequently strands a piece of furniture so far from the others that it has no communication with them. In summary, the Wrightian arrangement establishes its internal rhythms on the principle of continuity, the Miesian by dramatic contrast. Both are factors in contemporary culture.

FURNITURE

The various approaches to the task of creating a new twentieth-century environment indicated a need for rethinking the problems of furnishings as well as those of architecture. It was clear that new technologies, new economic and social conditions, and a new aesthetics pointed toward less expensive, more available, and less ornate productions.

Furniture in the twentieth century? It would not be a far cry to say that several considerations militated toward its obsolescence. Built-in furniture, the creed of omitting furniture to increase space, the cost of good pieces, the youthful preference for a cushion or a pad—all play their part. Expensive Mies van der Rohe chairs are likely to rest only in the foyers of art museums, and full-fledged contemporary houses often adhere to the lonely rocker school of equipment. I have heard one of America's leading architects declare that all furniture is unnecessary.

Although this picture has many virtues, it denies many facts. The most important is the evolution of a good modern style in furnishings that began with Art Nouveau and advanced to the point where suitable items may be obtained on the moderately priced market. Again there is man's persistent desire for comfort which precedes that for ideological beauty.

Figure 7.38 Settee, Hector Guimard, France, ca. 1898. Wood and tooled leather. Height, 94 cm, width, 1.71 m. Museum of Modern Art, New York. (Collection, The Museum of Modern Art. Greta Daniel Fund.)

Before World War I, the *English,* even with their most dedicated designers, were not prepared to depart far from the traditional. Mackintosh's cabinets and chairs, despite their straight lines, were in reality streamlined Carolean. Men like Frank Brangwyn, C. F. A. Voysey, Ernest Gimson, Ambrose Heal, Jr., M. H. Baillie Scott, and George Walton, so much in the press at the turn of the century, go but a short step beyond the arts and crafts approach.

The *French* were past masters in putting a new face on their royal styles. In the work of craftsman Louis Majorelle (1859–1916), designers Charles Plumet (1861–1928), J. E. Ruhlmann, and Tony Selmersheim, and architect Hector Guimard (Figure 7.38), Louis XV slides easily into Art Nouveau. The *Belgians* merged with the trend in the furniture of Gustave Serrurier-Bovy and the more outstanding creations of Victor Horta.

France played the important role of advertiser to the new. This was more than just the initial push given to Art Nouveau in Bing's studio. At twentieth-century exhibitions she popularized the movement known as *modern design.* This began with the 1900 Paris "L'Exposition Universelle," when Bing showed van de Velde's Art Nou-

veau rooms and the "Six" group (Plumet, Selmersheim, Charpentier, Moreau-Nelaton, Aubert, and Dampt) displayed their modern decorative art.

In 1901 the *Société des Artistes Décorateurs* was founded in Paris by Réné Guilleré. In 1913 he opened *le grand magazin Primavera,* which illustrated current fashion trends in the decorative arts. Later, when Guilleré's society enlarged its scope to become associated with *L'Union des Artistes Modernes,* it sponsored the periodic showing of the work of craftsmen and designers from all countries.

In 1903 the famous *Salon d'Automne* was inaugurated. This exhibition, the contemporary equivalent of which would be the *Milan Triennale* (see p. 373) or the *Venice Biennale,* was devoted to showing both fine and applied arts. The exhibits were chosen by jury action.

These famous "shows," and some of their beautifully rendered displays found their way into the French magazines such as *Les Arts de la Maison, Art et Décoration,* and *L'Art Décoratif.* Through such attention the style called *modern* was publicized.

A close liaison has existed between twentieth-century art movements and developments in the fine arts. This tie was nowhere more evident than in France. In 1906 Paris had an exhibition of Russian art followed in 1909 by a performance of the Russian ballet starring Diaghilev. Bakst and Benois collaborated on the costumes. In 1916 the ballet made its first crossing of the Atlantic. Although this scarcely can be said to have a direct relation to French furniture production, in retrospect we can see that it had a bearing on the unique function of France as a press agent for new conceptions. The richness of the color work displayed in these circumstances began to step up the industrial pallette and indirectly to increase the excitement over new ideas.

It was the *Dutch* van de Velde, in his work at Dresden, who led the way toward the rational approach that we now associate with modern furniture designing. His writings, if not always his performance, spoke of structure and function as basic determinants. In such a piece as the desk (1897), which he executed in ash, he incorporated the curved Art Nouveau line without denying its function as a vigorous support.

In keeping with the liaison between fine and applied art, the *Dutch* painter Gerrit Rietveld (1888–1964) demonstrated the impact that cubism had on the furniture world in his simple geometric chair with its colorful wood for body support (Figure 7.39).

We have already alluded to the group of young *German* designers who were practicing in Dresden at the time of van de Velde's arrival: Peter Behrens, August Endell, Bernard Pankok, and Richard Riemerschmid. Another should be mentioned—Bruno Paul (1874–1954). With Riemerschmid and Paul the early history of modern furniture may be said to have begun; with the first because of his social orientation and attempt to create furniture of simple machine fabrication that would be modest in price and with the second because he recognized the necessity for standardization in design.

Bruno Paul was a German printmaker and artist who turned industrial designer. In 1907 he was made principal of the Berlin School of Arts and Crafts. As a designer Paul did not discard all vestige of past styles. His furniture resembles simplified Neoclassic. Nevertheless, in 1906 he was a partner in the planning of the earliest machine-produced furniture of commensurable sizes. Except for some pilot work in the form of industrial bookcases made in the United States, he became the originator (1910) of examples of modular furniture of the same height or depth that could be fitted together to form unified compositions.

In *America* the earliest event important to furniture design was an exhibition of utilitarian objects at the Newark Art Museum, an almost unprecedented innovation for any American museum at that time. This was recognition of the fact that an industrialized economy should concern itself with the aesthetic value of everyday things, and it predated the famous Armory Show in New York (1913) that gave impetus to the cause of avant-garde painting.

Meanwhile, of course, Frank Lloyd Wright was designing furniture for his houses. With the straight backs of his chairs, similar to those that Mackintosh engineered (Figure 6.23) but fitted with narrow boards that stretched from almost floor level to well above the sitter's head, they are strange geometric pieces, examples of the general doctrine of uncomfortableness. There were others as well: three-legged chairs, folded and molded chairs, and chairs with half-circle backs. Frank Lloyd Wright wanted the furniture to fit into the architecture and actually it is a miniature shadow of the same. He said, "Furnishings should be consistent in design and construction, and used with style as an extension . . . of the building which they furnish."[16]

After World War I contemporary furniture entered on an expanded era. One significant date is that of the Paris Exhibition of 1925, *L'Exposition des Arts Décoratifs et Industriels*. This exposition, sponsored by the French government, was planned before the outbreak of World War I. In 1925 its theme was changed to demonstrate the advances that had occurred during the postwar years. Only wares made since the war were to be on display.

Art Deco is a popular name for the decorative art of the twenties and thirties (see Plate 13). It was assigned to the period in a retrospective exhibition held at the *Musée des Arts Décoratifs*, Paris, in 1966. It is a style dramatically characterized by diagonal thrusts and angular shapes, its inheritance from cubism, and indicative of the accelerating tempo of the times. Many of its displays were commercialized and, like much merchandise today, some were worthy, some interesting because they reflected the aura of the period, and many were "pretty bad."

Art Deco, in its superficial manifestations, was far more the result of merchandising than Art Nouveau had been. In retrospect we see Art Nouveau as a serious movement that inspired serious artists by belief in serious creeds. Art Deco, on the other hand, expressed no principle. It derived much of its superficial ornamental motifs from current topics of interest, such as Aztec-Mexican art, Erté's sets for the Folies Bergère, and the sensational discoveries that the Carner expedition had made at the tomb of Tutankhamun in Egypt. The accelerated pace of the times could be seen in its preference for animal forms that suggested fleetness (e.g., the gazelle). In the thirties, the decade preceding World War II, symbols became more forceful, and ominously so. The thirties nevertheless veered toward *exquisite* interior decoration for the wealthy and architecture took on the phase known as "modernistic,"

Figure 7.39 Armchair, Gerrit Rietveld, Holland, 1917. Painted wood. Height, 7.6 cm. Museum of Modern Art, New York. (Collection, The Museum of Modern Art, New York. Gift of Philip Johnson.)

which seemed conceived to be dramatically showy. It was the era of Elsie de Wolfe (Lady Mendl) and the French salons on the one hand and of "cubistic" gas stations, theater lobbies, and eating places on the other. All of this, however, is of the utmost importance to the historian and, if he searches carefully, he will find a reason—often an astonishing one—for these manifestations. This is Art Deco's ineradicable lesson, which is entirely divorced from the question whether it is good or bad art.

Germany can be represented by what the Bauhaus men showed at the 1925 exhibition. Their furniture was decried at the time as "nude." Le Corbusier had described modern design as streamlined, like a ship. So the press alluded to the tubular steel furniture as "steamer style." Reviewing the illustrations of the fair, the Bauhaus pieces did possess a sterile coldness in the atmosphere in which they were shown, so different from the polished work of the Austrians and the French in their plush settings.

The German approach to furniture design was totally different from the French. It was oriented toward new techniques, gave lip service to functionalism, and was certainly conceived in a sociological context, although hardly with an appropriate price. The Hungarian architect, Marcel Breuer (1902–), working in this program, produced the first modern tubular steel chair in 1925. Metal chairs had been manufactured in the nineteenth century and tubular metals had been in use since 1912. Breuer's, however, was the first in which the potentialities of the material were fully exploited in a design whose upholstery was cloth mesh rather than padded cushioning.

Breuer's chair was followed by one designed by Mies in 1927 in which the spring quality of the steel was used. A further extension of this principle can be seen in the Tugendhat chair at the fa-

Figure 7.40 The Barcelona Chair, Mies van der Rohe, 1929. Museum of Modern Art, New York. (Collection, The Museum of Modern Art, New York. The Mies Van Der Rohe Archives.)

mous house of that name. It was manufactured from resilient flat metal strips. The date 1929 is assigned to the creation of his Barcelona chair, which is peerless within its class (Figure 7.40). The back and seat form a ninety degree angle and are canted from the horizontal at almost thirty degrees. The front legs and back are a single geometric concave curve of flat banded, heavy-gauge stainless steel. The back legs flow up in a more subtle concave–convex curve to support the seat. The stout leather cushions of back rest and seat are laid on leather strips fastened to the frame. It is difficult to effect a translation of the suavity of the Greek klismos chair in terms more appropriate to today's needs. The chair fits into a neat 29-in. cubical package, which is scarcely the straight and narrow of Frank Lloyd Wright's. The Barcelona chair echoes the tautness of steel framing, the coldness of blue-gray, the polish of glass and metal, all of which relate it to architecture. Even its size and general proportions seem appropriate to provide an accent in a rectangular space. The curved outline, the warm coloring of the leather and its weight and textural porosity give just the right relief, which Wright's chairs fail to provide. As for function, neither would fit the average pocketbook. As for comfort, sit in one and judge.

The Germans were first in another technique, that of bending wood under the influence of chemicals and pressure to produce chairs with similar curvilinear shapes. Recall that the Greeks knew this method of fashioning but that it has not been common since. Such bentwood chairs were made during the early part of the nineteenth century by Michael Thonet in the Rhineland. The firm also manufactured metal furniture for rooms done by Gropius and Breuer at the 1930 Salon des Artistes Décorateurs in Paris.

In bending wood the grain is forced to follow the form. Hence, not being a curved shape cut from a straight block, it is much stronger and less likely to split with the grain. The Thonet firm in America is making sturdy furniture especially usable for institutional purposes. Since this pioneer achievement, and in the post-World War II decades, German furniture, now often of teak, beech, or rosewood, as well as steel, continues along sparse, clean-cut lines. In all there is a refreshing lack of striving for the theatrical. The spirit of the German designers remains clearly rational.

France and Austria were alike in orienting much of their after-the-war production toward a specialized market, one in which manufacture for a restricted clientele was important. France diverged toward an exclusive luxury trade with machine production but not mass industrial duplication. Traditional techniques were adhered to and metal mountings were used.

One French commercial firm, *Süe et Mare* (the architect Louis Süe and his partner André Mare), designed furniture that took its point of departure from the Louis Philippe style (1830, giving the late Empire style the name of the ruling monarch; see Chapter 6). J. E. Ruhlman added new elements to eighteenth-century designs. André Groult made some exquisitely chaste, straight-line cabinets which in their finish and simplicity were timeless masterpieces almost within an oriental context.

Robert Mallet-Stevens created interiors and furniture faintly reminiscent of Hoffmann's Stoclet in their straight-line, dark-on-light drama. The glass artist, Réné Lalique, was represented by some superlatively constructed rosewood cabinets in which the details would make any wood craftsman envious. In a French exhibit of 1937 the pieces of Maxine Old and Marcel Gascoin were similar.

Pierre Chareau, who was featured in the 1925 salons by a bibliothèque and a salle de repos, stood almost alone among the Frenchmen in illustrating the utilitarian point of view with pieces composed of movable and interchangeable parts.

The most forward-looking furniture in the French section of the 1925 exhibition was done by Le Corbusier and his cousin Jeanneret. Their predecessors on the Parisian architectural scene, Auguste and Gustav Perret, on the other hand, produced furniture in the outmoded classical vein.

Le Corbusier's fame rests on his reclining chair of these years. It was constructed with a tubular steel frame on a separate base, which gave the possibility of several positions with the tilt of the body weight. In 1927 he designed a tubular steel armchair supported on straight legs.

France has not been a large producer of furniture since World War II. When such men as Pierre Paulin do create in the new materials, we see curved forms in pieces both usable and pleasing. In general they adhere to older construction methods.

Austria was too postwar poor to invest in a program of industrialization and continued largely in a handicraft tradition. This emerged in furniture that smacked of Tyrolean country style with a bow to Mackintosh or Hoffmann. Hoffmann himself seems to have had a change of heart which transferred his lean elegance into overly upholstered but sturdy and taut plushness.

Austria sent the first missionaries of a "modern" movement abroad. We have mentioned Josef Maria Urban (see Chapter 6), who became manager of the outlet office opened by the Wiener Werkstätte in New York in 1919 and who later sponsored an exhibition of its work. Not finding the aesthetic climate responsive to Austrian production, Urban finally returned to Europe. Austria is not currently a large producer of furniture, although some creditable steel framing is being done.

Italy is divided into two camps with respect to modern design—one industrially oriented, the other rooted in handicraft, a combination that critics consider healthy for a civilization. The first centers around Milan, the industrial capital. The initial guiding spirit in the Italian enterprises was the architect Gio Ponti (1891–   ), editor of *Domus* and *Stile,* the architectural magazines he established, and member of Azucena, a group of architect designers in Milan. He created furniture for the firm of Cassina and for Chiesa. It was he who inaugurated the Milan Triennale, the *Institutione della Triennale d'Arte Decorativa,* an exhibition of the decorative arts that has been held in Milan every third year since 1923.

In 1950 a number of outstanding American designers, working under the direction of Meyric R. Rogers, then Curator of the Decorative and Industrial Arts, the Art Institute of Chicago, organized a touring exhibition of Italian arts and crafts which gave the American public its first taste of Italian design.[17]

An understanding of the artistic atmosphere of Italy developed from this viewing. Italy, which had been handicapped by her own brilliant past, had broken into the new. This "Second Resorgimento," as it is called, was facilitated by the fact that the artist in Italy had always been able to turn his hand to any form of art. Italy never broke completely with the handicraft tradition. Now, however, trained men possessed a certain versatility that enabled them to organize a new movement more easily than in countries in which art had been more regimented. In the country where *Futurism* was born and *Surrealism* (in painting) strongly represented we expect and find a furniture art modified in the direction of plasticity and movement and displaying a fertility of imagination.

Most of the industrially produced Italian furniture manufactured post-World War II was designed by the Azucena group. Production is active today. Names in the press have included Franco Albini, Augusto Bozzi, Carlo de Carli, Gianfranco Frattini, Angelo Mangiarotti, Ico Paresi, Carlo Ponzio, and Fabio De Sanctis. The proliferation of signatures confirms the Italian penchant for individualized work. In the category of hand made production we must mention such new-old materials as "grass"—furniture fashioned from wicker and similar native materials. A comparison of the Italian production in this medium with that of other countries reveals the elegant exuberance of the Latin. Curiously, in quite recent years Italian designers have led the way back to overinflated, overstuffed packages, without a modicum of skeletal structure evident, possibly the counterpart of "brutalism" but again allied to the formlessness and lack of formality of contemporary life.

Scandinavia, for our purposes, constitutes Denmark, Norway, Sweden, and Finland. So far these countries have been on the periphery of our story but now they come center front. Until recently a customary view of this northern civilization has been one assumed by the classical south. Only lately, as time goes, has there developed an appreciation of the artistic caliber of the men who fashioned the ships' prows of Oslo, the golden horns of Denmark, and the rock carvings of Ostergötland.

Scandinavian art, with its timbre of dramatic splendor, somber mystery, and consuming dynamic impulse, is to be seen in the museums of its capital cities. The names of Bartel Thorwaldsen and Kai Nielsen of Denmark, Anders Zorn and the American Carl Milles from Sweden, Edvard Munch and Gustav Vigeland from Norway, and Albert Edelfelt and Waine Altonene in Finland emphasize the fact that Scandinavian genius outreaches the crafts.

Of the latter, however, they have special reason to be proud, as displayed in permanent exhibitions to be visited at Den Permanente in Copenhagen, in Oslo the Forum, at Malmo the Svenskform, the Nordiska Museum for Crafts in Stockholm, and the Finnish Design Center in Helsinki. All Scandinavian applied art is characterized by a respect for craftsmanship and materials. If decoration is present, it is likely to mirror an animistic approach, often incorporating some representation of nature. To date it appears devoid of that voluptuousness so often seen in southern design. It is at once sturdy, tense, spare, and organically alive. It exhibits the substance of the man of toil, the propelling energy of the adventurous spirit, and occasionally an almost oriental fantasy verging on the demoniacal of a presumably harmless or pixie variety.

Finland. The most eastern portion of our present Scandinavia is Finland which lies north of the sixtieth parallel and much of which juts into the Arctic Circle—a land of boundless evergreens and six thousand lakes.

The Finnish background, like their language, differs from the rest of Scandinavia, a variance that may help to explain certain observable characteristics in their art. Keen analysts have traced in the spirit of the Finns a duality compounded at once of a respect for the economy of life and for manipulating it by craft techniques, as well as of an unaccountable recklessness and allowance for those things that serve spiritual needs through satisfactions to the aesthetic. The people of Finland seem to treasure a hidden and dedicated thrill to life that comes through as sparkle in their creations in a manner not quite approached by any other people on this earth. They can and will make a bauble out of tinsel and wood, which turns out to be folksy, bright and whimsical, and resplendent, all in one. And never gauche.

This preference for the aesthetics of the impractical almost proved their downfall. Finland was a late—after World War II—intruder on the industrial market. When she held a trade fair exhibit in Helsinki in 1949, her own critical press pointed out that the products had paid only lip service to functionalism, the talisman to success in the market in those days. With a quick right about face, the country geared into industrialization and designed factory-produced objects that emphasized utility. The leopard still retained his spots, however. These machined products were often designed with such delightfully extravagant imagination that the Finns were able to capture many of the coveted Milan Triennale prizes.

It was in Alvar Aalto's Finnish building in the 1939 World's Fair in New York—undoubtedly the most warmly inviting on the set—that the American public obtained a first look at that architect's laminated bentwood furniture. The patriarchal industrial designer Werner West (1870–1959) had already given Europe its first taste of Finnish furniture in which marquetry in native motifs was prominently featured. Aalto's pieces, and particularly his chairs of laminated bentwood (Figure 7.41), had no added ornament. They were ex-

Figure 7.41 Lounge chair, ca. 1934. Alvar Aalto designer; Artek OY, Finland, manufacturer. Molded and bent birch plywood. Height, 64.8 cm. Museum of Modern Art, New York. (Collection, The Museum of Modern Art, New York. Gift of Edgar Kaufmann, Jr.)

tremely comfortable, reasonably priced, and light and cheerful in tone. Aalto had designed his first chair of this sort in 1928, which was produced by the Finnish firm of Artek and for a time by the American Pascoe. Stacking pieces made their initial appearance in America at this time.

In America Eero Saarinen created his "leaf" chair in 1946 (Figure 7.42) and the plastic unipedestal chair and tables in 1957 (Figure 7.43). These pieces indicated at once his love affair with sculptured space and with new fabrication and materials.

The Finnish industry today, although not anonymous (for a good name enriches both merchant and designer), is fitting more into the general Scandinavian pattern. Men like Iimari Tapiovaara work in plywood and metal, always with a suave grace, not without fancy, but seldom with capriciousness. Antti Nurmesniemi, with his plastic

Figure 7.42 Chair, 1946. Eero Saarinen, designer; Knoll Associates, Inc., manufacturer. (Courtesy, Knoll International.)

Figure 7.43 Unipedestal chair, 1957. Eero Saarinen, designer; Knoll Associates, Inc., manufacturer. Molded plastic reinforced with fiberglass; aluminum, painted white. Height, 81.3 cm. Museum of Modern Art, New York. (Collection, The Museum of Modern Art, New York. Gift of the manufacturer.)

pieces, indicates that Finland does not lag behind in using new media.

Sweden. Across the Gulf of Bosnia lies Sweden, more mountainous than her eastern neighbor, but also more fertile, especially in the eastern and southern river valleys. Most southerly of the Scandinavian peninsulas, it stretches across the Kattergat toward Denmark.

Swedish modern design was first shown internationally at the Paris 1925 Exhibition. Considering the close ties between France and the Swedish royal house (the French Marshal Bernadotte was elected Crown Prince of Sweden in 1810), and Sweden's proximity to Denmark, it is not surprising that the 1925 showing was a watered-down classical version of the contemporary.

This bias was criticized by the Swedes themselves on economic and aesthetic grounds. It may be said in passing that these northern countries, indeed most of Europe, possess a press that is not hampered by advertising interests and is outspoken and considered in its objective criticism. Two magazines, *Svensk Form* and the annual *Kontur,* have not only stressed the duty owed by the manufacturer to the consumer but have suggested the advisability of having an enlightened consumer clientele. Where consumer education has been relegated to commercial interests, they describe unfortunate results.

Since this self-censure the more indigenous and practical point of view has dominated Swedish production. By the time of the Stockholm exhibition of 1930 Swedish modern had been reoriented along lines of functionalism. The exhibit was organized by the almost-century-old Swedish Society for Industrial Design (the Swedish craft guilds had been abolished in 1846).

Following the pioneering instruction of such teachers as Carl Malmsten (1888–) and the Viennese transplant, Josef Frank (1885–), the first generation of Swedish designers best known abroad may be said to have begun with Bruno Mathsson. His furniture has consistently used laminated wood for the bearing members and interwoven webbing for the borne, a clear distinction of the function of each being preserved. It is characterized by a bold dynamic line similar to that shown in the Aalto pieces. The producing firm carried his father's name, Karl Mathsson. Much of Mathsson's work is made of pine or walnut, as is Swedish furniture in general.

Lists are boring but frequently useful for reference. Other important names in Swedish furniture designing have been Axel Larsson, Karl Erik Ekselius, and Carl Axel Acking. Sven Kai-Larsen played with a geometric approach and a heavier hand, as if already sensing some of the tremendous forces of the post-World War II years. He returns to solid wood construction and gives it an unmodified squareness that agrees with aspects of current architecture. The wooden arms of his chairs, which completely encompass the back, provide durability and lateral support.

One innovation found first in Swedish furniture is the product of Alf Svensson and Folke Ohlsson, who specialize in dismountable pieces. Since

their introduction for the Fabrisken Dux, made in the town of Trellsborg, this type has had widespread acceptance.

Count Sigvard Bernadotte (1907–), son of King Gustav VI, is an industrial designer whose chair, known by his name, has deservedly won several of the American Good Design Awards.

Norway is also a mountainous land but with the narrowest of valleys and of great distances to travel along their course. Today a nominal monarchy, it is one of the world's truly classless societies. Its production, similar to Sweden's, is a mixture of handicraft and industrialization.

Furniture for the market has been a recent phenomenon. This occurred when the technical colleges began to train interior designers and wisely included cabinetry in their curricula. The output at first was largely of solid wood—teak or native oak—although the new materials are now being explored. Norwegian furniture is characterized by grace without contortion, and it boasts good, solid construction. Alf Sture is one of Norway's finest designers, whose work in the forties is well remembered. Although Norway does not at present loom large in the furniture industry, a new yearly furniture fair at Stavanger is creating an expanding market.

Denmark is the trade center of the Baltic. The Danes, surprisingly, have been relative newcomers to modern design. A review of the showings of the 1925 Paris Exposition indicate their orientation toward the somewhat theatrical style popular in the twenties that we have described as "art deco." More than any other Scandinavian country, their work will recurrently show influences from adjoining lands.

The Danes woke up when they saw what the Swedes had wrought in the 1930 Stockholm exhibition. The next Baltic exposition was in 1945 and it was Danish. Between these two dates much had changed in Denmark.

The Danish Academy of Art, motivated by the architect and designer Kaare Klint (1888–1951), established a Department of Furniture in 1924. Klint's was the concept of designing for industry. However, craftsmen continued to produce furniture in folk art tradition and to show their skill in yearly guild exhibits, the first of which was held in 1927. It was through these homely outlets that

Danish furniture first entered the world market. Soon the craftsmen invited architects to design the furniture they would make and exhibit. From such an alliance came Danish modern furniture.

Two of the continuing leaders are the architects Borge Mogensen and Hans Wegner. Both men have taken the basic and simple chair of native beech, oak, or teak, with rush or cane seat and continuous curved back support, adapted it to smaller spaces, and given it more contemporary lines. Wegner's "classic" chair (Figure 7.44), which was introduced in the Danish cabinet-maker's exhibition in 1949, was crafted by his friend, the cabinetmaker Johannes Hansen. It is one of the most beautiful pieces of sculptured

Figure 7.44 Armchair, 1949. Hans Wegner, designer; Johannes Hansen, Denmark, manufacturer. Oak and cane. Height, 76.2 cm. Museum of Modern Art, New York. (Collection, The Museum of Modern Art, New York. Gift of Georg Jensen, Inc.)

wood in the whole gamut of furniture history—a Barcelona of the forest. Since then Hansen's workshop of twenty-five skilled workers has turned out 9000 of these chairs. Would this be an industry or a handicraft? Hans Wegner now designs for eight Danish factories where his chairs are produced in larger numbers.

Most of today's Scandinavian furniture comes from the Danish market. One of the important earlier designers was Finn Juhl, the architect. He worked for the mass industrial market and for custom or craft designing. The crafted pieces were made in Denmark by Niels Vodder. Names that have recurred in the post-World War II period are Ib Kofod-Larsen, architect; Arne Jacobsen, whose molded plywood three-legged chair was so popular; and O. Molgaard-Nielsen, whose laminated demountable furniture was known as *Ax*. Vernor Panton has created some of the far-out designs.

Other European countries have entered the furniture market. Greece, Yugoslavia, the Netherlands, and Switzerland may be considered the latest arrivals. England continued to produce a volume of simple, stalwart wood (often bleached oak) and some steel furniture which does not defy tradition but nevertheless is streamlined. Canada is now competing.

America is one of the most important producers of modern furniture, some of which is designed by expatriate Europeans and much by native talent. The work is largely industrially manufactured, and except for a few notable craftsmen the individual designers remain anonymous.

How recently modern emphasis has been shown may be illustrated by the fact that when the United States was invited to participate in the Paris 1925 Exposition President Coolidge declined on the premise that this country had no significant contribution to make. And this was the home of Frank Lloyd Wright!

Nevertheless the European exhibition displays were avidly visited, and soon the American stores introduced wares, most of which were procured abroad and are now known as "Art Deco." Geared to quick merchandising, they were prime examples of what Giedion called the "transitory facts" in a culture[18]—a fashion which fastens onto whatever is out front in the current intellectual atmosphere and gives it a concrete body in a salable commodity. The weathercock but scarcely the wind.

Much of the furniture manufactured in the late twenties and early thirties in America was angular. It lacked a sense of rhythmic proportions, was heavily glossed, and labored under the delusion that machine-fabricated embellishment could substitute for good form.

The more plush designing of the two emigrant Viennese, Claude Bragdon (1866–1947) and Josef Urban, became popular in wealthy circles. Interiors done in America by the Germans—decorative painter Winold Reiis and designer Kem Weber—were Bauhaus garbled with "Art Deco." They appealed to the public taste for theatricality, so dominant after the harrowing experiences of the war. Paul Frankl of Vienna designed furniture in the same style, one from which he did not frequently depart throughout his successful career as producer and teacher at the University of Southern California. Nevertheless, his frequent use of steel and a modular system placed him in the ranks of the early functionalists.

Schools played their part in the introduction of modern. As early as 1925 Eliel Saarinen won the commission to design the forty-building complex for the Cranbrook Academy of Art, which became under his subsequent direction a nucleus for avant-garde designing. Bauhaus emigré László Moholy-Nagy (1895–1946), a Hungarian who had come to America in 1937 and taught at several eastern colleges, founded the Chicago School of Design in 1939. The name of this school was changed to the Institute of Design in 1944 and now is affiliated with the Illinois Institute of Technology. Black Mountain College in North Carolina offered a similar Bauhaus-type curriculum. The textile department in this southern school, under the direction of the famous weaver Anni Albers, began a trend toward handicrafting in that medium. The distinguished professor of art Josef Albers, who has contributed so much to the theories of color and shape at Yale University, began his American career at Black Mountain College. Walter Gropius and his staff pursued a more fundamentally Bauhaus curriculum at Harvard after the 1933 closing of the German school.

Nor should we forget that the Museum of Modern Art opened its doors in 1929 and that the Metropolitan had a significant showing of industrial art that same year. These are what Giedion would call "constituent facts"—those pregnant for the future.

The best American talent began to recognize that mere glossing of useful objects for quick merchandising would in the end prove an unsatisfying and ruinous course. Walter Dorwin Teague (1883–1960) was the first President and Fellow of the *Society of Industrial Designers,* an organization founded in 1938 which has consistently taken the lead in promoting modern design on a creative level and necessarily allied to the industrial processes.

The *American Institute of Interior Designers* was first founded in 1931 under the name of the *American Institute of Decorators.* This name was later changed to that of *Interior Designers* as a more accurate description of the work done by its members. The *National Society of Interior Designers* was organized in 1957 as the second group to engage in this endeavor. The two are now merged as the *American Society of Interior Designers.* Thus a stronger force involved in the planning and executing of the proximate environment was created. During the early years of these organizations the names of Elsie de Wolfe, Nancy McClelland, Dorothy Draper, and numerous others had great influence on the nature of interior design in America.

Russel Wright (1904–1976), who started his career as designer for the theater, found that he preferred to work in a more practical area of industrial art. His workshop of the twenties expanded to include furniture and accessories, especially ceramics. He was among the first to correlate a complete line of room furnishings at an economical price level. Beginning with the fantasy required and native to the theater, it is remarkable how this pioneer of modern design gradually turned toward a plain contemporary form that could retain its preeminence for another half century.

At the outbreak of World War II (several pavilions were closed on the eve of their opening), the New York World's Fair of 1939 may be considered a terminus of the first period of industrial design in America. Whereas the first World's Fair in Chicago had been called the architect's fair, the later one was aptly named the Industrial Designer's Fair. The Board of Design of that exhibition read as a roster of the leading pioneers in America. In addition to Walter Dorwin Teague, there was Norman Bel Geddes, Donald Deskey, Henry Dreyfuss, Lurelle Guild, Raymond Loewy, Gilbert Rohde, George Sakier, and Russel Wright. These men kept their positions as stars in the American designing firmament.

In 1941 the Museum of Modern Art sponsored a competition for good furniture design that used new industrialized techniques. The winning entry was a set of furniture by the young Eero Saarinen and his Cranbrook colleague, Charles Eames. Their line of seating furniture was constructed of laminated plywood pressed as a shell planned to suit the contours of the human body. It was articulated to the supports by a rubber joint that allowed flexibility of position. Upholstered in foam rubber and contemporary textiles, it was also light in weight. The chairs, subsequently produced by the Herman Miller Company of Zeeland, Michi-

gan, became the ancestors of a long line of distinguished seating pieces designed by Eames on some modification of the same principle (Figure 7.45).

Isamu Noguchi, son of a Japanese poet and professor and an American mother, is a sculptor of note who hand crafted a free-form low table as a custom piece. With glass top and ebonized base, it has been captured in essence and produced by the Herman Miller Company.

The first design director for this company was Gilbert Rohde. At his death the architect George Nelson succeeded to the position. He has also been a designer of interiors and of a highly successful line of modular furniture. The storage wall and the series of interlocking chairs for use in public spaces have been adopted throughout the commercial world. The stacking chair, first done by Alvar Aalto and further developed by Nelson, has proved a favorite. Nelson is an interesting and thoughtful spokesman for the modern cause.

The Baker Company of Holland, Michigan, which specializes in making fine furniture in the traditional styles, produced one line designed by the Dane Finn Juhl whose work we have already

Figure 7.45 Lounge chair and stool. Charles Eames, designer; Herman Miller Company, manufacturer. (Action Office System, Herman Miller, Inc., Zeeland, Michigan 49464.)

mentioned. Although Juhl's pieces were subsequently discontinued, they marked an introduction to Scandinavian design in America.

Jens Risom began his career in Copenhagen in the firm of his father, an architect. He came into furniture-design by the William Morris route, first creating for his own home. After a short working period in Sweden he came to America in 1938. At that time he said that he

> . . . found little in America to become excited about. The only two furniture designers who worked with the modern were Edward Wormley with the Dunbar Company, and Gilbert Rohde with Herman Miller.

Risom formed an acquaintance with Hans Knoll and together they planned the opening of a company that dealt with contemporary furniture for the architectural field. Jens Risom designed some of the first furniture for the new venture—the Hans Knoll Company. He worked for the firm until he went to war in 1943. Returning to practice in 1946, he opened his own establishment (Figure 7.52) which produced some of the finest contemporary furniture. The burgeoning postwar growth of skyscrapers and large commercial building complexes ensured firms that would satisfy the needs of a continuing sales outlet.

Knoll Associates was an American counterpart of the European Werkstätte and Werkbunds. It consisted of a group of associated designers dedicated to the production and merchandising of modern furnishings. It did not, however, include a scholastic program. In cooperation with the Knoll Planning Unit which coordinated designing in the field of interiors and of architecture, and which was under the direction of Mrs. Hans Knoll (Florence Knoll), herself an architect, the Knoll name has become synonymous with good contemporary work, especially in the International Style. Following the tragic death of Mr. Knoll in 1958, Florence S. Knoll (now Mrs. Bassett) carried on all aspects of the business until quite recently.

One type of furniture which the firm has produced features the use of the rigid steel frame from which fabric is hung for back and seat. The hammock is the ancestor of this idea, and designer Vietti who first made the chair in 1939 sus-

pended netting from an iron bar frame. A removable saddle leather was used in similar manner by designer Hardoy in 1941.

Eero Saarinen's shell or "leaf" chair has already been mentioned. It is another of Knoll's important chairs and was so named because, in its three-dimensional orientation, it resembled a bent leaf. With iron or steel supports, laminated shell, and synthetic foam upholstery, it has been a favored product of the firm. This is one of the first modern chairs that is interesting from whatever angle viewed, thus meriting the sobriquet—the silhouette chair. It is a modern counterpart of the wing chair in its quality of embracing the human form and giving it psychological shelter. Similar pieces fit well into the open space of contemporary interiors where furniture is no longer placed parallel to a wall. Saarinen's plastic unipedestal chair, which seems to hold the body aloft on such a slender support to provide the effect of weightlessness, is the latest of the group bearing his name. Saarinen said:

> A chair should look well as a piece of sculpture in a room. It should also look well when someone is sitting in it. And finally it should be flattering to the person sitting in it.[19]

These requirements set up a new category of functions.

Knoll markets some of the pieces designed by the Bauhaus group and the Barcelona of Mies van der Rohe in particular. It may then seem a little strange that the firm should favor the designs in solid wood done by George Nakashima. His respect for and expert craftsmanship with his medium has resulted in chairs that have the sturdy quality of early American prototypes with the slightly greater verve associated with today's models.

Harry Bertoia, the Italian-American sculptor in metal, was the designer of a series of chairs with metal mesh bodies and shaped frames that serve ideally for semioutdoor locations.

Speaking of one thing leads to another, and the degree of invisibility found in the Bertoias has been carried further in Estelle and Erwine Laverne's (a team of New York designers) production of the "invisible chair" of clear plastic. Their artistic output includes many other types of object, such as textiles and wallpapers.

It is no disparagement on the eminence of Edward Wormley as a designer that we have come to his story so late in this narrative of pioneers. His career with the Dunbar Furniture Company was so continuous and so linked with the firm's success that it merits unique attention. Since 1931 his furniture, which is at once easy for the traditionalist to enjoy and at the same time what a modernist with love for furniture suitable for contemporary spaces could wish—well made and elegant in an easy, straightforward masculine way—has held its position well near the central axis of preferment.

Many other men were prominent throughout the thirties and forties. There was the English-born Terence Harold Robsjohn-Gibbings, who opened his New York showroom as early as 1936 after a successful business in London. In his new location he designed on a custom basis and for industry. His approach was never marked with radical experimentation with new techniques. Rather his was a cleaned-up version of Neoclassic design done in light woods, which in late years he sharpened to historical accuracy in respect to Greek classical furniture. As an architectural student and designer in Britain, he planned room ensembles, and his atonal creations, in harmonies of blond, muted colors, created spacious-appearing backgrounds and became one of the fashionable trademarks of the early modern.

Paul McCobb, a designer with a similar approach, produced furniture that had a classical quality without appearing to be traditional. Some see Shaker influence in his work. This was in part achieved by new materials such as metal, stone, or plastic for parts or for ornament. He much favored an all-white scheme which added to the effect of preciosity.

One of the characteristics of American production has been the impermanence of its financial structure. Manufacturing and sales companies change ownership frequently and it requires regular visits to the wholesale markets to keep abreast not only of the new models but also of the new owners. There often seems to be no cataclysmic change in either and certainly no revolutionary trends such as the early part of the century wit-

nessed. The daily attritions, the small aberrations that change our culture so slowly, suddenly produce the new.

Where was modern furniture going after the fifties? Possibly not so far as the 1966 exhibition entitled "Fantasy Furniture" at New York's Museum of Contemporary Crafts would prepare us to believe. Here Fabio De Sanctis, with other artists, entertained with a sort of furniture theater of the absurd. Yet there is much of the current revolutionary doctrine in their words:

> We do not consider furniture as an end in itself, but as an experience, an extension of human feeling, freed from the limitations of functionalism and capable of restoring man to his own identity.[20]

The Knoll Gavina Group, taking its name from the recent acquisition of the Gavina group of Milan, introduced large pieces with amorphous leather cushioning as well as articles that are ingeniously modular foam-cushioned cubes with no rigid support. This latter is often, and even affectionately, called monkey island furniture, to be combined and located at will in open space.

On the one hand we see Warren Platner's (Knoll-produced) chair of bronzed steel wire (Figure 7.46) in the sculptured tradition of the "leaf," the rigid members of which create a pattern of light refraction and color as one moves. On the other, we regard the seemingly irrational examples (Figure 7.47) perpetrated by the Finn Yro Kukkapurous, the Dane Aagard Anderson, and the French Olivier Mourgue, as well as by the Italians. What is of tomorrow?

TEXTILES

Italy. As an impoverished nation, Italy could not forge to the front with modern textiles. Its tradition of luxury and complex silk patterns placed a damper on large-quantity production. The Italian color sense, however, and the inventive facility of her artists turned her emphasis toward printed fabrics. These were done on cottons and linens and on both fine and textured silks.

The Florentine printed silks of Emilio Pucci (as

Figure 7.46 Chair. Warren Platner, designer; Knoll International, manufacturer. Bronzed steel wire. (Courtesy of Knoll International.)

well as his carpets) displayed color ensembles that rivaled the palettes of many modern painters. The Venetian firm of Fortuny, in existence since the last century, with its process of multiple dyeing and printing has turned from old traditional patterns to create fabrics suited to the modern manner.

France. Since the early years when Paul Poiret drafted not only fabrics for women's clothes but also complex weaves for decorative uses, France has provided a succession of notable textile designers. Artists such as Raoul Dufy, Albert Lorenzi, Paul Vera, and Charles Martin created silk damasks, brocades, and hand-blocked linens for the firm of Bianchini-Ferier. Dufy's creations as pattern weaves and prints have a holiday, race-track air, roses, and beautiful people—just the milieu of the "effervescent twenties." Marie Laurencin, known for her portraiture of stylized young women with a distinctly French pink-and-blue femininity, produced wallpapers that conveyed the same feelings. Indeed the French were prone

to continue the use of *papier peintes.* As these were frequently used with curtains of the same design, many artists worked on fabrics and paper.

Jean Lurçat, who assumed the chairmanship of the International Tapestry Center, composed tapestries and embroideries as well as wall papers. The upsurge in the use and manufacture of *tapisseries* is not due solely to the money that the French government poured into the industry but is caused even more by the aesthetic appropriateness of tapestries in contemporary interiors. They can offer just the right amount of pattern and texture for hard surfaces of plaster and glass.

Lurçat was a one-time cubist painter who escaped from Paris after the Nazis burned his studio and killed his paratrooper son. He resettled at Aubusson where he found use for his talents by making cartoons for the local weavers whose stocks had been vandalized. With an artist's appreciation of the potentials of texture and broken color to be preserved in this art and with a twen-

Figure 7.47 *Lower left:* Lounge chair, 1968. Pierre Paulin, designer; Artifort Co., the Netherlands, manufacturer. Stretch fabric cover over urethane on steel frame. Height, 62.2 cm. Museum of Modern Art, New York. (Collection, The Museum of Modern Art, New York. Gift of the manufacturer and Turner T. Ltd., New York.) *Upper right:* Chaise, 1965. Olivier Mourgue, designer; Airborne International, France, manufacturer. Stretch fabric over urethane on steel frame. Length, 1.68 m. The Museum of Modern Art, New York. (Collection, The Museum of Modern Art, New York. Gift of George Tanier, Inc., New York.)

tieth-century outlook on style, he reduced the number of colors, coarsened the thread count, and gave an added dynamism to the pattern. His subjects center around nature or the les happy fate of modern man.

Some of the most prominent French painters shared in the making of these twentieth-century tapestries. Marcel Gromaire worked with Lurçat as an organizer of the movement. Fernand Léger, Maurice Andre, and Jean Picart Le Doux were well-known participants. Although many exhibitions showed these paintings on the loom, the response of the weaving world was not always enthusiastic. It was, in fact, rather easy to distinguish the cloths designed by the men who were masters of the loom and those who were primarily painters. Another unfortunate circumstance relates to the era in which the tapestry renaissance occurred. Jagged patterns of cubist derivation and typical symbols of the "Art Deco" world like those that appeared in Erté's (*nom de plume* for Romain de Tirtoff, 1892–, Petrograd) designs for tableaux in the Folies Bergère—minstrels, lyres, birds, symbolic landscapes emanating from surrealism—all detract from the monumental grandeur which could have been built into tapestry wall hangings.

In *England* such prominent painters as Graham Sutherland turned their talents to tapestry (e.g., the altar tapestry in Coventry Cathedral).

Scandinavia. The textile output of the Scandinavian countries is in the tradition of centuries of hand weaving. There is a sturdiness even in their sheers that reflects a bias toward practicality. Sometimes this is accomplished by tight beating on the loom. Again it relates to a deep, resilient pile (Figure 7.48) in the *Rya* technique, which is similar to oriental knotting done on prepared canvas, or it may be sheer but strong open weaves for the filtering of light at windows. Colors are generally pale and, except for some Finnish carousals which counterpoint reds and oranges in almost eastern splendor, they are inclined to ensemble around soft gray-blue. Northern cultures quite understandably use deep furs as textural foil.

Prominent *Finnish* weavers include the Triennale winner Dora Jung, who in 1957 showed a bleached linen damask which had interlacings of

thin, dark lines. Carpet weaving, in addition to the output of the Marimekko mills, is represented by many small enterprises. Marjatta Metsovaara-Nystrom had her own weaving studio. Eva Anttila's delicately etched patterns and Martaa Taipale's larger bolder designs have both been shown in America. In bidding for the foreign market, the firm of Printex made printed textiles that were popular for their clean-cut, fresh-colored, folk-art expressions.

Swedish textiles have also been influenced by handicrafts. A weaver of world renown was Astrid Sampe, who was associated with *Nordiska Com-*

Figure 7.48 Rug, *Deep River*, America, 1964. Brita Sjoman. Wool, Ghiordes knot. Length, 1.72 m, width, 1.07 m. Cleveland Museum of Art. (The Cleveland Museum of Art. Mary Spedding Milliken Memorial Fund.)

panet, Ltd., as director of textiles. This unique Stockholm store has a program of underwriting the designing and weaving of textiles for which it constitutes an outlet. Age Faith-ell handweaves her textiles in an old house in Vaxjo. Like so many artists, she feels the need to get away from cities and industry for her creative work. We may mention, among prominent Swedish weavers, Viola Grasten, and Barbro Nilsson, who was art director for Marta Maas-Fjetterstrom in Bastad where only hand weaving was done.

Norwegian art is predominantly that of textiles. The establishment of Norwegian Tapestries, Ltd., and the firm of Roros Tweed are the principal larger enterprises.

Denmark is much industrialized in its textile production. Screen printing was introduced as early as 1934 by Marie Gudme Leth, and impetus was given to showing large-scaled and clear-cut patterns. After World War II the Danes branched into woven cloths. Lis Ahlmann and Gerda Henning, who had worked with Kaare Klint, became the leaders of this renaissance.[21]

United States. Here as in England—industrialization. Nevertheless, it was handloom experimentation that paced progress. New uses—window hangings and room dividers—were created to give the warmth of art and handicraft to today's interiors (Figure 7.49). In the textile empire Dorothy Liebes (1899–1972) had undeniable right to the accolade First Lady of the Loom. Her handwoven fabrics and her machine production of similar weavings demonstrated a successful and artistic marriage of the two types of processes.

In printed fabric the designs of Ruth Reeves set the tone for patterns and colors, any motif of which might be used as a brilliant hanging. During the thirties Marion Dorn also designed for both printed textiles and for wallpapers.

The roster of the famous contains a large contingent of Europeans. Loja Saarinen (wife of Eliel) and Marianne Strengell Dusenbury, both from Finland, oriented the textile department at Cranbrook toward experimentation on the hand loom. Lili Blumenau from Germany studied with Anni Albers, director of weaving at Black Mountain College, among other prestigious institutions.

During the thirties and forties the sisters Mariska

Figure 7.49 Textile, *Pine Frost,* America, 1975. Dorothy Turobinski. Wool, Rayon, and Lurex. Length, 2.13 m, width, 76 cm. (Photo courtesy of Dorothy Turobinski.)

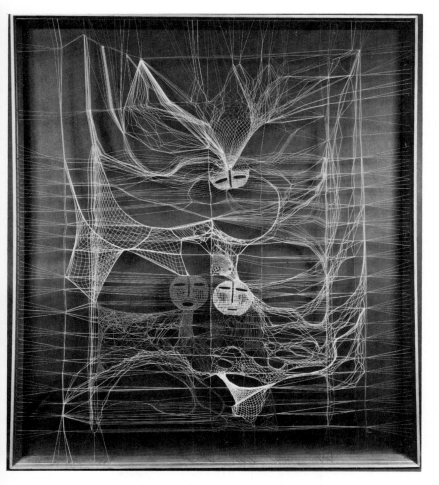

Figure 7.50 Fiber art, *Gemini*, Czechoslovakia, 1977. Luba Krejcí, fiber artist. Niták-knotted linen. Width, 140 cm, height, 120 cm. Cleveland Museum of Art. (The Cleveland Museum of Art. Gift of the Textile Arts Club.)

and Ilonka Karasz, working in textiles and papers, respectively, came from Hungary to enrich commercial offerings and museum collections in America. Mariska forged a reputation and a future tradition in the manner of creating and using large embroideries as wall and room dividers. Hers were abstract designs of the most subtle texture and color variations. One outcome has been the spate of macramé and the unique processes used by individual weavers to effect fantastic hangings and mobiles (Figure 7.50). Ilonka's cover designs for the New Yorker have endeared her and the cityscape to us all.

Jack Lenor Larsen, who includes the architec-

tural and design departments of the University of Washington as well as Cranbrook in his itinerary to fame, has become one of the top-ranking textile artists in America. He produces for industry today.

The patterned loomed textiles of Boris Kroll stand out as staunch contributions to upholstery needs. Kroll always advocated the use of the hand loom for experimentation. In his New York showroom he maintained one for the purpose of ironing out the bugs in texture and color schemes to be woven on the power loom.

Imported textiles from the Far East have contributed to the riches of contemporary output. They have also served to alter many a westerner's limited sense of color arrangements. James Thompson acted as entrepreneur for the "Thaibok" textiles of Thailand and Margit Pintar broke ground with her African textiles. Incidentally, Thompson is another of the war casualties whose fate is unknown.

Occasionally weavings designed in America have been produced on foreign and less expensive workshops. The carpets of Stanislav V'Soske, which were once subtle textural harmonies in traditional patterns, have taken on a twentieth-century cast since being woven on Puerto Rican looms (as well as in Grand Rapids, Michigan). Edward Fields is notable as a designer and producer of contemporary floor coverings.

Alexander Girard, born in New York City and graduated from the Royal Institute of British Architects in 1929, has been a designer of tableware and fabrics, the latter for the Herman Miller Company. His patterns for upholstery and curtains are frequently correlated.

Artist Ben Rose designed printed fabrics for his own industry in custom colors, a new market trend. Ruth Adler and Dan Cooper executed screen prints in the same manner. Silk screening, a stencil-type technique that blocks off areas to resist color, allows more economical production of smaller orders.

On the Pacific coast Michael Belangie of "menlo textiles" has operated power looms for custom weaves, a direction that seems sane in a market that needs some specialized products.

Tendencies which could never have crystallized except by large syndicates are those that feature the new synthetics (particularly the monofilament olefins), the plastics, the functionally oriented finishes, permanent three-dimensional fabric molding, and knitting (e.g., stretch fabrics), to name a few.

CERAMICS

Italy. It is said that if an Italian artist had twelve plates to decorate and was told to make them all alike each would be different, although they would form a compatible group. Colorful ceramics in glazed pottery of such individualized patterns, some intended for table use, some pure flights of decorative fancy, constitute much of the Italian repertoire. The Florentines Prisco and Urbano Zaccagnini and Lucio Fontana of Albisola have done sculptured pieces reminiscent of the Baroque in their emotional intensity, whereas Guido Gambone, also from the flower city on the Arno, showed forms that are Etruscan in their simplicity. Fausto Melotti of Milan fashioned his figures from sheets of clay, thereby creating shapes that in their attenuation resemble those of Giacometti.

The old firm of Ginori, just outside Florence, produces the most important porcelain currently made in Italy.

France. France is not noted for her twentieth-century ceramics, yet at Vallauris in the south, a long-time craft center and home of such potters as M. Picault, designing and ornamenting has been done by topflight artists like Arp, Chagall, Matisse, and Picasso. Old established firms have bowed to the contemporary in some of their lines; for instance, Haviland at Limoges has used Jean Dufy as a designer.

Germany. In Bavaria, close to France, hard-paste china in industrialized production is made at numerous factories. Most, such as Arzberg and Rosenthal, have adopted contemporary shapes and patterns.

Scandinavia. The Arabia Porcelain Company is the big ceramic name in Finland. Its processing is unique in that one artist may follow his production from the clay to the last glazing. Aune Siimes was one of the first artists to popularize Arabia's simplified contemporary shapes done in fine porcelain rather than in pottery or stoneware. The Austrian Friedl Kjellberg revived the old oriental process of rice porcelain at that factory. Rut Bryk is one of the more recent designers to gain fame with her trays and wall panels in heavily glazed nuances of texture and color. Michael Schilkin is known for his monumental architectural reliefs. The list of promising young talent at Arabia augurs well for the future.

The firm of Gustavsberg in Sweden makes hard paste. Professor Wilhelm Kage, the "grand old man of Swedish ceramics," was one of that company's early designers in the modern idiom. The factories of Rorstrand and the new Slojforeningen and the Upsala-Ekeby fall in line. Stig Lindberg and Tyra Lundgren helped with their skills.

In Norway, where Porsgrund is the only large factory, most of the contemporary work is done by individuals in private studios.

Denmark is an enterprising land of porcelain. Bing and Grondahl Porcelain emphasizes contemporary designing. Even the Royal Porcelain has at least curtsied to the modern. A unique ceramist is Nathalie Krebs, who through her chemical and technical knowledge has made Saxbo (a firm which grew from her 1929 workshop) stoneware famous. The well-known enterprise of Dansk has succeeded in many modern media and especially in the making of enameled steel ovenware. (Incidentally, Ireland is a runner-up.)

England and America. The long tradition of fine porcelain has been a deterrent to any English experimentation with new forms, but some breakthrough is evident. Indeed, Bernard Leach, one of the world's most famous potters, was from Cornwall. Studying in Japan in a companionship with the great Japanese potter, Shoji Hamadan, he not only perfected his technique but also developed his feeling for the aesthetic potential in ceramic art.

Henry Varnum Poor (1888–1970) was the dean of American ceramists who worked in the modern idiom. He operated his own kiln in New York in the twenties, when he added the vocation of potter to that of painter. Combining both skills, he threw and fired all the large vases done for the lounge of Radio City Music Hall in New York. They were decorated with human figures in an angular, stylized manner.

Russel Wright, as previously mentioned, arrived at ceramics via the stage-designing route. As fate would have it, he is best remembered for his simplified tableware, made from Georgia clay, heavily glazed in attractive colors and planned without any inner rims to plates and saucers for easy cleaning and greater useful space.

The European migration not only introduced potting as a handicraft skill appropriate to teaching in the schools but also provided an impetus to good modern design. Maija Grotell became head of the ceramics department at Cranbrook. Marianne von Allesch came from central Europe to be one of America's foremost designers. Eva Ziesel introduced fine dinnerware done in con-

Figure 7.51 Ceramic pot, America, 1958. Toshiko Takaezu. Copper-cobalt slip design on white mat glaze. Cleveland Museum of Art. (The Cleveland Museum of Art. The Mary Spedding Milliken Memorial Collection, Gift of William Mathewson Milliken.)

temporary feeling. She worked in a collaboration program between designer, producer (Castleton China Company), and the Museum of Modern Art. This was, in effect, America's answer to the art and industry conundrum.

Toshiko Takaezu (Figure 7.51), who studied under Grotell, ranks at the very top of that list of sensitive creators who, in the oriental tradition, effect a perfect and understated alliance between clay and art. Lisa McVey (Figure 7.52) and Thelma Franzier Winter of Ohio, Harvey Littleton of Wisconsin, Peter Voulkos of California—these are potters whose sculptured pieces echo the many facets of today's designs.

Names could be almost endless, for ceramics seem to satisfy the craving of many to form an intimacy with the earth and with the act of three-dimensional shaping. Careful discrimination will teach which of the practitioners have really attained a high standard of achievement. In this regard it is of interest that Stig Lindberg, in talking to the young Swedish dissenters who were protesting some of the classical principles handed down to them, said:

> You have to keep these things in bounds. I'd be very much concerned if we should see five hundred Swedish potters making things like Peter Voulkos.[22]

GLASS

Glass manufacture is certainly one of the great achievements of the twentieth century. Enormous strong sheets possess the ability to regulate rays—colored, diffused, or crystal clear. Glass can be fabricated for insulation. It is frequently heat-tempered and shatterproof. On it all manner of artistry can be practiced.

The upsurge in glass production closely correlates with the role that light, and particularly artificial light, plays in twentieth-century architecture. During the first part of the era, having at hand a new toy, designers used light in a visible housing as an element of artistry. Thus glass, in shades or screens, came into the picture. These were in the style of the period, fulsomely rounded, sharply angular, or straight tubular. Although more

Figure 7.52 Interior, home of Ernst Payer, architect. Ceramic vase, Lisa McVey; chair, Jens Risom; eighteenth-century Nepalese sculptures; Moroccan rug. (Courtesy of Ernst Payer, A. I. A.)

recent architectural thinking has favored concealed light sources, there is still need for luminaires and their patterning has been one of the newer opportunities for the artist.

Italy. Always a northern Italian craft, glass manufacture near Venice and Milan is experiencing an outstanding renaissance. The firms of Venini and Seguso on the Island of Murano and Fontane Arte in Milan are typical of those that produce art glass and lighting fixtures. Some of the shapes hark back to the soft blown glass forms of soda silica metal; others favor the sharp precision lines of the twenties and thirties. Enameled opaque glass often found in Italian lighting appliances introduced color and light diffusion. Architectural luminaires with steel or brass armatures were featured by designer Vittiuano and architect Cesare Lacca.

France. As the second ancient center of glass making, France has not lagged behind in today's production. The Daum Cristallerie, the Cie des Cristallerie de Baccarat, provide glass in traditional mode as well as in the fashionable manners of the period between the world wars, and in the more logical shapes that the fifties and sixties brought back to the medium.

The glass of René Lalique (1865–1940) is characteristic of the French temperament. Lalique began his career as a creator of jewelry in those days of custom work. Seeking a clear and less expensive medium for his settings, he turned to glass, certainly his mètier. His exhibits in 1925 catapulted him into world fame.

During World War II his Alsacian glass works were evacuated, leaving only a small factory at Coms-la-Ville, near Paris. Lalique presumably perished during the 1940 blackout but the enterprise has been continued by his family. The firm makes some pieces by the plastic mold process in which bits of broken glass (frit) are fired in a refractory mold. Lalique style generally favors the sinuous curves of Art Nouveau but gives its motifs—exotic vegetation, Art Deco animals such as the gazelle, and lithe maidens—a surprising sense of being entrapped in the vessel.

Maurice Marinot was another typical designer of the first part of the century. The Leerdam factory in Holland and the Belgian firm of Val Saint Lambert produce similar glass. Their figure sculptures are frequently so designed that frosted and clear glass interrelations display interesting rhythms of glowing masses when illumined from below.

Scandinavia. The glass industry of the north also has a long tradition. A. B. Notsjo Glasbruk of Finland was founded as a firm in 1793. It is now incorporated with the establishment known as Arabia. Finnish designers make superb use of the scintillating and fanciful character of glass. Riihimaki is a firm that enlisted the services of the artist Helena Tynell, who designed lighting fixtures in which glass bibelots, independently mounted on slender metal wires, throw moving shadows onto walls and ceiling. Her husband, Paavo, specialized in production for industrial lighting. Examples of his work are to be seen in the office of the Secretary-General of the United Nations.

The Karhula Iittala Glassworks of Finland are not only famous for their general output but also because they boast two original artists in the medium—Tapio Wirkkala and Timo Sarpaneva. Both are versatile and are at home with other materials. Wirkkala favors free sculptural form. He feels that a preordained shape might limit the spontaneous potentiality that springs unannounced from the blowpipe. He follows his work from start to finish, doing his own blowing. In wood his specialty is lamination, and he builds up a block from which he hews his tables, bowls, and sculptured abstracts. The artist uses the grains of the wood in the same manner that he uses the hollow bubbles of glass for free form.

It should be mentioned that before World War II some of the state factories in Germany were turning out creditable work not unlike that of their Finnish neighbors across the Baltic. Sharp, angular Art Deco movements marked much of their engraving.

Swedish and Norwegian glass is so well thought of that it scarcely requires comment. The Swedish firm of A. B. Kosta Glasbruk was founded in 1792. Victor Lindstrand has been the artistic head of Kosta since 1950. His conception that glass is the one material with intrinsic beauty has permeated the entire modern industry.

Orrefors Glasbruk is equally famous. *Bruk* is the name for glass factories in Sweden, and most of them are found far from the life in the large cities. Orrefors was bought almost by chance in 1913 by Johan Ekman because he had admired the vast forests on the estate. The small house on the grounds, which was engaged in blowing bottles and window glass, caught his fancy, and in 1916 he decided to place Simon Gate (1883–1945) in charge of its design. A year later he added Edward Hald, who came from Kosta. The name of Gate is associated with the *Graal* technique, which is the lineal descendant of Gallé's layering process. The etched, cut, or engraved patterns are slightly melted into the glass, thus providing opportunities for new color effects. His *Ariel* glass, with air bubbles incorporated, is likewise a trademark. Both *Graal* and *Ariel* bear the name of the artist.

Many young Swedish artists are helping to forge the image of fine glass. Erik Höglund, for instance, creates in glass and in bronze for Ab Boda Glasbruk. In addition to his smaller sculptures of figures poised in action and his many vitric witticisms, he has turned out large architectural installations. Höglund is another artist who sets colored glass into concrete walls (see later) and makes glass tiles to ornament wood. Bruno Mathsson planned the "House of Glass" for Kosta (1954), built on a 200-year-old foundation.

Hadelands is Norway in glass, and in Denmark, the Holmegaard Glassworks should be mentioned. Glass, however, is not the major star in either firmament.

In *America* both industrial manufacture and handcrafting are flourishing and distinct. The Steuben Division of the Corning Glass Company crosses over the lines, much like the small fur-

Figure 7.53 *Lunar vase.* David Dowler, designer. Blown lead glass with solid base. An air bubble appears to rise out of a cylindrical cut textured to a luminous tone of grey. (Courtesy, Steuben Glass, Corning, New York.)

naces in Scandinavia (Figure 7.53). Here in off-hand glass of the finest metal, the foremost artists, such as the architect John Monteith Gates and the sculptor Sidney Waugh, who inaugurated the artistic career of the company in 1933, design expensive as well as more modestly priced glass. Much of the output is intended to be of museum quality and new series of this caliber are constantly emerging from the furnaces. In 1940 one group boasted pieces by some of the world's leading artists, among whom were Henri Matisse, Salvador Dali, and Aristide Maillol. In 1950 the Englishman Sir Jacob Epstein, in 1954 Graham Sutherland, and in 1956 a famous coterie of Asian artists froze patterns in crystal. One cannot decry, among all these masterworks, Steuben's little animals that smile (Figure 7.54). They are little gems in their field.

The idea of the individual craftsman, working in glass from metal to the finished piece in his own small backyard furnace, has grown in America. The outstanding glass artist, Edris Eckhardt, has revived the lost technique of gold laminated between sheets of colored glass. The many layers of metals fired at different temperatures ensure refractions that are indescribably beautiful.

Harvey Littleton, already mentioned as a teacher and potter at the University of Wisconsin, has been instrumental in the revival of individual glass production in America. Like the fancies of Tapio Wirkkala, the creations of his pupils are marked by unprescribed shapes. Littleton's own pieces possess an integral beauty by virtue of the expanding bubble that he keeps in mind in determining the appropriate form.

In much of this glass the only reason to peg it as of one country or another is the location of the furnace. This is particularly true of modern stained glass. French *vitraux*, which were derived from Art Nouveau but with between-wars angularity, are illustrated by the windows and doors of Leon Barillet and Paul Vera. More recently, Marc Chagall, the expressionist painter, made the windows that illustrate the thirteen tribes of Israel for the Synagogue of the Hadassah Medical Center in Jerusalem. Today we are witnessing a renaissance in the production of stained glass art in the modern manner.

The architect Wallace K. Harrison used the concrete framing method in the windows of the First

Figure 7.54 Crystal cat with pointed ears and green tourmaline eyes. Height, 11.4 cm. (Courtesy, Steuben Glass, Corning, New York.)

Presbyterian Church at Stamford, Connecticut, in the manner of the powerful glass in the baptistry by Jean Bazaine (Plate 14) at Audincourt, France. The main church windows at Audincourt, which lack the force of those of the Baptistry, are by Fernand Léger. Experimentation with glass set into wood, with glass whose pattern is outlined in brass, and with glass bonded by clear epoxy-resin adhesives has opened new vistas in use of glass fragments in frames.

Because its future is just unfolding, we can only note the promising field of plastics as an art medium. Jan de Swart from Holland, now in California, pioneered much experimentation in this area.

METALS, ENAMELS, STONES

The stone mosaics, *pietra dura,* which were revived as an industry by the American Peter Blow on his estate at Montici, near Florence, have proved one of the highly decorative examples of contemporary crafts. The initial enterprise has fathered many similar ones, but the proximity to the great glass mosaics of Ravenna seems to have

given the Italians an edge on designing for flat pattern and dazzling color juxtaposition.

Despite Lindstrand's contention for the uniqueness of glass, the contemporary artist appreciates the integral beauty of stone (as indeed he appreciates wood). Isamu Noguchi, for instance, is using marble, porphyry, and granite in forms only slightly altered by the hand to make stunning fountains and equipment for semioutdoor settings. Notice here that the water usually jets (Figure 7.55), so different from the Baroque splashing of Rome's seventeenth-century waterworks but more in keeping with twentieth-century force.

Gio Ponti in Milan has produced copper and bronze utensils with the earmarks of Etruscan forging and with singular adaptation of old shapes to modernity.

In France the pioneer of the century's work in steel as an ornamental medium was Edgar Brandt. His earliest decorative grilles of steel and iron with their Art Deco motifs may now seem dated, but later pieces with a less realistic basis indicate the advance made by an artist who understood his material. Jean Puiforçat during the thirties wrought modern utilitarian silver, stressing plain surfaces and the diagonal thrust. The sculptors Jacques Lipchitz and Aristide Maillol often designed small articles such as andirons and screens, which had practical uses.

In the firm of Georg Jensen (1866–1935) and erstwhile partner Johan Rohde (?–1935) Danish silver attained the status of fine art. Silver is a native Norwegian specialty. Jacob Prytz (1886–1962) was the dean of Norwegian silversmiths. His daughter Greta Prytz Korsmo is one of Norway's leading enamelists.

The English silversmith Robert Welch has fabricated vessels of bold simplicity. He has also designed for industry in other metals.

American artists have been providing museum-quality accompaniments to interior design. The opening of the New York Museum of Contemporary Crafts provided the opportunity to view outstanding work. The silver of Frederick Miller (Figure 7.56) and the enamels of Kenneth Bates are superb examples.

Large enamel panels are the means of introducing color to exterior and interior. They have been made by such artists as Edward Winter and

Paul Hultberg to create individually designed sources for colored and patterned accents. Outdoors, they withstand exposure and combine well with modern architecture.

Abstractions in metal, such as the sculptured screen (70 × 18 ft) that Harry Bertoia made for the Manufacturer's Trust Company (1954) (New York) and again for the General Motors Technical Center (Detroit), serve as interest-getters in steel and glass buildings, which suit the rigidity of the lines of the architecture and join with the reflections from glass and metal yet provide a textural foil in the rough surface of the blocks.

DESCRIPTIVE SUMMARY

By the eighties of this century time has silenced the voices of many of the prophets of the new in architecture and environmental arts. Modern design, which began more than 100 years ago with the forms and symbols of earlier periods, has finally crystallized some positive images. What the leaders said and did has changed the landscape, set the norms, and enlarged the outlook of our world.

We have now arrived at a point of perspective at which we can claim some understanding of the results. Undoubted success has been obtained in the design of commercial, industrial, civic (Figures 7.57 and 7.58), and religious buildings which embody a cultural vision: on one side in relation to the Germanic sense of order, discipline, and science, on the other in terms of organic nature, the outcome of which is both magnificent and awesome (see Plate 16 and frontispiece). Even the great builders are beginning to appreciate that science and nature, and whatever it is that governs the universe, are not antithetical—indeed, they are closely interconnected.

The answer to creation for the private domain is always more complex and it is difficult to solve its problems by fiat. In the private world deep-rooted values, little-understood psychological sensitivities, and differing financial means suggest not one but many answers. In an industrial society training is required to help secure the ways in which our civilization can find its personal fulfillment. To find such norms is in reality the most serious problem we face. The twentieth century has made some brave tries at solutions but the problem has not yet been solved. Only when training is by teamwork and only when such training carries a big dose of education for the development of artistic sensitivity will any answer be found (Figure 7.59). And only today's generation can be equipped to find tomorrow's solutions.

Figure 7.55 Fountain in Cleveland's Erieview Development, 1966–1968. Harrison and Abramovitz, New York, architects. In the background is the Celebrezze Federal Building, 1966. Outcalt, Guenther, Rode and Bonebrake; Shafer, Flynn and Van Dijk; Dalton and Dalton, architects. (G. C. Ball.)

393

FINIS

As lives carry their own benediction, so a book should write its own confirmation. The following, therefore, is somewhat of a confession that this has not been done.

These two volumes have been an account of the struggle of western civilization for a satisfactory environment in which to live, work, and worship, a struggle that began before sedentary cultures. The method of meeting this goal has long been rooted in concepts that catered to man's practical sense, his notion of propriety, and his commitment to beauty. As new peoples, new ideas, and new skills were assimilated, this framework was given novel interpretation and new styles developed.

During the last two centuries western culture has expanded horizontally (geographically speaking) and vertically (economically speaking). At the same time the technique of creating an environment has been radically changed and the means of obtaining it has been commercialized. This is really an age of revolution, possibly peaceful because spread on so many fronts. Because of this, we cannot expect the environmental arts to descend solely from St. Denis or Versailles, nor yet from St. James, Dessau, Wiener Werkstätte, or Williamsburg. They will have traffic with the Kasbah, Hong Kong, and probably Bulawayo, possibly courtesy of Bloomingdale's.

Giacometti sculptured his metal image of man (Figure 7.60) in a lonely world where some scien-

Figure 7.56 (above) Pair of candlelabra, America, 1962. Frederick A. Miller, artist-craftsman. Silver with enameled bobeches and ebony leg tips. Height (without candles), 38 cm. (Courtesy of the artist; photograph by John Paul Miller.)

Figure 7.57 (below) The Garden Center of Greater Cleveland, 1966. William and Geoffrey Platt, architects. (Courtesy, The Garden Center of Greater Cleveland; C. W. Ackerman, photographer.)

Figure 7.58 The Eleanor Squire Library at the Garden Center of Greater Cleveland, 1966. (Courtesy, The Garden Center of Greater Cleveland; C. W. Ackerman, photographer.)

Figure 7.59 Living room at Windermere House, home of Hope L. Foote. (Courtesy of Hope L. Foote; house, carport, and lot by H. L. Foote). Hope L. Foote was Chairman of the Department of Interior Design, the University of Washington, Seattle. This school is one of an increasing number at which the teaching of architecture and interior design are coordinated.

Figure 7.60 *Walking Man,* Switzerland, 1947–1948. Alberto Giacometti. Bronze. Height, 67.3 cm. Hirshhorn Museum, Washington, D.C. (Hirshhorn Museum and Sculpture Garden, Smithsonian Institution.)

tists claim that space is encroaching on matter. We are inclined to think of matter as the only world of reality, things we can love and touch. But is it? It is the relation between space and matter—interrelations—that not only posses the supreme question for twentieth-century physics and gives art its encompassing rhythms but also provides life with whatever it has of meaning (Figure 7.61).

The Greek architect viewed his work with a sculptor's eye, perfecting its form; the Roman, with a potter's view, considered the interior of the vessel as well as its shell; the Gothic builder saw as the mystic, enervating his world with an inner vision that reached for the ineffable. The modern designer, who was born shortly after Galileo, looks with the aid of a telecamera that reveals space, mass, and time, a view that encompasses many worlds never seen before. In common with the scientist and the cleric, the architect ap-

Figure 7.61 *Genesis,* 1960. Donald Pollard, glass designer. Terry Haas, engraving designer. Height, 22.9 cm. (Courtesy, Steuben Glass, Corning, New York.) The rhythm of space and matter suggests the Creation and the music of the spheres.

Figure 7.62 Living room and dinette, home of Bertha Schaefer, New York. (Courtesy of Bertha Schaefer. Photographer, Bill Jackson. From *The Art of Interior Design,* © Victoria K. Ball, 1960, The Macmillan Company.) This contemporary setting features the harmonious use of furnishings and art from many periods and countries.

praises, as did Plato, the chances for stability and value in change. He is charged with producing its habitable image. In this task he must be an artist of his day.

Energy and matter—for two centuries scientific talk of movement and power has characterized their examination. We are prone to forget that the music of the spheres, the language of poetry, has also provided descriptions of great elegance, beauty, and subtlety (Figure 7.62). It is the function of the arts to reach across all manner of barriers and to unify understanding on the level of human experience. Where better than in the proximate environmental arts? And how better than in feeling and thinking through to solutions that come close to being for all—not as a sameness but as an alikeness?

To each age new routes to old ends.
To each generation—
To each life—

Honesty

Structure

Function—Expression—DESIGN (incorporating
Movement—Choice—Tension—Rest)

A whole

A meaning.

397

General References

There is no surer way for a writer to cut himself down to size than by attempting a bibliography. The lacunae in his own reading glare from every card index compendium. The basis for the inclusion of any book must be a combination of readability, availability, and quality—all neatly balanced by particular purpose. Neither date of publication nor of reprint can be certain guides. This list is offered with a modest hope that it will answer various purposes. As the text is intended to be no more than an introductory survey, so its bibliography should lead from there. This is a process of finding an interest and then going on to ever-widening horizons and deeper knowledge.

This bibliography takes us only into the first round. Many of the books can be bought on today's market without breaking the bank. Those with high prices or early publication dates may be found in libraries. Some of the best sources for up-to-date information are the magazines dedicated to the history of the arts which we are studying. The latest findings and viewpoints will naturally appear there before they can find their way into more expensive books. In the decorative arts the catalogs of noteworthy museum collections should be consulted and acquired whenever possible. Specialized bulletins of the leading museums are rich sources of erudite material. These entice one to travel in order to visit treasures at first hand. Such personal experience will give the serious student a lifetime of pleasure and can add a dimension that even the finest reproductions in books cannot convey.

Architecture

ALEXANDER, DRURY BLAKELY. *Texas Homes of the Nineteenth Century.* Austin, Texas: University of Texas Press, 1966.

ANDREWS, WAYNE. *Architecture, Ambition, and Americans.* London: Free Press and Collier-Macmillan, 1964.

BAYER, HERBERT, Walter Gropius, and Ise Gropius. *Bauhaus, 1919–1929.* Boston: Branford, 1952.

BEIRNE, R. R. and J. H. SCARFF. *William Buckland, 1734–1774, Architect of Virginia and Maryland.* Baltimore: Maryland Historical Society, 1958.

BLASER, WERNER. *Mies Van der Rohe, The Art of Structure.* New York: Praeger, 1965.

BORSI, FRANCO, and PAOLO PORTOGHESI. *Victor Horta.* New York: Wittenborn, 1970.

BRAUN, HUGH. *Old English Houses.* London: Faber & Faber, 1962.

BRIGGS, MARTIN SHAW. *Homes of the Pilgrim Fathers in England and America, 1620–1685.* London: Oxford University Press, 1932.

BURCHARD, JOHN E., and AIBERT BUSH-BROWN. *Architecture in America.* Boston: Little, Brown, 1961.

BUSH-BROWN, ALBERT. *Louis Sullivan.* New York: Braziller, 1960.

CANTACUZINO, SHERBAN. *European Domestic Architecture: Its Development from Early Times.* Great Britain: Dutton, Studio Vista, 1969.

————. *Modern Houses of the World*. New York: Dutton, Studio Vista, 1964.

CHOAY, FRANCOISE. *Le Corbusier*. New York: Braziller, 1960.

COLVIN, H. M. *A Biographical Dictionary of English Architects, 1660–1840*. Cambridge, Harvard University Press, 1954.

CONNOLLY, CYRIL, and JEROME ZERBE. *Les Pavillons*. New York: Macmillan, 1962.

De NOLHAC, PIERRE. *Versailles and the Trianons*. New York: Dodd, Mead, 1907.

DILL, ALONZO T. *Governor Tryon and His Palace*. Chapel Hill: University of North Carolina Press, 1955.

DREXLER, ARTHUR. *The Architecture of Japan*. New York: Museum of Modern Art, 1955.

————. *Ludwig Mies Van der Rohe*. New York: Braziller, 1960.

DUTTON, RALPH. *The Chateaux of France*. London: Batsford, 1957.

EBERLEIN, HAROLD DONALDSON and CORTLANDT VAN DYKE HUBBARD. *Historic Houses of George Town and Washington City*. Richmond, Virginia: Dietz Press, 1958.

ENGLE, HEINRICH. *The Japanese House*. Rutland, Vermont: Tuttle, 1964.

FITCH, JAMES MARSTON. *American Building: The Forces that Shape It*. Boston: Houghton Mifflin, 1948.

————. *Walter Gropius*. New York: Braziller, 1960.

FLEIG, KARL. *Alvar Aalto*. New York: Wittenborn, 1975.

FLEMING, JOHN, HUGH HONOUR, and NIKOLAUS PEVSNER. *The Penguin Dictionary of Architecture*. Harmondsworth: Penguin, 1966.

FLETCHER, BANISTER FLIGHT. *A History of Architecture by the Comparative Method*. 17th ed. New York: Scribner's, 1961.

FORD, JAMES, and KATHERINE MORROW. *The Modern House in America*. New York: Architectural Book, 1940.

FORD, KATHERINE MORROW, and THOMAS H. CREIGHTON. *The American House Today*. New York: Reinhold, 1951.

GALLET, MICHEL. *Stately Mansions: 18th Century Paris Architecture*. New York: Wittenborn, 1972.

GARVIN, AMEILA BEERS (WARNOCK). *Historic Houses of Canada*. Toronto: Ryerson, 1952.

GAUTHIER, JOSEPH-STANY. *Les Maisons Paysannes des Vielles Provinces de France*. Paris: Charles Massin, 1951.

GIEDION, SIEGFRIED. *The Eternal Present: The Beginnings of Architecture*. 2 vols. Princeton: Princeton University Press, 1962 and 1964.

GROPIUS, WALTER. *The New Architecture and the Bauhaus*. Cambridge: M.I.T. Press, 1965.

GROPIUS, WALTER, and others. *Katsura: Tradition and Creation in Japanese Architecture*. New Haven: Yale University Press, 1960.

GUINNESS, DESMOND, and WILLIAM BRYAN. *Great Irish Houses and Castles*. New York: Viking, 1978.

GUTHEIM, FREDERICK. *Alvar Aalto*. New York: Braziller, 1960.

HAMLIN, TALBOT. *Architecture, an Art for all Men*. New York: Columbia University Press, 1961.

————. *Greek Revival Architecture in America*. London: Oxford University Press, 1944.

HARRIS, JOHN. *Sir William Chambers: Knight of the Polar Star*. New York: Wittenborn, 1970.

HAYASHI, MASAKO. *House Design in Today's Japan*. New York: Wittenborn, 1969.

HILDEBRAND, GRANT. *Designing for Industry: The Architecture of Albert Kahn*. New York: Wittenborn, 1973.

HITCHCOCK, HENRY-RUSSELL. *Architecture: 19th and 20th Centuries*. 2nd ed. Baltimore: Penguin, 1963.

————. *The Architecture of H. H. Richardson and His Times*. Hamden, Connecticut: Archon, Shoestring, 1961.

————. *Boston Architecture 1637–1954*. New York: Reinhold, 1954.

————. *Early Victorian Architecture in Britain*. 2 vols. New Haven: Yale University Press, 1954.

————. *Gaudi*. New York: Museum of Modern Art, 1957.

HITCHCOCK, HENRY-RUSSELL, and PHILIP C. JOHNSON. *The International Style*. New York: Norton, 1932.

HONNOLD, DOUGLAS. *Southern California's Architecture 1767–1950*. New York: Reinhold, 1956.

HUNT, WILLIAM DUDLEY, Jr. *Encyclopedia of American Architecture*. New York: McGraw-Hill, 1980.

HUSSEY, CHRISTOPHER, and JOHN CORNFORTH. *English Country Houses*. 3 vols. New York: Oxford University Press, 1955–1958.

————. *English Country Houses Open to the Public*. 4th ed. London: Country Life, 1964.

HUXTABLE, ADA LOUISE. *Classic New York: Georgian Gentility to Greek Elegance*. New York: Doubleday, 1964.

————. *Pier Luigi Nervi*. New York: Braziller, 1960.

INN, HENRY. *Chinese Houses and Gardens*. Edited by S. C. Lee. New York: Hastings House, 1950.

JACOBUS, JOHN M., Jr. *Philip Johnson*. New York: Braziller, 1692.

JEANNERET-GRIS, CHARLES EDOUARD (Le Corbusier). *Le Corbusier, 1910–1960*. Zurich: Editions Girsberger, 1960.

JOHNSON, PHILIP C. *Architecture 1949–1965*. With an introduction by Henry-Russell Hitchcock. New York: Holt, Rinehart & Winston, 1966.

————. *Mies van der Rohe*. The Museum of Modern Art. New York: Simon & Schuster, 1947.

KELLY, JOHN FREDERICK. *Early Domestic Architecture of Connecticut*. Magnolia, Massachusetts: Peter Smith, 1964.

KIMBALL, FISKE. *The Creation of the Rococo*. Reprint of 1943 ed. Philadelphia Museum of Art. New York: Norton, 1964.

————. *Domestic Architecture of the American Colonies and of the Early Republic*. New York: Scribner's, 1927.

————. *Thomas Jefferson, Architect*. New York: Wittenborn, 1967.

KIRKER, HAROLD. *California's Architectural Frontier*. San Marino, California: Huntington Library, 1960.

KISHEDA, HIDETO. *Japanese Architecture*. Tokyo: Japan Travel Bureau, 1960.

LAVEDAN, PIERRE. *French Architecture*. Harmondsworth: Penguin, 1956.

LEWIS, OSCAR. *Here Lived the Californians*. New York: Holt, Rinehart and Winston, 1957.

LLOYD, NATHANIEL. *A History of the English House from Primitive Times to the Victorian Period*. New ed. London: Architectural Press, 1951.

LOCKWOOD, CHARLES. *Bricks and Brownstones: The New York Row House, 1783–1929*. New York: McGraw-Hill, 1972.

MAJOR, H. *The Domestic Architecture of the Early Republic, The Greek Revival*. Philadelphia: Lippincott, 1936.

MASSON, GEORGINA. *Italian Villas and Palaces*. New York: Abrams, 1959.

MAZZOTTI, GUISEPPE. *Venetian Villas*. Rome: Carlo Bestetti-Edizioni d'Arte, 1957.

MEEKS, CAROLL L. V. *Italian Architecture, 1715–1914*. New Haven: Yale University Press, 1965.

MOHOLY-NAGY, SYBIL. *Native Genius in Anonymous Architecture*. New York: Schocken, 1976.

MORRISON, HUGH. *Early American Architecture*. New York: Oxford University Press, 1952.

MORSE, EDWARD S. *Japanese Homes and Their Surroundings*. Magnolia, Massachusetts: Peter Smith, 1961.

MUMFORD, LEWIS. *The Roots of Contemporary American Architecture*. New York: Grove, 1959.

MURTAUGH, WILLIAM J. *Moravian Architecture and Town Planning, Bethlehem, Pa and Other 18th Century American Settlements*. Chapel Hill: University of North Carolina Press, 1967.

MUSGRAVE, CLIFFORD. *Royal Pavilion: An Episode in the Romantic*. Rev. enl. ed. London: L. Hill, 1959.

NEUTRA, RICHARD JOSEPH. *L'Architecture d'Aujourd'hui*. Translated by Helen Persitz. Boulogne, 1946.

NEWCOMB, REXFORD. *Architecture of the Old Northwest Territory*. Chicago: University of Chicago Press, 1950.

————. *Old Mission Churches and Historic Houses of California*. Philadelphia: Lippincott, 1925.

————. *Spanish-Colonial Architecture in the United States*. New York: Augustin, 1937.

PAULSSON, THOMAS. *Scandinavian Architecture*. London: L. Hill, 1958.

PEVSNER, NIKOLAUS. *An Outline of European Architecture*. Baltimore: Penguin, 1960.

PINKNEY, D. H. *Napoleon III and the Rebuilding of Paris*. Princeton, New Jersey: Princeton University Press, 1972.

PLACE, CHARLES A. *Charles Bulfinch, Architect and Citizen*. New York: Da Capo, 1968.

QUARMBY, ARTHUR. *Plastics in Architecture*. New York: Praeger, 1973.

REILLY, H. C. *McKim, Mead and White*. New York: Scribner's, 1924.

REYNOLDS, HELEN WILKINSON. *Dutch Houses in the Hudson Valley before 1776*. New York: Dover, 1965.

RICHARDS, J. M. *Introduction to Modern Architecture*. Baltimore: Penguin, 1962.

ROGERS, ERNEST N. *The Works of Pier Luigi Nervi*. New York: Praeger, 1957.

SAARINEN, ALINE B. *Eero Saarinen on His Work*. New Haven: Yale University Press, 1962.

SANDFORD, TRENT ELWOOD. *The Architecture of the Southwest*. New York: Norton, 1950.

SCULLY, VINCENT J., Jr. *Louis I. Kahn*. New York: Braziller, 1962.

————. *Modern Architecture, the Architecture of Democracy*. New York: Braziller, 1961.

————. *The Shingle Style: Architectural Theory and Design from Richardson to the Origins of Wright*. New Haven: Yale University Press, 1955.

SHURTLEFF, HAROLD ROBERT. *The Log Cabin Myth: A Study of the Early Dwellings of the English Colonists in North America*. Cambridge: Harvard University Press, 1939.

SITWELL, OSBERT, and MARGARET BARTON. *Brighton*. London: Faber & Faber, 1948.

SITWELL, SACHEVERELL. *Great Houses of Europe*. 2nd ed. New York: Putnam, 1964.

SMITH, G. E. KIDDER. *The New Architecture of Europe: An Illustrated Guidebook and Appraisal*. New York: World, 1961.

STANTON, PHOEBE. *Pugin*. With a Preface by Nikolaus Pevsner. London: Thames and Hudson, 1971.

STUBBLEBINE, JO. *The Northwest Architecture of Pietro Belluschi*. New York: Dodge, 1953.

SUMMERSON, JOHN. *Architecture in Britain: 1530–1830*. 4th rev. and enl. ed. Harmondsworth: Penguin, 1963.

————. *The Classical Language of Architecture*. Cambridge: M.I.T. Press, 1963.

401

TANGE, KENZO. *Katsura: Tradition and Creation in Japanese Architecture.* New Haven: Yale University Press, 1972.

TORROJA, EDUARDO. *Philosophy of Structures.* Translated by J. J. & Milos Polivka. Berkeley: University of California Press, 1958.

VAN RENSSELAER, MARIANA. *Henry Hobson Richardson, and His Works.* Boston: Houghton, Mifflin, 1888.

WATERMAN, THOMAS TILESTON. *The Dwellings of Colonial America.* Chapel Hill: University of North Carolina Press, 1950.

————. *Early Architecture of North Carolina.* Chapel Hill: University of North Carolina Press, 1947.

————. *The Mansions of Virginia. 1706–1776.* Chapel Hill: University of North Carolina Press, 1946.

WHITE HOUSE HISTORICAL ASSOCIATION. *The White House: An Historic Guide.* Washington, D.C.: White House Historical Association, 1963.

WILSON, SAMUEL, Jr. *New Orleans Architecture.* Gretna, Louisiana: Pelican, 1971.

WITTKOWER, RUDOLPH. *Art and Architecture in Italy: 1600–1750.* Baltimore: Penguin, 1965.

WRIGHT, FRANK LLOYD. *An American Architecture.* Edited by Edgar Kaufmann. New York: Horizon Press, 1955.

————. *An Autobiography.* New York: Duell, Sloan and Pearce, 1943.

————. *The Natural House.* New York: Horizon Press, 1954.

YOSHIDA, TETSURO. *The Japanese House and Garden.* New York: Praeger, 1955.

ZEVI, BRUNO, and EDGAR KAUFMANN, Jr. *F. Lloyd Wright's Falling Water.* 2nd ed. Milan: Etas Kompass, 1965.

Art History

ARNASON, H. H. *History of Modern Art: Architecture, Sculpture and Painting.* New York: Abrams, 1977.

CLARK, KENNETH. *The Gothic Revival: An Essay in the History of Taste.* New York: Harper & Row, Icon, 1974.

THE DETROIT INSTITUTE OF ARTS. *French Taste in the Eighteenth Century.* Exhibition Catalogue. Detroit: Detroit Institute of Arts, 1956.

FAULKNER, RAY, and EDWIN ZIEGFELD. *Art Today: An Introduction to the Visual Arts.* 5th ed. New York: Holt, Rinehart & Winston, 1969.

GARDNER, HELEN. *Gardner's Art Through the Ages.* 6th ed. Revised by Horst de la Croix and Richard G. Tansey. New York: Harcourt Brace Jovanovich, 1975.

GOWANS, ALAN. *Images of American Living: Four Centuries of Architecture and Furniture as Cultural Expression.* Philadelphia: Lippincott, 1964.

HILLIER, BEVIS. *Art Deco of the 20s and 30s.* Great Britain: Dutton, Studio Vista, n.d.

HOLT, ELIZABETH G., Ed. *A Documentary History of Art.* 2 vols. Garden City, New York: Doubleday, 1958.

————. *From the Classicists to the Impressionists: A Documentary History of Art and Architecture in the Nineteenth Century.* Garden City, New York: Doubleday, Anchor, 1966.

JANSON, H. W. *History of Art.* Rev. and enl. ed. Englewood Cliffs, New Jersey: Prentice-Hall, 1969.

LEE, SHERMAN E. *A History of Far Eastern Art.* Englewood Cliffs, New Jersey: Prentice-Hall; New York: Abrams, 1964.

————. *Japanese Decorative Style.* New York: Prentice-Hall, 1961.

LENNING, HENRY F. *The Art Nouveau.* The Hague: M. Nijhoff, 1951.

MAASS, JOHN. *The Gingerbread Age.* New York: Holt, Rinehart and Winston, 1957.

MUMFORD, LEWIS. *The Brown Decades: A Study of Arts in America, 1865–1895.* Magnolia, Mass.: Peter Smith, 1960.

PAINE, ROBERT TREAT, and ALEXANDER COBURN SOPER. *The Art and Architecture of Japan.* Baltimore: Penguin, 1955.

PEVSNER, NIKOLAUS. *High Victorian Design, A Study of the Exhibits of 1851.* London: Architectural, 1951.

————. *Pioneers of Modern Design.* Rev. ed. Baltimore: Penguin, 1964.

————. *The Sources of Modern Architecture and Design.* New York: Praeger, 1968.

POPE, ARTHUR U. *An Introduction to Persian Art Since the Seventh Century A.D.* Reprint of 1931 ed. Westport, Connecticut: Greenwood, 1972.

SCHMUTZLER, ROBERT. *Art Nouveau.* Translated by Edouard Roditi. New York: Abrams, 1964.

SELZ, PETER, and MILDRED CONSTANTINE, Eds. *Art Nouveau: Art and Design at the Turn of the Century.* Museum of Modern Art. Garden City, New York: Doubleday, 1959.

SICKMAN, LAURENCE C., and ALEXANDER COBURN SOPER. *The Art and Architecture of China.* 2nd ed. Baltimore: Penguin, 1960.

WARNER, LANGDON. *The Enduring Art of Japan.* New York: Grove, 1958.

WITTKOWER, RUDOLPH. *Art and Architecture in Italy: 1600–1750.* 2nd. rev. ed. Baltimore: Penguin, 1965.

Carpets

BODE, WILHELM von, and KÜHNEL. Translated by Charles Grant Ellis. *Antique Rugs from the Near East.* 4th rev. ed. Braunschweig: Klinkhardt and Biermann, 1958.

CALATCHI, ROBERT de. *Oriental Carpets.* New York: Wittenborn, 1967.

DILLY, ARTHUR URBANE. *Oriental Rugs and Carpets.* Revised by Maurice B. Dimond. Philadelphia: Lippincott, 1959.

DIMAND, M. S. *Oriental Rugs in the Metropolitan Museum of Art.* With a catalog of Rugs of China and Chinese Turkestan, by Jean Mailey. New York: Metropolitan Museum of Art, 1973.

ERDMANN, KURT. *Oriental Carpets.* New York: Universe, 1962.

HACKMARK, ADOLPH. *Chinese Carpets and Rugs.* New York: Dover, 1973.

HAWLEY, WALTER AUGUSTUS. *Oriental Rugs, Antique and Modern.* New York: Tudor, 1937.

JARRY, MADELAINE. *The Carpets of the Manufacture de la Savonnerie.* Leigh-on-Sea: F. Lewis, 1966.

LEWIS, GEORGE GRIFFIN. *The Practical Book of Oriental Rugs.* New rev. ed. Philadelphia: Lippincott, 1945.

MUMFORD, JOHN KIMBERLY. *Oriental Rugs.* New York: Scribner's, 1929.

REED, CHRISTOPHER DUNHAM. *Turkoman Rugs.* Cambridge: Fogg Art Museum, Harvard University, 1966.

ROSANSTIEL, HELENE von. *American Rugs and Carpets from the Seventeenth Century to Modern Times.* New York: Morrow, 1978.

Ceramics

BARRET, F. A. *Worcester Porcelain.* London: Faber & Faber, 1952.

BARRET, RICHARD CARTER. *Bennington Pottery and Porcelain.* New York: Crown, 1958.

BEURDELEY, MICHEL. *Chinese Trade Porcelain.* Translated by Diana Imber. Rutland, Vermont: Tuttle, 1962.

BOGER, LOUISE A. *Dictionary of World Pottery and Porcelain.* New York: Wittenborn, 1971.

BURTON, WILLIAM. *A General History of Porcelain.* 2 vols. London and New York: Cassell, 1921.

————. *History and Description of English Porcelain.* Elmsford, New York: British Book Center, reprint of 1924 ed.

CHAFFERS, WILLIAM. *Marks and Monograms on European and Oriental Pottery and Porcelain.* London: Reeves, 1954.

COX, W. E. *The Book of Pottery and Porcelain.* London: Batsford, 1947.

EBERLEIN, HAROLD DONALDSON, and ROGER WEARNE RAMSDELL. *The Practical Book of Chinaware.* New ed. enl. and rev. Philadelphia: Lippincott, 1948.

HANNOVER, EMIL. *Pottery and Porcelain.* Edited by Bernard Rackham. 3 vols. London: E. Benn, 1925.

HONEY, WILLIAM BOWYER. *English Pottery and Porcelain.* 5th ed. rev. London: A. C. Black, 1964.

HOOD, GRAHAM. *Bonnin and Morris of Philadelphia: The First American Porcelain Factory, 1770–1772.* Institute of Early American History and Culture at Williamsburg, Virginia. Chapel Hill: University of North Carolina Press, 1972.

KELLY, ALISON. *Decorative Wedgewood in Architecture and Furniture.* London: Country Life, 1965.

KOVEL, RALPH M., and TERRY H. KOVEL. *Dictionary of Marks: Pottery and Porcelain.* New York: Crown, 1953.

LANE, ARTHUR. *Early Islamic Pottery.* London: Faber & Faber, 1947.

————. *French Faience.* London: Faber & Faber, 1948.

————. *Later Islamic Pottery: Persia, Syria, Egypt, Turkey.* London: Faber & Faber, 1957.

LITCHFIELD, FREDERICK. *Pottery and Porcelain.* Revised and edited by Frank Tilly. New York: Barrows, 1963.

LIVERANI, G. *Five Centuries of Italian Majolica.* New York: McGraw-Hill, 1960.

MILLER, ROY ANDREW. *Japanese Ceramics.* After the text by Seiichi Okuda and others. Tokyo: Toto Shippan, 1960.

ORMSBEE, THOMAS H. *English China and Its Marks.* Great Neck, New York: Deerfield, 1959.

OSGOOD, C. *Blue and White Chinese Porcelain.* New York: Ronald Press, 1956.

PHILLIPS, J. G. *China-Trade Porcelain.* Cambridge: Harvard University Press, 1956.

RACKHAM, BERNARD. *Italian Majolica.* London: Faber & Faber, 1952.

SAVAGE, GEORGE. *Eighteenth Century English Porcelain.* London: Rockliff, 1952.

————. *Porcelain through the Ages.* Baltimore: Penguin, 1954.

————. *Pottery through the Ages.* New York: Barnes & Noble, 1964.

VYDROVA, JIRIKA. *Italian Majolica.* London: Spring House, 1960.

Clocks

BRITTEN, F. J. *Old Clocks and Watches and Their Makers.* 7th ed. G. H. Baillie, C. Clutton, and C. A. Ilbert, Eds. New York: Bonanza, 1956.

BRUTON, ERIC. *Clocks and Watches, 1400–1900.* New York: Praeger, 1967.

DREPPARD, CARL W. *American Clocks and Clockmakers.* Boston: Bransford, 1958.

LOOMES, BRIAN. *The White Dial Clock.* New York: Drake, 1975.

PALMER, BROOKS. *The Book of American Clocks.* New York: Macmillan, 1950.

Design Theory

BERENSON, BERNARD. *Aesthetics and History.* Garden City, New York: Doubleday, Anchor Books, 1948.

BREUER, M. *Sun and Shadow.* New York: Dodd, Mead, 1955.

EASTLAKE, CHARLES LOCKE. *Hints on Household Taste.* 3rd ed. London: Longmans, Green, 1872.

FRANKL, P. T. *Form and Reform.* New York: Harper, 1930.

FULLER, R. BUCKMINSTER. *Synergetics.* New York: Wittenborn, 1975.

GIEDION, SIEGFRIED. *Space, Time and Architecture.* 4th ed. enl. Cambridge: Harvard University Press, 1962.

GILBERT, KATHERINE EVERETT, and HELMUT KUHN. *A History of Aesthetics.* Rev. and enl. Bloomington: Indiana University Press, 1954.

GREENOUGH, HORATIO. *Form and Function: Remarks on Art, Design, and Architecture.* Edited by Harold A. Small. Berkeley and Los Angeles: University of California Press, 1966.

ITTEN, JOHANNES. *Design and Form: The Basic Course at the Bauhaus.* New York: Reinhold, 1963.

JEANNERET-GRIS, CHARLES EDOUARD (Le Corbusier). *New World of Space.* New York: Reynal and Hitchcock, 1948.

———. *Modulor: A Harmonious Measure to the Human Scale Universally Applicable to Architecture and Mechanics.* 2 vols. Cambridge: Harvard University Press, 1954–1958.

———. *Towards a New Architecture.* New York: Praeger, 1959.

KAUFMAN, EMILE. *Architecture in the Age of Reason.* Cambridge: Harvard University Press, 1955.

MALRAUX, ANDRÉ. *The Voices of Silence.* Translated by Stuart Gilbert. Princeton: Princeton University Press, 1978.

MORRIS, WILLIAM. *Hopes and Fears for Art.* London: Longmans, Green, 1917.

MUNRO, THOMAS. *The Arts and Their Interrelations.* New York: Liberal Arts Press, 1949.

REYNOLDS, SIR JOSHUA. *Discourses on Art.* With an introduction by Robert R. Wark. New York: Collier Books; London: Collier-Macmillan, 1966.

RUSKIN, JOHN. *The Seven Lamps of Architecture.* New York: E. P. Dutton, 1965.

SCOTT, GEOFFREY. *The Architecture of Humanism.* Garden City, New York: Doubleday, Anchor, 1954.

SULLIVAN, LOUIS L. *The Autobiography of an Idea.* New York: Dover, 1956.

TEAGUE, WALTER DORWIN. *Design this Day.* 2nd ed. New York: Harcourt, Brace and World, 1949.

WITTKOWER, RUDOLF. *Architectural Principles in the Age of Humanism.* Columbia University Studies in Art History and Archaeology. New York: Random House, 1965.

ZEVI, BRUNO. *Architecture as Space.* New York: Horizon Press, 1957.

Furniture

ANDREWS, EDWARD DEMING. *Shaker Furniture.* New York: Dover, 1950.

ANDREWS, EDWARD DEMING, and FAITH ANDREWS. *Shaker Furniture.* Magnolia, Massachusetts: Peter Smith, 1964.

ASLIN, ELIZABETH. *Nineteenth Century English Furniture.* New York: Yoseloff, 1962.

BJERKOE, E. H. *The Cabinet Makers of America.* Garden City, New York: Doubleday, 1957.

BRACKETT, OLIVER. *Thomas Chippendale, a Study of His Life, Work and Influence.* London: 1924.

BRUNHAMMER, YVONNE. *Meubles et ensembles epoque Louis XVI.* Paris: Massin, 1965.

———. *Meubles et ensembles epoque Regence et Louis XV.* Paris: Massin, 1965.

———. *Meubles et ensembles epoques directoire et empire.* Paris: Massin, 1965.

BURR, GRACE HARDENDORFF. *Hispanic Furniture.* 2nd ed. rev. and enl. New York: Archive, 1964.

CAMPKIN, MARIE. *Introducing Marquetry.* London: Batsford: 1969.

COLERIDGE, ANTHONY. *Chippendale Furniture: The Work of Thomas Chippendale and His Contemporaries in the Rococo Style.* London: Faber & Faber, 1968.

COMSTOCK, HELEN. *American Furniture: A Complete Guide to 17th, 18th, and Early 19th Century Styles.* New York: Viking, 1962.

CORNELIUS, CHARLES OVER. *Furniture Masterpieces of Duncan Phyfe.* Metropolitan Museum of Art. Garden City, New York: Doubleday, Page, 1922.

DE BELLAIQUE, G. *Furniture, Clocks, and Gilt Bronzes.* 2 vols. James A. de Rothschild Collection at Waddesdon Manor. London: National Trust, 1974.

DITZEL, N., and J. DITZEL. *Danish Chairs.* New York: Wittenborn, 1954.

DOMENECH, RAFAEL (Galissa), and LUIS PEREZ BUENO. *Antique Spanish Furniture.* New York: Archives, 1965.

DOWNS, JOSEPH. *American Furniture: Queen Anne and Chippendale Periods.* The Henry Francis du Pont Winterthur Museum. New York: Macmillan, 1952.

EBERLEIN, H. D., and A. MCCLURE. *The Practical Book of Period Furniture.* Philadelphia: Lippincott, 1914.

EDWARDS, RALPH. *The Shorter Dictionary of English Furniture.* London: Country Life, 1964.

EDWARDS, RALPH, and MARGARET JOURDAIN. *Georgian Cabinet-Makers.* Rev. ed. London: Country Life, 1955.

ELLSWORTH, ROBERT HATFIELD. *Chinese Furniture.* New York: Random House, 1971.

ERIKSEN, SVEND. *Early Neo-Classicism in France.* Translated by Peter Thornton. London: Faber & Faber, 1974.

FALES, DEAN A. *American Painted Furniture 1660–1880.* New York: Dutton, 1972.

FASTNEDGE, RALPH. *English Furniture Styles from 1500 to 1830.* New York: Barnes & Noble, 1964.

———. *Sheraton Furniture.* New York: Yoseloff, 1962.

FREEMAN, JOHN CROSBY. *The Forgotten Rebel:*

Gustav Stickley and His Craftsman Mission Furniture. Watkins Glen, New York: Century House, 1965.

GILBERT, CHRISTOPHER. *The Life and Work of Thomas Chippendale.* London: Christie's and Studio Vista, 1978.

GLOAG, JOHN. *The Englishman's Chair.* London: Allen and Unwin, 1964.

———. *A Short Dictionary of English Furniture.* Rev. and enl. London: Allen and Unwin, 1969.

GONZALES-PALACIOS, ALVAR. *Il Mobile nei secoli: I-III Italia.* Milan: Fratelli Fabbri, 1969.

GRANDJEAN, SERGE. *Empire Furniture.* London: Faber & Faber, 1966.

GREENLAW, BARRY A. *New England Furniture at Williamsburg.* Williamsburg, Virginia: Williamsburg Foundation, 1974.

HACKENBROCH, YVONNE. *English Furniture with Some Furniture of Other Countries in the Irwin Untermyer Collection.* Cambridge: Harvard University Press, 1958.

HARRIS, EILEEN. *The Furniture of Robert Adam.* London: Tiranti, 1963.

HARRIS, JOHN. *Regency Furniture.* London: Tiranti, 1961.

HAYWARD, CHARLES H. *Antique or Fake? The Making of Old Furniture.* London: Evans, 1970.

———. *English Period Furniture.* Rev. ed. London: Evans, 1971.

HAYWARD, HELENA, Ed. *World Furniture: A Pictorial History.* New York: McGraw-Hill, 1965.

HEAL, SIR AMBROSE. *The London Furniture Makers, from the Restoration to the Victorian Era, 1660–1840.* New York: Dover, 1972.

HIMMELHEBER, G. *Biedermeier Furniture.* Translated and edited by S. Jervis. London: Faber & Faber, 1974.

HIORT, ESBJORN. *Modern Danish Furniture.* New York: Architectural, 1956.

HONOUR, HUGH. *Cabinet Makers and Furniture Designers.* London: Weidenfeld and Nicholson, 1969.

HORNOR, WILLIAM MACPHERSON. *Blue Book, Philadelphia Furniture, 1682–1807.* Washington, D. C.: Highland House, 1977.

HUTH, HANS. *Lacquer of the West: The History of the Craft and an Industry 1550–1950.* Chicago and London: University of Chicago Press, 1971.

———. *Roentgen Furniture, Abraham and David Roentgen: European Cabinet-Makers.* London and New York: Sotheby Parke Bernet, 1974.

IVERSON, MARION DAY. *The American Chair 1630–1890.* New York: Hastings, 1957.

JOURDAIN, MARGARET. *Regency Furniture, 1795–1830.* Revised and edited by Ralph Fastnedge. London: Country Life, 1965.

KATES, GEORGE N. *Chinese Household Furniture.* New York: Dover, 1962.

KETTELL, RUSSELL HAWES. *The Pine Furniture of Early New England.* New York: Dover, 1949.

KOVEL, RALPH, and TERRY KOVEL. *American Country Furniture: 1780–1875.* New York: Crown, 1965.

LEDOUX-LEBARD, DENISE. *Les Ébénistes Parisiens: 1795–1830.* Paris: Librairie Grund, 1951.

LIZZANI, GOFFREDO. *Il mobile Romano.* Introduction by Alvar Gonzales Palacios. Milan: Görlich Editore, 1970.

LOCKWOOD, LUKE VINCENT. *Colonial Furniture in America.* Rev. ed. New York: Scribner's, 1957.

LUTHER, CLAIR FRANKLIN. *The Hadley Chest.* Hartford, Connecticut: Case, Lockwood and Brainard, 1935.

MCCLELLAND, NANCY VINCENT. *Duncan Phyfe and the English Regency.* New York: Scott, 1939.

MACQUOID, PERCY. *A History of English Furniture.* 4 vols. London: Lawrence and Bullen, 1938.

MARGON, LESTER. *Masterpieces of American Furniture, 1620–1840.* New York: Architectural, 1965.

———. *Masterpieces of European Furniture, 1380–1840.* New York: Architectural, 1967.

———. *World Furniture Treasures; Yesterday, Today, and Tomorrow.* New York: Reinhold, 1954.

MILLER, EDGAR GEORGE, Jr. *American Antique Furniture.* 2 vols. New York: Barrows, 1937.

MONTGOMERY, CHARLES F. *American Furniture, The Federal Period.* New York: Viking, 1966.

MOORE, MABEL ROBERTS. *Hitchcock Chairs.* Tercentenary Commission. Cambridge: Yale University Press, 1933.

MUSGRAVE, CLIFFORD. *Adam and Hepplewhite and other Neo-Classical Furniture.* London: Faber & Faber, 1966.

———. *Regency Furniture.* London: Faber & Faber, 1961.

NELSON, GEORGE. *Chairs.* New York: Whitney, 1953.

NUTTING, WALLACE. *Furniture of the Pilgrim Century (of American Origin) 1620–1720, with Maple and Pine to 1800.* 2 vols. Rev. and enl. New York: Dover, 1965.

———. *Furniture Treasury.* 4 vols. New York: Macmillan, 1948.

ODOM, WILLIAM M. *A History of Italian Furniture from the Fourteenth to the Early Nineteenth Centuries.* 2 vols. Reprint of 1918–1919 ed. New York: Archive, 1966.

OLIVER, J. L. *The Development and Structure of the Furniture Industry.* London: Pergamon, 1966.

ORMSBEE, THOMAS H. *Field Guide to American Victorian Furniture.* Boston: Little, Brown, 1964.

———. *The Windsor Chair.* London: W. H. Allen, 1962.

OTTO, CELIA JACKSON. *American Furniture of the Nineteenth Century.* New York: Viking, 1965.

RANDALL, RICHARD H., Jr. *American Furniture in the Museum of Fine Arts, Boston.* New York: October House, 1965.

RHODE ISLAND SCHOOL OF DESIGN. *Furniture by the Goddards and Townsends*. Providence, R. I.: Akerman-Standard, 1936.

ROE, FREDERICK G. *English Cottage Furniture*. London: Phoenix House, 1961.

————. *Victorian Furniture (English Victorian)*. London: Phoenix House, 1952.

SALVERTE, COMTE FRANCOIS de. *Les Ébénistes du XVIIIme Siècle*. 3me ed. Paris: Les Éditions d'art et d'histoire, 1923.

SIRONEN, MARTA KATRINA. *A History of American Furniture*. East Stroudsburg, Pennsylvania: Towse, 1936.

SOUCHAL, GENEVIEVE. *French Eighteenth-Century Furniture*. Translated by Simon Watson Taylor. New York: Putnam, 1961.

SPARKES, IVAN G. *The Windsor Chair: An Illustrated History of a Classic English Chair*. Levittown, New York: Transatlantic, 1975.

STONEMAN, VERNON C. *John and Thomas Seymour, Cabinetmakers in Boston, 1794–1816*. Boston: Special Publications, 1959.

SYMONDS, ROBERT WEMYSS, and B. B. WHINERAY. *Victorian Furniture*. New York: Taplinger, 1963.

VERLET, PIERRE. *Eighteenth Century in France—Society, Decoration, Furniture*. New York: Wittenborn, 1967.

————. *French Royal Furniture*. New York: Towse, 1963.

————. *Le Mobilier Royal Français*. 3 vols. Paris: Editions d'art et d'histoire, 1945.

WARD-JACKSON, PETER. *English Furniture Design in the Eighteenth Century*. London: Her Britannic Majesty's Stationery Office, 1958.

WATSON, F. J. B. *Furniture*. Wallace Collection Catalogues. London: Clowes, 1956.

————. *Louis XVI Furniture*. London: Tiranti, 1960.

WHITEHILL, WALTER MIUR, Ed. *Boston Furniture of the Eighteenth Century*. The Colonial Society of Massachusetts. Charlottesville, Virginia: University Press of Virginia, 1974.

Glass

BARBOUR, HARRIET BUXTON. *Sandwich, the Town that Glass Built*. Boston: Houghton, Mifflin, 1948.

THE CORNING MUSEUM OF GLASS. *The Story of Modern Pressed Glass of the Lacy Period: 1825–1850*. Corning, New York: Corning Museum, 1954.

DANIEL, DOROTHY. *Cut and Engraved Glass, 1771–1905: The Collector's Guide to American Wares*. New York: Barrows, 1950.

DAVIS, PEARCE. *The Development of the American Glass Industry*. Cambridge: Harvard University Press, 1949.

HARRINGTON, JEAN CARL. *Glassmaking at Jamestown, America's First Industry*. Richmond: Dietz, 1952.

HAYNES, E. BARRINGTON. *Glass through the Ages*. Baltimore: Penguin, 1964.

HONEY, W. B. *English Glass*. London: Collins, 1946.

HUNTER, FREDERICK WILLIAM. *Stiegel Glass*. New York: Dover, 1950.

KOCH, ROBERT. *Louis C. Tiffany, Rebel in Glass*. New York: Crown, 1964.

MCKEARIN, GEORGE S., and HELEN MCKEARIN. *American Glass*, New York: Crown, 1948.

MCKEARIN, HELEN. *Two Hundred Years of American Blown Glass*. Garden City, New York: Doubleday, 1950.

SALDERN, AXEL von. *German Enameled Glass*. Corning, New York: Corning Museum, 1965.

SCHRIJVER, ELKA. *Glass and Crystal*. 2 vols. New York: Universe, 1964.

SENNETT-WILSON, R. *The Beauty of Modern Glass*. London: Studio, 1958.

THORPE, W. A. *English and Irish Glass*. 3rd ed. New York: Barnes & Noble, 1961.

Interior Design

AMAYA, MARIO. *Art Nouveau*. London: Dutton, Studio Vista, 1966.

DREXLER, ARTHUR. *Introduction to 20th Century Design*. New York: Museum of Modern Art, 1959.

DUTTON, RALPH. *The English Interior, 1500–1900*. London: Batsford, 1948.

————. *The Victorian Home*. London: Batsford, 1959.

EDWARDS, R., and L. G. G. RAMSEY, Eds. *Connoisseur Period Guides: Tudor, Stuart, Early Georgian, Late Georgian, Regency, Early Victorian*. New York: Reynal, 1958.

FLEMING, JOHN. *Robert Adam and His Circle in Edinburgh and Rome*. Cambridge, Massachusetts: Harvard University Press, 1962.

FORD, JAMES, and KATHERINE MORROW FORD. *Design of Modern Interiors*. New York: Architectural, 1942.

FOWLER, JOHN, and JOHN CORNFORTH. *English Decoration in the 18th Century*. London: Barrie and Jenkins, 1974.

HATJE, GERD, and URSULA GERD. *Design for Modern Living*. New York: Abrams, 1962.

JOURDAIN, MARGARET. *English Interior Decoration, 1500–1830*. London: Batsford, 1950.

KAUFMANN, EDGAR, Jr. *What is Modern Interior Design?* New York: Museum of Modern Art, 1946.

LITTLE, NINA FLETCHER. *American Decorative Wall Painting, 1700–1860*. Old Sturbridge Village, Mass. New York: Studio, 1952.

MEYNELL, ESTHER. *Portrait of William Morris*. London: Chapman & Hall, 1947.

OGLESBY, C. *French Provincial Decorative Art*. New York: Scribner's, 1951.

GENERAL REFERENCES

PARK, EDWIN AVERY. *New Backgrounds for a New Age.* New York: Harcourt, Brace and World, 1927.

PEVSNER, NIKOLAUS. *Pioneers of Modern Design: From William Morris to Walter Gropius.* Rev. ed. Harmondsworth: Penguin, Pelican, 1960.

PRAZ, MARIO. Translated by William Weaver. *An Illustrated History of Furnishing from the Renaissance to the Twentieth Century.* New York: Braziller, 1964.

ROGERS, MEYRIC R. *American Interior Design.* New York: Norton, 1947.

————. *Italy at Work.* Italy: Compagnia Nationale Artigiane, 1950.

ROSENTHAL, RUDOLPH, and HELENA L. RATZKA. *The Story of Modern Applied Art.* New York: Harper, 1948.

WATKINSON, RAY. *William Morris as Designer.* New York: Wittenborn, 1967.

YARWOOD, DOREEN. *The English Home: A Thousand Years of Furnishing and Decoration.* New York: Scribner's, 1956.

ZAHLE, ERIK, Ed. *A Treasury of Scandinavian Design.* New York: Golden, 1961.

Metals

BOUQUET, A. C. *European Brasses.* New York: Wittenborn, 1967.

DAVIS, FRANK. *French Silver 1450–1825.* New York and Washington: Praeger, 1970.

DENNIS, FAITH. *Three Centuries of French Domestic Silver.* 2 vols. New York: Metropolitan Museum of Art, 1960.

ENSKO, STEPHEN, G. C. *American Silversmiths and Their Marks II.* New York: Robert Ensko, 1948.

FALES, MARTHA GANDY. *American Silver in the Henry Francis du Pont Winterthur Museum.* Winterthur, Delaware: Winterthur Museum, 1958.

FREDERICKS, J. W. *Dutch Silver, Renaissance through Eighteenth Century.* 4 vols. New York: Heineman, 1953–1961.

GARDNER, JOHN STARKIE. *English Ironwork of the XVII and XVIII Centuries.* New York: Blom, 1972.

GOODISON, NICHOLAS. *Ormolu: The Work of Matthew Boulton.* New York: Phaidon, 1974.

HAYWARD, J. F. *Huguenot Silver in England: 1688–1727.* Faber & Faber, 1959.

HIORT, ESBJØRN. *Modern Danish Silver.* New York: Museum Books, 1954.

KERFOOT, J. B. *American Pewter.* New York: Crown, 1942.

MCLANATHAN, RICHARD B. K., Ed. *Colonial Silversmiths, Masters and Apprentices.* Boston: Museum of Fine Arts, 1956.

MAY, EARL CHAPIN. *Century of Silver, 1847–1947.* New York: McBride, 1947.

PHILLIPS, P. A. S. *Paul de Lamerie.* London: Alsford, 1935.

ROBERTSON, R. A. *Old Sheffield Plate.* New York: Dover, 1957.

TAYLOR, GERALD. *Art in Silver and Gold.* London: Dutton, Studio Vista, 1964.

WENHAM, EDWARD. *Domestic Silver of Great Britain and Ireland.* London: Oxford University Press, 1931.

————. *The Practical Book of American Silver.* Philadelphia: Lippincott, 1949.

Miscellaneous

ACKERMAN, PHYLLIS. *Wallpaper, Its History, Design and Use.* New York: Tudor, 1938.

ANTIQUES MAGAZINE, EDITORS OF. *Antiques at Williamsburg.* New York: Hastings House, 1953.

BUTLER, JOSEPH T. *American Antiques, 1800–1900.* New York: Odyssey, 1965.

COMSTOCK, HELEN. *The Concise Encyclopedia of American Antiques.* New York: Hawthorne, 1958.

THE CONNOISSEUR. *The Concise Encyclopedia of Antiques.* New York: Hawthorne, 1955.

COSTANTINO, RUTH T. *How to Know French Antiques.* New York: Potter, 1961; London: P. Owen, 1963.

HEYDENRYK, H. *The Art and History of Frames.* New York: Heineman, 1969.

KOVEL, RALPH, and TERRY KOVEL. *Know Your Antiques.* New York: Crown, 1967.

LOESSER, ARTHUR. *Men, Women, and Pianos.* New York: Simon and Schuster, 1954.

MCCLELLAND, NANCY V. *Historic Wallpapers.* Philadelphia: Lippincott, 1924.

MAYER, RALPH. *The Artist's Handbook of Materials and Techniques.* New York: Viking, 1953.

PHIPPS, FRANCES. *The Collectors Complete Dictionary of American Antiques.* New York: Doubleday, 1974.

THORNE, J. O., Ed. *Chamber's Biographical Dictionary.* New York: St. Martin's, n.d.

THWING, LEROY. *Flickering Flames: A History of Domestic Lighting through the Ages.* Rutland, Vermont: Tuttle, 1957.

WATSON, F. J. B. *The Wrightsman Collection.* 2 vols. The Metropolitan Museum of Art. Greenwich, Connecticut: New York Graphic Society, 1966.

WATSON, F. J. B., and C. C. DAUTERMAN. *The Wrightsman Collection.* Vol. 3. Metropolitan Museum of Art, 1971.

WEIR, ALBERT E. *The Piano.* New York: Longmans, Green, 1940.

WILLS, G. *English Looking-Glasses (1670–1820).* Foreword by John Hayward. Cranbury, New Jersey: Barnes, 1965.

WINTERNITZ, EMANUEL. *Keyboard Instruments in the Metropolitan Museum of Art.* New York: Metropolitan Museum of Art, 1961.

GENERAL REFERENCES

Periodicals

Abitaire. Italy.

Antiques. New York.

Architectural Design. England.

Architectural Digest. Los Angeles.

Architectural Record. New York.

Architectural Review. England.

Bulletin de Liaison du Centre International d'Etude des Textiles Anciens. France.

Connaissance des Arts. France.

The Connoisseur. England.

Craft Horizons. New York.

Decorative Arts. Winterthur, Delaware

Domus. Italy.

Furniture History. England.

Interior Design. New York.

Interiors. New York

Journal of the Society of Architectural Historians. Philadelphia.

Journal of Interior Design Education and Research. Richmond, Va.

Studio International. England.

Social History

BRIDENBAUGH, CARL. *Cities in the Wilderness: Urban Life in America 1625–1742.* New York: Capricorn, 1964.

———. *The Colonial Craftsman.* Chicago: University of Chicago Press, Phoenix, 1950.

COULBORN, R. *The Origin of Civilized Societies.* Princeton, New Jersey: Princeton University Press, 1959.

LANGER, WILLIAM L., Ed. *Encyclopedia of World History.* Rev. ed. Boston: Houghton Mifflin, 1962.

SUMMERSON, JOHN NEWENHAM. *Georgian London.* New York: Scribner's, 1946.

Source Books

CHIPPENDALE, THOMAS. *The Gentleman and Cabinet-Maker's Director.* Reprint of 1762 ed. With biography and photographic supplement. New York: Dover, 1966.

DOWNING, ANDREW J. *Architecture of Country Houses.* Reprint of 1850 ed. Introduction by J. Stewart Johnson. New York: Dover, 1969.

———. *Cottage Residences or a Series of Designs.* Reprint of 1865 ed. St. Clair Shores, Mich.: Scholarly Books, 1977.

THE GREAT EXHIBITION—LONDON 1851. Facsimile of 1851 ed. New York: Crown, 1970.

HEPPLEWHITE, GEORGE. *Cabinet-Maker and Upholsterer's Guide.* Introduction by Joseph Aronson. Reprint of 1794 ed. New York: Dover, 1969.

HOPE, THOMAS. *Household Furniture and Interior Decoration.* Reprint of 1807 ed. Introduction by David Watkin. New York: Dover, 1971.

PALLADIO, ANDREA. *The Four Books on Architecture.* Reprint of 1738 Ware English ed. Introduction by A. Placzek. New York: Dover, 1965.

SHERATON, THOMAS. *The Cabinet Makers' and Upholsterers' Drawing Book.* Edited by Joseph Aronson. New York: Dover, 1972.

VAUX, CALVERT. *Villas and Cottages.* Reprint of 1864 ed. New York: Dover, 1970.

VIOLLET-LE-DUC, EUGÈNE E. *Discourses on Architecture.* 2 vols. New York: Grove, 1959.

VITRUVIUS, POLLIO MARCUS. *The Ten Books of Architecture.* Translated by Morris Hicky Morgan. New York: Dover, 1960.

Textiles

AMERICAN FABRICS MAGAZINE. *Encyclopedia of Textiles.* New York: Prentice-Hall, 1960.

CLOUZOT, HENRI, and FRANCES MORRIS. *Painted and Printed Fabrics: The History of the Manufactory at Jouy and Other Ateliers in France, 1760–1815, by Henri Clouzot: Notes on the History of Cotton Printing Especially in England and America by Francis Morris.* Metropolitan Museum of Art. Reprint of 1927 ed. New York: Arno, 1972.

DIGBY, GEORGE W. *French Tapestries.* London: Batsford, 1951.

FALKE, OTTO von. *Decorative Silks.* 3rd ed. London: Zwemmer, 1936.

HUNTER, GEORGE LELAND. *Decorative Textiles.* Philadelphia: Lippincott, 1918.

———. *The Practical Book of Tapestry.* Philadelphia: Lippincott, 1925.

JARRY, MADELEINE. *World Tapestry: From Its Origins to the Present.* New York: Putnam, 1969.

LEWIS, ETHEL. *The Romance of Textiles.* New York: Macmillan, 1953.

LITTLE, NINA FLETCHER. *Early American Textiles.* New York: Century, 1931.

LURÇAT, JEAN. *Designing Tapestry.* London: Rohcliff, 1950.

MAYER, CHRISTA. *Masterpieces of Western Textiles.* Chicago: Art Institute of Chicago, 1969.

MONTGOMERY, FLORENCE M. *Printed Textiles, English and American Cottons and Linens, 1700–1850.* A Winterthur Book. New York: 1970.

RODIER, PAUL. *The Romance of French Weaving.* New York: Stokes, 1931.

SANTANGELO, ANTONINO. *A Treasure of Great Italian Textiles.* New York: Abrams, 1964.

TAYLOR, LUCY D. *Know Your Fabrics.* New York: Wiley, 1951.

408

THOMSON, WILLIAM GEORGE. *A History of Tapestry from the Earliest Times until the Present Day.* London: Hodder & Houghton, 1960.

THORNTON, PETER. *Baroque and Rococo Silks.* New York: Taplinger, 1965.

WEIBEL, ADELE C. *Two Thousand Years of Textiles.* New York: Pantheon, 1952.

WEIGERT, ROGER-ARMAND. *La Tapisserie Française.* Paris: Larousse, 1956.

Notes

Chapter 1

1. Henry Steele Commager, Ed., *Documents of American History* (New York: Crofts, 1945), pp. 2–4.
2. Harold Robert Shurtleff, *The Log Cabin Myth* (Cambridge: Harvard University Press, 1939), p. 33.
3. J. Frederick Kelly, *Early Domestic Architecture of Connecticut* (New York: Dover, 1952).
4. Fiske Kimball, *Domestic Architecture of the American Colonies and of the Early Republic* (New York: Scribner's, 1922), p. 298.
5. Anne McVickar Grant, *Memoirs of an American Lady* (London: 1808; New York: Appleton, 1846), quoted by Helen Wilkinson Reynolds in *Dutch Houses in the Hudson Valley before 1776* (New York: Dover, 1928), p. 59.
6. Quoted by Esther Singleton in *Dutch New York* (New York: Dodd, Mead, 1909), pp. 8–9.
7. Quoted by J. Leander Bishop in *A History of American Manufactures 1608–1860,* 2 vols. (Philadelphia: Edward Young, 1864), 1:224.
8. Bishop, *A History of American Manufactures.*
9. Helen Wilkinson Reynolds, *Dutch Houses in the Hudson Valley Before 1776* (New York: Dover, 1928), pp. 149, 151.
10. Laurence Kocher, "Early Building with Brick," *Antiques,* 47 (July 1957).
11. Hazel S. Whipple, "Further Notes on the English Brick Myth," *Antiques,* 47–49 (July 1957).
12. Figures are from Thomas Tileston Waterman, *The Dwellings of Colonial America* (Chapel Hill: University of North Carolina Press, 1950), p. 213.
13. Waterman, *The Dwellings of Colonial America,* p. 125.
14. William Penn, "Information and Direction to such Persons as are Inclined to America, more Especially Those Related to the Province of Pennsylvania" (London, 1684). Copy in Pennsylvania Historical Society.
15. Kimball, *Domestic Architecture of the American Colonies,* p. 265, assigns the date of 1682 to the Letitia House.
16. John L. Cotter, "Jamestowne: Treasure in the Earth," *Antiques,* 44–46 (January 1957).
17. *Virginia a Guide to the Old Dominion* (New York: Oxford University Press, 1940), p. 194.
18. Adam Anderson, *History of British Commerce* (London, 1784).
19. Quoted by Robert W. Symonds in "The English Export Trade in Furniture to Colonial America, Part I," *Antiques,* 214–217 (June 1935).
20. Quoted by Richard B. Bailey in "Pilgrim Possessions 1620–1640," *Antiques* 236–239 (March 1952).
21. Luke Vincent Lockwood, *Colonial Furniture in America,* 2 vols. (New York: Castle Books, 1957), 2:5.
22. Lockwood, *Colonial Furniture in America,* 2:22.
23. The dates for American craftsmen (unless otherwise noted) are taken from Ethel Hall Bjerkoe, *The Cabinetmakers of America* (Garden City, New York: Doubleday, 1957).

24. Walter A. Dyer, "The Tulip and Sunflower Press Cupboard," *Antiques,* 140–143 (April 1935)
25. Bishop, *A History of American Manufactures,* 1:229.
26. Virginia Parslow, Crafts Expert, The Farmers' Museum, Cooperstown, New York, has written authoritative monographs on colonial dyes and dyeing.

Chapter 2

1. Quoted by John Fleming in *Robert Adam and His Circle* (Cambridge: Harvard University Press, 1962), p. 258.
2. Andrea Memmo, *Elementi dell'architettura Lodoliana* (Rome: 1786); Francesco Algarotti, *Saggio sopra l'Architettura* (Leghorn: 1764, 1765); see also Edgar Kaufmann, Jr., "Memmo's Lodoli," *The Art Bulletin, 56,* No. 2, 159–175 (June 1964).
3. Jacques-François Blondel, *Architecture Française,* Book 1, p. 21. As quoted by Emile Kaufmann in *Architecture in the Age of Reason* (New York: Archon Books, 1966), p. 252.
4. Fiske Kimball, *The Creation of the Rococo* (New York: Norton, 1964), p. 72.
5. Francis J. B. Watson, "The Furniture Guilds of Eighteenth Century Paris," *Antiques,* 465–469 (May 1958).
6. Henry H. Hawley, "Jean-Pierre Latz, Cabinetmaker," *The Bulletin of the Cleveland Museum of Art,* 203–259 (October 1970).
7. William M. Milliken, "Marquetry Bombé Commode," *The Bulletin of the Cleveland Museum of Art,* 117–118 (September 1943).
8. "Silks of Lyon," *Ciba Review* (February 1938).
9. Quoted by A. Juvet-Michel in "The Controversy over Indian Prints," *Ciba Review,* 1091 (March 1940).
10. William Chaffers, *Marks and Monograms on European and Oriental Pottery and Porcelain with Historical Notices of Each Manufactory,* 14th rev. ed. by Frederick Litchfield (London: Reeves & Turner, 1932).
11. Wilfred J. Sainsbury, "Soft-paste Biscuit of Vincennes-Sèvres," *Antiques,* 46–51 (January 1956).

Chapter 3

1. John Fleming, *Robert Adam and His Circle* (Cambridge: Harvard University Press, 1962), p. 127.
2. Fleming, *Robert Adam and His Circle,* p. 127.
3. Giovanni Battista Piranesi, *Antichità Romane de Tèmpi della Republica e de' primi Imperatori,* 1748.
4. Fleming, *Robert Adam and His Circle,* p. 132. Horace Mann, well known through his letters to Horace Walpole, was British minister at the Tuscan court. The Countess Salin was his wife.
5. Fleming, *Robert Adam and His Circle,* p. 227.

Chapter 4

1. In 1715 and 1717 Campbell published folios of classical buildings in Britain called *Vitruvius Britannicus.*
2. Quoted by John Summerson in *Architecture in Britain, 1530–1830,* 4th ed. rev. and enl. (Baltimore: Penguin Books, 1963), p. 183.
3. Rather than the brown one of the popular song.
4. Julia G. Longe, *Martha, Lady Giffard, Life and Letters* (London: George Allen, 1911), p. 15.
5. Quoted by John Fleming in *Robert Adam and His Circle* (Cambridge: Harvard University Press, 1962), p. 293.
6. As quoted by Nathaniel Lloyd, *A History of the English House* (London: Architectural Press, 1951), p. 133.
7. Quoted from Victoria and Albert Museum, "Guide to Osterley Park."
8. Lindsay Boynton and Nicholas Goodison, "Thomas Chippendale at Nostell Priory," *Furniture History,* Vol. 4, 17 (1968).
9. Edith A. Standen, "English Washing Furnitures," *The Metropolitan Museum of Art Bulletin,* November 1964, pp. 109–124.
10. Boynton and Goodison, "Thomas Chippendale at Nostell Priory," p. 47.
11. As quoted by Fleming in *Robert Adam and His Circle,* pp. 278–279.
12. William Hogarth, *The Analysis of Beauty* (London, 1753).
13. Ralph Edwards and Margaret Jourdain, *Georgian Cabinet-Makers* (London: Country Life, 1955), pp. 42–44.
14. As quoted by Edwards and Jourdain in *Georgian Cabinet-Makers,* p. 49.
15. As quoted by Anthony Coleridge in "A Reappraisal of William Hallett," *Furniture History,* Vol. I (1965), p. 13.
16. Documented reproductions of these appear in *Furniture History,* Vol. IV (1968).
17. Wilmarth S. Lewis, Ed., *Horace Walpole's Correspondence* (New Haven: Yale University Press, 1960), 20:382.
18. L. O. J. Boynton, "The Bed-bug and the 'Age of Elegance,'" *Furniture History,* Vol. I, 15–21 (1965).
19. Dates are those given in Edwards and Jourdain, *Georgian Cabinet-Makers.*
20. Eileen Harris, *The Furniture of Robert Adam* (London: Tiranti, 1963), p. 20.
21. As quoted by Ralph Fastnedge in *English Furniture Styles from 1500 to 1830* (Baltimore: Penguin Books, 1955), p. 74.
22. *Furniture History,* Vol. 4, p. 38 (1968).
23. *Furniture History,* Vol. 4, p. 88 (1968).
24. *Furniture History,* Vol. 4, pp. 77–80 (1968).
25. There is some obscurity about the dates of early English porcelain. Those quoted are for the most part from Frederick Litchfield, *Pottery and Porce-*

lain, 6th ed., rev. by Frank Tilley (New York: Barrows, n.d.).

Chapter 5

1. Alan Gowans, *Images of American Living* (Philadelphia and New York: Lippincott, 1964), p. 44.
2. Thomas Tileston Waterman, *The Mansions of Virginia, 1706–1776* (Chapel Hill: The University of North Carolina Press, 1946), p. 123.
3. Final destruction in fire of 1832.
4. Waterman, *The Mansions of Virginia* (Chapel Hill: The University of North Carolina Press, 1946), p. 246.
5. *New Letters of Abigail Adams 1788–1801,* Ed. Stewart Mitchell (Boston: Houghton Mifflin, 1947), p. 15.
6. E. T. Joy, "English Furniture Exports to America 1697–1830," *Antiques,* 92–98 (January 1964).
7. Alice G. B. Lockwood, "Furnishings and Embellishments of Boston Houses 1694–1770," *The Bulletin of the Society for the Preservation of New England Antiquities,* Vol. 30, No. 1, 15 (July 1939).
8. Edward Stratton Holloway, "Furniture Exclusively American," *Antiques,* 182–184 (May 1938).
9. All of the essential differences between American chairs from the various centers are definitively handled in Joseph Downs, *American Furniture: Queen Anne and Chippendale Periods* (New York: Macmillan, 1952); Charles F. Hummel, "Queen Anne and Chippendale Furniture in the Henry Francis du Pont Winterthur Museum," *Antiques* (June 1970, December 1970, January 1971); and John T. Kirk, *American Chairs: Queen Anne and Chippendale* (New York: Knopf, 1972).
10. David Stockwell, "Irish Influence in Pennsylvania Queen Anne Furniture," *Antiques,* 269–271 (March 1961).
11. Morrison H. Heckscher, "Form and Frame: New Thought on the American Easy Chair," 881–893 (December 1971).
12. Lockwood, "Furnishings and Embellishments of Boston Houses," pp. 15–24.
13. William Macpherson Hornor, *Blue Book, Philadelphia Furniture, 1682–1807* (Philadelphia: 1935), p. 105.
14. Helen Comstock, "Diversity in Connecticut Blockfronts," *Antiques,* 63–73 (July 1963).
15. Helen Comstock, "Aaron Roberts and the Southeastern Connecticut Cabinetmaking School," *Antiques,* 437–441 (October 1964).
16. For this and much similar data grateful acknowledgement is made to Ethel Hall Bjerkoe, *The Cabinet Makers of America* (Garden City, New York: Doubleday, 1957).
17. J. F. Reifsnyder (1846–1878) was a Philadelphia furniture manufacturer who owned these pieces.
18. Mabel M. Swan, "McIntire Vindicated," *Antiques,* 130–132 (October 1934); Helen Comstock, "McIntire in Antiques," *Antiques,* 338–341 (April 1957).
19. Rosamond Randall Beirne, "John Shaw, Cabinetmaker," *Antiques,* 554–558 (December 1960).
20. Bjerkoe, *The Cabinet Makers of America,* p. 288.
21. New International Encyclopedia, 31:103.
22. Hazel E. Cummin, "Tammies and Durants," *Antiques,* 153 (September 1942).
23. Jean Mailey, "Printed Textiles in America," *Antiques,* 422–427 (May 1956).
24. Mailey, "Printed Textiles in America."
25. Florence M. Montgomery, "Textile Printing in Eighteenth Century America," *Antiques,* 536–540 (October 1968).
26. Abbott Lowell Cummings, "Connecticut Homespun," *Antiques,* 206–209 (September 1954).
27. Hazel E. Cummin, "Colonial Dimities, Checked and Diapered," *Antiques,* 111–112 (September 1940); *idem,* "What was Dimity in 1790?" *Antiques,* 23–25 (July 1940).
28. Lockwood, "Furnishings and Embellishments of Boston Houses 1694–1770," pp. 15–24.
29. Anna Brightman, "Window Curtains in Colonial Boston and Salem," *Antiques,* 184–187 (August 1964).
30. Brightman, "Window Curtains in Colonial Boston and Salem," pp. 184–187.
31. Mildred B. Lanier, "(Williamsburg III) The Textile Furnishings," *Antiques,* 121–127 (January 1969).
32. *An Illustrated Handbook of Mount Vernon* (Mt. Vernon, Virginia: Mount Vernon Ladies' Association, 1936), p. 13.
33. Lockwood, "Furnishings and Embellishments of Boston Houses," pp. 15–24.
34. Lockwood, "Furnishings and Embellishments of Boston Houses."
35. Cornelia B. Faraday, "Rugs of the British Isles," *Good Furniture Magazine,* 253–258 (November 1927).
36. Margaret Swain, "A Note on Scotch Carpet," *Furniture History,* 1978, pp. 61–62.
37. Worth E. Shoults, "The Home of the First Farmer of America," *National Geographic Magazine,* 603–628 (May 1928).
38. Marian Day Iverson, "The Bed Rug in Colonial America," *Antiques,* 107–108 (January 1964).
39. Helen Comstock, "Eighteenth Century Floorcloths," *Antiques,* 48–49 (January 1955).
40. Joseph Leeming, *The White House in Picture and Story* (New York: George W. Stewart, 1953), p. 13.
41. Nina Fletcher Little, "(Cooperstown) The Painted Decoration," *Antiques,* 182–185 (February 1959).
42. Phyllis Ackerman, "Wallpapers from Old New England Houses," *Antiques,* 440–443 (May 1956).
43. Edward S. Holloway, *The Practical Book of American Furniture and Decoration, Colonial and Federal* (Philadelphia: Lippincott, 1937), p. 170.
44. Phyllis Ackerman, *Wallpaper—Its History, Design, and Use* (New York: Stokes, 1923), p. 70.
45. Eleanore M. Whitmore, "Origins of Pennsylvania Folk Art," *Antiques,* 106–110 (September 1940).

46. George S. and Helen McKearin, *American Glass* (New York: Crown, 1941), pp. 211–212.

47. Museum of Fine Arts, Boston, *Colonial Silversmiths, Masters and Apprentices* (Boston: Museum of Fine Arts, 1956), p. 19.

Chapter 6

1. Clay Lancaster, "Builders' Guide and Plan Books and American Architecture from the Revolution to the Civil War," *Antiques,* 16–22 (January 1948).

2. The November 1953 and January 1954 issues of *Antiques* are devoted to California architecture and furniture.

3. E. E. Viollet-le-Duc, *Dictionaire Raisoné de l'Architecture Française* (1854–1868); and Entretiens (2 vols.; 1863–1872).

4. A. C. Pugin and E. J. Willson, *Specimens of Gothic Architecture,* 2 vols. (London: 1821); and *Examples of Gothic Architecture* (London: 1831).

5. The building ordinances referred to here of the time of Louis Napoleon were an extension of those of the Emperor Napoleon Bonaparte. Their purpose was not only to create architecture of a uniform style but also, by height limitations, to provide for an extensive vista along the newly created boulevards. Uniformity, straight and wide avenues, and long views had become increasingly the classic ideal in French civic planning. In the nineteenth century this planning served pragmatic as well as aesthetic ends—favoring movement of organized troops and discouraging the barricading of narrow streets by mobs.

6. R. W. Burnham, R. M. Hanes, and C. J. Bartleson, *Color: A Guide to Basic Facts and Concepts* (New York: Wiley, 1963), p. 15. Chromaticness is the aspect of color that includes hue and saturation, apart from brightness.

7. Henry-Russell Hitchcock, *Architecture: Nineteenth and Twentieth Centuries* (Baltimore: Penguin Books, 1958), p. 227.

8. For example, Church of the Unity, Springfield, Mass., 1866–1869; Brattle Square Church, Boston, 1870–1872; Trinity Church, Boston, 1873–1877; Cheney Block, Hartford, 1875–1876; Ames Memorial Library, North Easton, 1877–1879; Allegheny Court House and County Jail, 1884–1888.

9. Richard H. Randall, Jr., "Sources of the Empire Style," *Antiques,* 452–453 (April 1963).

10. As quoted by Joseph T. Butler in "A Case Study in Nineteenth Century Color: Redecoration at Sunnyside," *Antiques,* 54 (July 1960).

11. Mario Praz, *An Illustrated History of Furnishing* (New York: George Braziller, 1964), p. 199.

12. As quoted by E. Maurice Bloch in "Regency styling, the Prince and the decorator, Frederick Crace at the Royal Pavilion, Brighton," *The Connoisseur,* 132 (June 1953).

13. Andrew Jackson Downing, *The Architecture of Country Houses* (New York: Dover, 1969, originally published in 1850), p. 405.

14. *Ciba Review,* No. 3, 84 (November 1937).

15. Downing, *The Architecture of Country Houses,* p. 368.

16. Butler, "A Case Study in Nineteenth Century Color," p. 54.

17. Lewis Mumford, *The Brown Decades: A Study of the Arts in America 1865–1895* (New York: Dover Publications, Inc., 1955), p. 8.

18. R. Glynn Grylls (Lady Mander), "Wightwick Manor—a William Morris Period-Piece," *The Connoisseur,* 3–12 (January 1962).

19. Probably the Duke of Westminster's private art gallery at Grosvenor House, in upper Grosvenor Street.

20. Madame de Staël, *On Politics, Literature and National Character,* Monroe Berger, translated and edited (Garden City, New York: Doubleday, Anchor Books, 1965), pp. 87–89.

21. Serge Grandjean, *Empire Furniture* (London: Faber & Faber, 1966), p. 60.

22. Derrick Worsdale, "Later Neo-Classical Florentine Furniture at Pallazo Pitti," *Furniture History,* 49–57 (1978).

23. Marie G. Kimball, "The Original Furnishings of the White House," *Antiques,* 32–38 (July 1952).

24. R. L. Raley, "Interior Designs by Benjamin Latrobe for the President's House," *Antiques,* 568–571 (1959).

25. Lorraine Waxman, "The Lannuier Brothers Cabinetmakers," *Antiques,* 141–143 (August 1957).

26. Francis James Dallett, "Michel Bouvier, Franco-American Cabinet-Maker," *Antiques,* 198–200 (February 1962).

27. Robert C. Smith, "Philadelphia Empire Furniture by Antoine Gabriel Quervelle," *Antiques,* 304–309 (September 1964); *idem,* "The Furniture of Anthony G. Quervelle, Parts I, II, and III," *Antiques,* 984–994 (May 1973), 90–99 (July 1973), and 261–268 (August 1973).

28. Ethel Hall Bjerkoe, *The Cabinetmakers of America* (Garden City, New York: Doubleday, 1957), p. 193.

29. As quoted by Mario Praz, in *An Illustrated History of Furnishing* (Milan, Italy: Longanesi, 1964), p. 197.

30. Praz, *History of Furnishings,* p. 197.

31. *Madame de Staël,* p. 90.

32. John N. Pearce, Lorraine W. Pearce, and Robert G. Smith, "The Meeks Family of Cabinetmakers," *Antiques,* 414–420 (April 1964); John Pearce and Lorraine Pearce, "More on the Meeks Cabinetmakers," *Antiques,* 69–72 (July 1966).

33. Louise Karr, "A Resume of Papier-Mâché, *Antiques,* 86–89 (March 1933).

34. Gordon Roe, "Victorian Papier-Mâché: A Reexamination," *Antiques,* 552–555 (December 1969).

35. Joseph T. Butler, "American Mid-Victorian Outdoor Furniture," *Antiques*, 564–567 (June 1959).
36. Clare Vincent, "John Henry Belter's Parlour Furniture," *Furniture History*, 92–99 (1967).
37. William Morris, *Hopes and Fears for Art* (London: Longmans, Green, 1905), p. 108.
38. Esther Meynell, *Portrait of William Morris* (London: Chapman & Hall, 1947), p. 131.
39. Arnold David Balch, *Elbert Hubbard, Genius of Roycroft* (New York: Stokes, 1940).
40. Elbert Hubbard, *A Catalogue and Some Comment* (East Aurora, New York: Roycrofters Shop, 1900).
41. Charles Lock Eastlake, *Hints on Household Taste* (London: Longmans, Green, 1872), p. 62.
42. Edna D. Pree Nelson, "When Is a Piano?" *Antiques*, 245–249 (June 1936).
43. *Ciba Review*, 1961, No. 1, "English Chintz."
44. *Ciba Review*, Vol. 12, No. 135 (December 1959), "Rouen-French Textile Center."
45. *Ciba Review*, 1961, No. 1, "English Chintz"; Peter Floud, "The Influence of William Morris," pp. 21–23. (Peter Floud was the well-known Morris expert with the Victoria and Albert.)
46. Mildred Davison, "Hand Woven Coverlets in the Chicago Institute of Art," *Antiques*, 734–740 (May 1970).
47. Constance Cary Harrison, *The Woman's Handiwork in Modern Homes* (New York: Scribner's, 1882), 46–50.
48. Joseph Leeming, *The White House in Picture and Story* (New York: W. Stewart, 1953), p. 13.
49. Edith Gaines, Ed., "Amberina: Legend and Lore," *Antiques*, 217, 218 (January 1972).
50. Kathryn Hait Dorflinger Manchee, "Dorflinger Glass," *Antiques*, Part I, 710–715 (April 1972); Part II, 1006–1011 (June 1972); Part III, 96–100 (July 1972).
51. N. M. Penzer, "Silver and Plate," *Connoisseur Period Guides: The Regency Period* (New York: Reynal, 1958), pp. 72–92.
52. Alston Deas, "Charleston Ornamental Ironwork," *Antiques*, 748–751 (May 1970).

Chapter 7

1. Louis L. Sullivan, *The Autobiography of an Idea* (New York: Press of the American Institute of Architects, 1924), p. 258. See also Henry T. Tuckerman, *Memorial of Horatio Greenough* (New York: Putnam, 1853) and Horatio Greenough, *Form and Function: Remarks on Art, Design, and Architecture*, Harold A. Small, Ed. (Berkeley and Los Angeles: University of California Press, 1966).
2. Gropius was Professor of Architecture at Harvard from 1937 to 1952; Mies van der Rohe was Director of Architecture at the Illinois Institute of Technology from 1938 to 1969.
3. Henry Russell Hitchcock and Philip C. Johnson, *The International Style, Architecture Since 1922* (New York: Norton, 1932).
4. Le Corbusier, *New World of Space* (New York: The Museum of Modern Art, 1947), p. 182.
5. Francois Bucher, Josef Albers, *Despite Straight Lines* (New Haven: Yale University Press, 1961), p. 33.
6. Frank Lloyd Wright, *An Autobiography* (New York: Duell, Sloan, and Pearce, 1943), p. 311.
7. Marcel Breuer, *Sun and Shadow* (New York: Dodd, Mead, 1955).
8. Frank Lloyd Wright, *An Autobiography*, p. 48.
9. R. Glynn Grylls (Lady Mander), "Wightwick Manor—a William Morris Period Piece," *Connoisseur*, 7 (February 1962).
10. Frank Lloyd Wright, *The Natural House* (New York: Horizon, 1954), p. 50.
11. The house is now part of the Western Pennsylvania Conservancy, 204 Fifth Avenue, Pittsburgh, Pennsylvania.
12. Sherman E. Lee, *A History of Far Eastern Art* (Englewood Cliffs, New Jersey: Prentice-Hall New York: Abrams, 1964), p. 18.
13. Conrad Brown, "Toshiko Takaezu," *Craft Horizons*, 26 (March/April, 1959).
14. Brown, "Toshiko Takaezu," p. 26.
15. *Time*, 46 (January 10, 1964).
16. Frank Lloyd Wright, *A Testament* (New York: Avon, 1972), p. 179.
17. Meyric R. Rogers, *Italy at Work* (Chicago: The Art Institute of Chicago, 1950).
18. Siegfried Giedion, *Space, Time, and Architecture* (Cambridge: Harvard University Press, 1946), pp. 17–19.
19. "Eero Saarinen Speaking," *Interiors*, 131 (October 1961).
20. "Fantasy Furniture," *Craft Horizons*, 10–16 (January/February 1966).
21. This material is found in Erik Zahle, Ed., *A Treasury of Scandinavian Design* (New York: Golden Press, 1962) and in Danish Handicraft Guild Publications, 1960–1963, as well as in *Craft Horizons* (March/April 1958).
22. "Scandinavia's Young Dissenters," *Craft Horizons* (March/April 1958).

Index